Reading Life
A Writer's Reader

INGE FINK
University of New Orleans

GABRIELLE GAUTREAUX
University of New Orleans

THOMSON
WADSWORTH

Australia   Canada   Mexico   Singapore   Spain   United Kingdom   United States

THOMSON

WADSWORTH

Reading Life: A Writer's Reader
Inge Fink, Gabrielle Gautreaux

Publisher: *Michael Rosenberg*
Acquisitions Editor: *Dickson Musslewhite*
Development Editor: *Aron Keesbury*
Managing Development Editor: *Karen Judd*
Senior Production Editor: *Lianne Ames*
Director of Marketing: *Elana Dolberg*
Marketing Manager: *Katrina Byrd*
Manufacturing Buyer: *Mary Beth Hennebury*

Compositor: *Publishers' Design and Production Services, Inc.*
Project Manager: *Kathy Smith*
Photography Manager: *Sheri Blaney*
Photo Researcher: *Sharon Donahue*
Cover/Text Designer: *Anne Carter*
Text Printer: *Maple Vail*
Cover Printer: Phoenix Color Corp.

Cover image © Taxi/Getty Images

Printed in the United States of America.
1 2 3 4 5 6 7 8 9 10   08 07 06 05 04

For more information, contact Thomson Wadsworth, 25 Thomson Place, Boston, Massachusetts 02210 USA, or you can visit our Internet site at http://www.wadsworth.com

Credits appear on pages 835-846, which constitute an extension of this copyright page.

For permission to use material from this text or product, submit a request online at http://www.thomsonrights.com Any additional questions about permissions can be submitted by email to thomsonrights@thomson.com

ISBN: 0-7593-9810-0 (InfoTrac® College Edition)

Library of Congress Control Number: 2004102716

CONTENTS

PART I A WRITER'S GUIDE

PART II A WRITER'S READER

12. LEARNING MATTERS *330*

IMAGE GALLERY

14. TALK THE TALK

IMAGE GALLERY

16. TO MARKET, TO MARKET 614

(IMAGE GALLERY)

(IMAGE GALLERY)

Rhetorical Table of Contents

NARRATION

DESCRIPTION

EXEMPLIFICATION AND ILLUSTRATION

PROCESS

CAUSE/EFFECT

COMPARISON/CONTRAST

DIVISION/CLASSIFICATION

DEFINITION

IRONY/SATIRE

About *Reading Life*

Reading Life makes a basic assumption about the writing process: Before writers can convey their experiences, ideas, and opinions effectively, they must be able to *read* life's texts—in a variety of forms, whether remembered, written, or visual. Writers are more successful when they focus on what they have to say before they worry about how to say it. And what they have to say springs from what they know, what they read, and what they see.

Emphasizing the sheer variety of texts—written and otherwise—and the integral relationship between reading texts and creating them, *Reading Life* aims to inform, inspire, and provoke. The definition of "reader" is expanded here to include an eclectic mix of writing and visuals. With its vast array of selections, varying widely in purpose, style, and tone, subject and genre, *Reading Life* can accommodate both "practical," contemporary approaches and more traditional approaches. It reinforces what we stress in the short, student-friendly writer's guide—that writing is creative, individual, empowering, powerful.

Eclectic Essays

Reading Life offers an eclectic reader, with classic and contemporary written texts—88 in all—that vary in length, genre, and degree of difficulty, providing exciting material for classroom discussion or private contemplation. While *Reading Life* includes many of the classic essays teachers have come to expect and rely on and the writing of several often-anthologized authors, it focuses on hipper, more contemporary reading selections, drawing from the *Best American Essays* series and similar essay collections, *The New Yorker, Rolling Stone, Harper's, Essence, Mother Jones,* and *The New York Times Magazine,* as well as other major newspapers and popular magazines and journals; many selections are by young, unknown writers.

We have tried to create the kind of reader that we have always wanted—one with a wide selection of fresh and new and of tried and trusted readings that appeal to both the seasoned veteran and the brand-new teaching assistant. We know that while their tastes may differ, they both value good writing. And, of course, we hope that *Reading Life* appeals to its most important audience, the students who will read and respond, question and challenge, reinterpret and reimagine, ultimately creating their own texts.

Provocative Themes

The ten thematic units in the book contain previously unanthologized essays on issues not often found in composition textbooks. These essays are integrated with more traditional themes, an approach that provides a fresh outlook on enduring questions and grounds new ideas in a tradition of historical thought and analysis. We hope students will be happy to see their concerns addressed in *Reading Life* and that teachers will embrace the opportunity to establish connections between the new and the old.

The thematic units in this book move from more personal issues (the body, relationships) in the early chapters to increasingly public issues (business and popular culture) in the later chapters. Timeless concerns for students and their teachers—personal relationships, body politics, and education matters—get fresh treatment. Other chapters consider particularly timely issues, whether the frontiers of science and technology, fraught with anxiety and possibility, or the fine line between government protection and government control. Overlapping themes invite cross-referencing and conversations between texts.

Extensive Gallery of Images

Reading Life offers a varied selection of intriguing visuals in both color and black-and-white. The 32-page insert of color photographs, covering a range of subjects relevant to the book's themes, can be treated as a separate unit for teaching visual rhetoric, or color images may be selected for use with each of the book's ten thematic units. In addition to the 32-page insert, each chapter includes a portfolio of black-and-white images chosen to help facilitate further analysis: They can serve to illustrate themes or can be used as subjects for composition themselves.

Apparatus Designed to Encourage Analysis

All reading and visual texts are accompanied by an unobtrusive apparatus designed to help students understand their content, their use of rhetorical and artistic techniques, and their connections to each other. These questions are meant to inspire students to discuss and write about the issues presented in the readings and images. Often students are overwhelmed when asked to analyze too many layers of meaning at once. They should find helpful the breakdown of questions into different categories: a *prereading* question before each written selection, as well as separate groups of questions asking students to *analyze what* writers are saying, *analyze how* they say it, *analyze the issue, analyze connections* to other texts, and *analyze visual rhetoric.* Teachers can assign these questions as homework for class preparation and use them as inspiration for class discussions and writing assignments, but they can easily substitute their own apparatus if they choose to do so.

Realistic Writer's Guide

Reading Life offers a hands-on, jargon-free, imminently practical guide to writing. We do not provide easy formulas—we've yet to discover one—but do try to demystify the writing process, breaking it into logical steps and showing how student writers plan and develop their writing projects, from idea to full-blown essay. We emphasize the importance of planning and the benefits of revision.

Like the reader, the writer's guide accommodates a variety of teaching styles; its rhetorical approach provides guidance without stifling writers or writing teachers. We hope that newer teachers will find the practical rhetoric and its exercises helpful as they develop their teaching styles, and that experienced teachers will appreciate that the writer's guide does not try to reinvent the wheel and interfere with the methods that work best for them.

First-of-Its-Kind Visual Rhetoric

Reading Life provides a basic introduction to engaging, analyzing, and writing about visuals, the first *rhetoric for visuals* in the composition market. While many current textbooks contain visuals for analysis, they don't actually teach students *what* to look for in a visual text or *how* to analyze images. Students are, of course, used to *looking* at pictures but not to thinking, talking, and writing about them. The final chapter of the writer's guide, based on the principles of art criticism but written straightforwardly, shows students how to consider different components in a visual image and draw conclusions about what they see so that they can understand it as text and write about it.

Practical Instructor's Manual

Reading Life is accompanied by a short instructor's manual designed to help first-time users and especially new teachers. Questions that appear in the apparatus are addressed in short summaries of each written and visual text.

User-Friendly Website

Reading Life is accompanied by a website (http://english.wadsworth.com/gautreaux_fink) that features Online Casebooks, each containing four or five InfoTrac links based on the book's themes. Other resources available on the website include a diction concept library, a grammar concept library, a mechanics concept library, a punctuation concept library, a research concept library, a writing concept library, and student paper libraries. If you have teaching suggestions after using Reading Life, please send them to the authors in care of the publisher, for possible incorporation into the website.

ACKNOWLEDGMENTS

We could never have completed *Reading Life* without the help of many others. Over the past several years, many of our colleagues at the University of New Orleans, too numerous to name, have brought essays and writers to our attention and shared ideas and concerns from their own classrooms with us. We are especially grateful to Kerri Barton, Amanda and Joseph Boyden, Jessica Emerson, Gabe Gomez, Carolyn Hembree, and Kim Martin for writing of their approaches to teaching some of the selections in *Reading Life*; their contributions can be found on the *Reading Life* website. Our thanks also go to Dan Doll for a suggestion that contributed significantly to the writer's guide; to Kim McDonald, with whom we discussed various ideas; to Jim Knudsen and Joanna Leake, who shared with us their experience coauthoring textbooks; and to Elizabeth Penfield, textbook author and writing teacher extraordinaire, who inspired us both. To our colleagues from the Fine Arts Department, Cheryl Hayes and Peggy McDowell, who lent art books, read portions of the manuscript, and were generally generous with their artistic expertise, we are particularly indebted.

Several outside reviewers offered constructive criticism, useful suggestions—and ultimate encouragement—during the early stages of our project. Their unjaundiced eyes helped us consider our project from a more objective vantage point. For their collective wisdom, thanks to Jesse Airubi of Baylor University, Beverly Braud of Southwest Texas University, Robert Happ of the University of Dubuque, Karen Hattaway of San Jacinto College North, Quentin Miller of Suffolk University, and Stuart Stelly of York College of Pennsylvania.

Our very productive relationship with Thomson/Wadsworth was born at a fortuitous dinner at 4Cs in Chicago, sponsored by the then-named Thomson/Heinle: one of us met—almost accidentally—Michael Rosenberg, our publisher, who, having been told of our project in a phone call from a local sales rep, Charlotte Strauser, noticed a name tag; the other had the good fortune to be seated next to Aron Keesbury, then on his first day as an employee of Thomson/Heinle, who became our development editor. In Michael, we have found a most supportive publisher. In Aron, we found a textbook author's dream editor. He is smart, sensitive, and innovative, and he is as responsible for the way this book has taken shape as we are. We refer to our other development editor, Karen Judd, as Wonder Woman: Her innate sense of organization and attention to detail transformed our hapless babe of a manuscript into a full-blown book. We are grateful to Dickson Musslewhite, our acquisitions editor, for having faith in our project in the first place. And we owe much to our production project manager, Lianne Ames, and to our project manager and excellent copy editor, Kathy Smith, who worked quietly and tirelessly during the final phase of our project. For hustling permissions under tight deadlines, we thank our permissions and photo researchers, Karyn Morrison and Sharon Donahue, and for an interior and cover design that we both love, we thank Anne Carter. Finally, for her encouragement and ceaseless good humor, we thank marketing manager Katrina Byrd, whom we knew before we knew anyone else at Thomson and whom we knew we wanted on our team.

Inge Fink would like to thank her husband, Todd Scurto, for his love, his patience, and his unwavering support of this and her many other projects. She would like to dedicate this book to him.

Gabrielle Gautreaux thanks her husband, David Allen, for his encouragement and support, for his tolerance for living among stacks of papers and books, and for his endurance of restaurants and take-out, all of which made completion of this book possible. She would also like to thank her mother for always telling her she could do anything she set her mind to; and she would like to dedicate this book to the memory of her father-in-law, fellow word traveler, who encouraged her in all her language and literary endeavors, and to her father, a man of few words, who died just as *Reading Life* was going to press, but who had monitored, proudly, its progress, and whose deeds and respect and encouragement continue to inspire her.

Finally, our greatest debt is to our students, past and present, who have challenged us daily to reread, rethink, revise—to read life anew.

PART

A Writer's Guide

1 GETTING STARTED

Student writers often are easily frustrated by their inability to sit down and write an essay. The problem is not that they can't write, but rather that they don't understand the writing *process*. Even the most accomplished writers don't produce polished drafts in a single sitting. They make preparations; they write drafts and revise; they edit.

Writing will be a much more manageable task if you break the process into steps. For many writers, the most difficult part is getting started. Many of your college writing assignments will require that you begin by reading—and many of the writing assignments you will get in the work world will also require some reading. Even if you are asked to write about a personal experience, reading is a good starting place: By reading others' accounts of their experiences, you are exposed to models that may trigger ideas for how to present your own experience. You may discover another angle for your own piece, or you may simply find out what you don't want to write.

Reading is an integral part of the writing process. The simple act of reading engages the mind and forces the reader to interact with texts, with words and phrases, with a variety of sentence shapes and sizes. It prepares us for the act of writing.

READING CRITICALLY

Many readers spend a lot more time reading than is necessary, usually because they aren't reading *actively*. They don't engage the text, they don't question the text, they don't take in much, and they quickly forget what they have read. An active, critical reader is an efficient reader. (For a more detailed discussion of how to analyze a text, see the beginning of Chapter 2, "Writing Analytically.")

Read once quickly to get a sense of what the piece is about and how it is organized. Then reread carefully, with a pencil. Underline key words; make notes in the margins. If you don't understand or you disagree with a point, put a question mark in the margin. Circle words you need to look up. Determine the **subject** of the piece you are reading: What is it about? Once you have identified the subject, determine the author's **thesis**. The thesis is the author's position, opinion, or stance on the subject. It is sometimes called the *main point* or *controlling idea*. Here are some tips for determining the main idea:

- The main idea is usually stated (or implied) early.
- Examples and evidence support the main idea.

- The main idea is almost always restated, explicitly or implicitly, in the final paragraphs.
- The title often contains a clue to the main idea.

Read the following short essay. First, determine the subject of the essay. Then, write out the thesis, using the writer's words if the thesis is explicit and your own words if the thesis is implied.

SHATTERED ILLUSIONS

I remember sitting in a literature class during my senior year in high school, bored practically to tears by the teacher's discussion of James Joyce—until he defined "epiphany" for us. He described it as a life-altering moment, a sudden realization that your life would be different from now on. Really different. Mr. Herrit was using the term in a literary context, but I understood it as it related to my own personal history, which I considered very tragic at the time. Little did I know that I had yet to experience a much greater epiphany.

When I was thirteen, my parents announced they were divorcing, and although I had heard them arguing, in hushed tones late at night, I was stunned. Divorce was no novelty in our circle: many of my friends' parents were divorced; I had divorced aunts and uncles; almost all the couples my parents knew contained at least one partner who had been divorced. Still, nothing prepared me for the way my life changed.

I was an only child, doted on by both my parents, truly indulged by my father. He was handsome, charming, athletic, playful, comfortably predictable. His work hours were more flexible than Mom's, so he drove me to school and picked me up. We always stopped on the way home for groceries and then for cookies or an ice-cream cone, for me. We played basketball in the driveway. He loved to cook, and on weekends, he experimented with exotic dishes. Just before the curry or the black bean soup or the seafood enchiladas were done, he would let me pour two glasses of wine for him and my mother and take a sip of his while my mother pretended to disapprove. I always hated the wine, but I loved that moment.

In the time it took my father to pack his things, it was all over. He lived an hour away, so my mother paid for me to join a carpool. He came and got me every other weekend. Sometimes we went to the zoo, to a movie, or walked around the mall. But everything was utterly changed.

The first time I went to my dad's apartment, I cried. There was a single tiny bedroom and hardly any furniture; when I stayed over, my dad slept on a cot in the living room that doubled as a couch. The tiny kitchen didn't have enough pots and pans for him to cook his elaborate meals; all the kitchen utensils had been left behind at our house. I never saw a bottle of wine there. And there was no driveway for shooting baskets.

Later I realized that the divorce was costly to my father. He could barely afford to pay our house note, my child support, and his own expenses. He traded in his new car for a cheaper, smaller, used one. My mother's lifestyle and mine didn't change much, but our life was different. Although she had kicked him out—that I knew from overhearing the end of their last big argument—my mother was depressed, withdrawn, snappish. When he came to pick me up, she wouldn't open the door for him, but instead called for me to come; she'd then kiss me quickly, say she loved me, and retreat to her bedroom before I had a chance to open the door. I grew to resent her for what she had reduced my father to, for the chill she had introduced into our household. I felt guilty for living in the house they had both been so proud of, with its shady yard, spacious rooms, big windows, and well-equipped kitchen. I saw my father—and myself—as a victim of her selfishness.

Two years after the divorce, my father remarried. I met Sara only a week before they left to get married. She was young and pretty and, most of all, cheerful; while I felt a pang of jealousy, I was glad that my dad's life was taking a turn for the better. When I told my mom about Sara, she went pale and made a funny gurgling sound, and I took mean-spirited pleasure in her pain.

Soon, Dad seemed to be doing better financially. He and Sara bought a house, a new car. And soon, Sara was pregnant. When I was sixteen, Dad and Sara welcomed Sammy, my baby brother, into their home, their family. I loved that baby like crazy, but every time I recognized my old dad, the pre-divorce dad, doting on his new son, it tore me up inside. I knew those feelings were immature and irrational, so I buried them.

I was in college and my brother was almost four when I had a knock-down, drag-out fight with my mother one weekend when she seemed hurt by my wanting to go to the beach with my other family instead of with her to visit my grandmother. I really let her have it, hurling insults as years of frustration and anger came pouring out. She wilted and didn't say anything else. I went to the beach, and a few months later, my aunt called me and told me what I now know is the truth. My mom had kicked my dad out, after she discovered he had been having an affair for over a year with one of her co-workers—Sara—whom he had met at an office party he attended with my mom. She had been devastated, believing, as I did, that we were the perfect family. She never could stand to cook in the kitchen after he left, her memories were so raw. Despite all that and despite her failure to maintain any illusion of normalcy in our home after Dad left, she was determined to protect the illusion I had of my father—and she did it at the expense of my illusion of her.

Once I processed my feelings after that revelation, I realized that my father had never even acknowledged my mother's existence after he left, that she became invisible to him as he pursued his own happiness after his betrayal of her. I realized that all the time I felt sorry for him—except for those weekends—he was enjoying the comforts and pleasures of romance while my mother was dying inside.

My parents' divorce was life-altering, for all of us. Looking back, I realize my mother made the largest sacrifice, paid the biggest price. I love both my parents, but the truth changed them utterly in my eyes—and changed me utterly.

WRITING SUMMARIES

Summarizing what you read is an excellent way to hone your skills of analysis. If you can summarize a reading accurately, you have read critically. A **summary** is a brief, nonjudgmental, restatement of the writer's main points. It uses neutral language and represents the *writer's* views fairly and accurately. Its goals are clarity and brevity.

By determining the subject and thesis of the above essay, you've written the briefest kind of summary, which may be sufficient for a short work or if you are simply making a note card or annotating a bibliography. Usually, however, the summary will also include a restatement of the writer's key points, arranged in the order of the work being summarized. Main ideas are combined into fewer sentences than in the original. Examples, illustrations, and anecdotes are left out. In a longer summary, of a long piece, important quotations may be included, but quotations are generally not included in summaries.

Before writing a summary, underline the writer's thesis and the **topic sentence** of each paragraph. Then see if you can leave out any of the topic sentences and combine others to effectively restate the writer's main points. Try it with the above essay.

GENERATING IDEAS FOR YOUR WRITING

So far we have been focusing on reading, often the first step in preparing to write an essay. Now we will talk about ways of coming up with ideas for your own essays and putting them on paper.

In class, your instructor will often point you toward the subject of your essay, asking you, for example, to write about a life-changing experience; or, your instructor may *give* you the subject of your essay, asking you to argue your views on gun control or capital punishment. Sometimes, however, you'll have to start from scratch.

Once you have determined a subject, it's time to start brainstorming for ideas that you can later work with, selecting and narrowing them down in order to come up with an angle or a position.

Writers all work differently, and there's no right or wrong way to get started. The two authors of your textbook, for example, work in completely different ways. One starts with neat lists that she quickly forms into outlines; the other uses a combination of rough lists and diagrams. Find a way that works for you.

FREEWRITING is a good technique to use when you can't think of anything to write about. Simply put your pen to paper and write, for about five minutes, on anything that comes into your mind. It won't seem logical or organized; it will be as varied and as disjointed as your thoughts. When the time is up, look at what you have written. Have you repeated any ideas? Can you make connections between ideas? In a more focused freewriting exercise, you begin with a subject or topic—your parents' divorce, say—and freewrite about anything that comes to mind when you think about it. The writer of the essay above, "Shattered Illusions," may have begun with a focused freewriting such as the one below:

```
When my parents divorced, I thought my life was over.
Depression. Loneliness. Guilt. Dad's sad little
```

```
apartment. Mom shell-shocked. Dad's betrayal. I blamed
Mom. Sometimes I wish I had known the truth about Sara,
but I probably would never have gotten over it and been
deprived of my brother and our relationship. Friends had
divorced parents, but mine seemed worse. I found out that
the truth isn't always the truth. Dad's curries, wine rit-
ual. Memories. Lies. Growing up. Children of divorce . . .
```

From this, the writer may begin to see a pattern or a focus: betrayal, lies, depression, the truth isn't always the truth. These could point the writer in a particular direction, just as some of the specific images (the apartment, the curries, and wine) could provide supporting detail.

LISTING is another easy way to get started, once you have a subject. If the writer of "Shattered Illusions" had started by listing ideas, she might have come up with something like this:

```
MY PARENTS' DIVORCE
The shock of their announcement
How things changed
Things about Dad I treasured: curries, playing basketball
Dad's apartment vs. our house
Mom's depression, my depression
Sara and Sammy
```

This list is organized somewhat chronologically, but often a list will seem more like freewriting arranged as a list. The important thing is to get some ideas and some details on paper and not to censor anything.

MAKING SATELLITES is a technique for generating ideas that may work for people who work less methodically, who have difficulty thinking in linear terms, particularly in the preliminary stages. Drawing diagrams may help them to connect related ideas and begin to organize. To make satellites, simply write your topic or subject in the middle of your page. Draw lines from the center (the topic, circled or boxed) that lead to related ideas or subtopics; circle or box those (your "satellites") and draw lines from those that lead to supporting details. Our "Shattered Illusions" writer, for example, might start with a circled "Parents' divorce" in the center of her page. Branching off from that, she might have five satellites: "predivorce memories," "postdivorce memories," "What I thought was true," "Truth," "What I learned." Then, branching off from her "postdivorce memories," she might have four satellites: "weekend visits," "Dad's apartment," "zoo, movies, mall," "Mom's reaction."

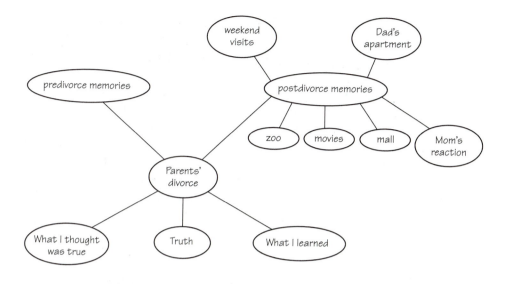

DEVELOPING A THESIS

A **thesis** is the writer's main point or controlling idea; it is not the writer's subject, but **the writer's position or opinion about or lesson learned from the subject.** In the case of the writer of "Shattered Illusions," the subject is her parents' divorce, but the main point of the essay is really what she learned through her experience, a painful lesson about the nature of illusion. Her thesis is **implied** in the final two sentences of her introductory paragraph. *Mr. Herrit was using the term in a literary context, but I understood it as it related to my own personal history, which I considered very tragic at the time. Little did I know that I had yet to experience a much greater epiphany.* Had she stated her thesis **explicitly,** she might have written: *My experiences after my parents' divorce taught me that illusions are powerful, that they obscure the truth and distort relationships, and that their dropping away can alter lives radically.*

How did she come up with her thesis? Probably by making connections between the ideas and details she jotted in her freewriting, her lists, or her satellite diagram. Like you, she may not have started with the same thesis she ended up with. Because writing is a process of discovery, she may not have realized what she really wanted to say until she began drafting or until she revised. Writers start with a working thesis, and often reshape and refine it as their ideas develop. The thesis, whether implicit or explicit, serves as the primary signpost, focusing the writer's ideas for readers, giving them an idea of exactly what to expect and why they should invest any time reading it.

OUTLINING

Not everyone uses an outline. Some people move immediately from thesis to drafting. Some simply jot down a word or phrase for each point they plan to develop. Others use brief but well-ordered lists as outlines. For those who may have trouble organizing their ideas, however, an outline can be very helpful. A good outline serves as map for the writer, getting her from beginning to end without detours.

An outline needn't be formal and painstakingly symmetrical, as some of us were once taught (there must be a Roman numeral II if there is a Roman numeral I, a small b if there is a small a, and so on). A good outline states the thesis, outlines the key supporting points, and then lists a word or phrase for each supporting example or detail under each supporting point. (Alternately, you can make a sentence outline: Write out your thesis, and then write the topic sentence for each paragraph you plan to include in the essay.)

The "Shattered Dreams" writer's outline may have looked like this:

Working thesis: My experiences after my parents' divorce taught me that illusions are powerful, that they obscure the truth and distort relationships, and that their dropping away can alter lives radically.

1. Parents' announcement and my shock
2. What is was like before the divorce
   • Dad taking me to and picking me up from school
   • Dad playing basketball with me
   • Dad's dinners and the wine ritual
3. What it was like after the divorce
   • Dad's apartment
   • Weekend visits, impersonal activities
   • Mom's reaction
   • My feelings toward Mom
4. Dad's remarriage
5. Illusions shattered: the truth comes out
   • The fight with Mom
   • Aunt J's call
   • My big epiphany

Although the writer's numbered ideas do not correspond paragraph with paragraph to the finished essay, the outline is detailed enough that she should have no trouble fleshing out these points to come up with a good first draft.

ORGANIZING YOUR ESSAY

While students get a lot of misinformation about how many paragraphs, and even sentences, are required in an essay, there really are no hard and fast rules about *numbers* of paragraphs *or* sentences in an essay. Flip through the reader in Part 2 of this book and you'll find few essays with only five paragraphs despite the popular five-paragraph formula. Instead, you'll see that the number of paragraphs varies greatly from essay to essay. What almost every essay does have, however, is three parts: an **introduction**, which may be one or several paragraphs and which serves as a hook for readers, introducing the subject and the controlling idea; a **body**, which may be one or several paragraphs and which develops and supports the controlling idea; and a **conclusion**, which be may one or several paragraphs and which restates the main point and perhaps challenges the reader to act. Each part of the essay should consist of paragraphs with clear topic sentences and relevant supporting details and examples, all of which help to develop the thesis.

How you select and arrange your details will depend on what your purpose is. In some cases, you'll want to arrange ideas and events chronologically or to determine causal relationships; in others, you may want to organize points comparatively or according to a classification system. If you have a good outline, your organizational plan should already be in place and you will be almost ready to write the first draft.

DETERMINING PURPOSE AND UNDERSTANDING AUDIENCE

Before you begin drafting, you should ask yourself: Why am I writing this essay? What do I hope to accomplish? You may be writing to share an important lesson you learned—about the power of illusion and its impact within a family, as the writer of "Shattered Illusions" did; you may be writing to inform—of the dangers associated with body piercing, perhaps; or you may be writing to convince someone to see things your way—to reject capital punishment, for example, or to support drilling for oil in the Alaskan wilderness.

Focusing on the purpose for your writing is something you should do at the very beginning of the process, once you've come up with a subject and begun to develop a thesis. You should come back to the question several times during the process so that you never lose sight of your reason for writing and your goal.

Considering your **audience** is often critical to your success as a writer. Sometimes you won't have a specific audience, especially in papers such as those assigned in classes, which often function primarily as exercises. In such cases, assume an academic audience that knows something about both the subject and the conventions of writing and that has high expectations—but is probably objective. (Don't assume your audience is only your instructor: You'll find yourself trying to second-guess the values and beliefs and expectations of someone about whom you probably know little, and you'll probably make wrong assumptions about the kind of language or tone the instructor expects.) If you are writing a letter to the editor of a large newspaper or writing an article for a newspaper, you can assume that you are writing for a general audience, united by little other than locale. Neutral language and an impartial tone are necessary to communicate effectively with such an audience.

When you have a specific audience, learn as much about its members as possible. How much do they know about your subject? Are they likely to be hostile? What are their values? Their biases? Knowing the answers to these questions will help you make informed choices in your writing.

Obviously, knowledge of your audience will affect what you say as well as how you say it.

EXERCISE: Analyzing Audience

Write a brief note to each of the following audiences explaining your decision to resign from your job as volunteer coordinator at the local hospital.

- The chief hospital administrator
- The volunteers
- Your best friend
- Your mother, a hospital employee, who got you the job

How do your knowledge and expectations of your audience affect the way you write each of those notes?

FINDING YOUR VOICE AND MANAGING TONE

Your writer's **voice** is your particular style, the language and syntax that is natural for you in your particular writing context. When you use language and syntax that is not your own, your writing will sound artificial. (This happens often when student writers mistakenly assume that their English teachers want them to use "big words" or florid prose.) Write only what you would be comfortable saying and you will find your own voice.

Just as your speaking voice varies in different speaking situations, so will your writing voice adjust to different writing situations—more emphatic here, less direct there. Even so, you should be writing in your own voice.

Tone, the particular language and syntax choices that reveal your attitude, is affected greatly by your subject, your audience, and the particular writing situation. While your writer's voice is constant, your tone changes often. Look again at the notes you wrote. The tone in a note to your mother, who may be disappointed in your resignation as volunteer coordinator, is likely to be more cautious than the tone in a note to your best friend, with whom you have no misgivings about being honest or venting your frustrations. The language will be different; the sentence structure will be different. Slang is likely to make it into your friend's note, but you're apt to be very formal in your letter to the hospital administrator.

WRITING A DRAFT

Now that you've planned and outlined, and taken into consideration your audience and the issues related to it, you're ready to begin writing a draft, a task that at this stage should not be too difficult. Like so many processes, much of the work is in the preparation.

2 | WRITING ANALYTICALLY

In the introduction to his short story "The Murders in the Rue Morgue," Edgar Allan Poe defines analysis as "that . . . activity which *disentangles*"—and then he presents the murder mystery as an illustration of this principle. Here are some of the grisly details: Two women are found brutally murdered in their house on Rue Morgue, by a perpetrator who seems to have superhuman strength and who apparently escaped from the scene of the crime even though the windows and doors are locked *from the inside*. Convinced that the police are looking too closely at the details to see the whole picture, C. Auguste Dupin, Poe's famous detective, solves the mystery by looking at the evidence from a different angle, allowing for the possibility that the murderer is not *super*human but, in fact, *non*human. Dupin's ability to think outside of the box, as we would say, has become a defining trait for scores of literary detectives, such as Agatha Christie's Hercule Poirot, who repeatedly boasts that he solves crimes with "the little gray cells of the mind."

Even though the writing we do in composition classes rarely solves murder mysteries, we can learn a good deal from these famous detectives: Both of them start by looking at the *evidence*, the factual details of a case. In addition, both detectives strive to look beyond the obvious; whereas lesser minds often jump to hasty conclusions before they have properly evaluated the facts, Dupin and Poirot try to find an explanation that will connect *all* the pieces of the puzzle, not just some. Most importantly, both detectives approach their cases with a fresh, unprejudiced mind, relying only on factual evidence and their "little gray cells" to disentangle the mystery.

ANALYSIS is the act of breaking a whole into its parts to facilitate further study; its goal is deeper understanding. And analysis isn't the sole prerogative of detectives, either. All of us break down things to understand them: Auto mechanics perform analyses when they test various functions of cars to determine their problems; laboratory technologists analyze blood samples by observing microscopically the different components in blood; bank loan officers analyze your credit-worthiness by breaking down your whole financial picture, looking closely at various aspects—your income, your debts, your assets, your credit history. Like detectives, these people examine bits and pieces of a "case" to solve a problem or to make a decision; in other words, they **read** the evidence.

READING ANALYTICALLY: THE KEY TO WRITING ANALYTICALLY

In Chapter 1, we talked about the importance of reading critically, which involves careful analysis. To analyze a text, you must do more than simply read it. You must look at and understand its individual parts if you are going to truly understand the sum of its parts, the whole. Analysis is rarely possible in one reading. To really understand a text, you have to **read it more than once**. As you reread, you'll begin to notice particular characteristics—perhaps repeated words or phrases, allusions to other texts, technical jargon, or a tone that reveals the writer's attitude. To keep track of these details, you should always **read with your pen**: Make notes in the margins (unless, of course, you are reading a library book, in which case you will have to use another note-taking method); put a star next to key passages; circle words you may need to look up and references to other texts you may need to research; write questions when you disagree or don't understand. **Read skeptically**, even when you find yourself agreeing with the writer; play "devil's advocate" so that you look at the issue from different perspectives. Consider carefully the writer's **introduction and conclusion**. If you don't get the writer's main point in the introduction, look again at the conclusion: Almost all writers will reiterate their key ideas in their final paragraphs. A piece's **title** often offers important clues to the writer's intent; it may put a particular spin on an interpretation, offer an irony, or establish an attitude. A simple **publication date** may load a work with historical significance. (Consider how knowing that an essay criticizing parents for dividing children's chores along traditional gender lines was published in 1955 instead of, say, 1995 would color your response to it.) Understanding a writer's intended **audience** also helps a reader understand the writer's purpose, the reasons for particular choices. As you become a more sophisticated reader, you will also detect characteristics that reveal a writer's tone and attitude. You'll see how **language choices** and **sentence length and patterns** contribute to a written work's impact. Finally, your analysis—and your understanding—deepen as you **discuss your responses** and interpretations with other readers and **read additional works** about the subject or by the author of the text.

Knowing how to analyze a text you are reading will make you a better writer; writing well always involves analysis. You must understand your subject—whether it be the secrets of your heart or gun control or rhetorical technique in Martin Luther King Jr.'s "I Have a Dream" speech—if you're going to write effectively about it. You must be able to write specifically, to break the subject into its parts. Your subject may be a written text or you may use several written texts to analyze a social problem or construct an argument; your "text" may in fact be something other than a written work—an experience, a painting, an advertisement, a movie. How you separate the components and then make connections between individual parts will color your larger understanding, help you draw conclusions, and determine the success of your expression.

Sometimes the "text" you read is your own experience or that of others: A written record of some events—in journals and diaries or family genealogies—may exist, but the experience may not be written down at all. Before writing about an experience, it is important that you read it as analytically as you would if you were working with a written text.

Consider as an example the essay "Shattered Illusions" (Chapter 1, "Getting Started"). The writer does not simply tell what happened after her parents divorced, compare her life before and after, or describe her feelings. She does all those things—she *analyzes* her experience—and draws conclusions about the larger impact of her parents' divorce on her and the universal truths about coming of age that she discovers. In that way, the piece transcends the mere recording of her personal history, a diary entry, and has significance for others in a way that a diary entry never could.

WRITING ANALYTICALLY: MAKING SENSE OF YOUR EVIDENCE

Like the famous literary detectives Dupin and Poirot, writers start by looking at the *evidence*, the things they know about a subject. If you are going to analyze a significant experience in your life (as the writer of "Shattered Illusions" does), your evidence may be mostly in your head: your memory of events and the feelings they inspired in you. If your history professor asks you to analyze the causes of the Civil War, however, you will have to gather facts and evidence in the library before you can evaluate them. Then, you may use any of a number of prewriting techniques introduced in Chapter 1 ("Getting Started") to start putting your ideas—whether you're transcribing memories or organizing research—on paper and begin making sense of your evidence. In both assignments, you will present the conclusions you draw from looking at the evidence in your thesis and topic sentences. Remember, though, that serious writers rarely start with conclusions and then look for "evidence" to back them up, a method that perpetuates prejudices (judgments formed without looking at the facts) and usually does not provide answers to genuine questions.

EXERCISE: Analyzing an Experience

Consider an experience in your life that changed everything—changed the way you viewed yourself, others, the world. "Read" and analyze it, looking for deeper meaning and broader significance, and write a brief essay explaining the significance of the event or experience.

WRITING ANALYTICALLY: UNDERSTANDING METHODS

Description, narration, and exemplification (discussed in Chapter 4) are ways of *telling* and *showing* your reader what you want to communicate. **Comparing** and **contrasting**, **examining causal relationships**, and **defining** are ways of *thinking*, methods of analysis.

COMPARISON-CONTRAST Humans naturally compare. We set people, things, and events next to those we are familiar with and observe similarities and distinctions to better understand ourselves and the world. We compare and contrast to each other what we don't know as well, in an effort to make informed judgments and come to informed conclusions. We do it when we buy cars, when we choose medical treatments, when we weigh job opportunities—almost any time we make choices or judgments. Writers use the method all the time: Almost every essay in this book uses comparison and contrast in some way (although sometimes it is so subtle or casual that you might not detect it—and that is usually the mark of a good writer). The methods a writer uses need not announce themselves to the reader. Since there is no reason to do comparison and contrast for its own sake and since it is always done to serve some other goal, comparison and contrast shouldn't be a self-conscious writing method.

Take, for example, the essay "Shattered Illusions," introduced in Chapter 1. In narrating her experience *before and after* her parents' divorce, the writer naturally contrasts the two periods; in that sense, much of her essay is concerned with comparing and contrasting. Although the comparison and contrast is embedded in the narrative, it is not the point of the paper, which is something much more important than the fact that the writer's life changed after her parents divorced.

Writers use two basic methods to compare and contrast: **block-by-block**, in which they discuss one subject of comparison first and then discuss the second, treating similar points or elements within each block, or **point-by-point**, which relates each point of comparison to other points before moving to discussion of the next point. Sometimes readers mix both types of organization, comparing-contrasting partly in blocks, partly according to points.

The organization used in "Shattered Illusions" is block-by-block.

Block-by-Block Comparison

Block 1: Pre-divorce

- Dad drove me to and from school
- We played basketball
- We spent weekends cooking, sharing meals at home
- Dad lived in a spacious, well-furnished family home

Block 2: Post-divorce

- I joined a car pool
- We no longer played basketball
- We spent weekends at the zoo, mall, movies
- Dad lived in a cramped, sparsely furnished apartment

If the writer had chosen to tell her story using point-by-point organization, the structure would be different.

Point-by-Point Comparison

Point 1: Transportation to school

- Pre-divorce: Dad
- Post-divorce: Car pool

Point 2: Father-daughter recreation

- Pre-divorce: Driveway basketball
- Post-divorce: No basketball

Point 3: Weekend activities

- Pre-divorce: Family meals at home
- Post-divorce: Father-daughter zoo, mall, movies

Point 4: Dad's living quarters

- Pre-divorce: Spacious, well-furnished family home and yard
- Post-divorce: Cramped, sparsely furnished apartment

Sometimes we use comparison-contrast to highlight distinctions; at other times we want to emphasize similarities. Start with the one you don't want to highlight. For example, if you want to establish common ground among neighbors feuding over a zoning issue, you may first want to establish the differences of opinion and then point to the ways in which you agree, emphasizing your similarities and ending on a positive note. But if you want to underscore the radical differences between homeschooling and private schooling to promote the former, you should begin by discussing the similarities—educational goals, close teacher-student relationships, lack of discipline problems—and then move to the bulk of your discussion, contrasting the two methods of educating children.

EXERCISE: Examining Comparison-Contrast Analysis

Read Roland Barthes's "A World of Wrestling" (p. 682). What parts of the essay involve comparison-contrast analysis? What kind of organization does Barthes use? What is the point of his comparison?

CAUSE-EFFECT Causal analysis examines the reasons for and the results of certain phenomena; it explains why something happens and predicts what else might happen. Because, as humans, we are always trying to understand why things happen, in order to either prevent them from happening again or make sure that they do, we are constantly exploring causal relationships. Thus, writers, whose realm is examination, discovery, and exploration, are natural cause-and-effect seekers. Causal analysis can be tricky, however. Be careful not to oversimplify or to confuse time sequence with causal relationships.

- Distinguish between causes and *influences.*
- Understand the possibility (and likelihood) of *more than one* cause.
- Know the difference between indirect and obvious causes.
- Know the difference between remote and immediate causes.
- Never assume that because one thing precedes another, it *causes* it.

Look again at "Shattered Illusions" (Chapter 1), the essay penned by a child of divorce. Throughout the essay, she enumerates the effects of her parents' divorce on each family member. Part of the point of the essay is to show how she had made a serious error in attributing to a faulty cause (her mother's "selfishness") the breakup of her parents' marriage. Part of her final "epiphany"—after discovering that her father's affair was a more immediate cause of the divorce— is the realization that her mother and her father were not the people she thought they were. The purpose of her narrative is not to explore the causes of her parents' divorce, but she does employ causal analysis (albeit perhaps simplistic— many other factors could have contributed to the deterioration of the marriage) in pursuit of her larger writing goal.

On the other hand, in "The Greening of Tony Soprano" (p. 692) Jeremiah Creedon's goal is to discover causes: He tries to get at the root of the television mob boss's psychic distress, to find out "what's wrong with Tony Soprano." After rejecting standard therapeutic explanations as well as Soprano's own psychiatrist's focus on family issues, Creedon points to a less obvious (and thus more interesting) reason: Soprano's disconnection from the natural world. In his last sentence, Creedon answers his introductory question and suggests a cause for our collective psychosocial ills: "We have to admit we're pretty much accomplices in the most dangerous form of organized crime today—our ruthless shakedown of the planet."

> **EXERCISE:** Identifying Causes and Effects

Think about a pivotal decision in your life. Make a list of all the causes, and try to determine the chief cause. Then make a list of the effects of that decision. Can you glean a lesson from the causal relationships? Come up with an idea for a personal experience essay.

DEFINITION   A definition explains a term or concept; it differentiates the term from others, and reveals its nuances. Writers rely on definitions not simply to explain words or phrases a reader may not know but often, in the case of **extended definition**, to expand on conventional definitions or limited understanding of words, phrases, or subjects, to illuminate concepts that are misunderstood or changing. An extended definition is analysis in that it explores its subject in depth, breaking it into parts and looking at relationships between those parts in addition to the subject's external relationships. Often dictionary definitions don't suffice. Consider the way some common terms—*love, family, feminism, patriotism*—are tossed about indiscriminately but, upon closer examination, mean very different things to the people using them. What, for example, does it mean to be *Jewish? Handicapped? Old?* The writer who attempts to define these terms broadens our understanding beyond the superficial or predictable.

In writing definitions, particularly extended ones, writers use other forms of analysis and various strategies for development. And while definition may indeed be the ultimate goal of a piece of writing, it is often used for some other purpose.

Consider again the writer of "Shattered Illusions." She begins her essay with a brief, English-teacher definition of *epiphany;* the point of that definition is, ostensibly, to clarify for her readers an unfamiliar term. But the essay is also an extended definition of *illusion,* and the subtlety of the narrative lies in the writer's use of the extended definition to discover *for herself* the nature of illusion. Again, the point of the essay is not to define "illusion," but to show how illusions can shape reality in important ways. For her, the gradual defining of *illusion,* the swapping it out with what she thought was *truth,* facilitates her growing up and her looking at the world from a different perspective.

Malcolm Gladwell's purpose in "The Physical Genius" (p. 765) is to define (or redefine) *genius,* expanding the definition beyond our traditional notion of a mental giant to include a person whose gift lies in motor skills as much as in mind. He begins by defining what genius is *not*—"something that can be ascribed to a single factor, a physical version of I.Q." He then demonstrates what physical genius *is,* supporting his points through three elaborate examples, neurosurgeon Charlie Wilson, star hockey player Wayne Gretzky, and cello virtuoso Yo-Yo Ma.

EXERCISE: Reading Definitions

Read Laura Pfefferle's "On Marriage: Lessons from a Work-in-Progress" (p. 152) What traditional definition of *marriage* does she refute? How does she define *marriage*? What methods of analysis and strategies of development does she use in her definition of marriage?

EXERCISE: Analyzing a Written Text

Choose one of the selections from Part 2 and analyze the writer's techniques. Start by summarizing what the writer says; then look at the methods and strategies the writer uses to make his or her points.

EXPANDED EXERCISE: Analyzing Two Hogarth Prints

Let's practice analysis as we examine two eighteenth-century engravings, William Hogarth's "Gin Lane" and "Beer Street" (pp. 22–23). Hogarth, a painter and printmaker who looked very carefully at the society he lived in, created two very different street scenes in these pictures.

Step 1. Finding Details

The first step in every analysis is to gather evidence, so look at the two pictures carefully and note the details in each. Make a list of the things you see in each picture. Your lists could start like this:

"Gin Lane"

- the woman in the foreground looks disheveled

- her baby is falling off the stairs; she does not pay attention

- (continue . . .)

"Beer Street"

- the two men on the left have big bellies

- there is a crate of books in the lower right corner

- (continue . . .)

Step 2. Discovering Meaning

As you look at your lists of details, it should be obvious that "Gin Street" and "Beer Lane" depict two very different neighborhoods and that your task calls for comparing and contrasting. Even though people in our century might think differently, people in Hogarth's time considered beer a very wholesome, healthy drink and gin a dangerous, addictive substance—similar to the way crack cocaine is viewed in our society. At the bottom of each picture, Hogarth's opinion of these two beverages appears in short poems. What do these verses suggest?

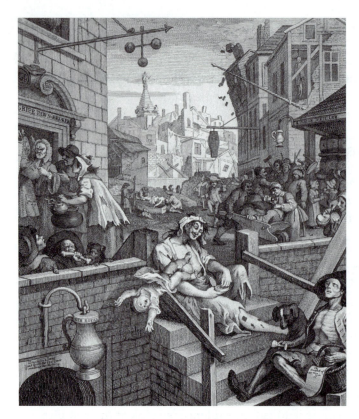

Gin cursed Fiend, with Fury
  fraught,
Makes human Race a Prey,
It enters by a deadly Draught,
And steals our life away.

Virtue and Truth, driv'n to
  Despair
It's Rage compels to fly
But cherishes, with hellish
  Care,
Theft, Murder, Perjury.

Damn'd Cup! that on the
  Vitals preys,
That liquid Fire contains
Which Madness to the Heart
  conveys,
And rolls it thro' the Veins.

Now that you know how Hogarth and his contemporaries viewed beer and gin, look at the list of details you drew up and note how each detail supports this attitude. Your lists could look like this:

"Gin Lane"

- the woman in the foreground looks disheveled (gin leads to poverty)
- her baby is falling off the stairs; she does not pay attention (gin causes women to neglect their children . . .)

"Beer Street"

- the two men on the left have big bellies (beer is nourishing)
- there is a crate of books in the lower right corner (beer drinkers are interested in learning . . .)

Step 3. Seeing a Pattern

As you look at your evidence, try to determine the areas of social life Hogarth comments on in these pictures: for example, "nutrition" and "building mainte-nance." Note how the artist's rendering of detail in these areas reveals contrast-ing patterns such as the abundance of ill-looking, starving people in "Gin Lane" and the obvious signs of prosperity on "Beer Street." From your lists of evidence, can you identify other social aspects upon which Hogarth comments in each pic-ture? How is the commentary different in each picture?

Beer, Happy Produce of our
    Isle
Can sinewy Strength impart,
And wearied with Fatigue and
    Toil
Can cheer each manly Heart.

Labor and Art upheld by Thee
Successfully advance,
We quaff the balmy Juice with
    Glee
And Water leave to France.

Genius of Health, the grateful
    Taste
Rivals the Cup of Jove,
And warms each English
    generous Breast
With Liberty and Love.

Step 4. Writing About Your Discoveries

When you write an analytical paper, your thesis presents the major conclusion you have come to about the subject you have studied. In a picture analysis such as this, your goal is to interpret (and explain to your reader) the artist's opinion on the subject.

Before we look at possible thesis statements, let's look at **what a thesis is not**:

A thesis is not a title.

Beer Street and Gin Lane
The Devil in the Gin Bottle
The Blessings of Beer

A title indicates the subject of an essay and often hints at its thesis, but it cannot take the place of the thesis.

A thesis is not an announcement of what you are going to do in your essay.

"In the following pages, I will compare and contrast 'Beer Street' and 'Gin Lane,' two engravings by the eighteenth-century artist William Hogarth."

"I will demonstrate that Hogarth sees gin as a dangerous drink."

Although a preview of the points you are going to make in the body of your essay can help your reader understand its overall structure, the preview cannot take the place of a thesis.

A thesis is not a statement of fact.

"Gin and beer are alcoholic beverages."

"People on Beer Street look healthy."

"There is a dead body in the foreground of Gin Lane."

Whereas facts provide the development of your paper as you demonstrate to your reader how your evidence has led you to the conclusions you present, facts cannot take the place of thesis statements.

So what is a good thesis? Besides being none of the above, **a good thesis reveals the writer's position. A good thesis is specific**; it makes a clear point about a clearly defined subject. **A good thesis is also complete**; it makes a point about the entire subject you have studied, not just a part of it. Keeping in mind that your task in this exercise is to write a comparative analysis of "Gin Lane" and "Beer Street," which of the following thesis statements suggests the writer's position and is specific and complete?

Gin is bad; beer is good.

Hogarth's pictures illustrate the devastating social consequences of gin addiction and contrast them to the healthy qualities of beer.

Stay away from gin; drink beer instead.

In his pictures, Hogarth tries to alert his audience to the dangers of gin.

Hogarth's "Beer Street" is an eighteenth-century version of a beer commercial.

FIND YOUR OWN THESIS AND TOPIC SENTENCES. Whereas your thesis expresses your main point about your subject, your **topic sentences** spell out various aspects of your topic, all of which support your thesis. Look at the list you made when you performed step 3 of this exercise. State your discoveries about nutrition, building maintenance, and/or the areas you have decided to look at in your own analysis as complete sentences and you will have your topic sentences.

PUTTING IT ALL TOGETHER. Your thesis and your **topic sentences** form the backbone of your essay. Your evidence will provide the "meat" attached to those bones. Your thesis should be part of your introduction (even though there is no law that says it has to be the last sentence in the first paragraph); your topic sentences should start your body paragraphs to help your reader understand which aspect of your topic each paragraph covers (although the topic sentence is not necessarily always the lead sentence in the paragraph). The evidence you present in each paragraph will show your reader how you came to the conclusion presented in the thesis and topic sentences. In a way, writing is a form of **"show and tell"**: The thesis and topic sentences do the telling, and the evidence does the showing.

In this chapter, we've examined several methods of analysis, and you've tried your hand at several of them. By now, you probably see that analysis involves a variety of skills and strategies, and that it is at the heart of any meaningful writing. We have directed you several times to the same essay, "Shattered Illusions," to make an important point: writers employ various methods of analysis in a single work. They determine *what* they want to say before they decide how to say it; they use narration to tell their stories, with description and examples to help illustrate them. They draft and revise and edit.

A FEW WORDS ABOUT DRAFTING AND REVISION

Many beginning writers have the mistaken notion that they can write successfully in one sitting, in a single draft. But in fact, most seasoned writers produce several drafts before they're satisfied. It often takes several drafts before a writer decides which organization, which approaches, and which techniques are most effective. Often it takes several drafts before writers discover what they really want to say.

Don't be afraid to revise, to tinker, to perfect: Revision usually results in improvement and refinement. You should consider your writing—your expression of yourself—as worthy of improvement as anything else you do. Just as you would rearrange the furniture if you weren't happy with a room, you may need to rearrange sentences or paragraphs, take something out or add something to your writing.

As a student, you will often get feedback, oral and written, from your instructors and from your peers. Those responses give you some idea of how you're being understood and provide opportunity for revision: for re-seeing, re-reading, re-thinking, and re-writing.

For a look at the whole writing process and an example of how a writer may do a substantive revision of his work—rearrange the furniture, hang a new picture, tidy up, so to speak—see Chapter 6, "A Writer at Work." Pay special attention to the way Travis, a student writer, takes his instructor's remarks and advice and rewrites his paper.

Revision is such an integral part of the writing process that it should be automatic. It should go without saying that anytime this text directs you to write, you should also revise.

3 | WRITING PERSUASIVELY

Except in diaries and private journals, writers strive to convince their readers that what they have to say is valid and true. Even if a subject is personal, writers try to *persuade* their readers to accept the conclusions they have drawn from their experience.

Take, for instance, an essay with the following thesis: "It was only after I changed my negative attitude about family reunions that I enjoyed spending time with my numerous relatives last Thanksgiving." The writer presents the reader with an insight into a personal situation, but it is a situation many of his readers have probably experienced. So by persuading them that one's enjoyment of family reunions depends on a person's attitude, the writer might actually teach readers something they did not know before.

Most writing you do in college and beyond is persuasive. The more radical an idea is, the more persuasion it will take to convince your reader that your opinion is valid and respectable. As a rule, avoid writing about subjects in which the arguments are obvious. "We should all be a bit nicer to other people" is a tired topic—who wouldn't agree, at least in theory? "Women should have the same voting rights as men" may have been a very controversial thesis a hundred years ago; however, when women were granted suffrage by constitutional amendment in 1920, the subject became a "has-been," at least where political debate is concerned. To persuade readers to see matters their way, writers have several techniques at their disposal. Note that these techniques rarely occur by themselves: Writers mix them to suit their subjects and their material.

It goes without saying that writers who do not know their subjects well cannot expect their readers to accept what they are saying. Who would buy a product from a vendor who does not know anything about the goods he sells? In a way, writers are merchants of ideas, and they have to prove to their readers that they know what they are talking about if they want to "make a sale." If you are going to be successful as a writer, you must *demonstrate that you are an authority on your subject.*

DEMONSTRATING AUTHORITY BY USING LOGIC AND REASON

A skilled writer is always logical and reasonable, relying on fair and ethical persuasive techniques. Before you decide how you are going to present your evidence, you must understand your issue and what kind of evidence it calls for.

Most arguments call for either examples or reasons as primary forms of support although many arguments contain a skillful mix of both. To determine the kind of support essential to proving your argument, examine your thesis. Does it ask you to first *show that something is true?* Or does it ask you to tell *why something is right or wrong?*

In "The Bully in the Mirror" (p. 207), Stephen S. Hall relies primarily on examples and illustrations from his own experience, the experience of Alexander Bregstein, and literature to *show that* adolescent boys are just as susceptible to negative body image as girls are. In "In Defense of Prejudice" (p. 499), Jonathan Rauch gives reasons, illustrated with examples, to *tell why* it is impossible to eradicate prejudice by legislating what people can and cannot say. If you are arguing that capital punishment should be abolished or that abortion is wrong, you will rely on reasons to *tell why* they are wrong.

Avoid logical errors:

- When relying on evidence—in examples, reports, statistics—make sure that you do not oversimplify or overgeneralize. Do not rely on a single example to prove a point; do not assume that your experience with the police, for example, proves a generalization about police.

- Do not assume that your opinions will automatically convince your reader just because they are important to *you;* you have to make a case for an opinion if you want your reader to "buy" it. Also, do not confuse restatement of your opinion with real support.

- Do not get diverted from the issue, arguing, for example, that someone would be a bad school board member because her brother is a drug addict.

DEMONSTRATING AUTHORITY BY USING EXAMPLES

Imagine that your best friend is about to make a huge mistake—a mistake that you have made yourself. How would you try to keep your friend from being foolish? You would tell him or her your own story and point out the benefits of avoiding the same mistake. Having been in the situation yourself makes you a kind of authority on the subject, one whose advice your friend may take. The same is true for your authority as a writer: If you can demonstrate to your reader that you have "been there, done that," your reader will be much more likely to accept what you have to say about your subject.

Besides convincing your reader that you know something about your subject, a good story of what happened to you or to somebody you know will give your essay "human interest." We all like to hear stories about other people, and if you can weave them into your essay, your reader will not be bored and will keep listening to what you have to say.

Some of the readings in this book are built almost entirely on personal experience. In "Carnal Acts" (p. 228), Nancy Mairs tells her readers how she has learned to live with multiple sclerosis, a debilitating disease. By her own admission, she wants her testimony of her struggles and victories to encourage others to break the barrier of embarrassed silence about the dysfunctions of their own bodies. The vivid (and not always pleasant) details she offers about her life with MS convince her readers that she knows what she is talking about and make them trust the conclusions she draws from her experience.

DEMONSTRATING AUTHORITY BY USING EVIDENCE FROM SOURCES

Granted, personal experience is a powerful agent in persuading your reader. But what if you are writing on a subject about which you have no personal experience (and do not want it, either)—drug addiction, let's say, or criminal justice, football, or terminal diseases? Writers who find they do not know a lot about their topics research them, which means they talk to people who have personal experience or they read what others have written on the subject. Using sources is a characteristic of academic writing, but it exists in journalistic writing as well.

Look at Stephen S. Hall's "The Bully in the Mirror" (p. 207). In his account of teenage boys' obsession with their body image, Hall combines the story of Alexander Bregstein, one of the boys he talks to in a gym, his own experiences, and the opinions of various experts on the subject:

> When you hear girls gawking at Abercrombie & Fitch about how hot the guy is on the bag—that makes an impression," Alexander told me one night on the phone.
>
> The "guy on the bag" turned out to be an exceptionally cute youth not wearing a shirt. "If I look this way," Alexander said, "I've got my foot in the door." This very heterosexual impulse, however, was elicited by a school of advertising whose genealogy follows a risque and decidedly homoerotic lineage.
> [Here follows a description of a Calvin Klein commercial]
> I don't think of myself as culturally squeamish, but the ad struck me as so creepy that when I screened it at home recently, I became concerned that my 15-month-old son, toddling around the room, might be paying attention. "The style, the look, the leering tone, even the 'chicken hawk' voice-over—Klein mimicked, closely, the style and tone of cheap basement gay pornography," says Bob Garfield, a columnist at Advertising Age and a longtime critic of what he calls Klein's "shockvertising" approach. If it is true, Garfield adds, that these commercials influence how boys think about their bodies, it reflects in part "the opening up of gay culture, where male objectification has almost nearly the effect that the objectification of females has had for time immemorial for women.

PERSUADING READERS BY SHOWING THAT YOU KNOW YOUR AUDIENCE

Do you remember the last time you had to "beg" something of your parents—to use the family car, for instance, or to extend your curfew? When you made your pitch, you probably used techniques that you knew would get you what you wanted, and, most likely, you approached your mom differently than you did your dad. Or, let's say, you have the difficult task of making a speech about abortion to a Catholic congregation or to the National Association of Women: Regardless of your opinion on the subject, you would go about persuading these two audiences in very different ways. The most important and probably most difficult skill in writing is to anticipate who will read your writing and to judge your writing from the reader's point of view.

Let us look at a couple of examples: Roland Barthes, a French scholar, addresses a very academic audience in his essay "The World of Wrestling" (p. 682). He assumes that his audience has the same solid education in French literature that he has and thus will be interested in the connections he draws between (neo)classical theater and amateur wrestling:

> There are people who think that wrestling is an ignoble sport. Wrestling is not a sport, it is a spectacle, and it is no more ignoble to attend a wrestled performance of Suffering than a performance of the sorrows of Arnolphe or Andromaque [both characters from neoclassical French plays].

Barbara Ehrenreich, on the other hand, has long been writing columns for *Time* and other magazines. Even though "Spudding Out" (p. 700), an essay about the influence of television on family life, is anything but shallow, her writing style indicates that she writes for an audience much less academic than that of Barthes.

> My husband was the first in the family to "spud out," as the expression now goes. Soon everyone wanted one of those zip-up "Couch Potato Bags," to keep warm during David Letterman. The youngest, and most thoroughly immobilized, member of the family relies on a remote that controls his TV, stereo, and VCR, and can also shut down the neighbor's pacemaker at fifteen yards.

PERSUADING READERS BY ESTABLISHING COMMON GROUND

Once you know who your readers are, you can anticipate their values and their ways of thinking and integrate them into your persuasive battle plan. You can, for instance, establish common ground with your readers whenever possible by pointing out the issues on which you and they agree. The message you send to your audience is something like, "We both really want the same thing, so you should consider my method of getting it."

Nancy Gibbs, in "If We Have it, Do We Use It?" (p. 409) takes a negative view on the prospect of enhancing an unborn child's intelligence through genetic engineering. Knowing that she is writing for the vast middle-class readership of *Time* magazine, an audience of people who believe in progress and want to give their children all the advantages they possibly can, she has to appeal to another value they hold equally sacred:

> The broader concern is one of fairness. Will such enhancement be available to everyone or only to those who can afford it? . . . If, as a parent, you haven't mortgaged the house to enhance your children, what sort of parent does that make you? Will a child one day be able to sue her parents for failing to do everything they could do for her?

PERSUADING READERS BY MOBILIZING THEIR EMOTIONS

Although many writers would rather not admit that their persuasive strategies are directed toward anything other than the readers' intelligence and reason, emotion is a powerful ingredient in persuasive approaches. The advertising industry (and the economy based on it) depends on advertisers' ability to manipulate the consumers' emotions. So does propaganda, a form of writing that appeals to the audience's feelings, not minds. Granted, ethical analytical and persuasive writing shies away from the overuse of emotional appeals, but a little emotion, carefully applied, can enliven and strengthen your appeal to your reader.

What exactly happens when writers mobilize their readers' emotions? Rather than just telling what something feels like, writers try to recreate this feeling for the readers through their words. Look at an excerpt from Scott Russell Sanders's "Under the Influence" (p. 295), an essay about his father's alcoholism. His purpose in this paragraph is to make the reader feel the misery of a child who somehow blames himself for his father's addiction:

> Left alone, our father prowls the house, thumping into furniture, rummaging in the kitchen, slamming doors, turning the pages of the newspaper with a savage crackle, muttering back at the late-night drivel from television. The roof might fly off, the walls might buckle from the pressure of his rage. Whatever my brother and sister and mother may be thinking on their own rumpled pillows, I lie there hating him, loving him, fearing him, knowing I have failed him. I tell myself he drinks to ease an ache that gnaws at his belly, an ache I must have caused by disappointing him somehow, a murderous ache I should be able to relieve by doing all my chores, earning A's in school, winning baseball games, fixing the broken washer and the burst

pipes, bringing in money to fill his empty wallet. He would not hide the green bottles in his tool box, would not sneak off to the barn with a lump under his coat, would not fall asleep in the daylight, would not roar and fume, would not drink himself to death, if only I were perfect.

PERSUADING READERS BY ANTICIPATING POSSIBLE OBJECTIONS

Another advantage of knowing your audience is being able to anticipate and "shoot down" (or refute) objections they may raise. "I know what you're going to say," you tell your reader, "and I have thought about it, and I have an answer to your objection."

Paul Keegan, in "Culture Quake" (p. 436), does exactly this when he attacks those who claim that the violence kids experience while playing "shooter" computer games "doesn't transfer over to reality":

> But how could it not? If media doesn't affect real-world behavior, there would be no such thing as advertising, which at last count was a $25 billion international business.

When Jonathan Rauch rejects arguments in favor of speech code laws in "In Defense of Prejudice" (p. 499), he points out how his opponents get so carried away battling verbal violence that they forget about physical violence:

> The fear engendered by [hate words] is real. The remedy is as clear and as imperfect as ever: protect citizens against violence. This, I grant, is something that American society has never done very well and now does quite poorly. It is no solution to define words as violence or prejudice as oppression, and then by cracking down on words or thoughts pretend that we are doing something about violence and oppressions. No doubt it is easier to pass a speech code or hate-crime laws and proclaim the streets safer than actually to make the streets safer, but the one must never be confused with the other.

ARRANGING IDEAS EFFECTIVELY

If we think of a writer as a seller of ideas who has to persuade his or her audience to "buy" the writer's opinion on a subject, we cannot ignore marketing strategies in the process. Anybody who has ever worked in retail knows that it is not just the product that is important or the seller's knowledge about that product, but also how that product is displayed in the shop. Does the product look attractive? Is it placed in such a way that customers are drawn to it? Writers have similar concerns when they set about marketing their ideas. Good writers take great pains to organize and present their material effectively.

Many textbooks give advice on organizing material: "Start with your weakest point and end with your strongest," some say. "Start with a 'bang' and then present your weaker material," others recommend. Some writers arrange their material so they can easily bridge from one point to the next, making their essay "flow" seamlessly from beginning to end; some writers like to juxtapose different points, counting on the effectiveness of the contrast. Unfortunately, there is no one formula that will work for every writer and every writing task; the only way to find out what works best for a particular essay is to arrange and rearrange your material until you are satisfied. Your subject, the degree of controversy, your desire to maintain suspense or to surprise—any or all of these factors may influence the way you present your ideas. It helps to let different people (peers, teachers) read your various drafts and comment on your organization.

The best way to learn to arrange your material effectively is to look at how experienced writers do it. By analyzing their organization, you may pick up some tricks of the trade that will make your own writing more professional and effective.

PRESENTING IDEAS DRAMATICALLY

When you present your evidence, do so by varying strategies: Mix direct speech with reported speech, long sentences with short, statements with occasional questions. Nothing turns a reader off more than eternal sameness in a writer's style. In her essay about what it is like to live with multiple sclerosis, Nancy Mairs makes her readers feel what it is like to be overlooked by those around her because she is seated on an electric scooter that helps her move about. Note how she uses different sentence types, and how she mixes statements with direct speech:

> At the same time, paradoxically, it [the scooter] renders me invisible, reducing me to the height of a seven-year-old, with a child's attendant low status. "Would she like smoking or nonsmoking?" the gate agent assigning me a seat asks the friend traveling with me. In crowds I see nothing but buttocks. I can tell you the name of every type of designer jeans ever sold. The wearers, eyes front, trip over me and fall across my handlebars into my lap. "Hey!" I want to shout to the lofty world. "Down here! There's a person down here!" But I'm not, by their standards, quite a person anymore.

A less accomplished writer than Nancy Mairs could have **told** her readers what it is like to be invisible; instead, Mairs chooses to **show** them what she experiences every day; she puts them right in the middle of her experience, and tells them, at the end of the paragraph, what this experience amounts to. This is dramatic presentation of evidence.

USING HUMOR AND IRONY

Humor is another way to "package" ideas. "If I can make you laugh," the writer seems to tell the reader, "you and I are friends, and friends agree with each other." Or, if writers use **irony**, a technique of saying the opposite of what they believe, readers become accomplices because they are in on the joke. However, be careful when you decide to use humor: Just as the corny jokes of the stereotypical used-car salesman turn off rather than attract potential customers, humor in writing can communicate the idea that a writer either is not serious about the subject or is trying to camouflage his or her ignorance. Also, keep in mind that certain (serious) subjects—such as abortion, for instance, or the death penalty—do not lend themselves to humorous treatment.

When it works, though, humor can greatly leaven a point or cast a new light on a commonplace idea. Natalie Kusz, in her essay "Ring Leader" (p. 223), recalls the embarrassment she suffered in school because she was overweight. Although her point has been made by many before her, it comes to life through her skillful use of humor:

> The rest of my anatomy did nothing to help matters. I come from a long line of famine-surviving ancestors—on my father's side, Polish and Russian, on my mother's everything from Irish to French Canadian—and thus I have an excellent, thrifty, Ebenezer Scrooge of a metabolism. I can ingest but a single calorie, and before quitting time at the Scrooge office, my system will have spent that calorie to replace an old blood cell, to secrete a vital hormone, to send a few chemicals around the old nervous system, and still have enough left over to deposit ten fat cells in my inner thigh—a nifty little investment for the future, in case the Irish potato famine ever recurs. These metabolic wonders are delightful if you are planning a move to central Africa, but for an American kid wiggling to Jane Fonda as if her life depended on it (which, in high school, it did), the luckiest people on earth seemed to be anorexics, those wispy and hollow-cheeked beings whose primary part in the locker room drama was to stand at the mirror and announce, "My God, I disgust myself, I am *so fat*."

Remember, almost everything you write makes some kind of argument and involves some persuasion on your part, some marketing of your ideas. How you accomplish your task will depend on your writing situation: your purpose, your subject, your audience.

4 DETERMINING STRATEGIES AND APPROACHES

Readers often ask of a writer: "So how do you *know* that what you say is true?" Only fools have opinions—prejudices, rather—on subjects they have not studied. Intelligent people do not form opinions until they have evidence that convinces them one way or the other. The writer's job is to convince the reader, but first, the writer must get the reader to pay attention and to read on. Once writers have assembled their evidence, their supporting details, how do they present it? What strategies do they use for developing essays, for writing introductions and conclusions?

Writers must make a lot of choices based on what they are trying to say, how, and to whom. The readings in this book show a range of strategies and approaches. Most works feature various types of analysis as well as narration, description, and examples.

When you write, you have several strategies at your disposal for convincing your reader of your trustworthiness: You can supply examples, both from personal experience and from your research; you can tell stories, both your own and those of others; and you can describe persons, things, and processes. You will occasionally see an essay that uses only one of these strategies throughout, but most writers mix them as their subjects demand.

MAKING POINTS THROUGH PERSONAL EXAMPLES AND EVIDENCE FROM SOURCES

Examples are specific cases that illustrate a larger principle. Let's say you have noticed that your grandmother led a busy, active life, and she remained sharp as a tack right up to her death at 97. If you observe the same phenomenon in other people's grandparents, you might conclude that older people who lead mentally active lives show fewer signs of senility. Your examples might not prove your point beyond the shadow of a doubt (there might be some elderly people out there, all very active, who develop Alzheimer's), but if you have a few good cases to back up your point, your readers will respect the conclusions you draw from your material; they will be convinced that you did not just make it up. If you can back up your personal examples with scientific studies, you can expand the validity of individual, anecdotal evidence. If, for instance, you can find a medical study based on hundreds or thousands of cases, that makes the same connection between active lives and mental alertness, this source would greatly support your own findings.

Although it will not always be possible, try to combine personal examples with scientific or scholarly evidence. The stories from your own life add color and human interest to your essays because you *know* the people you are talking about; evidence from sources, although often a bit dry, proves that your individual examples are, indeed, representative of larger groups or trends.

You can present a long, detailed example (an **extended example**) or a group of related, **brief examples** for support. (Remember, if you are trying to persuade your audience of the truth of a phenomenon, one example, long or otherwise, will not do it. When you are using examples to prove an argument, you need several.) Make sure that your paragraph always has a topic sentence that spells out the point of your example and that the relationship between your example and your main point is clear; examples rarely speak for themselves.

EXERCISE: Identifying Exemplification Technique

The following paragraphs give examples of how professional writers use examples to support their points. To sharpen your eye for their techniques, underline the topic sentence of each paragraph or write it in the margin, in your own words, if the writer implies rather than states it. Then analyze what type of examples the writer uses (extended or brief, personal or evidence from sources) and how he or she connects the different pieces of evidence:

> The fact is, I grew up ugly—no, worse than that, I grew up *unusual*, that unforgivable sin among youth. We lived in Alaska, where, despite what you might have heard about the Rugged Individualist, teenagers still adhere to the universal rules of conformity: if Popular Patty wears contact lenses, then you will by gum get contacts too, or else pocket those glasses and pray you can distinguish the girls' bathroom door from the boys'. The bad news was that I had only one eye, having lost the other in a dog attack at age seven; so although contacts, at half the two-eyed price, were easy to talk my parents into, I was still left with an eye patch and many facial scars, signs as gaudy as neon, telling everyone, "Here is a girl who is Not Like You." And Not Like Them, remember, was equivalent to Not from This Dimension, only half (maybe one third) as interesting.
>
> —*Natalie Kusz, "Ring Leader" (p. 223)*

> There was always a touch of seediness and sadness to pay phones, and a sense of transience. Drug dealers made calls from them, and shady types who did not want their whereabouts known, and otherwise respectable people planning assignations, and people too poor to have phones of their own. In the movies, any character who used a pay phone was either in trouble or

contemplating a crime. Pay phones came with their own special atmospherics and even accessories sometimes—the predictable bad smells and graffiti, of course, as well as cigarette butts, soda cans, scattered pamphlets from the Jehovah's Witnesses, and single bottles of beer (empty) still in their individual, street-legal paper bags. Mostly, pay phones evoked the mundane: "Honey, I'm just leaving. I'll be there soon." But you could tell that a lot of undifferentiated humanity had flowed through these places, and that in the muteness of each pay phone's little space, wild emotion had howled.

—Ian Frazier, "Dearly Disconnected" (pp. 405–406)

Recent figures on cosmetic surgery indirectly confirm the anecdotal sense that men are going to greater extremes to improve their appearances. Women still account for about 90 percent of all procedures, but the number of men undergoing cosmetic surgery rose about 34 percent between 1996 and 1998, with liposuction being the most sought service. "Basically, men in general are getting the same medicine that women have had to put up with for years, which was trying to match an unattainable ideal in terms of body image," says Pope [Harrison G. Pope Jr. of Harvard Medical School], who has focused his studies on college-age men just past adolescence. "Boys are much more prone at this point to worry about being beefed up, about having muscles," says Mary Pipher, a psychologist and the author of "Reviving Ophelia," a book about adolescent girls. "As we've commodified boys' bodies to sell products, with advertisement that shows boys as bodies without heads, we've had this whole business about focusing on the body." And, she adds, families move so often that teenagers "don't really know each other very well, so the only piece of information that's really accessible is your appearance."

—Stephen S. Hall, "The Bully in the Mirror" (p. 210)

MAKING POINTS THROUGH NARRATION

Narratives are simply stories writers tell to illustrate and support their points; in many cases, personal examples, as described above, take the form of brief narratives. Because we have listened to and told stories ever since we were children, narration comes naturally to most writers. However, sometimes writers forget to tell their readers what point a story supports: They get so carried away by their tales that they forget to remind readers of *why* they are telling a story in the first place. Make sure you always *show* and *tell* in your paragraphs: Specific evidence shows and topic sentences tell the point you are trying to communicate to your reader.

Writers can choose between telling their own stories or those of others; they can integrate direct speech into their stories; they can use one long story in an essay or a collection of brief anecdotes, as their subjects demand.

EXERCISE: Analyzing Narrative Technique

The following passages show how different writers use narrative to develop and support their points. As you read them, identify the stories' sources: Are they from the writers' own lives or from those of other people? Do the writers communicate clearly the overall points of these stories?

> The day of reckoning came in April 1998, during a spring-break vacation in Boca Raton, Fla. As his family was about to leave its hotel room to go to the beach, Alexander, then 15, stood in front of a mirror and just stared at the spectacle of his shirtless torso. "I remember the exact, like *moment* in my mind," he said. "Everything about that room is burned into my head, every little thing. I can tell you where every lamp was, where my father was standing, my mother was sitting. We are about to go out, and I'm looking in this mirror—me, with my gut hanging over my bathing suit—and it was, like: Who would want to look at this? It's part of me, and *I'm* disgusted! That moment, I realized that nobody was giving me a chance to find out who I was because of the way I looked.
>
> —*Stephen S. Hall, "The Bully in the Mirror" (pp. 208–209)*

> Afflicted by the general shame of having a body at all, and the specific shame of having one weakened and misshapen by disease, I ought not to be able to hold my head up in public. And yet I've gotten into the habit of holding my head up in public, sometimes under excruciating circumstances. Recently, for instance, I had to give a reading at the University of Arizona. Having smashed three of my front teeth in a fall onto the concrete floor of my screened porch, I was in the process of getting them crowned, and the temporary crowns flew out during dinner right before the reading. What to do? I wanted, of course, to rush home and hide till the dental office opened the next morning. But I couldn't very well break my word at this last moment. So, looking like Hansel and Gretel's witch, and lisping worse than the Wife of Bath, I got up on stage and read. Somehow, over the years, I've learned how to set shame aside and do what I have to do.
>
> —*Nancy Mairs, "Carnal Acts" (p. 233)*

> Charlie Wilson says that only once in his career has he allowed himself to become emotionally attached to a patient—attached to the point where the patient's death felt like that of a family member. "It was this beautiful girl who had a spinal tumor," he told me. "She was always bringing me cookies. It was a malignant tumor. She became a paraplegic, and then she got married." Wilson was talking softly and slowly. "It just tore me up. I couldn't help myself. I remember operating on her and crying, right there in the O.R." Charlie Wilson is a man who, when he operates, does not permit music or extraneous talking or the noise of beepers or phones, who is attuned to even the slightest hesitation on the part of his scrub nurse, who admits, in his

entire life, to just one day of depression, and who has the audacity and the control to take a No. 11 blade and slice down—just like that—to the basilar artery. But she was young, and it was tragic, and there was nothing he could do, and he has a daughter, too, so perhaps it touched a chord. He was sitting, as he talked, in his office at Moffitt Hospital with his Nike cross-trainers and surgical scrubs, thinking back to a moment when all certitude and composure escaped him. His performance on the day he operated on the girl's spinal tumor must have been compromised by his grief, he admitted. What did it matter? This was not a procedure that required great judgment or technical mastery. "It was an ugly operation," he said, pronouncing the word "ugly" with a special distaste. "Maybe that was part of it." Of course, it was. Charlie Wilson is one of the world's great neurosurgeons because he can fit some beauty in what he does—even in the midst of terrible illness. There was nothing beautiful there. "This lovely, lovely girl." He looked away. "Such a heart."

—Malcolm Gladwell, "The Physical Genius" (pp. 777–778)

MAKING POINTS THROUGH DESCRIPTION

Description paints a picture in words for the reader—a picture of a person, a place, a thing, or a process. As with narration, description never appears for its own sake: It is always part of a larger point a writer is trying to make. A brochure may describe a luxurious hotel room for the purpose of marketing the hotel; the writer of "Shattered Illusions" (p. 4) describes her father's apartment to make the point that his circumstances had been reduced considerably after his divorce from her mother. Writers may use description to establish atmosphere or setting in an introduction or to bring a person's physical presence to a reader. Detailed descriptions may take up quite a bit of space; writers often insert descriptive paragraphs in a larger essay, stating their overall point in the paragraphs surrounding the description.

Technical writers strive for absolute objectivity in their descriptions of machines and mechanical processes; however, writers of essays often select adjectives and other words because of their emotional quality (or their scientific detachment), thus commenting indirectly on the subjects they describe. As you examine the three passages below, you will see how the writers' different word choices put different spins on their detailed descriptions of surgical procedures.

Descriptive writers share a common goal: to paint a clear, precise picture for the reader, to make the reader a secondary eyewitness to what the writer has observed firsthand.

EXERCISE: Analyzing Descriptive Strategies

The three passages below all describe surgical procedures: insertion of a breast implant in the first, and the removal of a brain tumor in the second and third. These writers use adjectives and other words that reveal their attitudes toward their subjects. Underline the descriptive words that reveal these attitudes.

After a minute the breast and underlying muscle are loose, up. Reardon starts to rummage in. With a retractor light I can see the super-nudity of rib cage and this hollow pouch he has made behind her small pap. We strip-search it: crimson, lit, shaggy-fibered inside: a weird vest pocket. As you stuff throw pillows, Reardon has begun to push the colorless silicone implant in. Her bosom is swelling with false pride now. The implant, more sinuous than gelatin, a good female impersonator, squeezes through that two-inch gash. No, not large enough yet: she'll want, Reardon guesses, to be built better than this. Next size up, please. Her nub and gnarled nipple lolls, orange with antiseptic, while Reardon is coaxing the glib implant out. And I am disconcerted. There's so little blood: so little *to* a female breast, which things have long been the business and quick speculation of my male eye.

—D. Keith Mano, "Plastic Surgery" (p. 238)

Using small squares of cotton, he began to separate the tumor from very loose fibrous bands connecting it to the brain and to the right side of the part of the skull where the pituitary gland lies. The right optic nerve and carotid artery came into view, both displaced considerably to the right. The optic nerve had a normal appearance. He protected these structures with cotton compresses placed between them and the tumor. He began to raise the tumor from the skull and slowly to reach the point of its origin and attachment—just in front of the pituitary gland and medial to the left optic nerve, which still could not be seen. The small blood vessels entering the tumor were cauterized. The upper portion of the tumor was gradually separated from the brain, and the branches of the carotid arteries and the branches to the tumor were coagulated. The tumor was slowly and gently lifted from its bed, and for the first time the left carotid artery and optic nerve could be seen. Part of the tumor adhered to this nerve. The bulk of the tumor was amputated, leaving a small bit attached to the nerve. Very slowly and carefully the tumor fragment was resected.

—Roy C. Selby, Jr. "A Delicate Operation" (p. 248)

Wilson sat by the patient in what looked like a barber's chair, manipulating a surgical microscope with a foot pedal. In his left hand he wielded a tiny suction tube, which removed excess blood. In his right he held a series of instruments in steady alternation: Cloward elevator, Penfield No. 2, Cloward rongeur, Fulton rongeur, conchatome, Hardy dissector, Kurze scissors, and so on. He worked quickly, with no wasted motion. Through the microscope, the tumor looked like a piece of lobster flesh, white and fibrous. He removed the middle of it, exposing the pituitary underneath. Then he took a ring curette—a long instrument with a circular scalpel perpendicular to the handle—and ran it lightly across the surface of the gland, peeling the tumor away as he did so.

—Malcolm Gladwell, "The Physical Genius" (p. 766)

WRITING INTRODUCTIONS AND CONCLUSIONS

Many writers find writing introductions and conclusions especially challenging, probably because they realize how critical they are to the essay. The introduction is the first thing your readers read, and if you don't get their attention, they may stop reading. The conclusion is your last opportunity to make your point or to give your reader pause; a weak conclusion can make the difference between an excellent piece of writing and a merely adequate one.

Introductions and conclusions give writers the opportunity to exercise their creativity, to add a dash of panache to an essay that, on the face of it, may not seem very appealing. On the other hand, for writers who lament, "I'm not very creative," introductions and conclusions lend themselves to a host of strategies that borrow from other writers (quotes and paraphrases), from history (historical anecdote), from statistics (surprising facts) or from others' experience (stories).

The purpose of your **introduction**, which may range in length from a sentence to several paragraphs, is to hook the reader, create interest in your subject, and communicate (or hint at) your main point. Various approaches can accomplish these tasks; several examples follow:

- **Startling statement:** a statement of fact or a statistic that is sure to surprise your readers.

  I've often said that if polygamy didn't exist, the modern American career woman would have invented it.

  —Elizabeth Joseph, "Polygamy Now" (p. 143)

- **Narrative opening:** an effective strategy that even most beginning writers can master, the narrative may be in either first or third person.

  When Michael Wilkes left Sumter, S.C., two decades ago, he was trying to escape what he perceived to be his bloodstained fate. He was only 21, but he was already in trouble—in petty trouble with the law, in big trouble at home. He didn't want to end up like his father: a career criminal, a wife beater and dead by his wife's hand. So, baby-faced and jittery, Michael boarded a Greyhound for New York, fleeing an urge to exact vengeance on the step-mother who killed his father. He was running, too, from a failed, violence-ridden marriage of his own.

  —Deborah Sontag, "Fierce Entanglements" (p. 591)

- **Quoted (or paraphrased) remarks:** a no-brainer if you can get your hands on a book of quotations or a biography or history. Simply find a quote that is appropriate for your subject and thesis. A variation of this technique is to quote poetry or song lyrics.

It has been said that the greatest crime an advertisement can commit is to remain unnoticed.

> —*John Caples, "Layouts and Illustrations That*
> *Attract the Most Readers" (p. 640)*

- **Problems to be discussed or facts to be established:** a straightforward approach that wastes no time moving into the discussion at hand.

One problem advertisers have when they try to convince you that the product they are pushing is really different from other, similar products is that their claims are subject to some laws. Not a lot of laws, but there are some designed to prevent fraudulent or untruthful claims in advertising.

> —*William Lutz, "Weasel Words" (p. 661)*

- **(Rhetorical) Question:** a method too heavily relied upon by students, but which, when all else fails, can be effective.

What's the difference between mogul Sean "Puffy" Combs and the average Black man? Oh, about $100 million.

> —*Jean Morgan, "The Bad Boy" (p. 788)*

- **History or background:** a variation on the narrative opening, this can be a relevant historical anecdote.

Wedding announcements track American social history. Once they were the purview of the well-to-do, and the stereotypical division of roles was in the published details: the groom's work, the bride's gown. Point d'esprit, sweetheart neckline, Alençon lace: how quaint it all seems. In the blink of an eye, historically speaking, the dress disappeared and in its place was a working woman, sometimes one who was keeping her own name. The idealized gave way to the real. A previous marriage had ended in divorce. The ring bearer was the 5-year-old son of the bride and groom. And couples of all classes, religions and races eventually smiled out from the pages of the daily papers.

> —*Anna Quindlen, "Getting Rid of the Sex Police" (p. 583)*

EXERCISE: Analyzing Introductory Strategies

Read the following two introductions from student essays. Which of the above strategies do the writers use? Does each strategy clearly tie in with the stated or implied thesis? Does each introduction capture the reader's interest, introduce the subject, state the thesis?

1. "Gin, cursed fiend, with fury fraught, / Makes human race a prey," wrote William Hogarth in 1750 as part of a short poem about the evils of gin, which he printed at the bottom of his picture "Gin Lane." By contrast, he praises beer as a healthy drink, which "warms each English generous Breast / with liberty and love," praise illustrated in "Beer Street." The two engravings, designed as companion pieces in 1750, contrast the destructive powers of gin and the wholesomeness of beer: Gin destroys people's health and makes them too poor to buy (or care about) food; beer has the opposite effect—it nourishes people and makes them healthy in body and spirit. Because it is so powerfully addictive, gin destroys communities; the demise of social order is mirrored in the decay of the buildings. Beer, by contrast, leads to orderly communities within stately, well-kept buildings.

2. I remember sitting in a literature class during my senior year in high school, bored practically to tears by the teacher's discussion of James Joyce—until he defined "epiphany" for us. He described it as a life-altering moment, a sudden realization that your life would be different from now on. Really different. Mr. Herrit was using the term in a literary context, but I understood it as it related to my own personal history, which I considered very tragic at the time. Little did I know that I had yet to experience a much greater epiphany.

An essay's **conclusion**, which may range in length from a sentence to several paragraphs, reiterates the main idea and perhaps give the reader something to ponder. Various approaches can accomplish these tasks; several examples follow:

- **Summarize content:** a fairly obvious, straightforward technique, reiterating the point, but not restating the introduction *verbatim*, a mistake some writers make.

The current debate about whether we should have a national curriculum is phony. We already have a national curriculum locked up in the seven lessons I have just outlined. Such a curriculum produces physical, moral, and intellectual paralysis, and no curriculum of content will be sufficient to reverse its hideous effects. What is currently under discussion in our national hysteria about failing academic performance misses the point. Schools teach exactly what they are intended to teach and they do it well: how to be a good Egyptian and remain in your place in the pyramid.

> —*John Taylor Gatto, "The Seven-Lesson Schoolteacher" (p. 369)*

- **Repeat sentence or slogan or refer to title:** technique that cleverly repeats a catchy phrase or sentence, or, through repetition, creates interest in a phrase or slogan.

I have one wish for the Web site. In the words of the auctioneer: Going, going, gone!

> —*Ellen Goodman, "Beauty on the DNA Auction Block" (p. 415)*

- **Circle back to introductory example:** a closing technique that brings the piece full-circle, neatly tying beginning and ending.

Whether his motivation will be sufficiently powerful to overcome a lifelong pattern remains to be seen. For the moment, Michael and Sylvia are setting their sights on a more concrete goal: a vacation in the Poconos.

> —*Deborah Sontag, "Fierce Entanglements" (p. 606)*

- **Quotation:** an easy, reliable way to conclude, the quote may come from a song, poem, or other literary work, or from a famous person—or it may simply be a memorable remark from a not-so-famous person.

"Welcome to the Liberace Museum!" [Liberace] cried to the assembled multitude. "I don't usually wear diamonds in the afternoon, but this is a special occasion!"

> —*Dave Hickey, "A Rhinestone as Big as the Ritz" (p. 785)*

- **Announce the main point:** an effective technique when the writer withholds statement of the main point until the end of the essay.

I have now, after all, deliberately chosen a "facial flaw," a remarkable aspect of appearance. Somehow, now, the glances of strangers seem less invasive, nothing to incite me to nunhood; a long look is just that—a look—and what of it? I've invited it, I've made room for it, it is no longer inflicted upon me against my will.

> —*Natalie Kusz, "Ring Leader" (p. 226)*

- **Suggest the future for the subject:** a technique that attempts to answer questions like "where do we go from here?" or "what's next?"

What we need are fewer commentaries by self-promoting experts on network television, and more intelligent discussions by scholars and citizens in local media including local public-television stations. We need creative alternatives to the onslaught of talking heads, all saying much the same thing (as though they themselves were clones) to docile, sheep-like audiences waiting for others to address the most pressing moral issues of the day.

—*Leigh Turner, "The Media and the Ethics of Cloning" (p. 453)*

- **Leave the readers with a question to ponder:** a strategy that gives readers something to stop and consider, asks them to think beyond the subject.

But a question remains: Now that the shock of Littleton has subsided, will we simply return to a fantasy world where we can pretend that the ways we choose to entertain ourselves have no consequences, like some kid zoned out in front of a computer game? If so, game's over.

—*Paul Keegan, "Culture Quake" (p. 447)*

EXERCISE: Analyzing Concluding Strategies

Consider the following conclusions. Which of the above strategies do the writers use?

1. I imagine that across America there are groups of young women preparing to launch careers. They sit around tables, talking about the ideal lifestyle to support them in their aspirations for work, motherhood, and personal fulfillment. "A man would be nice," they might muse. "A Man on our own terms," they might add. What they don't realize is that there is an alternative that would allow their dreams to come true. That alternative is polygamy, the ultimate feminist lifestyle.

   —*Elizabeth Joseph, "Polygamy Now!" (p. 144)*

2. The campaigns to eradicate prejudice—all of them, the speech codes and workplace restrictions and mandatory therapy for accused bigots and all the rest—should stop, now. The whole objective of eradicating prejudice, as opposed to correcting and criticizing it, should be repudiated as a fool's errand. Salman Rushdie is right, Toni Morrison wrong, and minorities belong at his side, not hers.

   —*Jonathan Rauch, "In Defense of Prejudice" (p. 508)*

5 WRITING WITH SOURCES

In the academic world, we distinguish between two kinds of research: **primary** and **secondary**. The absent-minded professor blowing up things in his laboratory is a caricature of somebody involved in primary research: he tries to find answers to his questions by conducting experiments and observing how things (or animals or people) behave under certain circumstances. The term *field studies* summarizes the methods involved in primary research, which include conducting experiments, interviewing people, and inspecting sites.

The curious student working late hours in the library is an example of somebody involved in secondary research. Rather than going out and finding the data to analyze, she finds answers to her questions by reading up on the information gathered by primary researchers and evaluating the various sources.

When writing papers, you generally start out with primary research. Remember that dreaded first essay at the beginning of each school year "What I Did During My Summer Break"? To answer the question, you had to think back to your activities that summer and select the ones that would most interest your reader. Researching your memory is a form of primary research; because it is so very personal and subjective, however, you might want to check to see if other people have had similar experiences and if what happened to you is typical of a whole group. You can verify your experience by talking to other people (in interviews) or by reading what they have written, by doing secondary research.

The writing you do in your composition classes combines personal experience, primary research, and secondary research. This chapter will show you how to go about researching a topic and how to present your results in an interesting, readable way. Contrary to popular opinion, research is not a tedious process in which you search for a bunch of seemingly related sources and cut and paste them into a paper. Research is a natural process that comes out of curiosity, the desire to find answers to your questions. A writer who is not curious will never write anything of interest to a reader.

ASKING A GOOD TOPIC QUESTION

Often, teachers assign a topic to you: to analyze the causes of the Civil War, for instance, or to show how Hawthorne uses symbols in his short stories. Sometimes, however, they will let you choose your own topic, and with the freedom of choice comes the agony of decision, of narrowing your focus to a particular aspect of a topic you would like to investigate. Sometimes students resort to the type of paper that reports everything they have discovered about a topic. Although a good collection of facts is a great start for a paper, no reader will be satisfied with just facts. Your reader wants to see your *analysis* of these facts, to share a discovery you have made that goes beyond the material you have before you.

ANALYZING YOUR OWN EXPERIENCE OR THAT OF OTHERS

In order to find out what other people think about a subject, it's a good idea to conduct informal **interviews**. Simply draw up a list of questions (avoid yes/no questions if possible) and interview your friends and acquaintances to discover what they have to say. Although you'll probably treat these interviews informally, you should take along a note pad and write down what your friends say; you want to represent their experiences accurately in your paper.

FINDING SECONDARY SOURCES ONLINE

Besides collecting personal experiences, you also want to look in print sources for information on your topic. The essays in Part II of this book can serve as your sources for the suggested writing topics in the Your Turn sections at the end of each chapter. If your teacher asks you to find additional sources, the most convenient way to do it is electronically.

Most college and public libraries subscribe to a number of **databases** containing information that has been produced and edited by professionals. The difference between using these databases and surfing the Internet is that anybody can put stuff on the Web: from the famous Harvard professor to the tech-savvy fifth-grader. When you are new to a topic, it is often very difficult to tell the difference between reliable and unreliable information. If you use professional databases, however, somebody has already sorted through the pile, and you can feel confident that you are getting trustworthy information.

Some of these databases are **indexes**, lists of articles published on certain subjects within a given time frame. These indexes give you only the publication information about these sources, which you will then have to find through your college library's catalogue. Some databases offer **full-text** downloads, a service that will save you hours of time tracking down and xeroxing information. When it comes to finding information, all of these systems work the same way: As you put in a **search term** (a subject, a name, or a title), the computer searches the database's memory and flags all items that contain your search term. Keep in mind, though, that some search terms have synonyms (think of words like *drugstore, pharmacy, apothecary,* and *chemist*) and some writers might use one term but not the other. The *Library of Congress Subject Headings*, a formal listing of subject terms, is a valuable resource to help you find additional search terms. Ask your college librarian where you can find a copy.

Once you have found and printed/xeroxed your articles, read them carefully. Make sure you understand the article *as a whole* before you pick out bits and pieces that might (or might not) fit your topic. Again, this will take a while, but you will learn about your topic as you go—the most important requirement for any writer.

TAKING NOTES

Take notes to remind yourself about what kind of information you have gathered and where it came from (for example, title, publisher, location, and copyright year for a book; article title, journal name, volume number, and year for a journal). Not every paper requires notes, by the way: If you write largely about personal experience, you will likely not have to remind yourself of what you know. However, as soon as you use secondary sources, you have to keep track of where your information comes from to avoid that deadliest of academic sins, **plagiarism**. If you have only one or two brief articles, you might be able to use them without making notes; you can put the sources in front of you and consult them as you need to. However, if you cannot access your source information without shuffling pages, note "cards" help you keep track of your information without unnecessary clutter.

Traditionally, note cards are done on index cards, but you can do them on the computer just as well (and there is no need to make them *look* like index cards). As you take your notes, make sure you record individual ideas just as you would on index cards; put the source and page number next to every idea; double space between them. When you have taken all your notes, print a hard copy and cut the individual entries apart—you now have "note slips" that are just as flexible as index cards (and you can copy them into your paper as you go without rewriting them).

In order to take efficient notes, you must have a **question** in mind; without a question, you end up taking notes on everything that seems important, which might be just about everything you read.

Write your working question on a piece of paper and keep it visible at all times during the note-taking process. As you (re)read your sources, make notes only of those things that help answer your question; ignore everything else.

To avoid later confusion, write the name of the **author** and the **page number** of where the piece of information appears in the source on every note. This form of abbreviated citation saves a lot of time. The **works cited page** at the end of the paper will give your reader complete information as to where the source was published, so you can save yourself the trouble of writing it over and over.

When you take notes, you will **quote**, **paraphrase**, and/or **summarize** the material. Let's look at how each works.

QUOTATION

When writers quote, they copy parts of sentences, entire sentences, or short passages from their sources into their research papers. To make sure their readers know the difference between "borrowed" and original ideas, writers mark quotations with quotation marks and indicate the source in parentheses (we call this "documenting the source").

Here is an example of a note card using direct quotation. The source is Stephen S. Hall, "The Bully in the Mirror" (p. 207).

HALL 214

"Since the early 1990's, evidence has emerged suggesting that a small number of adult males suffer from extreme body-image disorders."

PARAPHRASE

When writers paraphrase, they use the original idea, but they put it in their own words. Since there are no quotation marks to show where the "borrowed" idea starts, writers introduce the source before the paraphrase and mark its end with **parenthetical documentation** (just as they do with quotes). Here are some phrases that work well in introducing a paraphrase: "According to So-and-so," "As Such-and-Such observes (states, believes, proves)."

Make sure you use your own words throughout the paraphrase: "Borrowing" any phrases from the original without quoting them is a form of plagiarism. Granted, it is difficult to come up with your own words right after you have read an idea in the author's words. Your best bet is to read the original until you have clearly understood the idea and then put it aside so you cannot look at it. Wait a couple of minutes, and then do the paraphrase from memory; you will still remember the idea but not the exact wording. Once you have finished the paraphrase, turn back to the original and check to see if you have left out anything or misrepresented something.

Here is an example of a note card using paraphrase. The source is the same as in the above example.

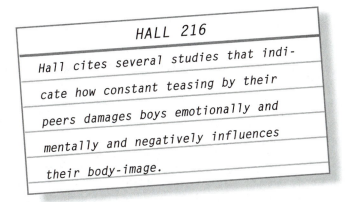

HALL 216

Hall cites several studies that indicate how constant teasing by their
peers damages boys emotionally and
mentally and negatively influences
their body-image.

SUMMARY

Paraphrasing is rendering someone else's ideas into your own words without excluding details from the original source. In a summary, a writer eliminates some details to paraphrase the main idea of a passage or a whole source. As in a paraphrase, you will use your own words, but your summary will be shorter than the original. Summary is especially useful when you use several sources in a paper. You may summarize an article to refute its position; you may summarize each of several articles that support your position; or you may summarize two different articles to establish two sides of a debate. You should document a summary the same way you document a paraphrase.

HOW TO QUOTE AND PARAPHRASE CORRECTLY

A **quotation** is a word-for-word repetition of a passage from a source. You mark it with quotation marks at the beginning and end. This sounds rather easy, doesn't it? Don't let appearances fool you, though. Even though putting quotes around a sentence or two does not require an advanced degree, *using* quotes properly is an art that distinguishes the pros from the amateurs.

Consider the following Ten Commandments of Quoting Correctly:

1. Quotations only *support* or *illustrate* a point; they cannot make the point.

2. Quotations have to fit the point they support. As a writer, you need to provide enough context so your reader can see the connection.

3. Quotes need to fit the grammar of the sentence into which they are

integrated. Put square brackets [ ] around words in the quotations that you have to change to fit the grammar of your sentence.

4. Avoid long quotes. Use partial sentences if possible and integrate them into your own sentences, your paraphrase of the larger context.

5. Shorten long quotes if possible. Use ellipses (. . .) to indicate where you took out words or phrases.

6. If you have to use a quote that's one or several sentences long, state the point of the quote in a sentence or two before you bring in the quote. Put a colon (:) between the "point" and the quote.

7. Quote accurately. Don't change or omit words without brackets or ellipses.

8. Put documentation after the quotation mark, before the end punctuation of the sentence: "Afflicted by the general shame of having a body at all, and the specific shame of having one weakened and misshapen by disease, I ought not to be able to hold my head up in public" (Mairs 233).

9. Introduce quotes and paraphrases by giving the name of the author; if possible, give the author's credentials when you first introduce his/her name. This will lend credibility to your quote:

Malcolm Gladwell, a reporter for the New Yorker, claims in "The Physical Genius" that we are tempted to "treat physical genius in the same way that we treat intellectual genius—to think of it as something that can be ascribed to a single factor, a physical version of I.Q." (767).

10. Indirect quotes must be identified as such: Let's say you are using Stephen S. Hall's "The Bully in the Mirror," in which he quotes from a book by Kindlon and Thomas. You want to use the Kindlon and Thomas quote, but you don't have access to the book. You can still use it, but you must introduce the quote with its authors' names and acknowledge the secondary source afterwards:

As Kindlon and Thomas point out, when men are asked about their adolescent body-image problems, "you've got two things against you. One is emotional literacy. They're not even in touch with their emotions, and they're doing things for reasons of which they're not even aware" (qtd. in Hall 212).

EXERCISE: Detecting Quotation Problems

Read the original quotation and then the passages that demonstrate unacceptable uses of quotation. Point out which rules these examples violate.

Original:

> To widen the rift between the self and the body, we treat our bodies as subordinates, inferior in moral status. Open association with them shames us. In fact, we treat our bodies with very much the same distance and ambivalence women have traditionally received from men in our culture.
>
> —*Mairs, "Carnal Acts" (p. 230)*

1. In her essay, Nancy Mairs shows her readers what it means to live with a disabling disease. "In fact, we treat our bodies with very much the same distance and ambivalence women have traditionally received from men in our culture (230)."

2. Many women "widen the rift between the self and the body" by treating "our bodies as subordinates, inferior in moral status (230)."

3. Nancy Mairs claims that "we treat our bodies with the same distance women have traditionally received from men in our culture" (230).

Unlike quotation, **paraphrases** present ideas or information from a source in your own words and sentence structures. Even documenting the source, "borrowing" words and phrases from the original, and substituting a few synonyms in the author's sentences constitutes plagiarism. Of course, *rewriting* and *rethinking* somebody's ideas without changing them is a much more challenging mental process than copying down words, but there are invaluable advantages in this. In order to paraphrase accurately, you have to *understand* the ideas presented in the source (which is not necessary in quotation); it is only once you have worked through an idea in this way that you can logically integrate it with your own ideas. Students who string together quotes in seemingly random fashion are not writing research papers; they are producing crazy quilts of other people's ideas.

In a quotation, the quotation marks show where the quote starts and ends. A paraphrase has no such obvious marker, and this is why you need to introduce each paraphrase with a reference to the source. Because you have already cited the source, the parentheses that mark the end of the paraphrase only contain the page number(s) from where the *idea* (in Mairs's original wording) appears:

> Nancy Mairs points out that women treat their bodies with the same kind of attitude they have experienced from men in our culture: they see their bodies as inferior and subservient (p. 230).

Let us look at an example of how to paraphrase properly:

Original:

> From what I've learned looking inside people, I've decided human beings
> are somewhere between a hurricane and an ice cube: in some respects, per-
> manently mysterious, but in others—with enough science and careful prob-
> ing—entirely scrutable.

—*Atul Gawande, "Final Cut" (p. 205)*

Unacceptable Paraphrase (Plagiarized)

> Human beings are similar to storms and ice cubes because they are perma-
> nently mysterious in some ways, but in other ways they are entirely scrutable
> (Gawande p. 205).

Acceptable Paraphrase

> According to Gawande, science can explain the workings of the human
> body—even though it will never reveal all of its mysteries (p. 205).

PLANNING YOUR PAPER

Once you have collected all your evidence (from your own experience, interviews
with others, and printed sources), look at the fruits of your research and see if
the various cards and notes come together at different points. You might find,
for example, that a personal story a friend told you connects with an article you
read or that several passages from different articles support the same point. Try
to group your material together (and don't worry if some does not fit).

Look at the question you started with: Can you answer it now? How do the
individual piles of material you have sorted out connect to it? From the information you have in front of you, write the answer to your question at the top of
a fresh sheet of paper. This is your **working thesis**, a central idea (that is not cast
in stone and can always be revised later).

With your working thesis in mind, summarize, in a sentence or two each, the
point of each "pile" of material. These are your **topic sentences**, and, like your
working thesis, they could change before you finish your paper. Write these sentences underneath your working thesis.

What you end up with is an **outline** of your paper, a basic (if informal) plan
of how you are going to organize your ideas in the first draft of your paper. Many
students are scared of outlines because they remember them as hugely complicated lists of ideas with Roman and Arabic numerals, with upper- and lower-

case letters, and fancy headings. Although formal outlines have their place in researched writing, they are unnecessary at this stage in your career. However, you need to plan your essay a bit before you start, knowing that your plan may shift and change as you develop your paper through its various drafts.

WRITING A FIRST DRAFT AND INTEGRATING SOURCES

Integrating sources into your writing means blending your own ideas with those of other people, making sure that your readers always know the difference between the two but still perceive them as one unit. Does this sound like an impossible task? It's not, even though many researchers will tell you that this is one of the hardest things they had to learn.

As you have learned in the previous chapter, writers integrate other people's ideas through **quotation** and **paraphrase**. Keep the following suggestions in mind.

- If possible, never quote an entire sentence; quote only pieces of sentences and **make them part of your own sentences.**

- Remember that **quotes never make points for you**; they only support a point you have already stated in your own language. If you find you have to quote a whole sentence, summarize the point of the quotation in the sentence preceding it.

- **Never quote anything you do not thoroughly understand.** If you can't make sense of it, your readers won't either. The penalty for confusing your readers is that they lose respect for you, the writer.

Because **paraphrasing** involves rewriting an idea completely in your own words and sentence structures, it is much harder to do. However, as you process an idea to recast it into your own language, you will understand it. Paraphrasing pretty much eliminates the problems that occur when writers quote things they do not fully understand. Remember, though, that you must mark a paraphrase by introducing the source at the beginning and by documenting it at the end.

REVISING YOUR PAPER

Contrary to popular opinion, **revising** a paper does not mean fixing what's wrong with it; that is the job of **editing**. Just as the word implies, *re-vision* means to see your topic again, in the light of what you have discovered by writing about it. Many writers do not really know what they think unless they write about it, and they know their topic much better after they have produced a first draft. Once writers understand their topics better, they also see the connections between their ideas more clearly and they discover that some ideas would be more effective if they were presented differently or in another place in the paper. So they set about rearranging and refocusing their papers, not because what they have said before is wrong, but because they have realized they can say it better.

It helps to have a critical reader—your teacher or one of your peers—to read and comment on your paper before you revise it. However, as you become a more experienced writer, you will also become your own best reader.

EDITING YOUR PAPER

Editing, the process of weeding out grammatical and stylistic errors, should occur once you are satisfied with your ideas and with the way you have arranged them. Since editing requires that you look not so much at what you have said but at how you said it, reading your paper backwards (starting with the last sentence and working your way up to the first) is a helpful trick. Your paper will not make any sense read backwards, and therefore, instead of seeing content and logic, you will see isolated sentences, and their flaws. (For some guidelines about stylistic revision, see Chapter 7.)

6 A WRITER AT WORK

To help you see the various steps involved in the writing process, Travis Lambert, one of our students, agreed to write a paper for this book. He used some of the readings from this book to explore a subject he had never much thought, let alone written, about. As you watch his paper unfold in the following chapters, you will see that the process of doing research and using sources is much more than a tedious assignment: It is a journey toward knowledge and understanding of a topic, a journey that involves a lot of different thinking skills.

To write his paper, Travis followed the steps outlined in the previous chapter.

ASKING A GOOD TOPIC QUESTION

Travis began his assignment by reading some of the essays included here. He found that he was interested in two aspects of the readings:

1. The importance of toys in the development of boys and girls.
2. The importance of role models for teenagers.

"If you read something that strikes you, it will strike the reader," he observed as he looked for a topic. "Don't write on anything you find boring."

ANALYZING YOUR OWN EXPERIENCE OR THAT OF OTHERS

Even though he was not sure exactly where his paper was going, Travis decided to interview some of his friends about the dolls they played with when they were children.

He asked his friends the following questions:

1. When you were a child, did you play with dolls? What kinds?
2. What did you like about these dolls? Did you find you wanted to be like them in any way?
3. Do you think that any of these dolls influenced the way you feel about yourself today?

From the answers he received from these informal interviews, he took the following notes:

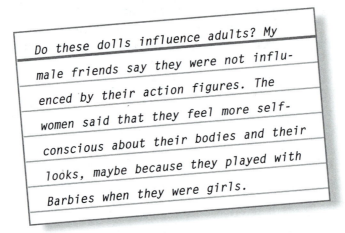

> *Boys like their action figures for the adventures they have; they are pro-active; their bodies are often very unrealistic. Girls like their Barbies because they are pretty; image is important, not action.*

> *Do these dolls influence adults? My male friends say they were not influenced by their action figures. The women said that they feel more self-conscious about their bodies and their looks, maybe because they played with Barbies when they were girls.*

READING UP ON THE SUBJECT AND TAKING NOTES

After he talked to his friends, Travis decided to focus his paper on the influence dolls have on boys and girls, looking at whether action figures influence boys in different ways than Barbie dolls do girls. His friends did not think their adult self-perception had been influenced much by their childhood dolls, but Travis was curious to see what professional writers had to say on the subject. He started looking for readings that address this question to see whether they supported or contradicted what his friends told him in the interviews. Most of his sources are included in this book.

As he started on his second tour through his sources, Travis's **topic question** became more specific: "Do dolls really influence the way children feel about themselves when they grow up?"

Here are some of the items he noted on cards as he looked for material that might answer his question. Note that he recorded the source for every idea he quoted or paraphrased and that he marked his own ideas with asterisks so as not to confuse them with those of the other writers. He used quotation marks to distinguish direct quotation from paraphrase, as in the following note, where all the information comes from Travis's source.

BORGER 40

"It's not Barbie's figure that's the big problem. It's her values." Barbie teaches girls that designer clothes and accessories are what count.

SHAPIRO

Shapiro points out some of the virtues she has learned from Barbie:

—tolerance (Barbie comes in different ethnic varieties; there are disabled Barbies; Barbie has all kinds of different jobs; yet, the dolls all seem to get along with each other.)

—independence (with only one male doll and a whole bunch of girls, Barbies teach how to get along without a man)

Shapiro's approach is tongue-in-cheek, though. Is she saying that Barbies do not teach these values? Or that these values do not really matter?

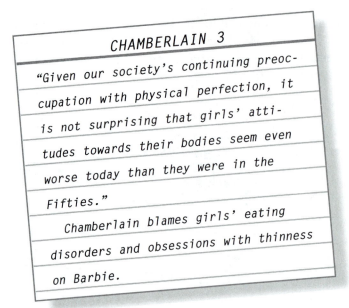

CHAMBERLAIN 3

"Given our society's continuing preoccupation with physical perfection, it is not surprising that girls' attitudes towards their bodies seem even worse today than they were in the Fifties."

Chamberlain blames girls' eating disorders and obsessions with thinness on Barbie.

POLLIT 46

Pollit does not deny that Barbie represents shallow values. But she says that these are societal values, not the doll's: "Yet to reject her is to say that what Barbie represents—being sexy, thin, stylish—is unimportant, which is obviously not true, and children know it's not true."

　** This seems to support what Borger says when she points out that it is not the children that complain about the doll but their mothers, "self-indulgent gen X-ers" and "the narcissistic (and aging) baby boomer" (Borger 40).

PLANNING YOUR PAPER

After reading a number of sources and taking a few notes, Travis decided he must organize the slew of material he found. He made a preliminary list of ideas:

Ideas about Barbie Dolls

Positive aspects of Barbie:

- Because Barbie is now available in different ethnic versions, girls can learn tolerance from her. There is even a wheelchair Barbie, although her wheelchair does not fit in the doll house.
- Because Barbie has a variety of jobs, girls learn that women work just as much as men.
- Barbie dolls create a sense of unity in the girls' peer groups; girls identify with the doll and each other.

Negative aspects of Barbie:

- Barbie teaches girls to be materialistic and that beauty alone will get a girl "stuff."
- Barbie has an unattainable body that never changes with age or disease.

The main differences between action figures and Barbie dolls:

Action figures	*Barbie dolls*
They are pro-active:	They are passive:
men are judged by what they do	women are judged by how they look
Unrealistic bodies:	Body more realistic:
mutant space creatures and mythic beings	even though unattainable, Barbie's body is closer to home than action figures

From his material, Travis made the following **outline** for his first draft:

WORKING THESIS: Children's toys act as role models, but they do not influence children a whole lot.

BODY P 1:   My own experience with Ninja turtles and other action figures: how they affected me, how they stirred my creativity, how I still like them today.

BODY P 2:   My interviews with my friends: men say they liked the adventure-aspect of action figures; women say that image was the most important thing with their Barbies.

BODY P 3:   The good influence of dolls (use some of the source material I have gathered): tolerance, imagination, role models for some.

BODY P 4:   The negative effects: Barbie may teach materialistic values and self-image (use some source material).

As you can see from this working outline, Travis was not quite sure yet of the exact focus in his essay: His working thesis was kind of vague, and his body grouped material more by source than by clear topic sentences. However, Travis knew that he would discover some more ideas as he wrote, and he had to see those ideas in writing before he could determine their exact relationship to each other.

Here is Travis's first draft, after his teacher has read and commented on it:

WRITING A FIRST DRAFT

A Child's Toy:

A Happy Childhood Aid or an Unattainable Idol with Kung-Fu Grip?

When I was a kid, Ninja Turtles were my world. I must have had enough action figures to fill a UNO dorm room. And contrary to the popular belief that children associate their self-image with their toys, I am proud to say that I never tried to cross-breed myself with a turtle, live in sewers, or battle evil on a weekly basis. Perhaps this is due in part to my childhood heroes being far from human role models. I never played with G.I. Joe's or Barbies (except for that one time a few weeks ago, but let's not get into that), but I'm sure I'd be a bit more influenced by toys resembling humans. A child's toy is a child's role model, and while they may only play a small role in shaping self-image, that role is a constant.

My Ninja Turtle addiction had its positive and negative sides. Throughout almost all of my childhood, I remember wanting nothing more than the Ninja Turtle's sewer play set. Unfortunately, my parents also know this was my sole desire, so they told me I couldn't have it until my grades were all A's. Alas, my brain was not up to the challenge, but I found a wonderful alternative. I started

Don't mention a story that you are not going to tell. It's not fair to your reader to raise expectations you are not going to fulfill.

I am not sure exactly what the main point of your essay is. Since the thesis is the core of your paper, you need to make it very clear.

I love these stories, but how do they support your thesis that toys act as role models for children?

taking cardboard boxes and constructing my own sewers. All I used were the boxes, markers, and various pieces of furniture that I stole from my sister's doll house. My sewer was huge. It had a dozen rooms all connected and was probably six feet long. The play set had two rooms. A few months later, I received the play set for Christmas. I never played with it, but I appreciated the box it came in. The Ninja Turtles are responsible for inspiring one of the most creative things I have ever done. As far as the negative aspect of my addiction goes, the Ninja Turtles are responsible for the most embarrassing story my parents have about me as a child. When I was four, I was waiting at the airport for my father to come home from a business trip. He arrived with a box in his hand. It was a Ninja Turtle pajama set. It was like a costume with a shell on the back and everything. I then took the box and removed the outfit. Then, I proceeded to remove all of my clothing in the middle of the airport so I could proudly wear the green colors of my Saturday morning heroes. My parents have told that story to every single friend and girlfriend I have ever had. And now you know, damnit.

    Unfortunately, not every child is fortunate enough to know the joy of the Ninja Turtle. When asked, my peers had varied answers as to what they played with as a child and how their toys have affected their self-image. Almost half of the men I asked said they favored G.I. Joe's when growing up. You would think watching such programming as a young child would lead to romantic associations with the military and eventually a desire to join one of the armed forces. Surprisingly, all who played with G.I. Joe's claimed they had no desire to enlist, and the extent of their romanticized attitudes goes only as far as war movies. Another toy that several guys said they played with as children was Transformers, action figures that can be changed into cars or robots. Some who played with these toys admitted they had a fixation with cars, and some even associate their masculinity with cars, perhaps because of the Transformers. A vast majority of women said they played with Barbies or similar dolls. Sadly, nearly every girl admitted to having some sort of complex due to playing with them. For example, those with smaller bust lines felt inadequate because of their large-breasted dolls, and those with a larger bust felt they were too big compared to Barbies's gravity-immune chest. But to be fair, if you can show me one

---

Are you talking about TV shows or action figures? Clarify your point here.

So those toys did have an influence on the boys that played with them? Explain how this proves your point about toys being role models!

I think you are dismissing your evidence a bit too lightly here: it seems that these women did expect to grow up to look like Barbie—and were disappointed when they didn't. Granted, many teenagers have body-image problems (for different reasons), but in the context of your paper, these image problems are connected with the dolls. Don't dismiss evidence that does not fit your expectations of what you were going to find: adjust your working thesis to fit the evidence you present in your essay!

teenager who never felt awkward about their body while growing up, I'll give you all of my Ninja Turtles.

Children's toys can bestow many positive virtues upon them at young ages. One example would be tolerance. Barbie may be the all-American, blond, blue-eyed queen, but her friends come in an endless variety of races, professions, and some are even handicapped. Plus, what Barbie collection would be complete without at least a few headless ones? If this doesn't teach children to accept people with physical deformities, I don't know what will. Toys can also teach independence. In the Barbie universe, there are countless scores of women in every profession imaginable, but only one Ken. With those kinds of odds, young girls must come to terms with the fact that a man is not required in their lives. Finally, a child's toys can teach the importance of unity. The favorite thing for any young boy to do with his toys is to wage war. Whether it be on his friend's toys, his sister's Barbies, or the family dog, war will be fought and unity must be learned to win the war (Shapiro).

As with anything, many virtues that a toy carries can be negative. Materialism is the strongest of them. Most toys, from Barbies to my beloved turtles, are accompanied by an endless line of sold-separately accessories. Modern Barbie dolls even come with name-brand clothes such as Gucci bags and Tommy Hilfiger pants (Borger). Without these accessories, Barbie is naked. And the designers hope that girls will feel the same without them as they grow up into today's consumers. The more obvious of the negative virtues that toys can have is that of their unattainable bodies. The Barbie, if measured to scale of the average female height, would be an imaginable 38-18-34. And this doesn't stop at girl toys. A new Batman figure, if projected onto a 5-foot-10 man, would have a 30-inch waist and a 27-inch biceps. Even more ridiculous, a new Wolverine figure from the X-Men movie would have a 32-inch biceps. That's larger than any body builder in history (Hall 35). But in all fairness, no children have come forward complaining about Barbie's thin waist or large breasts. It seems gen-Xers, Baby boomers, and feminists (the self-proclaimed liberated crowds who claim to be unaffected by Barbie) are the ones complaining (Borger).

You are taking an ironic stance in this paragraph (like Sharpio did in her article). Since you have not used irony up to this point, your reader is not prepared for this sudden switch in tone and gets confused.

Check your source: Shapiro does not make this point about unity, yet you attribute it to her.

Check your source: Borger uses different brand names for examples here.

What precisely is the point in this paragraph? Barbie's materialism? The unrealistic body proportions of Barbie and male action figures? The people that criticize Barbie— or your dismissal of them?

The effects that toys have on children may be irreversible, but they play only a small role when the children grow up. After all, I haven't grown up to be a mutated crossbreed whose diet consists exclusively of pizza, but I do love karate movies. Realistic toys are not the key to healthy self-esteem. Good parenting is. Just because little Jimmy plays with an army figure, he does not necessarily become a gun nut when he grows up, and little Tammy's playing with a large-breasted Barbie doesn't guarantee she'll get a boob job the day she turns eighteen. Our adult world is already chock-full of unimaginative, censored, "reality-based" crap. Let's not screw the kids like we've already screwed ourselves.

So are you saying that "unrealistic" toys are better than the harsh reality of the adult world? How does this support your thesis? Don't leave your reader hanging at the end of your essay; end with a clear statement.

End Comment:
This is a really good first draft: your stories are very interesting and you present quite a lot of evidence. However, it seems you designed the outline to accommodate all your material, not so much to state and support a main point. For your revision, you need to rethink your outline: start with a clear thesis. It seems to me that your evidence does support the thesis that dolls influence boys and girls who play with them—in different ways. Think about what these ways are: What do boys learn from action figures? What do girls learn from their Barbies? I think you have a very interesting paper here: a good revision will bring it out!

REVISING YOUR PAPER

Based on his teacher's comments, Travis revised his outline:

INTRO: Use pajama story for "attention grabber." Then add a "thesis paragraph."

THESIS: Action figures and Barbie dolls reinforce gender stereotypes, but it's questionable how much they influence the way adults think.

BODY P 1: Ninja turtles made me creative.

BODY P 2: Male action figures have muscular bodies, but what they do is more important than what they look like. Boys are interested in their dolls' actions, not in becoming like them.

BODY P 3: Barbie dolls are different from action figures. Girls want to *become* Barbie and wear all the dresses and stuff. Barbie does not really *do* anything, unlike action figures.

CONCLUSION: Even though dolls influence the kids that play with them somewhat, parents are still the children's most important role models.

Warriors and Clothes Horses:

Action Figures, Fashion Dolls, and the Question of Gender Stereotypes

When I was a kid, Ninja Turtles were my world. I must have had enough of their action figures to fill a UNO dorm room. Every Saturday morning the Turtles would protect me from such horrors as dog-sized brains named Krang and half-man, half-rhino street punks. Unfortunately, the Ninja Turtles are also responsible for my most embarrassing childhood story. When I was four, I was waiting at the airport for my father to come home from a business trip. He arrived with a box in his hand. It was a Ninja Turtle pajama set. It was like a costume with a shell on the back and everything. I proceeded to remove all of my clothing in the middle of the airport so I could proudly wear the green colors of my Saturday morning heroes. My parents have told that story to every single friend and girlfriend I have ever had. And now you know, damnit.

Obviously, the Ninja Turtles had a huge amount of influence on my life, and playing with them left me with many treasured memories. Some I'm proud of, some I'm not. But I can't help but wonder if I'd feel the same if I was a young girl playing with toys such as Barbie dolls. Male toys such as G. I. Joe and He-Man are action-oriented. They live for adventure, and their popularity often depends on how heroic they are or how much pain they inflict upon the bad guys while saving the galaxy. Male action figures are what they do. Female toys are a different story. Barbie has a much more limited agenda than G. I. Joe. Barbie shops, changes clothes, gets make-overs, and occasionally takes a drive in her convertible. The Barbie doll is basically a pint-sized mannequin for sold-separately merchandise. These dolls are defined by their bodies and their material possessions. Both boys and girls thus have toys that reinforce gender stereo-types, but do they really influence the way they think of themselves once they grow up? Do they make children obsessed with their bodies and material possessions?

One of my favorite Ninja Turtle memories suggests that they do not. I remember wanting nothing more than the Ninja Turtle's sewer play set when I was young. Unfortunately, my parents also knew this was my sole desire, so they told me I couldn't have it until my grades were all A's. Alas, my brain was not up to the challenge, but I found a wonderful alternative. I started taking cardboard boxes and constructing my own sewers. All I used were the boxes, markers, and various pieces of furniture I stole from my sister's doll house. My sewer was huge. It had a dozen rooms all connected and was probably six feet long. The play set had two rooms. A few months later, I received the play set for Christmas. I never played with it, but I appreciated the box it came in. The thing that mattered to me was action, not the paraphernalia that provided the backdrop.

Most action figures today have bodies that would make most NFL players feel like Screech. According to Harrison Pope and Roberto Olivardia, both psychiatrists who work on body-image issues in young men, the new Batman action figure, if projected onto a 5-foot-10 male, would have a 30-inch waist and a 27-inch biceps. Even more ridiculous, a new Wolverine figure from the X-Men movie would have a 32-inch biceps. That's "larger than any body builder in history" (qtd. in Hall 35). However, the bodies of male toys are not an important factor to the boys who play with them. It's what they do. I talked to some young men on campus about the doll toys they played with as children and how they think these toys influenced them. One man said he played with Transformers, action figures that can be changed into either cars or robots. He has not tried to engineer car/robot hybrids; he just likes cars now. A majority of the men I talked to admitted to playing with G. I. Joe's as children. Surprisingly, all who played with these toys claimed they had no desire to enlist, and the extent of their romanticized attitudes with the army goes only as far as war movies. It seems that action figures' activities are what interests boys; they do not seem to want to become like their toys.

The situation looks a bit different when we look at dolls marketed to girls. Fashion dolls in particular don't seem to have a positive, inspiring effect on their users. Unless you count shopping as a virtue. Barbies are accompanied by an endless line of sold-separately accessories. Modern Barbie dolls are "into labels," such as Ralph Lauren bags and Bill Blass and Christian Dior clothes

(Borger 2). Without these accessories, Barbie is naked. And the designers hope that girls will feel the same without them as they grow up into today's consumers. Parents should encourage their little Barbie fans to take a tip from yours truly, the cardboard architect, and show them how to make their own accessories and not to depend on the endless Mattel wardrobe.

Underneath—and because of—her wardrobe, Barbie's body is the focal point of the doll. Barbie, if measured on the scale of an average woman's height, would be an unimaginable 38-18-34 (Randolph 22). Most of the women I talked to said they played with Barbies or similar dolls when they grew up. Sadly, nearly every girl admitted to having some sort of complex due to playing with them. For example, those with smaller bust lines felt inadequate because of a large-breasted childhood role model, and those with a larger bust felt they were too big compared to the doll's gravity-immune chest. This is what makes Barbie's lack of adventure a danger. Since Barbie doesn't do much of anything besides lounging pool-side in Malibu with Ken, she becomes a role model for her body. She stands like a statue, saying (or doing) nothing. Barbie is her body, and this is what most teenage girls learn from her: women are their bodies.

Boys learn from their toys that men are active, in their adventures and perhaps their jobs. Girls learn that what matters in women is their physical appearance. So are our toys still teaching gender stereotypes we've been trying to overcome for so long? Action figures and fashion dolls seem to suggest that they do, but, fortunately, toys are not the only factor that determines our value system as adults. They may have some influence, but it's in no way more powerful than good parenting. Luckily, mom and dad are still more important role models than Barbies, Transformers, and sewer-dwelling Ninja Turtles.

Works Cited

Borger, Gloria. "Barbie's Newest Values." U.S. News and World Report 1 Dec.
        1997: 40.

Hall, Stephen S. "The Bully in the Mirror." The New York Times Magazine 22
        Aug. 1999. 31-35+.

Randolph, Laura B. "Living Dolls." Ebony Jan. 1998: 22.

You can see that Travis's approach was thoughtful and methodical. He did not write the paper in one sitting, but researched his topic through reading, asking questions of friends, and scouring his own memory. He took one step at a time so that he was never overwhelmed. He learned a lot in the process, answering questions and sharpening his focus. Writing his paper was an act of discovery.

You too will be a more successful writer once you realize that writing is a process of learning and discovery; few writers spit out polished drafts in a single sitting. Ideas evolve and develop. Start with whatever you have. In some cases, you may have a specific assignment in which your instructor or your boss has posed a question you must answer or a problem you must solve; sometimes you will have to come up with an initial question or topic yourself. Do some reading and brainstorming and start taking notes. From your notes, try to find an angle. Is a key point emerging, is a question taking shape? Remember, your thesis may be vague at this point. (Travis's was.) Further thinking and writing will help you refine it or perhaps change it altogether. That's all part of the process.

Once you have a draft, you're really on your way. While you're a student, you'll probably get feedback from a teacher or a peer; at work, it may be a boss or a co-worker. If no one is available to read your paper, set it down for a while so that when you do come back to it, you can read it objectively. Some drafts will require more radical revision than others, but don't be afraid to make major changes, rearrange sections, or leave out what doesn't seem to fit. You're discovering what you want to say and how you want to say it. It's hard work, but it's worth it.

7 A SHORT GUIDE TO STYLE

When we think about someone's *style*, we often think about how a person dresses or perhaps how that person relates to other people. A friend who regularly wears bow ties and tasseled loafers has a very different style from the friend with a pierced tongue and tattoos who favors black t-shirts, jeans, and boots. If the pierced-tongue, tattooed friend took to wearing pink oxford shirts and tasseled loafers, that person's style would be indeed distinctive—and perhaps confusing. And if you think about the conversational tactics of different people you know, you can easily recognize distinguishing traits. Some people tell long stories, making elaborate syntactical digressions without stopping for breath; others speak in short, clipped sentences; some show off extensive vocabularies; others never use any but the simplest words.

Most of us understand a person's *style*, whether sartorial or social or conversational, as a set of individualizing characteristics or markers. Similarly, **writing style** refers to those characteristics—word choices, punctuation, sentence patterns, among other things—that distinguish one writer's technique from that of another. And while we're not suggesting that any one style is *best*, as in anything, some styles are more effective than others. In writing, your goal should be a style that feels and sounds honest to you and that **facilitates clear communication**. While you'll have to worry about the first issue, we have included here a few simple ways to accomplish the second one. Changing your writing style completely would be difficult; improving your writing style is easy.

Consider the following:

> The meritorious completion of a race or competition of a person is in reverse proportion to his or her character idiosyncrasies, which is to say that the aforementioned person has a greatly increased likelihood of arriving at the projected goal with greater delay in time than the person or persons not possessed of virtuous righteousness.

From where do you think the above sentence comes? A legal document? A textbook? Surely, you have seen this kind of language before: It sounds very official and important, and if the reader has trouble understanding what it says, so much the better. This is language used to impress (intimidate?) a reader, not to express an idea. (By the way, once you strip the sentence of its excess verbiage, a simple idea emerges: "Good guys finish last.")

Unfortunately, because they are exposed to this kind of language every day, some beginning writers try to imitate it, assuming that teachers want it. By the time they get to college, many writers instinctively prefer a sentence like "We are experiencing precipitation" to the simpler "It is raining:" It sounds better, they think; it has a scientific ring to it that the everyday sentence lacks. And as they get better at writing "gobbledygook," as this pretentious guff is sometimes called, they discover that it can often disguise a banal idea as something academic and pseudosophisticated.

Good writers, however, learn at some point that gobbledygook works against them, not for them. They learn that, if they have nothing interesting to say, they have two options: shut up or find out something interesting about their subject. And once they have real ideas to communicate, writers want to be *understood* by their readers.

What follows are some simple techniques for avoiding vague and pretentious writing, and for making your prose clear and crisp.

USE REAL VERBS

The next time you read a passage in a newspaper or a textbook that seems utterly boring, grab a pencil and underline all the forms of the verb *to be* you can find. You will probably discover few verb forms besides *to be*, a verb that indicates not an action but a state of being. But readers want action, and good writers put as much action into their sentences as they can.

Take, for example, these few sentences from an essay written in response to the question "Should women have to decide between having a family and having a career?"

> There are certain critical developmental hurdles during the first few years of a child's life where direct participation by parents, i.e. mothers, is essential. At the foundation of cultivating a child's life, nutrition introduces necessary nutrients for biological progress. Much evidence is available to support that provisions of protein and vitamin balance is crucial. Our day care facilities are not able to provide the necessary freshness of foods, due to their volumes of mouths to fill and their attention to expense ratios. Canned food, which is a common institutional staple, has been proven to be insufficient on a constant basis.

Sound boring? You bet! Look at all the *to be* constructions in this paragraph: "There are certain critical developmental hurdles . . . Much evidence is available . . ." etc. Once we substitute real verbs for these constructions and cut out needless repetition, the above passage boils down to this:

> A small child needs his parents, especially his mother. To grow properly, children need a balanced diet that contains vitamins and protein. Day care centers cannot provide fresh food because they feed too many children. Canned food, commonly served in institutions, does not nourish children properly.

Forms of *to be* are not the only verbs we can easily replace with more energetic verbs. Many verbs do not provide much specific information about how something is done and thus rely on added adverbs or nouns and adjectives to communicate an idea clearly.

Consider this sentence:

> *Professor Pulaski* came *into the room.*

We get some information, but we get a lot more—about both the action and Professor Pulaski—if we replace *came* with any of the following: *charged, stole, staggered, sauntered, burst, shuffled, strutted, limped,* eliminating the need for follow-up phrases or sentences to explain a situation.

Sometimes writers or speakers stop at the vague verb, not providing the follow-up. Imagine a mother's bewilderment as a day care worker hands over her child, reporting that the baby has been *"making strange noises all day."* Consider the many different situations that would be more effectively communicated by replacing *making strange noises* with any of these: *gurgling, whining, wailing, shrieking, screeching, panting.*

Replacing verbs is one of the easiest revision techniques. After writing a draft, go over it, checking every verb and, if you can, replace it with one that is more vivid or more precise. You'll not only make your prose more lively, you'll likely be able to cut adverbs, adjectives, and qualifiers that may have been necessary to explain or describe. In the writing process, good verbs will carry a lot of the load.

USE ACTIVE VOICE

The passive voice deprives a sentence of live action. In a passive sentence, the grammatical subject does not perform an action but has an action performed upon it. Sound complicated? It's not. Here is an easy way to tell active and passive sentences apart: by answering the questions following the sample sentences, you can see the difference.

> *Chris donated two motorcycles.*

What is the grammatical subject of this sentence? *Chris.*

What is the action in the sentence? *Donating.*

Is the grammatical subject performing the action? *Yes.* Therefore this is an **active sentence**. The subject is actively doing something.

> *Two motorcycles were donated by Chris.*

What is the grammatical subject of this sentence? *Motorcycles.*

What is the action in the sentence? *Donating.*

Is the grammatical subject performing the action? *No.* Therefore this is a **passive sentence**. The subject is not doing something but having something done to it. In fact, Chris, the one performing the action, is not even grammatically necessary: *Two motorcycles were donated* is a grammatically complete sentence, but, lacking a live body and live action, it is rather stale.

The passive voice does have legitimate uses: for example, if we do not know who did something (*A man was murdered on Bourbon Street last night*) or if it does not matter who did it (*An intermission was added to the program*), the passive voice is a good choice. For most other sentences, however, use active verbs.

AVOID WORDINESS

Contrary to popular opinion, wordiness is not a matter of how many words a writer uses but of how many of those words are superfluous. Consider the following:

> *As a matter of fact,* many writers use long-winded sentences *due to the fact that, in a very real sense,* the word count is an essential *factor* in their grades. *In light of the fact that* the assignment said to write at least 400 words, *it seems that* students have a *tendency* to generate as many words as possible *in the process of their writing for the purpose of* fulfilling this goal. *In the event that* they fall short of the *type of* word quota that *exists* in the assignment, they *try to* insert *some* more *in a hasty manner. The point I am trying to make is that* although brevity is the soul of wit, as Shakespeare reminds us, his advice *has the appearance of going unheeded by* many students and their teachers.

The highlighted words and phrases in this passage are unnecessary. You do not need to preface a fact; *as a matter of fact, due to the fact that,* or *in light of the fact that* are long-winded ways of saying *because; for the purpose of* can be replaced by a simple *to; in the event that* and *in the case that* stand for *if;* and if your reader has not gotten the point you're trying to make because your writing is so unclear, announcing it at the end is not going to help matters much. Take a look at the revised passage.

> Many writers use long-winded sentences because the word count matters in their grades. Because the assignment says to write at least 400 words, students generate as many words as possible to fulfill this goal. If they fall short of the word quota in the assignment, they insert more hastily. Although brevity is the soul of wit, as Shakespeare reminds us, many students and their teachers ignore his advice.

USE SPECIFIC NOUNS

The following is an excerpt from a student essay on the topic of whether companies should have the right to forbid dating among employees.

> The idea of being professional encompasses the understanding of what is appropriate and what is not. The ultimate fact is when individuals are at work, they are there to complete specific tasks. When an individual is hired it is mainly because of character, knowledge, and competence. These are some characteristics that describe a professional.

The student wrote the essay "cold," without any preparation, and the paragraph is a typical example of the kind of writing this situation produces. As you look at the word choices, it becomes very obvious that the student lacks specific knowledge on the subject. Most of the words are abstract (*idea, understanding, fact, character, knowledge, competence, characteristics*); and the few concrete words (*individual, professional*) are not very specific—we do not know who this individual is or in what profession he or she works. Avoid abstract terms as much as possible, and wherever you use them, illustrate them with specific examples. In fact, writers who know what they are talking about rarely resort to B.S.—they want to share what they know with their readers, not camouflage their ignorance.

USE SUBORDINATION AND COORDINATION TO VARY SENTENCE PATTERNS

Sometimes, because they are afraid to make mistakes, students stick to short, simple sentences, all following the same basic sentence pattern and resulting in monotonous choppiness.

> My dad bought himself a Harley-Davidson on his fortieth birthday. I was eleven at the time. I was shocked. My mother was furious. Dad offered me a ride. I was too scared to go. Dad talked Mom into going for a spin. Mom ended up loving it. I was relieved. Dad was thrilled.

Skilled writing is fluid and graceful, the result of a variety of sentence lengths and patterns. Subordinating conjunctions such as *which, who,* and *that* can introduce less important ideas, subordinating them appropriately to the key ideas and achieving sentence fluidity and variety. Coordinating conjunctions such as *and, but,* and *for* are used to join clauses of equal weight, creating more flexible and more complex sentence patterns.

Consider the revised version of the above ten sentences.

> When I was eleven, I was shocked and my mother was furious when my dad bought himself a Harley-Davidson for his fortieth birthday. Dad offered me a ride, but I was too scared, so he talked Mom into going for a spin. When Mom ended up loving it, I was relieved. Dad was thrilled.

Ten sentences become four, and the effect is smoother and more natural sounding. The final sentence, a very short one, works well, balanced as it is against a longer, more complex pattern and bringing the paragraph to a close.

EXERCISE: Revising to Improve Style

Revise the following student essay to eliminate the stylistic errors discussed in this chapter.

My Recipe for Success

Taking for granted that in life I am determined to be extremely successful in whatever field I may decide upon, I will be in need of a formula for being successful. In order to achieve success, a pattern must be presented and followed throughout the course of study. Therefore, it is a must that at a particular time, my very best efforts must be put forth and I must be devoted to what will be my future.

The many steps involved in mapping out my future are as follows. I would be forced to attend only three days of schooling per week due to the ownership and management of my own business. Also, the determination to set forth all efforts to school would be acted out each and every day. On the three days, school would be attended the following up of out-of-school study will be made present. On the remaining days of the week, I will continue to contact future landscaping jobs, which will also help strengthen my future career.

On the other hand, my course of action is to strive upon being successful and to also be of guidance to others in the world who are not as fortunate as myself. In the present days my destination is partially unknown as to whether or not I want to continue in the landscaping field or to expand my knowledge in the engineering field. Although what I do realize is that the choice is mine whether I want to be a success in life or not.

In conclusion, I plan on mapping out my future by devoting myself to what will be known as my system and achieving success. On the side life I will continue to be a role model for younger children out there who need assistance and direction in their lives.

8 | WRITING ABOUT IMAGES

As you learned in the very first chapter in this book, critical readers read a text not only for *what* it says but also for *how* the writer says it: The techniques writers choose to express their ideas affect the messages they try to convey. The same is true for artists and the pictures they create.

For starters, every image is *about* something; in art, this "aboutness" is the **subject**[1] of the work. Often the title gives us a clue to the subject the artist had in mind. Norman Rockwell's "The Gossips" (p. 108), for instance, is about how gossip travels from mouth to mouth and how it can come back to its original source. The subject of an image is very much like the thesis in an essay: It is the main point, the central idea an artist wants to get across to the audience. And just as all the details in an essay (the topic sentences and examples) support the thesis, the technical details of an image come together to support its subject.

The things we recognize in a picture—faces, people, places—are called its **subject matter**. The subject matter of "The Gossips," for example, is a series of human heads in the process of passing on information to each other. We can tell by the expressions in these people's faces that the gossip must be juicy and that the original storyteller is shocked to have the tale come back to her. Sometimes artists produce works about the same subject ("love," for example), but they may choose different subject matters to express the idea of love (a mother and child, a man and a woman kissing, two puppies looking at each other with soulful eyes).

When you analyze an image, you should first look at its subject matter: What does the picture show? If there are people in the picture, what are they doing? What emotions do their facial expressions suggest? Where are these people: in a room, a street, an open landscape? What objects surround them? What might be the relationship between these people and their surroundings?

Once you have established what a picture shows, you are ready to determine its subject, its meaning. You are now ready to analyze the picture, to show how the individual details support the central idea. Just like writers, who have to decide what type of language or organization will be most effective in presenting their material, artists build images from various elements at their disposal. Some of these elements are line, shape, value, color, texture, and composition. Of course, none of these elements exists by itself, and they are not equally important in every picture: It is your task as the critical reader to discover how

---

[1]Definitions of *subject* and *subject matter* are drawn from Terry Barrett, *Interpreting Art: Reflecting, Wondering, and Responding.* New York: McGraw-Hill Education, 2003.

subject matter and technical elements come together to create the subject, the meaning of the image.

EXERCISE: Analyzing Subject

1. Describe the subject matter of Norman Rockwell's "After the Prom" (p. 91). Who are the people in the picture? Where are they? What would you say is the subject of this image, its main idea?

2. Look closely at William Hogarth's "Gin Lane" (p. 22). What is the setting of the picture? What are the people doing? What is Hogarth saying about Gin Lane and its inhabitants?

3. Describe the things you see in Walter Iooss's photograph of Michael Jordan (p. 121). What statement does the photographer make about Michael Jordan with this picture?

LINE

If you wanted to draw a house, you would make sure to outline its roof, its walls, and its windows to make sure that your reader recognized what your drawing represents. In essence, you would reproduce the edges of the architectural components as **lines**. Some of you would draw this house with very thin, faint lines, and some of you would make dark, bold strokes; some of you would draw wavy lines to indicate roof shingles, and some of you would draw a series of parallel lines to represents the slats on the window shutters. Individual artists approach line differently; the way they draw lines often becomes a kind of signature by which we can recognize the hand of a particular artist.

Photographs, too, have lines even though photographers do not draw them themselves; they take pictures of objects whose edges will translate into lines on the two-dimensional picture. Photographers and other artists are often attracted by the pattern of lines they see in nature, by the way various edges intersect with each other, and they (re)create these patterns in their pictures. In some pictures, vertical lines dominate; in others, it may be horizontal or diagonal lines. Some critics maintain that vertical lines are assertive, horizontal lines contemplative, and diagonals dynamic. A picture of tall, narrow skyscrapers with strong vertical lines affects us differently than a landscape, the lines of which echo the horizon in the background; pictures that show movement (sports photographs, for instance) often emphasize diagonal lines.

When you look at an image, you may discover certain line patterns. Do these patterns tie in with the subject of the picture? In Danny Lyon's photograph of a prisoner (p. 613), strong horizontal and vertical lines dominate: The prisoner in his white suit is standing up straight in front of a brick wall; the mortar between the bricks appears as a gridwork of horizontal and vertical lines. The photograph is taken through the spy-hole in the door, which forms a thick, black frame around the scene inside. It looks as if the prisoner is *caught* in the box formed by the cutout in the door, the lines of which echo the box-pattern on the wall behind him. The prison guard behind the prisoner is the only object in the picture that forms a diagonal as he raises his bent left arm and leans over to the right. This makes sense with regard to the subject: unlike the prisoner, who is trapped inside the vertical and horizontal lines of the picture, the guard is free to move at will.

EXERCISE: Analyzing Line

1. Describe the line patterns you see in Norman Rockwell's "After the Prom" (p. 91). How do these lines divide the picture into segments? If you follow the line patterns with your eyes, where do they lead your gaze?

2. Look at the line patterns in William Hogarth's "Gin Lane" (p. 22). How does he use vertical, horizontal, and diagonal lines?

3. Look at the line patterns in Michael Iooss's photograph of Michael Jordan (p. 121). How do the lines in this image tie in with the subject of the picture?

SHAPE

Who among us has not looked at the clouds in the sky and tried to determine what they look like—a camel, an elephant, a monster with two heads? When we do this, we look at clouds as **shapes**, as areas that can be distinguished from their surroundings, in this case by their color. Objects in pictures appear to us as patches of color or patches of light and darkness. If these shapes are rounded and have no sharp angles, we often call them *organic* shapes. If they have straight edges and precise angles, we refer to them as *geometric* shapes. Pictures with an abundance of soft, round shapes have a different impact on us than images with sharp, angular shapes do.

When you analyze pictures for shape, try to detect any patterns of shapes, just as you did with line, and see if you can link what you see to the subject of the picture. In Ernest Baker's "Albert Einstein" (p. 120), for instance, the shape of the mushroom cloud resembles the shape of the physicist's head. Since Einstein's work contributed to the development of the first atomic bomb, the similarity of the two shapes emphasizes the connection between his head and the cloud: His brain came up with the concepts that enabled engineers to build the bomb.

EXERCISE: Analyzing Shape

1. If you look at the shapes in Rockwell's "After the Prom," do you see any significant patterns that reinforce the subject of the picture?

2. How does Hogarth use and define shapes in "Gin Lane"?

3. How did Iooss use shape in his photograph of Michael Jordan?

VALUE

Value refers to tone, the distribution of brightness or darkness in an image. Value exists in both color and black-and-white pictures, but it might be easier to understand its principles by looking at a black and white image such as William Hogarth's "Gin Lane" (p. 23). In this picture, the artist has rendered the cityscape in the background in much lighter tones than those of the buildings closer to the front; the contrast creates the illusion of depth as things in the distance are not as clearly visible to us as things closer to the eye. The woman sitting on the steps is lighter than the scene behind her; it's almost as if she had a spotlight shining on her. The effect is the same as that of theatrical lighting: Because she is the brightest object in the foreground of the picture, she and her unfortunate child become the focal point of the image. And look at the vessel hanging from a hook in the bottom left corner. Can you see how it is darker on the edges and brighter in the middle? It is this distribution of light and shade that makes it look round rather than flat like the wall behind it. (When Renaissance artists discovered this effect, called *chiaroscuro*, it revolutionized art.)

When you analyze a picture, think of value as the light effects the artist has created: What parts of the picture are highlighted and thus stand out? What parts recede into the shade? What parts appear round or flat? Where do you see striking contrasts between light and dark that emphasize dark objects against a light background or the other way round? (If you have trouble seeing value in a color picture, a black-and-white xerox copy will give you a better idea of the distribution of light and shadow.) Once you have determined what light effects the artist has created, try to see if you can link them to the subject of the picture. Hogarth created "Gin Lane" to illustrate the destructive powers of gin. By putting a drunk woman, who does not notice that her baby is falling to his death, in the spotlit center of the picture, he delivers a powerful argument to his audience: A drink that makes mothers forget about their children is dangerous poison indeed.

EXERCISE: **Analyzing Value**

1. What light effects does Norman Rockwell create in "After the Prom"? What is the effect of the light?

2. How does Walter Iooss use light in his picture of Michael Jordan?

COLOR

"Everything looks worse in black and white," laments Paul Simon in his song "Kodachrome." Whereas many photographic artists would disagree with this statement, **colors** have a fascination for us that is hard to resist. Psychologists have tried to categorize the emotional effect colors have on us[2]: We perceive red as an energetic, impulsive color that might also signal danger or aggression. We see blue as a calm, soothing color that inspires confidence, and yellow as positive and cheerful. Since green is a dominant color in nature, we think of it in terms of youthfulness, hope, and vigor, but it can also symbolize danger and poison (green-faced witches at Halloween come to mind). Artists often refer to hues in terms of "cool" (blues and blueish greens) and "warm" (yellows and reds), a division that associates colors with tactile sensations.

Artists who work in advertising know about these emotional associations and use them in their ads and commercials. However, it would be wrong to reduce the color palette of every image to restricted symbolic meanings like those listed above, especially since the so-called experts do not always agree on the exact associations of each color. When you analyze an image, look primarily for color patterns and for effective contrasts: A brightly colored object in a picture of predominantly muted tones stands out, as does the chauffeur's sky-blue uniform in Annie Leibovitz's photograph of Liberace and Scott Thorson (p. 122). The glittery silver tones of the mirrored car, the sequins on the costumes, and the jewelry tie the two men and the car into a group that is separate from the dark background. The faces and hands of the men (the only parts of their bodies not completely covered by lavish materials) appear to be a strange orangey brown; their skin tone looks as artificial and made-up as their trappings, but their hands and faces stand out as warm patches of color, the only human element in the picture. Leibovitz's portrait renders the flamboyant artist as the epitome of Vegas-style entertainment and glitzy glamor; even his face and hands and those of his companion cannot quite escape the overall artificiality of this world.

EXERCISE: Analyzing Color

1. How does Norman Rockwell use color in "After the Prom"?

2. How does Walter Iooss use color in his picture of Michael Jordan?

TEXTURE

Texture refers to what an object or a surface feels like if you touch it. Since we normally *see* images rather than touch them, the accurate rendering of texture contributes to the realistic effect of a picture. Some objects in a picture may appear smooth, some rough. Some surfaces look like they would be cold to the touch, some warm. For example, many portrait artists of previous centuries worked very hard to reproduce the textures of splendid clothes—the rich bro-

---

[2]The following observations are drawn from William T. Squires, *Art, Experience, and Criticism*, Needham Heights, MA: Ginn Press, 1991.

cades, satins, and furs—their sitters wore because it was important to them that their portraits indicate the sitters' wealth and social power. Similarly, Leibovitz's portrait of Liberace and Scott Thorson emphasizes texture: the luxurious softness of Liberace's fur coat, the prickliness of the sequined designs on their clothes, the cold metallic smoothness of the mirror tiles on the car. Since most of us cannot afford such splendor, we recognize an air of upper-class exclusivity about the two men. However, the sheer abundance of rich materials makes them look fake and, well, a bit *tacky*, and this, too, is part of Leibovitz's point about the two men and the showbiz world they inhabit. Leibovitz could have shot this photograph in soft focus, emphasizing not the gaudiness but the luxuriousness of the textures; however, to make her audience see the tackiness of the Vegas lifestyle, she deliberately overemphasizes the opulent textures of her sitters' clothes.

EXERCISE: Analyzing Texture

1. How does Norman Rockwell render texture in "After the Prom"?
2. How does Hogarth use texture in "Gin Street"?
3. What does texture contribute to Walter Iooss's picture of Michael Jordan?

COMPOSITION

Composition refers to the overall arrangement of objects and shapes in a picture. Just as writers pay great attention to organization, the order in which they present information to their readers, artists arrange the things in their pictures to maximize the impact their images have on their audience. Just like an essay, an image has a *focal point*: an object, person, or shape that occupies the most important area of the picture and that is crucial to the overall meaning of the picture. As we have seen above, the woman too drunk to notice that her baby is falling down the stairs is the focal point in Hogarth's "Gin Lane." The other elements in the picture (the people and the buildings) are arranged around this woman. Hogarth (like many classically trained artists before and after him) presents his subject matter on three levels of the picture plane: the foreground (occupied by the woman, her baby, and the dead man in the bottom right), the middle ground (the groups of people on what appears to be a raised area behind the brick wall), and the background (the city-scape). Generally, the most important things in a picture are in the foreground and/or in the center because that is where the viewer's eye is naturally drawn. However, many artists choose to put their focal point elsewhere. When you look at an image, try to determine which part of the picture your eye comes back to again and again. Chances are, you have found the focal point of the picture.

An important concept in composition is *balance*, which refers to the distribution of shapes in a picture. The simplest type of balance is symmetry, which occurs when shapes are equally distributed on both sides of a vertical or a horizontal line. Leibovitz's portrait of the weightlifter Cheryl Haworth (p. 260) is a good example. The picture shows the young woman from the front; all the elements in the picture—the woman's body, her facial features, hands, and feet—are symmetrically lined up along a vertical line (this line, however, is not the middle of the picture—only one end of the barbell shows). However effective in some pictures, strict symmetry can get boring (that is why Leibovitz shifts the focus slightly to the right of the center), and thus many artists opt for an "easy symmetry"[3] in which the shapes around the focal point balance each other without being exactly identical. Hogarth's picture is a good example of this. The buildings on both sides of the picture are not the same, but they occupy roughly the same amount of space; they provide a frame of sorts for the cityscape in the background. Similarly, the group in the left middle ground (the figures around the man holding up a saw) balances the group on the opposite side, even though the latter has a larger number of figures, which appear smaller because they are at a greater distance. Simultaneously, the group around the man with the saw provides balance for the dead man at the bottom right. The drunk woman sits right in the middle of all these opposing shapes.

Sometimes artists choose compositions with which their audiences would be familiar from other pictures. Who has not seen the picture of the New York firefighters raising the American flag amidst the rubble of the World Trade Center after September 11, 2001? The image was immediately famous, partly because it recalled another, earlier picture: Joe Rosenthal's much-acclaimed photograph of American Marines raising the flag to celebrate victory in Iwo Jima, the site of a crucial battle in the Pacific during World War II. (Shortly after its publication, Felix DeWeldon turned the image into an equally famous sculpture.) In both pictures, the men and the flag post in the middle form a triangle, a compositional structure with which most of us are familiar from religious pictures of past centuries: Christ on the cross, surrounded by a group of figures around its base; the Virgin Mary and the child, with groups of adoring angels or saints at her feet. By using a triangular composition, the two contemporary photographers link their images to a long tradition of religious images and thus underscore the importance of the patriotic moments they portray.

When you analyze images for their composition, try to establish the focal point first and then examine how the shapes and things surrounding it are balanced with each other. Keep in mind that there is no set rule as to how much balance a picture has to have. Sometimes the *lack* of balance, the uneven distribution of shapes on the picture plane, is an important part of an artist's mes-

---

[3]William T. Squires's term.

sage. And, as always, keep in mind that technical details by themselves are not all that interesting: they gain significance only once you tie them to the subject of a picture.

EXERCISE: Analyzing Composition

1. What is the significance of Norman Rockwell's arrangement of objects and shapes in "After the Prom"?

2. How does Walter Iooss use composition in "Michael Jordan"?

A WRITER AT WORK: DAVE HICKEY WRITING ABOUT NORMAN ROCKWELL'S "AFTER THE PROM"

A long-time art critic and professor, Dave Hickey has written about countless images. His article "The Kids Are All Right: After the Prom," first published in the catalogue for a major Norman Rockwell exhibition, can teach us about the way pros write about images. Of course, Hickey draws from a great store of knowledge about art and art history; most of us would not know some of the things he says about the picture and its connections to European and American art history. This is why it is extremely important to take a look at the picture itself to see what *you* think of it before you read what Hickey has to say about it.

It would be excellent preparation to answer the questions about the picture that follow each of the elements discussed above. As a less time-consuming alternative, you might answer the following questions as a warming-up exercise:

- Rockwell titled his 1957 painting "After the Prom." What setting did he choose for his picture?

- Who are the people in the picture? What are they doing?

- Who is the man sitting on the left side of the picture? What clues do his clothes give us about him?

- What are the expressions on the faces of the people in the picture? What clue do they give us about Rockwell's subject, about the message the artist is trying to express with his picture?

- If you were to sum up the meaning of the picture, the statement Norman Rockwell makes with the soda fountain scene he created in this picture, what would it be?

The Kids Are All Right: After the Prom

DAVE HICKEY

The icons of a living culture do not begin as canonical works preserved in books and museums and taught in university classrooms. They begin as treasures of living memory, and when official canonization is not forthcoming, they either fade from that memory or remain and survive there, as Norman Rockwell's *After the Prom* has remained and survived in mine. I remember its first appearance on the cover of *The Saturday Evening Post* on May 25, 1957 (when I was as young as its young protagonists). Reconsidering it now, I find myself hard-pressed to come up with a better example of Rockwell's penchant for giving us, as John Updike put it, "a little more than the occasion strictly demands." With *After the Prom*, Rockwell has given us a great deal more than the occasion demands: a full-fledged, intricately constructed, deeply knowledgeable work that recruits the total resources of European narrative picture-making to tell the tiny tale of agape he has chosen to portray—all this for the cover of a weekly periodical whose pages will curl and melt before we have forgotten Rockwell's image.

The *Post* version of *After the Prom* is a reproduction of a painting in oil pigments on an easel-sized, rectangular canvas that is about 13 percent taller than it is wide. In the narrative of the painting, Rockwell has positioned us so we are at once inside and outside the story. We have just entered a small drugstore in an American town on an evening in the spring and now stand facing a 1950s-era soda fountain bathed in golden light and populated by local citizens in 1950s-era clothing. Three customers are sitting on stools in front of the counter. A soda jerk is on duty behind it. In the right center of the picture, a blond young woman in a white formal dress and a brown-headed boy in a white dinner jacket and dark slacks sit facing one another on counter stools so that we see them in profile.

The boy perches on the stool in an erect posture, holding the young woman's purse and gloves before him with her pale pink sweater draped across his forearm. He looks on proudly as the soda jerk leans across the counter to inhale the fragrance of the young woman's gardenia corsage. She lifts the flowers from her shoulder to present them to him. The third customer at the counter (partially cropped by the left-hand edge of the picture) sits on a stool with his back to us, holding a cup of coffee in his right hand. He glances over and smiles as the soda jerk sniffs the gardenia. A working man and almost certainly a war veteran, he wears a tattered bomber jacket, an Air Force cap with a visor, and khaki pants. A notebook and several pencils are stuffed into his back pocket. A ring of keys hangs from his belt.

The small-town consanguinity of the group is emphasized by the fact that all four figures in the painting bear a vague familial resemblance to one another. The boy and the soda jerk, who have the same nose, chin, and eyebrows, are almost certainly brothers. Everyone in the picture is smiling the same small smile, and we, as beholders at once inside and outside this cozy scene, are invited to smile as well. We are inside the store but not up at the counter—a part of the society but not a part of the community—but the open picture plane still welcomes us. It implies that even though it is best to be a part of the community, just being a part of the society is not so bad, because even though we cannot smell the gardenia, we can inhale the atmosphere of the benign tableau arranged around it. The clustered burst of white in the center of Rockwell's painting, created by the young woman's dress, the boy's jacket, and the soda jerk's hat and shirt, constitute *our gardenia*; we stand in the same relationship to that white blossom of tactile paint as the soda jerk does to the young woman's corsage.

To compose this scene before us, Rockwell has divided the vertical rectangle of his picture in the traditional European manner, by laying the short side of the rectangle off against its long side, creating two overlapping squares whose intersecting diagonals create the picture's armature. The bottom line of the upper square runs along the tile line at the base of the stools; the top line of the lower square runs exactly through the boy's sight line (marking one of the horizon lines in the bent space of the painting). The whole action of the picture occurs within the overlapping area of the two squares—just at, or just below, our eye level. The counter, the kick rail, and the floor tile create a harmonic sequence of strong horizontals that intersect the regular verticals of the stools, the wood paneling, and the signs on the wall behind the counter. This in turn creates an architectural grid into which the human figures are arranged in an intricate pattern of rhyming angles.

The forty-five-degree diagonals of the overlapping squares predominate. The front edge of the young woman's white dress, her upper arm, and the soda jerk's extended left forearm all lie on left-slanting forty-five-degree angles. The veteran's lower leg and the boy's upper leg lie on right-slanting forty-five-degree angles that reinforce the right-slanting forty-five-degree sight line of the soda jerk as he gazes at the gardenia. The boy's upper leg intersects the front of the young woman's dress at a right angle on the horizontal center line of the painting; this creates an inverted triangle that cradles the intimate action of the picture. The upper leg of the veteran and the boy's lower leg lie exactly on a falling thirty-degree line that traverses the picture, so their bent legs create two symmetrically opposed seventy-degree angles, like arrows, pointing to the young woman, who is the center of all their attention. The pencil behind the soda jerk's ear also lies on a thirty-degree angle; it points out the young woman, as well.

In his most elegant formal maneuver, Rockwell takes the right-pointing triangle created by the working man's bent leg and the left edge of the canvas and rotates it ninety degrees to the right so it reappears as the upward-pointing triangle created by the soda jerk's bent left arm and the top of the counter. In this way, Rockwell acknowledges and accommodates for the fact that he has taken the static, symmetrical, face-to-face encounter between the boy and the young woman and invested it with dynamic balance by shifting its center of gravity about 13 percent upward and to the right, as indicated by the direction of the pointing triangles, to a point marked by the inverted triangle that cradles the central action. This device, combined with Rockwell's cropping of the counter on the left and right, creates a picture that, although it is harmonious and delicately balanced within itself, does not feel self-enclosed or claustrophobic. It still opens out; it still includes us.

To achieve this peculiar blend of inclusion and exclusion, Rockwell employs a pictorial strategy invented in late-eighteenth-century France and subtly alters it to his own purposes. As Michael Fried pointed out in *Absorption and Theatricality* (1988), one of the idiosyncratic inventions of eighteenth-century French painting was the practice of inserting a surrogate beholder into narrative pictures—a character within the painting's space whose response to the action we may take as a cue to our own responses and through whose eyes we are presumed to see the scene portrayed in its optimum configuration. This device is employed as a naughty joke in Jean-Honoré Fragonard's *The Swing* where the surrogate beholder has a revealing view of the young lady in the swing that is not available to us. In Jacques-Louis David's *Belasarius Receiving Alms*, we see Justinian's great general, unfairly disgraced and blinded by the emperor, reduced to begging for alms in the street. One of Belasarius's soldiers stands in the background of David's painting facing us, witnessing the scene we see from the opposite side. His horror and alarm cue our own responses, and his presence renders the action of the painting self-enclosed, as if we were seeing this drama from outside the moment and behind the proscenium.

In *After the Prom*, the soda jerk performs the function of Belasarius's soldier. He is our surrogate beholder (or inhaler, in this case). His response is clearly a cue to our own, but with a difference. Eighteenth-century paintings of this sort, such as Jean-Baptiste Siméon Chardin's *House of Cards* or Fragonard's *Young Woman Reading*, insist on the *privacy* of the experience—of the young man building his house of cards or the young woman engrossed in her romantic novel. By extension, the private experience of absorbed beholder *inside* the painting is presumed to be analogous with that of the absorbed beholder *outside* the painting; both are presumed to be engaged in internal activities outside the realm of the social. In *After the Prom*, however, the soda jerk, who is our surrogate beholder (or inhaler), is not alone. He is *himself beheld* by the three other figures in the painting. He inhales the fragrance of the gardenia that is symbolic of young love, and he visibly responds; the other figures in the painting respond to his response, and to one another. We respond to the totality of these responses, but we are not alone either. We are but one of many citizens glancing at their weekly issue of *The Saturday Evening Post*.

The innocent relationship between the two young people, symbolized by the gardenia corsage, then, is less the subject of than the occasion for Rockwell's picture. The generosity of the characters' responses, and of our own, is the painting's true, argumentative moral subject, and this was especially true in 1957 when Rockwell's prescient visual argument that "the kids are all right" was far from de rigueur. Having been a kid in 1957, I can testify to the welcome reassurance of Rockwell's benediction. It was exactly what was needed because, even though we all remember that American children rebelled against their parents in the 1960s, we tend to forget that American parents rebelled against their own children in the 1950s—that in the midst of the postwar boom, they began to regard their offspring with jealousy and suspicion, as spoiled, hedonistic delinquents who had not fought World War II or suffered through the Great Depression and were now reaping the unearned benefits of their parents' struggle. This attitude is the target of the reproach implied by the veteran's response to the action in *After the Prom*. His benign smile seems to say: "This is what I was fighting for—this is the true consequence of that great historical cataclysm—this moment with the kids and the gardenia corsage."

Rockwell's picture, then, opposes the comfortable, suspicious pessimism of the 1950s and proposes, in its place, a tolerance for and faith in the young as the ground-level condition of democracy. And, strangely enough, this celebration of the historical promise of youth is probably the single aspect of Rockwell's work that distinguishes him as a peculiarly American artist. In all other aspects of his practice, Rockwell was a profoundly European painter, a painter of the bourgeois social world in an American tradition that has almost no social painters and very few paintings that even portray *groups* of people, except at ceremonial occasions in faux-democratic "history paintings" or as figures in a landscape. The high tradition of American art is that of portraits, landscapes, and still-life painting. Rockwell painted mercantile *society*, in the tradition of Hals, Hogarth, Grueze, Boilly, and Frith, but being an American, he painted a society grounded not in the wisdom of its elders, but in the promise of its youth.

This, I think, accounts for the perfect inversion of European convention in *After the Prom*. First, Rockwell was not painting a bucolic genre idyll, like one of François Boucher's romantic encounters of shepherd and shepherdess. He was investing this small-town flirtation with the seriousness of historical romance. In a comparable European painting, however, we would see earthbound adult lovers (Nicolas Poussin's *Venus and Adonis*, or Giovanni Battista Tiepolo's *Anthony and Cleopatra*) surrounded and celebrated by floating or gamboling infants. In Rockwell's painting, we have floating youths surrounded and celebrated by earthbound adults. Thus, the two adults in *After the Prom* are invested with considerable weight. The soda jerk leans theatrically on the counter. The veteran sits heavily on his stool, leans against the counter, and rests his foot on the kick rail. The force of gravity is made further visible by the draped sweater on the boy's arm and the hanging keys on the veteran's belt, while the two young people, in their whiteness and brightness, float above the floor, sitting perfectly erect on the pedestals of the counter stools—in one of the most complex, achieved emblems of agape, tolerance, and youthful promise ever painted. ■

ANALYZING ADS

Since most advertising combines images and words, writing about advertising requires skill at analyzing both. Like writers, photographers, or painters, ad designers make conscious choices to create the desired effect upon their audiences. In some ways, analyzing print ads is easier than analyzing images intended as art because the ad designer's ultimate goal is always to sell a product, service, or idea. In art, the subject and purpose of an image are not always immediately clear.

Because the goal of advertising is to sell, advertisers must employ particular strategies in designing ads. To familiarize yourself with these strategies, read John Caples's "Layouts and Illustrations That Attract the Most Readers" (p. 640). Now look closely at the ad for Phoenix Wealth Management on page 114 Does the ad adhere to the principles of advertising that Caples outlines? Does it violate any of those principles? What specific audience does the ad target? Make a list of features in the ad that correspond to those recommended by Caples for successful ad design. Then read the following analysis of the ad.

A NEW WORLD, A NEW WOMAN: PHOENIX
RISES TO THE CHALLENGE

In the top right corner of an ad for Phoenix Wealth Management, a woman dressed in Elizabethan finery sits erect, in an ornately carved chair. Her expression and her bearing are imperious: head at an angle, chin and nose tilted up, lips drawn, she looks down (her nose) at the viewer. The elaborate headdress, the ermine-and-jewel-trimmed gold brocade dress speak aristocracy, if not royalty.

The viewer's eye is drawn downward, to the bottom left corner of the ad, where a woman laughs openly, unapologetically, hands clasped gleefully close to her face. With chin down and a rebellious lock of hair grazing her cheek, she gazes directly, triumphantly, at the camera. Her attire—tiara and leather jacket—announces a risk-taker, someone unbound by rules or traditions.

What do an Elizabethan aristocrat and a thoroughly modern girl have in common? Money, the ad screams, but not much else. In fact, the ad is a study in contrasts, its theme announced in the large type: "Money. It's not what it used to be." What it used to be, the ad suggests, is stuffy and stiff, reserved and restricted, all corsets and heavy headdresses. What it *is* is bold, hip, liberating. The distinction between "old money," as represented

by the woman of dignified pose in the top portion of the
ad, and "new money," as suggested by the woman celebrating her good fortune in the bottom segment of the ad, is
clear. The sentence just below the large type, in smaller
type, reinforces the distinction: Some people still
inherit wealth; the rest of us have no choice but to earn
it. The distinction is drawn, then, not just between old
and new, but also between us and them. And who, the ad
asks, would want to be one of them? That severe-looking
noblewoman, weighted down by rank and privilege, is
clearly not having fun. But no *noblesse oblige*, the hefty
responsibility of the high-born, for our post-modern
babe; this girl earns her money—she's one of us.

   Positioning is crucial to the message here, beginning
with the obvious horizontal bisecting that clearly
divides the ad into two separate planes, one shot in rich
browns and golds, one in hip black and white, establishing class and time differences. While the eye lingers for
a moment on the top half of the page, the viewer's attention quickly moves to the bottom portion of the ad—where
the action is. Brighter and busier, this part of the ad
is dominated by a larger picture than the one at the top
part of the ad, so that we see more of the woman's face,
and it contains all but one word of the ad's text as
well as the all-important company logo. In pulling the
viewer downward, traditional hierarchies are rendered
invalid: although the regal figure is situated at the top
of the ad, it is clearly the woman on the bottom who is
on top. She has appropriated the "crown": While the headdress worn by the Elizabethan woman fades into the background, the apex of the tiara (rhinestones? diamonds?) is
positioned just below the end of the ad's most important
and prominently featured word, "Money," pulling it visu-
ally into the modern woman's space, suggesting the supplanting of wealth and power, by one of us.

   Of course, the ad targets an audience more specific
than us. Featuring women only, the ad clearly targets a
female audience, acknowledging that the acquisition of
riches, in the past a man's job (the only women who had
their own wealth were those privileged few born into it)
is now also the domain of women. But Phoenix Wealth

Management is marketing its services to a particular breed of women, women who earn their own money and have enough wealth to need management, "high-net-worth people," as we are told in the small type text.

While the Phoenix ad exploits contrasts—between blue bloods and the *nouveau riche*, the rule-bound and the rule-breakers, boredom and fun—to send the message that power without fun is no power indeed, it also uses an appeal to tradition to sell its product. In the small print message culminating in the large-type logo we are informed that Phoenix points people in "innovative new directions"—the only way for a modern moneyed gal to go—but, lest a potential customer worry about its track record, we are reminded that it has been doing so "for nearly 150 years." Phoenix uses traditional appeals—to money, power, and sex—but the message here is a feminist one, lending a decidedly contemporary edge, evident also in the ad's stark contrasts, in the cool black-and-white photography of its critical space, and in the ironic thwarting of traditional assumptions. The ad targets—and assumes—an audience of sophisticated, smart, successful women. This is a new world, with new ways: Phoenix rises to meet the New Woman and her new wealth.

EXERCISE: Analyzing a Magazine Ad

Find a full-page ad in a magazine that appeals to you (or use one of the ads reproduced in this book), and use what you learned from reading Caples and your own skills to analyze it. Look at the ad's overall design, and then look at its various parts. Consider pictures and illustrations, color type, visual lines, text. (You may find it easiest to organize your analysis according to these components.) Take notes, and then, using your sharpest descriptive skills, write an analysis of your ad. Be sure to consider *your* audience and purpose and how that might affect what you write. For example, you would probably approach your assignment somewhat differently if you were trying to sell a prospective ad to a company (in other words, you have designed the ad for the manufacturer of the product in the ad) than you would if you were using the ad to illustrate to a marketing class how advertising works. As in any other writing, your introduction and conclusion are critical areas of the text, and it is important that your thesis or controlling idea, whether stated explicitly or implicitly, is clear.

YOUR TURN: Writing About Images

1. Using your answers to the above questions about Norman Rockwell's "After the Prom," write a paper in which you analyze the meaning of the picture. You might want to start with a description of the subject matter so your reader gets an idea of what the paper looks like. Be sure to state the subject of the picture, its main idea, before you show how the individual elements work together to support this central idea.

2. Using your answers to the above questions about William Hogarth's "Gin Lane" and the sample analyses provided in the discussions of the picture's value and composition, write an analysis of the picture in which you show how the individual elements come together to support this central idea.

3. Using your answers to the above questions about Walter Iooss's portrait of Michael Jordan, take your material and put it together in an essay that analyzes the photograph as a whole. Again, for your reader's sake, you should discuss the subject matter before you state what you think the subject of the picture is, the central idea it conveys about the great athlete. The main part of your paper will probably consist of your detailed analysis of the individual elements and how they come together to articulate the subject of the photograph.

NORMAN ROCKWELL

After the Prom

Norman Rockwell's radiant scene of a young couple's stopover at a soda fountain on their way home from the prom first appeared on the cover of The Saturday Evening Post *on May 25, 1957. It remains a favorite among Rockwell's audience and critics, among them Dave Hickey, who chose it as the subject for "The Kids Are All Right: After the Prom," an essay included in the exhibition catalogue for a 1999 Norman Rockwell retrospective.*

1. Describe the scene Rockwell depicts in this painting. Who are the characters in this picture? What story does the picture tell?

2. What is the setting of this scene? How do you know?

3. How does Rockwell arrange lines and shapes in the composition of this image?

4. How does the artist use light and color in this painting?

5. What overall mood does Rockwell create in this picture? What emotions does he evoke in the viewer?

COLOR IMAGE GALLERY

[COLOR PLATE 1]

YANN ARTHUS-BERTRAND

Wedding Dress

The author of several books and a regular contributor to Figaro, GEO, *and* Newlook, *Yann Arthus-Bertrand lives in Paris, France. This photograph, published in* A Day in the Life of America *in 1986, captures a threshold moment between childhood and adulthood.*

1. Describe the style of Linda Scalese's wedding dress. Why do you think she is showing it to her friends?

2. What do the objects scattered around Linda's bedroom say about her?

3. How does the photographer use light and color in the picture?

4. What conclusions do you think the photographer ask us to draw about this picture?

RICHARD ELLIS

Close-up: James Carville

Louisiana-born James Carville was Bill Clinton's most powerful spin doctor, propelling the Arkansas governor to the presidency in 1992. Carville married Republican Mary Matalin, the manager of George H. W. Bush's unsuccessful reelection (pictured here, with Carville, on NBC's Meet the Press*), soon after the campaign. The couple's political disagreements and the concurrent success of their marriage has made them famous TV personalities; their 1994 book* All's Fair: Love, War and Running for President, *was a best-seller.*

1. What is the setting for this shot? How do you know? What commentary does the photographer make by shooting the couple in this environment and not, say, in their living room?

2. How do their facial expressions and body language reflect the political divide that James Carville and Mary Matalin represent?

3. What conclusions can you draw about these two individual personalities from the items in front of them, their clothes, and their body language?

IMAGE GALLERY

COLOR

ANNIE LEIBOVITZ

A Model and Her Son

Annie Leibovitz is known for her original and often poignant portraits of celebrities. Her photograph of Jerry Hall, ex-wife of Mick Jagger and mother of four of his children, with their youngest son, Gabriel, draws ironically upon the iconography of the Holy Virgin-and-Child tradition.

1. When you first look at the picture, does its depiction of a nursing mother surprise you? Are Hall's demeanor and body language consistent with those of a nursing mother?

2. What kind of clothes does Hall wear? What do they contribute to the image? How do the surroundings—the furniture and room accessories—contribute to the subject of the picture?

3. How does Leibovitz use color and texture in this photograph?

4. What is the effect of composition in this picture?

5. What references to art history does Leibovitz make in this picture, and how does she deviate from these models?

6. What comment about Hall does Leibovitz's photograph make?

ARTHUR GRACE

Workout

In this 1986 photograph of Amy Foote and her exercise partner Paul Neis, Arthur Grace captures an intense moment in an Albuquerque, New Mexico, aerobics class. Grace's photographs have appeared in Time, Life, Look, Newsweek, the London Sunday Times, *and* Paris-Match.

1. Describe the situation in the picture.

2. What do the woman's and the man's facial expressions say about this moment?

3. How does the photographer use color in this picture?

4. How does composition contribute to the effect of the photograph?

5. What does this photograph say about women and body image?

COLOR IMAGE GALLERY

COLOR

IMAGE GALLERY

LAUREN GREENFIELD

Ashleigh

Los Angeles photographer Lauren Greenfield garnered national attention when she won the National Press Photographers' Pictures of the Year contest with her 1997 documentary Fast Forward: Growing Up in the Shadow of Hollywood, *from which this image is taken. In her photographs, she captures the lives of young people as they try—in very different ways—to conform to the dream factory's standards of beauty and success.*

1. Describe the scene in the picture. What do you think is the story behind this photograph?

2. What do Ashleigh's clothes and her concern with the scale say about her?

3. What do her surroundings—the room, the objects—suggest about her social environment?

4. What commentary does Greenfield make about "growing up in the shadow of Hollywood" with this picture?

ANNIE LEIBOVITZ

Lenda Murray

In her 1999 book Women, _photographer Annie Leibovitz tells us that Lenda Murray "grew up in Detroit and majored in political science at Western Michigan University" and that she "began bodybuilding in 1984. She entered her first Ms. Olympia event in 1990 and won the competition—the pinnacle of women's bodybuilding—for six consecutive years."_

1. Leibovitz photographed Lenda Murray from the back, with her face only partially visible in profile. Why do you think she chose to shoot Murray from this angle?

2. Where was the photograph taken? What do the objects in the background contribute to the picture's overall effect?

3. What is the color scheme in the photograph? What does it contribute to the photograph's overall effect?

4. How does Lenda Murray's body compare to traditional definitions of female beauty?

COLOR

IMAGE GALLERY

CHRIS JOHNS

Shopping for Meat

Named Newspaper Photographer of the Year in 1979, Chris Johns took this picture of a modern-day cowboy and his family shopping at Dillon's Supermarket in Garden City, Kansas, in 1986, when Johns was working as a contract photographer with the National Geographic Society.

1. How does Johns emphasize the subject matter of this picture—meat?

2. What is ironic about Mike Hunter's clothes in connection with the meat packages in the cooler behind him?

3. What are the dominant colors in this picture? How is the color sym-bolism significant for the subject of this picture?

4. How does Johns's photograph comment on the shopping and eating habits of the average American family?

STEPHANIE MAZE

Lunch at Uncle Antonio's

Working in the United States, Mexico, Spain, and other countries, Stephanie Maze has freelanced for National Geographic since 1979. She has covered three Olympic Games and, in 1985, won a first-prize award from the White House Press Photographers Association.

1. What does this photograph say about food rituals in this Cuban family?

2. Does the photo suggest any clash of cultures or traditions? How?

3. What does the photograph say about the roles of men and women in this family?

4. How does Maze use composition in this photograph? What do the details of the dining room contribute to the composition?

IMAGE GALLERY

COLOR

IMAGE GALLERY

COLOR

KERRI McCAFFETY

Bourbon Street, New Orleans

This photograph is from Kerri McCaffety's 1998 book Obituary Cocktail, *a collection of photographs of famous (and infamous) New Orleans bars. New Orleanian McCaffety studied anthropology before becoming a full-time photographer.*

1. What do you know or have you heard about New Orleans's famed Bourbon Street? How does McCaffety's photograph support those descriptions? How does the picture go against the grain of what one associates with Bourbon Street?

2. How does McCaffety use color to create the mood in this photograph?

3. How does the photograph demonstrate McCaffety's eye for effective composition?

4. What does this photograph say about the way McCaffety sees New Orleans and Bourbon Street—its most famous tourist attraction?

STEVE LISS

Homework

Since 1976, Liss has photographed images of Americana for Time. *This photograph shows Diane Ruthazer and her children saying the Pledge of Allegiance as a part of their homeschooling routine.*

1. What items in this homeschool classroom are commonly found in a regular classroom? In what ways is the Ruthazer's schoolroom different from a regular classroom? Do the children in the picture look like children in a regular school? In what ways are they similar? Different?

2. Does it strike you as odd that the mother would pledge allegiance with her homeschooled children? Why or why not?

3. What is the focal point of the photograph?

4. What do you think the photographer is saying in this picture about homeschooling?

NORMAN ROCKWELL

The Problem We All Live With

When this painting of Ruby Bridges, the first African American girl to attend a forcibly desegregated New Orleans public school against the violent protests of white parents, was first published in Look *in 1964, Norman Rockwell was nationally known as a painter and illustrator of the kind of America his fans liked to see: big-hearted, generous, dedicated to family and community. Many of his admirers were therefore surprised when Rockwell took a stand on a politically charged subject and showed that there were some Americans, at least, who did not quite fit the cozy stereotype that had so long graced the covers of* The Saturday Evening Post.

1. How do you know that the situation depicted in Rockwell's painting is controversial?

2. Who are the men accompanying the little girl? What is their job? Why doesn't Rockwell include their heads in the picture?

3. How does Rockwell emphasize the symbolic significance of Ruby Bridges? What do the clothes she is wearing, her posture, and her facial expression say about the artist's attitude toward her and her ordeal?

4. What do color and composition contribute to the picture?

5. What is Rockwell telling his audience about desegregating public schools? Does he support or oppose it? How do you know?

6. How do you interpret the title of the picture?

MAX AGUILERA-HELLWEG

Reaching for Help

According to the editorial commentary in LIFE: Century of Change, *Aguilera-Hellweg's photograph chronicles a milestone in prenatal surgery: When Trish Switzer, of Maryland, found out that her unborn child had spina bifida, a crippling disease,* "she authorized Dr. Joseph Bruner of the Vanderbuilt University Medical Center to operate on the six-month fetus and close a lesion on its spinal cord." *At the time,* "the procedure had been performed successfully fewer than 50 times," *but when the little girl was born in 1999, she* "was expected to walk normally."

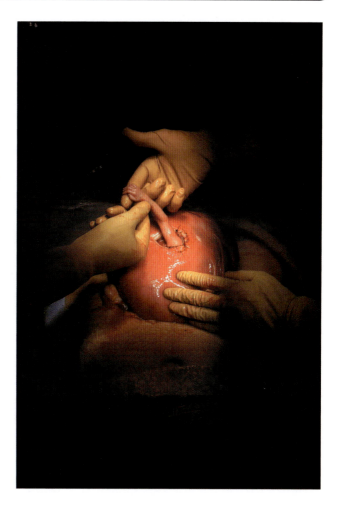

IMAGE GALLERY

COLOR

1. We have all seen photographs of operations. In what way does this photograph fit the genre? What makes it different?

2. How does the photographer use color and light effectively?

3. How does composition contribute to the picture's effectiveness? How would it have been different if the photographer had included objects outside the circle of hands?

4. How might this photograph be used to make a political or philosophical argument? How does it affect you most—artistically or ideologically?

BORIS ARTZYBASHEFF

The Computer in Society

Boris Artzybasheff (1899–1965) immigrated to the United States from Russia at the age of twenty-three. This pencil-and-tempera painting, one of his many images to grace the cover of Time, *was first published on April 2, 1965, and was part of a 1998 exhibit, "The Faces of* Time," *at the Smithsonian Institution in Washington, DC.*

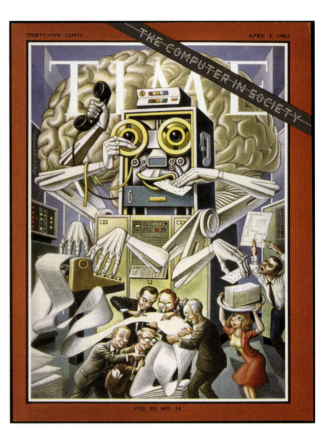

1. How does the painting portray the computer?

2. Why is the computer depicted with a face and human hands? What effect does the artist achieve by doing this?

3. How does this painting characterize the relationship between the computer and humans?

4. Artzybasheff's painting features six men and only one woman. What does the artist's rendering of the men and the woman—their faces, clothes, activities—say about his attitude toward gender equality in the computer age?

5. How are composition, line, and color used in this picture?

6. What details about this picture strike you as old-fashioned? What is still relevant today?

IMAGE GALLERY

COLOR

JOHN McGRAIL

Three-Mile-Island Atomic Power Plant

John McGrail, a professional photographer working out of New York and Philadelphia, specializes in aerial, aviation, maritime, architectural, and panorama photography. The picture included here shows the Three Mile Island nuclear power plant, which, in 1979, had been the site of a serious nuclear malfunction; the plant re-opened in 1985 while nuclear clean-up was still in progress.

1. How does the photograph portray the nuclear power station? Is this a typical "technical" picture of an industrial building complex?

2. How does the photographer use color in this picture? What effect does it have on the viewer?

3. How does he use composition?

4. What does the photograph suggest about the photographer's attitude toward nuclear power plants? Explain.

COLOR   IMAGE GALLERY

INGE FINK

Talk the Talk

A college English instructor and textbook author by trade, Inge Fink likes to take pictures in her spare time. She took this photograph in a parking lot just outside the French Quarter in New Orleans in 2003.

1. Try to decipher as many of the bumper stickers as possible. What recurring themes do you detect?

2. What relationship do you think there is between the car model, the little hut on the roof, and the stickers?

3. What kind of a person would you expect to drive this car? Why do you think someone would adorn a car this way?

4. Would you consider this car a work of art? Why or why not?

ANNIE LEIBOVITZ

Rebecca Denison

Rebecca Denison founded Women Organized to Respond to Life-threatening Diseases (WORLD) in 1991, a year after she was diagnosed with HIV. Leibovitz's portrait shows the activist engaged in spreading the message of her organization.

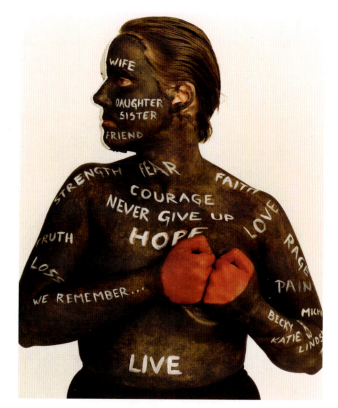

1. How do the words painted on Denison's body relate to the activities of WORLD, the AIDS organization she founded?

2. What do her hands, painted red, symbolize?

3. Why is Denison's body painted dark brown? Would the effect of the photograph have been the same if her skin had been any other color?

4. How does Leibovitz use color and composition in her photograph?

COLOR IMAGE GALLERY

NORMAN ROCKWELL

The Gossips

Rockwell's work is famous for its accurate portrayals of people to be found in virtually every community in America. In this humorous pictorial narrative, he drives home his message about spreading gossip. The picture was first published on the cover of The Saturday Evening Post *on March 6, 1948.*

1. How does Rockwell depict gossip—a speech act that is audible but not really visible?

2. What do the facial expressions of the characters in the painting reveal about the nature of the gossip they pass on? Do the men react differently from the women?

3. To what social class(es) do the characters belong? How do you know?

4. Who is the gossip about? How do you know?

5. What is Rockwell saying about the nature of gossip in this painting?

INFORMATION AWARENESS OFFICE

Information Awareness Office Logo

After widespread criticism for its Orwellian creepiness, the Information Awareness Office, formed in 2002 and housed in the Defense Advanced Research Projects Agency (DARPA), quickly abandoned its logo in favor of a text-only banner that no longer includes the phrase "Scientia est Potentia."

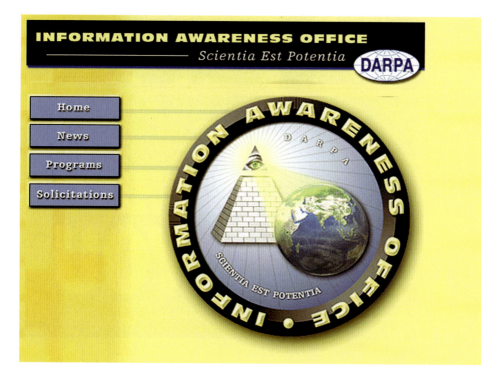

1. What is the effect of the eyeball atop the pyramid? Where does its gaze seem to be fixed?

2. What do you think the designers of the logo intended when they included the phrase *"Scientia est Potentia"*? Why do you think they left the phrase in Latin instead of translating it into English, "Knowledge Is Power"?

3. Consider this description from the opening chapter of George Orwell's *1984*: "The Ministry of Truth . . . was an enormous pyramidal structure of glittering white concrete, soaring up, terrace after terrace, 300 metres into the air." Do you think the IAO logo designers were aware of Orwell's book? Why or why not?

COLOR   IMAGE GALLERY

OFFICE FOR EMERGENCY MANAGEMENT

He's Watching You

This World War II-era poster, published by the United States Government Printing Office for the Office for Emergency Management, Division of Information, in 1942, warned the citizenry of German spies in their midst. Its ominous warning is a variation on the popular WWII slogan, "Loose lips sink ships."

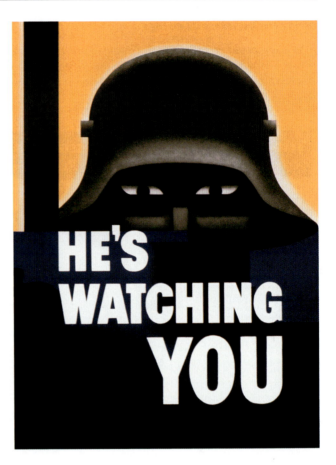

1. What is your first reaction to the image? Do you think the image has any contemporary significance?

2. Why do you think the designer chose a stylized image of a German soldier rather than a realistic image or a photograph?

Which features are emphasized, and why?

3. Comment on the significance of the poster's colors.

4. Note the poster's text. Why are the letters in "YOU" so much larger than those in the other words?

ANDREAS GURSKY

99 Cent

A celebrated contemporary photographer, Andreas Gursky is fascinated by patterns he sees in his environment, patterns he sometimes emphasizes by using large formats: his 1999 photograph of a convenience store on Sunset Boulevard measures almost 7 by 11 feet.

1. When you look at the picture, what do you notice first?

2. How do the line and composition of the picture contribute to its overall effect?

3. How does Gursky use color in this image? What are the dominant col-

ors? What is the effect of the color repetition?

4. What is the significance of the title?

5. What do you think inspired Gursky to take this picture? Is there a subject in all this subject matter?

IMAGE GALLERY

COLOR

COLOR   **IMAGE GALLERY** *(vertical left margin)*

PAUL CHESLEY

In the Pits

Freelance photographer Paul Chesley has contributed to major magazines such as Time, Esquire, *and* Fortune. *This photograph, taken for the 1986* A Day In the Life of America, *shows Matthew Barrall, a clerk at the Chicago Options Exchange, at the end of a long day of trading.*

1. What does the look of the trading pit at the end of the day indicate about the business of the stock exchange?

2. What is the purpose of having a single human being in the picture? How would it have been different if Chesley had included no one in the photograph? Or if he had taken the picture earlier in the day, when the room was full of other traders?

3. Why might the photographer have chosen Matthew Barrall and not someone older? How would you characterize his facial expression, and what does that contribute to the effect of the picture?

MEDICINE SHOPPING CART

This stock image of a shopping cart spilling over with pill bottles illustrates the relationship of pharmaceuticals and commerce, the big business of medicine, which has become a big headache for policymakers as many Americans have to choose between eating and paying rent or buying the medications they need.

1. How does the artist use composition in this picture? What does the downward slant of the cart suggest?

2. Clearly, the shopping cart and pill bottles are not to scale: either the shopping cart is miniaturized or the pill bottles are oversized. Why do you think the image's designer chose to present the objects in the picture as such?

3. What commentary on the state of healthcare does the image make?

COLOR IMAGE GALLERY

COLOR IMAGE GALLERY

PHOENIX WEALTH MANAGEMENT

Money. It's Just Not What It Used to Be

This ad was part of a series of ads for Phoenix Wealth Management that used variations on the theme of "old money" versus "new money."

Money.

It's just not what it used to be.

Some people still inherit wealth, the rest of us have no choice but to earn it. The good news is, a lot of us know how. But then what? Phoenix has been showing people innovative new directions for 150 years. We understand that making money—and knowing what to do with it—are two different skills. It's one reason high-net-worth people turn to Phoenix for help. To learn more about how Phoenix could be helping you, contact your financial advisor or visit www.phoenixwm.com.

⬥ PHOENIX
WEALTH MANAGEMENT

1. Describe the two women pictured in the ad. What do their clothes and facial expressions say about each woman and the social class to which she belongs?

2. How did the ad's designer arrange the images and the advertising copy? What is the focal point of the ad?

3. What does this ad say about money and its origin—in the past and in the present? How do the images and the advertising copy work together to deliver the ad's message?

4. What is the significance of color and tone in the ad?

5. Who is the target audience for this ad?

[COLOR PLATE 24]

ALAN BERNER

Man Photographing John DeAndrea's 'Linda'

An award-winning photojournalist and staff photographer for the Seattle Times, Alan Berner took this photo in 1986 at the Denver Art Museum, where John DeAndrea's life-like statue "Linda" is on display.

IMAGE GALLERY

COLOR

1. Berner's photograph features a lifelike sculpture being photographed by a man. What commentary on art—or genius—does Berner make by including the photographer in the picture?

2. What do the man's clothes, his paunch, and the fact that his face is obscured by his camera's flash suggest about this man? Whom might he represent?

3. What do the many contrasts in the photo—reality and illusion, the realistic sculpture and the abstract paintings, the man and the woman, the curves and the angles—suggest about the nature of art?

4. What does the composition of this picture say about the relationship between art and its audience?

5. What effect does Berner achieve with the colors he uses in his picture?

NEIL LEIFER

Cassius Clay Beats Sonny Liston

Legendary sports photographer Neil Leifer records the moment when Cassius Clay, who later changed his name to Muhammad Ali, knocks out Sonny Liston in the first round of their 1965 rematch for the world championship. According to Time's *original account, Clay beat Liston so fast that the fans in the arena chanted, "Fix! Fix! . . . Fake! Fake!" in protest. Later, Clay claimed to have used his secret "anchor punch" to accomplish this victory.*

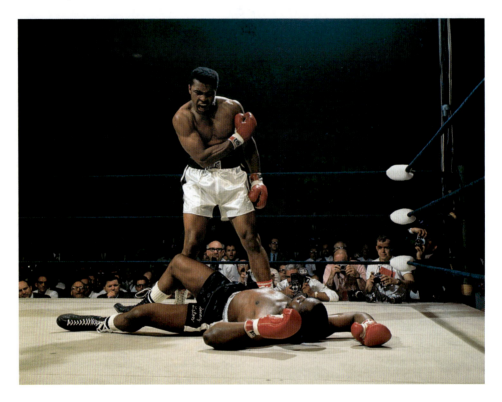

1. How do Clay's facial expression and the two boxers' body language testify to the significance of this moment?

2. How does Leifer use composition, color, and light effects in this picture?

3. Who are the people in the background? Are they just a coinciden-tal backdrop, or do their faces and gestures contribute to the image's overall effect? How?

4. Does this photo go beyond the mere recording of a significant moment in boxing history? Does it offer any commentary on the sport?

NORMAN ROCKWELL

Abstract & Concrete

Rockwell's painting, published on the cover of The Saturday Evening Post *on January 13, 1962, positions a dapper gentleman in front of a painting that mimics the style of abstract expressionist Jackson Pollock, who had died in a car crash six years before.*

1. Describe the painting the man is studying. How does its style contrast to the style of its viewer?

2. How is the man in front of the picture dressed? What social class do his clothes suggest?

3. We cannot see the man's face in the picture, but what do you think is his opinion of the painting he studies? Explain.

4. What story do you think Rockwell, known for his narrative paintings, is trying to tell in this picture?

IMAGE GALLERY

COLOR

FRED VUICH

Masterpiece

Fred Vuich's photograph shows Tiger Woods teeing off at the eighteenth hole during the 2001 Masters tournament in Augusta, Georgia, which Woods ended up winning (for the second time in a row). When interviewed by American Photo *magazine, Vuich, a professional sports photographer, declared that he was "shocked" when the picture made the cover of* Sports Illustrated *that month because it was so different from the usual victory pictures.* Sports Illustrated *photo editor Matt Ginella thought the shot looked "almost like a painting," which inspired him to run it with the headline "Masterpiece."*

1. How does the photographer use composition in this picture?

2. How do light and color contribute to the photograph's effect?

3. What does this photograph say about golfer Tiger Woods?

4. Explain the significance of the photograph's title.

TIMOTHY GREENFIELD-SANDERS

Be It Ever So Humble

In this photograph, which appeared in LIFE: Century of Change, *photographer Timothy Greenfield-Sanders portrays Martha Stewart, "that doyenne of domesticity," in her kitchen, at the height of her career, when her net worth was $232 million.*

1. What details in the photograph indicate the kitchen setting?

2. How does the kitchen in this photograph differ from one that most people would use for daily cooking?

3. Look carefully at Martha Stewart's clothes. Are they appropriate to the environment in which she is photographed? Why or why not?

4. How do the colors in the photograph affect your interpretation of it?

5. How are the items in the picture arranged? Does the composition remind you of patterns in other pictures?

6. What is the overall point the photographer is making about Martha Stewart in this picture?

COLOR IMAGE GALLERY

ERNEST HAMLIN BAKER

Albert Einstein

First reproduced as a Time *cover on July 1, 1946, when the memory of Hiroshima and Nagasaki was still fresh, Baker's painting of Albert Einstein features the great physicist in front of a mushroom cloud produced by an atomic explosion.*

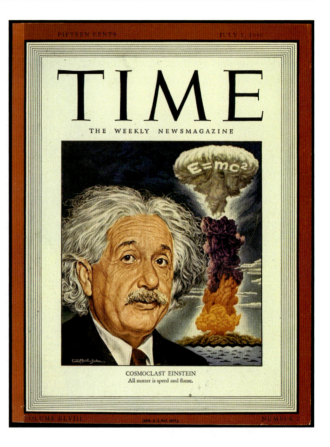

1. How would you describe the Einstein's facial expression in this painting? Based on the facial expression, how would you characterize the famous scientist?

2. Does anything in the artist's rendering suggest genius?

3. In this painting, Einstein's famous equation appears on the side of a mushroom cloud. What do you think Baker is suggesting about Einstein's work?

4. What is the significance of the tiny boats at the bottom right of the picture?

5. Does Baker's depiction of Einstein suggest that the scientist is aware of the implications of his work? If so, how?

6. What might be the significance of the dark gray background of the painting?

WALTER IOOSS JR.

Michael Jordan

Walter Iooss's photograph of Michael Jordan shows the great athlete in an uncharacteristic pose: hunched over a bucket in his hotel bathroom, soaking his injured ankle. Iooss's depiction of a vulnerable Jordan merited the photo's inclusion in the 1999 book Time: Great Images of the 20th Century.

1. In what way is Iooss's picture of Jordan soaking a sprained ankle in an Orlando hotel suite different from traditional sports pictures?

2. What effect does Iooss's photo have on our view of Jordan? What commentary on genius do the particular details of the photo make?

3. Why do you think the photographer positions Jordan off to the side with his back to the camera?

4. Even though Jordan is a small figure in the picture, he is still the center of attention. How does the composition of the picture, its lines and color scheme, make sure the viewer's eye is drawn to the figure on the chair in the bathroom?

COLOR IMAGE GALLERY

ANNIE LEIBOVITZ

COLOR IMAGE GALLERY

Liberace and Scott Thorson

Famous for her portraits of celebrities, Leibovitz photographed Las Vegas entertainer Liberace with his chauffer Scott Thorson in full regalia, posed in front of Liberace's Rolls Royce. The picture first appeared in Rolling Stone *on October 1, 1981.*

1. What does this portrait reveal about Liberace and his chauffeur? What do their clothes, jewelry, and the car in the background say about them?

2. Accept for a moment Liberace's "genius." What commentary on it does Scott Thorson's important positioning in the composition of the photograph make?

3. Scott Thorson was reportedly Liberace's lover for several years. Does knowing that change your interpretation of the photo at all?

4. How does the composition reinforce the overall message of the picture?

5. How does the photographer use color and texture in this picture?

[COLOR PLATE 32]

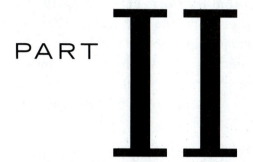

PART **II**

A Writer's Reader

WHEN HILLARY CLINTON SAID "IT takes a village to raise a child," she was drawing upon the wisdom of centuries and many cultures. The nuclear family—two parents and their children—as an ideal is a recent, relatively brief phenomenon.

> "Nobody has ever before asked the nuclear family to live all by itself in a box the way we do. With no relatives, no support, we've put it in an impossible situation."
>
> *Margaret Mead*

A photo herein, of a family a century ago, reminds us that throughout our history, the extended family was the norm: grandparents, in-laws, and cousins were as likely to sit at the table—and indeed share the home—as were mom, dad, and kids. Today, the family is again "extended," reinvented by social and economic changes in the wake of post–WWII prosperity, the Civil Rights Movement, the Women's Movement, the Vietnam era. The fifties ideal of the self-contained family unit, secured by the legal knot of marriage and rein-forced in a direct bloodline to offspring, has morphed into families inextri-cably linked through a bevy of "new" relationships—parents and stepchil-dren, stepparents and half-siblings, interracial marriages and biracial chil-dren, single parents supported by a network of family, friends, and commu-nity services, unmarried partners, whether straight or gay. Indeed, Donna Ferrato's photo of a family headed by a lesbian couple introduces a *new* nuclear family.

As the work here attests, negotiating such complexity requires great skill in diplomacy, great stores of emotional strength and of patience, great pow-ers of forgiveness; often, because we are human, we fail in those endeavors. Anndee Hochman challenges, even in her title, the myth of the "happy fam-ily." Melanie Thernstrom acknowledges the way money complicates the meaning of family "values" and puts a price tag on love while Carolyn Hwang explains the particular indebtedness felt by children of immigrants. Cornel West marvels at the miracle of his own father's paternal success against the backdrop of racism. Two other fathers, E. B. White and William C. Brisick, consider their relationships with their sons and contemplate mortality—one his own; one, sadly, his son's. Elizabeth Joseph and Laura Pfefferle offer dis-tinct takes on the subject of marriage. C. S. Lewis weighs in on the moral responsibility inherent in human relationships, and Marge Piercy questions the morality of patriarchy.

In the drama of life, it is our relationships that define us: we are whom we love, whom we hate, whom we nurture, whom we battle. Our interactions with people we care about are the source of our deepest satisfaction and our most searing pain. Death, divorce, feuds, couplings, births—they fracture and reconfigure our relationships, reassign our loyalties, render ever more com-plex our human condition. ✳

WARMING UP: *Can you recall an incident or event you shared with someone close to you that proved, in hindsight, to be a defining moment in your relationship?*

The Steep Cliffs of Life

By William C. Brisick

WILLIAM C. BRISICK

A former actor, William C. Brisick, has contributed essays, book reviews, profiles, and travel articles to numerous magazines and newspapers. Brisick lives in Los Angeles, where he now concentrates on fiction writing while working full-time in textbook publishing.

He walked slightly ahead of me, Kevin did. He had reversed the roles of childhood when I would have to slow down to let him catch up—and sometimes end up carrying him. My first-born was 23 years old now; his stride had lengthened, mine had shortened, and that is the way of life.

I am tempted to say he walked with a determined stride, but that wouldn't be true. The word saunter comes to mind; Kevin, after some minor triumphs in school, sports and music, had stopped taking life so seriously. He preferred its ironies; he was drawn to shadings rather than the black-and-white. In my own youth I thought it important "to hit life head-on"; my son, as I'd observed, was approaching it on a slant.

It was he who had suggested we take "a long hike" from Riomaggiore, the southernmost town in the Cinque Terre, the "five lands" stretching for eleven miles along Italy's Ligurian coast, the others, in order, Manarola, Corniglia, Vernazza and Monterosso al Mare. We'd arrived in late afternoon. It was a place removed, but not unlike the many we'd happened on in the course of our rental car meanderings.

With Kevin and my 14-year-old daughter, Jenny, I'd driven through Europe's big cities and small towns, gazed at its spectacular mountains and lush valleys. We had no itinerary; our days fell into place, each in turn, the leisurely drives punctuated by the sounds of the many cassette tapes we'd brought along, Kevin's favorite Beatles songs among them.

Something about Riomaggiore must have struck a chord with him: the cliffs 5 and mountains that isolate the town from its neighbors, the terraced slopes lined with grape arbors, the houses stacked up around a postage-stamp harbor, the precipitously steep walks that call for slow and carefully placed steps.

We had come to the end of the road: either turn around and go back to the more conventional tourist spot, nearby La Spezia an example, or try to find a place to stay. Jenny was thirsty, and made no bones about it. Large events often hinge on small needs. We set out in search of *aqua minerale*. And lodgings.

In a matter of minutes we'd found both. Our guest house was tucked away at the end of a narrow, terraced path flanked by fruit trees—peaches, apricots, and, of course, the ever-present grapes, destined to convert to the fine wines of the Cinque Terre.

Our room overlooked the sea. On the balcony we heard the rush and ebb of waves against the rocks; from lines strung from the balcony we pinned the T-shirts, jeans, underwear and socks we'd taken time to wash.

"We should do our hike in the morning, Kev," I said. Jenny was pressing for a shopping tour of the village, and by now it was after five. He agreed. We paused long enough to sample the wine I'd bought from our proprietor, Tonio by name; he'd decanted it from a gallon jug. We shopped, ate a leisurely dinner of calamari, then returned to our lodgings, the rhythm of the surf gentle in our ears.

At 6:30 AM Kevin and I were out of bed and onto the balcony. The sun sat 10 low, the air was cool, and Riomaggiore's shuttered houses looked pale in the morning light. At seven we were on our way, leaving behind a contentedly sleeping Jenny.

We walked past the railroad station, local transport serving the towns of the Cinque Terre. Our route would be less dependable, more adventurous: the *Via dell'Amore*, or "Walk of Love," a trail connecting to neighboring Manarola.

"Easy, so easy," I commented as we made our way, the path wide and flat, paved with stones, and for a long stretch it continued thus, till we were within sight of our destination. Then, as if to mark its inaccessibility, the trail lost itself in narrow, steep, foliage-shrouded steps, our only guide the faint blue-and-white flags planted at various points along the way. The sun edged higher; we began to sweat. But we trudged on, found Manarola, and for a few minutes walked along its shaded cobblestone. Lines of wash, looking much like ours, hung from windows; at the harbor we saw more boats than people, the lightweight craft scattered halfway up the steeply graded street. We decided to go on to Corniglia, remote, forbidding, on its own promontory, the sun's glint reflecting off its church, its cliffside houses stacked atop one another.

It *was* remote. And far off. Along the way the coastline softened; we spotted small, rock-strewn beaches, an occasional house, those sanctuaries reachable by trails descending from ours. We passed sleeping backpackers and maintained a respectful silence. Finally, Corniglia, smallest of the five towns, loomed ahead, a cluster of white and beige against the green hills.

I remarked to Kevin about the cars parked along the street leading to the train station. How did they get there? From what I'd read, no roads led to Corniglia, of the Cinque Terre towns the most difficult to reach either by land or sea. But 14th century Italian author Boccaccio found it, sampled—and praised—its wines. My son and I would forego such delights; what we needed was a café, an entrée into breakfast.

"It looks like Lombard Street," Kevin, mindful of the famous San Francisco 15
landmark, commented as we came upon a maze of steps zigzagging up the hill to the center of town. Three-hundred-seventy-seven in all (we counted), they were spaced to reduce the grade, but the Z patterns crisscrossed endlessly. At least on Lombard Street it was downhill. And you could drive.

I thought of that city, and of Berkeley where Kevin had made a start in what we hoped would be his academic blossoming. It ended after a year and a summer, the debilitation of drugs sapping his quest for knowledge. The struggles since then had often separated us, but all that was changing now, especially here during the trip, Kevin revisiting Europe, finding a quiet source of inspiration, and he and I, over countless rolls, coffee, pizzas and beer, finding each other again.

At the top of the steps we walked past a small piazza fronting the 14th century parish church, stopped in a café barely visible along one of Corniglia's cavernous, winding streets. We favored Cokes over coffee, and Kevin, who liked to sample exotic bolognas from all the "deli" stops we made, made do with a jelly doughnut. Refreshed, we bought a cold bottle of mineral water to take with us, then stepped outside to pursue our next destination: Vernazza.

Where exactly was it? we wondered, standing in the sunlight, surrounded by grape terraces at the edge of town. We could see no well-marked cliffside walk. Slightly eastward, and far, far up the hill stood a village, its church spire prominent. "Is that Vernazza?" I asked an elderly woman who had stopped to talk with a fellow villager. "San Bernardo," she replied, and with my sketchy knowledge of Italian I learned that Vernazza was on the other side of it, distant and unseen. I thought of Jenny, soon to wake up. "Shall we head back?"

Vernazza had eluded us, as it would later in the morning when we tried to reach the other towns by car. Jenny was in the back seat then, lost in her Walkman; Kevin was helping me navigate a torturously narrow road, one that for long stretches gave way to dirt and rock. Still another wrong turn.

We did get to Monterosso, the northernmost and largest of the "five lands" 20
and the only one to sport a bathing beach. We walked along its promenade, later enjoyed lunch in a cafeteria on the beach. The hundreds of tents and umbrellas filling the small space evoked an image of Mr. Hulot and his quintessential holiday. "I almost expect to see him darting about," I remarked to

Kevin—it was a film we'd shared years before. From our lunch spot, the view southward, we thought we might get a glimpse of the mysterious Vernazza, not unlike the one he and I had attempted hours earlier, from Corniglia, where we'd lingered beneath a steadily rising sun, and finally decided to retrace our steps.

Kevin found the blue-and-white flagged walk again, even after I'd questioned some of his moves. I was learning to trust his sense of direction; through large, sprawling cities—Vienna, Munich, Milan—he would drive our rental car, get us back to hotel or *pensione*.

He showed some of that sense of purpose now. I like to think he was heading *toward* something, a new goal, one he might have put aside. We talked about the trip, the inadequacies we both felt about European history, the many books out there for us to read. We spoke of working on languages again, listening to tapes. Kevin, who had studied German at Berkeley, had brought a textbook with him and was using every occasion to practice—"*Entschuldigen Sie*" (excuse me), he would say in his gentle voice.

My watch showed ten o'clock; we were again on the *Via dell'Amore*, Riomaggiore within view. Kevin began to talk about the future: his music, his hopes for creating something of value. "Whenever I start to write a song," he said, "it always sounds like one I've heard, and so I give it up."

I told him that there were only so many ideas out there, that the important thing was to take one and express it in your own way, and in the process find your voice. I spoke of my own writing, how I have to sit down, work at it, above all, give it time. Moments later we reached the end of the trail, looked up to see our house, the laundry flapping in the ocean air, Jenny still sleeping inside.

Time. It was something my son didn't have, and all the songs he might have written must remain forever in a corner of my imagination. We'd arrived back in Los Angeles on a Wednesday; two days later, the hour close to midnight, a sheriff's deputy rapped on my door, informed me that Kevin's drowned body had been found in a pond not far from our house. We hadn't even recovered from jet lag; the glow of the trip hadn't begun to mellow.

And it *would* mellow, I had promised him. We would talk about it, savor it in our minds for years to come. The places we visited, the meals we ate, the companionship we shared: all of it would amplify with new meaning as it filtered through the lens of memory.

Now, as I think of the conversations we had, and the many we didn't, the recollection is all too solitary, and filled with a haunting, searing poignancy I could not have imagined.

I intend to go back to the Cinque Terre some day and walk again along its steep cliffs. But in the words of Robert Frost, "knowing how way leads on to way," I understand that it may never happen.

On an evening however, twilight the best time, I can sit outside, perhaps to the accompaniment of a Beatles song, "Yesterday," or "Let It Be." There, in my mind's eye, I will see again his lean form striding ahead of me, and I will feel again the warm sun rising above the hills of Riomaggiore.

ANALYZING What the Writer Says

1. What does Brisick mean when he says of his son that he "was approaching [life] on a slant"?

2. Why does Brisick view the walk he takes with his son as a "large event"?

3. What is the significance of the Beatles song titles Brisick mentions at the end of his essay? How do they comment upon the nature of the father-son relationship?

ANALYZING How the Writer Says It

1. Note the many details—the steep walks, less-than-direct paths, and zig-zagged streets—that illustrate the nature of Brisick's family's European "meanderings." How do these references function as metaphor in the essay?

2. Given what happens to Kevin soon after the family returns from Europe, point to the irony in the essay's opening sentences.

ANALYZING the Issue

To what extent should parents try to guide their young-adult children, to push them down a particular path?

ANALYZING Connections Between Texts

1. Compare the opening sentences of Brisick's essay to the last in E. B. White's "Once More to the Lake" (p. 178). How does each author comment upon the natural cycle of life?

2. Compare Brisick's memories of his relationship with his son and his suggestions about the nature of fatherhood and the importance of parental encouragement, trust, and respect to the portrait of the relationship between Tiger Woods and his father as drawn by Gary Smith in "The Chosen One (p. 811)."

3. Compare Brisick's observations on the nature of the fatherhood to Dixie B. Vereen's photograph "Man and Child" (p. 193) What commentary on fatherhood do the writer and the photographer make?

WARMING UP: *Is there some place other than your home that evokes memories of your family at its best? What particular feature of the place do you associate with particular aspects of your family life?*

Growing Pains
Beyond "One Big Happy Family"

BY ANNDEE HOCHMAN

ANNDEE HOCHMAN

Hochman, a freelance writer, reflects on her childhood experiences at her extended family's beach house and considers how the open, honest, unpretentious aspects of the house itself and life inside it influenced her decision to be truthful—a decision that strains the ties of her "big happy family." The following essay is excerpted from her 1994 Everyday Acts and Small Subversions.

I remember waking up to the smell of salt.

Each August when I was little, my parents loaded the car with Bermuda shorts and groceries, beach towels and Scrabble board, and drove to the New Jersey shore. My great-uncle Bernie Ochman had bought a $16,000 bay-front house there in the mid-1950s; he imagined it as a sort of free-wheeling compound, where all the aunts, grandparents, and cousins of my mother's large extended family could gather each summer.

Bernie died before my parents were married, but my mother carried out his vision with her usual zest. She made sure the taxes on the house were paid quarterly, the water valve was turned on each May, and there were enough hamburgers for everyone on Memorial Day and the Fourth of July.

In August, my parents worked feverishly for two weeks, then packed up and headed to the shore for what my father used to call, with some sarcasm, "a little peace and quiet." We left at night to avoid traffic on the Atlantic City Expressway. I always fell asleep in the car and always woke up as we came over the bay bridge, where the smell of salt, moist and thick, would touch me like a mitten dipped in the ocean.

"Are we there yet?" I'd mumble from the back seat. 5

"Almost," my mom would say, and my dad would turn left, then left again, and park the car as close as he could to the big white house.

I loved the shore house because it was so different from home. The front steps tilted a little. Gray paint flaked off the window frames. Two daybeds in the living room were draped with pea green spreads, and the loveseats wore crunchy plastic slipcovers. The picket fence was red.

Even the architecture broke rules. The front room had been added as an afterthought, a low-budget job. The carpenters never removed what had once been the house's front window, now ridiculous in the wall between the front room and the kitchen. I used to sit on the stairs, tapping on the kitchen window and making faces until my mother or my grandmother or Aunt Sadie looked up from the dishes and waved at me. Then I would collapse in giggles.

Upstairs, there was no hall, no doors on the bedrooms. In fact, the bedrooms were not really separate rooms at all, just thin-walled divisions of the upper floor. The front stairs climbed right into the middle of Aunt Charlotte and Uncle Freddie's room; you could stand on the top step and almost tickle Uncle Freddie's feet.

Walk through that bedroom, and the next one, and the next, and you arrived   10 at the bathroom, which had its own quirks—a white claw-foot tub, a hasty shower rigged up with red rubber tubing, and two doors. When I was older, I would check the sliding locks on both doors several times before I dared to unpeel my damp, sandy bathing suit.

Aunt Sadie and Uncle Izzy slept in the larger of the two rear bedrooms, in twin beds pushed together to make one. The very back room was long and narrow, like a single-lane swimming pool, with windows that let in wet salty air off the bay. My grandparents—Bubie and Pop-pop—slept here.

My mother loves to tell the story of my father's first visit to this family compound, during their courtship. He recoiled at the upstairs setup; a private motel room, with a door that locked, was more what he had in mind. My mother informed him firmly that she was a package deal; if he loved her, he would learn to love her family—the father who smoked terrible cigars, the sister who rolled her hair in Kotex sanitary pads, the mother who stewed bruised peaches in the hot, tiny kitchen. And he could start loving them here, in their peculiar summer habitat.

I thought the house was wonderful. The connecting rooms reminded me of a maze, the sort of place where surprises could hunch in old dressers, under beds. Later I realized how the physical space shaped our time there, dissolving the barriers that, in most houses, separate adults from children, private from communal space, eating from work. At the shore, my friends and I played jacks in the middle of the living room, hide and seek in the freestanding metal closets. When people got hungry, they helped themselves from one of the three refrigerators. If I wanted to be alone, I opened a book.

There was one last room upstairs, an odd sixth bedroom lodged in the center of the house. It was the only bedroom with a door, and it belonged to my parents. When I was younger, I assumed they took that room out of generosity. It was small and dark and hot, and you had to grope for the light switch behind a high wooden headboard. It was also the only room in the house in which two people could have a private talk, or take a nap, without somebody else clomping through on her way to the bathroom.

Much later, the summer I was twenty-two, I finally grasped the full signifi-   15
cance of that room and made love with Jon Feldstein in it one June weekend when the family wasn't there. "Do you want to have sex?" he had asked, without expectation in his voice, as if it were a foregone conclusion. Later he said, "Well, you know, it gets better with practice."

I did not practice with Jon Feldstein again. In fact, I didn't practice with anyone until more than two years later. By then, I had fallen into a deep and surprising infatuation with one of my closest friends, driven my Datsun cross-country alone, and settled in Portland.

Early in the summer of 1987, I flew back east to tell my parents I was in love with a woman and believed I was destined to be in love with women throughout the foreseeable future. It was Memorial Day weekend, the time we traditionally turned on the water valve and began to inhabit the house at the shore. My mother and I drove there in her blue Honda.

"I think that's how it's going to be for me. With women, I mean," I told her.

"Well, your father thought so," she said finally. "He thought so back in November. I told him that was ridiculous, that you'd always had boyfriends."

She said a lot of other things after that, about not having grandchildren and   20
what a hard path I'd chosen and how she and my father weren't going to be around forever and had hoped to see me taken care of. I concentrated on driving and on the way blood was beating in my ankles, my thumbs, my neck, my ears. I wanted to go to sleep and not wake up until I smelled salt. When we came close to the bay, my mother asked me to pull into a parking lot so she could cry for a while. "I'm sorry," I said, but it didn't seem to help.

At the house, I walked around, touching things, while my mother told my father that he was right, I *was* having an affair with a woman. I wanted to eat something, anything, off the familiar mismatched dishes, play Scrabble until the stars came out, stand on the back porch and watch boats slip under the bridge, tap on the kitchen window until someone waved at me. Instead, I went into the bathroom and locked both doors.

About midnight, while I lay sleepless in Aunt Sadie and Uncle Izzy's room, my mother came in and crawled into the other twin bed. "I feel so empty," she said. "I feel empty inside. . . . I don't feel any joy anymore. I feel like the family is breaking apart. I remember how the family was when Uncle Bernie was alive, how this house was. . . ." And her voice, already thin, cracked like a bowl dropped on a tile floor—a splintering and then silence where something used to be.

2 A.M. 3 A.M. Everyone had trooped off to bed in pairs—cousins Joni and Gerry, cousins Debbie and Ralph. Except for my grandfather, who had always stayed up late to watch television and stayed up even later since my grandmother died three years before. Finally he switched off the set, and the house went dark and quiet.

"Don't you feel it's unnatural?" my mother asked. "Don't you feel it's just wrong, that it's weird?"

How can you ask me about being weird in this house, I wanted to shout. This house, with its bedrooms barging into each other and its mismatched dishes, its double-doored bathroom and its red picket fence. When I used to complain that our family wasn't like other families, you laughed and said, "Well, we may not be normal, but we have a lot of fun."

I didn't say these things. I only thought them. And it wasn't until much later, until very recently, that I began to understand why my mother could tolerate the quirks in that house. The madcap shell at the shore housed a solid, predictable center. Relatives came and went in pairs. Someday, presumably, I would join the procession; one of my children would tap on the kitchen window and giggle when I waved. The house might be a little cracked, but the family was predictable, enduring.

I understand why you are so upset, I could tell my mother now. The world has gone crazy and all the walls are too thin and your mother is dead and your sister divorced and your daughter loves women and everything is coming unglued and nothing turns out the way we plan.

4 A.M. 5 A.M. My mother stayed in my room all night, talking and weeping. Toward morning, as boats began to slosh in the bay, I fell into an exhausted, tear-stained sleep. When I woke up at noon, we ate tuna subs and drove back to Philadelphia.

The New Jersey beach house was never just a summertime shelter. It housed my family's favorite image of itself at our expansive best—gathered around the huge dining room table, traipsing through the bedrooms, one big happy family. Just like all the television shows I watched and worshipped.

It is no accident that this particular image clung. The picture of such charmed and cheerful families took hold in the decade proceeding my birth, a bit of postwar propaganda that paid homage to the supposedly idyllic families of Victorian times. Mass-marketed by television, the Cleaver clan and others were burned into our minds by millions of cathode-ray tubes.

The feminist movement challenged that postwar myth as women began to examine the contents inside the "happy family" cliché. Feminists of the late 1960s and 1970s urged their sisters to live authentic lives and to begin them at home. They insisted that personal choices had political import—that is, the daily, minute interactions of our lives *mattered,* not just for each of us alone, but potentially for everyone, for the world. "When a woman tells the truth," Adrienne Rich wrote, "she is creating the possibility for more truth around her."

Women pointed out that families maintained the illusion of happiness only by denying important facts—about adoptions, abortions, illness and illegitimate births, divorces and deaths. Some families devoted their lives to maintaining the secret of a son's homosexuality, a grandmother's alcoholism, a father's violent rage. Melancholy and despair split family members not only from outsiders but from each other; certain topics, one understood, were simply not discussed.

In consciousness-raising groups, women discovered the exhilaration of telling each other unvarnished stories of their bodies, relationships, and families. Back at home, in their kitchens and living rooms, they began to apply these feminist ideals; that *how* people talked meant as much as the conclusions they reached; that the only way to solve problems was to actively engage them; that keeping secrets cost too much.

It was feminism, in part, that prompted me to tell my own family a difficult truth, one I was sure would cause misunderstanding and pain. I was frightened to disturb the jovial peace that was a source of such family pride; at the same time, I could not visit that unpretentious house and pretend I was someone else. I wanted to be known, and seen, in the ways I had come to know and see myself.

I did it because I chose truth over tranquility. Because I had come to believe 35
that real families fight and resist, sob and explode, apologize and forgive. Beneath the fiction of happiness lies the raw, important tissue of human relationships.

And I did it because I had watched other women live without lying. For some, that meant no longer passing as heterosexual. For others, it meant acknowledging they did not want partners or children. Some urged their biological relatives and chosen kin to talk about subjects long considered taboo. Their example made my own convictions more fierce. Their bravery buoyed me.

"It's hard. We argue and struggle," Selma Miriam of the Bloodroot restaurant collective told me, with a glance around the room at her "cronies."

"You know each other's weaknesses," said Betsey Beaven, another Bloodroot member. "Love requires a lot of cultivation. It can be tenuous. You have to work on it all the time. It's very difficult at times, but so rewarding when you get through to the other side."

I remember my friend Susan's assessment, at the end of a long discussion about what separates family from friends. "Family," she said, "are the people I've struggled through things with."

Again, always, the personal becomes political. Women striving daily to make 40
plain the good and the bad of their lives also contribute to a larger change, the

breakdown of fictions that divide us from each other—white from black, lesbian from straight, old from young. Women who refuse to act out lies at home can turn the same honest scrutiny outside, demanding truth in their work, their education, their politics.

Maybe happiness, I have come to think, is a limiting proposition, a flat summary of human emotion in the same way a sitcom is a flat summary of real life. "Happy families" don't account for the ways people are knit by sorrow, the way bonds grow stronger through anger and grief.

This is it, I tell myself now; this mess is as real as it gets. I try to cherish flux—the mercurial moods, the feelings that flood and recede, the infinite chaos in which families become families.

Two days after I came out to my parents at the beach house, I returned to Portland, with my bicycle packed in a United Airlines baggage carrier and my grandmother's cameo ring on the pinky finger of my left hand. I'd found the ring in a jewelry box in my bedroom. It was delicate, a filigree setting with a small oblong cameo, the ivory-faced women profiled on a peach background.

The thin silver band barely eased over the knuckle on my pinky—lesbians' traditional ring-bearing finger. Wearing it, I felt marked, as though I were bringing contraband across the border in broad daylight, all my conflicting allegiances exposed.

My head ached. Would my relatives still love me if I failed to do my part by marrying and enlarging the family with children? Could I ever bring a woman lover to the shore? Where would we sleep? 45

How would I reconcile my relatives with the various families I developed as a writer, a Jew, a lesbian, a social worker, an East Coast expatriate in the Northwest? How far could everyone stretch without snapping, refusing wholeness, flying apart like shrapnel?

I stumbled off the plane at midnight into a solid hug from Marian, a coworker at the social service agency where I counseled street youth. At work that week, I walked numbly through my routine. On Friday, while cleaning up the drop-in center after the last round of kids, I looked at my left hand. Where the cameo of my grandmother's ring had been, a little rectangle of skin showed through the filigree window. In the agency's dim basement, I leaned against a paneled wall and sobbed.

All the rest of that summer my parents and I exchanged letters, envelopes full of anger and accusation, concern and caution, guilt and grief. I had been such a good child, cheerful, diligent, and brainy—good citizen awards in ninth grade, acceptance to Yale, an internship, then a job, at *The Washington Post*. It was bad enough that I had left the *Post* after two years, moved 3,000 miles away and begun to work with homeless teenagers. Now this! Where had I gotten such subversive ideas?

Perhaps in a certain south Jersey beach house, in a maze of doorless rooms.

From the West Coast, I glanced anxiously over my shoulder: Were my rela- 50 tives still there, with their shopping and their sweaters, their softening faces and their stiff resistance to change? If I returned, would I be swallowed up? If I stayed, would I be left adrift? Is that the brittle choice that, ultimately, forms the boundary line of every family: Be like us, or be alone?

I took off the empty ring and put it in a drawer. I spent that summer prowling my past, looking for signposts to help navigate the present. I heard voices, comforting and cautionary, joyous and pained, voices that chased in endless loops through my head.

"You can do anything you set your mind to."

"Don't leave."

"The world is full of interesting people and places."

"This family is the only safe spot on earth."   55

"Follow your dreams."

"Stay put."

I listened, and remembered, and wrote things down.

ANALYZING What the Writer Says

1. What connection does Hochman see between her family and the shore house?

2. How did the feminist movement affect Hochman's decision to tell her family the "difficult truth"?

3. How does Hochman's family react to her "coming out" to them? How do they resolve the conflict—or do they?

4. Hochman makes three references to her grandmother's ring in the last section of the essay. Analyze the significance of these references and what they suggest about Hochman's relationship to her family.

ANALYZING How the Writer Says It

1. Contrast the opening and closing sentences of the essay. How does the contrast reflect the changes that have occurred?

2. The essay is divided into four sections. Summarizing the main point of each, trace the way Hochman arranges and develops the piece.

3. Analyze Hochman's title. How does it suggest the myth of the happy family? To what does the phrase "growing pains" refer?

ANALYZING the Issue

Hochman suggests that speaking the truth inside the family will enable us to be more honest outside the family. Do you agree? Or are there some secrets that family members should keep from each other?

ANALYZING Connections Between Texts

1. Both Hochman and E. B. White ("Once More to the Lake," p. 178) associate family experience with a particular place and muse on things that change—and things that do not—in families. Despite their coming from very different generations, they come to similar conclusions about family life. What are those similarities? Where do they differ?

2. Hochman knows that some families maintain the illusion of happiness by keeping secret what would destroy the image—homosexuality, alcoholism, or violence, for instance—but she decides to come clean with her family. On the other hand, Scott Russell Sanders ("Under the Influence," p. 295) confesses: "Father's drinking became the family secret." Compare how the two writers describe their families and their dealing with their respective "difficult truths." Is it ultimately better to be honest about one's family even if it might involve shattering the "happy family" image?

3. Compare Donna Ferrato's photograph of a lesbian couple and their two children (p. 189) to the kind of family life Hochman describes in her essay. Does family happiness necessarily depend on how conventional a family is? Is family happiness possible (even more likely) in nontraditional families?

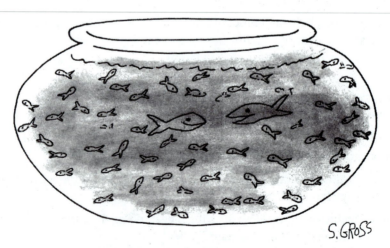

"I guess we'd be considered a family. We're living together, we love each other, and we haven't eaten the children yet."

WARMING UP: *How have your parents' expectations and dreams for you affected any of the important decisions you've made about your life?*

The Good Daughter

BY CAROLINE HWANG

CAROLINE HWANG

In a Newsweek *"My Turn" column in 1998, a daughter of immigrants wrestles with the question of to whom she owes her destiny—herself or her parents.*

The moment I walked into the dry-cleaning store, I knew the woman behind the counter was from Korea, like my parents. To show her that we shared a heritage, and possibly get a fellow countryman's discount, I tilted my head forward, in shy imitation of a traditional bow.

"Name?" she asked, not noticing my attempted obeisance.

"Hwang," I answered.

"Hwang? Are you Chinese?"

Her question caught me off-guard. I was used to hearing such queries from non-Asians who think Asians all look alike, but never from one of my own people. Of course, the only Koreans I knew were my parents and their friends, people who've never asked me where I came from, since they knew better than I.

I ransacked my mind for the Korean words that would tell her who I was. It's always struck me as funny (in a mirthless sort of way) that I can more readily say "I am Korean" in Spanish, German and even Latin than I can in the language of my ancestry. In the end, I told her in English.

The dry-cleaning woman squinted as though trying to see past the glare of my strangeness, repeating my surname under her breath. "Oh, *Fxuang*," she said, doubling over with laughter. "You don't know how to speak your name."

I flinched. Perhaps I was particularly sensitive at the time, having just dropped out of graduate school. I had torn up my map for the future, the one that said not only where I was going, but who I was. My sense of identity was already disintegrating.

When I got home, I called my parents to ask why they had never bothered to correct me. "Big deal," my mother said, sounding more flippant than I knew she intended. (Like many people who learn English in a classroom, she uses idioms that don't always fit the occasion.) "So what if you can't pronounce your name? You are American," she said.

Though I didn't challenge her explanation, it left me unsatisfied. The fact is,   10
my cultural identity is hardly that clear-cut.

My parents immigrated to this country 30 years ago, two years before I was born. They told me often, while I was growing up, that, if I wanted to, I could be president someday, that here my grasp would be as long as my reach.

To ensure that I reaped all the advantages of this country, my parents saw to it that I became fully assimilated. So, like any American of my generation, I whiled away my youth strolling malls and talking on the phone, rhapsodizing over Andrew McCarthy's blue eyes or analyzing the meaning of a certain upper-classman's offer of a ride to the Homecoming football game.

To my parents, I am all American, and the sacrifices they made in leaving Korea—including my mispronounced name—pale in comparison to the opportunities those sacrifices gave me. They do not see that I straddle two cultures, nor that I feel displaced in the only country I know. I identify with Americans, but Americans do not identify with me. I've never known what it's like to belong to a community—neither one at large, nor of an extended family. I know more about Europe than the continent my ancestors unmistakably come from. I sometimes wonder, as I did that day in the dry cleaner's, if I would be a happier person had my parents stayed in Korea.

I first began to consider this thought around the time I decided to go to graduate school. It had been a compromise: my parents wanted me to go to law school; I wanted to skip the starched-collar track and be a writer—the hungrier the better. But after 20-some years of following their wishes and meeting all of their expectations, I couldn't bring myself to disobey or disappoint. A writing career is riskier than law, I remember thinking. If I'm a failure and my life is a washout, then what does that make my parents' lives?

I know that many of my friends had to choose between pleasing their par-   15
ents and being true to themselves. But for the children of immigrants, the choice seems more complicated, a happy outcome impossible. By making the biggest move of their lives for me, my parents indentured me to the largest debt imaginable—I owe them the fulfillment of their hopes for me.

It tore me up inside to suppress my dream, but I went to school for a Ph.D. in English literature, thinking I had found the perfect compromise. I would be able to write at least about books while pursuing a graduate degree.

Predictably, it didn't work out. How could I labor for five years in a program I had no passion for? When I finally left school, my parents were disappointed, but since it wasn't what they wanted me to do, they weren't devastated. I, on the other hand, felt I was staring at the bottom of the abyss. I had seen the flaw in my life of halfwayness, in my planned life of compromises.

I hadn't thought about my love life, but I had a vague plan to make concessions there, too. Though they raised me as an American, my parents expect me to marry someone Korean and give them grandchildren who look like them. This didn't seem like such a huge request when I was 14, but now I don't know what I'm going to do. I've never been in love with someone I dated, or dated someone I loved. (Since I can't bring myself even to entertain the thought of marrying the non-Korean men I'm attracted to, I've been dating only those I know I can stay clear-headed about.) And as I near that age when the question of marriage stalks every relationship, I can't help but wonder if my parents' expectations are responsible for the lack of passion in my life.

My parents didn't want their daughter to be Korean, but they don't want her fully American, either. Children of immigrants are living paradoxes. We are the first generation and the last. We are in this country for its opportunities, yet filial duty binds us. When my parents boarded the plane, they knew they were embarking on a rough trip. I don't think they imagined the rocks in the path of their daughter who can't even pronounce her own name.

ANALYZING What the Writer Says

1. Why does Hwang feel she owes her parents an unusually large debt?

2. What contradictions in her upbringing make Hwang refer to herself and other children of immigrants as "living paradoxes"?

3. According to Hwang, how have her parents' expectations affected her romantic life?

ANALYZING How the Writer Says It

1. How does the essay's opening anecdote establish Hwang's key point?

2. What words, phrases, and images reflect Hwang's American-ness?

ANALYZING the Issue

1. Should children consider their parents' hopes and dreams when making professional or romantic choices? Why or why not?

2. Is Hwang's dilemma experienced primarily by children of immigrants? Explain.

ANALYZING Connections Between Texts

1. Both Hwang and Anndee Hochman ("Growing Pains," p. 131) discuss the dilemma children face if their lives turn out differently from what their parents had hoped for. Compare the conflicts both writers face and the conclusions they come to in their essays. How much do the families in these two essays value truth and honesty in resolving conflicts?

2. Compare Hwang's conflict with her immigrant parents to those Amy Tan describes in "Mother Tongue," (p. 515). In what way are both writers in a similar situation? How do they deal with their individual dilemmas?

3. In "Pledge of Allegiance" (p. 612), Dorothea Lange shows the patriotism of Asian girls as they recite the pledge against the backdrop of internment camps for Japanese-Americans during World War II. To what extent do the experiences of Hwang, Amy Tan, and other "hyphenated Americans" reflect the conflicts children of immigrants face in this country?

Polygamy Now!

BY ELIZABETH JOSEPH

ELIZABETH JOSEPH

Elizabeth Joseph, a Utah attorney and journalist, promotes polygamy as a feminist's dream-come-true in the following piece, delivered originally as a speech to the Utah chapter of the National Organization for Women in May 1997.

I've often said that if polygamy didn't exist, the modern American career woman would have invented it. Because, despite its reputation, polygamy is the one lifestyle that offers an independent woman a real chance to "have it all."

One of my heroes is Dr. Martha Hughes Cannon, a physician and a plural wife who in 1896 became the first woman legislator in any U.S. state or territory. Dr. Cannon once said, "You show me a woman who thinks about something besides cookstoves and washtubs and baby flannels, and I will show you nine times out of ten a successful mother." With all due respect, Gloria Steinem has nothing on Dr. Cannon.

As a journalist, I work many unpredictable hours in a fast-paced environment. The news determines my schedule. But am I calling home, asking my husband to please pick up the kids and pop something in the microwave and get them to bed on time just in case I'm really late? Because of my plural marriage arrangement, I don't have to worry. I know that when I have to work late my daughter will be at home surrounded by loving adults with whom she is comfortable and who know her schedule without my telling them. My eight-year-old has never seen the inside of a day care center, and my husband has never eaten a TV dinner. And I know that when I get home from work, if I'm dog tired and stressed out, I can be alone and guilt free. It's a rare day when all eight of my husband's wives are tired and stressed at the same time.

It's helpful to think of polygamy in terms of a free-market approach to marriage. Why shouldn't you or your daughters have the opportunity to marry the best man available, regard-less of his marital status?

I married the best man I ever met. The fact that he already had five wives did not prevent me from doing that. For twenty-three years I have observed how Alex's marriage to Margaret, Bo, Joanna, Diana, Leslie, Dawn, and Delinda has enhanced his marriage to me. The guy has hundreds of years of marital experience; as a result, he is a very skilled husband. 5

It's no mystery to me why Alex loves his other wives. I'd worry about him if he didn't. I did worry in the case of Delinda, whom I hired as my secretary when I was practicing law in Salt Lake City. Alex was in and out of my office a lot over the course of several months, and he never said a word about her. Finally, late one night on our way back from work, I said, "Why haven't you said anything about Delinda?"

He said, "Why should I?"

I said, "She's smart, she's beautiful. What, have you gone stupid on me?"

They were married a few months later.

Polygamy is an empowering lifestyle for women. It provides me the environment and opportunity to maximize my female potential without all the tradeoffs and compromises that attend monogamy. The women in my family are friends. You don't share two decades of experience, and a man, without those friendships becoming very special. 10

I imagine that across America there are groups of young women preparing to launch careers. They sit around tables, talking about the ideal lifestyle to support them in their aspirations for work, motherhood, and personal fulfill-ment. "A man would be nice," they might muse. "A man on our own terms," they might add. What they don't realize is that there is an alternative that would allow their dreams to come true. That alternative is polygamy, the ulti-mate feminist lifestyle.

ANALYZING | What the Writer Says

1. What are Joseph's reasons for advocating polygamy?

2. Joseph claims that polygamy allows her to live according to feminist ideals. How do you think Joseph would define feminism, and how would her defini-tion differ from most people's?

ANALYZING | How the Writer Says It

1. Joseph's piece was originally delivered as a speech to the Utah chapter of the National Organization of Women. What techniques make it especially appropri-ate as a speech? Are they equally effective in essay format?

2. In what ways does Joseph shape her argument to appeal to her audience?

3. How does Joseph anticipate negative reaction to her argument?

ANALYZING the Issue

Do you agree with Joseph's assertion that polygamy is especially beneficial to women?

ANALYZING Connections Between Texts

1. Several essays in this unit describe traditional nuclear—but dysfunctional—families. Is Joseph's model of a polygamous family (illegal though it is in this country) any worse than families that include unhappily married people, parents who make unfair demands of their children, family members who subject each other to painful "tests"—or even physical violence? Is Joseph's model—as well as other alternatives—worth considering? Why or why not?

2. In "From the Best of Japanese Families" (p. 351) Cathy Davidson describes how traditional Japanese girls, despite being provided rigorous educations, are still expected to become wives and mothers. In America, we have come to see this kind of traditionalism as restrictive for women, yet Elizabeth Joseph argues that polygamy would enable a woman to have a career and a family at the same time. Is Joseph's proposal as radically feminist as she claims—or is what she proposes simply a variation on the conservative values of the traditional Japanese families?

3. The Brown Brothers' picture included in this chapter (p. 188) shows an early twentieth-century family gathered around the parlor table. The family includes an elderly couple, three grown women, and three children. In the extended families of the past, several adult family members and their children would live under the same roof, sharing financial and household responsibilities. How were these extended families much different from the polygamous family Joseph describes? Would a model other than the nuclear family be a better option for today's families? Explain.

WARMING UP: *You probably know, or have known, of a marriage in which the partners are both unhappy, but they stay married for religious reasons or for children. If one of the partners is offered an opportunity for true happiness, should that person seize the opportunity despite how it might hurt the other partner or the children?*

We Have No "Right to Happiness"

BY C. S. LEWIS

C. S. LEWIS

A professor of medieval and Renaissance studies at Cambridge, C. S. Lewis (1890-1963) wrote extensively on literature, morality, and Christianity and was also the author of the beloved children's book series The Chronicles of Narnia. *Here, in his last work, he presents a carefully reasoned argument against the pursuit of happiness at the expense of "honesty," "loyalty," and "common humanity."*

"After all," said Clare, "they had a right to happiness."

We were discussing something that once happened in our own neighborhood. Mr. A. had deserted Mrs. A. and got his divorce in order to marry Mrs. B., who had likewise got her divorce in order to marry Mr. A. And there was certainly no doubt that Mr. A. and Mrs. B. were very much in love with one another. If they continued to be in love, and if nothing went wrong with their health or their income, they might reasonably expect to be very happy.

It was equally clear that they were not happy with their old partners. Mrs. B. had adored her husband at the outset. But then he got smashed up in the war. It was thought he had lost his virility, and it was known that he had lost his job. Life with him was no longer what Mrs. B. had bargained for. Poor Mrs. A., too. She had lost her looks—and all her liveliness. It might be true, as some said, that she consumed herself by bearing his children and nursing him through the long illness that overshadowed their earlier married life.

You mustn't, by the way, imagine that A. was the sort of man who nonchalantly threw a wife away like the peel of an orange he'd sucked dry. Her suicide was a terrible shock to him. We all knew this, for he told us so himself. "But what could I do?" he said. "A man has a right to happiness. I had to take my one chance when it came."

I went away thinking about the concept of a "right to happiness."

At first this sounds to me as odd as a right to good luck. For I believe—whatever one school of moralists may say—that we depend for a very great deal of our happiness or misery on circumstances outside all human control. A right to happiness doesn't, for me, make much more sense than a right to be six feet tall, or to have a millionaire for your father, or to get good weather whenever you want to have a picnic.

I can understand a right as a freedom guaranteed me by the laws of the society I live in. Thus, I have a right to travel along the public roads because society gives me that freedom; that's what we mean by calling the roads "public." I can also understand a right as a claim guaranteed me by the laws, and correlative to an obligation on some one else's part. If I have a right to receive £100 from you, this is another way of saying that you have a duty to pay me £100. If the laws allow Mr. A. to desert his wife and seduce his neighbor's wife, then, by definition, Mr. A. has a legal right to do so, and we need bring in no talk about "happiness."

But of course that was not what Clare meant. She meant that he had not only a legal but a moral right to act as he did. In other words, Clare is—or would be if she thought it out—a classical moralist after the style of Thomas Aquinas, Grotius, Hooker and Locke. She believes that behind the laws of the state there is a Natural Law.[1]

I agree with her. I hold this conception to be basic to all civilization. Without it, the actual laws of the state become an absolute, as in Hegel. They cannot be criticized because there is no norm against which they should be judged.

The ancestry of Clare's maxim, "They have a right to happiness," is august. In words that are cherished by all civilized men, but especially by Americans, it has been laid down that one of the rights of man is a right to "the pursuit of happiness." And now we get to the real point.

What did the writers of that august declaration mean?

It is quite certain what they did not mean. They did not mean that man was entitled to pursue happiness by any and every means—including, say, murder, rape, robbery, treason and fraud. No society could be built on such a basis.

They meant "to pursue happiness by all lawful means"; that is, by all means which the Law of Nature eternally sanctions and which the laws of the nation shall sanction.

_____

[1]**Thomas Aquinas . . . Natural Law** Lewis names some philosophers and theologians from the thirteenth through the eighteenth century who believed that certain basic moral principles are evident to rational people in all periods and in all cultures. (Editors' note)

Admittedly this seems at first to reduce their maxim to the tautology that men (in pursuit of happiness) have a right to do whatever they have a right to do. But tautologies, seen against their proper historical context, are not always barren tautologies. The declaration is primarily a denial of the political principles which long governed Europe: a challenge flung down to the Austrian and Russian empires, to England before the Reform Bills, to Bourbon France.[2] It demands that whatever means of pursuing happiness are lawful for any should be lawful for all; that "man," not men of some particular caste, class, status or religion, should be free to use them. In a century when this is being unsaid by nation after nation and party after party, let us not call it a barren tautology.

But the question as to what means are "lawful"—what methods of pursuing happiness are either morally permissible by the Law of Nature or should be declared legally permissible by the legislature of a particular nation—remains exactly where it did. And on that question I disagree with Clare. I don't think it is obvious that people have the unlimited "right to happiness" which she suggests.

For one thing, I believe that Clare, when she says "happiness," means simply and solely "sexual happiness." Partly because women like Clare never use the word "happiness" in any other sense. But also because I never heard Clare talk about the "right" to any other kind. She was rather leftist in her politics, and would have been scandalized if anyone had defended the actions of a ruthless man-eating tycoon on the ground that his happiness consisted in making money and he was pursuing his happiness. She was also a rabid teetotaler; I never heard her excuse an alcoholic because he was happy when he was drunk.

A good many of Clare's friends, and especially her female friends, often felt—I've heard them say so—that their own happiness would be perceptibly increased by boxing her ears. I very much doubt if this would have brought her theory of a right to happiness into play.

Clare, in fact, is doing what the whole western world seems to me to have been doing for the last forty-odd years. When I was a youngster, all the progressive people were saying, "Why all this prudery? Let us treat sex just as we treat all our other impulses." I was simple-minded enough to believe they meant what they said. I have since discovered that they meant exactly the opposite. They meant that sex was to be treated as no other impulse in our nature has ever been treated by civilized people. All the others, we admit, have to be bridled. Absolute obedience to your instinct for self-preservation is what we call cowardice; to your acquisitive impulse, avarice. Even sleep must be resisted if you're a sentry. But every unkindness and breach of faith seems to be condoned provided that the object aimed at is "four bare legs in a bed."

---

[2]**England . . . France** England before the bills that liberalized representation in Parliament in the nineteenth century, and France before the French Revolution of 1789–99. (Editors' note)

It is like having a morality in which stealing fruit is considered wrong—unless you steal nectarines.

And if you protest against this view you are usually met with chatter about the legitimacy and beauty and sanctity of "sex" and accused of harboring some Puritan prejudice against it as something disreputable or shameful. I deny the charge. Foam-born Venus . . . golden Aphrodite . . . Our Lady of Cyprus[3] . . . I never breathed a word against you. If I object to boys who steal my nectarines, must I be supposed to disapprove of nectarines in general? Or even of boys in general? It might, you know, be stealing that I disapproved of.

The real situation is skillfully concealed by saying that the question of Mr. A.'s "right" to desert his wife is one of "sexual morality." Robbing an orchard is not an offense against some special morality called "fruit morality." It is an offense against honesty. Mr. A.'s action is an offense against good faith (to solemn promises), against gratitude (toward one to whom he was deeply indebted) and against common humanity.

Our sexual impulses are thus being put in a position of preposterous privilege. The sexual motive is taken to condone all sorts of behavior which, if it had any other end in view, would be condemned as merciless, treacherous and unjust.

Now though I see no good reason for giving sex this privilege, I think I see a strong cause. It is this.

It is part of the nature of a strong erotic passion—as distinct from a transient fit of appetite—that it makes more towering promises than any other emotion. No doubt all our desires make promises, but not so impressively. To be in love involves the almost irresistible conviction that one will go on being in love until one dies, and that possession of the beloved will confer, not merely frequent ecstasies, but settled, fruitful, deep-rooted, lifelong happiness. Hence *all* seems to be at stake. If we miss this chance we shall have lived in vain. At the very thought of such a doom we sink into fathomless depths of self-pity.

Unfortunately these promises are found often to be quite untrue. Every experienced adult knows this to be so as regards all erotic passions (except the one he himself is feeling at the moment). We discount the world-without-end pretensions of our friends' amours easily enough. We know that such things sometimes last—and sometimes don't. And when they do last, this is not because they promised at the outset to do so. When two people achieve lasting happiness, this is not solely because they are great lovers but because they are also—I must put it crudely—good people; controlled, loyal, fairminded, mutually adaptable people.

20

25

---

[3]**Foam-born Venus . . . Aphrodite . . . Cyprus** The Roman goddess Venus was identified with the Greek goddess of love, Aphrodite. Aphrodite sprang from the foam (*aphros*), and was especially worshipped in Cyprus. (Editors' note)

If we establish a "right to (sexual) happiness" which supersedes all the ordinary rules of behavior, we do so not because of what our passion shows itself to be in experience but because of what it professes to be while we are in the grip of it. Hence, while the bad behavior is real and works miseries and degradations, the happiness which was the object of the behavior turns out again and again to be illusory. Everyone (except Mr. A. and Mrs. B.) knows that Mr. A. in a year or so may have the same reason for deserting his new wife as for deserting his old. He will feel again that all is at stake. He will see himself again as the great lover, and his pity for himself will exclude all pity for the woman.

Two further points remain.

One is this. A society in which conjugal infidelity is tolerated must always be in the long run a society adverse to women. Women, whatever a few male songs and satires may say to the contrary, are more naturally monogamous than men; it is a biological necessity. Where promiscuity prevails, they will therefore always be more often the victim than the culprits. Also, domestic happiness is more necessary to them than to us. And the quality by which they most easily hold a man, their beauty, decreases every year after they have come to maturity, but this does not happen to those qualities of personality—women don't really care twopence about our *looks*—by which we hold women. Thus in the ruthless war of promiscuity women are at a double disadvantage. They play for higher stakes and are also more likely to lose. I have no sympathy with moralists who frown at the increasing crudity of female provocativeness. These signs of desperate competition fill me with pity.

Secondly, though the "right to happiness" is chiefly claimed for the sexual impulse, it seems to me impossible that the matter should stay there. The fatal principle, once allowed in that department, must sooner or later seep through our whole lives. We thus advance toward a state of society in which not only each man but every impulse in each man claims *carte blanche*. And then, though our technological skill may help us survive a little longer, our civilization will have died at heart, and will—one dare not even add "unfortunately"—be swept away.

ANALYZING What the Writer Says

1. How does Lewis distinguish between *legal* rights and rights to happiness at the beginning of his discussion?

2. How does Lewis explain the constitutional right to happiness? What do you think the framers of the American constitution intended when they put the pursuit of happiness into a state document?

3. How is the "right to happiness," as the writer's friend Clare sees it, different from the constitutional right to happiness?

4. Why does Lewis disagree with Clare?

5. What two additional objections does Lewis raise at the end of his essay?

ANALYZING How the Writer Says It

1. Analyze Lewis's language and tone. Cite specific examples that might suggest weight or moral authority. How might you read the essay differently if Lewis's phrasing were more casual?

2. How does he use metaphor?

3. Why does Lewis enclose part of his title in quotes?

ANALYZING the Issue

1. Analyze Lewis's argument in light of current divorce rates.

2. In the penultimate paragraph, Lewis claims that "a society in which conjugal infidelity is tolerated must always be in the long run a society adverse to women" because they "are more naturally monogamous than men." Do you agree with this statement? Why or why not?

ANALYZING Connections Between Texts

1. Compare Lewis's argument with the points Laura Pfefferle raises in "On Marriage" (p. 152). In what sense do the two writers agree with each other?

2. In "Carnal Acts" (p. 228), how do Nancy Mairs's attitudes toward marriage, implicit in her description of her own marriage, compare to Lewis's philosophy?

3. To what degree does Patrick Tehan's photograph of the elderly man keeping vigil at his wife's sickbed (p. 191) illustrate what Lewis says about marriage?

WARMING UP: *Consider the marriages you know—your parents' or other family members', your friends', maybe even your own. What do you think makes a marriage successful? On the other hand, what makes marriages fail?*

On Marriage
Lessons from a Work-in-Progress

BY LAURA PFEFFERLE

LAURA PFEFFERLE

Laura Pfefferle, currently an attorney in Austin, Texas, was a University of New Orleans student majoring in Environmental Studies when she penned this essay on the challenges and triumphs of marriage for a writing class. She has discovered the "essence of happiness," she writes, but "it isn't love."

I met my husband Raymond in a bar; I was tending, he was drinking. I had just driven from Chicago to New Orleans with everything I owned in the back of my Chevy Vega wagon and a small travel trailer towed behind. It was June 9, 1981. On July 18th, the hottest day of that year, we were married. Realizing, that we have been together fifteen years, suddenly I feel old. I used to be the young person rolling my eyes at the adults who always seemed to talk in years: "it's been thirty years since I saw . . ." or "twenty years ago I. . . ." But now it's me speaking that language. Fifteen years. Together we've seen joy and catastrophe, birth and death, even divorce and remarriage. Sharing my life with Raymond has taught me about tolerance, communication, time, and so many things, but above all I have discovered the essence of happiness, and it isn't love.

That sticky New Orleans June when we met, Raymond was 46 and I had just turned 20. Some people call such pairings "May-December romances." There was some truth to that; I was born in May and Raymond in December, but beyond the coincidence, our age difference has had little effect on our lives. When I first saw Raymond, my sister and I had come in to her bar with po-boys we planned to eat before we tended bar for the evening. Raymond was sitting on a stool chatting with my sister's husband, who was seated nearby at a wobbly table. The doors, open to the heavy two-o'clock air, admitted scant light into the murky interior, where the lights were off and an oscillating fan droned in endless battle against the heat. In the summer in New Orleans, when the conditions of humidity and heat are just right, clocks don't have the energy to turn and time stands still. That day, only the four of us stirred, and just barely, in the doldrums before the evening rush. I remember thinking that Raymond looked just like a farmer who had been out in the fields on a tractor all day and had stopped in for a cold one before heading home to his wife and farmhouse full of kids. He had an open, friendly face and a personality to match; only a truly hard heart couldn't like him on sight. I sat at the bar a few stools away from him and sized up my po-boy. But he zeroed in on me, moving to the stool next to mine. Truthfully, I was concentrating on my sandwich, but I smiled at him and was friendly. He had had a few Schlitzes, and he got right to the point.

"Wanna go steady?" he asked.

"OK," I laughed back at him.

"Wanna have kids?" he pressed.   5

"Sure, how many?" I deadpanned. He closed in for the kill:

"Wanna get married?"

"OK, when?"

For him it was an actual case of love at first sight. After a few weeks, I took him up on his offer and said yes. Of course we barely knew each other, but we sensed an attraction we couldn't name but we knew was real. Neither of us had been married before, or had children. We knew nothing about long term commitment. Together, we would learn.

"Awkward" best describes the first years we were together. Raymond had been   10
a manager at a soft drink bottling plant but was permanently disabled, and I wasn't working, so we were together most of the time. In retrospect, time apart would have benefited us. We felt we wanted to have a child, but otherwise we had no clear goals. Raymond had been born with severe club feet and a single bone in each lower leg; people stared when he walked and, being immature, I felt uncomfortable. I was too young and we were essentially strangers unequipped for marriage and even less prepared to learn as a team. I hadn't fully grown up yet, and finally I decided that, though I loved Raymond, I wasn't "in love" with him. For a long while I didn't tell him, but one night he started talking about how we could be buried in his family plot when we died, and I knew it was time. Divorce was the last thing Raymond wanted, but he let me go because he loved me. Despite a "friendly divorce," inevitably there was anger and bitterness on both sides. Death is always sad, and our marriage was dead. The process of separating, mentally and physically, was one of the worst experiences of my life.

I moved 90 miles away to Baton Rouge and started working. Being single again was lonely and gave me plenty of time to think. The bruises in my heart healed slowly. Raymond kept in touch since parts of our lives were still

entwined, and because he was keeping our pets at the time. He would sometimes drive out to visit me on Saturdays. He was still in love with me, and
despite my resistance would not stop trying to win me back. After the ordeal
of the divorce, I was not anxious to open myself to more pain. But I slowly realized the attraction I felt had never disappeared. Unsure and still doubtful, I left
my job and moved back in with Raymond. He was overjoyed; I vowed to go
slowly. I wasn't sure we could make our relationship work, and I knew the
smoldering hot spots from the marriage could reignite unless we changed our
relationship and ourselves.

With the pressure of marriage off, and knowing each other much better than
we had the first time, we worked on rebuilding our partnership. We were wiser
and I had matured; my identity was more settled. We talked about all the issues
that had plagued our marriage, resolving many and declaring others off limits.
He agreed to stop obsessing about my past; I promised to be more patient. We
defined our goals more clearly, ruled out plans for children, included an eventual return to college for me. I found a job and made it clear that I needed to
keep working until school was possible. 1987 was winding down when I finally felt ready to try again. This time, there would be no rings, no fancy wedding
ceremony, no assuming Raymond's last name, and no illusions.

Our second marriage has been the antithesis of the first. Familiarity may bring
contempt to some, but we find comfort in being close. Over the years, we have
discovered what is vital to happiness in our marriage. The key is trust. Not just
trusting the other person to remain faithful, but trust in knowing that, even at
your worst, your partner will not forsake you in word or deed. Trust that, at your
best, your partner will be right behind you, not threatened by your success but
sharing in it, rightfully accepting credit as your main ally in achieving it. Crucial
to trusting is depending on your partner to keep promises, and to always act in
your best interests. No love will survive long without the support of trust, but
trust can stand alone and independent. Love is a fast growing willow that needs
to be propped and buttressed in life's storms, but trust grows slowly, like the oak,
and possesses great strength. No union based on love will survive long without
it, but a relationship based on trust provides an excellent foundation on which
love can flourish freely. We have been lucky enough to have both.

How do I describe what I have learned from being married? After all, our
relationship seems more like a work-in-progress than a marriage. The paper
that proclaims us "married" merely seals the deal; it is the cover on the book
of our lives, the title page of the story we are writing together. The plot would
lose nothing without that page; the book would read the same *sans* the cover.
Our tale is unique, formed of moments collected from our individual pasts,
our shared past, our now and our forever. Each day is another page, another
small but important piece of our magnum opus. Together we live the chapters
of the years, the central characters in a life story of our own creation. The marriage itself exists in his mind and mine, and in the charged particles that flow

between our eyes and etch moments into our memories that no force in time or space can erase. We are bound together with the strength of steel and the tenderness of gossamer.

I have learned much from Raymond's life story, as he has learned from mine, but his physical handicap has taught us valuable lessons about acceptance, tolerance, and will. He has told me of endless months spent in hospitals as a three- to five-year old, the experimental subject of Depression-era doctors attempting to learn to correct his condition. Through a haze of ether he felt them snap bones, sever tendons, skewer his feet with rods. Imprisoned by heavy casts in a hospital bed, he cried futilely for the comfort of parents able to visit only on weekends. He doesn't have to explain how minutes seem like hours to a small child, so the days between visits were eternities to that lost, lonely boy. But the handicap and the suffering in part made him who he is, made him tough enough to excel as a young man at boxing, baseball, and other sports, defying the doctors' predictions of life in a wheelchair. He learned to accept himself as he is and to make the most of that, a process not easily mastered. The inexorable turning and twisting of his feet pulls the tendons and muscles of his legs and back a little tighter each year. When I massage those scarred appendages and bandage their splits and bruises, he sometimes asks "how can you love a crippled-up guy like me?" and incredulous that he could still ask, I answer "how can I not?" I have learned that physical limitations are infinitely easier to overcome than many other difficulties in marriage. Experience dealing with imperfections of the body is excellent practice for surviving the first gray hair and wrinkle, and other inevitabilities of aging that begin sooner than you imagine possible. Raymond's handicap is insignificant to me now: I can't believe I was ever embarrassed by his walk. When I think of him, I forget he is handicapped. When I dream of him, he has no deformity. Because I love him, he needs no body at all.

I could say "my husband is a good, loving, kind, generous man," words that mean everything and nothing. Yes, he is all those things, but they mean nothing unless I explain that he knew why I cried every time it rained in the year after my favorite dog died. That he was "loving" enough to know she was terrified of storms and I cried because she was alone and past consoling by me. I could call "generous" his unquestioning agreement for me to spend whatever was necessary to cure or comfort her in her illness before she died. "Kind" certainly describes his driving fifty miles one evening to get medicine for her, a remedy he knew probably wouldn't save her. A good man does these things, but "good" is such an inadequate word. In my head, and my heart, is a feeling beyond words, a connection to him made of something outside of the realm of words. I feel a deep ache in my heart, a tightness in my throat, a smile on my soul.

Like any friendship, our marriage involves give and take. A willingness to compromise and to trade off or share unappealing tasks makes life more pleasant. We have learned to toss out gender roles and do what we do best, whether that is washing the car for me or doing the dishes for Raymond. Because of his handicap he can't stand or walk for very long, but he can easily kneel. We often split work according to whether it is "low" and easier for him, or "high" and better suited to me. When we go somewhere that involves much walking, I benefit from the exercise of pushing his wheelchair, and his feet are spared. We understand that a successful collaboration requires hard work and cooperation. Every day is not packed with excitement and page-turning suspense, but the abundance of average days makes the memorable ones more prominent. Even average days can be appreciated for the small rewards and accomplishments they bring. Several hours shared mowing, weeding, and trimming topped off by a cold iced tea, a cool dusk breeze, pleasantly tired muscles, and a lush, trim yard may not be heady excitement, but we settle happily for satisfaction.

Part of the fun of being married is collecting anecdotes to add to our chronicle. Several months after our dog died, the "dog place" in my heart was ready to be filled again. At first I couldn't accept that the place could be filled while there was still so much grief in my heart, but I found myself needing the soft fur, the flash of movement, the noise and confusion of a dog. Animal lovers know that some people are born with gaps that can only be filled by animals, and for me a dog is an excellent fit. So I convinced Raymond that the time had come, and almost immediately found two perfect matches. They were Chihuahua puppies, and we named them Joli and Menu for "pretty" and "small." Joli has blue eyes, and often sleeps soundly on her back with her legs in the air, snoring, on the recliner with Raymond. Menu is smaller and more reserved, but both are extremely affectionate. We cook dog food for "the girls" as we call them, so in the grocery store we always watch for bargain meat to put in to the next batch. One day I spotted a large package of discounted "old" ground meat, and I motioned to Raymond. He said "that's an awful lot of meat for just us two," and I exclaimed "no, not for us, for the GIRLS!" Well, a woman listening nearby jerked to attention and looked at us like the child abusers she obviously thought we were. When we realized how we had sounded, we knew instantaneously we had a perfect new anecdote for our story.

Because we don't have children, we appreciate the companionship of our pets even more. They don't take the place of children, but they add to our enjoyment of life. The pleasure of coming home is amplified by the tiny radiant faces and spinning tails that unerringly greet us at the gate. The gentleness of my husband's hands as he caresses their fragile forms testifies to the tenderness in his heart for all creatures. Our house is often visited by small guests that creep or dash along unfamiliar linoleum until captured by Raymond's careful hands, and returned, gently, to their native turf. Before we met, Raymond had had only a few dogs during his life, but together we have owned all sorts of livestock and pets. Through the sharing of my love of animals, he has come to milk goats, share our house with a Vietnamese potbelly pig, and build a pond for a school of goldfish, then name each one himself. He has been amazed to reach in to our aquarium and pet tame Oscar fish, and smiled at being welcomed home by the braying of our donkey. Together we have delivered everything from puppies to foals. The tolerance and patience we have learned from keeping animals have helped us to be more accepting and forgiving of each other. Watching Raymond's exquisite tenderness and compassion for animals, I know that hurting a human being would be just as alien to his nature.

One of the salient lessons I have learned about life from being married is to give much more importance to these little things. Major events, whether good fortune or disaster, inevitably receive all the attention necessary, but neglecting small happenings drains the richness out of life. My leading man never gives me flowers, but after a long day I come home to dinner hot and waiting. Each time I awoke from anesthesia, Raymond's concerned face was one of the first I saw. The one time he had surgery, I wasn't there when he woke because I had labored most of the night refinishing a loveseat as a surprise for him. But he held no resentment, just appreciation for my efforts. We have experienced fires, floods, and other tragedies, and have known the joy of good fortune. Each page we turn, each day we greet could bring upheaval and enormous change, but if we hold our breaths and cross our fingers waiting for those days, we would miss many of the best things in life. We avoid seriousness and revel in humor; we tease and flirt with each other and refuse to go by anyone's rules but our own. There are no dress rehearsals in life, so we savor all of it for its uniqueness before it slips forever from our grasp.

To paint this second marriage all in bright colors would be unrealistic, but we have discovered two ways to lessen the impact of the dark spots on the whole. The first way, at the outset, was to agree never to accept divorce as a possibility, no matter how bad things seemed. We don't suggest it, threaten it, speculate about it, or even say the word; that is how completely we have eliminated it from our consciousness. The other way we deal with the dark spots is to accept that every action and every word spoken becomes part of our book, and can never be unwritten. Without the possibility of quitting the marriage, any problem can be solved because we must solve it to go on. Arguments are ways to clear resentments and misunderstandings, but seldom become personal attacks because neither of us wants to be ashamed of contributing ugliness to our story. Speaking hurtful thoughts in anger gives them weight and permanence; not speaking them never results in regret, and they aren't entered on the pages of our book. Not surprisingly, we fight fair, and have the security of knowing that disagreements, though inevitable, do not represent the end of the marriage or even obstacles we can't overcome. With this strategy, trust thrives and love has stability.

I have recognized trust and happiness in other couples, and know they are hard at work writing their own stories. Sadly, the absence of happiness is conspicuous and common, too. I have attended weddings and known the marriage wouldn't last because the two were not suitable co-authors, or because they weren't yet ready to work on the task with another person. Some partners don't collaborate, but instead draft sad and lonely monologues in which their spouses are but minor characters. Many people pen a series of short stories, and perhaps a novella or two, before they find a partner for their book. Some are destined to a lifetime of poetry; others never find their voice. Many concentrate on the sub-plots of their children, achieving varying degrees of balance between them and the major plot with their co-author. What I find most incredible is the power of love that keeps some people writing with freshness and creativity for sometimes fifty years and even longer. What stories they must have, if only we could read them!

I have the great fortune of having found a partner with whom my soul is fulfilled and my words flow freely. Our story is a romance novel, an outrageous comedy, and a gripping drama, but at heart it is a love story, its theme the importance of trust. We have placed bookmarks at certain pages we love to reread; they are dog-eared with use. Other pages are folded over: we know what is written there but will never read it again. Sometimes Raymond agrees to crease and tuck a page of which I'm not too proud, and I in turn fold one on which there are things he would rather not have contributed. We learn from our mistakes this way, but stop castigating ourselves and each other for them. We cannot tear out pages with passages we don't like, because nothing in life can be un-lived, nothing spoken un-said. But it is our book and we have license to write it our way, to choose the characters, the locations, and the direction the story will take. Of course there are no guarantees; people and circumstances change; not all characters who begin a story are there when it ends. No one can tell us how many blank pages we have been allotted to continue the tale. My husband and I are writing our saga together, but at some point one of us will have to finish the final chapters alone. We both feel that the pain of being that lone writer would be worse than being the first of the two main characters to leave the story. Of course, the one remaining will suffer the loss until the end of the story, while the one who passes will suffer no more. That may be the sole comfort in being the last character, the one who pens the ending. Perhaps the true measure of love is feeling more pain at the thought of losing the one you love, than you feel at the thought of your own demise.

The world may not remember Raymond and me; ours will be just one of many great books never committed to paper, but written only in the consciousness of two people who loved. One day I may no longer have my husband, but my sadness will be eased because I will always have the treasure of our story, intact, unerasable. I have learned the joy of living lies in the writing of the story, not in the way it ends, because lives do not end in grand climaxes that suddenly give meaning to all that has gone before. The best ending one can hope for is one made happy because the life that preceded it was fulfilling.

Night has come; it is time to end another page. Freshly showered, we slip between 25
cool, clean-smelling sheets. Joli bounds into the room and Menu creeps behind her

with a hopeful expression. We slip them between the blankets, and I turn off the light. I mold myself against Raymond's strong back and put my arm around him, tucking my hand under his side in "lock." In the stillness, Joli begins to snore, and I feel Raymond's laugh. I squeeze him a little tighter, and know the ending will be happy.

ANALYZING **What the Writer Says**

1. The writer claims to have discovered "the essence of happiness, and it isn't love." What, according to the essay, *is* the essence of a happy marriage?

2. How do you think Pfefferle defines "love" when she says that it is not the essential ingredient for a happy marriage?

3. What principles of a happy marriage do the writer's examples illustrate?

ANALYZING **How the Writer Says It**

How does the writer use the metaphor of the "book" of their marriage throughout her essay? What does she gain from using this metaphor?

ANALYZING **the Issue**

Do you agree with Pfefferle that love is not the main component of a successful marriage? What do you consider the main ingredient?

ANALYZING **Connections Between Texts**

1. Compare Pfefferle's concepts of love and marriage to C.S. Lewis's ideas on marital happiness in "We Have No 'Right to Happiness'" (p. 146). In what way do the two writers agree? Where do they disagree?

2. Pfefferle describes her marriage to a man with a physical handicap. In "Carnal Acts" (p. 228) Nancy Mairs, who has multiple sclerosis, writes about the same issue from the point of view of the handicapped partner. What similar points do both writers make about marriage between an able-bodied and a physically challenged partner?

3. To what degree does Jay Ullal's 1983 picture "Bridal Couple in Beirut" (p. 192) illustrate the snares and pitfalls of marriage as Pfefferle (as well as C.S. Lewis) describes it? When the picture was published in *Time Great Images*, the caption identified the bride as Christian, the groom as Muslim, and the setting as the "green line" that split Beirut in the 1980s. Based on your reading, comment on other difficulties the bridal couple is likely to face.

WARMING UP: *Have you ever known a woman who was shaped by someone else's opinion about how she should act or what she should look like?*

A Work of Artifice

BY MARGE PIERCY

MARGE PIERCY

Winner of the 2000 Paterson Poetry Prize, Marge Piercy (b. 1936) has written numerous novels and books of poetry. In "A Work of Artifice" she comments on the stifling quality of patriarchal attitudes about female identity.

The bonsai tree
in the attractive pot
could have grown eighty feet
tall
on the side of a mountain   5
till split by lightning.
But a gardener
carefully pruned it.
It is nine inches high.
Every day as he   10
whittles back the branches
the gardener croons,
It is your nature
to be small and cozy,
domestic and weak;   15
how lucky, little tree,
to have a pot to grow in.
With living creatures
one must begin very early
to dwarf their growth: 20
the bound feet,
the crippled brain,
the hair in curlers,
the hands you
love to touch.   25

ANALYZING | What the Writer Says

1. What is the poem's operative metaphor, as established in the first seven lines? Who or what is represented by the bonsai tree? The gardener? The attractive pot?

2. What is the significance of the lines "how lucky, little tree / to have a pot to grow in"?

3. What do the images in the poem's final sentence suggest?

4. Put Piercy's point into a sentence.

ANALYZING | How the Writer Says It

Comment on how the poem's title informs the entire poem.

ANALYZING | the Issue

1. To what extent does our culture reinforce weak self-images in women?

2. Are the issues Piercy raises in this poem, published in 1982, still relevant? Cite examples to support your position.

"No, I don't want to change you, Darryl. But sure, it would be great if you were completely different."

ANALYZING Connections Between Texts

1. Show how Caroline Hwang's "The Good Daughter" (p. 139) confronts some of the same issues Piercy's poem raises.

2. How does Anna Quindlen's "Stretch Marks" (p. 242) echo points made by Piercy? What are the main differences?

3. Comment on how J. C. Duffy's cartoon reinforces Piercy's message—and the ways in which it contradicts it.

The Inheritance That Got Away

BY MELANIE THERNSTROM

MELANIE THERNSTROM

A Harvard graduate and professor of creative writing, Melanie Thernstrom has authored two "true crime" books, The Dead Girl *(1991) and* Halfway Heaven: Diary of a Harvard Murder *(1997). In the following piece she contemplates a kind of emotional crime in her personal history and ponders the degrees of culpability, concluding that "tests of love always end badly."*

It was at my grandmother's memorial service that a friend of hers mentioned that my sculpture—the one my grandmother had always promised to leave me— was worth $4 million. It was one of the few moments in my life I found myself wordless. It was her memorial service! I already disliked how the service seemed to resemble an art opening, with toastlike speeches, projected slides of her work and wine and cheese in the Art Students League building. And now we were talking about money?

Yet, in the midst of the floating emotions of the hour, the different kinds of grief, love and disappointment, here was something new: a number. It was as if I had been looking at a paperweight snow globe watching miniature snow petals fall in the miniature world and suddenly someone had flipped it over and exposed the price tag. My sculpture had represented so many things, incorporating so many realms of feeling, but here was a meaning I hadn't contemplated. And I knew that no matter how much I tried to banish the thought and right the globe, it would never look the same again.

The first time Grandma Dorothy suggested she might not leave me my sculpture was in a French restaurant a few blocks from her lower Fifth Avenue apartment. It was a gay late-April evening. I had just arrived from upstate, where I was in graduate school, and my grandmother embodied for me all the glamour of Old New York life. We took a turn in Washington Square Park, and then, sitting in Cafe Loup, I watched the elegant 87-year-old drink a glass of Lillet. With her dancer's posture and flapper's haircut and a topaz brooch at her throat, she looked far too attractively lofty to be interested in her plate of spaghetti.

"I am thinking of leaving 'Dorothy Taking Bath in Wheelbarrow' to the Cleveland Museum of Art," she announced. "It's an *extremely* valuable piece, and there's a young curator there who'd *love* to have it."

My sculpture is a small bronze abstraction of my grandmother as a young woman bathing in a wheelbarrow. Her first husband, David Smith, made it in 1940 on their farm in the Adirondacks. It's a remarkable piece. The woman whose body forms the cup of the wheelbarrow is not wholly human. Her head bulges forward like an insect, and she has multiple arms and tentacles for breasts. The work seems to summarize the narrative of their stormy 23-year marriage: she wanted to be an artist, and he wanted her to be art. Throughout her life, the sculpture sat in the entrance hall of her apartment, surrounded by dried red leaves; it was the first thing and the last thing I'd see on my many visits there. And for as long as I could remember, I'd always thought of it as mine.

Dorothy Dehner was my mother's stepmother from the time my mother was a teenager—her wicked stepmother, Dorothy liked to say, with a wicked look. And although she did treat my mother shabbily, she always bestowed her best attentions on me. I was her favorite, her real relative, she often told me conspiratorially—the next bather in the wheelbarrow. At dinner that night, she mentioned my rival heir—the museum—so coyly, it sounded less like a decision than a ploy of some kind. But what kind?

Did she want me to beg her for it? To tell her that it was my favorite favorite thing, that my heart was set on it and could not be reset? Or was this more of a King Lear test: would insisting that I wanted nothing but love from her prove me worthy of the marvelous thing?

I was 23 then and fancied myself a Cordelia type. I was infatuated with the idea of renunciation. I was Della, who cut off her hair in "The Gift of the Magi" and received true love in return. I was not someone whose treasure was something rust and moths could find. (I was studying Marxist literary theory, after all.) But since, unlike my literary heroines, I was actually filled with resentment, my speech came out like a parody of renunciation.

"What a good idea!" I declared. "The people of Cleveland will appreciate it! Why put a cultural treasure in private hands? Just because I'm your granddaughter doesn't mean I'm entitled to anything." As a final flourish, I picked the check off the table, saying "Oh, let me." The tab came to $84, I still recall. I took my time counting out the bills: a dollar for almost every year of her life. Loving her was like that, I thought: always having to pay for things that happened long before you were born.

The word "grandmother" has a noble ring. People—we like to think— 10
improve with time. Older people are said to be at peace with their pasts, as
memory loses its razor focus, blurring into an Impressionist painting of the
happiest occasions and the best weather. Striving, vanity and ambition pass
and are replaced by love—selfless love, charitas, giving. Had my head not been
so stuffed with idealized grandmother images, I might have seen my grandmother for who she was.

Whenever I'd visit her, the light in her room would flicker on and off until
dawn. She'd get up to pour herself Lillet. Her eyesight was failing; she no
longer had books for company. A century of loss, she would sometimes say,
the wars merging in her mind with the early death of her family. And this: two
fortunes—large fortunes, belonging to the two central figures in her life—had
slipped through her open fingers. She went over the details in her mind, again
and again, telling herself she didn't care; some people care about money, but
not Dorothy.

The first fortune belonged to her Aunt Cora. Dorothy was born in Cleveland
to a wealthy old American family of Dutch and German heritage on Christmas
Eve, 1901. Her parents and two siblings died by the time she was in her early
teens, leaving her in the care of her maiden aunts—Flo, the kind one, and
Cora, the terrible. Cora—the one she was close to—was a hot-tempered beauty involved in a long affair with a railroad baron who wouldn't leave his wife.
Dorothy decided to become an actress and moved to New York to play an
ingenue Off Broadway while she took classes at the Art Students League. At
her boardinghouse she met David Smith, an aspiring artist from Decatur, Ind.

"David was the first penniless man I married," Dorothy would say, "Your
mother's father was the second. But I didn't care. My life wasn't about
money—it was about art."

In all the times that she repeated this story, only once did I say, "But you had
inherited money from your mother to live on."

"I sewed all our clothes at Bolton Landing! And grew vegetables and canned 15
peaches and tomatoes while David sculpted."

It was clear to me, even as a teenager, that the sewing and growing were more
ideology than necessity: they were Communists, like many of their peer group.
(My grandmother always maintained that Stalin was the victim of unfair propaganda.) The income from her inheritance from her mother was always enough
to live on, and even during the Depression, they never had to worry.

Their farmhouse on Lake George in the Adirondacks was landscaped with
his colossal industrial-steel monuments. Dorothy wanted to sculpture but didn't
dare try while they were together. They visited the city frequently, hanging out
at the Cedar Tavern with John Graham, Arshile Gorky, Adolph Gottlieb, Mark
Rothko and Jackson Pollock—the whole macho gang of Abstract Expressionist
pioneers. Dorothy was "one of the wives." "Oh, the wives!" she would say, with
a sigh.

Like others in the gang, he had affairs. He began beating her, she said, and in 1951, when she was 50, she left him. Although she felt in his shadow professionally throughout her life, her work began to flower once she moved away. In her later years, her paintings and sculpture were sometimes clustered with other overlooked Abstract Expressionist-era wives like Lee Krasner and Elaine de Kooning.

After Dorothy left David, her Aunt Cora wanted her to move back in with her. Cora was an extremely rich woman by this point. Her baron lover had died, leaving her his railroad millions. But Dorothy didn't want to—she had just gotten out from her husband's domination. Cora was very offended. When she died soon after, she left her entire fortune to a mentally disabled girl from a poor family who had been put in her care.

But Dorothy lost an even greater fortune from the Smith estate. Like his friend Pollock, David died driving his car off the road, and the art whose production she had supported all those years was immensely valuable. Everyone advised Dorothy—who had never accepted alimony—to contest the will. She had a few drawings and sculptures that David had given her, but he left the entirety of his estate to his two young daughters from his second marriage. 20

"I didn't want the money," she would tell me over and over and over. "My life is about art. Money means nothing to me, you see."

As I got older, I began to see, but I didn't tell her what I saw. Although she didn't need the money, the fact that the two most important people in her life had left her nothing kept her awake nights.

Most people's grandparents aren't wealthy; many people support their parents in their old age. My father's parents didn't have money, although his mother, my Grandma Bea, left me some very fine English blue-pansy china and an Art Deco diamond engagement ring that I wear now. Last year, I made the decision to use the china too, and it makes me happy, several times a day. Since Bea didn't have money, money wasn't part of our relationship. And if my sculpture had been a teacup, maybe Grandma Dorothy would have given it to me. But when your teacups are David Smiths, what then?

From the night in the restaurant until the day she tumbled down some stairs to her death six years later, the fate of my sculpture was always an unspoken question. She seemed to toy with the idea of giving it to me, slipping sometimes into calling it "your sculpture," as in "Your sculpture has always been my favorite of all David's works." My heart would beat faster whenever she said this, but I steadfastly refused to respond. I knew she knew how badly I wanted it. I *refuse to be manipulated*, I told myself. I have pride. *I don't care*, I said, like Pierre to the lion.

This wasn't the first time I'd pretended not to care about something she 25 owned. When I was in college, my grandmother's building went co-op, and she was offered the insider price on her apartment. But as it was rent-controlled and her payments wouldn't decrease, she didn't want to buy it. My mother suggested she and my father might want to purchase it for me to live in after Dorothy died. It was the apartment my mother had grown up in, in which her own mother had died. But Dorothy said no; she didn't like the idea of anything being lived in after her death—"or anybody living," my mother added sardonically when she told me the story. I remembered how stunned I was. I didn't say anything to my grandmother (the idea of "unseemliness" held such weight with me then), but I kept asking my mother if she could have misunderstood. Didn't Grandma want me to have a life like hers? A life in which—from the vantage point of an antique and art-filled cordial-stocked apartment on lower Fifth—I, too, could say all I cared about was my art, and creating it without commercial considerations. Hadn't she always told me I was her heir in all senses of the word?

I liked all the same—costly—things she did. I liked accompanying her to the summer Bach festival in Madeira. And I would have liked to pop into delightful little bistros every night of the week dressed in splashy fabulous or cool drapey clothing with Victorian jewelry. Or spend my first years of marriage in the Virgin Islands and in Europe, as she and David had, and then buy 86 acres upstate. And even though I was still in college then, I already knew it took a great deal of money for money to be no object at all.

Yet she was always Lady Bountiful to people outside her family. She was godmother, honorary aunt or grandmother to literally dozens of others. "So delightful," they would tell me. "And so generous!" She especially relished wooing my boyfriends. Some of her gestures toward them were so provocative that it was as if she was daring me to say something. My college boyfriend and I loved one watercolor she made in the 40's. It was a playful, feminine work of delicately sketched squares melting into clouds of orange and violet. "I'll give it to you as your wedding present," my grandmother would always say. We weren't engaged, so the remark annoyed and embarrassed me, but that was a grandmother's prerogative, my boyfriend said. She was mad for that boyfriend, a writer, and she constantly compared us with her and David (a comparison we never quite knew what to make of). When we broke up, he moved to the Adirondacks near where my grandmother and David had lived. When he married, she told me that she sent the painting to him and his new wife to hang over their kitchen table.

She was every bit as seductive with my graduate-school boyfriend. She'd put on red lipstick and African jewelry, serve Mumm in Art Deco glasses and play the piano, determined to be more fabulous than any grandmother he had ever met. And although my sculpture was already on the scales by then, she seemed to have no hesitation about giving him a watercolor. Other paintings went to subsequent boyfriends.

Then a couple of years after our dinner, something unusual happened. Grandma had promised a Smith painting to my mother when she was a graduate student, if she finished her dissertation. Nineteen years passed. My mother was now a professor, the author of several books. The work was large with dark splashes of paint resembling a flock of angry, impersonal birds. My mother didn't especially admire it—she had, in fact, taken a dislike to modern art per se, and defiantly decorated her own walls with representational work my grandmother sniffed at. But she felt cheated. The slight grew in her mind, symbolizing all the ways the relationship had duped her. Finally, during a visit, she did something radical: she asked for it. And Grandma gave it to her.

Why didn't I just ask for my sculpture? I wondered at the time. Why didn't 30
I plead or argue or even get angry, and acknowledge what Grandma never would—that priceless art has a price and she had power for having it? While I knew she wanted me to ask, I didn't want to have to. I wanted her to have the kind of love that would make her want to give it to me.

But tests of love always end badly. Cordelia didn't get what she wanted. When I read "The Gift of the Magi" now, it seems to me a story about loss. I thought my grandmother was the one with the misbegotten tests, but I was testing her, too, with my silence.

ANALYZING What the Writer Says

1. What is the nature of the relationship between the author and her grandmother?

2. Why doesn't the author tell her grandmother that she really wants the sculpture?

3. Whom does the author blame for the sculpture's ultimate fate—in permanent storage at the Cleveland Museum? Whom do you see as most responsible?

4. Is appreciation of Thernstrom's essay limited to an audience that can relate to potential inheritances worth millions? Why or why not?

ANALYZING How the Writer Says It

1. Thernstrom suggests that she initially finds the discussion of money at her grandmother's memorial service unseemly, but the complex equation of the material value of one's possessions and one's love is quickly established as a theme in the essay. Point to words, phrases, and anecdotes that help articulate the *economy* of love Thernstrom has come to understand.

2. Identify the piece's tone. What words or phrases reveal the author's attitude toward her grandmother? Which reveal her attitude about her own role in the family drama?

ANALYZING the Issue

1. Family members may have an emotional claim to their departed loved ones' possessions. How might laws protect such rights, and should they be enacted?

2. What issues about family relationships does Thernstrom's piece raise? What do you think is the moral to this story?

3. Is Thernstrom's grandmother right to donate a valuable and possibly important work of art to an art museum? Does such work belong in museums?

ANALYZING Connections Between Texts

1. Analyze the last section of Anndee Hochman's "Growing Pains: Beyond 'One Big Happy Family'" (p. 131) in which she writes about finding her grandmother's cameo ring, wearing it in a symbolic act of defiance, and losing it. Compare the emotions and values tied to that family possession with those tied to the sculpture Thernstrom has always coveted.

2. The "lessons" in Thernstrom's essay and in Toni Cade Bambara's "The Lesson" (p. 332) are both occasioned by the coveting of valuable objects, although the principals in each piece come from very different backgrounds and life experience. Compare and contrast the lessons of these essays.

3. Look at Stephanie Maze's "Lunch at Uncle Antonio's" (p. 99) and compare the family values implicit in it with those of Thernstrom and her family.

On Black Fathering

By Cornel West

CORNEL WEST

Cornel West (b. 1953), an influential thinker and writer on religion, race, and social theory, recently returned to Princeton after serving as Professor of Religion and Afro-American Studies at Harvard for several years. His 1993 Race Matters *initiated a national dialogue on race issues. The following piece appeared in Andre C. Willis's* Faith of Our Fathers.

One of the most difficult tasks to accomplish in American society is to be a solid, caring, and loving black father. To be a good black father, first you have to negotiate all of the absurd attacks and assaults on your humanity and on your capacity and status as a human being. Second, you have to provide materially and economically, as well as nurture psychologically, personally, and existentially. All of this requires a deep level of maturity. By maturity I mean a solid understanding of who one is as a person, and a sense of sacrifice and courage. For black men to reach that level of maturity and understanding is almost miraculous given the dehumanizing context for black men, and yet millions and millions have done it. It is a tribute to fulfill the highest standards of fatherhood. When I think of my own particular case, I think of my father, my grandfather, and his father, because what they were able to do was to sustain some sense of dignity and sacrifice even as they dealt with all the arrows that were coming at them on every level in American society.

Let's consider the economic level. In America, generally speaking, patriarchal definitions of men in relation to the economic front mean you have a job and provide for your family. Many black men did not (and do not) make enough money to provide for their families adequately because of their exclusion from jobs with a living wage. They then oftentimes tended, and tend, to accent certain patriarchal identities (e.g., predatory or abusive behavior) in lieu of the fact that they could not perform the traditional patriarchal roles in American society.

Then on the home front, where black men had and have, oftentimes, wives who were and are subject to such white supremacist abuse, either at the white home where these sisters work(ed) or as a service worker in other parts of white society, most black men had to deal with the kinds of scars and bruises that come from knowing that you were supposed to protect your woman, as it were, which is also part of the patriarchal identity in America—a man ought to be able to protect his woman but could not protect her from the vicious abuse. Many black men also recognized that there was a relation between their not being able to get a job given the discrimination and segregation on the one hand and the tremendous power wielded by those white men who were often condoning the abuse of their own wives.

How children perceive their father is another interesting component of the dynamic that black fathers have to negotiate. How are black fathers able to convey to their children some affirmative sense of self, some sense of reality—given what is happening to these men on the economic front, given what many of them know is happening to their wives outside of the house, and given the perception by their own children that they are unable to fulfill the expected patriarchal role? In the tradition of the black father, the best ones—I think my grandfather and dad are good examples—came up with ways of negotiating a balance so that they would recognize that exclusion from the economic sphere was real, and recognize that possible abuse of their wives was real, and also recognize that they had to sustain a connection with their kids in which their kids could see the best in them despite the limited and dehumanizing circumstances under which they functioned.

My mother happened to be a woman who was not abused in the fashion   5
described above. I remember one incident when a white policeman disrespected my mother. Dad went at him verbally and, in the eyes of the police, ended up violating the law. At that point he just drew a line in the sand that said, "You're going too far." I thank God that a number of incidents like that didn't happen, or he would have ended up in jail forever—like so many other brothers who just do not allow certain levels of disrespect of their mother, wife, sister, or daughter. As a man, what I was able to see in Dad was his ability to transform his own pain with a sense of laughter, and a sense of empathy, and a sense of compassion for others. This was a real act of moral genius Dad accomplished, and I think that it is part of the best of a tradition of moral genius. Unfortunately, large numbers of black men do not reach that level because the rage and the anger are just too deep; they just burn them out and consume their soul. Fortunately, on the other hand, you do have many black men that achieve this level and some that go beyond it.

In my own case as a father, I certainly tried to emulate and imitate Dad's very ingenious ways of negotiating the balances between what was happening on these different fronts, but because of the sacrifices he and Mom made, I had access to opportunities that he did not. When my son Cliff was born, I was convinced that I wanted to try to do for him what Dad had done for me. But it was not to be—there was no way that I could be the father to my son that my dad was to me. Part of it was that my circumstances were very different. Another part was simply that I was not the man that my father was. My brother is actually the shining example of building on the rich legacy of my dad as a father much more than I am, because he gives everything—right across the board. He is there—whatever the circumstance—has spent time with the kids; he is always there in the same way that Dad was there for us. I'll always try to be a rich footnote to my brother, yet as a father I have certainly not been the person that he was. The effort has been there, the endeavor too, but the circumstances (as well as my not being as deep a person as he or my father) have not enabled me to measure up. On the other hand, my son Cliff turned out to be a decent and fascinating person—and he is still in process, of course.

The bottom line for my dad was always love, and he was a deeply Christian man—his favorite song was "I Will Trust in the Lord." He had a profound trust. His trust was much more profound than mine in some ways, even though I work at it. He had a deep love, and that's the thing I've tried to build on with Cliff. My hope and my inclination are that Cliff feels this love, but certainly it takes more than love to nurture and father a son or a daughter.

The most important things for black fathers to try to do are to give of themselves, to try to exemplify in their own behavior what they want to see in their sons and daughters, and, most important, to spend time with and give attention to their children. This is a big challenge, yet it is critical as we move into the twenty-first century.

The most difficult task of my life was to give the eulogy for my father. Everything else pales in the face of this challenge. Hence what Dad means to me—like my family, Cliff and Elleni—constitutes who and what I am and will be.

EULOGY

Clifton Lincoln West, Jr. What a man. What an individual. What a person. 10 What a servant. We gather here this afternoon in this sacred place and this consecrated space to say good-bye. To bid farewell to a good man, a great Christian who lived a grand and loving life. When I think of my father, I cannot but think of what he said to that reporter from the *Sacramento Bee* when they asked him, "What is it about you and what is it about your family—do you have a secret?" Dad said, "No, we live by Grace—in addition to that, me and his mother, we try to *be there*." I shall never forget that my father was not simply a man of quiet dignity, steadfast integrity, and high intelligence, but fundamentally and quintessentially he was a man of love, and love means being there for others. That's why when I think of Dad I recall that precious moment in the fifteenth chapter of John in the eleventh and twelfth verse: "These things have I given unto you that my joy might remain in you, and that your joy might be full. This is my commandment that ye love one another as I have loved you."

In the midst of Dad's sophistication and refinement he was always for real. He was someone who was down-to-earth because he took this commandment seriously, and it meant he had to cut against the grain in a world in which he was going to endure lovingly and with compassion. Isn't that what the very core of the gospel is about? The thirteenth chapter of I Corinthians—that great litany of love that Dr. King talked about—deals with it. Dad used to read it all the time. I will never forget when he took me to college in Cambridge, the first time I ever flew on an airplane (it cost about ninety-five dollars then). Dad told me, "Corn, we're praying for you, and always remember: 'Though I speak with the tongues of men and of angels and have not love, I become as a sounding brass or a tinkling cymbal. And though I have the gift of prophecy, and understand all mysteries, and all knowledge; and though I have all faith, so that I could remove mountains, and have not love, I am nothing.'"

As we stand here on these stormy banks of Jordan and watch Dad's ship go by, may I remind each and every one of you that we come from a loving family, a courageous people of African descent, and a rich Christian tradition. We have seen situations in which history has pushed our backs against the wall, and life has knocked us to our knees. In the face of despair and degradation sometimes we know that all we can do is sing a song, or crack a smile, or say a prayer. Yet we refuse to allow grief and misery to have the last word.

Dad was a man of love, and if I was to adopt his perspective at this very moment, he would say, "Corn, don't push me in the limelight, keep your mother in mind, don't focus on me, keep the family in mind—I'm just a servant passing through." That's the kind of father I had.

But he didn't come to it by himself, you see. He was part of a family, he was part of a people, he was part of a tradition that went all the way back to gut-bucket Jim Crow Louisiana, September 7, 1928. He was not supposed to make it, you see. Nobody would have believed that Clifton Lincoln West, Jr., the third child of C. L. West and Lovey West, would have been able to aspire to the heights that he did. No one would have predicted or projected that he would make it through the first three months in Louisiana—Cliff was not supposed to make that trip, you know. He was born the year before the stock market crashed. His family stayed three months in Louisiana, and Grandfather and Grandmother, with three young children in a snowstorm, journeyed on a train to Tulsa, Oklahoma. You all know what Tulsa, Oklahoma, was like. It was seven years after the major riot in this country in which over three hundred folks—black folks—were killed and Greenwood, Archer and Pine—that GAP corner—the Wall Street of black America was all burned out. But Grandmama had something else in mind, and the Lord did too.

Dad went on to Paul Laurence Dunbar Elementary School—to give you an   15
idea of what side of town they were living on—and George Washington Carver
Junior High School, and Booker T. Washington High School. It was there that
he got to choose the idea of pulling from the best of the world but remaining
not of the world. I like that about Dad. He wasn't so excessively pious or so
excessively rigid that he became naive and got caught up in narrow doctrines
and creeds and thought he was better than anybody else. That's not the kind
of man he was. No. His faith was grounded in a love because he knew that he
had fallen short of the glory of God. He knew he had inadequacies and shortcomings, but he was going to struggle anyhow; he was going to keep keeping
on anyway.

After high school he went on to the military for three years. He could have
easily given his life for this country. When he returned to Tulsa, Oklahoma, he
was refused admission at the University of Tulsa, and then went on to that
grand institution, Fisk University, where he met that indescribably wonderful,
beautiful, lovable honor student from Orange, Texas—Irene Bias. I'll never
forget when we were at Fisk together, he described the place right outside
Jubilee Hall where they met. I said, "Dad, that's a special place," and he said,
"Yes, that meeting was the beginning of the peak of my life." As their love
began to grow and multiply, the army grabbed him back again for eighteen
months, but in the years to come they had young Clifton, my brother, to whom
I'm just a footnote; myself, of course; and Cynthia and Cheryl. We moved from
Oklahoma through Topeka, Kansas, on our way to 8008 48th Avenue, Glen
Elder. Yes, how proud we were driving up in that bright orange Mercury. We
were at the cutting edge of residential breakdown in Sacramento, but along the
way, for almost a decade, Dad, and the men of Glen Elder—Mr. Peters, Mr.
Pool, Mr. Powell, Mr. Reed—these were black men who cared and who worked
together. These overworked yet noble men built the little league diamond by
themselves, and then they organized the league into ten teams—minor and
major leagues for the neighborhood. They provided a means by which character and integrity could be shaped among the young brothers. Then every
Sunday, onto Shiloh—"can't wait for the next sermon of Reverend Willie P.
Cooke, just hope that he didn't go too long"—but we knew that the Lord was
working in him. Dad would always tell us, "You know how blessed I am, how
blessed we are. Never think that we've come as far as we have on our own."

When we were in trouble, there was Mr. Fields, Mrs. Ray, and Mrs. Harris—
there were hundreds of folks who made a difference. You all remember when
Dad went to the hospital when he was thirty-one years old and the doctors had
given up on him. There was a great sadness on Forty-eighth Avenue because
he had left Mom with four little children. Granddad—the Reverend C. L. West,
left his church for months to come and be with Mom—Grandmom came as
well—and Dad was in the hospital in Oakland. They had given up on him; the
medical profession had reached its conclusion and said they could do nothing.

And we said, "We know the power. Let Him step in." We knew that Reverend Cook hadn't been preaching that "Jesus is a rock in a weary land, and water in dry places, and food when you are hungry, and a mind regulator and a heart fixer" for nothing. And we came to Calvary in prayer.

Can you imagine how different our lives would have been if we had lost Dad then, in 1961, rather than 1994? Even in the midst of our fear we rejoice. It would have been a different world for each and every one of us, especially the children. Dad kept going after his recovery. He worked at McClellan Air Force Base—steadily missed some of those promotions he should have got, but he stayed convinced that he was going to teach people right no matter what, even given his own situation.

That's another thing I loved about him. People always ask me, "West, why do you still talk about love? It's played out. Why when you talk about blackness is it always linked to white brothers and sisters and yellow brothers and sisters and red brothers and sisters and brown brothers and sisters?" And I tell them about John 15:11–12. I tell them that I dedicated my life a long time ago to the same Jesus that Dad dedicated his life to, to the same Jesus that Reverend C. L. West dedicated his life, to the same Jesus that my grandfather on my mother's side and my grandmother on my mother's side dedicated their lives to, but, more important, I saw in the concrete, with Dad and Mom, a love that transcends skin pigmentation. I saw it on the ground. Dad taught us that even as you keep track of the injustice, you don't lose track of the humanity. That's what love and being there are all about. Dad made it a priority and preference to be there for us. He made a choice. It meant that he would live a life of interruptions because those who are fundamentally committed to being there are going to be continually interrupted—your own agenda, your own project, are going to be interfered with. Dad was always open to that kind of interruption. He was able to translate a kind of unpredictable interruption into a supportive intervention in somebody else's life. More important, Dad realized that a being-there kind of love meant that you had to have follow up and follow through. One could not just show up—one has to follow up and follow through. This is the most difficult aspect of it. Love is inseparable from pain and hurt and sadness and sorrow and disappointment, but Dad knew that you had to have follow up and follow through. He knew that you had to struggle in the midst of that pain and that hurt—you had to have just not simply the high moments of love, but the funk of love, the stink and the stench of love. In all of his relationships Dad embodied precisely that struggle with the high moments of love and the low moments of love. He knew that the cross was not just about smiles and that it was not just about celebration—it was about sadness, stench, and funk. That is what the blood was about, not Kool-aid but blood. That's how inseparable scars, bruises, and wounds are from joy, affirmation, and wholeness. If you were serious about love, if you were serious about being there for people you were going to be there in in the midst of any situation, any circumstances, any condition. Dad realized that God being there for us in any situation and circumstances meant that if he was going to be Godlike, he had to be there in any situation for us. I've been alive now for forty years, and on Thursday I'll be forty-one years old, and *not once has my mother or father disappointed me*. They have always been there. That is a blessing, and I do not deserve it. It's a blessing, and I am thankful for it.

So as we bid farewell to Dad, I want you all to know that I am looking for- 20 ward to a family reunion. I am looking forward to union together on the other side of the Jordan. I am looking forward to seeing Dad in a place where the wicked will cease their troubling and the weary shall be at rest. I tell you when I get there, I'm going down Revelation Boulevard to the corner of John Street, right around the corner from Mark's place. But I want to go to Nahum's place. I don't want to be in Jeremiah's house, it would be too crowded. I don't even want to be down on Peter Street, too many people there—I want some quiet time. I want to sit down with C. L. West, I want to sit down with Nick Bias, and I want to sit down with Aunt Juanita, and I want to sit down with Aunt Tiny. And I want to sit down with Dad! I want to let them know that we did the best that we could to keep alive the best of the legacy of love that they left to us. And when we come together, we will come together in a way in which there will be no more tears, no more heartache, no more heartbreak, no more sadness and sorrow, no more agony and anguish. We shall sit at the feet of the Lord and be blessed, and our souls will look back and wonder how we got over, how we got over.

ANALYZING What the Writer Says

1. On what two fronts does West say it is particularly difficult for black men to develop their patriarchal identities?

2. What are the best black fathers able to do, according to West?

3. Why does West see race as the central component of black fatherhood?

4. What was the "act of moral genius" that West's own father was able to accomplish?

5. In the eulogy to his father, how does West define a father's love?

ANALYZING How the Writer Says It

1. Whereas the first section of West's piece is written in conventional essay form, the entire second portion comprises the eulogy West delivered at his father's funeral. Why do you think West uses this technique? In terms of West's overall argument, what does the eulogy offer?

2. Consider eulogies that you have heard (or read). How does West's compare to those? What other types of speeches does West's eulogy resemble?

ANALYZING the Issue

1. Do black men, in their struggle to be strong fathers, have more obstacles to overcome than men of other races or ethnicities?

2. What element or elements of good fathering transcend race?

ANALYZING Connections Between Texts

1. Both West and William C. Brisick ("The Steep Cliffs of Life," p. 126) write about the responsibilities of fathers for their children. How do their responsibilities differ? How are they similar?

2. In "Theme for English B" (p. 372) Langston Hughes describes the difficulty of being a black student in a white institution. Compare the situation of the poem's speaker to what West discusses: the particular challenges of being a black father in a white society.

3. Look at Dixie D. Vereen's "Man and Child" (p. 193). How does the photograph illustrate some of West's key points?

WARMING UP: *Describe a place that you and your family visited regularly when you were growing up. What were the reasons for your family's visits there? What emotional experiences do you connect with this place?*

Once More to the Lake

BY E. B. WHITE

E. B. WHITE

Essayist and beloved children's book author E. B. White (1899–1985) often celebrates the joyous side of life, but in "Once More to the Lake," a father's desire to recapture the summer lake experience of his own youth results in a meditation on the cyclical nature of life as he sees himself in his young son and confronts "the chill of death."

One summer, along about 1904, my father rented a camp on a lake in Maine and took us all there for the month of August. We all got ringworm from some kittens and had to rub Pond's Extract on our arms and legs night and morning, and my father rolled over in a canoe with all his clothes on; but outside of that the vacation was a success and from then on none of us ever thought there was any place in the world like that lake in Maine. We returned summer after summer—always on August 1st for one month. I have since become a salt-water man, but sometimes in summer there are days when the restlessness of the tides and the fearful cold of the sea water and the incessant wind which blows across the afternoon and into the evening make me wish for the placidity of a lake in the woods. A few weeks ago this feeling got so strong I bought myself a couple of bass hooks and a spinner and returned to the lake where we used to go, for a week's fishing and to revisit old haunts.

I took along my son, who had never had any fresh water up his nose and who had seen lily pads only from train windows. On the journey over to the lake I began to wonder what it would be like. I wondered how time would have marred this unique, this holy spot—the coves and streams, the hills that the sun set behind, the camps and the paths behind the camps. I was sure the tarred road would have found it out and I wondered in what other ways it would be desolated.

It is strange how much you can remember about places like that once you allow your mind to return into the grooves which lead back. You remember one thing, and that suddenly reminds you of another thing. I guess I remembered clearest of all the early mornings, when the lake was cool and motionless, remembered how the bedroom smelled of the lumber it was made of and of the wet woods whose scent entered through the screen. The partitions in the camp were thin and did not extend clear to the top of the rooms, and as I was always the first up I would dress softly so as not to wake the others, and sneak out into the sweet outdoors and start out in the canoe, keeping close along the shore in the long shadows of the pines. I remembered being very careful never to rub my paddle against the gunwale for fear of disturbing the stillness of the cathedral.

The lake had never been what you would call a wild lake. There were cottages sprinkled around the shores, and it was in farming country although the shores of the lake were quite heavily wooded. Some of the cottages were owned by nearby farmers, and you would live at the shore and eat your meals at the farmhouse. That's what our family did. But although it wasn't wild, it was a fairly large and undisturbed lake and there were places in it which, to a child at least, seemed infinitely remote and primeval.

I was right about the tar: it led to within half a mile of the shore. But when I got back there, with my boy, and we settled into a camp near a farmhouse and into the kind of summertime I had known, I could tell that it was going to be pretty much the same as it had been before—I knew it, lying in bed the first morning, smelling the bedroom, and hearing the boy sneak quietly out and go off along the shore in a boat. I began to sustain the illusion that he was I, and therefore, by simple transposition, that I was my father. This sensation persisted, kept cropping up all the time we were there. It was not an entirely new feeling, but in this setting it grew much stronger. I seemed to be living a dual existence. I would be in the middle of some simple act, I would be picking up a bait box or laying down a table fork, or I would be saying something, and suddenly it would be not I but my father who was saying the words or making the gesture. It gave me a creepy sensation.

We went fishing the first morning. I felt the same damp moss covering the worms in the bait can, and saw the dragonfly alight on the tip of my rod as it hovered a few inches from the surface of the water. It was the arrival of this fly that convinced me beyond any doubt that everything was as it always had been, that the years were a mirage and there had been no years. The small waves were the same, chucking the rowboat under the chin as we fished at anchor, and the boat was the same boat, the same color green and the ribs broken in the same places, and under the floor-boards the same fresh-water leavings and débris—the dead helgramite,[1] the wisps of moss, the rusty discarded fishhook,

---

[1] The nymph of the mayfly, used as bait. (Editor's note)

the dried blood from yesterday's catch. We stared silently at the tips of our rods, at the dragonflies that came and went. I lowered the tip of mine into the water, tentatively, pensively dislodging the fly, which darted two feet away, poised, darted two feet back, and came to rest again a little farther up the rod. There had been no years between the ducking of this dragonfly and the other one—the one that was part of memory. I looked at the boy, who was silently watching his fly, and it was my hands that held his rod, my eyes watching. I felt dizzy and didn't know which rod I was at the end of.

We caught two bass, hauling them in briskly as though they were mackerel, pulling them over the side of the boat in a businesslike manner without any landing net, and stunning them with a blow on the back of the head. When we got back for a swim before lunch, the lake was exactly where we had left it, the same number of inches from the dock, and there was only the merest sugges- tion of a breeze. This seemed an utterly enchanted sea, this lake you could leave to its own devices for a few hours and come back to, and find that it had not stirred, this constant and trustworthy body of water. In the shallows, the dark, water-soaked sticks and twigs, smooth and old, were undulating in clus- ters on the bottom against the clean ribbed sand, and the track of the mussel was plain. A school of minnows swam by, each minnow with its small indi- vidual shadow, doubling the attendance, so clear and sharp in the sunlight. Some of the other campers were in swimming, along the shore, one of them with a cake of soap, and the water felt thin and clear and unsubstantial. Over the years there had been this person with the cake of soap, this cultist, and here he was. There had been no years.

Up to the farmhouse to dinner through the teeming, dusty field, the road under our sneakers was only a two-track road. The middle track was missing, the one with the marks of the hooves and the splotches of dried, flaky manure. There had always been three tracks to choose from in choosing which track to walk in; now the choice was narrowed down to two. For a moment I missed terribly the middle alternative. But the way led past the tennis court, and some- thing about the way it lay there in the sun reassured me; the tape had loosened along the backline, the alleys were green with plantains and other weeds, and the net (installed in June and removed in September) sagged in the dry noon, and the whole place steamed with midday heat and hunger and emptiness. There was a choice of pie for dessert, and one was blueberry and one was apple, and the waitresses were the same country girls, there having been no passage of time, only the illusion of it as in a dropped curtain—the waitresses were still fifteen; their hair had been washed, that was the only difference— they had been to the movies and seen the pretty girls with the clean hair.

Summertime, oh summertime, pattern of life indelible, the fade-proof lake, the woods unshatterable, the pasture with the sweetfern and the juniper for- ever and ever, summer without end; this was the background, and the life along the shore was the design, the cottagers with their innocent and tranquil design, their tiny docks with the flagpole and the American flag floating against the white clouds in the blue sky, the little paths over the roots of the trees leading from camp to camp and the paths leading back to the outhouses and the can of lime for sprinkling, and at the souvenir counters at the store the miniature birch-bark canoes and the post cards that showed things looking a little better than they looked. This was the American family at play, escaping the city heat, wondering whether the newcomers in the camp at the head of the cove were "common" or "nice," wondering whether it was true that the people who drove up for Sunday dinner at the farmhouse were turned away because there wasn't enough chicken.

It seemed to me, as I kept remembering all this, that those times and those summers had been infinitely precious and worth saving. There had been jolli-ty and peace and goodness. The arriving (at the beginning of August) had been so big a business in itself, at the railway station the farm wagon drawn up, the first smell of the pine-laden air, the first glimpse of the smiling farmer, and the great importance of the trunks and your father's enormous authority in such matters, and the feel of the wagon under you for the long ten-mile haul, and at the top of the last long hill catching the first view of the lake after eleven months of not seeing this cherished body of water. The shouts and cries of the other campers when they saw you, and the trunks to be unpacked, to give up their rich burden. (Arriving was less exciting nowadays, when you sneaked up in your car and parked it under a tree near the camp and took out the bags and in five minutes it was all over, no fuss, no loud wonderful fuss about trunks.)

Peace and goodness and jollity. The only thing that was wrong now, really, was the sound of the place, an unfamiliar nervous sound of the outboard motors. This was the note that jarred, the one thing that would sometimes break the illusion and set the years moving. In those other summertimes all motors were inboard; and when they were at a little distance, the noise they made was a sedative, an ingredient of summer sleep. They were one-cylinder and two-cylinder engines, and some were make-and-break and some were jump-spark,[2] but they all made a sleepy sound across the lake. The one-lungers throbbed and fluttered, and the twin-cylinder ones purred and purred, and that was a quiet sound too. But now the campers all had outboards. In the daytime, in the hot mornings, these motors made a petulant, irritable sound; at night, in the still evening when the afterglow lit the water, they whined about one's ears like mosquitoes. My boy loved our rented outboard, and his great desire was to achieve singlehanded mastery over it, and authority, and he soon learned the trick of choking it a little (but not too much), and the adjustment of the needle valve. Watching him I would remember the things you could do with the old one-cylinder engine with the heavy flywheel, how you could have it eating out of your hand if you got really close to it spiritually. Motor boats in

---

[2]Methods of ignition timing. (Editor's note)

those days didn't have clutches, and you would make a landing by shutting off the motor at the proper time and coasting in with a dead rudder. But there was a way of reversing them, if you learned the trick, by cutting the switch and putting it on again exactly on the final dying revolution of the flywheel, so that it would kick back against compression and begin reversing. Approaching a dock in a strong following breeze, it was difficult to slow up sufficiently by the ordinary coasting method, and if a boy felt he had complete mastery over his motor, he was tempted to keep it running beyond its time and then reverse it a few feet from the dock. It took a cool nerve, because if you threw the switch a twentieth of a second too soon you would catch the flywheel when it still had speed enough to go up past center, and the boat would leap ahead, charging bull-fashion at the dock.

We had a good week at the camp. The bass were biting well and the sun shone endlessly, day after day. We would be tired at night and lie down in the accumulated heat of the little bedrooms after the long hot day and the breeze would stir almost imperceptibly outside and the smell of the swamp drift in through the rusty screens. Sleep would come easily and in the morning the red squirrel would be on the roof, tapping out his gay routine. I kept remembering everything, lying in bed in the mornings—the small steamboat that had a long rounded stern like the lip of a Ubangi, and how quietly she ran on the moon-light sails, when the older boys played their mandolins and the girls sang and we ate doughnuts dipped in sugar, and how sweet the music was on the water in the shining night, and what it had felt like to think about girls then. After breakfast we would go up to the store and the things were in the same place—the minnows in a bottle, the plugs and spinners disarranged and pawed over by the youngsters from the boys' camp, the fig newtons and the Beeman's gum. Outside, the road was tarred and cars stood in front of the store. Inside, all was just as it had always been, except there was more Coca-Cola and not so much Moxie and root beer and birch beer and sarsaparilla. We would walk out with a bottle of pop apiece and sometimes the pop would backfire up our noses and hurt. We explored the streams, quietly, where the turtles slid off the sunny logs and dug their way into the soft bottom; and we lay on the town wharf and fed worms to the tame bass. Everywhere we went I had trouble making out which was I, the one walking at my side, the one walking in my pants.

One afternoon while we were there at that lake a thunderstorm came up. It was like the revival of an old melodrama that I had seen long ago with childish awe. The second-act climax of the drama of the electrical disturbance over a lake in America had not changed in any important respect. This was the big scene, still the big scene. The whole thing was so familiar, the first feeling of oppression and heat and a general air around camp of not wanting to go very far away. In midafternoon (it was all the same) a curious darkening of the sky, and a lull in everything that had made life tick; and then the way the boats suddenly swung the other way at their moorings with the coming of a breeze out of the new quarter, and the premonitory rumble. Then the kettle drum, then the snare, then the bass drum and cymbals, then the crackling light against the dark, and the gods grinning and licking their chops in the hills. Afterward the calm, the rain steadily rustling in the calm lake, the return of light and hope and spirits, and the campers running out in joy and relief to go swimming in the rain, their bright cries perpetuating the deathless joke about how they were getting simply drenched, and the children screaming with delight at the new sensation of bathing in the rain, and the joke about getting drenched linking the generations in a strong indestructible chain. And the comedian who waded in carrying an umbrella.

When the others went swimming my son said he was going in too. He pulled his dripping trunks from the line where they had hung all through the shower, and wrung them out. Languidly, and with no thought of going in, I watched him, his hard little body, skinny and bare, saw him wince slightly as he pulled up around his vitals the small, soggy, icy garment. As he buckled the swollen belt suddenly my groin felt the chill of death.

ANALYZING | What the Writer Says

1. Upon returning to the lake where he had spent his childhood summers, White compares the old times with the new. What things seem to have remained the same? What things have changed?

2. "I seemed to be living a dual existence," White says in paragraph 4. What does he mean?

3. Why does White feel "the chill of death" as he watches his son prepare to go for a swim in the rain at the end of the essay?

ANALYZING | How the Writer Says It

1. What descriptive detail does White include in his description of the lake and its surroundings? Give examples of words and phrases that appeal to the five senses (sight, hearing, smell, touch, taste).

2. Pick a passage (a sentence or two) in which White integrates physical description and philosophical contemplation. Write out the sentence(s) and describe how White manages to go from one to the other; pay close attention to his transitions and word choice.

ANALYZING | the Issue

In what sense is White trying to relive his own youth? Do parents put undue pressure on children when they try to recreate experiences and feelings from their youth?

ANALYZING Connections Between Texts

1. Both White and William C. Brisick ("The Steep Cliffs of Life," p. 126) reflect on the relationship between fathers and sons and the transition of life from one generation to the other. In what sense do the two writers come to similar conclusions? In what way do they differ?

2. Compare the father-son relationship White describes to the one between Scott Russell Sanders ("Under the Influence," p. 295) and his alcoholic father. What are the most important differences? Similarities? Compare especially the last paragraphs in each essay.

3. In what way does Dixie D. Vereen's photograph "Man and Child" (p. 193) illustrate the same paternal concerns implicit in White's essay?

YOUR TURN: Suggestions for Writing About "Human Relations"

1. Several essays in this unit deal with the conflict that arises when children want to live their lives in ways different from what their parents dreamed for them. Drawing on your own experience and the readings you have done in this unit, write an essay in which you propose a workable solution for this conflict.

2. What makes families work? In the style of Laura Pfefferle, draw up a list of key "ingredients" that make a stable family and illustrate them with examples from your own experience and the readings in this unit.

3. Most parents sacrifice in some way so that their children can have lives better than theirs, and they are disappointed if their children do not show the proper gratitude. Write an essay in which you consider whether parents' sacrifices are always an act of selfless love—or whether they can be a way to make up for their own failures or to live vicariously through their children.

4. If parents fail to fulfill their responsibilities toward their children, should children have the right to "divorce" their parents? Write an essay in which you take a position on this issue.

5. In the style of William C. Brisick or E. B. White, write a narrative essay in which you show how an activity with one or both of your parents led you to a deeper understanding of the nature of your relationship with your parent(s).

6. Cornel West defines "being there" for his children as his father's most outstanding quality. Using a similar style (it does not have to be an obituary, but it could be), write an essay that demonstrates the most important quality or qualities that made one of your parents special.

7. Drawing on your own experience and the readings in this unit, write an essay in which you define the major responsibilities parents have toward their children. Illustrate your essay with real-life examples.

8. In the manner of Melanie Thernstrom, write an essay about a treasured family heirloom, one you already possess or one you hope to inherit one day. Tell your reader what the object is and why it is precious to you.

9. Taking Danny Lyon's picture "Visiting Room, Walls" as your point of departure, write an essay in which you analyze the meaning of family ties in difficult situations. Use your own experience and the readings in this chapter to show the importance of family loyalty in situations that threaten those loyalties—when family members die or go to prison, when they come out as homosexuals, or when they make choices of which other family members disapprove, for example.

10. Go to a greeting card store and find a *totally sentimental* picture of a mother and child (sappy Mother's Day cards or new-baby cards make good choices). Then compare this picture to Leibovitz's portrait of Jerry Hall and Gabriel Jagger. Pay close attention to the technical means the greeting card

photographer used to sentimentalize motherhood (soft focus lens, glowing light effects, soft colors, etc.)—and to how Leibovitz manages to avoid these stereotypes. You may want to consider the functions of greeting card photography and artistic photography in your analysis.

11. Write an essay in which you compare Yann Arthus-Bertrand's photograph of 18-year-old Linda Scalese as she shows off her wedding dress to her girlfriends to Jay Ullal's photo of a bridal couple in Beirut, analyzing the possible reasons the two photographers treated the wedding theme so differently.

12. Write an essay in which you compare Dixie D. Vereen's picture of a father and child to Annie Leibovitz's portrait of Jerry Hall and her infant son, paying close attention to how both photographers deviate from traditional stereotypes about parenting.

13. Find an old family picture—preferably from your own family—and write a paper in which you compare the family structure as it appears in the picture and the family as it is today. Alternately, compare the old photo to a recent photo, focusing on the differences between two eras of family life. Don't forget to make copies of the pictures and attach them to your paper.

IMAGE GALLERY 👁

BROWN BROTHERS

A Family Around the Table

When this photograph was included in the 2000 collection LIFE: Century of Change, *the editors commented: "On the farm in 1908, knittin' and spittin' constituted family entertainment for the three generations in this living room."*

1. What is the subject of this photograph?

2. How might the people in this picture be related to each other?

3. What are they doing? Speculate about their roles in the family.

4. What is the setting? What can we infer, from the interior of their house and the way the people are dressed, about the socioeconomic status of this family?

5. Look at the composition of the picture. How are the members of the family arranged? Which members are most visible? How does the picture on the wall figure into the overall arrangement?

6. How are light and shadow used?

7. What does the photo suggest about family life?

DONNA FERRATO

New Definitions

Photojournalist Donna Ferrato holds degrees in photography and sociology—and her work often records sociological themes. Ironically, while on a magazine assignment to document "love," Ferrato saw a man beat his wife, which spurred an interest in domestic abuse, resulting in her 1991 Living With the Enemy *and her founding a nonprofit organization, the Domestic Abuse Awareness project. In this photograph, she captures a happy albeit unconventional domestic scene, of Lisa Brodoff and her partner of 18 years, Lynn Grotsky, and their two children swimming.*

1. In what way is this photograph an ordinary family picture? In what way is it extraordinary?

2. What effect does the photographer's choice of black-and-white film have on the overall image? How does she manipulate light and shadow in this medium?

3. How does she arrange her subjects? What effect does her composition have on the overall meaning of the picture?

4. What commentary on "nontraditional" families does this photograph make?

DANNY LYON

Visiting Room, Walls

Daniel Joseph Lyon (b.1942) expresses a strong sense of social commitment in his pho-tographs and movies. In 1971 he published Conversations with the Dead: Photographs of Prison Life with the Letters and Drawings of Billy McCune, *from which this image is taken.*

1. Describe the situation revealed in the photograph. What is the setting for this scene? How do you know?

2. How would you characterize the relationship between the woman and the man in the picture? What do the expressions on their faces say about their attitude toward the situation?

3. How does the arrangement of the people and objects in the photo affect your interpretation of it?

4. How are lines important in this picture?

5. How does the photographer use light and shadow?

6. How does this picture make you feel? How do you think Danny Lyon is trying to get his audience to react to the image and the life it depicts?

PATRICK TEHAN

B. T. and Minnie Winkle

Prize-winning photographer Patrick Tehan's picture of B. T. "Bennie" Winkle, who, at 85, cares full-time for his invalid wife Minnie while still running his farm in Lebanon, Mississippi, was first published in 1986 in A Day in the Life of America.

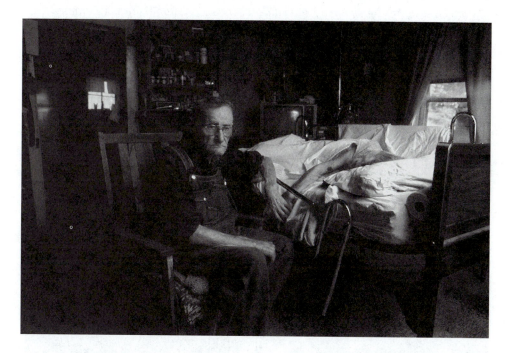

1. What can you tell about the man's life and profession from his clothes and the interior of the living room?

2. What in the picture indicates that the woman in the bed is not likely to recover?

3. What do the expression on the man's face and the couple's body language say about their situation?

4. How does the photographer use composition in the picture?

5. What message does this photograph send? What title would you give this photo?

JAY ULLAL

Bridal Couple in Beirut, 1983

When this photograph was published in Time: Great Images, *the editors added an explanation: The picture was taken during Lebanon's civil war (1975–1990), which was fought between the country's three dominant religious groups (Maronite Catholics and Sunni and Shi'ite Muslims). The bride in the picture is Christian, the groom, Muslim; they are crossing the "green line," a political boundary dividing Beirut at the time.*

1. When you first look at the picture, what strikes you as its most surprising or bizarre element?

2. Why do you think the photographer chose this setting for his unusual wedding picture?

3. How does the picture's composition underscore its subject?

4. The editors of *Time: Great Images* compare the couple in the picture to Romeo and Juliet. Comment upon the comparison.

DIXIE D. VEREEN

Man and Child

A photojournalist since her high school days in the 1970s, award-winning photographer Dixie Vereen contributed this 1990 image of a father and child to Songs of My People.

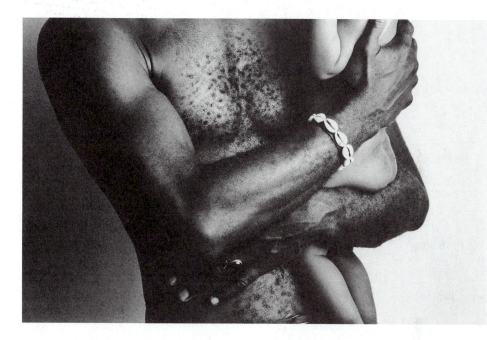

1. What is the subject of this picture?

2. Why did the photographer choose to crop the man's and baby's heads? In the absence of faces, what becomes the focal point of the picture?

3. The man in the picture does not wear a shirt, but he wears jewelry. Why did Vereen include these accessories?

4. The photograph shows skin texture very sharply. What is the effect of this technique?

5. How does this photograph refute stereotypes of fatherhood in general and black fatherhood in particular?

10 | BODY POLITICS

Americans have always been conflicted about their bodies. Even today, violence is more acceptable than nudity to television and film censors. In 2002, in a move reminiscent of the Puritans—if not the Taliban—U.S. Attorney General John

". . . I have a body/and I cannot escape from it."

—Anne Sexton
"The Poet of Ignorance"

Ashcroft had curtains draped over a statue in the Department of Justice, shielding audiences from its cast-aluminum breast. At the same time, more and more people express themselves by reshaping their bodies, through exercise and surgery, or adorning them with tattoos and piercings.

The title of a popular women's health book published in the early seventies—*Our Bodies, Our Selves*—helps to explain the near obsession we humans, both female and male, have with our bodies: body image and self-image are linked inextricably. And no wonder: the media bombards us with images of young, healthy, thin, sculpted bodies; studies show that height, weight, youth, and attractiveness are factors in employment.

It's hard to imagine that just a half-century ago, the physical ideal was completely different. For women, "curvaceous" was the coveted compliment; "skinny" was an insult. Today, Marilyn Monroe would be considered fat. And time was when the only men who pumped iron seriously were athletes. Today men and women flock to gyms, lifting and stretching, riding and climbing, dancing and kick-boxing their way to buffdom. The weight loss industry is big business; cosmetic surgery has become as routine as dental work.

The condition of our bodies, whether sized by genetics, scarred by accident, or crippled by disease, contributes greatly to our sense of identity, as Natalie Kusz, Alice Walker, and Nancy Mairs attest within these pages. (Consider that one of our most popular presidents, Franklin Delano Roosevelt, would not allow himself to be photographed with his crutches, for fear of appearing weak.) Stephen S. Hall reports on the growing phenomenon of an adolescent male version of body obsession, manifest in weight training and steroid use, and Anna Quindlen offers a humorous account of her own foray into fitness. With startling scientific precision, D. Keith Mano lays bare two common cosmetic surgical procedures, while Roy C. Selby, Jr. describes delicate, miraculous neurosurgery. Atul Gawande's essay on the decline of the practice of autopsy suggests that anxiety about the body extends into the grave.

Our bodies are the source of our most personal politics. How we understand and define physical limits, strengths, and rights: such is the stuff that selves are made of. ✷

WARMING UP: *Would you have any misgivings about doctors performing an autopsy on one of your loved ones?*

Final Cut

BY ATUL GAWANDE

ATUL GAWANDE

In this essay, first published in The New Yorker, *Atul Gawande, a surgeon, questions the decline of the practice of autopsy in the United States. Gawande (b. 1965), citing Lewis Thomas's* The Lives of a Cell *as a major influence, writes often about the human side of science. His 2002 collection of essays,* Complications: A Surgeon's Notes on an Imperfect Science, *was nominated for a National Book Award.*

Your patient is dead; the family is gathered. And there is one last thing that you must ask about: the autopsy. How should you go about it? You could do it offhandedly, as if it were the most ordinary thing in the world: "Shall we do an autopsy, then?" Or you could be firm, use your Sergeant Joe Friday voice: "Unless you have strong objections, we will need to do an autopsy, ma'am." Or you could take yourself out of it: "I am sorry, but they require me to ask, Do you want an autopsy done?"

What you can't be these days is mealy-mouthed about it. I once took care of a woman in her eighties who had given up her driver's license only to get hit by a car—driven by someone even older—while she was walking to a bus stop. She sustained a depressed skull fracture and cerebral bleeding, and, despite surgery, she died a few days later. So, on the spring afternoon after the patient took her last breath, I stood beside her and bowed my head with the fearful family. Then, as delicately as I could—not even using the awful word—I said, "If it's all right, we'd like to do an examination to confirm the cause of death."

"An *autopsy*?" a nephew said, horrified. He looked at me as if I were a buzzard circling his aunt's body. "Hasn't she been through enough?"

The autopsy is in a precarious state. A generation ago, it was routine; now it has become a rarity. Human beings have never quite become comfortable with the idea of having their bodies cut open after they die. Even for a surgeon, the sense of violation is inescapable.

Not long ago, I went to observe the dissection of a thirty-eight-year-old woman I had taken care of who had died after a long struggle with heart disease. The dissecting room was in the sub-basement, past the laundry and a loading dock, behind an unmarked metal door. It had high ceilings, peeling paint, and a brown tiled floor that sloped down to a central drain. There was a Bunsen burner on a countertop and an old-style grocer's hanging scale, with a big clockface red-arrow gauge and a pan underneath, for weighing organs. On shelves all around the room there were gray portions of brain, bowel, and other organs soaking in formalin in Tupperware-like containers. The facility seemed rundown, chintzy, low-tech. On a rickety gurney in the corner was my patient, sprawled out, completely naked. The autopsy team was just beginning its work.

Surgical procedures can be grisly, but dissections are somehow worse. In even the most gruesome operations—skin-grafting, amputations—surgeons maintain an attitude of tenderness and aestheticism toward their work. We know that the bodies we cut still pulse with life, and that these are people who will wake again. But in the dissecting room, where the person is gone and only the carcass remains, you find little of this delicacy, and the difference is visible in the smallest details. There is, for example, the simple matter of how a body is moved from gurney to table. In the operating room, we follow a careful, elaborate procedure for the unconscious patient, involving a canvas-sleeved rolling board and several gentle movements. We don't want so much as a bruise. Down here, by contrast, someone grabbed my patient's arm, another person a leg, and they just yanked. When her skin stuck to the stainless-steel dissecting table, they had to wet her and the table down with a hose before they could jerk her the rest of the way.

The young pathologist for the case stood on the sidelines and let a pathology assistant take the knife. Like many of her colleagues, the pathologist had not been drawn to her field by autopsies but by the high-tech detective work that she got to do on tissue from living patients. She was happy to leave the dissection to the PA, who had more experience at it anyway.

The PA was a tall, slender woman of around thirty with straight, sandy brown hair. She was wearing the full protective garb of mask, face shield, gloves, and blue plastic gown. Once the body was on the table, she placed a six-inch metal block under the back, between the shoulder blades, so that the head fell back and the chest arched up. Then she took a scalpel in her hand, a big number 6 blade, and made a huge Y-shaped incision that came down diagonally from each shoulder, curving slightly around each breast before reaching the midline, and then continued down the abdomen to the pubis.

Surgeons get used to the opening of bodies. It is easy to detach yourself from the person on the table and become absorbed by the details of method and anatomy. Nevertheless, I couldn't help wincing as she did her work: she was holding the scalpel like a pen, which forced her to cut slowly and jaggedly with the tip of the blade. Surgeons are taught to stand straight and parallel to their incision, hold the knife between the thumb and four fingers, like a violin bow, and draw the belly of the blade through the skin in a single, smooth slice to the exact depth desired. The PA was practically sawing her way through my patient.

From there, the evisceration was swift. The PA flayed back the skin flaps. [10] With an electric saw, she cut through the exposed ribs along both sides. Then she lifted the rib cage as if it were the hood of a car, opened the abdomen, and removed all the major organs—including the heart, the lungs, the liver, the bowels, and the kidneys. Then the skull was sawed open, and the brain, too, was removed. Meanwhile, the pathologist was at a back table, weighing and examining everything, and preparing samples for microscopy and thorough testing.

Despite all this, the patient came out looking surprisingly undisturbed. The PA had followed the usual procedure and kept the skull incision behind the woman's ears, where it was completely hidden by her hair. She had also taken care to close the chest and abdomen neatly, sewing the incision tightly with weaved seven-cord thread. My patient actually looked much the same as before, except now a little collapsed in the middle. (The standard consent allows the hospital to keep the organs for testing and research. This common and long-established practice is now causing huge controversy in Britain—the media have branded it "organ stripping"—but in America it remains generally accepted.) Families can still have an open-casket funeral, and most do. Morticians employ fillers to restore a corpse's shape, and when they're done you cannot tell that an autopsy has been performed.

Still, when it is time to ask for a family's permission to do such a thing, the images weigh on everyone's mind—not least the doctor's. You strive to achieve a cool, dispassionate attitude toward these matters. But doubts nevertheless creep in.

One of the first patients for whom I was expected to request an autopsy was a seventy-five-year-old retired New England doctor who died one winter night while I was with him. Herodotus Sykes (not his real name, but not unlike it, either) had been rushed to the hospital with an infected, rupturing abdominal aortic aneurysm and taken to emergency surgery. He survived it, and recovered steadily until, eighteen days later, his blood pressure dropped alarmingly and blood began to pour from a drainage tube in his abdomen. "The aortic stump must have blown out," his surgeon said. Residual infection must have weakened the suture line. We could have operated again, but the patient's chances were poor, and his surgeon didn't think he would be willing to take any more. He was right. No more surgery, Sykes told me. He'd been through enough. We called Mrs. Sykes, who was staying with a friend, about two hours away, and she set out for the hospital.

It was about midnight. I sat with him as he lay silent and bleeding, his arms slack at his sides, his eyes without fear. I imagined his wife out on the Mass Pike, frantic, helpless, with six lanes, virtually empty at that hour, stretching far ahead.

Sykes held on, and at two-fifteen A.M. his wife arrived. She turned ashen at the sight of him, but she steadied herself. She gently took his hand in hers. She squeezed, and he squeezed back, I left them to themselves.

At two-forty-five, the nurse called me in. I listened with my stethoscope, then turned to Mrs. Sykes and told her that he was gone. She had her husband's Yankee reserve, but she broke into quiet tears, weeping into her hands, and seemed suddenly frail and small. A friend who had come with her soon appeared, took her by the arm, and led her out of the room.

We are instructed to request an autopsy on everyone as a means of confirming the cause of death and catching our mistakes. And this was the moment I was supposed to ask—with the wife despondent and reeling with shock. But surely, I began to think, here was a case in which an autopsy would be pointless. We knew what had happened—a persistent infection, a rupture. We were sure of it. What would cutting the man apart accomplish?

And so I let Mrs. Sykes go. I could have caught her as she walked through the ICU's double doors. Or even called her on the phone later. But I never did.

Such reasoning, it appears, has become commonplace in medicine. Doctors are seeking so few autopsies that in recent years the *Journal of the American Medical Association* has twice felt the need to declare "war on the nonautopsy." According to the most recent statistics available, autopsies have been done in less than 10 percent of deaths; many hospitals do none. This is a dramatic turnabout. Through much of the twentieth century, doctors diligently obtained autopsies in the majority of all deaths—and it had taken centuries to reach this point. As Kenneth Iserson recounts in his fascinating almanac, *Death to Dust,* physicians have performed autopsies for more than two thousand years. But for most of history they were rarely performed, and only for legal purposes (if religions permitted them at all—Islam, Shinto, and the Greek Orthodox Church still frown on them). The Roman physician Antistius performed one of the earliest forensic examinations on record, in 44 B.C., on Julius Caesar, documenting twenty-three wounds, including a final, fatal stab to the chest. In 1410, the Catholic Church itself ordered an autopsy—on Pope Alexander V, to determine whether his successor had poisoned him. No evidence of this was found.

Even in the nineteenth century, long after church strictures had loosened, people in the West rarely allowed doctors to autopsy their family members for medical purposes. As a result, the practice was largely clandestine. Some doctors went ahead and autopsied hospital patients immediately after death, before relatives could turn up to object. Others waited until burial and then robbed the graves, either personally or through accomplices, an activity that continued into the twentieth century. To deter such autopsies, some families would post nighttime guards at the gravesite—hence the term "graveyard shift." Others placed heavy stones on the coffins. In 1878, one company in Columbus, Ohio, even sold "torpedo coffins," equipped with pipe bombs rigged to blow up if they were tampered with. Yet doctors remained undeterred. Ambrose Bierce's *The Devil's Dictionary,* published in 1906, defined "grave" as "a place in which the dead are laid to await the coming of the medical student."

By the turn of the century, however, prominent physicians such as Rudolf Virchow, in Berlin, Karl Rokitansky, in Vienna, and William Osler, in Baltimore, began to win popular support for the practice. They defended it as a tool of discovery, one that was used to identify the cause of tuberculosis, reveal how to treat appendicitis, and establish the existence of Alzheimer's disease. They showed that autopsies prevented errors—that without them doctors could not know when their diagnoses were incorrect. Most deaths were a mystery then, and perhaps what clinched the argument was the notion that autopsies could provide families with answers—give the story of a loved one's life a comprehensible ending. Once doctors had ensured a dignified and respectful dissection at the hospital, public opinion turned. With time, doctors who did *not* obtain autopsies were viewed with suspicion. By the end of the Second World War, the autopsy was firmly established as a routine part of death in Europe and North America.

So what accounts for its decline? It's not because families refuse—to judge from recent studies, they still grant that permission up to 80 percent of the time. Doctors, once so eager to perform autopsies that they stole bodies, have simply stopped asking. Some people ascribe this to shady motives. It has been said that hospitals are trying to save money by avoiding autopsies, since insurers don't pay for them, or that doctors avoid them in order to cover up evidence of malpractice. And yet autopsies lost money and uncovered malpractice when they were popular, too.

Instead, I suspect, what discourages autopsies is medicine's twenty-first-century, tall-in-the-saddle confidence. When I failed to ask Mrs. Sykes whether we could autopsy her husband, it was not because of the expense or because I feared that the autopsy would uncover an error. It was the opposite: I didn't see much likelihood that an error would be found. Today, we have MRI scans, ultrasound, nuclear medicine, molecular testing, and much more. When somebody dies, we already know why. We don't need an autopsy to find out.

Or so I thought. Then I had a patient who changed my mind.

He was in his sixties, whiskered and cheerful, a former engineer who had found success in retirement as an artist. I will call him Mr. Jolly, because that's what he was. He was also what we call a vasculopath—he did not seem to have an undiseased artery in him. Whether because of his diet or his genes or the fact that he used to smoke, he had had, in the previous decade, one heart attack, two abdominal aortic-aneurysm repairs, four bypass operations to keep blood flowing past blockages in his leg arteries, and several balloon procedures to keep hardened arteries open. Still, I never knew him to take a dark view of his lot. "Well, you can't get miserable about it," he'd say. He had wonderful children. He had beautiful grandchildren. "But, aargh, the wife," he'd go on. She would be sitting right there at the bedside, and would roll her eyes, and he'd break into a grin.

Mr. Jolly had come into the hospital for treatment of a wound infection in his legs. But he soon developed congestive heart failure, causing fluid to back up into his lungs. Breathing became steadily harder for him, until we had to put him in the ICU, intubate him, and place him on a ventilator. A two-day admission turned into two weeks. With a regimen of diuretics and a change in heart medications, however, his heart failure reversed, and his lungs recovered. And one bright Sunday morning he was reclining in bed, breathing on his own, watching the morning shows on the TV set that hung from the ceiling. "You're doing marvelously," I said. I told him we would transfer him out of intensive care by the afternoon. He would probably be home in a couple of days.

Two hours later, a code-blue call went out on the overhead speakers. When I got to the ICU and saw the nurse hunched over Mr. Jolly, doing chest compressions, I blurted out an angry curse. He'd been fine, the nurse explained, just watching TV, when suddenly he sat upright with a look of shock and then fell back, unresponsive. At first, he was asystolic—no heart rhythm on the monitor—and then the rhythm came back, but he had no pulse. A crowd of staffers set to work. I had him intubated, gave him fluids and epinephrine, had someone call the attending surgeon at home, someone else check the morning lab-test results. An x-ray technician shot a portable chest film.

I mentally ran through possible causes. There were not many. A collapsed lung, but I heard good breath sounds with my stethoscope, and when his x-ray came back the lungs looked fine. A massive blood loss, but his abdomen wasn't swelling, and his decline happened so quickly that bleeding just didn't make sense. Extreme acidity of the blood could do it, but his lab tests were fine. Then there was cardiac tamponade—bleeding into the sac that contains the heart. I took a six-inch spinal needle on a syringe, pushed it through the skin below the breastbone, and advanced it to the heart sac. I found no bleeding. That left only one possibility: a pulmonary embolism—a blood clot that flips into the lung and instantly wedges off all blood flow. And nothing could be done about that.

I went out and spoke to the attending surgeon by phone and then to the chief resident, who had just arrived. An embolism was the only logical explanation, they agreed. I went back into the room and stopped the code. "Time of death: ten-twenty-three A.M.," I announced. I phoned his wife at home, told her that things had taken a turn for the worse, and asked her to come in.

This shouldn't have happened; I was sure of it. I scanned the records for [30] clues. Then I found one. In a lab test done the day before, the patient's clotting had seemed slow, which wasn't serious, but an ICU physician had decided to correct it with vitamin K. A frequent complication with vitamin K is blood clots. I was furious. Giving the vitamin was completely unnecessary—just fixing a number on a lab test. Both the chief resident and I lit into the physician. We all but accused him of killing the patient.

When Mrs. Jolly arrived, we took her to a family room where it was quiet and calm, with table lamps instead of fluorescent lights and soft, plump chairs. I could see from her face that she'd already surmised the worst. His heart had stopped suddenly, we told her, because of a pulmonary embolism. We said the medicines we gave him may have contributed to it. I took her in to see him and left her with him. After a while, she came out, her hands trembling and her face stained with tears. Then, remarkably, she thanked us. We had kept him for her all these years, she said. Maybe so, but neither of us felt any pride about what had just happened. I asked her the required question. I told her that we wanted to perform an autopsy and needed her permission. We thought we already knew what had happened, but an autopsy would confirm it, I said. She considered my request for a moment. If an autopsy would help us, she finally said, then we could do it. I said, as I was supposed to, that it would. I wasn't sure I believed it.

I wasn't assigned to the operating room the following morning, so I went down to observe the autopsy. When I arrived, Mr. Jolly was already laid out on the dissecting table, his arms splayed, skin flayed back, chest exposed, abdomen open. I put on a gown, gloves, and a mask, and went up close. The PA began buzzing through the ribs on the left side with the electric saw, and immediately blood started seeping out, as dark and viscous as crankcase oil. Puzzled, I helped him lift open the rib cage. The left side of the chest was full of blood. I felt along the pulmonary arteries for a hardened, embolized clot, but there was none. He hadn't had an embolism after all. We suctioned out three liters of blood, lifted the left lung, and the answer appeared before our eyes. The thoracic aorta was almost three times larger than it should have been, and there was a half-inch hole in it. The man had ruptured an aortic aneurysm and had bled to death almost instantly.

In the days afterward, I apologized to the physician I'd reamed out over the vitamin, and pondered how we had managed to miss the diagnosis. I looked back through the patient's old x-rays and now saw a shadowy outline of what must have been his aneurysm. But none of us, not even the radiologists, had caught it. Even if we had caught it, we wouldn't have dared to do anything about it until weeks after treating his infection and heart failure, and that would have been too late. It disturbed me, however, to have felt so confident about what had happened that day and to have been so wrong.

The most perplexing thing was his final chest x-ray, the one we had taken during the code blue. With all that blood filling the chest, I should have seen at least a haze over the left side. But when I pulled the film out to look again there was nothing.

How often do autopsies turn up a major misdiagnosis in the cause of death? I would have guessed this happened rarely, in 1 or 2 percent of cases at most. According to three studies done in 1998 and 1999, however, the figure is about 40 percent. A large review of autopsy studies concluded that in about a third of the misdiagnoses the patients would have been expected to live if proper treatment had been administered. George Lundberg, a pathologist and former editor of the *Journal of the American Medical Association* who has done more than anyone to call attention to these figures, points out the most surprising fact of all: the rates at which misdiagnosis is detected have not improved in autopsy studies since at least 1938.

With all the recent advances in imaging and diagnostics, it's hard to accept that we not only get the diagnosis wrong in two out of five of our patients who die but that we have also failed to improve over time. To see if this could really be true, doctors at Harvard put together a simple study. They went back into their hospital records to see how often autopsies picked up missed diagnoses in 1960 and 1970, before the advent of CT, ultrasound, nuclear scanning, and other technologies, and then in 1980, after they became widely used. The researchers found no improvement. Regardless of the decade, physicians missed a quarter of fatal infections, a third of heart attacks, and almost two thirds of pulmonary emboli in their patients who died.

In most cases, it wasn't technology that failed. Rather, the physicians did not consider the correct diagnosis in the first place. The perfect test or scan may have been available, but the physicians never ordered it.

In a 1976 essay, the philosophers Samuel Gorovitz and Alasdair MacIntyre explored the nature of fallibility. Why would a meteorologist, say, fail to correctly predict where a hurricane was going to make landfall? They saw three possible reasons. One was ignorance: perhaps science affords only a limited understanding of how hurricanes behave. A second reason was ineptitude: the knowledge is available, but the weatherman fails to apply it correctly. Both of these are surmountable sources of error. We believe that science will overcome ignorance, and that training and technology will overcome ineptitude. The third possible cause of error the philosophers posited, however, was an insurmountable kind, one they termed "necessary fallibility."

There may be some kinds of knowledge that science and technology will never deliver, Gorovitz and MacIntyre argued. When we ask science to move beyond explaining how things (say, hurricanes) generally behave to predicting exactly how a particular thing (say, Thursday's storm off the South Carolina coast) will behave, we may be asking it to do more than it can. No hurricane is quite like any other hurricane. Although all hurricanes follow predictable laws of behavior, each one is continuously shaped by myriad uncontrollable, accidental factors in the environment. To say precisely how one specific hurricane will behave would require a complete understanding of the world in all its particulars—in other words, omniscience.

It's not that it's impossible to predict anything; plenty of things are completely predictable. Gorovitz and MacIntyre give the example of a random ice cube in a fire. Ice cubes are so simple and so alike that you can predict with complete assurance that an ice cube will melt. But when it comes to inferring exactly what is going on in a particular person, are people more like ice cubes or like hurricanes? 40

Right now, at about midnight, I am seeing a patient in the emergency room, and I want to say that she is an ice cube. That is, I believe I can understand what's going on with her, that I can discern all her relevant properties. I believe I can help her.

Charlotte Duveen, as we will call her, is forty-nine years old, and for two days she has had abdominal pain. I began observing her from the moment I walked through the curtains into her room. She was sitting cross-legged in the chair next to her stretcher and greeted me with a cheerful, tobacco-beaten voice. She did not look sick. No clutching the belly. No gasping for words. Her color was good—neither flushed nor pale. Her shoulder-length brown hair had been brushed, her red lipstick neatly applied.

She told me the pain had started out crampy, like a gas pain. But then, during the course of the day, it had become sharp and focused, and as she said this she pointed to a spot on the lower right side of her abdomen. She had developed diarrhea. She constantly felt as if she had to urinate. She didn't have a fever. She was not nauseated. Actually, she was hungry. She told me that she had eaten a hot dog at Fenway Park two days ago, and she asked if that might have anything to do with this. She had also seen the birds at the zoo a few days earlier. She has two grown children. Her last period was three months ago. She smokes half a pack a day. She used to use heroin but said she's clean now. She once had hepatitis. She has never had surgery.

I felt her abdomen. It could be anything, I thought: food poisoning, a virus, appendicitis, a urinary tract infection, an ovarian cyst, a pregnancy. Her abdomen was soft, without distension, and there was an area of particular tenderness in the lower right quadrant. When I pressed there, I felt her muscles harden reflexively beneath my fingers. On the pelvic exam, her ovaries felt normal. I ordered some lab tests. Her white-blood-cell count came back elevated. Her urinalysis was normal. A pregnancy test was negative. I ordered an abdominal CT scan.

I am sure I can figure out what's wrong with her, but, if you think about it, that's a curious faith. I have never seen this woman before in my life, and yet 45

I presume that she is like the others I've examined. Is it true? None of my other patients, admittedly, were forty-nine-year-old women who had had hepatitis and a drug habit, had recently been to the zoo and eaten a Fenway frank, and had come in with two days of mild lower-right-quadrant pain. Yet I still believe. Every day, we take people to surgery and open their abdomens, and, broadly speaking, we know what we will find: not eels or tiny chattering machines or a pool of blue liquid but coils of bowel, a liver to one side, a stomach to the other, a bladder down below. There are, of course, differences—an adhesion in one patient, an infection in another—but we have catalogued and sorted them by the thousands, making a statistical profile of mankind.

I am leaning toward appendicitis. The pain is in the right place. The timing of her symptoms, her exam, and her white-blood-cell count all fit with what I've seen before. She's hungry, however; she's walking around, not looking sick, and this seems unusual. I go to the radiology reading room and stand in the dark, looking over the radiologist's shoulder at the images of Duveen's abdomen flashing up on the monitor. He points to the appendix, wormlike, thick, surrounded by gray, streaky fat. It's appendicitis, he says confidently. I call the attending surgeon on duty and tell him what we've found. "Book the OR," he says. We're going to do an appendectomy.

This one is as sure as we get. Yet I've worked on similar cases—with identical results from the CT scan—in which we opened the patient up and found a normal appendix. Surgery itself is a kind of autopsy. "Autopsy" literally means "to see for oneself," and, despite our knowledge and technology, when we look we're often unprepared for what we find. I want to think that my patient's condition is as predictable as the sun's rising, as the melting of an ice cube, and maybe I have to. But I've been around long enough to know that in human beings the simplest certainties can be dashed.

Whether with living patients or dead, however, we cannot know until we look. Even in the case of Mr. Sykes's, I now wonder whether we put our stitches in correctly, or whether the bleeding had come from somewhere else entirely. Doctors are no longer asking such questions. Equally troubling, people seem happy to let us off the hook. In 1995, the National Center for Health Statistics stopped collecting autopsy statistics altogether. We can no longer even say how rare autopsies have become.

From what I've learned looking inside people, I've decided human beings are somewhere between a hurricane and an ice cube: in some respects, permanently mysterious, but in others—with enough science and careful probing—entirely scrutable. It would be as foolish to think we have reached the limits of human knowledge as it is to think we could ever know everything. There is still room enough to get better, to ask questions of even the dead, to learn from knowing when our simple certainties are wrong.

ANALYZING What the Writer Says

1. What are some of the reasons for the significant decline in the number of autopsies over the past century?
2. What made Gawande change his mind about autopsies?
3. What surprising statistic about autopsies does Gawande learn?
4. What is "necessary fallibility"?

ANALYZING How the Writer Says It

1. Gawande refers to five patients, four of whom have died. Why do you think he ends his essay with an anecdote about a patient, stricken only by appendicitis, who is obviously not a candidate for an autopsy?
2. Analyze the title. How many layers of meaning can you uncover?

ANALYZING the Issue

After reading Gawande's essay, are you convinced autopsies should be performed routinely? Why or why not?

ANALYZING Connections Between Texts

1. Compare Atul Gawande's descriptions of autopsies to Roy Selby's description of brain surgery in "A Delicate Operation" (p. 246).
2. Malcolm Gladwell ("The Physical Genius," p. 765) and Richard Selzer ("Imelda," p. 798) both write about gifted surgeons. In what way does Gawande offer similar insights into the medical profession?
3. Consider the implications of the photograph by Max Aguilera-Hellweg, "Reaching for Help" (p. 103). How might Gawande's essay and Aguilera-Hellweg's photograph be used to make the same argument?

WARMING UP: *Who in the world of fashion, sports, advertising, or entertainment do you think has the ideal body? Select a person or model and describe what it is about this person's body that makes it so outstanding.*

The Bully in the Mirror

BY STEPHEN S. HALL

STEPHEN S. HALL

Reporting on a group of teenage bodybuilders, Stephen Hall wonders what makes boys obsess about the way their bodies look, a phenomenon also widely observed in adolescent girls. Citing a number of studies on boys' and men's body-image problems, Hall concludes that boys try to change their bodies for the same reasons girls do: to fit in with a culture that champions a virtually unattainable ideal of the human body. This article was first published in The New York Times Magazine *in 1999.*

On an insufferably muggy afternoon in July, with the thermometer pushing 90 degrees and ozone alerts filling the airwaves, Alexander Bregstein was in a foul mood. He was furious, in fact, for reasons that would become clear only later. Working on just three hours of sleep, and having spent the last eight hours minding a bunch of preschool kids in his summer job as a camp counselor, Alexander was itching to kick back and relax. So there he was, lying on his back in the weight room of his gym, head down on an incline bench, earphones pitching three-figure decibels of the rock band Finger Eleven into his ears as he gripped an 85-pound weight in each hand and then, after a brief pause to gather himself, muscled them into the air with focused bursts of energy. Each lift was accompanied by a sharp exhalation, like the quick, short stroke of a piston.

The first thing you need to know about Alexander is that he is 16 years old, bright, articulate and funny in that self-deprecating and almost wise teen-age way. However, about a year ago, Alexander made a conscious decision that those weren't the qualities he wanted people to recognize in him, at least not at first. He wanted people to *see* him first, and what they see these days are thick neck muscles, shoulders so massive that he can't scratch his back, a powerful bulge in his arms and a chest that has been deliberately chiseled for the two-button look—what Alexander now calls "my most endearing fea-ture." He walks with a kind of cocky gravity-testing bounce in his step that derives in part from his muscular build but also from the confidence of knowing he looks good in his tank top and baggy shorts.

As his spotter, Aaron Anavim, looked on, Alexander lifted the 85-pound weights three more times, arms quivering, face reddening with effort. Each dumbbell, I realized as I watched, weighed more than I did when I entered high school. Another half-dozen teen-agers milled around the weight room, casting glances at themselves and one another in the mirror. They talked of looking "cut," with sharp definition to their muscles, and of developing "six-packs," crisp divisions of the abdominals, but of all the muscles that get a workout in rooms like these, the most important may be the ones that move the eyes in restless sweeping arcs of comparison and appraisal. "Once you're in this game to manipulate your body," Alexander said, "you want to be the best," likening the friendly competition in the room to a form of "whipping out the ruler." While we talked between sets of Alexander's 90-minute routine, his eyes wandered to the mirror again and again, searching for flaws, looking for areas of improvement. "The more you lift," he admitted, "the more you look in the mirror."

In this weight room, in a gym in a northern New Jersey suburb, the gym rats have a nickname for Alexander: Mirror Boy. That's a vast improvement over the nicknames he endured at school not long ago. "I know it sounds kind of odd to have favorite insults," he told me with a wry smile, munching on a pro-tein bar before moving on to his next set of lifts, "but Chunk Style always was kind of funny." And kind of appropriate. Until recently, Alexander carried nearly 210 pounds on a 5-foot-6 frame, and when I asked if he was teased about his weight, he practically dropped a dumbbell on my feet. "Oh! Oh, man, was I *teased*? Are you kidding?" he said in his rapid, agreeable patter. "When I was fat, people must have gone home and thought of nothing else except com-ing in with new material the next day. They must have had *study groups* just to make fun of people who were overweight." He even got an earful at home. "My parents—God bless them, but they would make comments *all the time*. My father would say, 'If you eat all that, you'll be as big as a house.' And I'm, like: 'Dad, it's a little late for that. What am I now? A mobile home?'"

The day of reckoning came in April 1998, during a spring-break vacation in Boca Raton, Fla. As his family was about to leave its hotel room to go to the beach, Alexander, then 15, stood in front of a mirror and just stared at the spec-tacle of his shirtless torso. "I remember the exact, like, *moment* in my mind," he said. "Everything about that room is burned into my head, every little thing. I can tell you where every lamp was, where my father was standing, my moth-er was sitting. We were about to go out, and I'm looking in this mirror—me, with my gut hanging over my bathing suit—and it was, like: Who would want to look at this? It's part of me, and *I'm* disgusted! That moment, I realized that nobody was giving me a chance to find out who I was because of the way I looked."

And so Alexander decided to do something about it, something drastic.

There is a kind of timeless, archetypical trajectory to a teen-ager's battle with body image, but in most accounts the teen-ager is female and the issue is anorexia or bulimia. As any psychologist knows, however, and as any sufficiently evolved adult male could tell you, boys have body-image problems, too. Traditionally, they have felt pressure to look not thin, but rather strong and virile, which increasingly seems to mean looking bulked up and muscular, and that is why I was interested in talking to Alexander.

Although more than 30 years in age separates us, hearing him give voice to his insecurities, to imagined physical flaws, reminded me all over again of my own tortured passage through adolescence, my own dissatisfaction with a body that seemed punitively untouched by any growth spurt and my own reluctant accommodation with certain inalienable facts of nature. Like me, Alexander had been teased and harassed about being short in stature. Like me, he had struggled to overcome his physical shortcomings as a member of the high-school wrestling team. Unlike me, he also battled a severe weight problem, but at a similar moment in life, we had both looked in the mirror and hadn't liked what we'd seen.

Still, a lot has changed since I was 15. Consider the current batch of cold messages from the culture at large. The new anabolic Tarzan. "Chicks dig the long ball." Littleton. (Buried beneath a ton of prose about gun control was the report that Eric Harris apparently felt dissatisfied with his height, repeatedly complaining that he was smaller than his brother.) Aggressive advertising campaigns showing half-naked men in which the Obsession could just as easily be about your own very toned body as about someone else's. Even a lawsuit at the higher echelons of American business peeled away the pretense of adult civility to show that the classic junior-high body-image put-down—Michael Eisner dissing Jeffrey Katzenberg as a "little midget"—is alive and well in the boardroom, as it has been in the locker room for decades. You would never know that for the past quarter-century feminist thought and conversation has created room for alternatives to traditional masculinity, in which toughness is equated with self-worth and physical stature is equated with moral stature.

No one can quite cite any data, any scientific studies proving that things are 10 different, but a number of psychologists with whom I spoke returned to the same point again and again: the cultural messages about an ideal male body, if not new, have grown more insistent, more aggressive, more widespread and more explicit in recent years.

Since roughly 90 percent of teen-agers who are treated for eating disorders are female, boys still have a way to go. Young girls have suffered greatly from insecurity about appearance and body image, and the scientific literature on anorexia and related body-image disorders depicts a widespread and serious health problem in adolescent females. But to hear some psychologists tell it, boys may be catching up in terms of insecurity and even psychological pathology. An avalanche of recent books on men and boys underlines the precarious nature of contemporary boyhood in America. A number of studies in the past decade—of men, not boys—have suggested that "body-image disturbances," as researchers sometimes call them, may be more prevalent in men than previously believed and almost always begin in the teen-age years. Katharine Phillips, a psychiatrist at the Brown University School of Medicine, has specialized in "body dysmorphic disorder," a psychiatric illness in which patients become obsessively preoccupied with perceived flaws in their appearance—receding hairlines, facial imperfections, small penises, inadequate musculature. In a study on "30 cases of imagined ugliness," Phillips and colleagues described a surprisingly common condition in males whose symptoms include excessive checking of mirrors and attempts to camouflage imagined deformities, most often of the hair, nose and skin. The average age of onset, Phillips says, is 15.

Two years ago, Harrison G. Pope, Jr., of Harvard Medical School, and his colleagues published a modest paper called "Muscle Dysmorphia: An Underrecognized Form of Body Dysmorphic Disorder" in a relatively obscure journal called Psychosomatics. The study described a group of men and women who had become "pathologically preoccupied" by their body image and were convinced that they looked small and puny, even though they were bulging with muscles. The paper got a lot of attention, and it led to an even more widely publicized study earlier this year from the same lab reporting how male action-figure toys like G.I. Joe and the "Star Wars" characters have bulked up over the years.

Recent figures on cosmetic surgery indirectly confirm the anecdotal sense that men are going to greater extremes to improve their appearances. Women still account for about 90 percent of all procedures, but the number of men undergoing cosmetic surgery rose about 34 percent between 1996 and 1998, with liposuction being the most sought service. "Basically, men in general are getting the same medicine that women have had to put up with for years, which was trying to match an unattainable ideal in terms of body image," says Pope, who has focused his studies on college-age men just past adolescence. "Boys are much more prone at this point to worry about being beefed up, about having muscles," says Mary Pipher, a psychologist and the author of "Reviving Ophelia," a book about adolescent girls. "As we've commodified boys' bodies to sell products, with advertisements that show boys as bodies without heads, we've had this whole business about focusing on the body." And, she adds, families move so often that teen-agers "don't really know each other very well, so the only piece of information that's really accessible is your appearance."

There is one trenchant piece of research that justifies the sudden new focus on male development. Inspired by the AIDS epidemic, Government-sponsored researchers began an enormous survey of sexual attitudes in teen-age boys called the 1988 National Survey of Adolescent Males. Joseph H. Pleck, a psychologist at the University of Illinois at Urbana-Champaign and one of the principal investigators of the study, reported in 1993 a factor called "masculinity ideology," which indicates the degree to which boys subscribe to the more traditional standards of male comportment: the need for respect from peers and spouses, a reliance on physical toughness, a reluctance to talk about problems, even a reluctance to do housework. "The more traditional the attitude about masculinity in adolescent males," Pleck found, "the higher their risk for risky sexual behavior, substance use, educational problems and problems with the law."

"This one variable is a really powerful predictor of behavior," says Dan   15 Kindlon, a researcher at the School of Public Health at Harvard and co-author, with Michael Thompson, of "Raising Cain." "When you look at the kinds of kids who are in trouble in terms of—you name it—drugs and alcohol, suicide, attention-deficit disorder and learning disabilities, the prevalent statistics are so skewed toward boys that it's enough to knock you over. And when they looked at kids over time, the kids who had the highest risk were the highest in terms of this masculinity ideology." Since this ideology is so pervasive in boys, Kindlon says, it creates a kind of social pecking order based on physical size and the *appearance* of toughness.

The confusions that arise in young males as they try to reconcile the traditional masculine values of their fathers, for example, with a post-feminist culture that celebrates sensitivity and openness have created a "national crisis of boyhood," according to some psychologists—as well as a boomlet of academic interest in boys and a burst of popular literature on the subject. In addition to "Raising Cain," there is William S. Pollack's "Real Boys," Michael Gurian's "Wonder of Boys" and James Garbarino's "Lost Boys," as well as a spate of books and magazines about male fitness. Many of these books were inspired by the groundbreaking research in the 1970's and 80's by Carol Gilligan, of Harvard's Graduate School of Education, who charted the psychological and moral development of adolescent girls. Now Gilligan and Judy Chu, her research associate, are listening to boys' voices too. And one of the most eagerly awaited books this fall is "Stiffed," an account of the "masculinity crisis," by Susan Faludi, author of "Backlash."

Some academics claim to have seen the crisis coming for years. After the recent outbreaks of school violence in Littleton, Jonesboro and Springfield, Pollack said, "It's boys who are doing this, because of this code about what they can say and can't say, how they feel about their body self, how they feel about their self-image, how they feel about themselves in school," There's "no coincidence," he added, that boys are unleashing this violence in school.

You don't have to buy the alarmism implicit in Pollack's point to appreciate that body-image concerns form part of a larger, more complex and in some ways changeless ethos of male adolescence that would be trite and obvious if it weren't so true: boys, like girls, are keenly aware of, and insecure about, their physical appearance. Boys, unlike some girls, do not talk about it with their parents, other adults or even among themselves, at least in part for fear of being perceived as "sensitive," a code word for "weak." Indeed, they tease each other, on a scale from casually nasty to obsessively cruel, about any perceived flaws, many of which involve some physical difference—size, shape, complexion, coordination—and since adolescent teasing begs for an audience, much of this physical ridicule occurs in school. If you don't change the "culture of cruelty," as Kindlon and Thompson put it in their book, you'll never defuse the self-consciousness and concerns about body image in boys.

"When you go to ask men questions about psychological issues," Kindlon says, "you've got two things going against you. One is emotional literacy. They're not even in touch with their emotions, and they're doing things for reasons of which they're not even aware. You're not getting the real story because *they* don't even know the whole story. And even if they did, a lot of them would underrepresent what the problem was, because you're not supposed to ask for help. If you can't ask for directions when you're lost in a foreign city, how are you going to ask for help about something that's really personal? Especially if you're an eighth grader."

Getting boys to talk about their bodies is not an easy thing to do, as I learned   20
when I met with several groups of teen-agers. On one occasion, six middle-school boys and I sat around a table on a warm afternoon very close to the end of the school year at a Manhattan public school in Chelsea. I asked them to describe the feelings they have when they look at themselves alone in the mirror, and for its sheer confused candor, it was tough to top the remark of Mickey, a 13-year-old who begins the ninth grade in a public school early next month.

"I don't know," he said at first. "I can't even tell what stage of puberty I'm in. Some parts, I'm sure about, but"—he added with an impish smile—"other parts, I'm not so sure."

We went around the table. Dwayne, mentioning that he appeared younger than his 13 years, looked forward to the effect this would have later in life. Bernie, lean and a little more satisfied than the others, said he didn't want muscles and would never use steroids. James saw a chubby 13-year-old in his mirror. ("I just want to be skinnier," he said plaintively.) Adel, who shot up six inches and gained 24 pounds in the last 14 months, monitored acne outbreaks with the avidity of a D.E.A. agent. Willie, a powerfully built 15-year-old with impressive biceps, derived no solace from his solid athletic build. "When I look in the mirror, I wish my ears were bigger and my feet were smaller. I wear size 11 1/2 shoes. My behind is big, too. But," he added, "girls like it." In retrospect, the most interesting thing about the conversation was how the older, bigger boys dominated the discussion while the younger, smaller boys deferred: size cued the communication.

Take any half-dozen boys and you'll probably get close to hitting the same cross section: the fat one, the skinny one, the one who's self-conscious about being tall and the one who's self-conscious about being short, the jock and the kid who plays in the band. No one here looked like Mark Wahlberg. They slouched in the body language of feigned boredom, although that may just have been another way of expressing wary curiosity, as if body image is something they think about *all the time* and talk about almost never.

Mickey, the eighth grader, captured the problem well. "When you're at this stage," he observed, "it's all about fitting in to something, cliques and stuff. And when you're not at the same stage of life as other kids, it's harder to fit in." He was using "fit," of course, in its metaphorical sense, but it was exceptionally apt: the essence of the word is physical, of shapes and interactions and congruence. For boys in the midst of the exotic and uncontrollable incongruence of puberty, growing up in an internal world flooded with hormones and an external world flooded with idealized male images, the fit may be tighter than ever before.

In seventh and eighth grades, Alexander Bregstein didn't fit in at all. "I was picked on in every single class," he recalled, "every single day, walking the hallways. It was beyond belief. They would do things like hide your bag, turn your bag inside out, tie your shoelaces together. Some of the stuff I just can't repeat, it was so awful." They called him Fat Boy. They thought he was lazy, that something was wrong with him. He knew it wasn't true, but he also realized that his physical appearance made him a social outcast and a target—neither of which is a good thing to be in early adolescence.

When you visit the office of Harrison (Skip) Pope, in a grim institutional building on the rolling grounds of McLean Hospital in Belmont, Mass., the first thing you notice are the calipers hanging on the wall—partly as objets d'art, but partly as a reminder that what we subjectively consider attractive can sometimes yield to objective measurement. Pope, after all, was one of the scientists who devised what might be called the Buff Equation, or: $FFMI = W \times (1\text{-}BF/100) \times h2 + 6.1 \times (1.8 - H)$.

The formula is ostensibly used to calculate a person's Fat-free Mass Index; it has sniffed out presumed steroid use by Mr. America winners, professional body-builders and men whose unhealthy preoccupation with looking muscular has induced them to use drugs.

Pope is a wiry, compact psychiatrist who can squat 400 pounds in his spare time. ("You can reach me pretty much all day except from 11 A.M. to 2 P.M.," he told me, "when I'm at the gym.") I had gone to see him and his colleague

Roberto Olivardia not only because they were the lead authors on the G.I. Joe study, but also because their studies of body-image disorders in slightly older postadolescent men may be the best indicator yet of where male body-image issues are headed.

Shortly after I arrived, Olivardia emptied a shopping bag full of male action dolls onto a coffee table in the office. The loot lay in a heap, a plastic orgy of superhero beefcake—three versions of G.I. Joe (Hasbro's original 1964 version plus two others) and one G.I. Joe Extreme, Luke Skywalker and Han Solo in their 1978 and mid-1980's versions, Mighty Morphin Power Rangers, Batman, Superman, Iron Man and Wolverine. The inspiration for the whole study came from . . . an adolescent girl. Pope's 13-year-old daughter, Courtney, was surfing the Web one night, working on a school project on how Barbie's body had radically changed over the years, and Pope thought to himself, There's got to be the male equivalent of that.

Once Pope and Olivardia gathered new and "vintage" action figures, they measured their waist, chest and biceps dimensions and projected them onto a 5-foot-10 male. Where the original G.I. Joe projected to a man of average height with a 32-inch waist, 44-inch chest and 12-inch biceps, the more recent figures have not only bulked up, but also show much more definition. Batman has the equivalent of a 30-inch waist, 57-inch chest and 27-inch biceps. "If he was your height," Pope told me, holding up Wolverine, "he would have 32-inch biceps." Larger, that is, than any bodybuilder in history. 30

Now let it be said that measuring the styrene hamstrings of G.I. Joe does not represent 20th-century science at its most glorious. But Pope says it's a way to get at what he calls "evolving American cultural ideals of male body image." Those ideals, he maintains, create "cultural expectations" that may contribute to body-image disorders in men. "People misinterpreted our findings to assume that playing with toys, in and of itself, caused kids to develop into neurotic people as they grew up who abused anabolic steroids," Pope said. "Of course that was not our conclusion. We simply chose the toys because they were symptomatic of what we think is a much more general trend in our society."

Since the early 1990's, evidence has emerged suggesting that a small number of adult males suffer from extreme body-image disorders. In 1993, in a study of steroid use among male weight lifters, Pope discovered that 10 percent of the subjects "perceived themselves as physically small and weak, even though they were in fact large and muscular." Researchers termed this syndrome "reverse anorexia nervosa" and started looking for more cases. Two years ago, the Pope group renamed this disorder "muscle dysmorphia," the more specialized condition that involves an obsessive preoccupation with muscularity. Men who were clearly well developed and, by anyone's standards, exceedingly muscular, repeatedly expressed the feeling that they were too small, too skinny and too weak, to the point that their obsessive quest to build up their bodies began to interfere with work and relationships—in short, their entire lives.

"It's very hard to document trends like this in quantitative terms," Pope said, "because people who are insecure about their body appearance are unlikely to come out of the woodwork to confess that they're insecure about their body appearance. And so it is an epidemic which by definition is covert. But it clearly has become a much more widespread concern among men in the United States."

Alexander said he felt that insecurity at a visceral level. He was not only overweight, but also undersize. "I've been called short umpteen times," he said during a pause in his routine, and the only time I saw a hint of visible anger in his face was when he talked about being discriminated against because of being short.

"Kids are *so* self-conscious," Kindlon says. "One of the reasons that this body-image stuff is so powerful is because there's such an increase in self-consciousness as you move into puberty. I don't know anybody who has a good neurological explanation for it, but clearly there's real egocentricity, especially in early adolescence. Everything revolves around *you*. You walk into a room and you think everybody is looking at you. These kids are petrified because they always feel like they're onstage. Clothes at least are something that you can change. Fat kids and short kids are the ones who get it the most." 35

Another factor tends to complicate the sense of feeling like an outsider. Girls usually reach puberty earlier than boys, and the starting line is starkly marked by menstruation. Boys, by contrast, beginning around the age of 11, suddenly find themselves awash in hormones, but without any navigational landmarks. The amount of testosterone in the bloodstream rises roughly 100-fold in boys during puberty. (It also rises in girls, though not nearly so much.) And yet biology is not behavioral destiny, according to the research of Richard Tremblay, director of the Research Unit on Children's Psychosocial Maladjustment at the University of Montreal. In a long-term study that has followed boys from kindergarten through high school, Tremblay's group has shown that the most aggressive boys at age 13 actually had *lower* than average levels of testosterone, although the most socially dominant boys had the highest levels of the hormone.

"The real damage gets done in middle school," Pollack says, "when boys and girls are most out of sync with each other in their development." He tells of a group of mothers, including feminists, who yanked their sons out of public school and put them in single-sex schools because they were getting harassed by girls. "They weren't physically harassing them. But they were calling them on the phone, wanting to talk to them. They were wanting to be romantic, and some of them wanting to be sexual. In an assertive way, not in an aggressive way. And these were little shrimp boys, as I call them, who wanted to play

Nintendo and basketball and weren't ready for this level of development. They were two years behind. When this goes on for two or three years at the middle school and then you're throwing them into the environment of high school, then you've got this revved-up negative experience from middle school that gets over-aggressified in high school. And it just gets worse."

I can vouch for that. In 1965, just shy of 14, I was not only the shortest kid in my freshman gym class, but also the new kid in school, my family having just moved to a suburb west of Chicago. It had rained heavily the day before, and there were huge puddles on the fields around which we were ordered to take the obligatory lap at the end of calisthenics. As I was running along, two larger boys—football players, it turned out—came up behind me, knocked me down and then, each taking a leg as if grabbing a wishbone, dragged my 4-foot-9, 82-pound frame along the ground and through several pond-size puddles. It is part of the dynamic of stoic boyhood, of suffering the routine bullying and hazing in resentful silence, that my parents will learn of this incident for the first time when they read this article.

As I spoke with adolescent boys and psychologists, it became clear that of all body-image issues, size is the most important, in part because it leads to a kind of involuntary self-definition. One morning I met with a group of boys attending a summer session at the Chelsea Center of the McBurney Y.M.C.A. in Manhattan. I asked them if they had nicknames, and almost every name referred to a physical quality. Mouse. String Bean. Little J. Leprechaun. Shortie. Half Pint. Spaghetti.

These insults, even the benign ones, seem to have the half-life of nuclear waste for kids. Adel, now a hulking and self-confident 6-foot-2 10th grader at the public school in Chelsea, recalled specific insults about his size and clumsiness dating back to the 4th grade. Another boy, who will attend Friends Seminary, in Manhattan, this fall, told me he has always been teased about being tall; he recalled with painful precision what was said, when and by whom—eight years earlier. Rob, who will begin boarding school in the fall, was the shortest in his class, and he could barely contain a fidgety, amusingly self-aware impatience. "Can I talk about feeling insecure about being short?" he piped up at one point. "I'm insecure about being short, because all the bigger kids think, correctly, that they can beat me up." 40

Harmless teasing? Psychologists have begun to suggest that the stress of all this taunting and hazing may have significant biological effects on boys during puberty. Kindlon, for example, cites the research of Bruce McEwen, a Rockefeller University neuroscientist who has shown in animal studies that prolonged and chronic stress leads to biochemical and structural changes in the brain that compromise the development of cognitive functions like memory. And Katharine Phillips, the Brown University psychiatrist who specializes in body dysmorphic disorder, says that some adolescent boys may have a biological susceptibility to teasing, which in extreme cases can lead to psychiatric illness. Men who suffer from B.D.D. may believe they are so ugly or unattractive that they refuse to leave their homes—they become, in effect, body-image agoraphobics, and they almost always date the onset of this insecurity to adolescence.

Leaving such extreme pathology aside, the point remains that a boy's body image is shaped, if not determined, by the cruelest, most unforgiving and meanest group of judges imaginable: other boys. And even if you outgrow, physically and emotionally, the body image that oppressed you as an adolescent, it stays with you in adult life as a kind of subdermal emotional skin that can never be shed, only incorporated into the larger person you try to become. I think that's what Garry Trudeau, the formerly small cartoonist, had in mind when he described life as a tall adult as that of a "recovering short person."

It was during his sophomore year, getting "the daylights pounded out of him" in wrestling and gaining even more weight, that Alexander began what he calls, with justification, his "drastic transformation." He started by losing 30 pounds in one month. For a time, he consumed only 900 calories a day, and ultimately got down to 152 pounds. He began to lift weights seriously, every day for three months straight. He started to read magazines like *Flex* and *Men's Fitness*. He briefly dabbled with muscle-building supplements like creatine. He got buff, and then beyond buff.

By the time his sophomore year in high school began, Alexander had packaged his old self in a phenomenally new body, and it has had the desired effect. "My quality of social life changed dramatically when I changed my image," he said. He still maintained friendships with the guys in the computer lab, still programmed, still played Quake with dozens of others. But he worked out at the gym at least five times a week. He shifted his diet to heavy protein. He pushed himself to lift ever-heavier weights. Until an injury curtailed his season, he brought new strength to his wrestling. Still, he wasn't satisfied. When I asked him if he ever felt tempted to try steroids during his effort to re-make his physical image, he denied using them, and I believe him. But he wasn't coy about the temptation. "When someone offers you a shortcut," he replied, "and it's a shortcut you want so bad, you're willing to ignore what it might be doing to your insides. I wanted to look better. Who cares if it's going to clog up my kidneys? Who cares if it'll destroy my liver? There was so much peer pressure that I didn't care."

Alexander was especially pleased by the good shape he was in—although he didn't care for aerobics, his resting heart rate was low, he ran a mile under six minutes and seemed to have boundless energy. But fitness was only part of what he was after. As he put it: "No one's looking for a natural look, of being thin and in shape. It's more of looking toward a level beyond that." He added that "guys who work out, especially guys who have six-packs and are really cut up, are the ones girls go after."

To be honest, I was a little dubious about this until I spoke with an admittedly unscientific sampling of teen-age girls. It turned out that they not only agreed with the sentiment, but also spoke the same lingo. "If you're going swimming or something like that, girls like the stomach best," said Elizabeth, a 14-year old. "Girls like it if they have a six-pack, or if they're really ripped, as they say. That's the most important thing. And arms too."

"But not too much," added her friend Kate, also 14. "You don't like it if the muscles are too huge."

"It changes your perspective on them if they have a flabby stomach," Elizabeth continued. "And the chest is important too."

There is nothing inherently dangerous about weight lifting. "It's great exercise," says Dr. Linn Goldberg, professor of medicine at Oregon Health Sciences University and an authority on muscle-enhancing substances in high-school athletes, who lifts weights with his 18-year-old son. "Here's the problem, though. Our studies show that supplements are gateway substances to steroid use, and kids who use them are at greater risk for using anabolic steroids." Goldberg noted that 50 percent of males participate in athletics at some point between the 9th and 12th grades, and a recent study of more than 3,000 boys in Oregon and Washington by Goldberg and his colleagues showed that 78 percent of high-school athletes use supplements, which include creatine, ginseng, ma-huang and androstenedione, the supplement made famous by Mark McGwire, who recently renounced its use.

Many of the kids with whom I spoke were well aware of the health risks 50 associated with the use of anabolic steroids, especially the fact that the testicles shrink with prolonged use. (Steroids also increase the risk of cardiovascular diseases and some forms of cancer.) Despite a great deal more scientific uncertainty about the risks—and benefits—of the supplements, however, Charles Yesalis, an expert on steroid abuse at Penn State University, estimated that "creatine use is epidemic at the junior-high-school level, and ubiquitous at the high-school level."

In my conversations with boys, it began to dawn on me that male adolescents pass through two distinct stages. During the early phase, when self-consciousness is at its peak, boys tend to look inward, think asexually and act like, well, boys. As they get older, their field of view enlarges, and they start to pay more sophisticated attention to cultural images and their own sexuality. And they become very interested in whatever their objects of romantic attraction are interested in. So if you ask 13-year-old boys what catches their eyes, they'll say "The Simpsons" and "Revenge of the Nerds" and ads for Mountain Dew. If you ask 16-year-olds the same question, they tend to mention "Dawson's Creek" and "American Pie" and fashion advertising.

"When you hear girls gawking at Abercrombie & Fitch about how hot the guy is on the bag—that makes an impression," Alexander told me one night on the phone.

The "guy on the bag" turned out to be an exceptionally cut youth not wearing a shirt. "If I look this way," Alexander said, "I've got my foot in the door." This very heterosexual impulse, however, was elicited by a school of advertising whose genealogy follows a risqué and decidedly homoerotic lineage.

In the slow male striptease known as men's fashion advertising, there have been plenty of landmark cultural images in recent years. Calvin Klein, which until recently developed all of its advertising in-house, has been pushing the boundary of taste navel-ward and beyond ever since 1980, when a 15-year-old Brooke Shields teasingly announced that nothing came between her and her Calvins. There was Bruce Weber's photo of the model Jeff Aquilon splayed on a boulder for Calvin Klein in 1982 and Mark Wahlberg (then known as Marky Mark) prancing in Calvin Klein underwear in 1992. But the ad that made sociologically explicit what had been implicit all along is what detractors have called Calvin Klein's "basement porn" campaign of 1995.

These television spots—they were, almost incidentally, for jeans—featured a deliberately cheesy, amateurishly lighted basement-like setting with cheap wall paneling. They began with an adult male voice posing questions to youthful and shirtless boys. The models were, of course, beautiful, but only in retrospect do you realize how toned and buff their bodies were—and how the ads made sure you noticed. In one commercial, the off-camera voice says: "You have a lovely body. Do you like your body?" In another, a boy who has both the looks and indifferent demeanor of a young James Dean sits on a ladder, wearing jeans and a white T-shirt.

"You got a real nice look," an adult male voice says off-camera. "How old are   55
you?"

"Twenty-one," the boy says.

"What's your name?"

"August."

"Why don't you stand up?"

When the boy complies, the man continues, "Are you strong?"   60

"I like to think so."

"You think you could rip that shirt off of you," The boy pulls down on the T-shirt with both hands and suddenly rips it off his body, revealing an extremely lean and well-developed chest. "It's a nice body!" the man exclaims. "Do you work out?"

"Uh-huh." The boy nods again.

"Yeah, I can tell."

I don't think of myself as culturally squeamish, but the ad struck me as so   65
creepy that when I screened it at home recently, I became concerned that my 15-month-old son, toddling around the room, might be paying attention. "The

style, the look, the leering tone, even the 'chicken hawk' voice-over—Klein mimicked, closely, the style and tone of cheap basement gay pornography," says Bob Garfield, a columnist at Advertising Age and a longtime critic of what he calls Klein's "shockvertising" approach. If it is true, Garfield adds, that these commercials influence how boys think about their bodies, it reflects in part "the opening up of gay culture, where male objectification has almost nearly the effect that the objectification of females has had for time immemorial for women."

This point is not lost on researchers. "The feminist complaint all along has been that women get treated as objects, that they internalize this and that it damages their self-esteem," says Kelly D. Brownell, director of the Yale Center for Eating and Weight Disorders. "And more and more, guys are falling into that same thing. They're getting judged not by who they are, but how they look."

There is no way to plug popular culture into an equation and see what effect it has on mass psychology, of course, but there is widespread sentiment that these provocative images of buff males have really upped the ante for boys. Writing of both men and women in her new book, "The Male Body," Susan Bordo notes that "in an era characterized by some as 'postfeminist,' beauty seems to count more than it ever did before, and the standards for achieving it have become more stringent, more rigorous, than ever." Some of the research on body-image disorders in males indirectly makes the connection to cultural images.

Olivardia, who conducted extensive interviews with men suffering from body dysmorphic disorder, says the patients bring up Hollywood movie stars all the time. "Arnold Schwarzenegger, Stallone, Jean-Claude Van Damme. And Calvin Klein—that name has been brought up quite a lot of times." If you pick up an issue of Gentleman's Quarterly or Men's Health or Teen People . . . , you'll see the trickle-down effect: a boy removes a tank top for Guess jeans. Firemen drop trou for jockey shorts. Even the recent ads for "Smart Start" cereals by Kellogg's feature a naked torso. Consider: a six-pack in a cereal ad!

Indeed, the bare, hairless, ripped chest has become so ubiquitous as a cultural icon that it occurred to me that contemporary advertising may have completely reinvented—or at least relocated—the physiological epicenter of male insecurity. Once, the defining moment of terror in a boy's life came in the locker room at shower time—the place, as a boy at the Chelsea school put it, "where there's nowhere to hide." There's still plenty of angst about penis size; many boys simply don't take showers after gym class these days, but I heard genuine fear in the voices of older boys when they spoke about the impending horror of going to camp or the beach and having to appear in public *without a shirt.*

After Alexander finished his workout that hot July day, we stopped to get something to drink at the gym's cafe. "I feel pretty good right now," Alexander   70 admitted, "and I was furious when I went in there." It turned out that the night before, he had a conversation with a girl that took a decidedly unsatisfying turn at the end.

At a time when the collective amount of American body fat is enough to stretch the jaws of Skip Pope's calipers from coast to coast, when so many adults amble about like fatted calves and so many children are little more than couch potatoes in training, it's hard to find fault with disciplined, drug-free efforts by teen-age boys to add a bit of muscle; weight lifting is not a sport with shortcuts, and it has become an essential adjunct to contemporary athletic performance. But there is a psychological side to all this heavy lifting that may be as unhealthy and undermining on the inside as it seems fit on the outside. And it resides not in that telltale mirror, but in how we see ourselves.

"I look in the mirror and I don't see what other people see," Alexander told me. "I look in the mirror, and I see my flaws. People go, 'Oh, you're narcissistic.' I go, 'No, I was looking at how uneven my pecs are,' although I know that in reality, they're, like, a nanometer off. And I have three friends who do exactly the same thing. They look and they go, 'Look how *uneven* I am, man!' And I go: '*What* are you talking about! They look pretty even to me.' It's not narcissism—it's lack of self-esteem."

I'm not so worried about kids like Alexander—he clearly has demonstrated both the discipline to remake his appearance and the psychological distance not to take it, or himself, too seriously. But there will be many other boys out there who cannot hope to match the impossibly raised bar of idealized male body image without resorting to the physically corrosive effects of steroids or the psychologically corrosive effects of self-doubt. Either way, the majority of boys will be diminished by chasing after the golden few.

Moreover, this male preoccupation with appearance seems to herald a dubious, regressive form of equality—now boys can become as psychologically and physically debilitated by body-image concerns as girls have been for decades. After all, this vast expenditure of teen-age male energy, both psychic and kinetic, is based on the premise that members of the opposite sex are attracted to a retro, rough-hewn, muscular look, and it's a premise that psychologists who study boys have noticed, too. "While girls and women say one thing, some of them continue to do another," Pollack says. "Some of them are still intrigued by the old male images, and are attracted to them."

Because he's a perceptive kid, Alexander recognizes how feckless, how disturbing, how *crazy* this all is. "I tell you, it's definitely distressing," he said, "the fact that as much as girls get this anorexic thing and they're going through these image things with dolls and stuff, guys are definitely doing the same." True, he admitted, his social life has never been better. "But in a way it depresses me," he said, before heading off to a party; "that I had to do this for people to get to know me."

75

ANALYZING What the Writer Says

1. What made Alexander Bregstein decide to start working out at the gym?

2. Why is research into the body-image problems of boys a fairly new thing? Why, according to researchers, is such study necessary?

3. How are boys different from girls in the way they deal with body-image problems?

4. What is "body dysmorphic disorder" or "muscle dysmorphia," as the disorder is also known? What do those suffering from it believe?

5. How has advertising aggravated body-image problems in boys and young men?

6. What does Hall see as the most serious dangers of the current emphasis on muscular male bodies?

ANALYZING How the Writer Says It

Throughout the article, Hall balances personal with quotes and paraphrases from scientific studies and interviews with researchers. How does this mix of evidence support his points more than if he had used just one or the other by itself?

ANALYZING the Issue

1. Body-image disorders in young girls, such as anorexia and bulimia, have been widely studied. Hall alerts us to similar problems in young boys. Have you observed similar phenomena? Are you worried about the trend Hall describes in his essay?

2. Almost every day we hear about the growing problem of obesity in America and its attendant health problems; on the other hand, advertising and the fashion industry champion a body style for both men and women that is virtually unattainable for the average person. How do you explain the presence of these two trends—bulging waistlines on the one hand, anorexia and muscle dysmorphia on the other? What does this seeming paradox say about our society?

ANALYZING Connections Between Texts

1. In "Stretch Marks" (p. 242) Anna Quindlen discusses body image from the point of view of a middle-aged woman. Compare her anxieties to those of Alexander Bregstein. About whom are you more concerned. Why?

2. Marge Piercy refers to the feminine ideal as "a work of artifice" in her poem of the same title (p. 160). To what extent is the body Alexander Bregstein desires also a work of artifice? Are the situations of Piercy's subject and Bregstein analogous? Explain.

3. How does the spoof ad "Reality for Men" (p. 263) lampoon some of the issues Hall raises in "The Bully in the Mirror"?

Ring Leader

BY NATALIE KUSZ

NATALIE KUSZ

Kusz's essay, first pub-lished in Allure, *describes her personal transforma-tion from an insecure ado-lescent to a confident adult. Having suffered for "being different" in her native Alaska and feeling similarly alienated as a junior professor at a mid-western university, she experiences a personal breakthrough when she embraces her difference—and celebrates by getting her nose pierced.*

I was thirty years old when I had my right nostril pierced, and back-home friends fell speechless at the news, lapsing into long telephone pauses of the sort that June Cleaver would employ if the Beave had ever called to report, "Mom, I'm married. His name's Eddie." Not that I resemble a Cleaver or have friends who wear pearls in the shower, but people who have known me the longest would say that for me to *draw* attention to my body rather than to work all out to *repel* it is at least as out of character as the Beave's abrupt urge for his-and-his golf ensembles. A nose ring, they might tell you, would be my last choice for a fashion accessory, way down on the list with a sag-enhancing specialty bra or a sign on my butt reading "Wide Load."

The fact is, I grew up ugly—no, worse than that, I grew up *unusual*, that unforgivable sin among youth. We lived in Alaska, where, despite what you might have heard about the Rugged Individualist, teenagers still adhere to the universal rules of conformity: if Popular Patty wears contact lenses, then you will by gum get contacts too, or else pocket those glasses and pray you can distinguish the girls' bathroom door from the boys'. The bad news was that I had only one eye, having lost the other in a dog attack at age seven; so although contacts, at half the two-eyed price, were easy to talk my parents into, I was still left with an eye patch and many facial scars, signs as gaudy as neon, telling everyone, "Here is a girl who is Not Like You." And Not Like Them, remember, was equivalent to Not from This Dimension, only half (maybe one third) as interesting.

The rest of my anatomy did nothing to help matters. I come from a long line of famine-surviving ancestors—on my father's side, Polish and Russian, on my mother's, everything from Irish to French Canadian—and thus I have an excellent, thrifty, Ebenezer Scrooge of a metabolism. I can ingest but a single calorie, and before quitting time at the Scrooge office, my system will have spent that calorie to replace an old blood cell, to secrete a vital hormone, to send a few chemicals around the old nervous system, and still have enough left over to deposit ten fat cells in my inner thigh—a nifty little investment for the future, in case the Irish potato famine ever recurs. These metabolic wonders are delightful if you are planning a move to central Africa, but for an American kid wiggling to Jane Fonda as if her life depended on it (which, in high school, it did), the luckiest people on earth seemed to be anorexics, whose wispy and hollow-cheeked beings whose primary part in the locker room drama was to stand at the mirror and announce, "My God, I disgust myself, I am *so fat*." While the other girls recited their lines ("No, Samantha, don't talk like that, you're beautiful, you really *are!*"), I tried to pull on a gym shirt without removing any other shirt first, writhing inside the cloth like a cat trapped among the bedsheets.

Thus, if you add the oversized body to the disfigured face, and add again my family's low income and my secondhand wardrobe, you have a formula for pure, excruciating teenage angst. Hiding from public scrutiny became for me, as for many people like me, a way of life. I developed a bouncy sense of humor, the kid that makes people say, "That Natalie, she is always so *up*," and keeps them from probing for deep emotion. After teaching myself to sew, I made myself cheap versions of those Popular Patty clothes or at least the items (*never* halter tops, although this was the seventies) that a large girl could wear with any aplomb. And above all, I studied the other kids, their physical posture, their music, their methods of blow-dryer artistry, hoping one day to emerge from my body, invisible. I suppose I came as close to invisibility as my appearance would allow, for if you look at the yearbook photos from that time, you will find on my face the same "too cool to say 'cheese'" expression as on Popular Patty's eleven-man entourage.

But at age thirty, I found myself living in the (to me) incomprehensible   5
politeness of America's Midwest, teaching at a small private college that I found suffocating, and anticipating the arrival of that all-affirming desire of college professors everywhere, that professional certification indicating you are now "one of the family": academic tenure. A first-time visitor to any college campus can easily differentiate between tenured and nontenured faculty by keeping in mind a learning institution's two main expectations: (1) that a young professor will spend her first several years on the job proving herself indispensable (sucking up), working to advance the interests of the college (sucking up), and making a name for herself in the field of study (sucking up); and (2) that a senior, tenured professor, having achieved indispensability,

institutional usefulness, and fame will thereafter lend her widely recognized name to the school's public relations office, which will use that name to attract prospective new students and faculty, who will in turn be encouraged to call on senior professors for the purpose of asking deep, scholarly questions (sucking up). Thus, a visitor touring any random campus can quickly distinguish tenured faculty from nontenured ones simply by noting the habitual shape and amount of chapping of their lips.

I anticipated a future of senior-faculty meetings with academia's own version of Popular Patty—not a nubile, cheerleading fashion plate, but a somber and scholarly denture wearer who, under the legal terms of tenure, cannot be fired except for the most grievous unprofessional behavior, such as igniting plastique under the dean's new Lexus. When that official notice landed in my In box, my sucking-up days would be over. I would have arrived. I would be family.

I couldn't bear it. In addition to the fact that I possessed all my own teeth, I was unsuited to Become As One with the other tenured beings because I was by nature boisterous, a collector of Elvis memorabilia, and given to not washing my car—in short, I was and always would be from Alaska.

Even in my leisure hours, my roots made my life of that period disorienting. Having moved to the immaculate Midwest from the far-from-immaculate wilderness, I found myself incapable of understanding, say, the nature of cul-de-sacs, those little circles of pristine homes where all the children were named Chris, and where all the parents got to vote on whether the Johnsons (they were all Johnsons) could paint their house beige. I would go to potluck suppers where the dishes were foreign to me, and twelve people at my table would take a bite, savor it with closed eyes, and say, "Ah, Tater Tot casserole. Now *that* takes me back." It got to the point where I felt defensive all the time, professing my out-of-towness whenever I was mistaken for a local, someone who understood the conversational subtexts and genteel body language of a Minnesotan. Moreover, I could never be sure what I myself said to these people with my subtextual language or my body. For all I knew, my posture during one of those impossible kaffeeklatsches proclaimed to everyone, "I am about to steal the silverware," or "I subscribe to the beliefs of Reverend Sun Myung Moon."

I grew depressed. Before long, I was feeling nostalgic for Alaskan eccentricities I had avoided even when I had lived there—unshaven legs and armpits, for example, and automobiles held together entirely by duct tape. I began decorating my office with absurd and nonprofessional items: velvet paintings, Mr. Potato Head, and a growing collection of snow globes from each of the fifty states. Students took to coming by to play with Legos, or to blow bubbles from those little circular wands and a wish started to grow in my brain, a yearning for some way to transport the paraphernalia around with me, to carry it along as an indication that I was truly unconventional at heart.

So the week that I received tenure, when they could no longer fire me 10
and when a sore nose would not get bumped during the course of any future
sucking-up maneuver, I entered a little shop in the black-leather part of town
and emerged within minutes with my right nostril duly pierced. The gesture
was, for me, a celebration, a visible statement that said, "Assume nothing. I
might be a punk from Hennepin Avenue, or a belly dancer with brass knuckles in my purse." Polite as was the society of that region, my colleagues never
referred to my nose, but I could see them looking and wondering a bit, which
was exactly the thing I had wanted—a lingering question in the minds of the
natives, the possibility of forces they had never fathomed.

After this, my comfort level changed some, and almost entirely for the better.
I had warned my father, who lived with me those years, that I was thinking of
piercing my nose. When I arrived home that day and the hole was through the
side instead of the center—he had expected, I found out, a Maori-style bone
beneath the nostrils—he looked at me, his color improved, and he asked if I
wanted chicken for dinner. So that was all fine. At school, students got over
their initial shock relatively quickly, having already seen the trailer-park
ambiance of my office, and they became less apt to question my judgment on
their papers; I could hear them thinking, She looks like she must understand
something about where I'm coming from. And my daughter—this was the best
part of all—declared I was the hippest parent she knew, and decided it was
O.K. to introduce me to her junior high friends; even Cool Chris—the Mid-
western variety of Popular Patty—couldn't boast a body-pierced mom.

I have since moved away from Minnesota, and old friends (those of the
aforementioned June Cleaver-type stunned silence) have begun to ask if I have
decided to stop wearing a nose stud now that my initial reason for acquiring it
has passed. And here, to me, is the interesting part: the answer, categorically,
is no. Nonconformity, or something like it, may have been the initial reason
behind shooting a new hole through my proboscis, but a whole set of side
effects, a broad and unexpected brand of liberation, has provided me a reason
for keeping it. Because the one-eyed fat girl who couldn't wear Popular Patty's
clothes, much less aspire to steal her boyfriends, who was long accustomed to
the grocery-store stares of adults and small children ("Mommy, what happened to that fat lady's face?"), who had learned over the years to hide whenever possible, slathering her facial scars with cover stick, is now—am I dreaming?—in charge. I have now, after all, deliberately chosen a "facial flaw," a
remarkable aspect of appearance. Somehow now, the glances of strangers
seem less invasive, nothing to incite me to nunhood; a long look is just that—
a look—and what of it? I've invited it, I've made room for it, it is no longer
inflicted upon me against my will.

ANALYZING What the Writer Says

1. Kusz suggests that "be[ing] from Alaska" is for her much more than an acknowledgment of her geographical roots. What else does it represent for her?
2. Why does Kusz get her nose pierced?
3. How does Kusz's nose ring change others' perception of her? Her perception of herself?

ANALYZING How the Writer Says It

1. What is the impact of Kusz's early revelation, "The fact is, I grew up ugly"?
2. Considering the youthful pain and trauma she relates, how does Kusz keep the reader from pitying her?
3. What is the significance of the essay's title?

ANALYZING the Issue

1. Do bold body adornments or fashion statements truly empower people? If so, how?
2. Are body piercings, brandings, or tattoos forms of speech—or simply fashion choices? Should employers, for example, dictate the ways in which individuals adorn their bodies by insisting that tattoos be covered or nose rings be removed before employees come to work?

ANALYZING Connections Between Texts

1. Both Natalie Kusz and Alice Walker ("Beauty," p. 250) suffered an eye injury that made them overly conscious of the way others perceived their appearance. How do the two women cope with their injuries? Do they come to similar insights about beauty and self-worth in the end?
2. Read Deborah Tannen's "Marked Women" (p. 521). How does Natalie Kusz use the social system of marking that Tannen discusses to defy it?
3. How does Leibovitz's portrait of Sidney Silver (p. 261) reinforce some of the insights Kusz presents in her essay?

WARMING UP: *Does society think differently about a body (male or female) "crippled" by disease or accident than about a "healthy" body? What words or phrases do we use to speak about it differently?*

Carnal Acts

BY NANCY MAIRS

NANCY MAIRS

Much of Nancy Mairs's writing is informed by her struggle with multiple sclerosis. In "Carnal Acts," from her 1990 book of the same title, she explains the connection between her body, weakened and deformed by disease, and her voice as a writer, which allows her to speak out against the perceived "shame" of her body.

Inviting me to speak at her small, liberal arts college during Women's Week, a young woman set me a task: "We would be pleased," she wrote, "if you could talk on how you cope with your MS disability, and also how you discovered your voice as a writer." Oh, Lord, I thought in dismay, how am I going to pull this one off? How can I yoke two such disparate subjects into a coherent presentation, without doing violence to one, or the other, or both, or myself? This is going to take some fancy footwork, and my feet scarcely carry out the basic steps, let alone anything elaborate.

To make matters worse, the assumption underlying each of her questions struck me as suspect. To ask *how* I cope with multiple sclerosis suggests that I *do* cope. Now, "to cope," *Webster's Third* tells me, is "to face or encounter and to find necessary expedients to overcome problems and difficulties." In these terms, I have to confess, I don't feel like much of a coper. I'm likely to deal with my problems and difficulties by squawking and flapping around like that hysterical chicken who was convinced the sky was falling. Never mind that in my case the sky really *is* falling. In response to a clonk on the head, regardless of its origin, one might comport oneself with a grace and courtesy I generally lack.

As for "finding" my voice, the implication is that it was at one time lost or missing. But I don't think it ever was. Ask my mother, who will tell you a little wearily that I was speaking full sentences by the time I was a year old and could never be silenced again. As for its being a writer's voice, it seems to have become one early on. Ask Mother again. At the age of eight I rewrote the Trojan War, she will say, and what Nestor was about to do to Helen at the end doesn't bear discussion in polite company.

Faced with these uncertainties, I took my own teacherly advice, something, I must confess, I don't always do. "If an idea is giving you trouble," I tell my writing students, "put it on the back burner and let it simmer while you do something else. Go to the movies. Reread a stack of old love letters. Sit in your history class and take detailed notes on the Teapot Dome Scandal. If you've got your idea in mind, it will go on cooking at some level no matter what else you're doing." "I've had an idea for my documented essay on the back burn- er," one of my students once scribbled in her journal, "and I think it's just boiled over!"

I can't claim to have reached such a flashpoint. But in the weeks I've had the   5 themes "disability" and "voice" sitting around in my head, they seem to have con- verged on their own, without my having to wrench them together and bind them with hoops of tough rhetoric. They *are* related, indeed interdependent, with an intimacy that has for some reason remained, until now, submerged below the surface of my attention. Forced to juxtapose them, I yank them out of the depths, a little startled to discover how they were intertwined down there out of sight. This kind of discovery can unnerve you at first. You feel like a giant hand that, pulling two swimmers out of the water, two separate heads bobbling on the iri- descent swells, finds the two bodies below, legs coiled around each other, in an ecstasy of copulation. You don't quite know where to turn your eyes.

Perhaps the place to start illuminating this erotic connection between who I am and how I speak lies in history. I have known that I have multiple sclero- sis for about sixteen years now, though the disease probably started long before. The hypothesis is that the disease process, in which the protective cov- ering of the nerves in the brain and spinal cord is eaten away and replaced by scar tissue, "hard patches," is caused by an auto-immune reaction to a slow- acting virus. Research suggests that I was infected by this virus, which no one has ever seen and which therefore, technically, doesn't even "exist," between the ages of four and fifteen. In effect, living with this mysterious mechanism feels like having your present self, and the past selves it embodies, haunted by a capricious and mean-spirited ghost, unseen except for its footprints, which trips you even when you're watching where you're going, knocks glassware out of your hand, squeezes the urine out of your bladder before you reach the bath- room, and weights your whole body with a weariness no amount of rest can relieve. An alien invader must be at work. But of course it's not. It's your own body. That is, it's you.

This, for me, has been the most difficult aspect of adjusting to a chronic incurable degenerative disease: the fact that it has rammed my "self" straight back into the body I had been trained to believe it could, through high-minded acts and aspirations, rise above. The Western tradition of distinguishing the body from the mind and/or the soul is so ancient as to have become part of our collective unconscious, if one is inclined to believe in such a noumenon, or at least to have become an unquestioned element in the social instruction we impose upon infants from birth, in much the same way we inculcate, without reflection, the gender distinctions "female" and "male." I *have* a body, you are likely to say if you talk about embodiment at all; you don't say, I *am* a body. A body is a separate entity possessible by the "I"; the "I" and the body aren't, as the copula would make them, grammatically indistinguishable.

To widen the rift between the self and the body, we treat our bodies as subordinates, inferior in moral status. Open association with them shames us. In fact, we treat our bodies with very much the same distance and ambivalence women have traditionally received from men in our culture. Sometimes this treatment is benevolent, even respectful, but all too often it is tainted by outright sadism. I think of the body-building regimens that have become popular in the last decade or so, with the complicated vacillations they reflect between self-worship and self-degradation: joggers and aerobic dancers and weightlifters all beating their bodies into shape. "No pain, no gain," the saying goes. "Feel the burn." Bodies get treated like wayward women who have to be shown who's boss, even if it means slapping them around a little. I'm not for a moment opposing rugged exercise here. I'm simply questioning the spirit in which it is often undertaken.

Since, as Hélenè Cixous points out in her essay on women and writing, "Sorties," thought has always worked "[t]rough dual, hierarchical oppositions,"[1] the mind/body split cannot possibly be innocent. The utterance of an "I" immediately calls into being its opposite, the "not-I," Western discourse being unequipped to conceive "that which is neither 'I' nor 'not-I' "; "that which is both 'I' and 'not-I' "; or some other permutation which language doesn't permit me to speak. The "not-I" is, by definition, other. And we've never been too fond of the other. We prefer the same. We tend to ascribe to the other those qualities we prefer not to associate with our selves: It is the hidden, the dark, the secret, the shameful. Thus, when the "I" takes possession of the body, it makes the body into an other, direct object of a transitive verb, with all the other's repudiated and potentially dangerous qualities.

At the least, then, the body had best be viewed with suspicion. And a woman's body is particularly suspect, since so much of it is in fact hidden, dark, secret, carried about on the inside where, even with the aid of a speculum, one can never perceive all of it in the plain light of day, a graspable whole. I, for one, have never understood why anyone would want to carry all that del-

10

---

[1]Hélène Cixous, "Sorties," in *The Newly Born Women: Theory and History of Literature, Volume 24,* trans. Betsy Wing (Minneapolis: University of Minnesota Press, 1986), p. 64.

icate stuff around on the outside. It would make you awfully anxious, I should think, put you constantly on the defensive, create a kind of siege mentality that viewed all other beings, even your own kind, as threats to be warded off with spears and guns and atomic missiles. And you'd never get to experience that inward dreaming that comes when your flesh surrounds all your treasures, holding them close, like a sturdy shuttered house. Be my personal skepticism as it may, however, as a cultural woman I bear just as much shame as any woman for my dark, enfolded secrets. Let the word for my external genitals tell the tale: my pudendum, from the Latin infinitive meaning "to be ashamed."

It's bad enough to bear your genitals like a sealed envelope bearing the cipher that, once unlocked, might loose the chaotic flood of female pleasure—*jouissance,* the French call it—upon the world-of-the-same. But I have an additional reason to feel shame for my body, less explicitly connected with its sexuality: It is a crippled body. Thus it is doubly other, not merely by the homosexual standards of patriarchal culture but by the standards of physical desirability erected for every body in our world. Men, who are by definition exonerated from shame in sexual terms (this doesn't mean that an individual man might not experience sexual shame, of course; remember that I'm talking in general about discourse, not folks), may—more likely must—experience bodily shame if they are crippled. I won't presume to speak about the details of their experience, however. I don't know enough. I'll just go on telling what it's like to be a crippled woman, trusting that, since we're fellow creatures who've been living together for some thousands of years now, much of my experience will resonate with theirs.

I was never a beautiful woman, and for that reason I've spent most of my life (together with probably at least ninety-five percent of the female population of the United States) suffering from the shame of falling short of an unattainable standard. The ideal woman of my generation was . . . perky, I think you'd say, rather than gorgeous. Blond hair pulled into a bouncing ponytail. Wide blue eyes, a turned-up nose with maybe a scattering of golden freckles across it, a small mouth with full lips over straight white teeth. Her breasts were large but well-harnessed high on her chest; her tiny waist flared to hips just wide enough to give the crinolines under her circle skirt a starting outward push. In terms of personality, she was outgoing, even bubbly, not pensive or mysterious. Her milieu was the front fender of a white Corvette convertible, surrounded by teasing crewcuts, dressed in black flats, a sissy blouse, and the letter sweater of the Corvette owner. Needless to say, she never missed a prom.

Ten years or so later, when I first noticed the symptoms that would be diagnosed as MS, I was probably looking my best. Not beautiful still, but the ideal had shifted enough so that my flat chest and narrow hips gave me an elegantly attentuated shape, set off by a thick mass of long, straight, shining hair. I had terrific legs, long and shapely, revealed nearly to the pudendum by the fashionable miniskirts and hot pants I adopted with more enthusiasm than delicacy of taste. Not surprisingly, I suppose, during this time I involved myself in several pretty torrid love affairs.

The beginning of MS wasn't too bad. The first symptom, besides the pernicious fatigue that had begun to devour me, was "foot drop," the inability to raise my left foot at the ankle. As a consequence, I'd started to limp, but I could still wear high heels, and a bit of a limp might seem more intriguing than repulsive. After a few months, when the doctor suggested a cane, a crippled friend gave me quite an elegant wood-and-silver one, which I carried with a fair amount of panache. The real blow to my self-image came when I had to get a brace. As braces go, it's not bad: lightweight plastic molded to my foot and leg, fitting down into an ordinary shoe and secured around my calf by a Velcro strap. It reduces my limp and, more important, the danger of tripping and falling. But it meant the end of high heels. And it's ugly. Not as ugly as I think it is, I gather, but still pretty ugly. It signified for me, and perhaps still does, the permanence and irreversibility of my condition. The brace makes my MS concrete and forces me to wear it on the outside. As soon as I strapped the brace on, I climbed into trousers and stayed there (though not in the same trousers, of course). The idea of going around with my bare brace hanging out seemed almost as indecent as exposing my breasts. Not until 1984, soon after I won the Western States Book Award for poetry, did I put on a skirt short enough to reveal my plasticized leg. The connection between winning a writing award and baring my brace is not merely fortuitous; being affirmed as a writer really did embolden me. Since then, I've grown so accustomed to wearing skirts that I don't think about my brace any more than I think about my cane. I've incorporated them, I suppose: made them, in their necessity, insensate but fundamental parts of my body.

Meanwhile, I had to adjust to the most outward and visible sign of all, a three-wheeled electric scooter called an Amigo. This lessens my fatigue and increases my range terrifically, but it also shouts out to the world, "Here is a woman who can't stand on her own two feet." At the same time, paradoxically, it renders me invisible, reducing me to the height of a seven-year-old, with a child's attendant low status. "Would she like smoking or nonsmoking?" the gate agent assigning me a seat asks the friend traveling with me. In crowds I see nothing but buttocks. I can tell you the name of every type of designer jeans ever sold. The wearers, eyes front, trip over me and fall across my handlebars into my lap. "Hey!" I want to shout to the lofty world. "Down here! There's a person down here!" But I'm not, by their standards, quite a person anymore.

My self-esteem diminishes further as age and illness strip from me the features that made me, for a brief while anyway, a good-looking, even sexy, young woman. No more long, bounding strides: I shuffle along with the timid gait I remember observing, with pity and impatience, in the little old ladies at Boston's Symphony Hall on Friday afternoons. No more lithe, girlish figure: my belly sags from the loss of muscle tone, which also creates all kinds of intestinal disruptions, hopelessly humiliating in a society in which excretory functions remain strictly unspeakable. No more sex, either, if society had its way. The sexuality of the disabled so repulses most people that you can hardly get a doctor, let alone a member of the general population, to consider the issues it raises. Cripples simply aren't supposed to Want It, much less Do It. Fortunately, I've got a husband with a strong libido and a weak sense of social propriety, or else I'd find myself perforce practicing a vow of chastity I never cared to take.

Afflicted by the general shame of having a body at all, and the specific shame of having one weakened and misshapen by disease, I ought not to be able to hold my head up in public. And yet I've gotten into the habit of holding my head up in public, sometimes under excruciating circumstances. Recently, for instance, I had to give a reading at the University of Arizona. Having smashed three of my front teeth in a fall onto the concrete floor of my screened porch, I was in the process of getting them crowned, and the temporary crowns flew out during dinner right before the reading. What to do? I wanted, of course, to rush home and hide till the dental office opened the next morning. But I couldn't very well break my word at this last moment. So, looking like Hansel and Gretel's witch, and lisping worse than the Wife of Bath, I got up on stage and read. Somehow, over the years, I've learned how to set shame aside and do what I have to do.

Here, I think, is where my "voice" comes in. Because, in spite of my demurral at the beginning, I do in fact cope with my disability at least some of the time. And I do so, I think, by speaking about it, and about the whole experience of being a body, specifically a female body, out loud, in a clear, level tone that drowns out the frantic whispers of my mother, my grandmothers, all the other trainers of wayward childish tongues: "Sssh! Sssh! Nice girls don't talk like that. Don't mention sweat. Don't mention menstrual blood. Don't ask what your grandfather does on his business trips. Don't laugh so loud. You sound like a loon. Keep your voice down. Don't tell. Don't tell. Don't tell." Speaking out loud is an antidote to shame.

I want to distinguish clearly here between "shame," as I'm using the word, and "guilt" and "embarrassment," which, though equally painful, are not similarly poisonous. Guilt arises from performing a forbidden act or failing to perform a required one. In either case, the guilty person can, through reparation, erase the offense and start fresh. Embarrassment, less opprobrious though not necessarily less distressing, is generally caused by acting in a socially stupid or awkward way. When I trip and sprawl in public, when I wet myself, when my front teeth fly out, I feel horribly embarrassed, but, like the pain of childbirth, the sensation blurs and dissolves in time. If it didn't, every child would be an only child, and no one would set foot in public after the onset of puberty, when embarrassment erupts like a geyser and bathes one's whole life in its bitter stream. Shame may attach itself to guilt or embarrassment, complicating their resolution, but it is not the same emotion. I feel guilt or embarrassment for something I've done; shame, for who I am. I may stop doing bad or stupid things, but I can't stop being. How then can I help but be ashamed? Of the three conditions, this is the one that cracks and stifles my voice.

I can subvert its power, I've found, by acknowledging who I am, shame and all, and, in doing so, raising what was hidden, dark, secret about my life into the plain light of shared human experience. What we aren't permitted to utter holds us, each isolated from every other, in a kind of solipsistic thrall. Without any way to check our reality against anyone else's, we assume our fears and shortcomings are ours alone. One of the strangest consequences of publishing a collection of personal essays called *Plaintext* has been the steady trickle of letters and telephone calls saying essentially, in a tone of unmistakable relief, "Oh, me too! Me too!" It's as though the part I thought was solo has turned out to be a chorus. But none of us was singing loud enough for the others to hear.

Singing loud enough demands a particular kind of voice, I think. And I was wrong to suggest, at the beginning, that I've always had my voice. I have indeed always had *a* voice, but it wasn't *this* voice, the one with which I could call up and transform my hidden self from a naughty girl into a woman talking directly to others like herself. Recently, in the process of writing a new book, a memoir entitled *Remembering the Bone House*, I've had occasion to read some of my early writing, from college, high school, even junior high. It's not an experience I recommend to anyone susceptible to shame. Not that the writing was all that bad. I was surprised at how competent a lot of it was. Here was a writer who already knew precisely how the language worked. But the voice . . . oh, the voice was all wrong: maudlin, rhapsodic, breaking here and there into little shrieks—almost, you might say, hysterical. It was a voice that had shucked off its own body, its own homely life of Cheerios for breakfast and seventy pages of Chaucer to read before the exam on Tuesday and a planter's wart growing painfully on the ball of its foot, and reeled now wraithlike through the air, seeking incarnation only as the heroine who enacts her doomed love for the tall, dark, mysterious stranger. If it didn't get that part, it wouldn't play at all.

Among all these overheated and vaporous imaginings, I must have retained some shred of sense, because I stopped writing prose entirely, except for scholarly papers, for nearly twenty years. I even forgot, not exactly that I had written prose, but at least what kind of prose it was. So when I needed to take up the process again, I could start almost fresh, using the vocal range I'd gotten used to in years of asking the waiter in the Greek restaurant for an extra anchovy on my salad, congratulating the puppy on making a puddle outside rather than inside the patio door, pondering with my daughter the vagaries of female orgasm, saying goodbye to my husband, and hello, and goodbye, and hello.

This new voice—thoughtful, affectionate, often amused—was essential because what I needed to write about when I returned to prose was an attempt I'd made not long before to kill myself, and suicide simply refuses to be spoken of authentically in high-flown romantic language. It's too ugly. Too shameful. Too strictly a bodily event. And, yes, too funny as well, though people are sometimes shocked to find humor shoved up against suicide. They don't like the incongruity. But let's face it, life (real life, I mean, not the edited-for-television version) is a cacophonous affair from start to finish. I might have wanted to portray my suicidal self as a languishing maiden, too exquisitely sensitive to sustain life's wounding pressures on her soul. (I didn't want to, as a matter of fact, but I might have.) The truth remained, regardless of my desires, that when my husband lugged me into the emergency room, my hair matted, my face swollen and gray, my nightgown streaked with blood and urine, I was no frail and tender spirit. I was a body, and one in a hell of a mess.

I "should" have kept quiet about that experience. I know the rules of polite discourse. I should have kept my shame, and the nearly lethal sense of isolation and alienation it brought, to myself. And I might have, except for something the psychiatrist in the emergency room had told my husband. "You might as well take her home," he said. "If she wants to kill herself, she'll do it no matter how many precautions we take. They always do." *They* always do. I was one of "them," whoever they were. I was, in this context anyway, not singular, not aberrant, but typical. I think it was this sense of commonality with others I didn't even know, a sense of being returned somehow, in spite of my appalling act, to the human family, that urged me to write that first essay, not merely speaking out but calling out, perhaps. "Here's the way I am," it said. "How about you?" And the answer came, as I've said: "Me too! Me too!"

This has been the kind of work I've continued to do: to scrutinize the details of my own experience and to report what I see, and what I think about what I see, as lucidly and accurately as possible. But because feminine experience has been immemorially devalued and repressed, I continue to find this task terrifying. "Every woman has known the torture of beginning to speak aloud," Cixous writes, "heart beating as if to break, occasionally falling into loss of language, ground and language slipping out from under her, because for woman speaking—even just opening her mouth—in public is something rash, a transgression."[2]

The voice I summon up wants to crack, to whisper, to trail back into silence. "I'm sorry to have nothing more than this to say," it wants to apologize. "I shouldn't be taking up your time. I've never fought in a war, or even in a schoolyard free-for-all. I've never tried to see who could piss farthest up the barn wall.

[2]Ibid., p. 92.

I've never even been to a whorehouse. All the important formative experiences have passed me by. I was raped once. I've borne two children. Milk trickling out of my breasts, blood trickling from between my legs. You don't want to hear about it. Sometimes I'm too scared to leave my house. Not scared *of* anything, just scared: mouth dry, bowels writhing. When the fear got really bad, they locked me up for six months, but that was years ago. I'm getting old now. Misshapen, too. I don't blame you if you can't get it up. No one could possibly desire a body like this. It's not your fault. It's mine. Forgive me. I didn't mean to start crying. I'm sorry . . . sorry . . . sorry. . . ."

An easy solace to the anxiety of speaking aloud: this slow subsidence beneath the waves of shame, back into what Cixous calls "this body that has been worse than confiscated, a body replaced with a disturbing stranger, sick or dead, who so often is a bad influence, the cause and place of inhibitions. By censuring the body," she goes on, "breath and speech are censored at the same time."[3] But I am not going back, not going under one more time. To do so would demonstrate a failure of nerve far worse than the depredations of MS have caused. Paradoxically, losing one sort of nerve has given me another. No one is going to take my breath away. No one is going to leave me speechless. To be silent is to comply with the standard of feminine grace. But my crippled body already violates all notions of feminine grace. What more have I got to lose? I've gone beyond shame. I'm shameless, you might say. You know, as in "shameless hussy"? A woman with her bare brace and her tongue hanging out.

I've "found" my voice, then, just where it ought to have been, in the body-warmed breath escaping my lungs and throat. Forced by the exigencies of physical disease to embrace my self in the flesh, I couldn't write bodiless prose. The voice is the creature of the body that produces it. I speak as a crippled woman. At the same time, in the utterance I redeem both "cripple" and "woman" from the shameful silences by which I have often felt surrounded, contained, set apart; I give myself permission to live openly among others, to reach out for them, stroke them with fingers and sighs. No body, no voice; no voice, no body. That's what I know in my bones.

ANALYZING | What the Writer Says

1. How has multiple sclerosis changed the way Nancy Mairs thinks about the connection between herself—her "I"—and her body?
2. In our culture, how do we treat the body—especially the female body?
3. In what ways does a "crippled" body increase the shame a woman already feels?
4. How does Nancy Mairs's responsibility as a writer mesh with the shame she

---

[3]Ibid., p. 97.

feels for her body? In what ways has her disability been a liberating force as well?

5. How is her adult voice, informed as it is by disease, different from her youthful voice as a writer, and how is it a more appropriate instrument for what she has to say?

ANALYZING How the Writer Says It

1. What is the significance of the title?
2. Nancy Mairs claims that she must overcome the shame about her body to speak the truth as she knows it. How do her choice of language and subject in this essay help her?

ANALYZING the Issue

How does Mairs's essay change the way you look at disability, at "crippled bodies"?

ANALYZING Connections Between Texts

1. Compare Mairs's description of how she copes with the ravages of disease to the insights Alice Walker presents in "Beauty: When the Other Dancer is the Self" (p. 250). In what way do the two writers' attitudes toward their bodies resemble each other? How are they different?

2. How has Mairs's disease liberated her from the fate Marge Piercy describes in "A Work of Artifice" (p. 160)?

3. Norman Rockwell's "Girl at the Mirror" (p. 262) has just discovered "beauty" as a standard manufactured by others, a standard she and most other women will never achieve. How does Nancy Mairs, her own body image compromised by multiple sclerosis, come to terms with these standards as she learns to live with her ever-weakening body? What could Mairs tell the girl at the mirror about beauty that the girl has yet to discover?

WARMING UP: *Would you ever consider having surgery for purely cosmetic reasons?*

Plastic Surgery

BY D. KEITH MANO

D. KEITH MANO

In graphic, excruciating detail, Mano, a contributor to Playboy *and* The National Review, *describes two cosmetic procedures as he observes a plastic surgeon at work. This article first appeared in 1981 in the* National Review.

Her right breast is cut: slit open like fresh tallow beneath: a two-inch incision under the hang of it. Dr. James Reardon has spread her wound for me. Red fat tissue, the meat of breasts, is glossy there: not good eating, I think: over-rich. With an electric scalpel-cautery, Reardon will slice and slice through this ragged human packing. The instrument snaps blue sparks out: cut, coagulate, cut. Occasionally some minute vessel will spray fine blood, then stanch.

After a minute the breast and underlying muscle are loose, up. Reardon starts to rummage in. With a retractor light I can see the super-nudity of rib cage and this hollow pouch he has made behind her small pap. We strip-search it: crimson, lit, shaggy-fibered inside: a weird vest pocket. As you stuff throw pillows, Reardon has begun to push the colorless silicone implant in. Her bosom is swelling with false pride now. The implant, more sinuous than gelatin, a good female impersonator, squeezes through that two-inch gash. No, not large enough yet: she'll want, Reardon guesses, to be built better than this. Next size up, please. Her snub and gnarled nipple lolls, orange with antiseptic, while Reardon is coaxing the glib implant out. And I am disconcerted. There's so little blood: so little *to* a female breast, which things have long been the business and quick speculation of my male eye.

I am, after all, in a strange protectorate: sterile mayhem is customary here. The kind assumptions we hold about flesh—personal nature, erotic value, tenderness—do not prevail in an operating room. I touch my scrub-suited arm. Skin plates us over: muscle can engage and disengage power: the breast is, well, an appendage not often of use. Dr. Reardon has practiced plastic surgery for 11 years: you, she may trust his deft bloodshed. Nothing I say is meant to judge or impugn him: I admire his frankness and generosity. Yet, being not native to the land, I find it all grotesque: that female breast stuff can be holed in such dispassion: the way, once, I slit calfskin with a child's leather-working kit. This woman will never, except before God, be so hugely undressed. She is lying now, unsutured still, phony-glamorous: alluring to all men but we four who know. From each flesh rip, as from a socket, I watch one glassy silicone eye blear out. It alienates me. She has begun to look mechanical: unalive inside. Flesh just a housing for some android gadgetry.

"That black bag," I ask the anaesthetist, "why d'you keep squeezing it?"

"Well, her diaphragm is paralyzed now. I have to breathe for her. See." He will clutch at the bag. Her servile ribs fan out: aaaah, she is inspired by him. A hobgoblin moment: I think what enormous surrogate forces are around me. But I don't experience outrage for her: she of the manipulated wind. By a Silastic voluptuousness this woman intends to paralyze and cause swelling in men. For that power, I find it all appropriate, she should trade some of her nature away.

Their patter—surgeon, assistant, anaesthetist—has the tick-whirr that fine clock escapements have. Unemphatic, even in tenor: low: a good beat to thread skin by. It is, I think, the way we talk among foreigners: expressionless, so that they cannot translate face or tone: this foreign body here, for one. And the irreverence, the M*A*S*H note, will disinvolve. "Let's stuff her with raisins and walnuts, huh?" "Has the guy from NATIONAL REVIEW fainted yet?" "Great, great: she can hire out as a ship's figurehead now." I like their irony: it settles me down. I trust them more, certainly, than I do the patient: who is torn and mindless: who would admonish my complacent flesh. This group-practiced chat is, anyhow, preferable to silence. Silence might announce tension. As when, later, we do a nose job.

"Rhinoplasts aren't my favorite," the anaesthetist has told me. "They're messy. The patient's fairly light at that point—we put them to sleep only actually for the injections. Then they're awake after the nose is all numbed. But they're groggy. They usually have no recall, but they're on spontaneous respiration. They're responsive if you talk to them. Where he breaks the bone a bit—that's the part where I usually whistle or sing or something. And usually—they tease me about it—I look; the other way."

Live Cartilage comes out: a thick, red toenail paring of it. I see blood froth. Reardon is cutting within the nose tip: he carves a sort of human rind away. The woman has been moaning: her nostrils are flared almost inside out: she will hawk phlegm up. The surgical hardware seems, to me, almost burlesque: mallet, chisel, rasp: tools for sullen carpentry. They do not banter now. Forty-five minutes have gone by: longer, I judge, than Reardon might expect. A bump on her nose bridge won't shear off. Reardon points the chisel, and his assistant—it is grisly, gristly this procedure—will start to hit with a mallet: rap, rap, rap, rap, *rap*. My anaesthetist friend has looked some other way. The woman is guzzling spit: a hopeless knee has risen in half-conscious protest: nnnnn, she can just say. Reardon asks again for the largest metal rasp: I note one in his voice. He sticks it far up the nostril and, with full body weight down, begins to saw. I have never heard such a monstrous sound: bone or cartilage abrades, shreds. But it is done. Reardon asks for my approval. Yes, different: yes, if you will, better. And now, to form a cast, doughy gauze-plaster strips are laid down. As you would put wet cloth over sculpted clay.

   I sit after. Not giddy: disorganized, rather, by what I have seen. I must withdraw from it and very soon: so that I can see a face as face. Or, some night, touch my wife's breast with naïve lust again.

ANALYZING What the Writer Says

1. What surprises the author most about plastic surgery? What does he fear will happen after his experience?
2. How does Mano characterize the demeanor of the medical professionals present for the surgical procedures?

ANALYZING How the Writer Says It

1. What is the effect of the author's precise, exact description of the procedures he witnesses?
2. Throughout the essay, Mano combines words that seem incompatible with each other, such as "sterile mayhem" and "deft bloodshed." He also uses words that seem out of place in an operating room, such as "strip-search" and "rummage." Can you find other examples? What do these juxtapositions reveal about the author's attitude toward his subject?
3. What is the connection between the first and last sentences of the essay?

ANALYZING the Issue

What is Mano's purpose in writing this essay? Is he making some argument about cosmetic surgery?

ANALYZING Connections Between Texts

1. How does Mano's description of plastic surgery differ from Roy Selby's account of brain surgery in "A Delicate Operation" (p. 246)? What attitudes toward the different procedures do the writers' descriptions reveal?

2. Read Richard Selzer's "Imelda" (p. 798). Compare and contrast the motives of Imelda's mother and the patients about whom Mano writes. What are the doctor's motives?

3. Look at Annie Leibovitz's portrait of bodybuilder Lenda Murray (p. 97). Does her muscular body represent an alternative to conventional female beauty? Does Murray's decision to transform her body through weight training make her any different from women who pay plastic surgeons to transform their bodies?

"He has the rough outline of a good body but none of the details."

WARMING UP: *Have you ever joined a gym or tried some physical activity that made you laugh at yourself?*

Stretch Marks

By Anna Quindlen

ANNA QUINDLEN

Pulitzer Prize-winning journalist, novelist, social critic, and children's book author Anna Quindlen (b. 1953) currently writes for Newsweek. *In "Stretch Marks," from her 1988 best-selling collection of* New York Times *op-ed columns* Living Out Loud, *Quindlen employs her trademark humor to share her experiences in the gym.*

For most of my life I have pursued a policy toward my body that could best be characterized as benign neglect. From the time I could remember until the time I was fifteen it looked one way, and from the time I was fifteen until I was thirty it looked another way. Then, in the space of two years, I had two children and more weight changes than Ted Kennedy, and my body headed south without me.

This is how I began to work out. I work out for a very simple reason, and it is not because it makes me feel invigorated and refreshed. The people who say that exercise is important because it makes you feel wonderful are the same people who say a mink coat is nice because it keeps you warm. Show me a woman who wears a mink coat to keep warm and who exercises because it feels good and I'll show you Jane Fonda. I wear a mink coat because it is a mink coat, and I work out so that my husband will not gasp when he runs into me in the bathroom and take off with an eighteen-year-old who looks as good out of her clothes as in them. It's as simple as that.

So I go to this gym three times a week, and here is how it works. First I go into the locker room. On the wall is an extremely large photograph of a person named Terri Jones wearing what I can only assume is meant to be a bathing suit. The caption above her body says Slim Strong and Sexy.

It is accurate. I check to make sure no one else is in the locker room, then I take my clothes off. As soon as I've done this, one of two people will enter the locker room: either an eighteen-year-old who looks as good out of her clothes as in them who spontaneously confides in me that she is having an affair with a young lawyer whose wife has really gone to seed since she had her two kids, or a fifty-year-old woman who has had nine children, weighs 105 and has abdominal muscles you could bounce a quarter off and who says she can't understand why, maybe it's her metabolism, but she can eat anything she wants, including a pint of Frusen Glädjé Swiss chocolate almond candy ice cream, and never gain a pound. So then I go out and exercise.

I do Nautilus. It is a series of fierce-looking machines, each designed, according to this book I have, to exercise some distinct muscle group, which all happen in my case never to have been exercised before. Nautilus was allegedly invented by Arthur Jones, husband of the aforementioned slim strong and sexy Terri, who is his seventeenth wife, or something like that. But I think anyone who comes upon a Nautilus machine suddenly will agree with me that its prototype was clearly invented at some time in history when torture was considered a reasonable alternative to diplomacy. Over each machine is a little drawing of a human body—not mine, of course—with a certain muscle group inked in red. This is so you can recognize immediately the muscle group that is on fire during the time you are using the machine.

There is actually supposed to be a good reason to do Nautilus, and it is sup-posed to be that it results in toning without bulk: that is, you will look like a dancer, not a defensive lineman. That may be compelling for Terri Jones, but I chose it because it takes me only a little more than a half hour—or what I like to think of as the time an average person burning calories at an average rate would need to read Where the Wild Things Are, Good Night, Moon and The Cat in the Hat twice—to finish all the machines. It is also not social, like aerobics classes, and will not hold you up to widespread ridicule, like running. I feel about exercise the same way that I feel about a few other things: that there is nothing wrong with it if it is done in private by consenting adults.

Actually, there are some of the Nautilus machines I even like. Call it old-fashioned machisma, but I get a kick out of building biceps. This is a throw-back to all those times when my brothers would flex their arms and a mound of muscle would appear, and I would flex mine and nothing would happen, and they'd laugh and go off somewhere to smoke cigarettes and look at dirty pictures. There's a machine to exercise the inner thigh muscles that bears such a remarkable resemblance to a delivery room apparatus that every time I get into it I think someone is going to yell push! and I will have another baby. I feel comfortable with that one. On the other hand, there is another machine on which I am supposed to lift a weight straight up in the air and the most I ever manage is to squinch my face up until I look like an infant with bad gas: My instructor explained to me that this is because women have no upper body strength, which probably explains why I've always found it somewhat difficult to carry a toddler and an infant up four flights of stairs with a diaper bag over one shoulder while holding a Big Wheel.

Anyhow, the great thing about working out is that I have met a lot of very nice men. This would be a lot more important if I weren't married and the mother of two. But of course if I were single and looking to meet someone, I would never meet anyone except married men and psychopaths. (This is Murphy's Other Law, named after a Doreen Murphy, who in 1981 had a record eleven bad relationships in one year.) The men I have met seem to really get a kick out of the fact that I work out, not unlike the kick that most of us get out of hearing very small children try to say words like hippopotamus or chauvinist. As one of the men at my gym said, "Most of the people here are guys or women who are uh well hmm umm. . . ."

"In good shape," I said.

"I wouldn't have put it like that," he answered.   10

Because I go to the gym at the same time on the same days, I actually see the same men over and over again. One or two of them are high school students, which I find truly remarkable. When I was in high school, it was a big deal if a guy had shoulders, never mind muscles. So when I'm finished I go back into the locker room and take a shower. The eighteen-year-old is usually in there, and sometimes she'll say something like, "Oh, that's what stretch marks look like." Then I put on my clothes and go home by the route that does not pass Dunkin' Donuts. The bottom line is that I really hate to exercise, but I have found on balance that this working out is all worth it. One day we were walking down the street and one of the guys from my gym—it was actually one of the high school guys, the one with the great pecs—walked by and said, "How ya doing?" My husband said, "Who the hell is that guy?" and I knew that Nautilus had already made a big difference in my life.

ANALYZING What the Writer Says

1. What reasons does Quindlen cite for joining a gym?
2. What initially makes Quindlen uncomfortable about working out at a gym?
3. What unexpected benefits does Quindlen reap from her experiences at the gym?

ANALYZING How the Writer Says It

1. Quindlen uses self-deprecating humor to muse about what, for many, is a nightmarish experience. How does that technique help her to connect with her readers?
2. What is the significance of the title?

...THE MANY FACES of THE BOTOX BABE...

HAPPY · SAD · WORRIED · EXCITED · DEPRESSED · ASLEEP

ANALYZING the Issue

How is Quindlen's attitude about her body and self-consciousness in the gym a product of a body-obsessed culture? How does what drives Quindlen to the gym resemble the fear that results in eating disorders, in chronic dissatisfaction with our physical selves?

ANALYZING Connections Between Texts

1. Both Quindlen and Stephen S. Hall ("The Bully in the Mirror," p. 207) see in the health club a means of obtaining the kind of body nature has failed to give us. In what regard is Alexander Bregstein's situation similar to Quindlen's? How is it different?

2. How does Quindlen both mock and affirm the social pressures Marge Piercy describes in "A Work of Artifice" (p. 160)?

3. In what way does Amy Foote, the woman doing oblique crunches in Arthur Grace's photograph (p. 95), resemble Anna Quindlen as she describes herself in "Stretch Marks"?

A Delicate Operation

BY ROY C. SELBY, JR.

ROY C. SELBY, JR.

Selby describes, step by step, delicate brain surgery and the risks involved. This article first appeared in Harper's Magazine *in 1975.*

In the autumn of 1973 a woman in her early fifties noticed, upon closing one eye while reading, that she was unable to see clearly. Her eyesight grew slowly worse. Changing her eyeglasses did not help. She saw an ophthalmologist, who found that her vision was seriously impaired in both eyes. She then saw a neurologist, who confirmed the finding and obtained X-rays of the skull and an EMI scan—a photograph of the patient's head. The latter revealed a tumor growing between the optic nerves at the base of the brain. The woman was admitted to the hospital by a neurosurgeon.

Further diagnosis, based on angiography, a detailed X-ray study of the circulatory system, showed the tumor to be about two inches in diameter and supplied by many small blood vessels. It rested beneath the brain, just above the pituitary gland, stretching the optic nerves to either side and intimately close to the major blood vessels supplying the brain. Removing it would pose many technical problems. Probably benign and slow-growing, it may have been present for several years. If left alone it would continue to grow and produce blindness and might become impossible to remove completely. Removing it, however, might not improve the patient's vision and could make it worse. A major blood vessel could be damaged, causing a stroke. Damage to the undersurface of the brain could cause impairment of memory and changes in mood and personality. The hypothalamus, a most important structure of the brain, could be injured, causing coma, high fever, bleeding from the stomach, and death.

The neurosurgeon met with the patient and her husband and discussed the various possibilities. The common decision was to operate.

The patient's hair was shampooed for two nights before surgery. She was given a cortisonelike drug to reduce the risk of damage to the brain during surgery. Five units of blood were cross-matched, as a contingency against hemorrhage. At 1:00 P.M. the operation began. After the patient was anesthetized, her hair was completely clipped and shaved from the scalp. Her head was prepped with an organic iodine solution for ten minutes. Drapes were placed over her, leaving exposed only the forehead and crown of the skull. All the routine instruments were brought up—the electrocautery used to coagulate areas of bleeding, bipolar coagulation forceps to arrest bleeding from individual blood vessels without damaging adjacent tissues, and small suction tubes to remove blood and cerebrospinal fluid from the head, thus giving the surgeon a better view of the tumor and surrounding areas.

A curved incision was made behind the hairline so it would be concealed when the hair grew back. It extended almost from ear to ear. Plastic clips were applied to the cut edges of the scalp to arrest bleeding. The scalp was folded back to the level of the eyebrows. Incisions were made in the muscle of the right temple, and three sets of holes were drilled near the temple and the top of the head because the tumor had to be approached from directly in front. The drill, powered by nitrogen, was replaced with a fluted steel blade, and the holes were connected. The incised piece of skull was pried loose and held out of the way by a large sponge.

Beneath the bone is a yellowish leatherlike membrane, the dura, that surrounds the brain. Down the middle of the head the dura carries a large vein, but in the area near the nose the vein is small. At that point the vein and dura were cut, and clips made of tantalum, a hard metal, were applied to arrest and prevent bleeding. Sutures were put into the dura and tied to the scalp to keep the dura open and retracted. A malleable silver retractor, resembling the blade of a butter knife, was inserted between the brain and skull. The anesthesiologist began to administer a drug to relax the brain by removing some of its water, making it easier for the surgeon to manipulate the retractor, hold the brain back, and see the tumor. The nerve tracts for smell were cut on both sides to provide additional room. The tumor was seen approximately two-and-one-half inches behind the base of the nose. It was pink in color. On touching it, it proved to be very fibrous and tough. A special retractor was attached to the skull, enabling the other retractor blades to be held automatically and freeing the surgeon's hands. With further displacement of the frontal lobes of the brain, the tumor could be seen better, but no normal structures—the carotid arteries, their branches, and the optic nerves—were visible. The tumor obscured them.

A surgical microscope was placed above the wound. The surgeon had select-ed the lenses and focal length prior to the operation. Looking through the microscope, he could see some of the small vessels supplying the tumor and he coagulated them. He incised the tumor to attempt to remove its core and thus collapse it, but the substance of the tumor was too firm to be removed in this fashion. He then began to slowly dissect the tumor from the adjacent brain tissue and from where he believed the normal structures to be.

Using small squares of cotton, he began to separate the tumor from very loose fibrous bands connecting it to the brain and to the right side of the part of the skull where the pituitary gland lies. The right optic nerve and carotid artery came into view, both displaced considerably to the right. The optic nerve had a normal appearance. He protected these structures with cotton compresses placed between them and the tumor. He began to raise the tumor from the skull and slowly to reach the point of its origin and attachment—just in front of the pituitary gland and medial to the left optic nerve, which still could not be seen. The small blood vessels entering the tumor were cauterized. The upper portion of the tumor was gradually separated from the brain, and the branches of the carotid arteries and the branches to the tumor were coagulated. The tumor was slowly and gently lifted from its bed, and for the first time the left carotid artery and optic nerve could be seen. Part of the tumor adhered to this nerve. The bulk of the tumor was amputated, leaving a small bit attached to the nerve. Very slowly and carefully the tumor fragment was resected.

The tumor now removed, a most impressive sight came into view—the pitu-itary gland and its stalk of attachment to the hypothalamus, the hypothalamus itself, and the brainstem, which conveys nerve impulses between the body and the brain. As far as could be determined, no damage had been done to these structures or other vital centers, but the left optic nerve, from chronic pressure of the tumor, appeared gray and thin. Probably it would not completely recov-er its function.

After making certain there was no bleeding, the surgeon closed the wounds [10] and placed wire mesh over the holes in the skull to prevent dimpling of the scalp over the points that had been drilled. A gauze dressing was applied to the patient's head. She was awakened and sent to the recovery room.

Even with the microscope, damage might still have occurred to the cerebral cortex and hypothalamus. It would require at least a day to be reasonably cer-tain there was none, and about seventy-two hours to monitor for the major postoperative dangers—swelling of the brain and blood clots forming over the surface of the brain. The surgeon explained this to the patient's husband, and both of them waited anxiously. The operation had required seven hours. A glass of orange juice had given the surgeon some additional energy during the closure of the wound. Though exhausted, he could not fall asleep until after two in the morning, momentarily expecting a call from the nurse in the inten-sive care unit announcing deterioration of the patient's condition.

At 8:00 A.M. the surgeon saw the patient in the intensive care unit. She was alert, oriented, and showed no sign of additional damage to the optic nerves or the brain. She appeared to be in better shape than the surgeon or her husband.

ANALYZING What the Writer Says

1. What is Selby's purpose in writing this essay?
2. List the places in Selby's essay that acknowledge human emotion.

ANALYZING How the Writer Says It

1. After two long paragraphs detailing the patient's symptoms, diagnosis, and considerable surgical risk, Selby concludes with the essay's shortest paragraph, writing that after consultation among patient, husband, and doctor, "The common decision was to operate." What is the effect of the succinct statement? What does it suggest about human nature?
2. The essay's tone is detached and clinical, with precise description of brain surgery. Is the essay's final sentence in keeping with the overall tone? Why or why not? What does it offer the reader that may have been inappropriate at some other point in the essay?

ANALYZING the Issue

Should doctors advise surgery when it is extremely risky and delicate? Should insurance companies be required to pay in such cases?

ANALYZING Connections Between Texts

1. Compare Selby's account of brain surgery to Keith D. Mano's description of plastic surgery (p. 238). What are the fundamental differences in the two writers' attitudes toward the procedures they witness?
2. Compare the description of brain surgery presented by Selby to that of Malcolm Gladwell in "The Physical Genius, (p. 765)" What do the two essays say about the writers' attitude toward brain surgery and the doctors performing it?
3. In what way does Max Aguilera-Hellweg's picture "Reaching for Help" (p. 103) illustrate the concept of a "delicate operation"? What aspect of medicine does the photographer include in his image that is absent from Selby's description?

WARMING UP: *Is there something about your looks that you perceive as flawed? What is it? Do you know anyone whose character or emotional life has been shaped by a physical scar?*

Beauty: When the Other Dancer Is the Self

BY ALICE WALKER

ALICE WALKER

Alice Walker (b. 1944) is probably best known for her novel The Color Purple *(1982); the following essay comes from her 1983 collection,* In Search of Our Mothers' Gardens. *Here she recalls mourning the loss of her childhood identity—being cute—to an accident that leaves her eye permanently scarred. She doesn't truly recover until her young daughter helps her discover the "world" in her eye.*

It is a bright summer day in 1974. My father, a fat, funny man with beautiful eyes and a subversive wit, is trying to decide which of his eight children he will take with him to the county fair. My mother, of course, will not go. She is knocked out from getting most of us ready: I hold my neck stiff against the pressure of her knuckles as she hastily completes the braiding and the beribboning of my hair.

My father is the driver for the rich old white lady up the road. Her name is Miss Mey. She owns all the land for miles around, as well as the house in which we live. All I remember about her is that she once offered to pay my mother thirty-five cents for cleaning her house, raking up piles of her magnolia leaves, and washing her family's clothes, and that my mother—she of no money, eight children, and a chronic earache—refused it. But I do not think of this in 1947. I am two and a half years old. I want to go everywhere my daddy goes. I am excited at the prospect of riding in a car. Someone has told me fairs are fun. That there is room in the car for only three of us doesn't faze me at all. Whirling happily in my starchy frock, showing off my biscuit-polished patent-leather shoes and lavender socks, tossing my head in a way that makes my ribbons bounce, I stand, hands on hips, before my father. "Take me, Daddy," I say with assurance; "I'm the prettiest!"

Later, it does not surprise me to find myself in Miss Mey's shiny black car, sharing the back seat with the other lucky ones. Does not surprise me that I thoroughly enjoy the fair. At home that night I tell the unlucky ones all I can remember about the merry-go-round, the man who eats live chickens, and the teddy bears, until they say: that's enough, baby Alice. Shut up now, and go to sleep.

It is Easter Sunday, 1950. I am dressed in a green, flocked, scalloped-hem dress (handmade by my adoring sister, Ruth) that has its own smooth satin petticoat and tiny hot-pink roses tucked into each scallop. My shoes, new T-strap patent leather, again highly biscuit-polished. I am six years old and have learned one of the longest Easter speeches to be heard that day, totally unlike the speech I said when I was two: "Easter lilies/pure and white/blossom in/the morning light." When I rise to give my speech I do so on a great wave of love and pride and expectation. People in the church stop rustling their new crinolines. They seem to hold their breath. I can tell they admire my dress, but it is my spirit, bordering on sassiness (womanishness), they secretly applaud.

"That girl's a little *mess*," they whisper to each other, pleased.   5

Naturally I say my speech without stammer or pause, unlike those who stutter, stammer, or, worst of all, forget. This is before the word "beautiful" exists in people's vocabulary, but "Oh, isn't she the *cutest* thing!" frequently floats my way." "And got so much sense!" they gratefully add . . . for which thoughtful addition I thank them this day.

> *It was great fun being cute. But then, one day, it ended.*

I am eight years old and a tomboy. I have a cowboy hat, cowboy boots, checkered shirt and pants, all red. My playmates are my brothers, two and four years older than I. Their colors are black and green, the only difference in the way we are dressed. On Saturday nights we all go to the picture show, even my mother; Westerns are her favorite kind of movie. Back home, "on the ranch," we pretend we are Tom Mix, Hopalong Cassidy, Lash LaRue (we've even named one of our dogs Lash LaRue); we chase each other for hours rustling cattle, being outlaws, delivering damsels from distress. Then my parents decide to buy my brothers guns. They are not "real" guns. They shoot "BBs," copper pellets my brothers say will kill birds. Because I am a girl, I do not get a gun. Instantly I am relegated to the position of Indian. Now there appears a great distance between us. They shoot and shoot at everything with their new guns. I try to keep up with my bow and arrows.

One day while I am standing on top of our makeshift "garage"—pieces of tin nailed across some poles—holding my bow and arrow and looking out toward the fields, I feel an incredible blow in my right eye. I look down just in time to see my brother lower his gun.

Both brothers rush to my side. My eyes sting, and I cover it with my hand. "If you tell," they say, "we will get a whipping. You don't want that to happen, do you?" I do not. "Here is a piece of wire," says the older brother, picking it up from the roof; "say you stepped on one end of it and the other flew up and hit you." The pain is beginning to start. "Yes," I say, "Yes, I will say that is what happened." If I do not say this is what happened, I know my brothers will find ways to make me wish I had. But now I will say anything that gets me to my mother.

Confronted by our parents we stick to the lie agreed upon. They place me on   10
a bench on the porch and I close my left eye while they examine the right. There is a tree growing from underneath the porch that climbs past the railing to the roof. It is the last thing my right eye sees. I watch as its trunk, its branches and then its leaves are blotted out by the rising blood.

I am in shock. First there is intense fever, which my father tries to break using lily leaves bound around my head. Then there are chills: my mother tries to get me to eat soup. Eventually, I do not know how, my parents learn what has happened. A week after the "accident" they take me to see a doctor. "Why did you wait so long to come?" he asks, looking into my eye and shaking his head. "Eyes are sympathetic," he says. "If one is blind, the other is likely to become blind too."

This comment of the doctor's terrifies me. But it is really how I look that bothers me the most. Where the BB pellet stuck there is a glob of whitish scar tissue, a hideous cataract, on my eye. Now when I stare at people—a favorite pastime, up to now—they will stare back. Not at the "cute" little girl, but at her scar. For six years I do not stare at anyone, because I do not raise my head.

Years later, in the throes of mid-life crisis, I ask my mother and sister whether I changed after the "accident." "No," they say, puzzled. "What do you mean?"

What do I mean?

I am eight, and for the first time, doing poorly in school, where I have been   15
something of a whiz since I was four. We have just moved to the place where the "accident" occurred. We do not know any of the people around us because this is a different county. The only time I see friends I knew is when we go back to our old church. The new school is the former state penitentiary. It is a large stone building, cold and drafty, crammed to overflowing with boisterous, ill-disciplined children. On the third floor there is a huge circular imprint of some partition that has been torn out.

"What used to be here?" I ask a sullen girl next to me on our way past it to lunch.

"The electric chair," says she.

At night, I have nightmares about the electric chair, and about all the people reputedly "fried" in it. I am afraid of the school, where all the students seem to be budding criminals.

"What's the matter with your eye?" they ask, critically.

When I don't answer (I cannot decide whether it was an "accident" or not), they shove me, insist on a fight.   20

My brother, the one who created the story about the wire, comes to my rescue. But then brags so much about "protecting" me, I become sick.

After months of torture at the school, my parents decide to send me back to our old community, to my old school. I live with my grandparents and the teacher they board. But there is no room for Phoebe, my cat. By the time my grandparents decide there *is* room, and I ask for my cat, she cannot be found. Miss Yarborough, the boarding teacher, takes me under her wing, and begins to teach me to play the piano. But soon she marries an African—a "prince," she says—and is whisked away to his continent.

At my old school there is at least one teacher who loves me. She is the teacher who "knew me before I was born" and bought my first baby clothes. It is she who makes life bearable. It is her presence that finally helps me turn on the one child at the school who continually calls me "one-eyed bitch." One day I simply grab him by the coat and beat him until I am satisfied. It is my teacher who tells me my mother is ill.

My mother is lying in bed in the middle of the day, something I have never seen. She is in too much pain to speak. She has an abscess in her ear. I stand looking down on her, knowing that if she dies, I cannot live. She is being treated with warm oils and hot bricks held against her cheek. Finally a doctor comes. But I must go back to my grandparents' house. The weeks pass but I am hardly aware of it. All I know is that my mother might die, my father is not so jolly, my brothers still have their guns, and I am the one sent away from home.

"You did not change," they say.   25

Did I imagine the anguish of never looking up?

I am twelve. When relatives come to visit I hide in my room. My cousin Brenda, just my age, whose father works in the post office and whose mother is a nurse, comes to find me. "Hello," she says. And then she asks, looking at my recent school picture, which I did not want taken, and on which the "glob" as I think of it, is clearly visible, "You still can't see out of that eye?"

"No," I say, and flop back on the bed over my book.

That night, as I do almost every night, I abuse my eye. I rant and rave at it, in front of the mirror. I plead with it to clear up before morning. I tell it I hate and despise it. I do not pray for sight. I pray for beauty.

"You did not change," they say.   30

*　*　*

I am fourteen and baby-sitting for my brother Bill, who lives in Boston. He is my favorite brother and there is a strong bond between us. Understanding my feelings of shame and ugliness he and his wife take me to a local hospital, where the "glob" is removed by a doctor named O. Henry. There is still a small bluish crater where the scar tissue was, but the ugly white stuff is gone. Almost immediately I become a different person from the girl who does not want to raise her head. Or so I think. Now that I've raised my head I win the boyfriend of my dreams. Now that I've raised my head I have plenty of friends. Now that I've raised my head classwork comes from my lips as faultlessly as Easter speeches did, and I leave high school as valedictorian, most popular student, and *queen*, hardly believing my luck. Ironically, the girl who was voted most beautiful in our class (and was) was later shot twice through the chest by a male companion, using a "real" gun, while she was pregnant. But that's another story in itself. Or is it?

"You did not change," they say.

It is now thirty years since the "accident." A beautiful journalist comes to visit and to interview me. She is going to write a cover story for her magazine that focuses on my latest book. "Decide how you want to look on the cover," she says. "Glamorous, or whatever."

Never mind "glamorous," it is the "whatever" that I hear. Suddenly all I can think of is whether I will get enough sleep the night before the photography session: if I don't, my eye will be tired and wander, as blind eyes will.

At night in bed with my lover I think up reasons why I should not appear on the cover of a magazine. "My meanest critics will say I've sold out," I say. "My family will now realize I write scandalous books."   35

"But what's the real reason you don't want to do this?" he asks.

"Because in all probability," I say in a rush, "my eye won't be straight."

"It will be straight enough," he says. Then, "Besides, I thought you'd made your peace with that."

And I suddenly remember that I have.

I remember: 40

I am talking to my brother, Jimmy, asking if he remembers anything unusual about the day I was shot. He does not know I consider that day the last time my father, with his sweet home remedy of cool lily leaves, chose me, and that I suffered and raged inside because of this. "Well," he says, "all I remember is standing by the side of the highway with Daddy, trying to flag down a car. A white man stopped, but when Daddy said he needed somebody to take his little girl to the doctor, he drove off."

I remember:

I am in the desert for the first time. I fall totally in love with it. I am so overwhelmed by its beauty, I confront for the first time, consciously, the meaning of the doctor's words years ago: "Eyes are sympathetic. If one is blind, the other will likely become blind too." I realize I have dashed about the world madly, looking at this, looking at that, storing up images against the fading of the light. *But I might have missed seeing the desert!* The shock of that possibility —and gratitude for over twenty-five years of sight—sends me literally to my knees. Poem after poem comes—which is perhaps how poets pray.

On Sight

I am so thankful I have seen
The Desert
And the creatures in the desert
And the desert Itself.   45

The desert has its own moon
Which I have seen
With my own eye.
There is no flag on it.

Trees of the desert have arms   50
All of which are always up
That is because the moon is up

The sun is up
Also the sky
The stars   55

Clouds
None with flags

If there *were* flags, I doubt
the trees would point.
Would you?   60

But mostly, I remember this:

I am twenty-seven, and my baby daughter is almost three. Since her birth I have worried about her discovery that her mother's eyes are different from other people's. Will she be embarrassed? I think. What will she say? Every day she watches a television program called "Big Blue Marble." It begins with a picture of the earth as it appears from the moon. It is bluish, a little battered-looking, but full of light, with whitish clouds swirling around it. Every time I see it I weep with love, as if it is a picture of Grandma's house. One day when I am putting Rebecca down for her nap, she suddenly focuses on my eye. Something inside me cringes, gets ready to try to protect myself. All children are cruel about physical differences, I know from experience, and that they don't always mean to be is another matter. I assume Rebecca will be the same.

But no-o-o-o. She studies my face intently as we stand, her inside and me outside her crib. She even holds my face maternally between her dimpled little hands. Then, looking every bit as serious and lawyer-like as her father, she says, as if it may just possibly have slipped my attention: "Mommy, there's a *world* in your eye." (As in, "Don't be alarmed, or do anything crazy.") And then, gently, but with great interest: "Mommy, where did you *get* that world in your eye?"

For the most part, the pain left then. (So what, if my brothers grew up to buy even more powerful pellet guns for their sons and to carry real guns themselves. So what, if a young "Morehouse man"[1] once nearly fell off the steps of Trevor Arnett Library because he thought my eyes were blue.) Crying and laughing I ran to the bathroom, while Rebecca mumbled and sang herself to sleep. Yes indeed, I realized, looking into the mirror. There *was* a world in my eye. And I saw that it was possible to love it: that in fact, for all it had taught me of shame and anger and inner vision, I *did* love it. Even to see it drifting out of orbit in boredom, or rolling up out of fatigue, not to mention floating back at attention in excitement (bearing witness, a friend has called it), deeply suitable to my personality, and even characteristic of me.

That night I dream I am dancing to Stevie Wonder's song "Always" (the name of the song is really "As," but I hear it as "Always"). As I dance, whirling and joyous, happier than I've ever been in my life, another bright-faced dancer joins me. We dance and kiss each other and hold each other through the night. The other dancer has obviously come through all right, as I have done. She is beautiful, whole and free. And she is also me. 65

ANALYZING What the Writer Says

1. What, besides unmarred beauty, does the writer lose after her accident?
2. Cite examples from the essay to illustrate how the writer's sense of luck and success and love are linked to her sense of her beauty.
3. As a teenager, Walker has the scar tissue removed from her eye, minimizing her scar and restoring her confidence. What triggers her insecurity, briefly, years later? What squelches it?
4. What is the point of the author's digression about her classmate who was "voted most beautiful" but later was shot, while pregnant, by a boyfriend?
5. When Walker's daughter says, "Mommy, there's a *world* in your eye," she speaks literally but offers Walker a metaphor for the ways her physical imperfection has shaped her experience. What significance is attached to "*world* in your eye"?

---

[1]A student at Morehouse College in Atlanta, Georgia. (Editor's note)

ANALYZING | How the Writer Says It

1. Walker uses a series of flashbacks ("It is . . . 1947"; "I am eight years old"; "I am fourteen") to chronicle her journey from cute child to scarred adolescent to confident adult. What does this technique contribute to the telling that straight narration might not?

2. What does the subtitle mean?

3. What is the significance of the refrain of the writer's mother and sister, "You did not change."

4. What is the significance of the italicized phrases and sentences?

ANALYZING | the Issue

After her accident, Walker prays for beauty rather than sight. Why is that reaction understandable in our culture?

ANALYZING | Connections Between Texts

1. Alice Walker describes how, due to the sudden loss of her childhood "cuteness," she is forced to redefine herself and the way she sees her body. Compare the ways Walker, Alexander Bregstein (in Stephen S. Hall's "The Bully in the Mirror," p. 207) and Anna Quindlen (in "Stretch Marks," p. 242) address their body issues.

2. In "Beauty on the DNA Auction Block" (p. 413), Ellen Goodman discusses how the importance of physical attractiveness in our society has led some people to consider ethically questionable maneuvers in order to give their children the advantage of beauty. What do you think Alice Walker would tell parents considering genetic manipulation to ensure their unborn children's beauty?

3. Annie Leibovitz's portraits of Lenda Murray (p. 97) and Cheryl Haworth (p. 260) show female bodies that do not conform to the Barbie-doll ideal. In what way does the photographer share Alice Walker's ideas about female beauty?

YOUR TURN: Suggestions for Writing About "Body Politics"

1. Are there moral and ethical reasons that doctors shouldn't perform autopsies? Or do you agree with Atul Gawande's position? Write an essay in which you argue for or against routine autopsies.

2. Body-image disorders in young girls, such as anorexia and bulimia, have been widely studied. Hall alerts us to similar problems in young boys. Does your experience support his observations? Write an essay in which you show how crucial a muscular body is for teenage boys in our culture.

3. Is trying to alter one's body through diet, exercise, or plastic surgery a sign of subservience to a commercial ideal of beauty? After considering your own experience and some of the essays in this unit, write an essay in which you discuss why it is or is not important for women to look a certain way.

4. Several articles in this unit talk about "body modification," the (temporary or permanent) altering of one's look through tattoos, body piercing, and the like. Write an essay in which you analyze why so many young people today participate in "bod mod."

5. Given the popularity of tattoos and body piercing among young people, do you still consider them a sign of rebellion? Write an essay in which you examine the degrees of social acceptability in different kinds of body modification.

6. Should employers dictate the ways in which individuals adorn their bodies by insisting that tattoos be covered or nose rings be removed before employees come to work? Write an employment policy arguing why such steps are necessary.

7. Compare the ways in which Alice Walker and Natalie Kusz deal with the physical imperfections that result from accidents in early childhood. In your essay analyze the similarities and differences in the two women's attitudes toward their bodies.

8. Using the Calvin Klein spoof ads included in this unit as a springboard, write an essay in which you analyze destructive trends in advertising, particularly where the body is concerned.

9. Write an essay in which you analyze the growing industry in medical and surgical procedures—botox injections, liposuction, etc.—to alter appearance and fight the aging process.

IMAGE GALLERY 👁

BLACK-AND-WHITE PORTFOLIO

COLOR PORTFOLIO

ANNIE LEIBOVITZ

Cheryl Haworth

Acclaimed for her work in Rolling Stone *and* Vanity Fair, *Annie Leibovitz is best known for her edgy celebrity portraits. This photograph of Cheryl Haworth appears in her 1999 book* Women. *According to* Women, *Haworth, who holds records in several weight lifting disciplines, is "the strongest woman weight lifter in the United States."*

1. How do you read Cheryl Haworth's facial expression in this photograph?

2. Leibovitz chose to have Ms. Haworth pose as she is about to lift a massive barbell. How does the young woman's posture—and the composition of the image—contribute to the overall effect of the picture?

3. What commentary do you think Leibovitz intends with this photograph?

4. Compare this photograph to Leibovitz's portrait of bodybuilder Lenda Murray (p. 97). What are the major differences between these two pictures? How do the bodies of these two athletes jibe with social expectations of what women's bodies should look like?

ANNIE LEIBOVITZ

Sidney Silver

Famous for her brash, often startling portraits, Annie Leibovitz included this photograph of Sidney "Squid" Silver, an actress, tattoo artist, and founding member and bass player for the Lunachicks, in her 1999 collection, Women.

1. If you had never have heard of the Lunachicks, what kind of music would you guess the band plays? What details in the photograph suggest clues?

2. What do Sidney Silver's facial expression and her body language say about her?

3. How does Leibovitz's choice of black and white contribute to the effect of the photograph? How would the picture have been different if she had shot it in color?

4. Comment on the effectiveness of composition in this photograph.

NORMAN ROCKWELL

Girl at the Mirror

This picture of a girl gazing at herself in the mirror, by popular American painter and illustrator Norman Rockwell (1894–1978), appeared on the March 6, 1954, cover of The Saturday Evening Post.

1. What do the girl's facial expression and body language reveal about her attitude about what she sees in the mirror?
2. What is the function of the magazine in the girl's lap?
3. What do the girl's clothes and the objects surrounding her—the doll, the brush, the lipstick—contribute to the image?
4. What is Rockwell's point in this picture? Does his 1954 message strike you as dated today? Why or why not?

ADBUSTERS

Spoof ads

Adbusters, a Canadian organization working to make us aware of the power of advertising, lampoons enormously successful Calvin Klein campaigns in these two spoof ads.

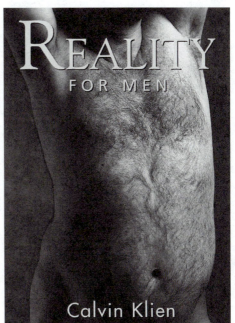

1. What does the "Obsession" spoof ad have in common with the original advertising campaign?
2. What is the young woman in the "Obsession" spoof ad doing? Why?
3. What commentary is Adbusters making in the "Obsession" spoof ad? How is the name of the product used ironically in this context? At whom or what is the satire directed?

4. What is your reaction to the "Reality for Men" ad? Why? Is your reaction to this spoof ad different from your feelings about the "Obsession" ad?
5. What message does Adbusters convey in the "Reality for Men" spoof ad? How does it differ from that in the "Obsession" ad?

11 APPETITES AND ADDICTIONS

An obesity epidemic, high rates of alcohol and drug abuse, and relentless smoking even as the tobacco-dependent have been exiled to the street all suggest that the line between appetite and addiction is a very fine one. For reasons not fully

> "A well governed appetite is the greater part of liberty."
>
> —Lucius Annaeus Seneca
> *Letters from a Stoic*

understood—perhaps psychological, physical, environmental, or even genetic—some of us cannot stop feeding our hungers despite sometimes serious consequences.

Enslaved by their appetites, addicts, of whatever type, often wreak havoc in their personal lives, for their addictions control not just them but their families, as Scott Russell Sanders recalls in a poignant account of his father's alcoholism. Renee Graham wonders if Hollywood can resist glamorizing cigarette smoking in films, while Stanton Peele argues that fear tactics, fueled by flawed views of addiction as "disease," are ineffective in the treatment of adolescent substance abuse. As Eric Schlosser sees it, a whole nation has been changed by the fast food industry—if not addicted to its product. Sure to *suppress* appetites is the U.S. Food and Drug Administration list, included here, of unacceptable food contamination levels.

The flip side of appetite, however, is pleasure. Satisfying our cravings, whether for cigarettes or chocolate, makes us happy, at least temporarily. The preparation of and enjoyment of food involves more than the satisfaction of physical hunger: culinary rituals feed the psyche and the soul. In the following pages, Billy Collins, Laurie Colwin, and Calvin Trillin celebrate food for its comfort, its sensuality, its social and cultural currency.

Our appetite for food and drink is surely linked to our appetite for love and warmth, our yearning for contentment, so it is no wonder that so many people overindulge. For those able to strike a balance, however, to satisfy desires without becoming prisoners to them, the reward is great. As Shakespeare tells us in *The Merchant of Venice*, "He is well paid that is well satisfied." ❖

WARMING UP: *Can you remember meals that have satisfied you in ways that have gone well beyond the alleviation of hunger? If so, what sorts of feelings did they inspire in you?*

Osso Buco

BY BILLY COLLINS

BILLY COLLINS
A popular and critically acclaimed poet, Billy Collins has authored several collections of poems. In his service as America's Poet Laureate, a post to which he was appointed in 2001, Collins, a Professor of English at City University of New York, launched Poetry 180, *a program designed to let school students hear one poem each day. He ponders the meaning of pleasure and contentment in "Osso Buco," from his 1995* The Art of Drowning.

I love the sound of the bone against the plate
and the fortress-like look of it
lying before me in a moat of risotto,
the meat soft as the leg of an angel
who has lived a purely airborne existence.   5
And best of all, the secret marrow,
the invaded privacy of the animal
prized out with a knife and swallowed down
with cold, exhilarating wine.

I am swaying now in the hour after dinner,   10
a citizen tilted back on his chair,
a creature with a full stomach—
something you don't hear much about in poetry,
that sanctuary of hunger and deprivation.
You know: the driving rain, the boots by the door,   15
small birds searching for berries in winter.

But tonight, the lion of contentment
has placed a warm, heavy paw on my chest,
and I can only close my eyes and listen

to the drums of woe throbbing in the distance   20
and the sound of my wife's laughter
on the telephone in the next room,
the woman who cooked the savory osso buco,
who pointed to show the butcher the ones she wanted.
She who talks to her faraway friend   25
while I linger here at the table
with a hot, companionable cup of tea,
feeling like one of the friendly natives,
a reliable guide, maybe even the chief's son.

Somewhere, a man is crawling up a rocky hillside   30
on bleeding knees and palms, an Irish penitent
carrying the stone of the world in his stomach;
and elsewhere people of all nations stare
at one another across a long, empty table.

But here, the candles give off their warm glow,   35
the same light that Shakespeare and Izaac Walton wrote by,
the light that lit and shadowed the faces of history.
Only now it plays on the blue plates,
the crumpled napkins, the crossed knife and fork.

In a while, one of us will go up to bed   40
and the other one will follow.
Then we will slip below the surface of the night
into miles of water, drifting down and down
to the dark, soundless bottom
until the weight of dreams pulls us lower still,   45
below the shale and layered rock,
beneath the strata of hunger and pleasure,
into the broken bones of the earth itself,
into the marrow of the only place we know.

ANALYZING What the Writer Says

1. In a phrase, describe the speaker's feelings.

2. What, according to the speaker, is unusual about this poem? Of what reality is he only vaguely aware?

3. What do you think the speaker is talking about when he refers in the last line to "the marrow of the only place we know"?

ANALYZING How the Writer Says It

1. Collins relies heavily on contrasting images in "Osso Buco." Point to several examples of contrast.

2. Point to images of the jungle or the hunt in the poem. Why do you think Collins uses these images? How does he manipulate the images to serve the purposes of the poem?

3. Identify words and phrases Collins uses to introduce the element of guilt into the poem.

ANALYZING the Issue

Collins brings up the issue of guilt—and seems to reject it. Do you think enjoyment and contentment are guilty indulgences when there is so much starvation, deprivation, and suffering in the world? Explain.

ANALYZING Connections Between Texts

1. In "How to Fry Chicken" (p. 269) Laurie Colwin describes what for her is clearly an important ritual. How does Collins capture the importance of ritual in his poem?

2. In "The Steep Cliffs of Life" (p. 126), William C. Brisick often mentions the food and drink he shared with his son in their travels. Consider the ways in which Collins and Brisick suggest food's psychic, as well as physical, nourishment.

3. Chris Johns's photograph of a family surveying an array of red meat (p. 98) suggests the unapologetic carnivorous quality of the average family. Compare Collins's treatment of carnivorousness in "Osso Buco."

How to Fry Chicken

BY LAURIE COLWIN

LAURIE COLWIN

After a successful career in publishing, in which she edited and translated the works of Isaac Bashevis Singer, Laurie Colwin (1944–92) became a successful novelist whose opinionated food writing won her many additional admirers. In "How to Fry Chicken," which first appeared as one of her columns in Gourmet, *Colwin pronounces on the "correct method" of preparing an American classic.*

As everyone knows, there is only one way to fry chicken correctly. Unfortunately, most people think their method is best, but most people are wrong. Mine is the only right way, and on this subject I feel almost evangelical.

It is not that I am a bug on method—I am fastidious about results. Fried chicken must have a crisp, deep (but not too deep) crust. It must be completely cooked, yet juicy and tender. These requirements sound minimal, but achieving them requires technique. I have been frying chicken according to the correct method for about ten years, and I realize that this skill improves over time. The last batch fried was far, far better than the first. The lady who taught my sister and me, a black woman who cooked for us in Philadelphia, was of course the apotheosis: no one will ever be fit to touch the top of her chicken fryer.

I have had all kinds of nasty fried chicken served to me, usually with great flourish: crisp little baby shoes or hockey pucks turned out by electric frying machines with names such as Little Fry Guy. Beautifully golden morsels completely raw on the inside. Chicken that has been fried and put into the fridge, giving the crust the texture of a wet paper towel.

I have also had described to me Viennese fried chicken, which involves egg and bread crumbs and is put in the oven after frying and drizzled with butter. It sounds very nice, but it is *not* fried chicken.

To fry chicken that makes people want to stand up and sing "The Star-   5
Spangled Banner," the following facts of life must be taken seriously.

- Fried chicken should be served warm. It should never be eaten straight
  from the fryer—it needs time to cool down and set. Likewise, fried
  chicken must never see the inside of a refrigerator because this turns
  the crisp into something awful and cottony.
- Contrary to popular belief, fried chicken should not be deep-fried.
- Anyone who says you merely shake up the chicken in a bag with flour
  is fooling himself. (More on this later.)
- Fried chicken must be made in a chicken fryer—a steep-sided frying
  pan with a domed top.
- It must never be breaded or coated with anything except flour (which
  can be spiced with salt, pepper and paprika). No egg, no crumbs, no
  crushed Rice Krispies.

Now that the basics have been stated, the preparation is the next step. The
chicken pieces should be roughly the same size—this means that the breast is
cut into quarters. The breast is the hardest to cook just right as it tends to get
dry. People who don't quarter the breast usually end up with either a large,
underdone half, or they overcompensate and fry it until it resembles beef jerky.

The chicken should be put in a dish and covered with a little water or milk.
This will help to keep the flour on. Let the chicken stand at room temperature.
It is not a good thing to put cold raw chicken into hot oil.

Meanwhile, the flour should be put into a deep, wide bowl, with salt, pepper
and paprika added to taste. I myself adore paprika and feel it gives the chick-
en a smoky taste and a beautiful color.

To coat the chicken, lay a few pieces at a time in the bowl and pack the flour
on as if you were a child making sand pies. Any excess flour should be packed
between the layers. It is important to make sure that every inch of chicken has
a nice thick cover. Now heat the oil and let the chicken sit.

And now to the frying. There are people who say, and probably correctly, that   10
chicken should be fried in lard and Crisco, but I am not one of these people.
Fried food is bad enough for you. I feel it should not be made worse. The lady
who taught me swore by Wesson oil, and I swear by it, too, with the addition
of about one-fourth part of light sesame oil. This gives a wonderful taste and
is worth the added expense. It also helps to realize that both oils are polyun-
saturated in case one cannot fry without guilt.

The oil should come up to just under the halfway mark of your chicken fryer.
Heat it slowly until a piece of bread on a skewer fries as soon as you dip it. If
it does, you are ready to start.

Carefully slip into the oil as many pieces as will fit. The rule is to crowd a little. Turn down the heat at once and *cover*. The idea of covering frying chicken

makes many people squeal, but it is the only correct method. It gets the chick-en cooked through. Remember that the chicken must be just done—juicy and crisp. About six minutes or so per side—and you must turn it once—is prob-ably about right, although dark meat takes a little longer. A sharp fork makes a good tester.

When the chicken just slips off the fork, it is done inside. Take the cover off, turn up the heat, and fry it to the color of Colonial pine stain—a dark honey color. Set it on a platter and put it in the oven. If your oven is gas, there is no need for any more warmth than that provided by the pilot light. If electric, turn it up a lit-tle in advance and then turn it off. You have now made perfect fried chicken.

And you have suffered. There are many disagreeable things about frying chicken. No matter how careful you are, flour gets all over everything and the oil splatters far beyond the stove. It is impossible to fry chicken without burn-ing yourself at least once. For about twenty-four hours your house smells of fried chicken. This is nice only during dinner and then begins to pall. Waking up to the smell of cooking fat is not wonderful.

Furthermore, frying chicken is just about the most boring thing you can do.   15 You can't read while you do it. Music is drowned out by constant sizzling. Finally, as you fry you are consumed with the realization that fried food is ter-rible for you, even if you serve it only four times a year.

But the rewards are many, and when you appear with your platter your fam-ily and friends greet you with cries of happiness. Soon your table is full of ecstat-ic eaters, including, if you are lucky, some delirious Europeans—the British are especially impressed by fried chicken. As the cook you get to take the pieces you like best. As for me, I snag the backs, those most neglected and delectable bits, and I do it without a trace of remorse. After all, I did the cooking.

Not only have you mastered a true American folk tradition, but you know that next time will be even better.

ANALYZING What the Writer Says

1. What are the characteristics of properly fried chicken, according to Colwin?

2. Why do you think Colwin maintains that there is only one *right* way to fry chicken?

3. What associations, other than with simple tastiness, does correctly fried chicken have for Colwin?

ANALYZING How the Writer Says It

1. Colwin opens her essay with a pronouncement: "As everyone knows, there is only one way to fry chicken correctly." How does she maintain her authoritative tone throughout the piece? Point to examples.

2. How does Colwin temper or lighten her authoritative tone?

"I'm not eating. I'm self-medicating."

ANALYZING the Issue

How important are rules and ritual in "classic" preparations?

ANALYZING Connections Between Texts

1. Compare and contrast Colwin's piece to Calvin Trillin's exposé on Cajun boudin (p. 317). What attitudes toward food do the two authors share? How are they different?

2. Compare Colwin's piece to Roy Selby, Jr.'s "A Delicate Operation" (p. 246). How are their analyses of a process similar? Different?

3. How do Colwin's notions of domesticity conflict with the image of domesticity Timothy Greenfield-Sanders captures in his photograph "Be It Ever So Humble" (p. 119)?

WARMING UP: *How do (old) Hollywood movies depict characters who smoke? Which actors or actresses are hard to imagine without their cigarettes? What message about smoking did their characters (or their creators) send?*

Can Hollywood Kick the Habit?

BY RENEE GRAHAM

RENEE GRAHAM

A staff writer for the Globe, Renee Graham asks whether Hollywood script writers (such as newly reformed nonsmoker Joe Eszterhas) should stop glamorizing smoking in their movies. This essay first appeared in 2002.

In one of my favorite scenes from one of my favorite movies, "The Great Escape," wily prisoner of war James Garner sidles up to gullible German guard Robert Graf. Blowing cigarette smoke in the guard's direction—Graf practically swoons in the cloud—Garner offers Graf a cigarette, then slides a few more into the chest pocket of the guard's uniform. Accepting the cigarettes could be viewed as fraternizing, yet they are a pleasure these two men, made enemies by war, can share. Soon the two are talking casually in the lazy haze of smoke.

Garner intends to bribe and blackmail the guard, but it all plays as if Garner were picking Graf up in a bar. For all intents and purposes, it's a subtle seduction scene, and one that would not have been as persuasive without the cigarettes.

And therein lies the problem.

In reality, smoking is a nasty addiction linked to a bevy of medical problems. Yet in Hollywood, tobacco products remain a favorite prop. In scripted scenes, they serve as accent marks and exclamation points. For actors, they are as character-defining as a lisp or a way of walking—try to imagine Humphrey Bogart without a cigarette dangling from his lips.

In a century of moviemaking, cigarettes have made tangible the doomed cool of James Dean, the carnivorous conniving of Bette Davis, and the urbane 5 sophistication of superspy James Bond. When Olivia Newton-John's virginal Sandy in "Grease" turns teased and Spandex-clad bad girl, a cigarette becomes a potent accessory. And in 1992's "Basic Instinct," Sharon Stone became a star as the underwear-averse femme fatale who, when told by police she's not allowed to smoke in an interrogation room, utters the line, "What are you going to do? Charge me with smoking?"

That line was written by Joe Eszterhas, once a self-described "militant smoker." Now, the screenwriter, stricken with throat cancer 18 months ago, is challenging Hollywood to finally kick the habit.

In a *New York Times* opinion piece, Eszterhas wrote, "Smoking was an integral part of many of my screenplays because I was a militant smoker. It was part of a bad-boy image I'd cultivated for a long time—smoking, drinking, partying, rock 'n' roll." By featuring smoking in his films, including "Flashdance" and "Jagged Edge," Eszterhas said, "I have been an accomplice to the murders of untold numbers of human beings. I am admitting this only because I have made a deal with God. Spare me, I said, and I will try to stop others from committing the same crimes I did."

It's easy to be cynical, even dismissive, about Eszterhas's epiphany—this, after all, is the man who wrote "Showgirls." But he makes a salient point. At a time when cities are considering smoking bans in all public establishments, Hollywood remains tantalized by tobacco. In such recent films as "In the Bedroom," "The Royal Tennenbaums," and "Vanilla Sky," characters smoke like chimneys.

According to a 2001 study by the University of California at San Francisco, cigarette products appeared in 1990s films an average of every three to five minutes, as compared with every 10 to 15 minutes in movies from the 1970s and 1980s. In a random sampling of top box-office hits between 1990 and 1996, researchers found that 57 percent of lead characters smoked.

Certainly, Hollywood should curb its love affair with tobacco. But then there are lots of things Hollywood should do—such as create more meaningful roles for women and people of color, and convince 72-year-old Clint Eastwood to stop doing love scenes with women less than half his age.

So far there hasn't been a chorus of voices joining Eszterhas in condemning on-screen smoking, although Rob Reiner, who directed 1986's "Stand by Me," which features a prominent scene with a quartet of prepubescent boys smoking, is now an outspoken antismoking advocate.

It's unfortunate, but hardly surprising. Hollywood types may pride themselves on having a ready eye and ear for trends, but they're usually slow to recognize and respond to social changes—for example, there wasn't a major studio film about AIDS until 1993's "Philadelphia," 11 years into the epidemic.

With the fervor of a revival tent preacher, Eszterhas has proclaimed that his "hands are bloody" and "so are Hollywood's." Now the same town that offered Eszterhas millions for mediocre scripts has all but ignored the most meaningful words he's ever written. Eszterhas may have had an about-face, but right now it seems pretty unlikely that on-screen smoking will ever go up in smoke.

Still, it's worth remembering that the same cigarettes that helped define Bogart's iconic cool and world-weary insouciance for generations also killed him, when he died from throat cancer in 1957.

ANALYZING What the Writer Says

1. How has Hollywood influenced the way we view cigarette smoking?

2. Who is Joe Eszterhas? What is his crusade?

3. What does Graham think about the likelihood that Hollywood will become instrumental in curbing nicotine addiction?

ANALYZING How the Writer Says It

1. Graham starts her essay by describing movie clips featuring smokers. How do these descriptions make the introduction more effective?

2. How does the last paragraph of the essay relate to the introduction?

ANALYZING the Issue

Do you think the movie and television industry should make an effort to show the reality of nicotine addiction rather than glamorize smoking? Why or why not?

ANALYZING Connections Between Texts

1. Read Stanton Peele's "Running Scared" (p. 279) What would Peele say about Eszterhas's demand that Hollywood "kick its habit"?

2. In "Ozzy Without Harriet: What *The Osbournes* Tells Us About Drugs" (p. 704), Jonah Goldberg maintains that the popular reality show effectively warns the young MTV audience about the dangers of drugs. Do you think the popular media actually influence viewers about dangerous addictive behavior? Explain. Would Goldberg agree with Graham's point? Why or why not?

3. How does the poster distributed in 1918 by the Our Boys in France Tobacco Fund ("I Need Smokes More than Anything Else," p. 326) illustrate the issue Graham raises?

WARMING UP: *Did you ever find anything or hear about someone who found something in a commercial food product that had no business there—a hair, maybe, or a dead insect? Did it make you wonder about the kinds of controls established to prevent such things from happening?*

Passed by a Hair

PASSED BY A HAIR

According to the October 2002 edition of Harper's Magazine, *the following piece is taken from "The Food Defect Action Levels," "a guide published by the U.S. Food and Drug Administration listing unacceptable contamination levels for food products."*

APPLE BUTTER
Average of 4 or more rodent hairs per 100 grams of apple butter

ASPARAGUS, CANNED OR FROZEN
Ten percent by count of spears or pieces are infested with 6 or more attached asparagus beetle eggs and/or sacs

BERRIES, CANNED AND FROZEN
Average mold count is 60 percent or more
Average of 4 or more larvae per 500 grams
Average of 10 or more whole insects or equivalent per 500 grams

CHERRIES, BRINED AND MARASCHINO
Average of 5 percent or more pieces are rejects due to maggots

CHERRIES, FRESH, CANNED, OR FROZEN
Average of 4 percent or more pieces are rejects due to insects other than maggots

COCOA BEANS
Average of 10 milligrams or more mammalian excreta per pound

CURRANTS
Five percent or more wormy in the average of the subsamples

5

FIG PASTE
Contains 13 or more insect heads per 100 grams of fig paste in each of two or more subsamples

FISH, FRESH OR FROZEN
Sixty parasitic cysts per 100 fish
Three percent of the fillets examined contain one or more copepods accompanied by pus pockets

PLUMS, CANNED
Average of 5 percent or more plums with rot spots larger than the area of a circle 12 millimeters in diameter

POPCORN
Twenty or more gnawed grains per pound and rodent hair is found in 50 percent or more of the subsamples

TOMATO PASTE, PIZZA, AND OTHER SAUCES
Average of 30 or more fly eggs per 100 grams

WHEAT
Average of 9 milligrams or more rodent excreta pellets and/or pellet fragments per kilogram

ANALYZING | What the Writer Says

The list presented in this piece details *unacceptable* contamination levels in food products. What does this list say about the food industry in general?

ANALYZING | How the Writer Says It

Harper's published this piece without further comment other than a brief explanation of its provenance. What effect does the editors' choice *not* to say anything about it have on the audience?

ANALYZING | the Issue

1. Would you just as soon not have read this list of what's unacceptable in commercial food? Why or why not?
2. Is food contamination an unavoidable side effect of food preparation? How would "homecooking" eliminate the risk of contamination?

"Yes, but take away the rodent droppings and the occasional shard of glass, and you've still got a damn fine product."

ANALYZING Connections Between Texts

1. Do you think food enthusiasts like Calvin Trillin ("Missing Links," p. 317) are aware of contamination issues? Is their belief in the natural goodness of ethnic food naive? Or are food purists too sensitive about contamination issues?

2. Consider William Lutz's "Weasel Words" (p. 661) in light of publications such as the Food and Drug Administration's "The Food Defect Action Levels." How might advertisers such as those employing the techniques described by Lutz use it to advertise food that is contaminated, but not "unacceptabl[y]" so?

3. How does Jack Ziegler's cartoon (above) illustrate the issue raised in "Passed By a Hair"? What does the cartoon say about the food industry's attitude toward contamination?

WARMING UP: *Do you think "Just Say No" and abstinence approaches to fighting drug abuse in adolescents work?*

Running Scared

By STANTON PEELE

STANTON PEELE

Social psychologist and attorney Stanton Peele has authored several books on the nature of addiction, among them the widely read and controversial Diseasing of America: Addiction Treatment Out of Control, *in which he argues that the conventional wisdom on treating addictive behaviors—including that of popular twelve-step programs—is scientifically flawed and fueled by social denial of the root causes of addiction.*

ABSTRACT

Contemporary America is obsessed with self destructive drug and alcohol use. However, our policies are based entirely on erroneous epidemiological, pharmacological and clinical beliefs about drug use and alcoholism. Adolescents are special targets for our anti-drug efforts, since they are a high-risk group both for substance abuse and for other kinds of self-destructive behavior. Nonetheless, our main prevention efforts—to instill more fear of drugs and alcohol—seem not to have persuaded most young people to avoid drug and alcohol intoxication or to have prevented the small group of potential addicts from their immersion in lives built around drugs. Rather than dealing with what in fact underlies such behavior, we are preoccupied with seeking biological explanations for our personal and social sense of loss and searching for medical cures for our cultural failures and existential malaise. This elaborate social defense mechanism, which at times achieves the level of psychosis, masks and ultimately exacerbates our deepest fears that we cannot cope with our worlds.

INTRODUCTION

When US college basketball star Len Bias died in 1986 while inhaling cocaine, cries went out for increased surveillance against drug use. In fact, the University of Maryland athletic program of which Bias was a part already had a model drug-testing program in place. Obviously, Bias circumvented this program while he regularly took massive amounts of cocaine. However, a reliable indicator was readily available that Bias was not fully engaged in university life—he didn't pass a single course in his last year of college.[1]

Bias's behavior and death contrast with the experiences of the large number of cocaine users in American universities. In 1985, 17% of American college students used cocaine and most students said the drug was fairly easy to obtain. Yet only 0.1% of students (or 1 in 170 of those who used cocaine) used it daily for as long as a month (Johnston *et al.*, 1986). Apparently, most students resist the addictive lure of cocaine, even after having sampled the drug, because school obligations and other values they hold prevent them from consistently savoring the drug's effects. It would seem that drug addiction is best resisted through an involvement in activities and values—such as achievement at school—that are incompatible with continued drug intoxication.

However, American society has not been able to inculcate such values adequately, particularly in certain key high-risk groups of people. Bias actually represents a class of people with similar problems. Bias's basketball coach, Lefty Driesell (who was removed as coach but became assistant athletic director at the University after Bias's death), noted about the athletic conference Maryland participated in: 'Cocaine has been a continuing problem among Atlantic Coast Conference players and former players. Five of the best players we've ever had have all admitted having drug problems: Bias, David Thompson, John Lucas, Phil Ford, and Walter Davis.' Meanwhile, "asked if he had been made a scapegoat for Bias's death (by Maryland), Driesell ducked the question with a smile, 'I'm still being paid by that school' " (Driesell reflects, 1987).[2]

Driesell called David Thompson 'the best player I ever saw in the conference'. Thompson, after having been investigated for cocaine use and for beating his wife while he was a professional basketball player, has since retired and was recently sentenced to jail for criminal assault (*Woes for Thompson*, 1987). Thompson played for a college team that emphasized God and community spirit (although this team was banned from tournament play because of violations it committed in recruiting Thompson from high school), and Thompson was thought to be a model citizen in college. Bias, too, was from an extremely religious family. Driesell said about Bias, 'He was one of the nicest young men I have ever known . . . I didn't even think he drank beer'. Bias's mother currently lectures around the US on the dangers of drugs. All of the five men

5

---

[1]Since reviewing this paper, we have become aware that the interpretation of these facts is in some dispute. A source at the University of Maryland informs us that although Bias did not complete his University course, he was academically successful and completed his eligibility for the University as far as his final year. At this point Bias apparently joined a professional basketball team; a not uncommon occurrence amongst college 'stars'. The implication that his failure to graduate was entirely due to drug problems is disputed.

[2]A source at the University of Maryland points out that Driesell had recently signed a ten year contract. Consequently although he was demoted, his appointment could not be terminated.

Driesell discussed were blacks who came from rural sections of the southern US and from extremely abstemious backgrounds.[3]

Driesell and others seemed to have mistaken the kinds of values and preparation that are necessary to prevent self-destructive drug use. A dedication to abstemiousness and God does not seem adequate for the job. In common with most Americans, Driesell conceives of drug abuse as an external force that surprises otherwise good young people. The solution, of course, is to avoid any contact with drugs. Once someone uses drugs, in this view, anything can happen (no matter what the user's previous disposition). For those stricken with the 'disease' of drug abuse, medical treatment emphasizes biological causation but recommends something very much like religious conversion to keep the individual away from drugs—however tenuous the person's self-control and however ready for relapse the person remains as long as he or she lives.

FACING THE FACTS

It is not true that several decades of widespread drug use in the United States have made us more aware of the facts about, and nature of, drug use. Rather, the contrary has occurred, and totally unsupportable assertions about drugs are made and accepted without question. We have witnessed in the United States a gradual growth in recreational drug use until more high school seniors nationwide have tried illicit drugs than have not done so (Johnston et al., 1986). In many areas and among many groups, such drug use is a norm, and not to use drugs is abnormal. Such statistics are, of course, horribly alarming to parents and others. Nonetheless, as indicated in the 1985 college student cocaine use data, the rather large majority of young drug users are casual or occasional users. Less well known is that even those young people who use drugs heavily will generally desist or cut back this use before the age of 30, even when the drug in question is heroin (O'Donnell et al., 1976).

The American reaction to data indicating that many young people have used drugs has been increasingly alarmist (Clymer, 1986), even though there have not been clear indications that abusive drug use has grown. For example, daily marijuana use declined among high school seniors in the mid-1980s (Johnston et al., 1986), even while marijuana continued to be widely available and most adolescents have used the drug by the time they enter college. The one sign of regular drug intoxication among the young occurs in the case of alcohol. Fifty-nine percent of 1985 male college students (along with 34% of female students) reported having had five drinks or more in one sitting in the previous two weeks.

---

[3] Again, we are informed by a source at the University of Maryland that Bias himself did not accord with this description. Bias apparently lived in a lower-middle-class urban environment approximately one mile from the University.

Anti-drug and anti-alcohol propaganda have exploded in America in the 1980s. This represents more of a change in the case of alcohol than it does for drug use, which, despite some claims that drug use became acceptable in the US, has been portrayed in continuously negative tones since drug experimentation first appeared on college campuses in the 1960s. Even so, anti-drug campaigns have been stepped up along with anti-drinking programs in recent years, including now regular celebrity anti-drug and anti-alcohol messages, testimonials from former drug abusers and alcoholics, anti-drug and anti-alcohol school programs, and widespread advertising by and for private treatment centers.

These campaigns seem to have inspired fear in many young people (drugs were the number one concern of elementary children polled by the *Weekly Reader*). In the case of declining daily marijuana use, this approach might seem to be quite effective. However, drug use continues at extremely high levels in the US, compared with other Western nations and with pre-1970 levels. Cocaine use has risen among young people (although it involves far fewer users than marijuana). Overall, it is hard to imagine the circumstances that would return the United States to pre-1970 drug usage levels. At the time when President Nixon announced Operation Intercept in 1969 (the first in a series of massive US government drug interception programs), perhaps 15 million Americans had used marijuana. By 1982, 22 million had taken cocaine and 80 million had used marijuana (Miller *et al.*, 1984). Following President Reagan's 1982 War on Drugs, tailored specifically for cocaine, use of that drug did not decline (Peele, 1987a).

As new generations of drug-using students graduate, we have a population that has largely been exposed to drugs, and somewhat higher levels of drug use throughout the life cycle (considering most people quit or reduce drug use in adulthood). Along with these continued high levels of drug use, we also display greater official concern and more negative public attitudes toward drugs. It may be that those who heed dire drug warnings are those least likely to become problematic users under any circumstances. At the same time, many young people describe drug use as dangerous while continuing to use drugs. Most young people, in fact, continue to ignore messages that they should never take a drug or get drunk. They apparently reject anti-drug messages because these messages deny the multifarious types of drug use they observe around them.

The most important question is how our scare tactics affect the small minority that uses drugs regularly and the smaller minority still whose drug use totally dominates their lives. Heavy drug users may have the same negative beliefs about drugs as their peers and still persist in taking drugs. They are likely to misuse a whole host of substances at the same time; those who smoke cigarettes have the highest probability of smoking marijuana regularly and using cocaine (Clayton, 1985). These young people are those least involved in school and other achievement and pro-social activities (Peele, 1987b). On the one hand, this describes a small but intractable minority of children from middle-class backgrounds. On the other, it characterizes a larger group of inner-city and minority youths. In this way, substance abuse problems grow out of social problems like an evolving underclass with which the US has been unable to come to grips, and which may be growing worse.

Our inability to engage many youngsters in meaningful achievement activity or to provide a large number with a minimal degree of social integration vitiates our drug education programs for the groups we are most concerned to reach. National news programs in the States carried the story on June 8, 1987 of First Lady Nancy Reagan's visit to a Swedish program that induces young mothers to desist from drug use. This intensive residential program teaches mothers coping and child-care skills in highly supervised homes, and costs the Swedish government $75,000 per client. Staff of the Swedish program rightly point out that this investment is repaid if it reorients children's and mothers' lives. Unfortunately, the sheer number of children and mothers such programs would need to reach in New York City and elsewhere in the US makes such cost prohibitive. While Sweden reports 18,000 addicts nationwide (mainly amphetamine users) in its homogeneous population, New York City alone (with a population slightly smaller than Sweden's) claims 200,000 addicts (Lohr, 1987). As a result, we need to ask what comparable public health and social policies might be adopted at a lower cost that will help high-risk groups develop constructive values, activities and skills.

THE TREATMENT TRAP

I must confess that I am discouraged when our First Lady endorses the Swedish program with a seeming lack of awareness of the basic conditions of drug use in her home country. In hearing Mrs Reagan enthuse that ghetto children and others should 'Just Say No' to drugs and sex, I cannot help but think of Marie Antoinette explaining that those without bread should simply eat cake. One erroneous deduction Mrs Reagan and other observers made from the contrast between US and Swedish policies is that the US does not spend nearly enough on this problem. Although in their far smaller country Swedes spend twice as much per capita on drug programs as the US, American expenditures in this area are fantastically high and growing: they have doubled since 1981 to 3 billion dollars. This does not take into account astronomical costs for drug law enforcement and interdiction efforts, large expenditures for alcoholism, and far higher expenditures by the private sector for treatment than occur in European countries.

Sweden's drug program is entirely non-medical in nature and is government-funded, while in the US alcohol and drug programs are nearly always under private medical supervision. Growth in American private sector treatment accelerated in the mid-1970s, when the federal government encouraged private contractors to care for alcoholics and addicts, and as third-party (insurance) reimbursement for such treatment grew. This expansion has accelerated in the 1980s; for example, the hospitalization of teenagers has more than quadrupled since 1980 (Peele, 1986). A few large organizations such as CompCare dominate the treatment industry, engage in hostile takeovers of smaller centers, and mount aggressive marketing efforts to engage clients and their families in treatment. At the same time, the courts and corporate Employee Assistance Programs have become the largest sources of clients for the private treatment system (Weisner, 1987).

This situation differs dramatically from Britain and most other European nations. In the case of alcoholism, according to British psychiatrist Robin Murray (1986), Dean of the Bethlem Royal and Maudsley Hospitals' Institute of Psychiatry, 'British clinicians have shown that the effect of treatment is only marginal, and, in contrast to their American counterparts, have decided against a major expansion of in-patient treatment facilities'. At the same time, Murray remarks, 'It is perhaps worth noting that whether or not alcoholism is considered a disease, and how much treatment is offered, has no bearing on the remuneration of British doctors'. In Britain, Murray notes, 'Even R.E. Kendall, one of the British psychiatrists most interested in categorical diagnostic systems, states that for alcoholism it is increasingly clear that most of the assumptions of the 'disease model' are unjustified and act as a barrier to a more intelligent and effective approach to the problem'.

American hospital treatment has demonstrated no greater success than that found in the UK, and remission rates for outpatient counseling in the US are typically at least as good as those resulting from hospital stays (Miller and Hester, 1986). As Murray indicates, the tremendous emphasis on medical treatment and insurer payments in the face of unmeasurable treatment benefits is closely tied to the economics of the private enterprise medical system in America. Having established for insurers and in public opinion that alcoholism is a treatable disease, the American alcoholism movement now draws more and more individuals into treatment. These alcoholics are freshly discovered; that is, street inebriates are no more attractive as patients than they have ever been. Instead, well-placed and financially secure alcoholics, often women with rather mild drinking problems combined with reliance on sedatives (epitomized by former First Lady Betty Ford) now fill fancy psychiatric and other private facilities for one-month stays that can cost as much as $25,000.

Young people provide the other major areas of growth for treatment in what is termed 'chemical dependence' (both alcohol and drug abuse). CompCare and other organizations frequently present school staffs and parents with the frightening specter of the results of the untreated diseases of alcohol and drug abuse. Such organizations contract to teach school counseling staffs to conduct 'interventions' in which suspected drug users are confronted by friends, teaching and school counseling staff, and family members who together insist the student immediately enter treatment. Families may be encouraged to sell their houses in order to raise funds to ensure their children receive such treatment, without which, they may be convinced, their children will die. In the treatment setting itself, if the child should claim not to be chemically dependent, counselors attribute this to denial—an inescapable Catch-22.

DRUG HYSTERIA

The American political and social system has been dramatically affected by the current drug scare. That is, convinced we are in the throes of a drug epidemic, frightened that we cannot control the effects of drugs that are everywhere around us and are regularly consumed, Americans rely increasingly on drug-testing and other unAmerican invasions of privacy (Clymer, 1986) and on involuntary treatment of those found to have been using drugs. Any degree of police intervention is justified since drugs are destroying our society, any degree of medical intervention is justified on the grounds that the drug user has a disease that would result in death if left untreated. Drug-treatment advocates like Gold (1984) unabashedly argue for greater freedom for involuntary commitments, such as that allowed for by a model Connecticut law whereby 'a relative or police official who believes that a person is drug dependent may petition a court for compulsory treatment' (p. 70).

Of course, who is to be involuntarily treated on the grounds of being chemically dependent turns out to be quite vague. Star baseball player Dwight Gooden tested positive for cocaine use and was instantaneously spirited off to a hospital program. After he was released, Gooden indicated that he was not actually addicted and that he never took the drug while pitching. "When he was asked how he could regulate the use of cocaine after taking it in the winter, he said: 'I wasn't addicted, so I was able to lay off it during the baseball season. But once you take it the first time, you're starting to be addicted'" (*Gooden tells of cocaine use*, 1987). For what was Dwight Gooden being treated—starting to be addicted? In this way, in an horrific Orwellian atmosphere, people are tested for drugs, declared drug dependent if discovered to have used one, and compelled into treatment from which they may be released only when the treatment center finds they have passed muster. In Gooden's words: 'I cried a lot before I went to bed at night. It was embarrassing because whether you had a problem or not, you're there'.

Those who object to the CompCare-type approach or the treatment of people like Gooden (who, after all, accepted his fate as a necessity for his return to baseball) are not well-received in the US today. After a national television news program revealed CompCare's conduct described above, an unrepentant Vice-President of that company declared to the investigators: 'I don't know why you think that when you're done, the mafia, NORML and all those supporting drug abuse in the world won't have you . . . as their champions'. This man noted that parents weren't concerned 'about treatment professionals doing something wrong with their child. They are worried about their kid dying because of lack of professional help' (Adolescent treatment debate rages, 1986).

If drugs are killing our young, then anyone found to be insufficiently negative toward drugs, or who questions the indiscriminate hospitalization of young drug users, is in danger of being branded as insensitive or, worse, an abettor of drug smugglers or a killer. When rational discourse about a topic that is so much on our minds becomes impossible, and to weigh the pros and cons of different courses of action becomes an invitation to personal attack, we surely do have a problem! If children do come to view drugs as having magical powers to corrupt and control, they will have learned this from the general social environment. And those young people least adept at making informed decisions and beneficial discriminations in their lives (that is, those who most closely mirror the general social irrationality) will be those most liable to drug abuse.

THE BLIND LEADING SIGHTED

Betty Ford has become the poster woman for the new age of treatment for alcoholism and chemical dependence. When she initially was promoted to First Lady, Mrs Ford offhandedly announced that she used tranquilizers several times daily. This announcement was printed throughout the American press without comment. But when Mrs Ford learned through intensive medical therapy that she wasn't using tranquilizers wisely (even though they were prescribed by her physician) but was actually addicted to them, she stopped all drug use and drinking, and now lectures as a drug addiction and alcoholism expert. Yet, one might be most struck in Mrs Ford's history by how utterly unable she has been from the first to come to grips with the emotional meaning of her use of drugs and alcohol.

I participated in a television program with Monica Wright, who now directs a New York treatment center and who described her 20 years of alcoholism. Ms. Wright's alcoholic drinking coincided with her raising six children, four of whom became substance abusers and the other two of whom entered treatment as children of an alcoholic. Ms. Wright and the moderator were not in the least abashed by this information, for the program claimed Monica had inherited her alcoholism from her father. Today, based on theories that alcoholism and addiction are biologically and genetically caused, addicts are presented as passive victims of their disease. Who is better qualified to discuss the nature and side-effects of the disease? Thus Betty Ford is relied on equally as much for her insights into tranquilizer addiction as into the experience of breast cancer, because she has suffered from both of these medical problems.

The careers of Monica Wright and Betty Ford are simply two examples of the reliance on people who abused drugs and alcohol as instructors on drugs and alcohol. For instance, school children regularly hear from Alcoholics Anonymous members of young drug abusers about the effect of drugs and alcohol and the nature of drinking and drug-taking behavior. What would happen if someone suggested instead that basketball star Kareem Abdul Jabbar talk about his drug use? Jabbar revealed in his autobiography that he sampled psychedelic drugs while he was in college but gradually abandoned the habit as his professional basketball career, family and spiritual life took the forefront for him. Indeed, most young people have taken drugs and drink without becoming addicted, leading us to wonder what they should learn from those less successful than they at managing their lives.

The idea that we should seek knowledge about addictive substances from addicts grows from the temperance lecture, a popular nineteenth-century stage entertainment in the United States and the UK. Now, claiming the mantle of science, the sinner who has seen the light has come to be a moral instructor cum addiction expert. How Mrs Ford, Ms Wright, and other alcoholics or addicts have become models for children and others, while we ignore people who have drunk and lived moderately, is quite a remarkable phenomenon. Is our society undergoing a psychotic episode, where failure is conceived as success, where loss of control is thought to be the path to control, and where we are so unconcerned about wrongdoing that we make drug-abusing criminals (the majority of felons) our heroes? The *New York Times* reported (October 14, 1986, p. 30):

> Thomas (Hollywood) Henderson, the former Dallas Cowboy linebacker who has been jailed in California since 1984 on sex charges involving two teenage girls, will be released this week and has already been scheduled for a paid speaking tour to talk against drug and alcohol abuse. Henderson was an admitted drug user.

ABUSING THE YOUTHFUL DRUG ABUSER

The same system that elevates out-of-control people to positions of prestige and command victimizes others. The most common victims are the young.

> Programs intended to 'resocialize' troubled or troubling youth sometimes have resorted to holding youth incommunicado, refusing to allow them to wear street clothes, keeping them in isolation for prolonged periods of time, or forcing them to wear self-derogatory signs, engage in other humiliation rituals, or submit to intense and prolonged group confrontation.
>
> Such 'treatments', which have been all too common in juvenile justice and substance abuse programs, are based on dubious psychological theory . . . attempts to strip away a supposedly 'missocialized' or antisocial character structure through intense confrontation or humiliation may destroy the youngster's already fragile self-esteem. The effects of such treatment are thus much more likely to be iatrogenic than ameliorative (Melton and Davidson, 1987, p. 174).

This article argues that children need to be protected from therapy and government agencies!

The fundamental model for drug education programs in the US is the lecture by the recovered addict who indicates that anyone who takes drugs will follow the same route to perdition as the addict. The body of the lecture (as was the case in the temperance lecture) is devoted to recounting the horrors of the addiction, the addict's misbehavior, and especially the addict's lack of self-control. The lectures, from temperance to the modern drug scare program, are completely noninteractive. Both in form and content, the program assails the audience, impressing especially those whose self-management and self-image are already weak. Although these programs dominate the American scene, they have been shown to be ineffective. According to the chief of the prevention research branch of the National Institute on Drug Abuse: 'Those programs that use scare tactics, moralizing and information alone may actually have put children at increased risk' (*Some school drug efforts faulted*, 1986).

Why do such programs remain so popular? They are no doubt very self-gratifying for the lecturer, and they give vent to the anxieties of parents and authorities who wish nothing so much as to act forcefully, even without assessing the consequences. The goal seems most clearly to be to have the audience admire and emulate the speaker. A favorite program of this type for combatting crime in the US has been the so-called 'Lifer's Juvenile Awareness Program', in which recidivist criminals are allowed a free hand in lecturing youngsters (who may or may not have already committed offenses themselves) about the fruits of crime. A film entitled *Scared Straight!* (which won a special Academy Award) depicted criminals screaming at and threatening children, who often then break down. A follow-up of the program entitled *Scared Straight! Ten Years Later*, recently shown on American television, advertised as follows: 'If you resist, you will be raped. If you report us, they'll put you in solitary. If they let you out, we'll kill you'.

The original film and the follow-up made outlandish claims of success for the program (90–95 % of the children are typically said never to have engaged in further delinquent or criminal activities). In fact, nearly every evaluation of the Lifer's (or similar) programs has failed to show their efficacy. Indeed, several comparisons of children sent through prison 'awareness' programs and those not sent found outcomes that favored the control group. In one systematic comparison of a treated and untreated group, twice as many delinquent children who went through the program committed a crime in the following six months as did those in a comparable group who did not receive the training. Even a study favorable to the program indicated that 85% of participants committed delinquent acts afterwards [for a review see Finckenauer (1982)].

Nonetheless, the popularity of the Lifer's program remains high nationwide. The 1987 follow-up *Scared Straight!* film interviewed participants in the program, all of whom reported they had really been impressed by it. Why is the program such a failure and yet Pollyanna results such as these are accepted so uncritically? Convicts physically intimidating children is really more of the same of what got them where they are, while to the extent they impress children, these children are most likely to emulate the convicts' hyper-aggressiveness and brutishness. Meanwhile, the audience masks its own feelings of ineffectuality with a moralistic faith that deterrence works and browbeating children will bring them to their senses, even though most such supporters could never imagine acting this way toward children they knew personally. Do the film's on-screen stars (Peter Falk and Whoopie Goldberg) and producers humiliate and threaten to maim their own children when their youngsters do something wrong?

FEAR ITSELF

Albert Stunkard and his colleagues (1986) have recently claimed in investigations of adopted children that obesity is largely inherited. This result seemed to contradict work Stunkard conducted as part of the famous Midtown Manhattan study, research that indicated lower socioeconomic status (SES) girls were nine times as likely to be obese by age 6 as upper SES girls (Gold-blatt et al., 1956). Overall, Stunkard in that research found SES was a powerful predictor of obesity, so much so that when people changed social classes their weights approximated the norm of the group they entered (Stunkard et al., 1972). A British group replicated Stunkard's several decades of work by claiming both that obesity was largely genetic and depended on social class. In this study, permanent obesity appeared in people's 20s rather than childhood. Nonetheless, the onset of obesity was linked to poor education and lower SES, and people often changed their physiques when they rose in social class (Braddon et al., 1986).

Assertions that obesity is largely genetic, is greatly influenced by social class, and changes with changing life circumstances are confusing. Should people worry about their weight and should we try to do something about obesity, or should we just accept it? The question is especially crucial because in the US, childhood obesity is rampant and growing distinctly worse. 'Data from four national surveys indicate pronounced increases in the prevalence of pediatric obesity in the United States . . . (including, since the mid-1960s) a 54% increase in the prevalence of obesity among children 6–11 years old and 98% increase in the prevalence of superobesity' (Gortmaker et al., 1987). Whatever role genes play in obesity, this role seems to have been overridden by a general trend toward fatness in America. What is more, this trend has appeared despite a preoccupation with physical fitness that has overtaken American society.

Why should obesity be increasing so rapidly and why do our science and our public policies and popular attitudes have so little positive effect on the problem? One strong relationship with childhood obesity is television viewing, a positive correlation that withstands statistical controls for prior obesity, race, SES, region and a variety of family variables. Dietz and Gortmaker (1985) reported: 'We have shown that the association of television viewing and obesity in children fulfills the criteria necessary to establish a causal association. These criteria include . . . that television viewing precedes obesity, even when controlled for confounding variables, that the relationship is unidirectional, that a dose-response effect occurs, and that a mechanism exists by which this association can be explained' (p. 811).

An obvious connection between television viewing and obesity is that television is a passive, sedentary activity (a description that fits drug taking and drinking as well). However, since 'television viewing precedes obesity', another variable must account for differences in amount of television children watch in the first place. One candidate is another factor strongly associated with television viewing: fear. Heavy television viewers overestimate the number of crimes and the danger in their environments (Gerbner and Gross, 1976). Television emphasizes antisocial conduct that not only encourages violent behavior, but makes the viewer more fearful. Is our world more dangerous today than 20 years ago? Certainly, our awareness of child abuse, drugs, kidnapping, crime and violence has been exacerbated in the last 20 years. Regardless of whether these events are actually more common, television has made them seem so.

Is a more dangerous world, or a world we consider more dangerous, a root cause of obesity, and while we're at it, of the drug use patterns that have developed since the 1960s (cf. Zinberg, 1972)? In this analysis, we need to consider the possibility that fear precedes excessive television viewing and thus obesity, along with drug and alcohol excess. The link is that fear prevents the child from experiencing his or her environment directly, thereby encouraging alternate, 'safer' (i.e. less challenging) means of modifying experience. If fear fosters television viewing and substance abuse, we would need, in order to combat obesity and other addictions, both to create a safer society and to help Americans get control of fears about their environments which, in many cases, have run amok. Consider, for example, the idea that a child should never speak to a stranger. In this view, the bulk of humanity are to be feared as hostile agents who would harm one if only they had the opportunity!

At the same time that we, as parents and a society, must control our irrational fears, we need to make our children less afraid and more capable of facing their environments. This, too, is a formidable task, and one on which we seem to be losing ground rather than making progress. After all, we constantly strive to make children more afraid of drugs (among a number of other things). In this, we simply reflect our own fears. In the US today, we have given up the ghost that children (and adults) can be counted on to regulate their consumption of drugs, and instead dedicate ourselves to an escalating war to eliminate all exposure to drugs. If our goal were to create people competent to deal with their environments and content enough to resist self-destructive temptations, our current efforts would prove we have already lost the war on drugs.

The disease theory of alcoholism and addiction is an elaborate defense mechanism to prevent us from examining those things that, individually and as a society, we fear too much and do not believe we can deal with (Fingarette, 1985). Unfortunately, as in the classic addiction syndrome, relying on this disease fantasy exacerbates the very problems from which we recoil. Put simply, we don't have the courage to confront the dilemma that addiction is transmitted through fundamental family and societal processes (including such daily socially sanctioned activities as television viewing), and cannot be eradicated without examining and seeing the beast within. If we cannot create a world worth living in, and people who want to live in this world, then the disease of addiction will continue to typify our age.

Nevertheless, we and our children are not so helpless as we make out. Most of the young and we ourselves have already resisted a host of potential addictions to which we have been exposed. Most ghetto young people have avoided addiction under quite remarkable circumstances of deprivation and environmental assault. What we mean to do by falsely convincing ourselves that we are at the mercy of every new drug that comes down the pike is beyond me. As I argued in *The Meaning of Addiction:*

> Our conventional view of addiction, aided and abetted by science, does nothing so much as convince people of their vulnerability. It is one more element in a pervasive sense of loss of control that is the major contributor to drug and alcohol abuse, along with a host of other maladies of our age. We feel we must warn people against the dangers of the substances our society has banned, or attempted to curtail, but cannot eradicate. This book argues that our best hope is to convey these dangers realistically, by rationally pointing out the dangers of excess and, more importantly, by convincing people of the benefits of health and positive life experience.

AFTERWORD (NOVEMBER, 1996):

For the only time in my life, the editors sent out something I had written to the [40] authorities whom I criticized to get their reactions. In [the footnotes], the University of Maryland justifies why Len Bias was still permitted to complete university despite having ceased attending classes, why Bias's coach Lefty Driesell was smugly still employed by the University—though he had been demoted—, and why all the cocaine addicts discovered in the Atlantic Coast Conference were black scholarship students from less well-off economically but religious backgrounds. Interestingly, I have more than once seen the editor who invited my article and who got the University's response, John Davis, speak about the insidious role of institutions in controlling academic content.

REFERENCES

Adolescent treatment debate rages. (1986, June) *U.S. Journal of Drug and Alcohol Dependence*, pp. 4, 16.

Braddon, F.E. et al. (1986) Onset of obesity in a 36 year birth cohort study. *British Medical Journal*, **293**, 299-303.

Clayton, R.R. (1985) In Kozel, N.J. and Adams, E.H. (eds), *Cocaine Use in America: Epidemiological and Clinical Perspectives* (DHHS Pub. No. ADM 85-1414, pp. 8-34). US Government Printing Office, Washington, DC.

Clymer, A. (1986) Public found ready to sacrifice in drug fight. *New York Times*, September 2, pp. 1, D16.

Dietz, W.H. and Gortmaker, S.L. (1985) Do we fatten our children at the television set? *Pediatrics*, **75**, 807-812.

Driesell reflects. (1987, June 8) *New York Times*, p. C2.

Finckenauer, J.O. (1982) *'Scared Straight' and the Panacea Phenomenon*. Prentice-Hall, Englewood Cliffs, New Jersey.

Fingarette, H. (1985) In Martin, M.W. (ed.), *Self-Deception and Self-Understanding*. University of Kansas, Lawrence, KS, pp. 52-67.

Gerbner, G. and Gross, L. (1976, April, 17). The scary world of the TV's heavy viewer. *Psychology Today*, pp. 41-45.

Gold, M.S. (1984) *800-Cocaine*. Bantam, New York.

Goldblatt, P.N., Moore, M.E. and Stunkard, A.J. (1965) Social factors in obesity. *Journal of the American Medical Association*, **192**, 1039-1044.

Gooden tells of cocaine use. (1987, June 26) *New York Times*, p. D17.

Gortmaker, S.L. *et al.* (1987) Increasing pediatric obesity in the United States. *American Journal of Diseases of Children*, **141**, 535-540.

Johnston, L.D., O'Malley, P.M. and Bachman, J.G. (1986) Drug use among American high school students, college students, and other young adults (DHSS Publication No. ADM 86-1450). US Government Printing Office, Washington, DC.

Lohr, S. (1987, June 10) First lady views Sweden drug plan. *New York Times*, p. A13.

Melton, G.B. and Davidson, A. (1987) Child protection and society. *American Psychologist*, **42**, 172-175.

Miller, J.D. *et al.* (1984) National survey on drug abuse: main findings 1982 (DHHS Pub. No. ADM 84-1263). US Government Printing Office, Washington, DC.

Miller, W.R. and Hester, R.K. (1986) Inpatient alcoholism treatment: who benefits? *American Psychologist*, **41**, 794-805.

Murray, R.M. *et al.* (1986, March) Economics, occupation and genes: a British perspective. Paper presented at the American Psychopathological Association, New York.

O'Donnell, J.A. et al. (1976) Young men and drugs: a nationwide survey (DHEW Pub. No. ADM 76-311). US Government Printing Office, Washington, DC.

Peele, S. (1985) *The Meaning of Addiction: Compulsive Experience, and its Interpretation*. Lexington Books, Lexington, MA.

Peele, S. (1986) *The cure for adolescent drug abuse: worse than the problem? Journal of Counseling and Development*, **65**, 23-24.

Peele, S. (1987a) The notations of control-of-supply models for explaining and preventing alcoholism and drug addiction. *Journal of Studies on Alcohol*, **48**, 61-77.

Peele, S. (1987b) *A moral vision of addiction: how people's values determine whether they become and remain addicts. Journal of Drug Issues*, **17**, 187-215.

Some school drug efforts faulted. (1986, September 17) *New York Times*, pp. B1, B6.

Stunkard, A.J. et al. (1972) Influence of social class on obesity and thinness in children. *Journal of the American Medical Association*, **221**, 579-584.

Stunkard, A.J. et al. (1986) An adoption study of human obesity. *New England Journal of Medicine,* 314, 193-198.

Weisner, C. (1987) The social ecology of alcohol treatment in the United States. In Galanter, M. (ed.), *Recent Developments in Alcoholism.* Plenum Press, New York, Vol. 5, pp. 203-243.

Woes for Thompson. (1987, June 7) *New York Times,* p. 8.

Zinberg, N.E. (1972) Why now? Drug use as a response to social and technological change. *Contemporary Drug Problems,* 1, 747-782.

ANALYZING What the Writer Says

1. What does Peele view as the best way to prevent drug addiction? What does he cite as a typical, but mistaken, belief about how to prevent drug abuse?

2. What, according to Peele, is wrong with the "Just Say No" approach to battling drug abuse?

3. What is the "treatment trap" as Peele sees it?

4. How do policymakers and treatment programs cultivate Americans' fear of drugs? What are some of the common myths and misconceptions about drug addiction?

5. What, according to Peele, is flawed about using addicts to teach others about addiction?

6. How does defining drug addiction as a "disease"—with genetic and biological causes—hinder, rather than help, in the fight against drug abuse? How do these theories let policymakers, and indeed the whole society, off the hook?

7. How does fear exacerbate addictive behaviors?

ANALYZING How the Writer Says It

1. Peele's article appeared in 1987 in *Health Education Review,* an academic journal. What characteristics of the article suggest his appeal to an academic audience? What aspects would appeal to a popular audience as well?

2. How do Peele's section headings reveal his attitudes toward popular approaches to combating addiction?

ANALYZING the Issue

1. Is instilling fear in young people an effective means of getting them to control their behavior? Why or why not?

2. Are twelve-step programs—and their insistence on the acknowledgment by individuals of forces beyond their control—ultimately healthy approaches to combating drug and alcohol abuse? Explain.

ANALYZING Connections Between Texts

1. Read Scott Russell Sanders's account of his father's alcoholism ("Under the Influence," p. 295). How do you think Sanders would respond to Peele's points?

2. How would Peele assess the approach of Miss Moore, the teacher in Tony Cade Bambara's "The Lesson," (p. 332) in combating social ills?

3. How does Carrie Mae Weems's photograph ("Jim, if you choose to accept, the mission is to land on your own two feet," p. 329) reinforce Peele's argument about battling addiction?

WARMING UP: *Do you know anyone who has had to hide a family secret? How has keeping that secret affected individuals in the family and the family as a whole?*

Under the Influence

BY SCOTT RUSSELL SANDERS

SCOTT RUSSELL SANDERS
*In this 1989 piece, a wide-
ly anthologized essayist
confronts his father's legacy and reveals the family
secret: alcoholism and
its effects on those who
live with, and love, the
alcoholic.*

My father drank. He drank as a gut-punched boxer gasps for breath, as a starving dog gobbles food—compulsively, secretly, in pain and trembling. I use the past tense not because he ever quit drinking but because he quit living. That is how the story ends for my father, age sixty-four, heart bursting, body cooling and forsaken on the linoleum of my brother's trailer. The story continues for my brother, my sister, my mother, and me, and will continue so long as memory holds.

In the perennial present of memory, I slip into the garage or barn to see my father tipping back the flat green bottles of wine, the brown cylinders of whisky, the cans of beer disguised in paper bags. His Adam's apple bobs, the liquid gurgles, he wipes the sandy-haired back of a hand over his lips, and then, his bloodshot gaze bumping into me, he stashes the bottle or can inside his jacket, under the workbench, between two bales of hay, and we both pretend the moment has not occurred.

"What's up, buddy?" he says, thick-tongued and edgy.

"Sky's up," I answer, playing along.

"And don't forget prices," he grumbles. "Prices are always up. And taxes." ⁵

In memory, his white 1951 Pontiac with the stripes down the hood and the Indian head on the snout jounces to a stop in the driveway; or it is the 1956 Ford station wagon, or the 1963 Rambler shaped like a toad, or the sleek 1969 Bonneville that will do 120 miles per hour on straightaways; or it is the robin's-egg blue pickup, new in 1980, battered in 1981, the year of his death. He climbs out, grinning dangerously, unsteady on his legs, and we children interrupt our game of catch, our building of snow forts, our picking of plums, to watch in silence as he weaves past into the house, where he slumps into his overstuffed chair and falls asleep. Shaking her head, our mother stubs out the cigarette he has left smoldering in the ashtray. All evening, until our bedtimes, we tiptoe past him, as past a snoring dragon. Then we curl in our fearful sheets, listening. Eventually he wakes with a grunt, Mother slings accusations at him, he snarls back, she yells, he growls, their voices clashing. Before long, she retreats to their bedroom, sobbing—not from the blows of fists, for he never strikes her, but from the force of words.

Left alone, our father prowls the house, thumping into furniture, rummaging in the kitchen, slamming doors, turning the pages of the newspaper with a savage crackle, muttering back at the late-night drivel from television. The roof might fly off, the walls might buckle from the pressure of his rage. Whatever my brother and sister and mother may be thinking on their own rumpled pillows, I lie there hating him, loving him, fearing him, knowing I have failed him. I tell myself he drinks to ease an ache that gnaws at his belly, an ache I must have caused by disappointing him somehow, a murderous ache I should be able to relieve by doing all my chores, earning A's in school, winning baseball games, fixing the broken washer and the burst pipes, bringing in money to fill his empty wallet. He would not hide the green bottles in his tool box, would not sneak off to the barn with a lump under his coat, would not fall asleep in the daylight, would not roar and fume, would not drink himself to death, if only I were perfect.

I am forty-two as I write these words, and I know full well now that my father was an alcoholic, a man consumed by disease rather than by disappointment. What had seemed to me a private grief is in fact a public scourge. In the United States alone some ten or fifteen million people share his ailment, and behind the doors they slam in fury or disgrace, countless other children tremble. I comfort myself with such knowledge, holding it against the throb of memory like an ice pack against a bruise. There are keener sources of grief: poverty, racism, rape, war. I do not wish to compete for a trophy in suffering. I am only trying to understand the corrosive mixture of helplessness, responsibility, and shame that I learned to feel as the son of an alcoholic. I realize now that I did not cause my father's illness, nor could I have cured it. Yet for all this grown-up knowledge, I am still ten years old, my own son's age, and as that boy I struggle in guilt and confusion to save my father from pain.

Consider a few of our synonyms for drunk: tipsy, tight, pickled, soused, and plowed; stoned and stewed, lubricated and inebriated, juiced and sluiced; three sheets to the wind, in your cups, out of your mind, under the table, lit up, tanked up, wiped out; besotted, blotto, bombed, and buzzed; plastered, polluted, putrified; loaded or looped, boozy, woozy, fuddled, or smashed; crocked and shit-faced, corked and pissed, snockered and sloshed.

It is a mostly humorous lexicon, as the lore that deals with drunks—in jokes and cartoons, in plays, films, and television skits—is largely comic. Aunt Matilda nips elderberry wine from the sideboard and burps politely during supper. Uncle Fred slouches to the table glassy-eyed, wearing a lamp shade for a hat and murmuring, "Candy is dandy but liquor is quicker." Inspired by cocktails, Mrs. Somebody recounts the events of her day in a fuzzy dialect, while Mr. Somebody nibbles her ear and croons a bawdy song. On the sofa with Boyfriend, Daughter giggles, licking gin from her lips, and loosens the bows in her hair. Junior knocks back some brews with his chums at the Leopard Lounge and stumbles home to the wrong house, wonders foggily why he cannot locate his pajamas, and crawls naked into bed with the ugliest girl in school. The family dog slurps from a neglected martini and wobbles to the nursery, where he vomits in Baby's shoe. 10

It is all great fun. But if in the audience you notice a few laughing faces turn grim when the drunk lurches on stage, don't be surprised, for these are the children of alcoholics. Over the grinning mask of Dionysus, the leering mask of Bacchus, these children cannot help seeing the bloated features of their own parents. Instead of laughing, they wince, they mourn. Instead of celebrating the drunk as one freed from constraints, they pity him as one enslaved. They refuse to believe *in vino veritas,* having seen their befuddled parents skid away from truth toward folly and oblivion. And so these children bite their lips until the lush staggers into the wings.

My father, when drunk, was neither funny nor honest; he was pathetic, frightening, deceitful. There seemed to be a leak in him somewhere, and he poured in booze to keep from draining dry. Like a torture victim who refuses to squeal, he would never admit that he had touched a drop, not even in his last year, when he seemed to be dissolving in alcohol before our very eyes. I never knew him to lie about anything, ever, except about this one ruinous fact. Drowsy, clumsy, unable to fix a bicycle tire, throw a baseball, balance a grocery sack, or walk across the room, he was stripped of his true self by drink. In a matter of minutes, the contents of a bottle could transform a brave man into a coward, a buddy into a bully, a gifted athlete and skilled carpenter and shrewd businessman into a bumbler. No dictionary of synonyms for *drunk* would soften the anguish of watching our prince turn into a frog.

Father's drinking became the family secret. While growing up, we children never breathed a word of it beyond the four walls of our house. To this day, my brother and sister rarely mention it, and then only when I press them. I did not confess the ugly, bewildering fact to my wife until his wavering walk and slurred speech forced me to. Recently, on the seventh anniversary of my father's death, I asked my mother if she ever spoke of his drinking to friends. "No, no, never," she replied hastily. "I couldn't bear for anyone to know."

The secret bores under the skin, gets in the blood, into the bone, and stays there. Long after you have supposedly been cured of malaria, the fever can flare up the tremors can shake you. So it is with the fevers of shame. You swallow the bitter quinine of knowledge, and you learn to feel pity and compassion toward the drinker. Yet the shame lingers in your marrow, and, because of the shame, anger.

For a long stretch of my childhood we lived on a military reservation in Ohio, an arsenal where bombs were stored underground in bunkers, vintage airplanes burst into flames, and unstable artillery shells boomed nightly at the dump. We had the feeling, as children, that we played in a mine field, where a heedless footfall could trigger an explosion. When Father was drinking, the house, too, became a mine field. The least bump could set off either parent.

The more he drank, the more obsessed Mother became with stopping him. She hunted for bottles, counted the cash in his wallet, sniffed at his breath. Without meaning to snoop, we children blundered left and right into damning evidence. On afternoons when he came home from work sober, we flung ourselves at him for hugs, and felt against our ribs the telltale lump in his coat. In the barn we tumbled on the hay and heard beneath our sneakers the crunch of buried glass. We tugged open a drawer in his workbench, looking for screwdrivers or crescent wrenches, and spied a gleaming six-pack among the tools. Playing tag, we darted around the house just in time to see him sway on the rear stoop and heave a finished bottle into the woods. In his good night kiss we smelled the cloying sweetness of Clorets, the mints he chewed to camouflage his dragon's breath.

I can summon up that kiss right now by recalling Theodore Roethke's lines about his own father in "My Papa's Waltz":

> The whisky on your breath
> Could make a small boy dizzy;
> But I hung on like death:
> Such waltzing was not easy.

Such waltzing was hard, terribly hard, for with a boy's scrawny arms I was trying to hold my tipsy father upright.

For years, the chief source of those incriminating bottles and cans was a grimy store a mile from us, a cinder block place called Sly's, with two gas pumps outside and a moth-eaten dog asleep in the window. A strip of flypaper, speckled the year round with black bodies, coiled in the doorway. Inside, on rusty metal shelves or in wheezing coolers, you could find pop and Popsicles, cigarettes, potato chips, canned soup, raunchy postcards, fishing gear, Twinkies, wine, and beer. When Father drove anywhere on errands, Mother would send us kids along as guards, warning us not to let him out of our sight. And so with one or more of us on board, Father would cruise up to Sly's, pump a dollar's worth of gas or plump the tires with air, and then, telling us to wait in the car, he would head for that fly-spangled doorway.

Dutiful and panicky, we cried, "Let us go in with you!"

"No," he answered. "I'll be back in two shakes." 20

"Please!"

"No!" he roared. "Don't you budge, or I'll jerk a knot in your tails!"

So we stayed put, kicking the seats, while he ducked inside. Often, when he had parked the car at a careless angle, we gazed in through the window and saw Mr. Sly fetching down from a shelf behind the cash register two green pints of Gallo wine. Father swigged one of them right there at the counter, stuffed the other in his pocket, and then out he came, a bulge in his coat, a flustered look on his red face.

Because the Mom and Pop who ran the dump were neighbors of ours, living just down the tar-blistered road, I hated them all the more for poisoning my father. I wanted to sneak in their store and smash the bottles and set fire to the place. I also hated the Gallo brothers, Ernest and Julio, whose jovial faces shone from the labels of their wine, labels I would find, torn and curled, when I burned the trash. I noted the Gallo brothers' address, in California, and I studied the road atlas to see how far that was from Ohio, because I meant to go out there and tell Ernest and Julio what they were doing to my father, and then, if they showed no mercy, I would kill them.

While growing up on the back roads and in the country schools and cramped 25 Methodist churches of Ohio and Tennessee, I never heard the word *alcoholism*, never happened across it in books or magazines. In the nearby towns, there were no addiction treatment programs, no community mental health centers, no Alcoholics Anonymous chapters, no therapists. Left alone with our grievous secret, we had no way of understanding Father's drinking except as an act of will, a deliberate folly or cruelty, a moral weakness, a sin. He drank because he chose to, pure and simple. Why our father, so playful and competent and kind when sober, would choose to ruin himself and punish his family, we could not fathom.

Our neighborhood was high on the Bible, and the Bible was hard on drunkards. "Woe to those who are heroes at drinking wine, and valiant men in mixing strong drink," wrote Isaiah. "The priest and the prophet reel with strong drink, they are confused with wine, they err in vision, they stumble in giving judgment. For all tables are full of vomit, no place is without filthiness." We children had seen those fouled tables at the local truck stop where the notorious boozers hung out, our father occasionally among them. "Wine and new wine take away the understanding," declared the prophet Hosea. We had also seen evidence of that in our father, who could multiply seven-digit numbers in his head when sober, but when drunk could not help us with fourth-grade math. Proverbs warned: "Do not look at wine when it is red, when it sparkles in the cup and goes down smoothly. At the last it bites like a serpent, and stings like an adder. Your eyes will see strange things, and your mind utter perverse things." Woe, woe.

Dismayingly often, these biblical drunkards stirred up trouble for their own kids. Noah made fresh wine after the flood, drank too much of it, fell asleep without any clothes on, and was glimpsed in the buff by his son Ham, whom Noah promptly cursed. In one passage—it was so shocking we had to read it under our blankets with flashlights—the patriarch Lot fell down drunk and slept with his daughters. The sins of the fathers set their children's teeth on edge.

Our ministers were fond of quoting St. Paul's pronouncement that drunkards would not inherit the kingdom of God. These grave preachers assured us that the wine referred to during the Last Supper was in fact grape juice. Bible and sermons and hymns combined to give us the impression that Moses should have brought down from the mountain another stone tablet, bearing the Eleventh Commandment: Thou shalt not drink.

The scariest and most illuminating Bible story apropos of drunkards was the one about the lunatic and the swine. Matthew, Mark, and Luke each told a version of the tale. We knew it by heart: When Jesus climbed out of his boat one day, this lunatic came charging up from the graveyard, stark naked and filthy, frothing at the mouth, so violent that he broke the strongest chains. Nobody would go near him. Night and day for years this madman had been wailing among the tombs and bruising himself with stones. Jesus took one look at him and said, "Come out of the man, you unclean spirits!" for he could see that the lunatic was possessed by demons. Meanwhile, some hogs were conveniently rooting nearby. "If we have to come out," begged the demons, "at least let us go into those swine." Jesus agreed. The unclean spirits entered the hogs, and the hogs rushed straight off a cliff and plunged into a lake. Hearing the story in Sunday school, my friends thought mainly of the pigs. (How big a splash did they make? Who paid for the lost pork?) But I thought of the redeemed lunatic, who bathed himself and put on clothes and calmly sat at the feet of Jesus, restored—so the Bible said—to "his right mind."

When drunk, our father was clearly in his wrong mind. He became a stranger, as fearful to us as any graveyard lunatic, not quite frothing at the mouth but fierce enough, quick-tempered, explosive; or else he grew maudlin and weepy, which frightened us nearly as much. In my boyhood despair, I reasoned that maybe he wasn't to blame for turning into an ogre. Maybe, like the lunatic, he was possessed by demons. I found support for my theory when I heard liquor referred to as "spirits," when the newspapers reported that somebody had been arrested for "driving under the influence," and when church ladies railed against that "demon drink."

If my father was indeed possessed, who would exorcise him? If he was a sinner, who would save him? If he was ill, who would cure him? If he suffered, who would ease his pain? Not ministers or doctors, for we could not bring ourselves to confide in them; not the neighbors, for we pretended they had never seen him drunk; not Mother, who fussed and pleaded but could not budge him; not my brother and sister, who were only kids. That left me. It did not matter that I, too, was only a child, and a bewildered one at that. I could not excuse myself.

On first reading a description of delirium tremens—in a book on alcoholism I smuggled from the library—I thought immediately of the frothing lunatic and the frenzied swine. When I read stories or watched films about grisly metamorphoses—Dr. Jekyll becoming Mr. Hyde, the mild husband changing into a werewolf, the kindly neighbor taken over by a brutal alien—I could not help seeing my own father's mutation from sober to drunk. Even today, knowing better, I am attracted by the demonic theory of drink, for when I recall my father's transformation, the emergence of his ugly second self, I find it easy to believe in possession by unclean spirits. We never knew which version of Father would come home from work, the true or the tainted, nor could we guess how far down the slope toward cruelty he would slide.

How far a man *could* slide we gauged by observing our back-road neighbors— the out-of-work miners who had dragged their families to our corner of Ohio from the desolate hollows of Appalachia, the tightfisted farmers, the surly mechanics, the balked and broken men. There was, for example, whiskey-soaked Mr. Jenkins, who beat his wife and kids so hard we could hear their screams from the road. There was Mr. Lavo the wino, who fell asleep smoking time and again, until one night his disgusted wife bundled up the children and went out-side and left him in his easy chair to burn; he awoke on his own, staggered out coughing into the yard, and pounded her flat while the children looked on and the shack turned to ash. There was the truck driver, Mr. Sampson, who tripped over his son's tricycle one night while drunk and got so mad that he jumped into his semi and drove away, shifting through the dozen gears, and never came back. We saw the bruised children of these fathers clump onto our school bus, we saw the abandoned children huddle in the pews at church, we saw the stunned and battered mothers begging for help at our doors.

Our own father never beat us, and I don't think he ever beat Mother, but he threatened often. The Old Testament Yahweh was not more terrible in his wrath. Eyes blazing, voice booming, Father would pull out his belt and swear to give us a whipping, but he never followed through, never needed to, because we could imagine it so vividly. He shoved us, pawed us with the back of his hand, as an irked bear might smack a cub, not to injure, just to clear a space. I can see him grabbing Mother by the hair as she cowers on a chair during a nightly quar-rel. He twists her neck back until she gapes up at him, and then he lifts over her skull a glass quart bottle of milk, the milk running down his forearm, and he yells at her, "Say just one more word, one goddamn word, and I'll shut you up!" I fear she will prick him with her sharp tongue, but she is terrified into silence, and so am I, and the leaking bottle quivers in the air, and milk slithers through the red hair of my father's uplifted arm, and the entire scene is there to this moment, the head jerked back, the club raised.

When the drink made him weepy, Father would pack a bag and kiss each of us children on the head, and announce from the front door that he was moving out. "Where to?" we demanded, fearful each time that he would leave for good, as Mr. Sampson had roared away for good in his diesel truck. "Someplace where I won't get hounded every minute," Father would answer, his jaw quivering. He stabbed a look at Mother, who might say, "Don't run into the ditch before you get there," or "Good riddance," and then he would slink away. Mother watched him go with arms crossed over her chest, her face closed like the lid on a box of snakes. We children bawled. Where could he go? To the truck stop, that den of iniquity? To one of those dark, ratty flophouses in town? Would he wind up sleeping under a railroad bridge or on a park bench or in a cardboard box, mummied in rags, like the bums we had seen on our trips to Cleveland and Chicago? We bawled and bawled, wondering if he would ever come back.

He always did come back, a day or a week later, but each time there was a sliver less of him.

In Kafka's *The Metamorphosis*, which opens famously with Gregor Samsa waking up from uneasy dreams to find himself transformed into an insect, Gregor's family keep reassuring themselves that things will be just fine again, "When he comes back to us." Each time alcohol transformed our father, we held out the same hope, that he would really and truly come back to us, our authentic father, the tender and playful and competent man, and then all things would be fine. We had grounds for such hope. After his weepy departures and chapfallen returns, he would sometimes go weeks, even months without drinking. Those were glad times. Joy banged inside my ribs. Every day without the furtive glint of bottles, every meal without a fight, every bedtime without sobs encouraged us to believe that such bliss might go on forever.

Mother was fooled by just such a hope all during the forty-odd years she knew this Greeley Ray Sanders. Soon after she met him in a Chicago delicatessen on the eve of World War II, and fell for his butter-melting Mississippi drawl and his wavy red hair, she learned that he drank heavily. But then so did a lot of men. She would soon coax or scold him into breaking the nasty habit. She would point out to him how ugly and foolish it was, this bleary drinking, and then he would quit. He refused to quit during their engagement, however, still refused during the first years of marriage, refused until my sister came along. The shock of fatherhood sobered him, and he remained sober through my birth at the end of the war and right on through until we moved in 1951 to the Ohio arsenal, that paradise of bombs. Like all places that make a business of death, the arsenal had more than its share of alcoholics and drug addicts and other varieties of escape artists. There I turned six and started school and woke into a child's flickering awareness, just in time to see my father begin sneaking swigs in the garage.

He sobered up again for most of a year at the height of the Korean War, to celebrate the birth of my brother. But aside from that dry spell, his only breaks from drinking before I graduated from high school were just long enough to raise and then dash our hopes. Then during the fall of my senior year—the time of the Cuban missile crisis, when it seemed that the nightly explosions at the munitions dump and the nightly rages in our household might spread to engulf the globe—Father collapsed. His liver, kidneys, and heart all conked out. The doctors saved him, but only by a hair. He stayed in the hospital for weeks, going through a withdrawal so terrible that Mother would not let us visit him. If he wanted to kill himself, the doctors solemnly warned him, all he had to do was hit the bottle again. One binge would finish him.

Father must have believed them, for he stayed dry for the next fifteen years. 40 It was an answer to prayer, Mother said, it was a miracle. I believe it was a reflex of fear, which he sustained over the years through courage and pride. He knew a man could die from drink, for his brother Roscoe had. We children never laid eyes on doomed Uncle Roscoe, but in the stories Mother told us he became a fairy-tale figure, like a boy who took the wrong turning in the woods and was gobbled up by the wolf.

The fifteen-year dry spell came to an end with Father's retirement in the spring of 1978. Like many men, he gave up his identity along with his job. One day he was a boss at the factory, with a brass plate on his door and a reputation to uphold; the next day he was a nobody at home. He and Mother were leaving Ontario, the last of the many places to which his job had carried them, and they were moving to a new house in Mississippi, his childhood stomping grounds. As a boy in Mississippi, Father sold Coca Cola during dances while the moonshiners peddled their brew in the parking lot; as a young blade, he fought in bars and in the ring, seeking a state Golden Gloves championship; he gambled at poker, hunted pheasants, raced motorcycles and cars, played semiprofessional baseball, and, along with all his buddies—in the Black Cat Saloon, behind the cotton gin, in the woods—he drank. It was a perilous youth to dream of recovering.

After his final day of work, Mother drove on ahead with a car full of begonias and violets, while Father stayed behind to oversee the packing. When the van was loaded, the sweaty movers broke open a six-pack and offered him a beer.

"Let's drink to retirement!" they crowed. "Let's drink to freedom! to fishing! hunting! loafing! Let's drink to a guy who's going home!"

At least I imagine some such words, for that is all I can do, imagine, and I see Father's hand trembling in midair as he thinks about the fifteen sober years and about the doctors' warning, and he tells himself *Goddamnit, I am a free man,* and *Why can't a free man drink one beer after a lifetime of hard work?*

and I see his arm reaching, his fingers closing, the can tilting to his lips. I even supply a label for the beer, a swaggering brand that promises on television to deliver the essence of life. I watch the amber liquid pour down his throat, the alcohol steal into his blood, the key turn in his brain.

Soon after my parents moved back to Father's treacherous stomping ground, my wife and I visited them in Mississippi with our five-year-old daughter. Mother had been too distraught to warn me about the return of the demons. So when I climbed out of the car that bright July morning and saw my father napping in the hammock, I felt uneasy, for in all his sober years I had never known him to sleep in daylight. Then he lurched upright, blinked his blood-shot eyes, and greeted us in a syrupy voice. I was hurled back helpless into childhood. 45

"What's the matter with Papaw?" our daughter asked.

"Nothing," I said. "Nothing!"

Like a child again, I pretended not to see him in his stupor, and behind my phony smile I grieved. On that visit and on the few that remained before his death, once again I found bottles in the workbench, bottles in the woods. Again his hands shook too much for him to run a saw, to make his precious miniature furniture, to drive straight down back roads. Again he wound up in the ditch, in the hospital, in jail, in treatment centers. Again he shouted and wept. Again he lied. "I never touched a drop," he swore. "Your mother's making it up."

I no longer fancied I could reason with the men whose names I found on the bottles—Jim Beam, Jack Daniels—nor did I hope to save my father by burning down a store. I was able now to press the cold statistics about alcoholism against the ache of memory: ten million victims, fifteen million, twenty. And yet, in spite of my age, I reacted in the same blind way as I had in childhood, ignoring biology, forgetting numbers, vainly seeking to erase through my efforts whatever drove him to drink. I worked on their place twelve and sixteen hours a day, in the swelter of Mississippi summers, digging ditches, running electrical wires, planting trees, mowing grass, building sheds, as though what nagged at him was some list of chores, as though by taking his worries on my shoulders I could redeem him. I was flung back into boyhood, acting as though my father would not drink himself to death if only I were perfect.

I failed of perfection; he succeeded in dying. To the end, he considered himself not sick but sinful. "Do you want to kill yourself?" I asked him. "Why not?" he answered. "Why the hell not? What's there to save?" To the end, he would not speak about his feelings, would not or could not give a name to the beast that was devouring him. 50

In silence, he went rushing off the cliff. Unlike the biblical swine, however, he left behind a few of the demons to haunt his children. Life with him and the loss of him twisted us into shapes that will be familiar to other sons and daughters of alcoholics. My brother became a rebel, my sister retreated into shyness, I played the stalwart and dutiful son who would hold the family together. If my father was unstable, I would be a rock. If he squandered money on drink, I would pinch every penny. If he wept when drunk—and only when drunk—I would not let myself weep at all. If he roared at the Little League umpire for calling my pitches balls, I would throw nothing but strikes. Watching him flounder and rage, I came to dread the loss of control. I would go through life without making anyone mad. I vowed never to put in my mouth or veins any chemical that would banish my everyday self. I would never make a scene, never lash out at the ones I loved, never hurt a soul. Through hard work, relentless work, I would achieve something dazzling—in the classroom, on the basketball floor, in the science lab, in the pages of books—and my achievement would distract the world's eyes from his humiliation. I would become a worthy sacrifice, and the smoke of my burning would please God.

It is far easier to recognize these twists in my character than to undo them. Work has become an addiction for me, as drink was an addiction for my father. Knowing this, my daughter gave me a placard for the wall: WORKAHOLIC. The labor is endless and futile, for I can no more redeem myself through work than I could redeem my father. I still panic in the face of other people's anger, because his drunken temper was so terrible. I shrink from causing sadness or disappointment even to strangers, as though I were still concealing the family shame. I still notice every twitch of emotion in the faces around me, having learned as a child to read the weather in faces, and I blame myself for their least pang of unhappiness or anger. In certain moods I blame myself for everything. Guilt burns like acid in my veins.

I am moved to write these pages now because my own son, at the age of ten, is taking on himself the griefs of the world, and in particular the griefs of his father. He tells me that when I am gripped by sadness he feels responsible; he feels there must be something he can do to spring me from depression, to fix my life. And that crushing sense of responsibility is exactly what I felt at the age of ten in the face of my father's drinking. My son wonders if I, too, am possessed. I write, therefore, to drag into the light what eats at me—the fear, the guilt, the shame—so that my own children my be spared.

I still shy away from nightclubs, from bars, from parties where the solvent is alcohol. My friends puzzle over this, but it is no more peculiar than for a man to shy away from the lions' den after seeing his father torn apart. I took my own first drink at the age of twenty-one, half a glass of burgundy. I knew the odds of my becoming an alcoholic were four times higher than for the sons of nonalcoholic fathers. So I sipped warily.

I still do—once a week, perhaps, a glass of wine, a can of beer, nothing 55 stronger, nothing more. I listen for the turning of a key in my brain.

ANALYZING **What the Writer Says**

1. How does Sanders come to view his father's alcoholism? Why does he refer to biblical drunks and warnings?

2. Why is Sanders's brief reference to Kafka's *Metamorphosis* especially appropriate to this discussion of alcoholism?

3. How are the "father's sins visited upon the son"? In what sense has Sanders copied his father's behavior?

ANALYZING **How the Writer Says It**

1. Beginning with the second paragraph of the essay, why does Sanders use the present tense although he is writing about the past?

2. Why does Sanders begin the essay with such a short, simple sentence?

3. Look at Sanders's conclusion. How does its tone document the truth of his point about alcoholism's effect on children who live under its influence?

ANALYZING **the Issue**

What is the purpose of writing about such personal pain? Do you think the kind of writing Sanders is doing in "Under the Influence" is helpful to others? Or is it simply therapeutic for the writer?

ANALYZING **Connections Between Texts**

1. In "Can Hollywood Kick the Habit?" (p. 273) Renee Graham points out how, for many years, the movie industry has made smoking look glamorous, thus contributing to many smokers' addiction. How does Sanders's account of alcoholism dispel any notions of glamour?

2. In "Growing Pains" (p. 131), Anndee Hochman describes how some families "devote their lives" to keeping some shameful secret, only to discover "that keeping secrets [costs] too much." How does Sanders's family fit this pattern? What is the price the family members pay for keeping the father's alcoholism a secret?

3. Eugene Richards's photograph "Crack for Sale" (p. 328) depicts the seedy reality of the crack cocaine trade. In what way is middle-class alcoholism, as Sanders describes it, different from Richards's vision? In what way is it similar?

WARMING UP: *How often do you eat fast food? What do you like (or dislike) about fast food?*

Fast Food Nation

BY ERIC SCHLOSSER

ERIC SCHLOSSER

Published in 2001, Eric Schlosser's Fast Food Nation *became a national best seller. The book investigates the American fast-food industry and the far-reaching social, cultural, and economic changes it has wrought. Schlosser, an award-winning investigative journalist, is also the author of the 2003* Reefer Madness, and Other Tales from the American Underground.

INTRODUCTION

Cheyenne Mountain sits on the eastern slope of Colorado's Front Range, rising steeply from the prairie and overlooking the city of Colorado Springs. From a distance, the mountain appears beautiful and serene, dotted with rocky outcroppings, scrub oak, and ponderosa pine. It looks like the backdrop of an old Hollywood western, just another gorgeous Rocky Mountain vista. And yet Cheyenne Mountain is hardly pristine. One of the nation's most important military installations lies deep within it, housing units of the North American Aerospace Command, the Air Force Space Command, and the United States Space Command. During the mid-1950s, high-level officials at the Pentagon worried that America's air defenses had become vulnerable to sabotage and attack. Cheyenne Mountain was chosen as the site for a top-secret, underground combat operations center. The mountain was hollowed out, and fifteen buildings, most of them three stories high, were erected amid a maze of tunnels and passageways extending for miles. The four-and-a-half-acre underground complex was designed to survive a direct hit by an atomic bomb. Now officially called the Cheyenne Mountain Air Force Station, the facility is entered through steel blast doors that are three feet thick and weigh twenty-five tons each; they automatically swing shut in less than twenty seconds. The base is closed to the public, and a heavily armed quick response team guards against intruders. Pressurized air within the complex prevents contamination by radioactive fallout and biological weapons. The buildings are mounted on gigantic steel springs to ride out an earthquake or the blast wave of a thermonuclear strike. The hallways and staircases are painted slate gray, the ceilings are low, and there are combination locks on many of the doors. A narrow escape tunnel, entered through a metal hatch, twists and turns its way out of the mountain through solid rock. The place feels like the set of an early James Bond movie, with men in jumpsuits driving little electric vans from one brightly lit cavern to another.

Fifteen hundred people work inside the mountain, maintaining the facility and collecting information from a worldwide network of radars, spy satellites, ground-based sensors, airplanes, and blimps. The Cheyenne Mountain Operations Center tracks every manmade object that enters North American airspace or that orbits the earth. It is the heart of the nation's early warning system. It can detect the firing of a long-range missile, anywhere in the world, before that missile has left the launch pad.

This futuristic military base inside a mountain has the capability to be self-sustaining for at least one month. Its generators can produce enough electricity to power a city the size of Tampa, Florida. Its underground reservoirs hold millions of gallons of water; workers sometimes traverse them in rowboats. The complex has its own underground fitness center, a medical clinic, a dentist's office, a barbershop, a chapel, and a cafeteria. When the men and women stationed at Cheyenne Mountain get tired of the food in the cafeteria, they often send somebody over to the Burger King at Fort Carson, a nearby army base. Or they call Domino's.

Almost every night, a Domino's deliveryman winds his way up the lonely Cheyenne Mountain Road, past the ominous DEADLY FORCE AUTHORIZED signs, past the security checkpoint at the entrance of the base, driving toward the heavily guarded North Portal, tucked behind chain link and barbed wire. Near the spot where the road heads straight into the mountainside, the delivery man drops off his pizzas and collects his tip. And should Armageddon come, should a foreign enemy someday shower the United States with nuclear warheads, laying waste to the whole continent, entombed within Cheyenne Mountain, along with the high-tech marvels, the pale blue jumpsuits, comic books, and Bibles, future archeologists may find other clues to the nature of our civilization—Big King wrappers, hardened crusts of Cheesy Bread, Barbeque Wing bones, and the red, white, and blue of a Domino's pizza box.

WHAT WE EAT

Over the last three decades, fast food has infiltrated every nook and cranny of American society. An industry that began with a handful of modest hot dog and hamburger stands in southern California has spread to every corner of the nation, selling a broad range of foods wherever paying customers may be found. Fast food is now served at restaurants and drive-throughs, at stadiums, airports, zoos, high schools, elementary schools, and universities, on cruise ships, trains, and airplanes, at K-Marts, Wal-Marts, gas stations, and even at hospital cafeterias. In 1970, Americans spent about $6 billion on fast food; in 2000, they spent more than $110 billion. Americans now spend more money on fast food than on higher education, personal computers, computer software, or new cars. They spend more on fast food than on movies, books, magazines, newspapers, videos, and recorded music—combined.

Pull open the glass door, feel the rush of cool air, walk in, get on line, study the backlit color photographs above the counter, place your order, hand over a few dollars, watch teenagers in uniforms pushing various buttons, and moments later take hold of a plastic tray full of food wrapped in colored paper and cardboard. The whole experience of buying fast food has become so routine, so thoroughly unexceptional and mundane, that it is now taken for granted, like brushing your teeth or stopping for a red light. It has become a social custom as American as a small, rectangular, hand-held, frozen, and reheated apple pie.

This is a book about fast food, the values it embodies, and the world it has made. Fast food has proven to be a revolutionary force in American life; I am interested in it both as a commodity and as a metaphor. What people eat (or don't eat) has always been determined by a complex interplay of social, economic, and technological forces. The early Roman Republic was fed by its citizen-farmers; the Roman Empire, by its slaves. A nation's diet can be more revealing than its art or literature. On any given day in the United States about one-quarter of the adult population visits a fast food restaurant. During a relatively brief period of time, the fast food industry has helped to transform not only the American diet, but also our landscape, economy, workforce, and popular culture. Fast food and its consequences have become inescapable, regardless of whether you eat it twice a day, try to avoid it, or have never taken a single bite.

The extraordinary growth of the fast food industry has been driven by fundamental changes in American society. Adjusted for inflation, the hourly wage of the average U.S. worker peaked in 1973 and then steadily declined for the next twenty-five years. During that period, women entered the workforce in record numbers, often motivated less by a feminist perspective than by a need to pay the bills. In 1975, about one-third of American mothers with young children worked outside the home; today almost two-thirds of such mothers are employed. As the sociologists Cameron Lynne Macdonald and Carmen Sirianni have noted, the entry of so many women into the workforce has greatly increased demand for the types of services that housewives traditionally perform: cooking, cleaning, and child care. A generation ago, three-quarters of the money used to buy food in the United States was spent to prepare meals at home. Today about half of the money used to buy food is spent at restaurants—mainly at fast food restaurants.

The McDonald's Corporation has become a powerful symbol of America's service economy, which is now responsible for 90 percent of the country's new jobs. In 1968, McDonald's operated about one thousand restaurants. Today it has about twenty-eight thousand restaurants worldwide and opens almost two thousand new ones each year. An estimated one out of every eight workers in the United States has at some point been employed by McDonald's. The company annually hires about one million people, more than any other American organization, public or private. McDonald's is the nation's largest purchaser of beef, pork, and potatoes—and the second largest purchaser of chicken. The McDonald's Corporation is the largest owner of retail property in the world. Indeed, the company earns the majority of its profits not from selling food but from collecting rent. McDonald's spends more money on advertising and marketing than any other brand. As a result it has replaced Coca-Cola as the world's most famous brand. McDonald's operates more playgrounds than any other private entity in the United States. It is one of the nation's largest distributors of toys. A survey of American schoolchildren found that 96 percent could identify Ronald McDonald. The only fictional character with a higher degree of recognition was Santa Claus. The impact of McDonald's on the way we live today is hard to overstate. The Golden Arches are now more widely recognized than the Christian cross.

In the early 1970s, the farm activist Jim Hightower warned of "the McDonaldization of America." He viewed the emerging fast food industry as a threat to independent businesses, as a step toward a food economy dominated by giant corporations, and as a homogenizing influence on American life. In *Eat Your Heart Out* (1975), he argued that "bigger is *not* better." Much of what Hightower feared has come to pass. The centralized purchasing decisions of the large restaurant chains and their demand for standardized products have given a handful of corporations an unprecedented degree of power over the nation's food supply. Moreover, the tremendous success of the fast food industry has encouraged other industries to adopt similar business methods. The basic thinking behind fast food has become the operating system of today's retail economy, wiping out small businesses, obliterating regional differences, and spreading identical stores throughout the country like a self-replicating code.

America's main streets and malls now boast the same Pizza Huts and Taco Bells, Gaps and Banana Republics, Starbucks and Jiffy-Lubes, Foot Lockers, Snip N' Clips, Sunglass Huts, and Hobbytown USAs. Almost every facet of American life has now been franchised or chained. From the maternity ward at a Columbia/HCA hospital to an embalming room owned by Service Corporation International—"the world's largest provider of death care services," based in Houston, Texas, which since 1968 has grown to include 3,823 funeral homes, 523 cemeteries, and 198 crematoriums, and which today handles the final remains of one out of every nine Americans—a person can now go from the cradle to the grave without spending a nickel at an independently owned business.

The key to a successful franchise, according to many texts on the subject, can be expressed in one word: "uniformity." Franchises and chain stores strive to offer exactly the same product or service at numerous locations. Customers are drawn to familiar brands by an instinct to avoid the unknown. A brand offers a feeling of reassurance when its products are always and everywhere the same. "We have found out . . . that we cannot trust some people who are nonconformists," declared Ray Kroc, one of the founders of McDonald's, angered by some of his franchisees. "We will make conformists out of them in a hurry . . . The organization cannot trust the individual; the individual must trust the organization."

One of the ironies of America's fast food industry is that a business so dedicated to conformity was founded by iconoclasts and self-made men, by entrepreneurs willing to defy conventional opinion. Few of the people who built fast food empires ever attended college, let alone business school. They worked hard, took risks, and followed their own paths. In many respects, the fast food industry embodies the best and the worst of American capitalism at the start of the twenty-first century—its constant stream of new products and innovations, its widening gulf between rich and poor. The industrialization of the restaurant kitchen has enabled the fast food chains to rely upon a low-paid and unskilled workforce. While a handful of workers manage to rise up the corporate ladder, the vast majority lack full-time employment, receive no benefits, learn few skills, exercise little control over their workplace, quit after a few months, and float from job to job. The restaurant industry is now America's largest private employer, and it pays some of the lowest wages. During the economic boom of the 1990s, when many American workers enjoyed their first pay raises in a generation, the real value of wages in the restaurant industry continued to fall. The roughly 3.5 million fast food workers are by far the largest group of minimum wage earners in the United States. The only Americans who consistently earn a lower hourly wage are migrant farm workers.

A hamburger and french fries became the quintessential American meal in the 1950s, thanks to the promotional efforts of the fast food chains. The typical American now consumes approximately three hamburgers and four orders of french fries every week. But the steady barrage of fast food ads, full of thick juicy burgers and long golden fries, rarely mentions where these foods come from nowadays or what ingredients they contain. The birth of the fast food industry coincided with Eisenhower-era glorifications of technology, with optimistic slogans like "Better Living through Chemistry" and "Our Friend the Atom." The sort of technological wizardry that Walt Disney promoted on television and at Disneyland eventually reached its fulfillment in the kitchens of fast food restaurants. Indeed, the corporate culture of McDonald's seems inextricably linked to that of the Disney empire, sharing a reverence for sleek machinery, electronics, and automation. The leading fast food chains still embrace a boundless faith in science—and as a result have changed not just what Americans eat, but also how their food is made.

The current methods for preparing fast food are less likely to be found in   15
cookbooks than in trade journals such as *Food Technologist* and *Food Engineering*. Aside from the salad greens and tomatoes, most fast food is delivered to the restaurant already frozen, canned, dehydrated, or freeze-dried. A fast food kitchen is merely the final stage in a vast and highly complex system of mass production. Foods that may look familiar have in fact been completely reformulated. What we eat has changed more in the last forty years than in the previous forty thousand. Like Cheyenne Mountain, today's fast food conceals remarkable technological advances behind an ordinary-looking façade. Much of the taste and aroma of American fast food, for example, is now manufactured at a series of large chemical plants off the New Jersey Turnpike.

In the fast food restaurants of Colorado Springs, behind the counters, amid the plastic seats, in the changing landscape outside the window, you can see all the virtues and destructiveness of our fast food nation. I chose Colorado Springs as a focal point for this book because the changes that have recently swept through the city are emblematic of those that fast food—and the fast food mentality—have encouraged throughout the United States. Countless other suburban communities, in every part of the country, could have been used to illustrate the same points. The extraordinary growth of Colorado Springs neatly parallels that of the fast food industry: during the last few decades, the city's population has more than doubled. Subdivisions, shopping malls, and chain restaurants are appearing in the foothills of Cheyenne Mountain and the plains rolling to the east. The Rocky Mountain region as a whole has the fastest-growing economy in the United States, mixing high-tech and service industries in a way that may define America's workforce for years to come. And new restaurants are opening there at a faster pace than anywhere else in the nation.

Fast food is now so commonplace that it has acquired an air of inevitability, as though it were somehow unavoidable, a fact of modern life. And yet the dominance of the fast food giants was no more preordained than the march of colonial split-levels, golf courses, and manmade lakes across the deserts of the American West. The political philosophy that now prevails in so much of the West—with its demand for lower taxes, smaller government, an unbridled free market—stands in total contradiction to the region's true economic underpinnings. No other region of the United States has been so dependent on government subsidies for so long, from the nineteenth-century construction of its railroads to the twentieth-century financing of its military bases and dams. One historian has described the federal government's 1950s highway-building binge as a case study in "interstate socialism"—a phase that aptly describes how the West was really won. The fast food industry took root alongside that interstate highway system, as a new form of restaurant sprang up beside the new off-

ramps. Moreover, the extraordinary growth of this industry over the past quarter-century did not occur in a political vacuum. It took place during a period
when the inflation-adjusted value of the minimum wage declined by about 40
percent, when sophisticated mass marketing techniques were for the first time
directed at small children, and when federal agencies created to protect workers
and consumers too often behaved like branch offices of the companies that
were supposed to be regulated. Ever since the administration of President
Richard Nixon, the fast food industry has worked closely with its allies in
Congress and the White House to oppose new worker safety, food safety, and
minimum wage laws. While publicly espousing support for the free market, the
fast food chains have quietly pursued and greatly benefited from a wide variety
of government subsidies. Far from being inevitable, America's fast food industry in its present form is the logical outcome of certain political and economic
choices.

In the potato fields and processing plants of Idaho, in the ranchlands east of
Colorado Springs, in the feedlots and slaughterhouses of the High Plains, you
can see the effects of fast food on the nation's rural life, its environment, its
workers, and its health. The fast food chains now stand atop a huge food-
industrial complex that has gained control of American agriculture. During
the 1980s, large multinationals—such as Cargill, ConAgra, and IBP—were
allowed to dominate one commodity market after another. Farmers and cattle
ranchers are losing their independence, essentially becoming hired hands for
the agribusiness giants or being forced off the land. Family farms are now
being replaced by gigantic corporate farms with absentee owners. Rural communities are losing their middle class and becoming socially stratified, divided between a small, wealthy elite and large numbers of the working poor.
Small towns that seemingly belong in a Norman Rockwell painting are being
turned into rural ghettos. The hardy, independent farmers whom Thomas
Jefferson considered the bedrock of American democracy are a truly vanishing
breed. The United States now has more prison inmates than full-time farmers.

The fast food chains' vast purchasing power and their demand for a uniform
product have encouraged fundamental changes in how cattle are raised,
slaughtered, and processed into ground beef. These changes have made meat-
packing—once a highly skilled, highly paid occupation—into the most dangerous job in the United States, performed by armies of poor, transient immigrants whose injuries often go unrecorded and uncompensated. And the same
meat industry practices that endanger these workers have facilitated the introduction of deadly pathogens, such as E. coli 0157:H7, into America's hamburger meat, a food aggressively marketed to children. Again and again,
efforts to prevent the sale of tainted ground beef have been thwarted by meat
industry lobbyists and their allies in Congress. The federal government has the
legal authority to recall a defective toaster oven or stuffed animal—but still
lacks the power to recall tons of contaminated, potentially lethal meat.

I do not mean to suggest that fast food is solely responsible for every social 20 problem now haunting the United States. In some cases (such as the malling and sprawling of the West) the fast food industry has been a catalyst and a symptom of larger economic trends. In other cases (such as the rise of franchising and the spread of obesity) fast food has played a more central role. By tracing the diverse influences of fast food I hope to shed light not only on the workings of an important industry, but also on a distinctively American way of viewing the world.

Elitists have always looked down at fast food, criticizing how it tastes and regarding it as another tacky manifestation of American popular culture. The aesthetics of fast food are of much less concern to me than its impact upon the lives of ordinary Americans, both as workers and consumers. Most of all, I am concerned about its impact on the nation's children. Fast food is heavily marketed to children and prepared by people who are barely older than children. This is an industry that both feeds and feeds off the young. During the two years spent researching this book, I ate an enormous amount of fast food. Most of it tasted pretty good. That is one of the main reasons people buy fast food; it has been carefully designed to taste good. It's also inexpensive and convenient. But the value meals, two-for-one deals, and free refills of soda give a distorted sense of how much fast food actually costs. The real price never appears on the menu.

The sociologist George Ritzer has attacked the fast food industry for celebrating a narrow measure of efficiency over every other human value, calling the triumph of McDonald's "the irrationality of rationality." Others consider the fast food industry proof of the nation's great economic vitality, a beloved American institution that appeals overseas to millions who admire our way of life. Indeed, the values, the culture, and the industrial arrangements of our fast food nation are now being exported to the rest of the world. Fast food has joined Hollywood movies, blue jeans, and pop music as one of America's most prominent cultural exports. Unlike other commodities, however, fast food isn't viewed, read, played, or worn. It enters the body and becomes part of the consumer. No other industry offers, both literally and figuratively, so much insight into the nature of mass consumption.

Hundreds of millions of people buy fast food every day without giving it much thought, unaware of the subtle and not so subtle ramifications of their purchases. They rarely consider where this food came from, how it was made, what it is doing to the community around them. They just grab their tray off the counter, find a table, take a seat, unwrap the paper, and dig in. The whole experience is transitory and soon forgotten. I've written this book out of a belief that people should know what lies behind the shiny, happy surface of every fast food transaction. They should know what really lurks between those sesame-seed buns. As the old saying goes: You are what you eat.

ANALYZING What the Writer Says

1. In what ways has the fast food industry transformed American life and the American economy?

2. What economic changes in the last thirty years have fueled the growth of the American fast food industry?

3. "The Golden Arches are now more widely recognized than the Christian cross," says Schlosser. What does he mean by this statement?

4. What does Schlosser say is the purpose behind his writing this book?

ANALYZING How the Writer Says It

1. Schlosser begins his book on fast food with a description of Cheyenne Mountain and the "top-secret, underground combat operations center" it contains. How effective is this "hook"?

2. A good introduction presents the subject of an essay (or book) and sets up its structure for the reader. How does Schlosser do this in his introduction to *Fast Food Nation*?

3. "The whole experience of buying fast food," says Schlosser, "has become a social custom as American as a small, rectangular, hand-held, frozen, and reheated apple pie." What effect does the writer achieve by adding a string of adjectives to the proverbial "as American as apple pie"?

ANALYZING the Issue

1. "You are what you eat," says Schlosser at the end of the introduction to *Fast Food Nation*. In what ways has fast food changed us and our culture? Is this change necessarily for the worse? Explain.

2. Many ecologists and animal-rights activists have protested the changes the fast food industry has effected in how animals are raised for food: the razing of large areas of rain forests to make grazing pastures for cattle, the use of hormones to promote growth in cattle and poultry, and the confinement of animals in small cages until they have acquired the desired weight for slaughter. Do you think these protesters have a point? Or do you think the changes in our farm industry are simply the price we must pay for progress? Explain.

ANALYZING Connections Between Texts

1. Compare Schlosser's statements about fast food and the way it is made to the attention Laurie Colwin ("How to Fry Chicken," p. 269) lavishes on frying

chicken just right. Are cooks like Colwin dying out in our fast food nation—or are they being replaced by scientists devising newer and better ways to process (and sell) food to an ever-increasing clientele? Explain.

2. What does Matthew Blakeslee's "Madison Avenue and Your Brain" (p. 632) add to Schlosser's analysis of the runaway success of the fast-food industry?

3. How does Chris Johns's photograph of a family shopping for groceries (p. 98) tie in with Schlosser's revelations about the fast food industry? Does Johns's image support or contradict what Schlosser says? Why?

WARMING UP: *Is there a food you crave that is not available where you live? To how much trouble would you go to get it?*

Missing Links

BY CALVIN TRILLIN

CALVIN TRILLIN

Humorist and columnist Calvin Trillin has written regularly for Time, *the* New Yorker, *and* USA Today. *He has appeared on many morning and late-night television news shows and written and produced a one-man show on Broadway. This essay appeared in the* New Yorker *in 2002.*

Of all the things I've eaten in the Cajun parishes of Louisiana—an array of foodstuffs which has been characterized as somewhere between extensive and deplorable—I yearn most often for boudin. When people in Breaux Bridge or Opelousas or Jeanerette talk about boudin (pronounced "boo-DAN"), they mean a soft, spicy mixture of rice and pork and liver and seasoning which is squeezed hot into the mouth from a sausage casing, usually in the parking lot of a grocery store and preferably while leaning against a pickup. ("Boudin" means blood sausage to the French, most of whom would probably line up for immigration visas if they ever tasted the Cajun version.) I figure that about eighty per cent of the boudin purchased in Louisiana is consumed before the purchaser has left the parking lot, and most of the rest of it is polished off in the car. In other words, Cajun boudin not only doesn't get outside the state; it usually doesn't even get home. For Americans who haven't been to South Louisiana, boudin remains as foreign as *gado-gado* or *cheb;* for them, the word "Cajun" on a menu is simply a synonym for burnt fish or too much pepper. When I am daydreaming of boudin, it sometimes occurs to me that of all the indignities the Acadians of Louisiana have had visited upon them—being booted out of Nova Scotia, being ridiculed as rubes and swamp rats by neighboring Anglophones for a couple of centuries, being punished for speaking their own language in the schoolyard—nothing has been as deeply insulting as what restaurants outside South Louisiana present as Cajun food.

The scarcity of boudin in the rest of the country makes it all the more pleasurable to have a Louisiana friend who likes to travel and occasionally carries along an ice chest full of local ingredients, just in case. I happen to have such a friend in James Edmunds, of New Iberia, Louisiana. Over the past twenty years or so, James's visits to New York have regularly included the ritualistic unpacking of an ice chest on my kitchen table. His custom has been to bring the ice chest if he plans to cook a meal during the visit—crawfish étouffée, for instance, or gumbo or his signature shrimp stew. On those trips, the ice chest would also hold some boudin. I was so eager to get my hands on the boudin that I often ate it right in the kitchen, as soon as we heated it through, rather than trying to make the experience more authentic by searching for something appropriate to lean against. In lower Manhattan, after all, it could take a while to find a pickup truck.

Then there came the day when I was sentenced to what I think of as medium-security cholesterol prison. (Once the cholesterol penal system was concessioned out to the manufacturers of statin drugs, medium-security cholesterol prison came to mean that the inmate could eat the occasional bit of bacon from the plate of a generous luncheon companion but could not order his own B.L.T.) James stopped bringing boudin, the warders having summarily dismissed my argument that the kind I particularly like—Cajun boudin varies greatly from maker to maker—was mostly just rice anyway.

I did not despair. James is inventive, and he's flexible. Several years ago, he decided that an architect friend of his who lives just outside New Iberia made the best crawfish étouffée in the area, and, like one of those research-and-development hot shots who are always interested in ways of improving the product, he took the trouble to look into the recipe, which had been handed down to the architect by forebears of unadulterated Cajunness. James was prepared for the possibility that one of the secret ingredients of the architect's blissful étouffée was, say, some herb available only at certain times of the year in the swamps of the Atchafalaya Basin Spillway. As it turned out, one of the secret ingredients was Campbell's cream-of-mushroom soup. (Although crawfish étouffée, which means smothered crawfish, is one of the best-known Cajun dishes, it emerged only in the fifties, when a lot of people assumed that just about any recipe was enhanced by a can of Campbell's cream-of-mushroom soup.) During ensuing étouffée preparations in New York, there would come a moment when James said, in his soft South Louisiana accent, "I think this might be a good time for certain sensitive people to leave the kitchen for just a little while." Then we'd hear the whine of the can opener, followed by an unmistakable *glub-glub-glub*.

A few years after my sentence was imposed, James and I were talking on the telephone about an imminent New York visit that was to include the preparation of one of his dinner specialties, and he told me not to worry about the problem of items rattling around in his ice chest. I told him that I actually hadn't

given that problem much thought, what with global warming and nuclear proliferation and all. As if he hadn't heard me, he went on to say that he'd stopped
the rattling with what he called packing-boudin.

"Packing-boudin?"

"That's right," James said.

I thought about that for a moment or two. "Well, it's got bubble wrap beat,"
I finally said. "And we wouldn't have to worry about adding to this country's
solid-waste-disposal problem. Except for the casing." The habit of tossing aside
the casing of a spent link of boudin is so ingrained in some parts of Louisiana
that there is a bumper sticker reading "Caution: Driver Eating Boudin"—a way
of warning the cars that follow about the possibility of their windshields being
splattered with what appear to be odd-looking insects. From that visit on, I
took charge of packing-boudin disposal whenever James was carrying his ice
chest, and I tried not to dwell on my disappointment when he wasn't.

Not long ago, I got a call from James before a business trip to New York
which was not scheduled to include the preparation of a Louisiana meal—that
is, a trip that would ordinarily not include boudin. He asked if he could store a
turducken in my freezer for a couple of days; he was making a delivery for a
friend. I hesitated. I was trying to remember precisely what a turducken is,
other than something Cajuns make that seems to go against the laws of nature.

James, perhaps thinking that my hesitancy reflected some reluctance to take   10
on the storage job, said, "There'd be rental-boudin involved, of course."

"Fair's fair," I said.

What led to my being in Louisiana a couple of weeks later for something that
James insisted on calling a boudin blitzkrieg is rather complicated. As a matter of convenience, James had picked up the rental-boudin at the same place
he'd bought the turducken, Hebert's Specialty Meats, in Maurice, Louisiana.
Hebert's is a leading purveyor of turducken, which it makes by taking the
bones out of a chicken and a duck and a turkey, stuffing the chicken with stuffing, stuffing the stuffed chicken into a similarly stuffed duck, and stuffing all
that, along with a third kind of stuffing, into the turkey. The result cannot be
criticized for lacking complexity, and it presents a challenge to the holiday
carver almost precisely as daunting as meat loaf.

The emergence of turducken, eight or ten years ago, did not surprise Cajuns.
When it comes to eating, they take improvisation for granted. Some people in
New Iberia, for instance, collect the sludge left over from mashing peppers at
the McIlhenny Tabasco plant and use it to spice up the huge pots of water they
employ to boil crawfish. When Thanksgiving approaches, they fill the same
huge pots with five or six gallons of lard instead of water and produce deep-fried
turkey—a dish that is related to the traditional roast turkey in the way that *soupe
au pistou* in Provence or *ribollita* in Tuscany is related to the vegetable soup that
was served in your high-school cafeteria. James's wife, Susan Hester, who

works at the Iberia Parish Library, once heard a deputy sheriff who was lecturing on personal defense recommend buying water-based rather than oil-based pepper spray not only because it comes off the clothing easier but because it is preferable for flavoring the meat being grilled at a cookout.

Although I didn't want to appear ungrateful for the rental-boudin, I reminded James that his buying boudin in Maurice, which is more than twenty miles from New Iberia, flies in the face of the rule promulgated by his old friend Barry Jean Ancelet, a folklorist and French professor at the University of Louisiana at Lafayette: in the Cajun country of Louisiana, the best boudin is always the boudin closest to where you live, and the best place to eat boiled crawfish is always extraordinarily inconvenient to your house. James is aware that this theory has a problem with internal consistency—it means, for instance, that for him the best boudin is at Bonin's meat market, in New Iberia, and for Barry Jean Ancelet it's at The Best Stop Supermarket, in Scott— but he reconciles that by saying that Barry, being a folklorist, has a different notion of objective truth than some other people.

We had never talked much about the source of the boudin James brought to   15 New York, except that I knew it had changed once, some years ago, when a purveyor named Dud Breaux retired. Once his purchase of boudin in Maurice raised the subject, though, James assured me that under ordinary circumstances he follows the Ancelet Dictum: before leaving for New York, he stocks up at Bonin's, assuming that the proprietor happens to be in what James called "a period of non-retirement." The proprietor's name is Waldo Bonin, but he is known in New Iberia as Nook. He is a magisterial man with white hair and a white mustache and a white T-shirt and a white apron. Nook Bonin has not retired as many times as Frank Sinatra did, but he is about even with Michael Jordan.

Like one of those boxers who bid farewell to the ring with some regularity, Bonin comes back every time with a little less in his repertoire. For nearly fifty years, he and his wife, Delores, ran a full-service meat market that also included a lot of Cajun specialties. The first time they came out of retirement, they had dropped everything but boudin and cracklins (crunchy pieces of fatback that are produced by rendering lard from a hog) and hogshead cheese, plus soft drinks for those who weren't going to make it back to their cars with their purchases intact. The second time, when the Bonins started appearing only on Friday afternoons and Saturday mornings, they had dropped the cracklins. As a matter of policy, James doesn't actually eat cracklins—"I just think it's good to know that there's a line out there you're not going to cross," he has said— but, as someone who depends on Nook Bonin's boudin, he had to be disturbed by what appeared to be a trend. "I wouldn't mind losing the Cokes," he has said, when envisioning what might be dropped in the Bonins' next comeback. "But it is getting kind of scary."

The recipe for the boudin sold at Bonin's is a secret. In fact, it has occurred to James that the proprietor himself may not know the secret: people customarily speak of Nook Bonin's boudin, but it is actually made by Delores Bonin, who goes heavy on the rice and uses an array of spices that, I would be prepared to testify under oath, owe nothing to the test kitchens of the Campbell's Soup Company. Although the Bonins have two daughters, neither of them chose to go into the family business. Anna is an administrator in a special-education program, and Melissa is an artist. James and Susan happen to be longtime admirers of Melissa's work—some years ago, they bought the first painting she ever sold—but James can't help thinking that if she had chosen to put her creative energies into boudin-making rather than art, the community would not now be beset by the tension brought on by her parents' stairstep retirements. At this point, James and Susan have pinned their hopes on the Bonins' only grandchild—Melissa's son, Emile. Unfortunately, Emile is only ten years old. James was cheered, though, when we walked into the Bonins' store on a Saturday morning and Delores Bonin reached over the meat case to hand us a photograph of Emile posing behind the device that stuffs boudin into sausage casing. Emile was smiling.

Even assuming that Emile decides to cast his lot with boudin, though, it will be a number of years before he's old enough to take over the business. James and I discussed that situation in the sort of conversation I can imagine a working team from State and Defense having about whether sufficient steps have been taken to guarantee that this country maintains a secure and unbroken supply of cobalt in the face of any contingency. We decided that, just in case the Bonin family line of succession does get broken, I should sample some of the possibilities for what I suppose you'd have to call replacement-boudin. This is why Susan, who was carrying a cutting board and a kitchen knife, and James and I were driving around on a sunny weekend, tasting what Nook Bonin had to offer and testing out, in a judicious way, the work of other purveyors. At least, that's what I would tell the penal authorities if the question ever came up.

By Sunday night, we had tried the boudin from, among other places, Legnon's Boucherie, in New Iberia, and Bruce's U-Need-A-Butcher, in Lafayette, and Poche's Meat Market and Restaurant, in Poche Bridge, and Heleaux's Grocery, also in Lafayette, and, of course, The Best Stop, in Scott. We hadn't by any measure exhausted the supply of even highly recommended boudin purveyors. For instance, we hadn't tried Johnson's Grocery, in Eunice, or Billeaud's, in Broussard, a town near Lafayette that used to have an annual boudin festival. A friend of mine in New Orleans, Randy Fertel, after tracking down the source of the boudin that he looks forward to eating every year at the New Orleans Jazz Fest, had recommended Abe's Cajun Market, in Lake Charles, which is practically in Texas, but there hadn't been time. Still, I had tasted enough contenders for replacement-boudin to tell James that I hoped Nook and Delores Bonin truly understood that for people who have been active all their lives retirement can be a trap.

I had to admit to Barry Jean Ancelet, who joined us at The Best Stop, that   20
his local purveyor makes a distinguished link of boudin—moderate, shading
toward meaty, when it comes to the all-important rice/meat ratio. Lawrence
Menard, who opened The Best Stop in 1986, told us that he now sells between
sixty-five hundred and seven thousand pounds of boudin a week. In a conversation that began, appropriately, at The Best Stop and continued later that
evening in a restaurant called Bubba Frey's, Barry explained the Ancelet
Dictum to us in more detail. A link of boudin, he said, is a clean food, essentially treated by Cajuns as "an enclosed lunch"; it's even cleaner if you eat the
casing, which Lawrence Menard himself always does. Boiled crawfish, on the
other hand, is notoriously messy, leaving a table piled with shells and crawfish
heads. It stands to reason that you'd want to leave that kind of mess far from
your lair. He pointed out that for boiled crawfish he and James both favor a
place called Hawk's, whose location is inconvenient to both of them and to
practically everybody else. In a book called "Cajun Country Guide," Macon Fry
and Julie Posner wrote that the reason Hawk's is so good is that Hawk
Arceneaux puts his crawfish through a twenty-four-hour freshwater purging
process, but, then again, they're not folklorists.

Since the "e" in Frey is silent, Bubba Frey's sounds at first like a succinct
description of Southern cooking rather than a restaurant. It is a restaurant,
though—a bright, knotty-pine place with a Cajun combo that, on the night we
were there, included Bubba Frey himself as one of its fiddlers. We went there
after a performance of "Rendezvous des Cadiens," a Cajun radio show that Barry
m.c.s every Saturday at the Liberty Theatre in Eunice—a town in an area known
as the Cajun Prairies. For some time, Bubba Frey has run a general store in a
nearby hamlet called Mowata—a name I don't intend to investigate, just in case
it is unconnected with a floor or the discovery of a particularly capacious well—
and not long ago he decided to add a restaurant next door. Boudin balls were listed as an appetizer. Boudin isn't commonly served by restaurants, although Café
des Amis, in Breaux Bridge, offers something called *oreille de cochon*—beignet
dough that is baked in the shape of pigs' ears, covered with powdered sugar, and,
for an extra dollar, stuffed with boudin. It's a dollar well spent.

Boudin balls are made by rolling boudin into balls, coating them with something like Zatarain's Fish Fry, and frying away. At Bubba Frey's, they were
delicious, and the proprietor, who came over to our table between sets, told us
that the boudin was made at his store next door. I told James that the next time
he happened to be on the Cajun Prairies he might consider finding out what
Bubba's boudin tasted like unfried. Then it occurred to me that if James liked
it better than he liked Nook Bonin's boudin he might feel obligated to move to
Mowata. James did not seem enthusiastic about that prospect. He and Susan
have both lived in New Iberia virtually all their lives, and have a lot of friends
there. Also, James subscribes to the theory that, perhaps because the French
settlement of the Cajun Prairies included a strong admixture of Germans, peo-

ple there are a bit stiffer than the people who live in the Cajun bayous. I don't know how stiffness in Cajuns would manifest itself. Maybe they use only two kinds of stuffing in their turduckens.

A couple of weeks later, I heard from James: the boudin at Bubba Frey's store was, as we suspected, excellent—"a commendable second place to Nook," James wrote, "but still not with the transcendent special taste." Moving to Mowata was not on the table. Also, he and Susan and the Bonins' daughter Melissa had gone to dinner together and, as it happened, had fallen into a little chat about the future. "I told her that if Emile learned the recipe and learned how to make boudin he'd never starve," James said. "And neither, it goes without saying, would we."

ANALYZING What the Writer Says

1. What is the point of Trillin's piece on cajun boudin? What does he associate with the enjoyment of the decidedly—and specifically—Cajun delicacy?

2. What is "turducken," and how does Trillin acknowledge its particular Cajun-ness?

3. What is Trillin's opinion of Cajuns? Why do you think he finds Cajun food so appealing?

ANALYZING How the Writer Says It

1. What is the purpose of the humor Trillin uses throughout his piece?

2. Analyze the layers of meaning in Trillin's title.

ANALYZING the Issue

1. How do particular gastronomic specialties comment on a place, its people, and its culture?

2. Do you think there is a connection between attitudes toward food and character? Explain.

ANALYZING Connections Between Texts

1. Does Trillin's piece reinforce or contradict fears raised by Eric Schlosser in the introduction to *Fast Food Nation* (p. 307)?

2. How does Trillin echo some of the points Amy Tan makes in "Mother Tongue" (p. 515)?

3. Which of Trillin's points does Stephanie Maze's photograph "Lunch at Uncle Antonio's" (p. 99) illustrate?

YOUR TURN: Suggestions for Writing About "Appetites and Addictions"

1. In the manner of Laurie Colwin, write an essay instructing your reader on the best way to prepare a favorite dish. Be sure to convey in your essay your love for the dish and its significant associations.

2. Describe and discuss the significance of a particular dish or meal connected to a family or cultural tradition.

3. The old adage goes, "some people eat to live; others live to eat." How important is the preparation and consumption of food? Write an essay exploring the importance of food and food rituals to a culture.

4. Write an essay analyzing recent food trends and how they reflect a changing culture.

5. Obsession with food can, of course, be very unhealthy, as reflected in many of the health issues recently spotlighted by the media—such as anorexia, bulimia, and obesity. Write an essay exploring one of these problems and its connection to food.

6. Should the media warn the public against addictive behaviors or substance abuse? Write an essay in which you take a position on this issue.

7. Should fast food corporations be held responsible for obesity and other health problems associated with the consumption of their products? Write an essay in which you take a position on this issue.

8. Do works such as Eric Schlosser's *Fast Food Nation* or even the publication by *Harper's* of the FDA's standards of food purity ("Passed by a Hair") promote irrational fear of food? Or do they serve an important public service? Write an essay to defend your answer.

9. Write an essay exploring the root causes of addictive behavior; Stanton Peele and Scott Russell Sanders are potential sources.

10. After reading Stanton Peele's "Running Scared," write an essay analyzing recent popular approaches to battling drug and alcohol abuse among adolescents.

11. Write an essay in which you analyze how drug and/or alcohol abuse is dealt with in recent films.

IMAGE GALLERY 👁

I NEED SMOKES MORE THAN ANY THING ELSE

According to Harper's Magazine, *this poster begging contributions to improve life in the trenches for Americans fighting in WWI was distributed in 1918 by the Our Boys in France Tobacco Fund.*

1. Of what popular iconography does this poster remind you?

2. How does the poster's design attract attention?

3. What does this 1918 poster say about the public's attitude toward smoking at the time? How would a twenty-first century audience react differently to this message?

JIM ARBOGAST

Shopping Spree

The photograph captures a stylish young woman on a shopping spree.

1. What is the model in the photograph wearing? What is the connection between her clothes and the bags she is carrying?

2. Is there a reason why there aren't any (visible) logos on the bags?

3. How would your response to the photo be different if the model's face and upper body were visible?

4. Would you react differently to this photograph if the model had been middle-aged or overweight?

5. How does the choice of background enhance the photograph's overall effect?

6. In what other reading unit in this book might this photograph be appropriate?

EUGENE RICHARDS

Crack for Sale

Throughout his career, Eugene Richards has tried to record a reality that many Americans would prefer not to acknowledge. In 1990 he took this picture of "Kojak," a 13-year-old crack dealer in North Philadelphia, as he permits a customer to inspect his merchandise.

1. What is the focal point of this picture? How does it fit into the photograph's overall composition scheme?

2. What do the two men in the background contribute to the overall effect of the picture?

3. Compare the young woman in the foreground to the two men behind her.

4. How do the setting and background comment on the crack deal depicted in the foreground of the picture?

5. How does the photographer use light and shadow in this image?

6. Do you feel that this photograph merely records a drug transaction, or does it make a statement about drug trafficking and drug addiction in general? What does Richards want you to think about drug addiction?

CARRIE MAE WEEMS

The Mission

Carrie Mae Weems (b. 1953) addresses issues of race, identity, class, and gender in her photographs and installations. This 1987 photograph seems to debunk not only racial stereotypes but simplistic notions of addiction and cure.

Jim, if you choose to accept, the mission is to land on your own two feet.

1. What is the man in the picture doing? Why is a phone lying face down on the table? Why is he listening to the tape recorder?

2. The caption, "Jim, if you choose to accept, the mission is to land on your own two feet," is a significant part of the image. How does it contribute to the photograph's subject?

3. How does the photographer use light effects in this photograph? What does the white oval of light above the man's head symbolize? What does the cloud of smoke symbolize?

4. How does composition contribute to the impact of this image?

12 | LEARNING MATTERS

Considering recent report cards on American education, our system is failing. Students, especially in poor, urban school systems, lack basic math and reading skills and perform poorly on standardized tests—no big surprise given that education funding is so often based on property tax. So affluent kids who live in

> "**Education**, *n.*
> That which disguises to the wise and disguises from the foolish their lack of understanding."
>
> —Ambrose Bierce
> *The Devil's Dictionary*

areas that generate high property taxes attend better schools, while children of the underclass go to underfunded schools. And even in better schools, violence is increasing. More and more parents, disenchanted with public education, either support vouchers—thus transferring already skimpy public funding to private schools—or opt for home schooling.

The state of higher education, some argue, is not much better. Increasing costs keep college education out of reach for many people. Those in college complain about overworked instructors who are stretched too thin, or research-obsessed professors for whom teaching is not a priority; some professors, like Roberta F. Borkat and Jacob Neusner, in these pages, lament the grade inflation, decline of standards, and lack of motivation they see resulting from current administrative practices in higher education. And what of the championing of political correctness on college campuses? Does it promote sensitivity? Or choke intellectual debate?

Enumerating the major lessons taught in schools, John Taylor Gatto's essay suggests that Ambrose Bierce's cynicism is neither dated nor erroneous. Mike Rose uses his own experience in a vocational education track to point out some of the flaws inherent in public education. Toni Cade Bambara's young protagonist learns an important lesson about class—not in a classroom but on a fashionable Manhattan street. Robert Coles questions the ability of art to accurately represent the ugliness of Ruby Bridges's experience as a child on the front lines of school integration, while Langston Hughes describes a black student's sense of alienation in a white institution. Questioning Japanese culture, Cathy Davidson wonders whether the rigorous education imposed on its daughters is wasted on girls who are expected only to marry and raise children. Joe Queenan directs a withering gaze toward Baby Boomer parents panicked about which colleges accept their offspring, and Norman Atkins satirizes the man who invented Cliffs Notes, the ubiquitous guides more likely than not to stand in, at one time or another in the educational experience of Boomers' kids, for actual literature.

A photograph in this chapter, "Golden Rules," captures a schoolroom in an earlier era, a time when—if the fingernail inspection is any indication—cleanliness was up there with reading, writing, and arithmetic, a time when, no doubt, the concept of education was understood in simpler terms. But one truth is timeless: education is an ongoing process, and most education takes place outside the classroom. The wisest among us are those willing to learn. ❄

WARMING UP: *Can you think of an important lesson you learned at a time and place in which you were caught completely off guard?*

The Lesson

BY TONI CADE BAMBARA

TONI CADE BAMBARA

Educated in New York, Florence, and Paris, Toni Cade Bambara (1939–95) published her first short story in 1960 and published several collections of short stories, along with novels and screenplays. The following story of a young girl's initiation into harsh social reality comes from Gorilla My Love *(1972).*

Back in the days when everyone was old and stupid or young and foolish and me and Sugar were the only ones just right, this lady moved on our block with nappy hair and proper speech and no makeup. And quite naturally we laughed at her, laughed the way we did at the junk man who went about his business like he was some big-time president and his sorry ass horse his secretary. And we kinda hated her too, hated the way we did the winos who cluttered up our parks and pissed on our handball walls and stank up our hallways and stairs so you couldn't halfway play hide-and-seek without a goddamn gas mask. Miss Moore was her name. The only woman on the block with no first name. And she was black as hell, cept for her feet, which were fish-white and spooky. And she was always planning these boring-ass things for us to do, us being my cousin, mostly, who lived on the block cause we all moved North the same time and to the same apartment then spread out gradual to breathe. And our parents would yank our heads into some kinda shape and crisp up our clothes so we'd be presentable for travel with Miss Moore, who always looked like she was going to church, though she never did. Which is just one of the things the grown ups talked about when they talked behind her back like a dog. But when she came calling with some sachet[1] she'd sewed up or some gingerbread she'd made or some book, why then they'd all be too em-

---

[1] A small bag or packet of aromatic powder used to scent clothes in a closet. (Editor's note)

barrassed to turn her down and we'd get handed over all spruced up. She'd been to college and said it was only right that she should take responsibility for the young ones' education, and she not even related by marriage or blood. So they'd go for it. Specially Aunt Gretchen. She was the main gofer in the family. You got some ole dumb shit foolishness you want somebody to go for, you send for Aunt Gretchen. She been screwed into the go-along for so long, it's a blood-deep natural thing with her. Which is how she got saddled with me and Sugar and Junior in the first place while our mothers were in a la-de-da apartment up the block having a good ole time.

So this one day Miss Moore rounds us all up at the mailbox and it's puredee hot and she's knockin herself out about arithmetic. And school suppose to let up in summer I heard, but she don't never let up. And the starch in my pinafore scratching the shit outta me and I'm really hating this nappy-head bitch and her goddamn college degree. I'd much rather go to the pool or to the show where it's cool. So me and Sugar leaning on the mailbox being surly, which is a Miss Moore word. And Flyboy checking out what everybody brought for lunch. And Fat Butt already wasting his peanut-butter-and-jelly sandwich like the pig he is. And Junebug punchin on Q.T.'s arm for potato chips. And Rosie Giraffe shifting from one hip to the other waiting for somebody to step on her foot or ask her if she from Georgia so she can kick ass, preferably Mercedes'. And Miss Moore asking us do we know what money is, like we a bunch of retards. I mean real money, she say, like it's only poker chips or monopoly papers we lay on the grocer. So right away I'm tired of this and say so. And would much rather snatch Sugar and go to the Sunset and terrorize the West Indian kids and take their hair ribbons and their money too. And Miss Moore files that remark away for next week's lesson on brotherhood, I can tell. And finally I say we oughta get to the subway cause it's cooler and besides we might meet some cute boys. Sugar done swiped her mama's lipstick, so we ready.

So we heading down the street and she's boring us silly about what things cost and what our parents make and how much goes for rent and how money ain't divided up right in this country. And then she gets to the part about we all poor and live in the slums, which I don't feature. And I'm ready to speak on that, but she steps out in the street and hails two cabs just like that. Then she hustles half the crew in with her and hands me a five-dollar bill and tells me to calculate 10 percent tip for the driver. And we're off Me and Sugar and Junebug and Flyboy hangin out the window and hollering to everybody, putting lipstick on each other cause Flyboy a faggot anyway, and making farts with our sweaty armpits. But I'm mostly trying to figure how to spend this money. But they all fascinated with the meter ticking and Junebug starts laying bets as to how much it'll read when Flyboy can't hold his breath no more. Then Sugar lays bets as to how much it'll be when we get there. So I'm stuck. Don't nobody want to go for my plan, which is to jump out at the next light and run off the first bar-b-que we can find. Then the driver tells us to get the hell out cause we there already. And the meter reads eighty five cents. And I'm stalling to figure out the tip and Sugar say give him a dime. And I decide he don't need it bad as I do, so later for him. But then he tries to take off with Junebug foot still in the door so we talk about his mama something ferocious. Then we check out that we on Fifth Avenue[2] and everybody dressed up in stockings. One lady in a fur coat, hot as it is. White folks crazy.

"This is the place," Miss Moore say, presenting it to us in the voice she uses at the museum. "Let's look in the windows before we go in."

"Can we steal?" Sugar asks very serious like she's getting the ground rules   5 squared away before she plays. "I beg your pardon," say Miss Moore, and we fall out. So she leads us around the windows of the toy store and me and Sugar screamin, "This is mine, that's mine, I gotta have that, that was made for me, I was born for that," till Big Butt drowns us out.

"Hey, I'm goin to buy that there."

"That there? You don't even know what it is, stupid."

"I do so," he say punchin on Rosie Giraffe. "It's a microscope."

"Whatcha gonna do with a microscope, fool?"

"Look at things."   10

"Like what, Ronald?" ask Miss Moore. And Big Butt ain't got the first notion. So here go Miss Moore gabbing about the thousands of bacteria in a drop of water and the somethinorother in a speck of blood and the million and one living things in the air around us is invisible to the naked eye. And what she say that for? Junebug go to town on that "naked" and we rolling. Then Miss Moore ask what it cost. So we all jam into the window smudgin it up and the price tag say $300. So then she ask how long'd take for Big Butt and Junebug to save up their allowances. "Too long," I say. "Yeh," adds Sugar, "outgrown it by that time." And Miss Moore say no, you never outgrow learning instruments. "Why, even medical students and interns and," blah, blah, blah. And we ready to choke Big Butt for bringing it up in the first damn place.

"This here costs four hundred eighty dollars," say Rosie Giraffe. So we pile up all over her to see what she pointin out. My eyes tell me it's a chunk of glass cracked with something heavy, and different-color inks dripped into the splits, then the whole thing put into a oven or something. But for $480 it don't make sense.

"That's a paperweight made of semi-precious stones fused together under tremendous pressure," she explains slowly, with her hands doing the mining and all the factory work.

"So what's a paperweight?" asks Rosie Giraffe.

---

[2]New York's Fifth Avenue has always been associated with the fashionably dressed and upscale shopping. F. A. O. Schwarz, perhaps America's best known toy store, is located on Fifth Avenue; nearby is Central Park (both are mentioned below). (Editor's note)

"To weigh paper with, dumbbell," say Flyboy, the wise man from the East.   15
"Not exactly," say Miss Moore, which is what she say when you warm or way off too. "It's to weigh paper down so it won't scatter and make your desk untidy." So right away me and Sugar curtsy to each other and then to Mercedes who is more the tidy type.

"We don't keep paper on top of the desk in my class," say Junebug, figuring Miss Moore crazy or lyin one.

"At home, then," she say. "Don't you have a calendar and a pencil case and a blotter and a letter-opener on your desk at home where you do your homework?" And she know damn well what our homes look like cause she nosys around in them every chance she gets.

"I don't even have a desk," say Junebug. "Do we?"

"No. And I don't get no homework neither," says Big Butt.   20

"And I don't even have a home," say Flyboy like he do at school to keep the white folks off his back and sorry for him. Send this poor kid to camp posters, is his specialty.

"I do," says Mercedes. "I have a box of stationery on my desk and a picture of my cat. My godmother bought the stationery and the desk. There's a big rose on each sheet and the envelopes smell like roses."

"Who wants to know about your smelly-ass stationery," say Rosie Giraffe fore I can get my two cents in.

"It's important to have a work area all your own so that . . ."

"Will you look at this sailboat, please," say Flyboy, cuttin her off and pointin   25
to the thing like it was his. So once again we tumble all over each other to gaze at this magnificent thing in the toy store which is just big enough to maybe sail two kittens across the pond if you strap them to the posts tight. We all start reciting the price tag like we in assembly. "Handcrafted sailboat of fiberglass at one thousand one hundred ninety-five dollars."

"Unbelievable," I hear myself say and am really stunned. I read it again for myself just in case the group recitation put me in a trance. Same thing. For some reason this pisses me off. We look at Miss Moore and she lookin at us, waiting for I dunno what.

"Who'd pay all that when you can buy a sailboat set for a quarter at Pop's, a tube of glue for a dime, and a ball of string for eight cents? It must have a motor and a whole lot else besides," I say. "My sailboat cost me about fifty cents."

"But will it take water?" say Mercedes with her smart ass.

"Took mine to Alley Pond Park once," say Flyboy. "String broke. Lost it. Pity."

"Sailed mine in Central Park and it keeled over and sank. Had to ask my   30
father for another dollar."

"And you got the strap," laugh Big Butt. "The jerk didn't even have a string on it. My old man wailed on his behind."

Little Q.T. was staring hard at the sailboat and you could see he wanted it bad. But he too little and somebody'd just take it from him. So what the hell. "This boat for kids, Miss Moore?"

"Parents silly to buy something like that just to get all broke up," say Rosie Giraffe.

"That much money it should last forever," I figure.

"My father'd buy it for me if I wanted it."   35

"Your father, my ass," say Rosie Giraffe getting a chance to finally push Mercedes.

"Must be rich people shop here," say Q.T.

"You are a very bright boy," say Flyboy. "What was your first clue?" And he rap him on the head with the back of his knuckles, since Q.T. the only one he could get away with. Though Q.T. liable to come up behind you years later and get his licks in when you half expect it.

"What I want to know is," I says to Miss Moore though I never talk to her, I wouldn't give the bitch that satisfaction, "is how much a real boat costs? I figure a thousand'd get you a yacht any day."

"Why don't you check that out," she says, "and report back to the group?"   40
Which really pains my ass. If you gonna mess up a perfectly good swim day least you could do is have some answers. "Let's go in," she say like she got something up her sleeve only she don't lead the way. So me and Sugar turn the corner to where the entrance is, but when we get there I kinda hang back. Not that I'm scared, what's there to be afraid of, just a toy store. But I feel funny, shame. But what I got to be shamed about? Got as much right to go in as anybody. But somehow I can't seem to get hold of the door, so I step away for Sugar to lead. But she hangs back too. And I look at her and she looks at me and this is ridiculous. I mean, damn, I have never ever been shy about doing nothing or going nowhere. But then Mercedes steps up and then Rosie Giraffe and Big Butt crowd in behind and shove, and next thing we all stuffed into the doorway with only Mercedes squeezing past us, smoothing out her jumper and walking right down the aisle. Then the rest of us tumble in like a glued together jigsaw done all wrong. And people lookin at us. And it's like the time me and Sugar crashed into the Catholic church on a dare. But once we got in there and everything so hushed and holy and the candles and the bowin and the handkerchiefs on all the drooping heads, I just couldn't go through with the plan. Which was for me to run up to the altar and do a tap dance while Sugar played the nose flute and messed around in the holy water. And Sugar kept givin me the elbow. Then later teased me so bad I tied her up in the shower and turned it on and locked her in. And she'd be there till this day if Aunt Gretchen hadn't finally figured I was lyin about the boarder taken a shower.

Same thing in the store. We all walking on tiptoe and hardly touchin the games and puzzles and things. And I watched Miss Moore who is steady watchin us like she waitin for a sign. Like Mama Drewery watches the sky and sniffs the air and takes note of just how much slant is in the bird formation. Then me and Sugar bump smack into each other, so busy gazing at the toys, 'specially the sailboat. But we don't laugh and go into our fat-lady bump-stomach routine. We just stare at that price tag. Then Sugar run a finger over the whole boat. And I'm jealous and want to hit her. Maybe not her, but I sure want to punch somebody in the mouth.

"Watcha bring us here for, Miss Moore?"

"You sound angry, Sylvia. Are you mad about something?" Giving me one of them grins like she tellin a grown-up joke that never turns out to be funny. And she's lookin very closely at me like maybe she plannin to do my portrait from memory. I'm mad, but I won't give her that satisfaction. So I slouch around the store bein very bored and say, "Let's go."

Me and Sugar at the back of the train watchin the tracks whizzin by large then small then gettin gobbled up in the dark. I'm thinkin about this tricky toy I saw in the store. A clown that somersaults on a bar then does chin-ups just cause you yank lightly at his leg. Cost $35. I could see me askin my mother for a $35 birthday clown. "You wanna who that costs what?" she'd say, cocking her head to the side to get a better view of the hole in my head. Thirty-five dollars could buy new bunk beds for Junior and Gretchen's boy. Thirty-five dollars and the whole household could go visit Granddaddy Nelson in the country. Thirty-five dollars would pay for the rent and the piano bill too. Who are these people that spend that much for performing clowns and $1000 for toy sailboats? What kinda work they do and how they live and how come we ain't in on it? Where we are is who we are, Miss Moore always pointin out. But it don't necessarily have to be that way, she always adds then waits for somebody to say that poor people have to wake up and demand their share of the pie and don't none of us know what kind of pie she talkin about in the first damn place. But she ain't so smart cause I still got her four dollars from the taxi and she sure ain't gettin it. Messin up my day with this shit. Sugar nudges me in my pocket and winks.

Miss Moore lines us up in front of the mailbox where we started from, seem like years ago, and I got a headache for thinkin so hard. And we lean all over each other so we can hold up under the draggy-ass lecture she always finishes us off with at the end before we thank her for borin us to tears. But she just looks at us like she readin tea leaves. Finally she say, "Well, what did you think of F.A.O. Schwarz?"

Rosie Giraffe mumbles, "White folks crazy."

"I'd like to go there again when I get my birthday money," says Mercedes, and we shove her out the pack so she has to lean on the mailbox by herself.

"I'd like a shower. Tiring day," say Flyboy.

Then Sugar surprises me by saying, "You know, Miss Moore, I don't think all of us here put together eat in a year what that sailboat costs." And Miss Moore lights up like somebody goosed her. "And?" she say, urging Sugar on. Only I'm standin on her foot so she don't continue.

"Imagine for a minute what kind of society it is in which some people can   50
spend on a toy what it would cost to feed a family of six or seven. What do you
think?"

"I think," say Sugar pushing me off her feet like she never done before,
cause I whip her ass in a minute, "that this is not much of a democracy if you
ask me. Equal chance to pursue happiness means an equal crack at the dough,
don't it?" Miss Moore is besides herself and I am disgusted with Sugar's
treachery. So I stand on her foot one more time to see if she'll shove me. She
shuts up, and Miss Moore looks at me, sorrowfully I'm thinkin. And somethin
weird is going on, I can feel it in my chest.

"Anybody else learn anything today?" lookin dead at me. I walk away and
Sugar has to run to catch up and don't even seem to notice when I shrug her
arm off my shoulder.

"Well, we got four dollars anyway," she says.

"Uh hunh."

"We could go to Hascombs and get half a chocolate layer and then go to the   55
Sunset and still have plenty money for potato chips and ice cream sodas."

"Uh hunh."

"Race you to Hascombs," she say.

We start down the block and she gets ahead which is O.K. by me cause I'm
going to the West End[3] and then over to the Drive[4] to think this day through.
She can run if she want to and even run faster. But ain't nobody gonna beat
me at nuthin.

ANALYZING   What the Writer Says

1. What kind of person is Sylvia? Why does she resist Miss Moore as much as she does?

2. What kind of person is Miss Moore? Why does she spend her summers teaching the neighborhood kids even though she must know that they are not very enthusiastic about her lessons?

3. What is the lesson Miss Moore tries to teach her students? Does Sylvia learn the lesson? How do you know?

ANALYZING   How the Writer Says It

Bambara has Sylvia narrate the story in her own language. What does Bambara accomplish by this method? How would the story have been different had Miss Moore been the narrator, or had there been an objective third-person narrator?

---

[3]A bar near Columbia University. (Editor's note)

[4]Riverside Drive on New York's west side, along the Hudson River. (Editor's note)

ANALYZING the Issue

"Ignorance is bliss," says an old proverb. Considering that Sylvia seems to be happy in her world, do you think Miss Moore does her a favor by introducing her to larger social issues and to the power of money—of which Sylvia's family has very little? Why or why not?

ANALYZING Connections Between Texts

1. Compare the lesson of Bambara's story to the lesson of Langston Hughes's "Theme for English B" (p. 372).

2. How different is the "lesson" Sylvia learns from the reality Natalie Kusz ("Ring Leader," p. 223) is forced to accept as she grows up? Are their responses more similar than different?

3. How might Elliott Erwitt's photograph of three children (p. 399) serve to illustrate Bambara's essay?

WARMING UP: *Have you ever tried to get a teacher to raise a grade—even when you knew you had not worked as hard as you could have for it?*

A Liberating Curriculum

By Roberta F. Borkat

ROBERTA F. BORKAT

As a professor of English and comparative literature at San Diego State University, Borkat is only too familiar with students complaining about low grades and high academic standards. Her "liberating curriculum" is a modest proposal for abandoning grades and teaching altogether and rewarding all students with straight As. This essay appeared as a "My Turn" column in Newsweek *on April 12, 1993.*

A blessed change has come over me. Events of recent months have revealed to me that I have been laboring as a university professor for more than 20 years under a misguided theory of teaching. I humbly regret that during all those years I have caused distress and inconvenience to thousands of students while providing some amusement to my more practical colleagues. Enlightenment came to me in a sublime moment of clarity while I was being verbally attacked by a student whose paper I had just proved to have been plagiarized from "The Norton Anthology of English Literature." Suddenly, I understood the true purpose of my profession, and I devised a plan to embody that revelation. Every moment since then has been filled with delight about the advantages to students, professors and universities from my Plan to Increase Student Happiness.

The plan is simplicity itself: at the end of the second week of the semester, all students enrolled in each course will receive a final grade of A. Then their minds will be relieved of anxiety, and they will be free to do whatever they want for the rest of the term.

The benefits are immediately evident. Students will be assured of high grade-point averages and an absence of obstacles in their march toward graduation. Professors will be relieved of useless burdens and will have time to pursue their real interests. Universities will have achieved the long-desired goal of molding individual professors into interchangeable parts of a smoothly operating machine. Even the environment will be improved because education will no longer consume vast quantities of paper for books, compositions and examinations.

Although this scheme will instantly solve countless problems that have plagued education, a few people may raise trivial objections and even urge universities not to adopt it. Some of my colleagues may protest that we have an obligation to uphold the integrity of our profession. Poor fools, I understand their delusion, for I formerly shared it. To them, I say: "Hey, lighten up! Why make life difficult?"

Those who believe that we have a duty to increase the knowledge of our students may also object. I, too, used to think that knowledge was important and that we should encourage hard work and perseverance. Now I realize that the concept of rewards for merits is elitist and, therefore, wrong in a society that aims for equality in all things. We are a democracy. What could be more democratic than to give exactly the same grade to every single student?

One or two forlorn colleagues may even protest that we have a responsibility to significant works of the past because the writings of such authors as Chaucer, Shakespeare, Milton and Swift are intrinsically valuable. I can empathize with these misguided souls, for I once labored under the illusion that I was giving my students a precious gift by introducing them to works by great poets, playwrights and satirists. Now I recognize the error of my ways. The writings of such authors may have seemed meaningful to our ancestors, who had nothing better to do, but we are living in a time of wonderful improvements. The writers of bygone eras have been made irrelevant, replaced by MTV and *People* magazine. After all, their bodies are dead. Why shouldn't their ideas be dead, too?

If any colleagues persist in protesting that we should try to convey knowledge to students and preserve our cultural heritage, I offer this suggestion: honestly consider what students really want. As one young man graciously explained to me, he had no desire to take my course but had enrolled in it merely to fulfill a requirement that he resented. His job schedule made it impossible for him to attend at least 30 percent of my class sessions, and he wouldn't have time to do much of the reading. Nevertheless, he wanted a good grade. Another student consulted me after the first exam, upset because she had not studied and had earned only 14 points out of a possible 100. I told her that, if she studied hard and attended class more regularly, she could do well enough on the remaining tests to pass the course. This encouragement did not satisfy her. What she wanted was an assurance that she would receive at least a B. Under my plan both students would be guaranteed an A. Why not? They have good looks and self-esteem. What more could anyone ever need in life?

I do not ask for thanks from the many people who will benefit. I'm grateful to my colleagues who for decades have tried to help me realize that seriousness about teaching is not the path to professional prestige, rapid promotion and frequent sabbaticals. Alas, I was stubborn. Not until I heard the illuminating explanation of the student who had plagiarized from the anthology's introduction to Jonathan Swift did I fully grasp the wisdom that others had been generously offering to me for years—learning is just too hard. Now, with a light heart, I await the plan's adoption. In my mind's eye, I can see the happy faces of university administrators and professors, released at last from the irksome chore of dealing with students. I can imagine the joyous smiles of thousands of students, all with straight-A averages and plenty of free time.

My only regret is that I wasted so much time. For nearly 30 years, I threw away numerous hours annually on trivia: writing, grading and explaining examinations; grading hundreds of papers a semester; holding private conferences with students; reading countless books; buying extra materials to give students a feeling for the music, art and clothing of past centuries; endlessly worrying about how to improve my teaching. At last I see the folly of grubbing away in meaningless efforts. I wish that I had faced facts earlier and had not lost years because of old-fashioned notions. But such are the penalties for those who do not understand the true purpose of education.

ANALYZING What the Writer Says

1. What is Borkat's "Plan to Increase Student Happiness"?
2. Who would be most liberated by Borkat's plan?
3. What, according to Borkat, do students want? What do university administrators want? What does Borkat want?
4. Who or what has replaced the great writers of the past?

ANALYZING How the Writer Says It

1. Cite examples from the essay that help you identify Borkat's tone.
2. How would Borkat's piece have been different if she had written it straightforwardly, without irony?

ANALYZING the Issue

1. Do you agree with Borkat's assessment of the modern student's plight: "learning is just too hard"?
2. Given the hectic schedules of students today, should universities expect less of students than they once did and lower their standards?

"English lit—how about you?"

ANALYZING Connections Between Texts

1. Compare Borkat's piece to Jacob Neusner's "The Speech the Graduates Didn't Hear" (p. 375). On what points do they agree? Disagree? What is the main difference in their approaches?

2. How do Steven Reiss and James Wiltz ("Why America Loves Reality TV," p. 734) and Katie Roiphe ("Profiles Encouraged," p. 737) help explain or support Borkat's conclusions about college students today?

3. The University of Louisville photo "Golden Rules" (p. 400) clearly illustrates that educational goals and values change as times change. How does Borkat's essay address changing educational values?

WARMING UP: *Look at Rockwell's picture "The Problem We All Live With" (p. 102). How do you think Ruby Bridges, the little girl in the picture, must have felt at that moment?*

Ruby Bridges and a Painting

BY ROBERT COLES

ROBERT COLES

As an (accidental) eyewitness to Ruby Bridges's ordeal as the first African-American child to attend a forcibly desegregated grammar school in New Orleans, Robert Coles investigates the dynamics of scapegoating—and the power of art as an instrument to bring about change of mind. This essay was included in the 1999 Norman Rockwell: Pictures for the American People, *the exhibition catalogue for a Rockwell retrospective that included his famous 1963 picture "The Problem We All Live With."*

A fateful coincidence changed my life in the fall of 1960—and gave me, eventually, an unforgettable acquaintance with a Norman Rockwell painting. I was on my way to a medical conference in New Orleans when suddenly a police barricade confronted me and others trying to make our way toward that cosmopolitan city. All of us were told that because a nearby school was being desegregated by federal court order, we were not going to be allowed further travel—a blockade had been established to give the police control over some of the city's neighborhoods. Suddenly, unexpectedly, I had a lot of time on my hands. I could have turned around and returned to Biloxi, Mississippi, where I then lived as an Air Force physician, in the military under the old doctors' draft law. Instead, I walked a few blocks, and soon enough I was in the presence of a large crowd of men, women, and children, who were not only milling around but occasionally uniting in a shouted refrain: "Two, four, six, eight, we don't want to integrate!"

Again and again I heard those words, directed at the yellow brick and cement building, the William Frantz School. Police were standing here and there, some of them, I noticed, joining in the screaming. I asked a middle-aged woman who seemed friendly what was happening. She told me right away—with words I'll never stop hearing in my head: "They're trying to bring a nigger kid into our school—it'll be over our dead bodies!" I was stunned—a well-dressed, fine-spoken woman who had descended into a panicky malice, who couldn't seem to help herself, who was ranting on a street corner to a Yankee stranger.

In about five minutes, just as I was about to walk away then drive away, I heard a hush, an almost audible spell of silence—as all eyes were directed toward several cars which, out of nowhere it seemed, had arrived in front of the school. Out of them, a number of men jumped quickly, warily, and out of one car, two men and a small girl dressed in white, with a white bow in her hair and a lunch box in her right hand. Suddenly, as the men and the child approached the school, walked up its steps, the crowd got back its collective voice and started the chant I'd already heard, kept repeating it, interrupted by cuss words, threats, terrible curses. The girl didn't look back; the men kept walking and, I noticed, were armed.

In no time, Ruby and her protectors (who were federal marshals mobilized by the Justice Department in Washington) had disappeared, though the mob was reluctant to follow suit. I left—drove away toward my home near Keesler Air Force Base, lost in melancholy thought. Not long afterward, in a way, my working life began: I determined it was my job to try to get to know Ruby Bridges, that girl I'd seen, and the three other girls, also aged six, who faced mobs standing outside another New Orleans school, McDonogh 19, and in the years following, a host of African American children who initiated school desegregation in city after city of the deep South during the early and middle 1960s.

Of all those children, Ruby was most familiar to me. For one thing, I knew   5
her and her parents the longest—and then, her ordeal was literally singular: unlike others in New Orleans and elsewhere, she was all alone as she encountered those daily mobs, and the people on the street hurling epithets knew it, because they persisted far longer than those who shouted at the three girls who began attending the McDonogh school. I was often, as a white man wearing an Air Force officer's uniform, able to stand and listen to those people as they heckled Ruby, and in time I got to know some of them, interviewed them in their homes, even as I was meeting Ruby and her family in their home.

In a sense, it was Ruby's father who got me to do those interviews with the various white people I'd seen as I watched the drama in front of the Frantz School unfold. (A total boycott lasted months, so that Ruby had the school all to herself.) One day, Abon Bridges, while contemplating his daughter's school life (the struggles she experienced in order to arrive there and leave there, always in the company of federal marshals, and the experiences she had there as the sole student), offered these telling remarks: "You know, Ruby isn't learning only from her teacher at Frantz. She's learning from what's going on outside that building. She's learning all about people, human nature you could say—she's taking a *course* in human nature. What do I mean? I mean that this is a tough world, and people are always worrying about what's ahead, whether they'll keep their job, and be able to make ends meet—at least most people. You look at those folks on television, shouting at my little girl, and you can't help but wonder what they're really shouting about! I tell Ruby—you have to feel sorry for folks who can't help themselves: they leave their homes to come to the school, even in the heavy rain, just so they can tell this little girl that they hate her, and she'll 'get it,' and they hate the government, their own government, and it'll 'get it,' too. Now I ask you, isn't there something real sick about that—and what is it, what in the world is it that makes people get like that? Ruby has asked that so many times; she wants to know why, why, why—and I keep telling her that we should feel real sorry for people who behave like that, because they're telling you something. When she asks me *what* they're telling us, I try to get her to stop and think. I say, honey, when someone's shouting at a little child they don't know, at a stranger trying to go to the first grade, then you can be sure there's someone else they want to shout at, or there's something on their mind that's upsetting them real, real, bad and they don't know how to get it out, how to say it, even to themselves—what's bothering them so bad—and then you come along, and they just go and use you, that's what they're doing: they're going after you, so they won't have to figure out what's wrong in their life, and what's wrong in the country."

As I heard such words, realized their import, I decided I ought try to learn more from the people whose predicament Mr. Bridges had so shrewdly evoked for his daughter, for me. In time, I came to know a family whose six-year-old daughter would have been Ruby's classmate, had not the following line of reasoning prevailed—relayed to me by a father almost the same age as Ruby's dad, and whom I had gotten to know reasonably well: "You probably wonder why we won't just ignore that kid, and let our own [children] return. [I had been asking him and his wife about their daughter's educational future, and that of her younger brother, when he became of school age, if the boycott persisted.] Well, let me tell you something: it's a matter of pride, that's how I'd put it to you. There's a lot of things that will happen to you in this life, there's all these problems that you have, and you've just got to learn to live with them, and it can be hard. I've lost my job twice in the past couple years, and I've had to go and find a new one each time; and my folks, they're getting old, and they're sick, and you have to pay the doctors and there's no money you have, so you borrow, and then there's big interest, and you feel everything is ready to crash in on you. Then, all of a sudden, some big-shot federal judge, on a big, life-time salary, comes and tells you that everything is going to change, that what is right and wrong is now going to be different, and *you're* the one to take the lead on all this, not the rich folks, living in the fancy neighborhoods, no sir: they got protection—[if] worse comes to worse, they'll send their kids to private schools. It's all unfair, and that's why there comes a time when you just have taken so much, and now it's all come here to roost right in your own neighborhood, and they're coming at your own child's life, *her* school, and giving it to someone else, just because someone up there in Washington, D.C., says it's got to happen, and someone down here, that judge, goes along."

The longer I listened to him and others like him, the more I realized the truth of Abon Bridges's observations, a biblical truth, really: the scapegoat as an instrument of persecutory self-expression—the mob's anger, in this instance, deflected from its own social and economic vulnerability onto Ruby's situation, her presence and her jeopardy as a symbolic version of a day-to-day jeopardy experienced by her tormentors. Of course, it is one thing to know that, and quite another to be in Ruby's position, as even her dad, so intent on comprehending the world and explaining it to his daughter, well knew: "I try to help my little girl know what's going on, and why it's turned out like this. But there will be times when she looks at me, and she's clearly in trouble, because no matter what I tell her, she's got to listen to those folks saying their mean, mean words and she has every right to be upset. I'm telling her we've all got our problems, including those people screaming their heads off, and she's thinking that she's the one who has the biggest problem of all, what with the marshals the only white ones in New Orleans who are in any way looking out for her."

Ruby's father and the white father of a girl who was kept out of school for months because of a segregationist defiance of a federal judge's ruling both talked of their serious problems, and they shared those problems, which are in general to be found across the color line. No wonder that in early 1964, when the centerfold of *Look* magazine showed Norman Rockwell's *The Problem We All Live With* [p. 102], there was an intense interest among both the white and the African American families I had come to know, and certainly an attentive, even aroused response from both fathers I have just quoted, not to mention from Ruby herself. Ruby was less expansively talkative, of course, than her dad, not to mention the white dad just summoned here. When she saw the picture of a "Negro child," as she heard herself described at the time by polite people, friendly people, as opposed to long-time hecklers, she looked carefully and for some time, but had no words to offer. She did, an hour or so later, ask her mother whether the picture was meant to be of her. In the mother's words: "She said, 'Mama, do you think that's supposed to be someone like me, maybe me?'" The mother said yes, that her experience had become well known to many people across the nation, hence that picture.

When I had a chance to sit with Ruby, we had a more extended discussion 10 of the picture. Of course she had been drawing pictures of herself for me all along; and she had even tried to draw a picture not unlike, in subject matter, the one Norman Rockwell did for *Look*. (In child psychiatry we often ask children to draw, paint—and learn, thereby, what is on their minds, no matter their not-rare reluctance to speak about the worries or fears besetting them.) As we looked at the Rockwell picture together and at her own pictures that dealt with the same theme (a girl escorted by grown-ups into a school in the face of evident or implied danger, a pioneer's lonely act on behalf of certain ideals), Ruby mused aloud about several matters: "I sure wish I could draw the way he does! He's got it down, what's happening, Daddy said, and he's right. I thought of the picture the other day, when I went to school, and I wondered what the men would say—if they saw the picture. [By then the marshals were not needed at the school.] I'll bet one of the marshals would say that his wife thought that if everyone in that crowd saw the picture, it might make a difference—they'd stop being so mean. (Daddy said that, and one of the marshals, maybe, would agree with him, and he'd mention his wife, because he always did.) But I'll bet the other marshal would say he wasn't sure [that would happen], because you've got a lot of angry people out there. That's what one marshal kept saying a lot—that there were a lot of angry people out there. If you look at the [Rockwell] picture in the magazine, you'll see things going all right, nice and quiet, but if you looked at the television, back then, it was real bad."

That was an extraordinary moment for me, listening to Ruby: in her own way, with the help of what she'd heard in the past from her dad and those marshals, she'd become a knowing social critic, and also an art critic. She had figured out the difference between television's documentary footage and the work of an artist—a painter's kindly but firm evocation of a moral moment in a nation's history, as contrasted to the first-hand, sometimes only thinly edited camera work that appeared on home screens. For Ruby, eventually, it came down to this: "That picture [by Rockwell] is about me, I guess—and what you see in the news is about the trouble on the street."

The white man who has been one of our witnesses here, and who surely caused some of the "trouble" Ruby rather tactfully mentioned, also got to see the Rockwell picture in *Look,* and had this to say: "That magazine tells you to 'look,' and I sure did; I thought 'there she is, the nigra kid.' You look at her and you begin to feel sorry for her—a lot of people will, I'm sure. It's not *her* we were against, you know. It's the interference in our life by those folks up North, that's what it was, that's what we were saying."

A shift in his language and his sentiment or ideology, so I noticed. For him, "nigra" was a less hostile or insulting or demeaning characterization—as opposed to the word "nigger" which, heretofore, he'd all the time used. Moreover, he was now (as never before was the case) letting Ruby herself off the hook, directing his considerable ire at his nation's political life, at a region rather than a person. I couldn't help but feel then that a magazine's picture had somehow touched his heart, had given him some psychological if not moral pause. In a strange way, of course, Rockwell's picture, with its title of *The Problem We All Live With,* had brought together African American and white antagonists, each of whom (two fathers of six-year-old girls) had already said virtually the same thing: that there was indeed "a problem" or two with which they had to contend. The picture's quiet drama, its mix of affection and social candor, and its title worthy of a Trollope novel had somehow had an impact on a wide range, indeed, of those caught in such a difficult and scary and prolonged confrontation—all of which I had the pleasure and honor to tell Norman Rockwell in person when I got to know him in the late 1960s, as we worked together on a children's book, *Dead End School,* which I wrote and he illustrated. It was a book about school desegregation, only up north in Boston. How well I remember his interest in, as he put it, "the real Ruby," as opposed to the girl he gave to all of us—though I kept telling him that he, in fact, had caught and rendered for all of us some of the "real Ruby": after all, I had her word for it.

ANALYZING What the Writer Says

1. Briefly sketch the historical situation Robert Coles has chosen for his essay. What was happening in New Orleans in 1960?

2. How does Abon Bridges, Ruby's father, explain the hatred his daughter has to face every day as she goes to school?

3. When Coles interviews one of the white children's fathers, the writer "realize[s] the truth of Abon Bridges's observations." What convinced Coles that Bridges was right?

4. When Ruby Bridges first sees the picture of herself, what is her reaction? In what ways does the picture not do justice to her experience?

5. How does seeing Norman Rockwell's "The Problem We All Live With" in *Look* in 1964 change the white father's attitude toward Ruby and the integration controversy? How much of his change of mind does Coles attribute to the picture?

ANALYZING How the Writer Says It

1. How effective is Coles's narrative introduction?

2. After he witnessed her daily ordeal, Coles "determined that it was [his] job to try to get to know Ruby Bridges." His decision to interview her father makes good sense in this context, but what about his decision to talk to some of the white fathers who kept their children out of school out of protest? What do his interviews with Ruby's tormentors contribute to his subject?

ANALYZING the Issue

1. When Ruby first sees Rockwell's painting, she notices that "you'll see things going all right, nice and quiet," which is not how she remembers her ordeal. What does her observation about herself as a subject in Rockwell's painting say about the function of art? Should art accurately portray reality as it is—or must artists transcend eyewitness reportage to make a larger moral point?

2. As the title indicates, Coles's essay combines social commentary and art criticism. Should he have stuck to one or the other? Why or why not?

ANALYZING Connections Between Texts

1. Compare what Langston Hughes describes in "Theme for English B" (p. 372) to what Coles describes.

2. In "On Black Fathering" (p. 170), Cornel West talks about the difficulties his father overcame, as an African American, in fulfilling the patriarchal role our society expects of fathers. Compare the situations of the two fathers—Cornel West's and Ruby Bridges's—and the ways in which they raise their children against the backdrop of racism.

3. Compare Coles's account of Ruby's ordeal to Rockwell's painting "The Problem We All Live With" (p. 102). Do you agree with Coles's statement that the artist only partially captured "the real Ruby" in the picture?

WARMING UP: *Have you ever spent time among a group of people from a completely different culture and been surprised by some of their habits and beliefs? Did it make you rethink your own habits and values?*

From the Best of Japanese Families

By Cathy Davidson

CATHY DAVIDSON

An American educator and author of numerous books, Cathy Davidson spent time teaching in Japan, documenting her experience in her 1993 Thirty-Six Views of Mount Fuji: On Finding Myself in Japan, *from which the following excerpt is taken.*

In some ways Kansai Women's University is an exception to many of the rules about college life in Japan. A private university with rigorous admissions standards, KWU was founded by American missionaries who were alumnae of one of the Seven Sisters schools[1] and is also modeled on the liberal arts ideals of prestigious American women's colleges. The women who go to KWU study hard, American-style, during their four years of college. They are brilliant students from, we were told, "the best families," typically the daughters of professional people. Many are on their way to being wives and mothers of future business leaders and statesmen, the country's elite. Some cherish hopes of being business and civic leaders themselves.

Many of the English majors at KWU are fluent in English. Often they have spent time abroad, sometimes only a few months but sometimes as much as six or eight years. Many of their courses are conducted entirely in English, whether taught by Japanese teachers of English or by native English speakers.

Unlike many Japanese students, KWU students do not enter college with the anticipation of a four-year vacation. On the contrary, for KWU students, their

---

[1]Radcliffe, Vassar, Bryn Mawr, Barnard, Wellesley, Mt. Holyoke, and Smith, all founded as women's private liberal arts colleges. (Editor's note)

college years may be the busiest time in their lives. They take over fifteen courses each semester and can spend thirty to forty hours a week in the classroom. After class, their time is filled with other lessons: tea ceremony, *koto* (Japanese harp), *ikebana* (flower arrangement), piano or violin, tennis, French, aerobics, Chinese cooking, French cooking, and kimono dressing (no easy task, especially learning to wrap and tie the twelve-foot-long *obi* sash). All of these accomplishments become part of the young woman's "dossier" as she and her family set out to find her the perfect life partner, through an adaptation of the ancient custom of *omiai*, the formal meeting between the couple, parents, and go-between preparatory to arranged marriage. Nearly 85 percent of upper-class Japanese still go through at least a loose form of *omiai*, and KWU students are no exception. It is almost a truism that the English majors at KWU make perfect, cosmopolitan wives, able to function effortlessly in any environment, East or West.

Yet despite the exceptional intelligence of the KWU students, they did not perform in the classroom with anything like the articulateness and liveliness of my American students. Twelve years of a more passive educational system, coupled with a basic Japanese idea that one should not show off in front of one's peers, made it difficult to elicit the kind of classroom discussion that I prize in my American students.

The only way I found to break through this pattern of passive learning was   5 by using Japanese group consciousness and "team spirit," as they say, to an American end. I divided my classes into rows and asked each row to pick a group leader. I'd ask a question ("What does the image of the wall suggest to you in Robert Frost's 'Mending Wall'?") and have the rows work in teams to see who could come up with the best answer. In my advanced classes, I asked that all discussion in the group be conducted in English. I'd give them a time limit, two or three minutes.

At first, there were faint murmurings, barely audible even within the row, and self-conscious answers from the team leader. But as I encouraged them to be more freewheeling and gave them permission to do something they weren't used to doing in the classroom, hesitant whispers gave way to a flurry of excited discussion. They would argue strenuously in their group and then the team captain would report what the group had come up with. I've seldom encountered more insightful, sensitive responses to poetry.

By the end of the year, students were coming up with their own team questions and answering them. Sometimes, on their own, they would challenge one another, never in a combative or even competitive way, but with seriousness, as if this discussion of modern American poetry really mattered.

It was exhilarating. Once given a mechanism by which they could adapt American-style dialogue to their Japanese group patterns, these Japanese overachievers were spectacularly articulate.

*   *   *

There was only one course in which Professor Sano, my department head, thought I might have trouble. I was assigned to teach Oral English for Non-English Majors, the B class, and Professor Sano made a point of warning me that these students would be very different from my English majors. Few, if any, would have had any contact with English except through the traditional Japanese educational system. Intelligent young women, they still would have learned English the way my young friend Kenji had—lots of "who" and "whom," virtually nothing resembling practical conversational English. Most never would have heard a native speaker of English, except in Hollywood movies.

The "English" taught in their Japanese schoolrooms was actually *katakana*, 10 the Japanese syllabary for foreign words, a way of transliterating all foreign sounds into the forty-six basic Japanese sound patterns: *r* becomes *l*, *v* becomes *b*, each consonant (except *n*) must be followed by a vowel. *Rocket* is *rokketo* (pronounced "locketo"), *ventillator* is *benchirētā*, and, the classic example, *blacklist* is the six-syllable *burakku-risuto*.

Perhaps because I was struggling so hard to learn even the most rudimentary Japanese, I was eager to teach these students English. My dislike of the traditional Japanese way of teaching English also made me feel almost a missionary zeal upon entering my Oral English course at KWU. I'd never taken any courses in the field of TOESL, Teaching of English as a Second Language, but I certainly knew from colleagues that the way English is taught in the Japanese schools is exactly the *wrong* way to encourage people to really communicate in a new language.

I tried a different tack, beginning with the conscious demotion of *sensei*.[2] Unlike many language teachers who refuse to speak anything but the language being taught, I delighted in speaking to the students in my execrable Japanese. Partly this was selfish; I practiced more Japanese in beginner's Oral English class than anywhere else. But it was also pedagogical. I figured if they realized that *sensei* wasn't ashamed to make mistakes, they certainly didn't have a right to be—a way of using the Japanese proclivity for authoritarianism and punctiliousness against itself. To show what I expected on the first formal presentation, a requirement in all of the Oral English sections, I initially prepared the same assignment—in Japanese. At first I thought I'd intentionally throw in a few mistakes, but quickly realized my Japanese was quite bad enough on its own without my having to invent errors.

I came up with a whopper. It is the kind of mistake often made by native English-speakers, who have a hard time differentiating between repeated

---

[2]The teacher. (Editor's note)

consonants. Mine, I found out later, was already a famous mistake; it happened when an American introduced the oldest and most revered woman in the Japanese parliament on national television. The American meant to say that this legislator was not only "very distinguished" but also "very feminine" (*onna-rashii*). She ended up saying the legislator was both distinguished and *onara shi* (which means, roughly, to cut a fart).

"That double *n* is hard for foreigners," I said when one of my students started to giggle. "We can't really hear the difference between *onna ra* and *onara*."

The students were now all laughing, but in polite Japanese-girl fashion, a hand covering the mouth.

"*Wait!*" I shouted in my sternest voice. "This is Oral English class!"

The laughter stopped. They looked ashamed.

"No, no. In this class, you must *laugh* in English. Think about it. You've all seen American movies. How do you laugh in English?"

I could see a gleam in Miss Shimura's eyes, and I called on her. "Would an American woman ever put her hand over her mouth when she laughed, Miss Shimura?"

"No, *sensei*—I mean, teacher."

"Show, me. Laugh like an American movie star."

Miss Shimura kept her hands plastered at her side. She threw back her head. She opened her mouth as far as it would go. She made a deep, staccato sound at the back of her throat. *Hanh. Hanh. Hanh.*

We all laughed hysterically.

"Hands down!" I shouted again. "This is Oral English!"

They put their hands at their sides and imitated Miss Shimura's American head-back, open-mouth plosive laugh.

"What about the body?" I asked.

I parodied a Japanese laugh, pulling my arms in to my sides, bowing my head and shoulders forward, putting a hand coyly to my mouth.

Again they laughed. This time it was American-style.

"Oral English is about bodies too, not just words." I smiled.

Miss Kato raised her hand.

"*Hai?*" (Yes?).

"Americans also laugh like this." She put her head back, opened her mouth, and rocked her upper body from side to side, her shoulders heaving and dodging, like Santa Claus.

There were gleeful shouts of "Yes! Yes!" and again a roomful of American-style laughter. It would start to die down, then someone would catch her friend doing the funny American laugh, and she'd break into hysterics again, the hand going to her mouth, me pointing, her correcting herself with the Santa Claus laughter. I continued to laugh Japanese-style, which made them laugh even louder, bouncier. We were off and running, laughing in each other's languages.

I'm convinced shame kills language learning faster than anything, even more so in Japan, where shame lurks so close to the surface of every social interaction. The laughing routine was a childish exercise, but then all language learning is childish, inherently infantilizing, a giving up and a giving in, a loss of control. Learning a language means returning to a state of near idiocy.

And honesty. Language learning is so consuming, there's no energy left over for invention. Ask someone to tell you their height and weight in a beginning foreign language class, and you'll likely get a much more reliable answer than the one on her driver's license.

This quickly became the case in beginners Oral English, where I learned aspects of Japanese life that the sophisticated, cosmopolitan students in the advanced classes at KWU would not have revealed, under normal circumstances, to a *gaijin*.[3] My beginners talked in English the way they might talk in Japanese, among friends. They didn't know enough about Western culture to anticipate what we might consider strange or exotic, controversial or even reprehensible. Consequently, they spoke without excessive censoring, something I never experienced later on, when I taught an Advanced Oral English class.

My advanced students often dodged my questions with polite evasions. "The Japanese myth of racial homogeneity is as erroneous as the American myth of the melting pot" offered a student who had spent several years in the States. I had thought my opening question, "What is racism?", would provoke a heated debate that would lead us around, by the end of the class period, to addressing each country's particular brand of racism. Typically, Japanese are happy to discuss American racism but blind to the equivalent prejudice in their own country. The student's pointed answer effectively short-circuited the lesson I had hoped to make that day by anticipating what my own point of view might be. The rest of the class period was filled with platitudes and bored and knowing nods. The students in the advanced class knew exactly where to fudge.

After summer break, I require students in beginning Oral English for Non-Majors to give a brief presentation on what they've done over the vacation. It's designed to be simple, to ease them back into the term. They've been in Oral English since April, the beginning of the Japanese school year. They have had six weeks off for the summer, and now must return to classes for three more weeks before the grueling end-of-semester exams in late September.

I call on the first student.

"I was constipated most of the way to Nikko," a lovely young woman in a Kenzo flower-print jumper begins her talk.

I set my face like a Japanese mask, careful to express no emotion, and steal glances around the room. No one seems even remotely surprised at this

---

[3] Foreigner. (Editor's note)

beginning except me, and I know that it is absolutely mandatory that I act as if this is the most ordinary opening in the world.

"I was with the tennis club, and my *sensei* made sure I ate *konnyaku* for my constipation."

At this point she gets flustered. She is obviously embarrassed.

"It's okay," I jump in hastily, searching for my most soothing and encouraging Japanese. "You're doing very well. Please go on."

"It's just," she stammers, also in Japanese, "I don't know the English for 45 *konnyaku*. Do you know?"

I assure her that there's no American equivalent. *Konnyaku* is a glutinous substance, made from the root of a plant that seems to grow only in Japan. In America, I tell her, most people eat bran to cure constipation or we take over-the-counter medicines such as Ex Lax.

"Ecks Racks," she repeats solemnly, then breaks into giggles (American-style). So does everyone.

The word sounds so funny. It becomes the class joke for the next few weeks. If anyone forgets a word in English, someone else inevitably whispers to a friend, loud enough for the rest of us to hear, "Ecks Racks!"

Three of four other speeches that morning give blow-by-blow reports of near gastrointestinal crises and how they were averted, usually by the wise intervention of some *sensei*.

What surprises me most about the morning is how embarrassed *I* am, although 50 I think I've concealed it pretty well. These students would wilt with shame if they had any inkling that this is not something we would talk about in America, and I find myself in a quandary. They trust me to tell them about Western culture, but I know that if I tell them it's not considered polite to talk about one's bowel movements in Western society, it will destroy the easy camaraderie I've worked so hard to foster this year. But if I don't tell them, I'm violating a trust.

I decide to resolve this by keeping a list of things they bring up that wouldn't be acceptable in the West. All semester I've been working to correct certain Japanese misconceptions and stereotypes, especially their idea that English is a completely logical and direct language, and that Americans always say exactly what they mean, regardless of social status or power relationships. Often my students say things that sound very rude because they've been taught that English lacks the politeness levels of Japanese. These are topics we discuss all the time, so it will work just fine to devote the last week of the semester to lecturing, in my comical Japanese, about misconceptions and cultural differences that I've discovered during my year in Japan. I can tell them about how surprised I was the first time I used a public restroom that turned out to be coed or about bathing Japanese-style with a group of women I barely knew or having a male colleague slip around a corner on the way home from a party. I started to follow, then realized he was taking a quick pee. I know I can act out my own surprise, making my Westerner's prudishness about bodily functions

seem funny but also relevant. This is as close as I can come to having my pedagogical cake and eating it too.

From my beginning non-English majors in Oral English, I learn a great deal
about Japan, including the rituals and superstitions that have not been effaced
by the rampant capitalism of modern, urban Japanese life. They tell of phone
numbers one can call for horoscopes, fortunes, curses, cures. Rituals for marriages, pregnancies, births, divorces. A kind of Japanese voodoo that takes
place in the forest on a certain kind of night. Number symbolism. Lucky and
unlucky days, lucky and unlucky years, lucky and unlucky directions ("Never
sleep with your head to the North, the way the dead are buried"). Blood-type
matchmaking. Tengu, the wicked long-nosed trickster goblin. Kappa, the
amphibious river imp. Tanuki, the raccoonlike creature with the money bag
and enormous testicles, a symbol of plenty. Dragons, supernatural foxes, thun-
der gods, long-life noodles, boiled eels for stamina on hot summer days, chewy
mochi rice cakes for strength and endurance on the New Year, the ashes of a
burnt *imori* (salamander) served to someone you want to make fall in love with
you. They talk seriously about prejudice and injustice toward the *burakumin*
(Japan's untouchable caste), the Ainu (the indigenous people, now almost
extinct), and Koreans (who must take Japanese names before being allowed
citizenship or who are denied citizenship even two or three generations after
their family immigrated to Japan and who must carry alien registration papers
with their thumbprint, like foreigners). They talk of burial customs, going to
the crematorium with the long chopsticks to pick out the vertebra that goes in
the urn in the family altar at home.

When they talk of *omiai* and arranged marriage, one woman starts to cry.
Her friends comfort her. It's the only time I've ever seen someone express personal sorrow in a Japanese classroom. Several students insist that they will
never marry an eldest son, because they do not want to be responsible for taking care of his aged parents. Two say they will never have children because
they do not want their children to hate them the way they hated their mothers
all through school. One young woman says if she marries, it will be to a foreigner because she knows from the movies that foreign husbands help around
the house. Another protests that she wouldn't want to marry a *gaijin,* because
she doesn't want a *gokiburi teishu* (a cockroach husband), some man scurrying
around underfoot in her kitchen. Funny or serious, they talk with candor. And,
mostly, they talk. In English.

"There was so much laughing going on in the next room this semester, I
checked the schedule," sniffs one of the part-time teachers. "It's your Oral
English class. My students are getting jealous. All we hear from your room is
laughter. Is anyone learning anything at all in there?"

I've had conversations before with this woman, none of them pleasant. She
teaches at one of the more conventional Japanese universities and comes to

Kansai Women's University only one day a week. I've heard her say more than once that she's been here so long that now "she's more Japanese than the Japanese."

We're sitting and talking together over our *bentō* boxes, eating our lunch in the faculty room. I tell her, proudly, that my students are learning to speak English very well, and, maybe more important, they are learning to speak freely and confidently.

"And you think that's a good thing?" she asks rhetorically. "They graduate and get to be OLs[4] for a while. Then they're married off to some jerk of a *sarariiman*.[5] But it's okay, you've taught them how to 'speak freely.'"

I am not liking this woman. I am not liking the insinuation in her voice or the smirk on her face. But I can't ignore her comment. I've thought about it myself, many times, especially on the train to and from the university, as I watch the faces of older Japanese women and think about where and how my students will fit in.

Most of these KWU students will graduate and they will, indeed, work as OLs for a few years before marriage, smiling politely and serving tea for busy male executives in Japanese firms. The closest they will come to real "business" might be working the Xerox machine or the paper shredder. Since only about a quarter of the population at four-year colleges in Japan is female (compared to well over half in the United States), there are lots of women available to work after the completion of secondary school. OLs are perpetually replenishable, an eternally young group of women. Most quit—or are fired—once they are married or after they become pregnant.

The KWU women are the crème de la crème of Japanese female students. 60 Some well might advance further in corporate life than the OLs. A few might even achieve their dreams. One of my students wants to be a composer. Another wants to be an international news correspondent. Still others want to be doctors, lawyers. The odds are stacked against them, but the very fact that they are here shows that they are good at overcoming odds.

"My dream is to be a housewife and a mother," one of my Oral English students said in class one day. "But when I am a mother, I will give my children a *choice* of whether or not they want to go to *juku*.[6] I will help to improve Japanese society by allowing my children to be free."

To be free. It's a phrase I've heard a lot this year, and I suspect some of this is just student grandstanding to please the *gaijin* teacher. Some of it is probably wishful thinking. Many of these smart, polished young women will become

---

[4]Office Ladies, a derisive term reflecting the decorative function and lowly position accorded to most women in Japanese business firms. (Editor's note)

[5]Salary man, the typical Japanese male office worker. (Editor's note)

[6]Cram school, which helps students prepare for the rigorous university entrance exams. (Editor's note)

thoroughly conventional upper-middle-class housewives and mothers. It's hard for me to understand the point of all their study, all their years of deprivation, all those hours in *juku* cramming for "examination hell," just so one day they, too, can become "education moms," sending their young sons and daughters off under the falling cherry blossoms, the whole cycle beginning again with a new generation.

"We are told Japanese workers are better than American," one of my students says in an assignment about the work ethic. "We are told this so that we keep working—hard, harder, and hardest. Even as children, we're told to work hard. We Japanese work ourselves to death."

She is as startled as the rest of us by the burning quality of her speech. Her accent isn't perfect and her vocabulary has its limits but her eloquence is unmistakable. We have heard her. She returns to her seat, flushed with attention.

When I take the train home to my apartment in Nigawa that afternoon, I can't help noticing that the only men on the train are elderly, retired. The train is filled with mothers coming home from shopping and with schoolchildren in uniform, finished with one more day of regular school and now on their way to *juku*.

I find myself asking the big question, the dangerous question. What am I really doing here? My students are having fun, they're learning English, but what is my role here? I have learned a lot teaching at Kansai Women's University, and I know my students have learned things too. I don't think it's romanticizing to say we've touched one another, shown each other glimpses of one another's culture. Is that enough?

I can tell sometimes, as I look out over the classroom, that something like love is happening in there. It scares me. My students are convinced I look like a Western movie star. If I wear my shoulder-length hair up in a twist on a hot day, I can predict that at least a dozen of them will have their hair in a twist the next week. If I roll my jacket sleeves, they will roll theirs. My Oral English class has fun imitating my American slang, especially my habit of saying "Oh wow!" They have fun telling me their culture's secrets. They have fun making jokes and laughing and speaking English, hair in a twist, jacket sleeves rolled.

Maybe that's my function. Not very consequential but perhaps necessary. "Visiting Foreign Teacher" is the official title on my visa. The students call me "*sensei*," but I'm not like other *sensei* in the Japanese scheme of things. I am exotic and I am temporary. My embittered colleague might be right. In the sum total of their existence, it doesn't matter greatly that their English has improved. At my most cynical, I think of myself as a diversion, a respite from frenetic Japanese life, the pedagogical equivalent of the *sarariiman's* whiskey.

But I don't think you can be a teacher unless you believe in the possibility of change. When I'm feeling optimistic, I like to think I give my Japanese students the same thing I try to give my American students back home: a space in which to speak and be heard.

Sometimes I look at middle-aged women in Japan and I'm filled with awe. 70 Often they *look* middle-aged—not engaged in the frantic and self-defeating American quest to look forever young—and often they look happy. Their children grown, many become adventurous. For some, it's ballroom dancing or traditional Japanese *koto,* hobbies given up during the busy childrearing years. For others, it's running for local government or working for school reform or in the peace or environmental movements. KWU recently started accepting "returning women"—older women, including mothers whose children are grown—into its graduate program, and the success rate, both in school and for subsequent employment, has been impressive.

That's what I think about when I teach the brilliant young women of Kansai Women's University. I think about their future, and hope that someday, soon or late, they will stop and hear the sound of their own voices and remember their young fire.

ANALYZING What the Writer Says

1. How are the students of Kansai Woman's University "an exception" among many of their Japanese peers?

2. How, according to Davidson, are they different from their American colleagues?

3. What motivated Davidson to teach her Oral English class the way she did? What did she accomplish that other teachers failed to do?

4. What does Davidson learn from her students about Japan and its culture?

5. Why does one of her colleagues, an American woman who has been in Japan so long she considers herself "more Japanese than the Japanese," criticize Davidson's attempts to teach her students to speak freely?

6. What does Davidson, at the end of her essay, decide her function is as a temporary teacher at a prestigious Japanese university?

ANALYZING How the Writer Says It

1. Davidson uses narration as one of her main persuasive tools. How effective is this technique? How would her essay have been different had she substituted scholarly analysis for the stories she tells?

2. In several places throughout the essay, Davidson uses Japanese words and explains them in footnotes. Would using the English term have been more effective? What does Davidson gain from including foreign terms that she knows her audience will not understand?

ANALYZING the Issue

In her second sentence, Davidson tells her readers that Kansai Women's University "was founded by American missionaries," all graduates of prestigious American women's liberal arts colleges. Do you think Davidson's attempts to get her Japanese students to "speak freely" are inspired by a missionary zeal to impose American cultural values on a culture that has no use for them? Or do you think Davidson's students will profit from their experience in her classroom in the long run? Explain.

ANALYZING Connections Between Texts

1. In "The Seven-Lesson Schoolteacher" (p. 362), John Taylor Gatto complains that American schools systematically discourage students from thinking for themselves, turning them into obedient citizens who do what they are told. How are Davidson's observations similar to Gatto's? How are they different?

2. In "Me Talk Pretty One Day" (p. 510), David Sedaris describes the experience of learning a foreign language. How are his experiences similar to Davidson's and her students'?

3. How does the photograph "German Schoolboys Salute" (p. 401) illustrate some of Davidson's concerns about the Japanese university classroom?

WARMING UP: *As a child, did you ever complain that you no longer wanted to go to school? What arguments did your parents make about why you had to keep going?*

The Seven-Lesson Schoolteacher

BY JOHN TAYLOR GATTO

JOHN TAYLOR GATTO
An award-winning long-time schoolteacher, John Gatto argues that compulsory schooling does not provide children with an education but teaches them to become a part of the hierarchical society we inhabit. The following is an excerpt from his 1992 book Dumbing Us Down: The Hidden Curriculum of Compulsory Education.

I

Call me Mr. Gatto, please. Twenty-six years ago, having nothing better to do with myself at the time, I tried my hand at schoolteaching. The license I have certifies that I am an instructor of English language and English literature, but that isn't what I do at all. I don't teach English, I teach school—and I win awards doing it.

Teaching means different things in different places, but seven lessons are universally taught from Harlem to Hollywood Hills. They constitute a national curriculum you pay for in more ways than you can imagine, so you might as well know what it is. You are at liberty, of course, to regard these lessons any way you like, but believe me when I say I intend no irony in this presentation. These are the things I teach, these are the things you pay me to teach. Make of them what you will.

1. Confusion

A lady named Kathy wrote this to me from Dubois, Indiana the other day:

> What big ideas are important to little kids? Well, the biggest idea I think they need is that what they are learning isn't idiosyncratic—that there is some system to it all and it's not just raining down on them as they helplessly absorb. That's the task, to understand, to make coherent.

Kathy has it wrong. *The first lesson I teach is confusion. Everything* I teach is out of context. I teach the un-relating of everything. I teach disconnections. I teach too much: the orbiting of planets, the law of large numbers, slavery, adjectives, architectural drawing, dance, gymnasium, choral singing, assemblies, surprise guests, fire drills, computer languages, parents' nights, staff-development days, pull-out programs, guidance with strangers my students may never see again, standardized tests, age-segregation unlike anything seen in the outside world. . . . What do any of these things have to do with each other?

Even in the best schools a close examination of curriculum and its sequences turns up a lack of coherence, full of internal contradictions. Fortunately the children have no words to define the panic and anger they feel *at constant violations of natural order and sequence* fobbed off on them as quality in education. The logic of the school-mind is that it is better to leave school with a tool kit of superficial jargon derived from economics, sociology, natural science, and so on, than with one genuine enthusiasm. But quality in education entails learning about something in depth. Confusion is thrust upon kids by too many strange adults, each working alone with only the thinnest relationship with each other, pretending, for the most part, to an expertise they do not possess.

Meaning, not disconnected facts, is what sane human beings seek, and education is a set of codes for processing raw data into meaning. Behind the patchwork quilt of school sequences and the school obsession with facts and theories, the age-old human search for meaning lies well concealed. This is harder to see in elementary school where the hierarchy of school experience seems to make better sense because the good-natured simple relationship between "let's do this" and "let's do that" is just assumed to mean something and the clientele has not yet consciously discerned how little substance is behind the play and pretense.

Think of the great natural sequences—like learning to walk and learning to talk; the progression of light from sunrise to sunset; the ancient procedures of a farmer, a smithy, or a shoemaker; or the preparation of a Thanksgiving feast—all of the parts are in perfect harmony with each other, each action justifies itself and illuminates the past and the future. School sequences aren't like that, not inside a single class and not among the total menu of daily classes. School sequences are crazy. There is no particular reason for any of them, nothing that bears close scrutiny. Few teachers would dare to teach the tools whereby dogmas of a school or a teacher could be criticized, since everything must be accepted. School subjects are learned, if they *can* be learned, like children learn the catechism or memorize the Thirty-nine Articles of Anglicanism.

I teach the un-relating of everything, an infinite fragmentation the opposite of cohesion; what I do is more related to television programming than to making a scheme of order. In a world where home is only a ghost, because both parents work, or because of too many moves or too many job changes or too

5

much ambition, or because something else has left everybody too confused to maintain a family relation, I teach you how to accept confusion as your destiny. That's the first lesson I teach.

2. Class Position

The second lesson I teach is class position. I teach that students must stay in the class where they belong. I don't know who decides my kids belong there but that's not my business. The children are numbered so that if any get away they can be returned to the right class. Over the years the variety of ways children are numbered by schools has increased dramatically, until it is hard to see the human beings plainly under the weight of numbers they carry. Numbering children is a big and very profitable undertaking, though what the strategy is designed to accomplish is elusive. I don't even know why parents would, without a fight, allow it to be done to their kids.

In any case, that's not my business. My job is to make them like being   10
locked together with children who bear numbers like their own. Or at the least to endure it like good sports. If I do my job well, the kids can't even *imagine* themselves somewhere else, because I've shown them how to envy and fear the better classes and how to have contempt for the dumb classes. Under this efficient discipline the class mostly polices itself into good marching order. That's the real lesson of any rigged competition like school. You come to know your place.

In spite of the overall class blueprint, which assumes that ninety-nine percent of the kids are in their class to stay, I nevertheless make a public effort to exhort children to higher levels of test success, hinting at eventual transfer from the lower class as a reward. I frequently insinuate the day will come when an employer will hire them on the basis of test scores and grades, even though my own experience is that employers are rightly indifferent to such things. I never lie outright, but I've come to see that truth and schoolteaching are, at bottom, incompatible, just as Socrates said thousands of years ago. The lesson of numbered classes is that everyone has a proper place in the pyramid and there is no way out of your class except by number magic. Failing that, you must stay where you are put.

3. Indifference

The third lesson I teach is indifference. I teach children not to care too much about anything, even though they want to make it appear that they do. How I do this is very subtle. I do it by demanding that they become totally involved in my lessons, jumping up and down in their seats with anticipation, competing vigorously with each other for my favor. It's heartwarming when they do that; it impresses everyone, even me. When I'm at my best I plan lessons very carefully in order to produce this show of enthusiasm. But when the bell rings I insist they drop whatever it is we have been doing and proceed quickly to the next work station. They must turn on and off like a light switch. Nothing important is ever finished in my class nor in any class I know of. Students never have a complete experience except on the installment plan.

Indeed, the lesson of bells is that no work is worth finishing, so why care too deeply about anything? Years of bells will condition all but the strongest to a world that can no longer offer important work to do. Bells are the secret logic of schooltime; their logic is inexorable. Bells destroy the past and future, rendering every interval the same as any other, as the abstraction of a map renders every living mountain and river the same, even though they are not. Bells inoculate each undertaking with indifference.

4. Emotional Dependency

The fourth lesson I teach is emotional dependency. By stars and red checks, smiles and frowns, prizes, honors, and disgraces, I teach kids to surrender their will to the predestined chain of command. Rights may be granted or withheld by any authority without appeal, because rights do not exist inside a school—not even the right of free speech, as the Supreme Court has ruled—unless school authorities say they do. As a schoolteacher, I intervene in many personal decisions, issuing a pass for those I deem legitimate, or initiating a disciplinary confrontation for behavior that threatens my control. Individuality is constantly trying to assert itself among children and teenagers so my judgments come thick and fast. Individuality is a contradiction of class theory, a curse to all systems of classification.

Here are some common ways it shows up: children sneak away for a private 15 moment in the toilet on the pretext of moving their bowels, or they steal a private instant in the hallway on the grounds they need water. I know they don't, but I allow them to "deceive" me because this conditions them to depend on my favors. Sometimes free will appears right in front of me in pockets of children angry, depressed, or unhappy about things outside my ken; rights in such matters cannot be recognized by schoolteachers, only privileges that can be withdrawn, hostages to good behavior.

5. Intellectual Dependency

The fifth lesson I teach is intellectual dependency. Good students wait for a teacher to tell them what to do. It is the most important lesson, that we must wait for other people, better trained than ourselves, to make the meanings of our lives. The expert makes all the important choices; only I, the teacher, can determine what my kids must study, or rather, only the people who pay me can make those decisions, which I then enforce. If I'm told that evolution is a fact instead of a theory, I transmit that as ordered, punishing deviants who resist what I have been told to tell them to think. This power to control what children will think lets me separate successful students from failures very easily.

Successful children do the thinking I assign them with a minimum of resistance and a decent show of enthusiasm. Of the millions of things of value to study, I decide what few we have time for, or actually it is decided by my faceless employers. The choices are theirs, why should I argue? Curiosity has no important place in my work, only conformity.

Bad kids fight this, of course, even though they lack the concepts to know what they are fighting, struggling to make decisions for themselves about what they will learn and when they will learn it. How can we allow that and survive as schoolteachers? Fortunately there are tested procedures to break the will of those who resist; it is more difficult, naturally, if the kids have respectable parents who come to their aid, but that happens less and less in spite of the bad reputation of schools. No middle-class parents I have ever met actually believe that *their* kid's school is one of the bad ones. Not one single parent in twenty-six years of teaching. That's amazing, and probably the best testimony to what happens to families when mother and father have been well-schooled themselves, learning the seven lessons.

Good people wait for an expert to tell them what to do. It is hardly an exaggeration to say that our entire economy depends upon this lesson being learned. Think of what might fall apart if children weren't trained to be dependent: the social services could hardly survive; they would vanish, I think, into the recent historical limbo out of which they arose. Counselors and therapists would look on in horror as the supply of psychic invalids vanished. Commercial entertainment of all sorts, including television, would wither as people learned again how to make their own fun. Restaurants, the prepared-food industry, and a whole host of other assorted food services would be drastically down-sized if people returned to making their own meals rather than depending on strangers to plant, pick, chop, and cook for them. Much of modern law, medicine, and engineering would go too, the clothing business and schoolteaching as well, unless a guaranteed supply of helpless people continued to pour out of our schools each year.

Don't be too quick to vote for radical school reform if you want to continue getting a paycheck. We've built a way of life that depends on people doing what they are told because they don't know how to tell *themselves* what to do. It's one of the biggest lessons I teach.

6. Provisional Self-Esteem

The sixth lesson I teach is provisional self-esteem. If you've ever tried to wrestle into line kids whose parents have convinced them to believe they'll be loved in spite of anything, you know how impossible it is to make self-confident spirits conform. Our world wouldn't survive a flood of confident people very long, so I teach that a kid's self-respect should depend on expert opinion. My kids are constantly evaluated and judged.

A monthly report, impressive in its provision, is sent into a student's home to elicit approval or mark exactly, down to a single percentage point, how dissatisfied with the child a parent should be. The ecology of "good" schooling depends on perpetuating dissatisfaction, just as the commercial economy depends on the same fertilizer. Although some people might be surprised how little time or reflection goes into making up these mathematical records, the cumulative weight of these objective-seeming documents establishes a profile that compels children to arrive at certain decisions about themselves and their futures based on the casual judgment of strangers. Self-evaluation, the staple of every major philosophical system that ever appeared on the planet, is never considered a factor. The lesson of report cards, grades, and tests is that children should not trust themselves or their parents but should instead rely on the evaluation of certified officials. People need to be told what they are worth.

7. One Can't Hide

The seventh lesson I teach is that one can't hide. I teach students they are always watched, that each is under constant surveillance by myself and my colleagues. There are no private spaces for children, there is no private time. Class change lasts exactly three hundred seconds to keep promiscuous fraternization at low levels. Students are encouraged to tattle on each other or even to tattle on their own parents. Of course, I encourage parents to file reports about their own child's waywardness too. A family trained to snitch on itself isn't likely to conceal any dangerous secrets.

I assign a type of extended schooling called "homework," so that the effect of surveillance, if not that surveillance itself, travels into private households where students might otherwise use free time to learn something unauthorized from a father or mother, by exploration, or by apprenticing to some wise person in the neighborhood. Disloyalty to the idea of schooling is a devil always ready to find work for idle hands.

The meaning of constant surveillance and denial of privacy is that no one can be trusted, that privacy is not legitimate. Surveillance is an ancient imperative, espoused by certain influential thinkers, a central prescription set down in *The Republic*, in *The City of God*, in the *Institutes of the Christian Religion*, in *New Atlantis*, in *Leviathan*,[1] and in a host of other places. All these childless men who wrote these books discovered the same thing: children must be

25

---

[1] *The Republic*, in *The City of God* . . . *Leviathan:* Famous political and philosophical writings by authors like Plato, St. Augustine, and Thomas Hobbes. (Editor's note)

closely watched if you want to keep a society under tight central control. Children will follow a private drummer if you can't get them into a uniformed marching band.

II

It is the great triumph of compulsory government monopoly mass-schooling that among even the best of my fellow teachers, and among even the best of my students' parents, only a small number can imagine a different way to do things. "The kids have to know how to read and write, don't they?" "They have to know how to add and subtract, don't they?" "They have to learn to follow orders if they ever expect to keep a job."

Only a few lifetimes ago things were very different in the United States. Originality and variety were common currency; our freedom from regimentation made us the miracle of the world; social-class boundaries were relatively easy to cross; our citizenry was marvelously confident, inventive, and able to do much for themselves independently, and to think for themselves. We were something special, we Americans, all by ourselves, without government sticking its nose into and measuring every aspect of our lives, without institutions and social agencies telling us how to think and feel. We were something special, as individuals, as Americans.

But we've had a society essentially under central control in the United States since just before the Civil War, and such a society requires compulsory schooling, government monopoly schooling, to maintain itself. Before this development schooling wasn't very important anywhere. We had it, but not too much of it, and only as much as an individual *wanted*. People learned to read, write, and do arithmetic just fine anyway; there are some studies that suggest literacy at the time of the American Revolution, at least for non-slaves on the Eastern seaboard, was close to total. Thomas Paine's *Common Sense*[2] sold 600,000 copies to a population of 3,000,000, twenty percent of whom were slaves, and fifty percent indentured servants.

Were the colonists geniuses? No, the truth is that reading, writing, and arithmetic only take about one hundred hours to transmit as long as the audience is eager and willing to learn. The trick is to wait until someone asks and then move fast while the mood is on. Millions of people teach themselves these things, it really isn't very hard. Pick up a fifth-grade math or rhetoric textbook from 1850 and you'll see that the texts were pitched then on what would today be considered college level. The continuing cry for "basic skills" practice is a

---

[2]*Common Sense:* Paine's fifty-page pamphlet, published January 10, 1776, was recognized as the war-cry of the American revolutionary movement. (Editor's note)

smoke screen behind which schools preempt the time of children for twelve years and teach them the seven lessons I've just described to you.

The society that has come increasingly under central control since just 30 before the Civil War shows itself in the lives we lead, the clothes we wear, the food we eat, and the green highway signs we drive by from coast to coast, all of which are the products of this control. So too, I think, are the epidemics of drugs, suicide, divorce, violence, cruelty, and hardening of class into caste in the United States products of the dehumanization of our lives, the lessening of individual, family, and community importance, a diminishment that proceeds from central control. The character of large compulsory institutions is inevitable; they want more and more until there isn't any more to give. School takes our children away from any possibility of an active role in community life—in fact it destroys communities by relegating the training of children to the hands of certified experts—and by doing so it ensures our children cannot grow up fully human. Aristotle taught that without a fully active role in community life one could not hope to become a healthy human being. Surely he was right. Look around you the next time you are near a school or an old people's reservation if you wish a demonstration.

School as it was built is an essential support system for a model of social engineering that condemns most people to be subordinate stones in a pyramid that narrows as it ascends to a terminal of control. School is an artifice that makes such a pyramidical social order seem inevitable, although such a premise is a fundamental betrayal of the American Revolution. From Colonial days through the period of the Republic we had no schools to speak of—read Benjamin Franklin's *Autobiography* for an example of a man who had no time to waste in school—and yet the promise of democracy was beginning to be realized. We turned our backs on this promise by bringing to life the ancient pharaonic dream of Egypt: compulsory subordination for all. That was the secret Plato reluctantly transmitted in *The Republic* when Glaucon and Adeimantus extort from Socrates the plan for total state control of human life, a plan necessary to maintain a society where some people take more than their share. "I will show you," says Socrates, "how to bring about such a feverish city, but you will not like what I am going to say." And so the blueprint of the seven-lesson school was first sketched.

The current debate about whether we should have a national curriculum is phony. We already have a national curriculum locked up in the seven lessons I have just outlined. Such a curriculum produces physical, moral, and intellectual paralysis, and no curriculum of content will be sufficient to reverse its hideous effects. What is currently under discussion in our national hysteria about failing academic performance misses the point. Schools teach exactly what they are intended to teach and they do it well: how to be a good Egyptian and remain in your place in the pyramid.

ANALYZING What the Writer Says

1. In your own words, sum up the seven "lessons" Gatto (and, by extension, every schoolteacher) teaches his students.

2. Why do you think Gatto emphasizes in his introduction that he "intend[s] no irony"?

3. In what way are the "seven lessons" political, not educational?

4. In what way, according to Gatto, was the education system in Colonial America superior to the educational systems of the rest of the world? What changed just before the Civil War?

5. What is Gatto's suggestion for improving our children's education?

ANALYZING How the Writer Says It

1. What is the effect of Gatto's opening sentence—"Call me Mr. Gatto, please"?

2. How does Gatto's format—the presentation of seven points—reinforce his thesis?

ANALYZING the Issue

1. Gatto sums up his evaluation of the American school system as follows: "School as it was built is an essential support system for a model of social engineering that condemns most people to be subordinate stones in a pyramid that narrows as it ascends to a terminal of control." Do you agree with his opinion that the education we receive in our schools makes us prisoners of a system rather than free individuals who make their own choices? Why or why not?

2. Gatto claims that social problems (drugs, violence, divorce, etc.) exist partially because American society "has come increasingly under central control." What do you think Gatto means by this statement? Given his arguments in the essay, how would he support such a statement? Do you think he is right? Explain.

3. Gatto claims that "only a few lifetimes ago," the American educational method was the envy of the Western world. Today, American schoolchildren perform much worse than children from other industrialized nations on standardized exams. How would Gatto explain this phenomenon based on the premises he laid down in his essay? Do you agree with this explanation? Why or why not?

ANALYZING Connections Between Texts

1. Compare the approach of Gatto, who emphasizes that his argument is *not* to be misunderstood as tongue-in-cheek, to that of Roberta F. Borkat ("A Liberating Curriculum," p. 340). How are the fundamental beliefs of these writers similar? How do they differ?

2. In "Politics and the English Language" (p. 487), George Orwell argues that governmental authorities use deliberately sloppy language to anesthetize citizens and stifle thought. In what ways, according to Gatto, does compulsory education have similar goals? Choose a sentence from the piece that makes the same point Orwell does.

3. Explain how the photograph "German Schoolboys Salute" (p. 401) illustrates Gatto's points.

Theme for English B

BY LANGSTON HUGHES

The instructor said,

> Go home and write
> a page tonight.
> And let that page come out of you—
> Then, it will be true.   5

I wonder if it's that simple?
I am twenty-two, colored, born in Winston-Salem.
I went to school there, then Durham, then here
to this college on the hill above Harlem.
I am the only colored student in my class.   10
The steps from the hill lead down into Harlem,
through a park, then I cross St. Nicholas,
Eighth Avenue, Seventh, and I come to the Y,
the Harlem Branch Y, where I take the elevator
up to my room, sit down, and write this page: 15

It's not easy to know what is true for you or me
at twenty-two, my age. But I guess I'm what
I feel and see and hear, Harlem, I hear you:
hear you, hear me—we two—you, me, talk on this page.
(I hear New York, too.) Me—who?   20
Well, I like to eat, sleep, drink, and be in love.
I like to work, read, learn, and understand life.
I like a pipe for a Christmas present,
or records—Bessie, bop, or Bach.
I guess being colored doesn't make me *not* like   25
the same things other folks like who are other races.

LANGSTON HUGHES

A figure at the forefront of the Harlem Renaissance, Langston Hughes (1902–67) wrote eloquently about the experience of being black in America. The following poem, first published in 1926, depicts the alienation of a black student in a predominantly white school system—an experience Hughes must have had when he attended Columbia University from 1921 to 1922.

So will my page be colored that I write?
Being me, it will not be white.
But it will be
a part of you, instructor.   30
You are white—
yet a part of me, as I am a part of you.
That's American.
Sometimes perhaps you don't want to be a part of me.
Nor do I often want to be a part of you.   35
But we are, that's true!
I guess you learn from me—
although you're older—and white—
and somewhat more free.

This is my page for English B.   40

ANALYZING What the Writer Says

1. How does the assignment the speaker got relate to the reality of his life? What does the speaker mean when he says that "it's not easy to know what is true for you or me"? What insights about the relationship between reader and writer does this statement imply?

2. What does the speaker mean when he says that the page he writes will be "a part of you, instructor. / . . . / yet a part of me, as I am a part of you. / That's American"?

3. "I guess you can learn from me," says the speaker toward the end of the poem. What do you think the instructor can learn from his student? What can we, the readers, learn from the poem?

ANALYZING How the Writer Says It

The poem begins with the speaker quoting his instructor's assignment and ends with the speaker's "This is my page for English B." What is the effect of framing the speaker's monologue and his remarks to his instructor in this fashion?

ANALYZING the Issue

1. Imagine you are the speaker's instructor in English B. Do you think the student fulfills the assignment? Why or why not?

2. Langston Hughes had first-hand experience being a minority student at Columbia University from 1921 to 1922. What similar experiences do minority students today have?

ANALYZING Connections Between Texts

1. Compare and contrast the instructor of Hughes's poem to the generic school-teacher of which Gatto writes (p. 362). Do Hughes and Gatto make similar points?

2. What experiences are shared by Hughes's speaker and Carolyn Hwang ("The Good Daughter," p. 139)? Cite sentences from each to illustrate your point.

3. Look at Inge Fink's photo "Talk the Talk" (p. 106) How is Hughes's poem analogous to the sticker-adorned vehicle?

What do you remember about your high school graduation? What kinds of things did the graduation speaker tell your class? What do you expect to hear when you graduate from college?

The Speech the Graduates Didn't Hear

BY JACOB NEUSNER

JACOB NEUSNER

Formerly a professor at Brown University, Jacob Neusner must have heard a great number of gradua- tion speeches in the course of his career. The follow- ing speech was never deliv- ered—at least not to any graduating class—because it lays bare the failings rather than the triumphs of higher education.

We the faculty take no pride in our educational achievements with you. We have prepared you for a world that does not exist, indeed, that cannot exist. You have spent four years supposing that failure leaves no record. You have learned at Brown that when your work goes poorly, the painless solution is to drop out. But starting now, in the world to which you go, failure marks you. Confronting difficulty by quitting leaves you changed. Outside Brown, quitters are no heroes.

With us you could argue about why your errors were not errors, why mediocre work really was excel- lent, why you could take pride in routine and slipshod presentation. Most of you, after all, can look back on honor grades for most of what you have done. So, here grades can have meant little in distinguishing the excellent from the ordinary. But tomorrow, in the world to which you go, you had best not defend errors but learn from them. You will be ill-advised to demand praise for what does not deserve it, and abuse those who do not give it.

For four years we created an altogether forgiv- ing world, in which whatever slight effort you gave was all that was demanded. When you did not keep appointments, we made new ones. When your work came in beyond the deadline, we pretended not to care.

Worse still, when you were boring, we acted as if you were saying something important. When you were garrulous and talked to hear yourself talk, we listened as if it mattered. When you tossed on our desks writing upon which you had not labored, we read it and even responded, as though you earned a response. When you were dull, we pretended you were smart. When you were predictable, unimaginative, and routine, we listened as if to new and wonderful things. When you demanded free lunch, we served it. And all this why?

Despite your fantasies, it was not even that we wanted to be liked by you. It was that we did not want to be bothered, and the easy way out was pretense: smiles and easy Bs.   5

It is conventional to quote in addresses such as these. Let me quote someone you've never heard of: Professor Carter A. Daniel, Rutgers University (*Chronicle of Higher Education*, May 7, 1979):

> College has spoiled you by reading papers that don't deserve to be read, listening to comments that don't deserve a hearing, paying attention even to the lazy, ill-informed, and rude. We had to do it, for the sake of education. But nobody will ever do it again. College has deprived you of adequate preparation for the last fifty years. It has failed you by being easy, free, forgiving, attentive, comfortable, interesting, unchallenging fun. Good luck tomorrow.

That is why, on this commencement day, we have nothing in which to take much pride.

Oh, yes, there is one more thing. Try not to act toward your coworkers and bosses as you have acted toward us. I mean, when they give you what you want but have not earned, don't abuse them, insult them, act out with them your parlous relationships with your parents. This too we have tolerated. It was, as I said, not to be liked. Few professors actually care whether or not they are liked by peer-paralyzed adolescents, fools so shallow as to imagine professors care not about education but about popularity. It was, again, to be rid of you. So go, unlearn the lies we taught you. To Life!

ANALYZING What the Writer Says

1. Summarize the main points the speaker makes about how the school of the speech has *not* prepared its graduates for the real world.

2. As Neusner complains about the students' many shortcomings, what is he implying about the faculty? To whom is Neusner's criticism directed more pointedly—teachers or students?

ANALYZING How the Writer Says It

1. Pick out the "loaded" words and phrases Neusner uses to describe students and teachers. Explain them.

2. What kind of evidence does Neusner use to support his points? Does he show convincingly how he knows the things he tells his audience? Does he present the evidence from which he draws his conclusions?

3. Who is Neusner's intended audience?

4. How is an address to a live audience different from a written paper? What characteristics of a speech do you recognize in Neusner's piece?

5. In what ways can Neusner's essay be described as ironic?

ANALYZING the Issue

1. Do you agree with Neusner's idea that easy teachers and easy grades cheat students out of the education they paid to get in college? Explain.

2. Do you think that rules in college should be different from those in the real world—that it should be okay in college to have flexible deadlines, less responsibility, and a forgiving attitude from those who evaluate a student's performance? Why or why not?

3. How would you defend the (student) behavior that Neusner attacks in his "speech"?

ANALYZING Connections Between Texts

1. Compare John Taylor Gatto's conclusions about the failings of the American school system (p. 362) to those of Neusner.

2. In "Scandal 101: Lessons from Ken Lay" (p. 672) Julie Schlosser lists university courses designed to teach business ethics, suggesting that universities, like any other business, follow market trends to make themselves more attractive to their customers. How does Neusner imply similar market concerns in his "speech"?

3. Compare Neusner's conclusions about the American university to the sentiments expressed in the picture "Graduation Day" (p. 398).

WARMING UP: *Did you and/or your parents, or anyone else you know, spend a lot of time worrying about which college you would attend?*

Matriculation Fixation

BY JOE QUEENAN

JOE QUEENAN

Queenan, who has written for Spy, GQ, *and* The New York Times, *among others, has little patience for the self-absorption of baby boomers, and his humorous* Balsamic Dreams: A Short but Self-Important History of the Baby Boomer Generation *(2001) takes a book-length jab at his own generation. In the following piece, which appeared on November 11, 2001, in the "Endpaper" from the Education Life Supplement to the* New York Times Magazine, *Queenan fixes a cynical eye on a typical boomer obsession: which colleges will take their kids.*

Two years ago, I was languishing in the waiting room of a Philadelphia hospital when a complete stranger unexpectedly began telling me about his daughter's college plans. As my 79-year-old mother was recovering from major surgery that afternoon, I could not give him my complete and undivided attention. But as the briefing session wore on, I did manage to garner most of the relevant details.

The girl, bright but not brilliant, had been accepted to a first-tier university without financial aid but had also been accepted to a local, second-echelon university where she was promised a free ride. Money being tight, with other college-bound children in the family queue, the man had persuaded his daughter to accept the second university's offer. Now he was worried that she would one day rue this decision. Because she would be graduating from a less prestigious institution, fewer contacts would be made and fewer doors would be opened. Her degree would put her within striking distance of the yellow brick road, but not physically on the road itself. Did this make her father the spawn of Satan?

As a man of the world accustomed to being told the most intimate details about complete strangers' marriages, careers and hobbies, I had long ago acquired the requisite skills to mediate this crisis. I told the man that many of my high school chums had graduated from the second-tier university in question and had gone on to live rich, full lives.

I told him that I myself had graduated from a second-echelon Philadelphia university not unlike the one his daughter was entering, and had managed to carve out a nice little niche for myself. I told him that my college days had been among the happiest of my life, that the sun never set without my thanking God for the illumination and inspiration provided by my talented, dedicated professors. Pressed for biographical data, I explained that I was a freelance writer, ticked off a list of my credentials and said I was pretty happy with the way my career had turned out.

The man had never heard of me, had never read anything I'd written. Though he tried to feign interest in my pathetic curriculum vitae, I could see that he was devastated. By following an academic path similar to mine, his daughter, who was also planning a career in journalism, was going to end up as big a failure as I.

I never did find out why he was visiting the hospital.

I mention this incident because it illustrates the neurotic gabbiness that afflicts parents when it comes time to send their children to college. I know whereof I speak. Next fall, my daughter goes to college. Three years later my son will follow suit. I will be sorry to see them go; over the years they have proved to be remarkably amusing. But every dark cloud has a silver lining. Once my children have left the house, I will never again have to participate in a mind-numbing discussion about where my children or my friends' children or my neighbors' children are going to college, and why. On this subject, I am completely tapped out.

This lack of interest does not stem from pure selfishness or unalloyed contempt for other people's offspring. Rather, I feel this way because I find almost all conversations about the college selection process to be banal, self-aggrandizing, self-flagellatory or punitive. I'd rather talk about cribbage.

The most infuriating conversation is the one where the parent clearly seeks a decisive, career-validating moment of emotional closure. Such individuals believe that securing admission to a top-flight university provides a child with an irrevocable passport to success, guaranteeing a life of uninterrupted economic mirth. Parents such as these upwardly mobile chuckleheads exude an almost Prussian belligerence when announcing their children's destinations, congratulating themselves on a job well done, while issuing a sotto voce taunt to parents of the less gifted. For them, the hard part of child rearing is now over. Junior went to the right prep school, made the right friends, signed up for the right activities and is now headed for the right school. Now we can get the heck out of here and move to Tuscany.

But in reality, life doesn't end at age 17. Or 21. In real life, some children get the finest educations but still become first-class screw-ups. My own profession is filled with people who went to the right school but ended up in the wrong career. (They should have been flacks; the phone ringing in the next room is not and never will be the Pulitzer committee.) Some of those boys and girls most likely to succeed are going to end up on welfare or skid row. At which point they'll need parental input. Or cash. A parent's responsibility doesn't end once the kids leave. A parent's responsibility never ends. That's why Nature gives you the job.

A second, far more numerous class of obsessives consists of people who suddenly realize that their Brand X children aren't going to make the cut. Seventeen years of unread textbooks, unvisited museums and untaken A.P. courses are now finally taking their toll, and those grandiose delivery-room dreams of Amherst, Bard and Duke are suddenly going up in smoke. Bashfully, shamefacedly, miserably, these parents now mumble the names of the glamourless institutions their progeny are skulking off to. Invariably, they are colleges you never heard of in towns no one wants to visit in states whose capitals only repeat winners on "Jeopardy" can name. The market has spoken, the glum parental expressions seem to say. My child is an idiot.

But once again, reality has a way of upsetting the worst-laid plans of mice and Mensa. Some kids are late bloomers. Some kids are better off in a less competitive environment. Lots of people achieve huge success in this society without a degree from a prestigious university. Just because your child has failed to clear the first, or even the 20th, hurdle doesn't mean you should disown him. Matisse didn't get rolling until he was in his 40's. Bill Gates, David Geffen, Michael Dell, Graydon Carter and Madonna are all college dropouts. Ronald Reagan attended tiny Eureka College, while Warren Buffet went to Football U in Lincoln, Neb. Despite what you may have read in F. Scott Fitzgerald (who dropped out of Princeton in 1917), life doesn't have just one act. There is often Act II. And Act V. Not to mention the sequels.

Matriculation fixation reaches its dottiest form during the obligatory campus visit. Here it is never entirely clear what parents are looking for, particularly in high-profile institutions whose renown has in some way preceded them. During a recent visit to M.I.T., I watched the first 30 seconds of an admissions office video poking fun at the university's reputation as a nerd factory. While my wife and daughter watched the rest of the video, which assured applicants that M.I.T. nerds were hard to find, I took a stroll around the campus. I saw a lot of nerds. And I do not mean this as a criticism.

Later that morning, a guide showed a bunch of us around campus. At one juncture, she pointed out a restaurant where students could grab a fast, inexpensive meal. "How much?" asked one high-strung mother. "About eight bucks," she was told. The woman shuddered, noting that forking over $8 for dinner every night could get pretty darned expensive.

"It's going to cost you 40 grand to send your kid to school here," I interjected. "Don't start worrying about dinner prices." 15

Since that visit this fall, this incident has become an invaluable part of my repertory. Now, whenever I am dragooned into the 30,000th interminable conversation about the college selection process I indicate that sedulous mon-

itoring of on-campus restaurant prices should be a vital component of the win-
nowing procedure, particularly vis-à-vis panini. People who hear me say things
like this can't decide whether I am insensitive or ornery or flat-out dumb. Well,
let's just put it this way: I was never M.I.T. material.

ANALYZING What the Writer Says

1. Why does Queenan spend the first six paragraphs of his essay on an anecdote
   about a stranger he meets in a hospital waiting room and the stranger's daughter's college plans?

2. Why, according to Queenan, do parents put so much stock into which colleges
   will accept their kids?

3. What realities of human nature does the "matriculation fixation" ignore?

ANALYZING How the Writer Says It

1. Cite several phrases or sentences that reveal Queenan's attitude toward his
   subject.

2. What is the effect of Queenan's self-deprecating humor?

ANALYZING the Issue

1. Do you agree that the college a person attends is a significant factor in that person's success? Why or why not?

2. Many parents encourage grueling study habits and lots of extracurricular activities during high school, often in the guise of offering their children "opportunities" but nonetheless nudging them toward getting into the best colleges. Is it
   healthy for parents to pressure their children to succeed on the parents' terms?
   Explain.

ANALYZING Connections Between Texts

1. Compare the parental pressure Queenan describes to what Cathy Davidson discusses in "From the Best of Japanese Families" (p. 351).

2. How are the expectations of Caroline Hwang's immigrant parents ("The Good
   Daughter," p. 139) similar to the those of baby boomer parents of college-age
   offspring?

3. How does the "Mostly Mozart . . ." cartoon (p. 787) illustrate Queenan's points?

WARMING UP: *Have you ever had a teacher who really made a difference in your life, who changed your opinion of yourself and your abilities?*

I Just Wanna Be Average

BY MIKE ROSE

MIKE ROSE

A UCLA professor of education, prolific writer Mike Rose recalls the time he spent in the vocational education track in high school. This piece comes from his 1989 Lives on the Boundaries: The Struggles and Achievements of America's Underprepared.

It took two buses to get to Our Lady of Mercy. The first started deep in South Los Angeles and caught me at midpoint. The second drifted through neighborhoods with trees, parks, big lawns, and lots of flowers. The rides were long but were livened up by a group of South L.A. veterans whose parents also thought that Hope had set up shop in the west end of the county. There was Christy Biggars, who, at sixteen, was dealing and was, according to rumor, a pimp as well. There were Bill Cobb and Johnny Gonzales, grease-pencil artists extraordinaire, who left Nembutal-enhanced[1] swirls of "Cobb" and "Johnny" on the corrugated walls of the bus. And then there was Tyrrell Wilson. Tyrrell was the coolest kid I knew. He ran the dozens[2] like a metric halfback, laid down a rap that outrhymed and outpointed Cobb, whose rap was good but not great—the curse of a moderately soulful kid trapped in white skin. But it was Cobb who would sneak a radio onto the bus, and thus underwrote his patter with Little Richard, Fats Domino, Chuck Berry, the Coasters,[3] and Ernie K-Doe's mother-in-law, an awful woman who was "sent from down below." And so it was that Christy and

---

[1] Trade name for pentobarbital, a sedative drug. (Editor's note)

[2] A verbal game of African origin in which competitors try to top each other's insults. (Editor's note)

[3] Popular black musicians of the 1950s. (Editor's note)

Cobb and Johnny G. and Tyrrell and I and assorted others picked up along the way passed our days in the back of the bus, a funny mix brought together by geography and parental desire.

Entrance to school brings with it forms and releases and assessments. Mercy relied on a series of tests, mostly the Stanford-Binet,[4] for placement, and somehow the results of my tests got confused with those of another student named Rose. The other Rose apparently didn't do very well, for I was placed in the vocational track, a euphemism for the bottom level. Neither I nor my parents realized what this meant. We had no sense that Business Math, Typing, and English—Level D were dead ends. The current spate of reports on the schools criticizes parents for not involving themselves in the education of their children. But how would someone like Tommy Rose, with his two years of Italian schooling, know what to ask? And what sort of pressure could an exhausted waitress apply? The error went undetected, and I remained in the vocational track for two years. What a place.

My homeroom was supervised by Brother Dill, a troubled and unstable man who also taught freshman English. When his class drifted away from him, which was often, his voice would rise in paranoid accusations, and occasionally he would lose control and shake or smack us. I hadn't been there two months when one of his brisk, face-turning slaps had my glasses sliding down the aisle. Physical education was also pretty harsh. Our teacher was a stubby ex-lineman who had played old-time pro ball in the Midwest. He routinely had us grabbing our ankles to receive his stinging paddle across our butts. He did that, he said, to make men of us. "Rose," he bellowed on our first encounter; me standing geeky in line in my baggy shorts. " 'Rose'? What the hell kind of name is that?"

"Italian, sir," I squeaked.

"Italian! Ho. Rose, do you know the sound a bag of shit makes when it hits   5
the wall?"

"No, sir."

"Wop!"[5]

Sophomore English was taught by Mr. Mitropetros. He was a large, bejeweled man who managed the parking lot at the Shrine Auditorium. He would crow and preen and list for us the stars he'd brushed against. We'd ask questions and glance knowingly and snicker, and all that fueled the poor guy to brag some more. Parking cars was his night job. He had little training in English, so his lesson plan for his day work had us reading the district's required text, *Julius Caesar,* aloud for the semester. We'd finished the play way before the twenty weeks was up, so he'd have us switch parts again and again and start again: Dave Snyder, the fastest guy at Mercy, muscling through

---

[4]An IQ test. (Editor's note)

[5]Derogatory term for Italian. (Editor's note)

Caesar to the breathless squeals of Calpurnia, as interpreted by Steven Fusco, a surfer who owned the school's most envied paneled wagon. Week ten and Dave and Steve would take on new roles, as would we all, and render a water-logged Cassius and a Brutus that are beyond my powers of description.

Spanish I—taken in the second year—fell into the hands of a new recruit. Mr. Montez was a tiny man, slight, five foot six at the most, soft-spoken and delicate. Spanish was a particularly rowdy class, and Mr. Montez was as prepared for it as a doily maker at a hammer throw. He would tap his pencil to a room in which Steve Fusco was propelling spitballs from his heavy lips, in which Mike Dweetz was taunting Billy Hawk, a half-Indian, half-Spanish, reed-thin, quietly explosive boy. The vocational track at Our Lady of Mercy mixed kids traveling in from South L.A. with South Bay surfers and a few Slavs and Chicanos from the harbors of San Pedro. This was a dangerous miscellany: surfers and hodads[6] and South-Central blacks all ablaze to the metronomic tapping of Hector Montez's pencil.

One day Billy lost it. Out of the corner of my eye I saw him strike out with   10
his right arm and catch Dweetz across the neck. Quick as a spasm, Dweetz was out of his seat, scattering desks, cracking Billy on the side of the head, right behind the eye. Snyder and Fusco and others broke it up, but the room felt hot and close and naked. Mr. Montez's tenuous authority was finally ripped to shreds, and I think everyone felt a little strange about that. The charade was over, and when it came down to it, I don't think any of the kids really wanted it to end this way. They had pushed and pushed and bullied their way into a freedom that both scared and embarrassed them.

Students will float to the mark you set. I and the others in the vocational classes were bobbing in pretty shallow water. Vocational education has aimed at increasing the economic opportunities of students who do not do well in our schools. Some serious programs succeed in doing that, and through exceptional teachers—like Mr. Gross in *Horace's Compromise*[7]—students learn to develop hypotheses and troubleshoot, reason through a problem, and communicate effectively—the true job skills. The vocational track, however, is most often a place for those who are just not making it, a dumping ground for the disaffected. There were a few teachers who worked hard at education; young Brother Slattery, for example, combined a stern voice with weekly quizzes to try to pass along to us a skeletal outline of world history. But mostly the teachers had no idea of how to engage the imaginations of us kids who were scuttling along at the bottom of the pond.

And the teachers would have needed some inventiveness, for none of us was groomed for the classroom. It wasn't just that I didn't know things—didn't

---

[6]Nonsurfers. (Editor's note)

[7]A book on American education by Theodore Sizer. (Editor's note)

know how to simplify algebraic fractions, couldn't identify different kinds of clauses, bungled Spanish translations—but that I had developed various faulty and inadequate ways of doing algebra and making sense of Spanish. Worse yet, the years of defensive tuning out in elementary school had given me a way to escape quickly while seeming at least half alert. During my time in Voc. Ed., I developed further into a mediocre student and a somnambulant problem solver, and that affected the subjects I did have the wherewithal to handle: I detested Shakespeare; I got bored with history. My attention flitted here and there. I fooled around in class and read my books indifferently—the intellectual equivalent of playing with your food. I did what I had to do to get by, and I did it with half a mind.

But I did learn things about people and eventually came into my own socially. I liked the guys in Voc. Ed. Growing up where I did, I understood and admired physical prowess, and there was an abundance of muscle here. There was Dave Snyder, a sprinter and halfback of true quality. Dave's ability and his quick wit gave him a natural appeal, and he was welcome in any clique, though he always kept a little independent. He enjoyed acting the fool and could care less about studies, but he possessed a certain maturity and never caused the faculty much trouble. It was a testament to his independence that he included me among his friends—I eventually went out for track, but I was no jock. Owing to the Latin alphabet and a dearth of Rs and Ss, Snyder sat behind Rose, and we started exchanging one-liners and became friends.

There was Ted Richard, a much-touted Little League pitcher. He was chunky and had a baby face and came to Our Lady of Mercy as a seasoned street fighter. Ted was quick to laugh and he had a loud, jolly laugh, but when he got angry he'd smile a little smile, the kind that simply raises the corner of the mouth a quarter of an inch. For those who knew, it was an eerie signal. Those who didn't found themselves in big trouble, for Ted was very quick. He loved to carry on what we would come to call philosophical discussions: What is courage? Does God exist? He also loved words, enjoyed picking up big ones like *salubrious* and *equivocal* and using them in our conversations—laughing at himself as the word hit a chuckhole rolling off his tongue. Ted didn't do all that well in school—baseball and parties and testing the courage he'd speculated about took up his time. His textbooks were *Argosy* and *Field and Stream*, whatever newspapers he'd find on the bus stop—from the *Daily Worker* to pornography—conversations with uncles or hobos or businessmen he'd meet in a coffee shop, *The Old Man and the Sea*. With hindsight, I can see that Ted was developing into one of those rough-hewn intellectuals whose sources are a mix of the learned and the apocryphal, whose discussions are both assured and sad.

And then there was Ken Harvey. Ken was good-looking in a puffy way and 15 had a full and oily ducktail and was a car enthusiast . . . a hodad. One day in religion class, he said the sentence that turned out to be one of the most memorable of the hundreds of thousands I heard in those Voc. Ed. years. We were talking about the parable of the talents, about achievement, working hard, doing the best you can do, blah-blah-blah, when the teacher called on the restive Ken Harvey for an opinion. Ken thought about it, but just for a second, and said (with studied, minimal affect), "I just wanna be average." That woke me up. Average? Who wants to be average? Then the athletes chimed in with the clichés that make you want to laryngectomize them, and the exchange became a platitudinous melee. At the time, I thought Ken's assertion was stupid, and I wrote him off. But his sentence has stayed with me all these years, and I think I am finally coming to understand it.

Ken Harvey was gasping for air. School can be a tremendously disorienting place. No matter how bad the school, you're going to encounter notions that don't fit with the assumptions and beliefs that you grew up with—maybe you'll hear these dissonant notions from teachers, maybe from the other students, and maybe you'll read them. You'll also be thrown in with all kinds of kids from all kinds of backgrounds, and that can be unsettling—this is especially true in places of rich ethnic and linguistic mix, like the L.A. basin. You'll see a handful of students far excel you in courses that sound exotic and that are only in the curriculum of the elite: French, physics, trigonometry. And all this is happening while you're trying to shape an identity, your body is changing, and your emotions are running wild. If you're a working-class kid in the vocational track, the options you'll have to deal with this will be constrained in certain ways: you're defined by your school as "slow"; you're placed in a curriculum that isn't designed to liberate you but to occupy you, or, if you're lucky, train you, though the training is for work the society does not esteem; other students are picking up the cues from your school and your curriculum and interacting with you in particular ways. If you're a kid like Ted Richard, you turn your back on all this and let your mind roam where it may. But youngsters like Ted are rare. What Ken and so many others do is protect themselves from such suffocating madness by taking on with a vengeance the identity implied in the vocational track. Reject the confusion and frustration by openly defining yourself as the Common Joe. Champion the average. Rely on your own good sense. Fuck this bullshit. Bullshit, of course, is everything you —and the others—fear is beyond you: books, essays, tests, academic scrambling, complexity, scientific reasoning, philosophical inquiry.

The tragedy is that you have to twist the knife in your own gray matter to make this defense work. You'll have to shut down, have to reject intellectual stimuli or diffuse them with sarcasm, have to cultivate stupidity, have to convert boredom from a malady into a way of confronting the world. Keep your vocabulary simple, act stoned when you're not or act more stoned than you are, flaunt ignorance, materialize your dreams. It is a powerful and effective defense—it neutralizes the insult and the frustration of being a vocational kid and, when perfected, it drives teachers up the wall, a delightful secondary effect. But like all strong magic, it exacts a price.

My own deliverance from the Voc. Ed. world began with sophomore biology. Every student, college prep to vocational, had to take biology, and unlike
the other courses, the same person taught all sections. When teaching the
vocational group, Brother Clint probably slowed down a bit or omitted a little
of the fundamental biochemistry, but he used the same book and more or less
the same syllabus across the board. If one class got tough, he could get
tougher. He was young and powerful and very handsome, and looks and physical strength were high currency. No one gave him any trouble.

I was pretty bad at the dissecting table, but the lectures and the textbook were
interesting: plastic overlays that, with each turned page, peeled away skin, then
veins and muscle, then organs, down to the very bones that Brother Clint, point-
er in hand, would tap out on our hanging skeleton. Dave Snyder was in big trouble, for the study of life—versus the living of it—was sticking in his craw. We
worked out a code for our multiple-choice exams. He'd poke me in the back:
once for the answer under *A,* twice for *B,* and so on; and when he'd hit the right
one, I'd look up to the ceiling as though I were lost in thought. Poke: cytoplasm.
Poke, poke: methane. Poke, poke, poke: William Harvey. Poke, poke, poke,
poke: islets of Langerhans. This didn't work out perfectly, but Dave passed the
course, and I mastered the dreamy look of a guy on a record jacket. And something else happened. Brother Clint puzzled over this Voc. Ed. kid who was rack-
ing up 98s and 99s on his tests. He checked the school's records and discovered the error. He recommended that I begin my junior year in the College
Prep program. According to all I've read since, such a shift, as one report put it,
is virtually impossible. Kids at that level rarely cross tracks. The telling thing is
how chancy both my placement into and exit from Voc. Ed. was; neither I nor
my parents had anything to do with it. I lived in one world during spring semester, and when I came back to school in the fall, I was living in another.

Switching to College Prep was a mixed blessing. I was an erratic student. I   20
was undisciplined. And I hadn't caught onto the rules of the game: why work
hard in a class that didn't grab my fancy? I was also hopelessly behind in math.
Chemistry was hard; toying with my chemistry set years before hadn't prepared me for the chemist's equations. Fortunately, the priest who taught both
chemistry and second-year algebra was also the school's athletic director.
Membership on the track team covered me; I knew I wouldn't get lower than
a C. U.S. history was taught pretty well, and I did okay. But civics was taken
over by a football coach who had trouble reading the textbook aloud—and
reading aloud was the centerpiece of his pedagogy. College Prep at Mercy was
certainly an improvement over the vocational program—at least it carried
some status—but the social science curriculum was weak, and the mathemat-
ics and physical sciences were simply beyond me. I had a miserable quantitative background and ended up copying some assignments and finessing the
rest as best I could. Let me try to explain how it feels to see again and again
material you should once have learned but didn't.

You are given a problem. It requires you to simplify algebraic fractions or to multiply expressions containing square roots. You know this is pretty basic material because you've seen it for years. Once a teacher took some time with you, and you learned how to carry out these operations. Simple versions, anyway. But that was a year or two or more in the past, and these are more complex versions, and now you're not sure. And this, you keep telling yourself, is ninth- or even eighth-grade stuff.

Next it's a word problem. This is also old hat. The basic elements are as familiar as story characters: trains speeding so many miles per hour or shadows of buildings angling so many degrees. Maybe you know enough, have sat through enough explanations, to be able to begin setting up the problem: "If one train is going this fast . . ." or "This shadow is really one line of a triangle . . ." Then: "Let's see . . ." "How did Jones do this?" "Hmmmm." "No." "No, that won't work." Your attention wavers. You wonder about other things: a football game, a dance, that cute new checker at the market. You try to focus on the problem again. You scribble on paper for a while, but the tension wins out and your attention flits elsewhere. You crumple the paper and begin daydreaming to ease the frustration.

The particulars will vary, but in essence this is what a number of students go through, especially those in so-called remedial classes. They open their textbooks and see once again the familiar and impenetrable formulas and diagrams and terms that have stumped them for years. There is no excitement here. *No* excitement. Regardless of what the teacher says, this is not a new challenge. There is, rather, embarrassment and frustration and, not surprisingly, some anger in being reminded once again of long-standing inadequacies. No wonder so many students finally attribute their difficulties to something inborn, organic: "That part of my brain just doesn't work." Given the troubling histories many of these students have, it's miraculous that any of them can lift the shroud of hopelessness sufficiently to make deliverance from these classes possible.

Through this entire period, my father's health was deteriorating with cruel momentum. His arteriosclerosis progressed to the point where a simple nick on his shin wouldn't heal. Eventually it ulcerated and widened. Lou Minton would come by daily to change the dressing. We tried renting an oscillating bed—which we placed in the front room—to force blood through the constricted arteries in my father's legs. The bed hummed through the night, moving in place to ward off the inevitable. The ulcer continued to spread, and the doctors finally had to amputate. My grandfather had lost his leg in a stockyard accident. Now my father too was crippled. His convalescence was slow but steady, and the doctors placed him in the Santa Monica Rehabilitation Center, a sun-bleached building that opened out onto the warm spray of the Pacific. The place gave him some strength and some color and some training in walking with an artificial leg. He did pretty well for a year or so until he slipped and broke his

hip. He was confined to a wheelchair after that, and the confinement contributed to the diminishing of his body and spirit.

I am holding a picture of him. He is sitting in his wheelchair and smiling at   25
the camera. The smile appears forced, unsteady, seems to quaver, though it is
frozen in silver nitrate. He is in his mid-sixties and looks eighty. Late in my
junior year, he had a stroke and never came out of the resulting coma. After
that, I would see him only in dreams, and to this day that is how I join him.
Sometimes the dreams are sad and grisly and primal: my father lying in a bed
soaked with his suppuration,[8] holding me, rocking me. But sometimes the
dreams bring him back to me healthy: him talking to me on an empty street,
or buying some pictures to decorate our old house, or transformed somehow
into someone strong and adept with tools and the physical.

Jack MacFarland couldn't have come into my life at a better time. My father
was dead, and I had logged up too many years of scholastic indifference. Mr.
MacFarland had a master's degree from Columbia and decided, at twenty-six,
to find a little school and teach his heart out. He never took any credentialing
courses, couldn't bear to, he said, so he had to find employment in a private
system. He ended up at Our Lady of Mercy teaching five sections of senior
English. He was a beatnik who was born too late. His teeth were stained, he
tucked his sorry tie in between the third and fourth buttons of his shirt, and
his pants were chronically wrinkled. At first, we couldn't believe this guy,
thought he slept in his car. But within no time, he had us so startled with work
that we didn't much worry about where he slept or if he slept at all. We wrote
three or four essays a month. We read a book every two to three weeks, starting with the *Iliad* and ending up with Hemingway. He gave us a quiz on the
reading every other day. He brought a prep school curriculum to Mercy High.

MacFarland's lectures were crafted, and as he delivered them he would pace
the room jiggling a piece of chalk in his cupped hand, using it to scribble on the
board the names of all the writers and philosophers and plays and novels he was
weaving into his discussion. He asked questions often, raised everything from
Zeno's paradox to the repeated last line of Frost's "Stopping by Woods on a
Snowy Evening." He slowly and carefully built up our knowledge of Western
intellectual history—with facts, with connections, with speculations. We learned
about Greek philosophy, about Dante, the Elizabethan world view, the Age of
Reason, existentialism. He analyzed poems with us, had us reading sections
from John Ciardi's *How Does a Poem Mean?,* making a potentially difficult book
accessible with his own explanations. We gave oral reports on poems Ciardi didn't
cover. We imitated the styles of Conrad, Hemingway, and *Time* magazine. We
wrote and talked, wrote and talked. The man immersed us in language.

Even MacFarland's barbs were literary. If Jim Fitzsimmons, hung over and
irritable, tried to smart-ass him, he'd rejoin with a flourish that would spark the

---

[8]Discharge from wounds. (Editor's note)

indomitable Skip Madison—who'd lost his front teeth in a hapless tackle—to flick his tongue through the gap and opine, "good chop," drawing out the single "o" in stinging indictment. Jack MacFarland, this tobacco-stained intellectual, brandished linguistic weapons of a kind I hadn't encountered before. Here was this *egghead*, for God's sake, keeping some pretty difficult people in line. And from what I heard, Mike Dweetz and Steve Fusco and all the notorious Voc. Ed. crowd settled down as well when MacFarland took the podium. Though a lot of guys groused in the schoolyard, it just seemed that giving trouble to this particular teacher was a silly thing to do. Tomfoolery, not to mention assault, had no place in the world he was trying to create for us, and instinctively everyone knew that. If nothing else, we all recognized MacFarland's considerable intelligence and respected the hours he put into his work. It came to this: the troublemaker would look foolish rather than daring. Even Jim Fitzsimmons was reading *On the Road* and turning his incipient alcoholism to literary ends.

There were some lives that were already beyond Jack MacFarland's ministrations, but mine was not. I started reading again as I hadn't since elementary school. I would go into our gloomy little bedroom or sit at the dinner table while, on the television, Danny McShane was paralyzing Mr. Moto with the atomic drop, and work slowly back through *Heart of Darkness,* trying to catch the words in Conrad's sentences. I certainly was not MacFarland's best student; most of the other guys in College Prep, even my fellow slackers, had better backgrounds than I did. But I worked very hard, for MacFarland had hooked me. He tapped my old interest in reading and creating stories. He gave me a way to feel special by using my mind. And he provided a role model that wasn't shaped on physical prowess alone, and something inside me that I wasn't quite aware of responded to that. Jack MacFarland established a literacy club, to borrow a phrase of Frank Smith's, and invited me—invited all of us—to join.

There's been a good deal of research and speculation suggesting that the acknowledgment of school performance with extrinsic rewards—smiling faces, stars, numbers, grades—diminishes the intrinsic satisfaction children experience by engaging in reading or writing or problem solving. While it's certainly true that we've created an educational system that encourages our best and brightest to become cynical grade collectors and, in general, have developed an obsession with evaluation and assessment, I must tell you that venal though it may have been, I loved getting good grades from MacFarland. I now know how subjective grades can be, but then they came tucked in the back of essays like bits of scientific data, some sort of spectroscopic readout that said, objectively and publicly, that I had made something of value. I suppose I'd been mediocre for too long and enjoyed a public redefinition. And I suppose the workings of my mind, such as they were, had been private for too long. My linguistic play moved into the world; . . . these papers with their circled, red B-pluses and A-minuses linked my mind to something outside it. I carried them around like a club emblem.

One day in the December of my senior year, Mr. MacFarland asked me where I was going to go to college. I hadn't thought much about it. Many of the students I teach today spent their last year in high school with a physics text in one hand and the Stanford catalog in the other, but I wasn't even aware of what "entrance requirements" were. My folks would say that they wanted me to go to college and be a doctor, but I don't know how seriously I ever took that; it seemed a sweet thing to say, a bit of supportive family chatter, like telling a gangly daughter she's graceful. The reality of higher education wasn't in my scheme of things: no one in the family had gone to college; only two of my uncles had completed high school. I figured I'd get a night job and go to the local junior college because I knew that Snyder and Company were going there to play ball. But I hadn't even prepared for that. When I finally said, "I don't know," MacFarland looked down at me—I was seated in his office—and said, "Listen, you can write."

My grades stank. I had A's in biology and a handful of B's in a few English and social science classes. All the rest were C's—or worse. MacFarland said I would do well in his class and laid down the law about doing well in the others. Still, the record for my first three years wouldn't have been acceptable to any four-year school. To nobody's surprise, I was turned down flat by USC and UCLA. But Jack MacFarland was on the case. He had received his bachelor's degree from Loyola University, so he made calls to old professors and talked to somebody in admissions and wrote me a strong letter. Loyola finally accepted me as a probationary student. I would be on trial for the first year, and if I did okay, I would be granted regular status. MacFarland also intervened to get me a loan, for I could never have afforded a private college without it. Four more years of religion classes and four more years of boys at one school, girls at another. But at least I was going to college. Amazing.

In my last semester of high school, I elected a special English course fashioned by Mr. MacFarland, and it was through this elective that there arose at Mercy a fledgling literati. Art Mitz, the editor of the school newspaper and a very smart guy, was the kingpin. He was joined by me and by Mark Dever, a quiet boy who wrote beautifully and who would die before he was forty. MacFarland occasionally invited us to his apartment, and those visits became the high point of our apprenticeship: we'd clamp on our training wheels and drive to his salon.

He lived in a cramped and cluttered place near the airport, tucked away in the kind of building that architectural critic Reyner Banham calls a *dingbat*. Books were all over: stacked, piled, tossed, and crated, underlined and dog eared, well worn and new. Cigarette ashes crusted with coffee in saucers or spilling over the sides of motel ashtrays. The little bedroom had, along two of its walls, bricks and boards loaded with notes, magazines, and oversized books. The kitchen joined the living room, and there was a stack of German newspapers under the sink. I had never seen anything like it: a great flophouse of language furnished by City Lights and Café le Metro. I read every title. I flipped through paperbacks and scanned jackets and memorized names: Gogol, *Finnegans Wake,* Djuna Barnes, Jackson Pollock, *A Coney Island of the Mind,* F.O. Matthiessen's *American Renaissance,* all sorts of Freud, *Troubled Sleep,* Man Ray, *The Education of Henry Adams,* Richard Wright, *Film as Art,* William Butler Yeats, Marguerite Duras, *Redburn, A Season in Hell, Kapital.* On the cover of Alain-Fournier's *The Wanderer* was an Edward Gorey drawing of a young man on a road winding into dark trees. By the hotplate sat a strange Kafka novel called *Amerika,* in which an adolescent hero crosses the Atlantic to find the Nature Theater of Oklahoma. Art and Mark would be talking about a movie or the school newspaper, and I would be consuming my English teacher's library. It was heady stuff. I felt like a Pop Warner[9] athlete on steroids.

Art, Mark, and I would buy stogies and triangulate from MacFarland's apart- 35 ment to the Cinema, which now shows X-rated films but was then L.A.'s premier art theater, and then to the musty Cherokee Bookstore in Hollywood to hobnob with beatnik homosexuals—smoking, drinking bourbon and coffee, and trying out awkward phrases we'd gleaned from our mentor's bookshelves. I was happy and precocious and a little scared as well, for Hollywood Boulevard was thick with a kind of decadence that was foreign to the South Side. After the Cherokee, we would head back to the security of MacFarland's apartment, slaphappy with hipness.

Let me be the first to admit that there was a good deal of adolescent passion in this embrace of the avant-garde: self-absorption, sexually charged pedantry, an elevation of the odd and abandoned. Still it was a time during which I absorbed an awful lot of information: long lists of titles, images from expressionist paintings, new wave shibboleths,[10] snippets of philosophy, and names that read like Steve Fusco's misspellings—Goethe, Nietzsche, Kierkegaard. Now this is hardly the stuff of deep understanding. But it was an introduction, a phrase book, a Baedeker[11] to a vocabulary of ideas, and it felt good at the time to know all these words. With hindsight I realize how layered and important that knowledge was.

It enabled me to do things in the world. I could browse bohemian bookstores in far-off, mysterious Hollywood; I could go to the Cinema and see events through the lenses of European directors; and, most of all, I could share an evening, talk that talk, with Jack MacFarland, the man I most admired at the time. Knowledge was becoming a bonding agent. Within a year or two, the persona of the disaffected hipster would prove too cynical, too alienated to last. But for a time it was new and exciting: it provided a critical perspective on society, and it allowed me to act as though I were living beyond the limiting boundaries of South Vermont.[12]

---

[9] A nationwide youth athletics organization. (Editor's note)

[10] Trendy phrases or jargon. (Editor's note)

[11] Travel guide. (Editor's note)

[12] A street in an economically depressed area of Los Angeles. (Editor's note)

ANALYZING What the Writer Says

1. Referring to his parents' decision to bus him across Los Angeles to a Catholic school, Rose writes that they "thought Hope had set up shop in the west end of the county." What does this say about his parents? Is Rose being ironic?

2. What is Rose's opinion of vocational education? Where does he state it?

3. What skills are truly important, according to Rose, for economic opportunity?

4. What happens when Rose is moved into the College Prep track at Mercy? What finally makes a real difference in Rose's life?

5. What common notion about student satisfaction and motivation does Rose refute?

ANALYZING How the Writer Says It

1. Analyze the implications of the title of the piece.

2. While Rose is making an argument, he relies heavily on personal narrative and examples of colorful characters. How does this approach advance his argument?

3. The essay's opening sentences and its last allude to place, to travel, and to boundaries. How are these references appropriate to the story Rose tells?

"Keep your eyes on your own screen."

ANALYZING the Issue

1. Should schools segregate students into separate tracks or programs such as "vo-tech," "college prep," "special ed," "gifted and talented," etc.?

2. How should schools deal with incompetent teachers?

ANALYZING Connections Between Texts

1. What assumptions about students do Roberta F. Borkat (p. 340) and Jacob Neusner (p. 375) make in their pieces that Rose refutes?

2. How do the methods by which Rose and many of his peers were classified as inferior students compare to the profiling Adnan R. Khan describes in "Bordering on Panic" (p. 555)?

3. How does Elliott Erwitt's "Three Children" (p. 399) illustrate some of the concerns Rose addresses in his essay?

YOUR TURN: Suggestions for Writing About "Learning Matters"

1. Gatto claims that our school system teaches children their place in the hierarchy without offering much of a way to improve their situation. In Bambara's short story, Miss Moore teaches the economically disadvantaged students in her care that money rules the world, a world from which poor people are largely excluded. Write an essay in which you defend or criticize Miss Moore's behavior in the light of Gatto's arguments.

2. Write a paper in which you support or refute Gatto's arguments about the "hidden curriculum" in the American school system.

3. Argue for or against Gatto's assertion that we should not teach a child anything that child does not ask to be taught.

4. Do our school systems give everyone an equal chance at success? Write an essay in which you show how our schools do or do not discriminate against students on the basis of social class, race, or ethnicity. Consider the works by Bambara, Hughes, and Rose when writing your essay.

5. Write an ironic essay, in the style of Borkat, from a student's perspective.

6. In the style of Neusner's "speech," write a valedictorian speech in which you voice your discontent with the high school you attended before you went to college.

7. Write an essay in which you support or refute Neusner's points, using specific examples from the teachers you had in high school.

8. Using Mike Rose as a source, write an essay in which you argue for or against separate tracks in schools: "vo-tech," "college prep," and "gifted and talented," for example.

9. Using personal experience and your readings, write an essay in which you define the "ideal teacher." You may describe an actual teacher you have had or support the various characteristics of your ideal teacher with examples that come from different teachers.

10. Research the growing phenomenon of prepping kids for college application beginning as early as in the preschool years, the "matriculation fixation" Queenan writes about. Write an analysis of the high-pressure situation so many children face.

11. If you have ever attended school in another country, write an essay in which you compare the two systems. Consider the questions of what makes a good teacher and what makes a good student for each culture.

12. Research the advantages and disadvantages of home schooling, and write an essay in which you answer this question: Is homeschooling a viable alternative to traditional schools?

13. Gatto's essay and some of the photos in this chapter suggest that schools train children to conform. Based on your own experience and your reading, pick one side of the debate and write an essay: "Our education system is concerned primarily with teaching students to conform," or "Our education system is concerned primarily with teaching students to think for themselves."

IMAGE GALLERY

GRADUATION DAY

This photo, which could easily adorn a greeting card congratulating the new graduate, captures the sentiment associated with graduation day.

1. What idea does this photograph communicate about college graduation?

2. What does the sculpture in the background contribute to the photograph's overall theme?

3. What is the symbolic significance of the graduate's binoculars?

4. How does the photographer use shapes (triangles, circles) in the photo's overall composition?

ELLIOTT ERWITT

Three Children

Born in 1928 in Paris, Elliott Erwitt immigrated to the United States with his Russian parents in 1939. In 1954 he became a member of the prestigious Magnum photographic agency. Noted for both its humor and humanity, Erwitt's portfolio spans subjects ranging from architecture to animals. A wide array of his black-and-white images are collected in the 2001 Snaps. *He snapped this shot from that collection in Kissimmee, Florida, in 1997.*

1. What are the children in this picture doing?

2. What do the children's clothes say about their social background?

3. How do you interpret the expressions on the children's faces?

4. How does Erwitt use light and shadow in this picture?

5. How does Erwitt use line and composition?

6. Does this photograph tie in to any of the readings included in the "Learning Matters" chapter of this book? How?

7. Erwitt did not title this photograph. What title would you give it? Explain your choice.

UNIVERSITY OF LOUISVILLE, CAUFIELD AND SHOOK COLLECTION

Golden Rules

As the careful fingernail check proves, grooming was still an important issue in this Louisville school around 1920, in the days before educational reform.

1. Why did the photographer choose to record the fingernail-check routine in the picture of a Louisville classroom? What would today's audiences find strange about this activity?

2. How does the furniture of the classroom reflect an educational philosophy that is different from our own? What does the chart in the background suggest about educational priorities of the era?

3. Why did the photographer pose the teacher in the back corner with an open book and a piece of chalk in her hand? What does her pose and her place in the overall composition of the picture say about her importance in the classroom?

CULVER PICTURES

German Schoolboys Salute

This photo, taken during the Nazi era by an unknown photographer, says on the back: "Schoolchildren do not pour out of schools at the end of the day, whooping and rejoicing at being set free, but march out in military formation."

1. What are the boys in the picture doing? What can you tell about the picture's historical context from their gestures?

2. What do the boys' clothes and the group's formation say about school discipline?

3. Do the children's faces indicate that they understand what they are doing?

4. At the left edge of the picture, we see an adult's arm and part of his jacket. Who do you think this person is? What effect does the photographer's choice not to include him in the picture have on the overall meaning of the picture?

5. How does the photographer use light and composition effectively in this picture?

6. What is the photographer saying in this picture about educational institutions under totalitarian governments?

13 FUTURE SHOCK

The rate of technological change has been exponential indeed. People born at the beginning of the twentieth century would have, by age 50, witnessed extraordinary developments in science and technology: their lives were no doubt changed rather dramatically by automobiles, airplanes,

> "Future shock [is] the shattering stress and disorientation that we induce in individuals by subjecting them to too much change in too short a time."
>
> —Alvin Toffler
> *Future Shock*

telephones, television. But a person born in 1950 would, at age 50, likely take for granted not only air travel but space travel, would as likely have mail delivered over the Internet as by a postal worker. To a child starting school today, a phonograph record is an historical artifact, but the computer is as commonplace as the microwave oven.

The grandparents who watch bewilderedly as their preschool grandchild surfs the Internet are experiencing what Alvin Toffler described in his 1970 best seller, *Future Shock*. Not only is the technology currently at our disposal sometimes overwhelming, it is often downright frightening. The implications of stem cell research, genetic engineering, and cloning scare some people so much that they are willing to forego possible cures for maladies ranging from diabetes to infertility. In the following pages, Nancy Gibbs, Ellen Goodman, and Leigh Turner consider various aspects of the questions raised by these technologies. A nineteenth-century story by Nathaniel Hawthorne of an overreaching scientist in pursuit of cosmetic perfection offers a prescient allegory, one that resonates in our technology-driven society. The social disconnect that Toffler predicted in 1970 resurfaces in Ellen Ullman's concerns about the anti-community of cyberspace. Self-described romantic Ian Frazier laments the supplanting of the solid, stationary pay phone—a symbol of ordinary lives in simpler times—by the "sleek little phones in our pockets." Paul Keegan worries about the connection between computer games and teen violence; a review of KABOOM!, an electronic game featuring a suicide bomber, puts a spotlight on an ugly intersection of entertainment and technology.

Like any phenomenon, rapid growth in science and technology has brought both blessing and curse: the low hum of our personal computers and Palm Pilots and the ringing of so many cell phones have resulted in a kind of white noise, masking the buzz of humanity, its greed, its evil, its simple blindness. But the idyllic complacency that modern technology affords us has been punctuated by catastrophe—at Three Mile Island and Love Canal, in two space shuttle disasters. It was the advanced technology of the modern jetliner that toppled a monumental feat of architecture and engineering on September 11, 2001—but it was, as it has always been, human evil that manipulated that technology, human blindness that missed the warnings.✣

WARMING UP: *Can you remember an event in your life that was closely associated with a pay phone? What was it? Where do you see pay phones now? What kinds of people use them, and what kinds of calls are they making? Do people use cell phones any differently from how they used to use pay phones?*

Dearly Disconnected

BY IAN FRAZIER

IAN FRAZIER

In this essay, published in the January/February 2000 issue of Mother Jones, *Ian Frazier, former staff writer for the* New Yorker *and the author of several books, contemplates the personal and cultural implications of the disappearance of phone booths as cell phones become increasingly popular.*

Before I got married I was living by myself in an A-frame cabin in northwestern Montana. The cabin's interior was a single high-ceilinged room, and at the center of the room, mounted on the rough-hewn log that held up the ceiling beam, was a telephone. I knew no one in the area or indeed the whole state, so my entire social life came to me through that phone. The woman I would marry was living in Sarasota, Florida, and the distance between us suggests how well we were getting along at the time. We had not been in touch for several months; she had no phone. One day she decided to call me from a pay phone. We talked for a while, and after her coins ran out I jotted the number on the wood beside my phone and called her back. A day or two later, thinking about the call, I wanted to talk to her again. The only number I had for her was the pay phone number I'd written down.

The pay phone was on the street some blocks from the apartment where she stayed. As it happened, though, she had just stepped out to do some errands a few minutes before I called, and she was passing by on the sidewalk when the phone rang. She had no reason to think that a public phone ringing on a busy street would be for her. She stopped, listened to it ring again, and picked up the receiver. Love is pure luck; somehow I had known she would answer, and she had known it would be me.

Long afterwards, on a trip to Disney World in Orlando with our two kids, then aged six and two, we made a special detour to Sarasota to show them the pay phone. It didn't impress them much. It's just a nondescript Bell Atlantic pay phone on the cement wall of a building, by the vestibule. But its ordinariness and even boringness only make me like it more; ordinary places where extraordinary events have occurred are my favorite kind. On my mental map of Florida that pay phone is a landmark looming above the city it occupies, and a notable, if private, historic site.

I'm interested in pay phones in general these days, especially when I get the feeling that they are about to go away. Technology, in the form of sleek little phones in our pockets, has swept on by them and made them begin to seem antique. My lifelong entanglement with pay phones dates me; when I was young they were just there, a given, often as stubborn and uncongenial as the curbstone underfoot. They were instruments of torture sometimes. You had to feed them fistfuls of change in those pre-phone-card days, and the operator was a real person who stood maddeningly between you and whomever you were trying to call. And when the call went wrong, as communication often does, the pay phone gave you a focus for your rage. Pay phones were always getting smashed up, the receivers shattered to bits against the booth, the coin slots jammed with chewing gum, the cords yanked out and unraveled to the floor.

You used to hear people standing at pay phones and cursing them. I remember the sound of my own frustrated shouting confined by the glass walls of a phone booth—the kind you don't see much anymore, with a little ventilating fan in the ceiling that turned on when you shut the double-hinged glass door. The noise that fan made in the silence of a phone booth was for a while the essence of romantic, lonely-guy melancholy for me. Certain specific pay phones I still resent for the unhappiness they caused me, and others I will never forgive, though not for any fault of their own. In the C concourse of the Salt Lake City airport there's a row of pay phones set on the wall by the men's room just past the concourse entry. While on a business trip a few years ago, I called home from a phone in that row and learned that a friend had collapsed in her apartment and was in the hospital with brain cancer. I had liked those pay phones before, and had used them often; now I can't even look at them when I go by.

There was always a touch of seediness and sadness to pay phones, and a sense of transience. Drug dealers made calls from them, and shady types who did not want their whereabouts known, and otherwise respectable people planning assignations, and people too poor to have phones of their own. In the movies, any character who used a pay phone was either in trouble or contemplating a crime. Pay phones came with their own special atmospherics and even accessories sometimes—the predictable bad smells and graffiti, of course, as well as cigarette butts, soda cans, scattered pamphlets from the Jehovah's Witnesses, and single bottles of beer (empty) still in their individual, street-legal paper bags. Mostly, pay phones evoked the mundane: "Honey, I'm just leaving. I'll be there soon." But you could tell that a lot of undifferentiated humanity had flowed through these places, and that in the muteness of each pay phone's little space, wild emotion had howled.

Once, when I was living in Brooklyn, I read in the newspaper that a South American man suspected of dozens of drug-related contract murders had been arrested at a pay phone in Queens. Police said that the man had been on the phone setting up a murder at the time of his arrest. The newspaper story gave the address of the pay phone, and out of curiosity one afternoon I took a long walk to Queens to take a look at it. It was on an undistinguished street in a middle-class neighborhood, by a florist's shop. By the time I saw it, however, the pay phone had been blown up and/or firebombed. I had never before seen a pay phone so damaged; explosives had blasted pieces of the phone itself wide open in metal shreds like frozen banana peels, and flames had blackened everything and melted the plastic parts and burned the insulation off the wires. Soon after, I read that police could not find enough evidence against the suspected murderer and so had let him go.

The cold phone outside a shopping center in Bigfork, Montana, from which I called a friend in the West Indies one winter when her brother was sick; the phone on the wall of the concession stand at Redwood Pool, where I used to stand dripping and call my mom to come and pick me up; the sweaty phones used almost only by men in the hallway outside the maternity ward at Lenox Hill Hospital in New York; the phone by the driveway of the Red Cloud Indian School in South Dakota where I used to talk with my wife while priests in black slacks and white socks chatted on a bench nearby; the phone in the old wood-paneled phone booth with leaded glass windows in the drugstore in my Ohio hometown—each one is as specific as a birthmark, a point on earth unlike any other. Recently I went back to New York City after a long absence and tried to find a working pay phone. I picked up one receiver after the next without success. Meanwhile, as I scanned down the long block, I counted half a dozen or more pedestrians talking on their cell phones.

It's the cell phone, of course, that's putting the pay phone out of business. The pay phone is to the cell phone as the troubled and difficult older sibling is to the cherished newborn. People even treat their cell phones like babies, cradling them in their palms and beaming down upon them lovingly as they dial. You sometimes hear people yelling on their cell phones, but almost never yelling at them. Cell phones are toylike, nearly magic, and we get a huge kick out of them, as often happens with technological advances until the new wears off. Somehow I don't believe people had a similar honeymoon period with pay phones back in their early days, and they certainly have no such enthusiasm for them now. When I see a cell-phone user gently push the little antenna and fit the phone back into its brushed-vinyl carrying case and tuck the case inside his jacket beside his heart, I feel sorry for the beat-up pay phone standing in the rain.

People almost always talk on cell phones while in motion—driving, walking   10 down the street, riding on a commuter train. The cell phone took the transience the pay phone implied and turned it into VIP-style mobility and speed. Even sitting in a restaurant, the person on a cell phone seems importantly busy and on the move. Cell-phone conversations seem to be unlimited by ordinary constraints of place and time, as if they represent an almost-perfect form of communication whose perfect state would be telepathy.

And yet no matter how we factor the world away, it remains. I think this is what drives me so nuts when a person sitting next to me on a bus makes a call from her cell phone. Yes, this busy and important caller is at no fixed point in space, but nevertheless I happen to be beside her. The job of providing physical context falls on me; I become her call's surroundings, as if I'm the phone booth wall. For me to lean over and comment on her cell-phone conversation would be as unseemly and unexpected as if I were in fact a wall; and yet I have no choice, as a sentient person, but to hear what my chatty fellow traveler has to say.

Some middle-aged guys like me go around complaining about this kind of thing. The more sensible approach is just to accept it and forget about it, because there's not much we can do. I don't think that pay phones will completely disappear. Probably they will survive for a long while as clumsy old technology still of some use to those lagging behind, and as a backup if ever the superior systems should temporarily fail. Before pay phones became endangered I never thought of them as public spaces, which of course they are. They suggested a human average; they belonged to anybody who had a couple of coins. Now I see that, like public schools and public transportation, pay phones belong to a former commonality our culture is no longer quite so sure it needs.

I have a weakness for places—for old battlefields, car-crash sites, houses where famous authors lived. Bygone passions should always have an address, it seems to me. Ideally, the world would be covered with plaques and markers listing the notable events that occurred at each particular spot. A sign on every pay phone would describe how a woman broke up with her fiance here, how a young ballplayer learned that he had made the team. Unfortunately, the world itself is fluid, and changes out from under us; the rocky islands that the pilot Mark Twain was careful to avoid in the Mississippi are now stone outcroppings in a soybean field. Meanwhile, our passions proliferate into illegibility, and the places they occur can't hold them. Eventually pay phones will become relics of an almost-vanished landscape, and of a time when there were fewer of us and our stories were on an earlier page. Romantics like me will have to reimagine our passions as they are—unmoored to earth, like an infinitude of cell-phone messages flying through the atmosphere.

ANALYZING What the Writer Says

1. What emotional experiences does Frazier associate with pay phones?

2. In what sense are cell phones fundamentally different from pay phones, according to Frazier?

3. "Like public schools and public transportation, pay phones belong to a former commonality our culture is no longer quite so sure it needs," Frazier says toward the end of the essay. What do you think he means by this statement? Upon what evidence does he base this conclusion?

ANALYZING How the Writer Says It

1. The essay is separated into two parts. What is the purpose of each? What does Frazier accomplish by this division?

2. Frazier relates several anecdotes in his essay. Why does he do that? Does it work?

ANALYZING the Issue

Frazier regrets that the old-fashioned pay phone is making way for the more mobile cell phone. Having read his essay, do you think that he is merely a sentimental old fogy who had better "get with the program," or do you think there is some merit in his analysis? Defend your choice.

ANALYZING Connections Between Texts

1. Frazier thinks that the cell phone has changed human communication forever. What dangers does Ellen Ullman ("The Museum of Me," p. 455) see in the development of the Internet as a vehicle of communication? How are the points the two writers make similar? How are they different?

2. Compare Frazier's argument to Michael Kinsley's in "Orwell Got It Wrong" (p. 559). How do the two writers regard innovations in communication technology?

3. How does Frazier's analysis of telephone communication mesh with Norman Rockwell's rendering of a story circulating among a small group of people in "The Gossips" (p. 108)? What difference would it make in the painting's interpretation if Rockwell's characters were using cell phones?

WARMING UP: *If you knew that your unborn child would be born with a major defect, but discovered that new gene technology could fix the problem, would you agree to it? What if your doctor offered gene technology that would make your baby much smarter than it would be otherwise?*

If We Have It, Do We Use It?

BY NANCY GIBBS

NANCY GIBBS

First published in Time *in September 1999, Gibbs's piece looks at genetic engineering as a means of enhancing the intelligence of unborn babies and raises several questions about its medical and ethical implications. Gibbs, a* Time *editor, has written numerous cover stories for the magazine.*

We've seen these visions glinting in the distance for some time—the prospect that one day parents will be able to browse through gene catalogs to special-order a hazel-eyed, redheaded extrovert with perfect pitch. Leave aside for the moment whether scientists actually found an "IQ gene" last week or the argument over what really constitutes intelligence. Every new discovery gives shape and bracing focus to a debate we have barely begun. Even skeptics admit it's only a matter of time before these issues become real. If you could make your kids smarter, would you? If everyone else did, would it be fair not to?

It's an ethical quandary and an economic one, about fairness and fate, about vanity and value. Which side effects would we tolerate? What if making kids smarter also made them meaner? What if only the rich could afford the advantage? Does God give us both the power to re-create ourselves and the moral muscles to resist? "The time to talk about it in school and churches and magazines and debate societies is now," says bioethicist Arthur Caplan of the University of Pennsylvania. "If you wait, five years from now the gene doctor will be hanging out the MAKE A SMARTER BABY sign down the street."

What makes the conversation tricky is that we're already on the slippery slope. Doctors can screen fetuses for genetic diseases like cystic fibrosis and Duchenne muscular dystrophy; one day they may be able to treat them in utero. But correcting is one thing, perfecting is another. If doctors can someday tinker with a gene to help children with autism, what's to prevent them from tinkering with other genes to make "normal" children smarter? Technology always adapts to demand; prenatal sex-selection tests designed to weed out inherited diseases that strike one gender or the other—hemophilia, for instance—are being used to help families have the son or daughter they always wanted. Human-growth hormone was intended for children with a proven severe deficiency, but it came to be used on self-conscious short kids—if their parents could afford as much as $30,000 for a year's injections.

Self-improvement has forever been an American religion, but the norms about what is normal keep changing. Many parents don't think twice about straightening their kids' crooked teeth but stop short of fixing a crooked nose, and yet, in just the past seven years, plastic surgery performed on teens has doubled. As for intellectual advantages, parents soak their babies in Mozart with dubious effect, put a toy computer in the crib, elbow their way into the best preschools to speed them on their path to Harvard. Infertile couples advertise for an egg donor in the *Yale Daily News*, while entrepreneurs sold the sperm of Nobel laureates.

"What, if anything, is the difference between getting one's child in a better 5 school and getting one's child a better gene?" asks Erik Parens of the Hastings Center, a bioethics think tank. "I think the answer has to do with the difference between cultivating and purchasing capacities." Buying a Harvard education may enhance a child's natural gifts, he argues, but it's not the same as buying the gifts.

Every novel, every movie that updates *Frankenstein* provides a cautionary tale: these experiments may not turn out as we expect. Genetic engineering is more permanent than a pill or a summer-school class. Parents would be making decisions over which their children had no control and whose long-term impact would be uncertain. "Human organisms are not things you hang ornaments on like a Christmas tree," says Thomas Murray, Hastings' director. "If you make a change in one area, it may cause very subtle changes in some other area. Will there be an imbalance that the scientists are not looking for, not testing for, and might not even show up in mice?"

What if it turned out that by enhancing intellectual ability, some other personality trait changed as well? "Everything comes at a price," argues UCLA neurobiologist Alcino Silva. "Very often when there's a genetic change where we improve something, something else gets hit by it, so it's never a clean thing." The alarmists, like longtime biotech critic Jeremy Rifkin, go further. "How do you know you're not going to create a mental monster?" he asks. "We may be on the road to programming our own extinction."

The broader concern is one of fairness. Will such enhancement be available to everyone or only to those who can afford it? "Every parent in the world is going to want this," says Rifkin. "But who will have access to it? It will create a new form of discrimination. How will we look at those who are not enhanced, the child with the low IQ?" Who would have the right to know whether your smarts were natural or turbo-charged? How would it affect whom we choose to marry—those with altered genes or those without? If, as a parent, you haven't mortgaged the house to enhance your children, what sort of parent does that make you? Will a child one day be able to sue her parents for failing to do everything they could for her?

But just for the sake of argument, suppose raising IQ didn't require any permanent, expensive genetic engineering at all. Scientists are studying brain-boosting compounds. Suppose they found something as cheap and easy as aspirin: one pill and you wake up the next morning a little bit brighter. Who could argue with that?

Some people are worried about the trend toward making people more   10
alike—taller, thinner, smarter. Maybe it's best for society as a whole to include those with a range of needs and talents and predispositions, warts and all. "As someone who morally values diversity," says ethicist Elizabeth Bounds of Emory University's Candler School of Theology, "I find this frightening. We run the risk of shaping a much more homogeneous community around certain dominant values, a far more engineered community." What sort of lottery would decide who is to leap ahead, who is to be held back for an overall balance? At the moment, nature orchestrates our diversity. But human nature resists leaving so much to chance, if there is actually a choice.

The debate raises an even more basic question: Why would we want to enhance memory in the first place? We may imagine that it would make us happier, except that we all know smart, sad people; or richer, except that there are wildly successful people who can't remember their phone number. Perhaps it would help us get better grades, land a better job, but it might also take us down a road we'd prefer not to travel. "You might say yes, it would be wonderful if we could all have better memories," muses Stanford University neuropsychiatrist Dr. Robert Malenka. "But there's a great adaptive value to being able to forget things. If your memory improves too much, you might not be a happier person. I'm thinking of rape victims and soldiers coming back from war. There's a reason the brain has evolved to forget certain things."

In the end it is the scientists who both offer the vision and raise the alarms. People with exceptional, photographic memories, they note, sometimes complain of mental overload. "Such people," says University of Iowa neurologist Dr. Antonio Damasio, "have enormous difficulty making decisions, because every time they can think of 20 different options to choose from." There is luxury and peace in forgetting, sometimes; it literally clears the mind, allows us to focus on the general rather than the specific and immediate evidence in front of us. Maybe it even makes room for reflection on questions like when better is not necessarily good.

ANALYZING What the Writer Says

1. Why would some parents be tempted to use genetic engineering on their unborn children if it were widely available?

2. What are the concerns Gibbs mentions that speak against genetic enhancement of a person's intelligence?

ANALYZING How the Writer Says It

1. Gibbs asks a series of questions throughout the essay, questions she does not always answer. What effect does she achieve by doing this?

2. Why does Gibbs quote a number of authorities on genetic engineering in her essay? How would the article have been different if she had not?

ANALYZING the Issue

1. After reading Gibbs's argument, is your opinion of genetic engineering any different?

2. If genetic enhancement of a child's looks and intelligence were widely available and a lot of parents were to use it on their unborn children, would it be fair to a child whose parents refused to do it? Is it the duty of parents to give their children all the advantages they can afford? Explain.

ANALYZING Connections Between Texts

1. Ellen Goodman, ("Beauty on the DNA Auction Block," p. 413) follows Gibbs's concerns, pointing to the inevitable practical applications of gene technology. Is the manipulation of genes to ensure good looks any different from the altering of genes to increase intelligence?

2. Malcolm Gladwell, Richard Selzer, and Gary Smith (pp. 765, 798, 811) each write about the contributions extraordinarily gifted individuals have made to humanity. If you thought you had a chance, through genetic manipulation, to produce a child who could make a similar contribution, would you avail yourself of the technology?

3. Max Aguilera-Hellweg's photograph "Reaching for Help" (p. 103) shows a team of surgeons operating on a fetus. Do you think Nancy Gibbs would approve of such surgery? Why or why not?

WARMING UP: *Do you consider looks—particularly our society's ideal of beauty—an important advantage for children? Would you consider paying for genetic technology to ensure that your child was born with certain physical attributes?*

Beauty on the DNA Auction Block

By Ellen Goodman

ELLEN GOODMAN

A longtime writer for the Boston Globe, *syndicated columnist Ellen Goodman (b. 1941) has authored several collections of essays, often addressing women's and family issues. In the following article, published in the* Globe *in October 1999, she takes aim at the marketing of genetic technology to prospective parents to ensure beautiful offspring.*

Now it's time for a pop quiz in genetics.

What happens when you combine the sperm of Internet entrepreneurship and the egg of a beauty-obsessed culture and then enhance this embryo with a few extra genes of gall?

Congratulations! You have just given birth to rons angels.com, the Web site allegedly set up to auction off the eggs of beautiful babes to the highest bidder.

This is the brainchild, or brain ovum if you prefer, of Ron Harris, a fashion photographer, Arabian horse breeder and purveyor of soft-core exercise videos.

Ron is himself more a creature of nurture than nature. His career path in beauty, sex and breeding led inexorably to the idea of a prenatal, indeed pre-conceptual, market in beauty. 5

Having grown up in a culture that makes beauty a commodity, he developed the Web site philosophy that "Choosing eggs from beautiful women will profoundly increase the success of your children and your children's children for centuries to come."

Or, as he said to one reporter, "What mother wants an ugly child?"

It's not clear whether Ron is an Internet hustler trying to get folks to ante up their $24.95 a month for a peek at the babes who could be moms of their babes or whether these women will really auction off their genetic maternity. But Ron's Internet egg market has gotten attention for the simplest of reasons. It was predictable. It was inevitable.

Let us go back to those wonderful yesteryears in the annals of reproductive technology when a California entrepreneur first opened up a sperm bank of Nobel Prize winners. It turned out that dozens of women wanted a brief, if artificial, encounter that might result in a genius.

Just last spring, someone placed an ad in Ivy League college newspapers   10
offering $50,000 to a 5-foot-10 Ivy Leaguer with a combined SAT score of 1400. Many were willing to trade an egg for a nest egg.

Today, you can point and click to any number of infertility dot.coms that offer physical descriptions of their would-be "donors"—a word now hopelessly perverted beyond its altruistic roots—and check out the merchandise. Looks are part of the package set before all the "customers."

What is a surprise is not the free enterprise system at work on the Net. It's the entire direction of the market economy in selling better and better products, i.e., children.

Once upon a time, says Lori Andrews, a law professor and author of "The Clone Age," "infertile couples wanted children who looked as much like them as possible, right down to the acne." Now it's assumed that would-be parents want or should want, as Ron says, "to give their children an advantage."

The beauty egg auction, whether it turns out to be real or a scam, is only a modest example of what may happen when gene therapy takes off. We are moving toward genetic technology that may allow us to add selective traits to an embryo. As Andrews says, "parents may be able to pay to give their children traits they don't have."

Not long ago, a Louis Harris poll reported that 43 percent of parents would use   15
genetic enhancement to make their children more attractive. If we can make a kid taller or prettier, if we can eliminate baldness or obesity, will we? In a world of competitive parenting, will those who want "the best" for their children come to see genetic engineering more like tennis lessons or private school?

"We actually do start down the road of treating people like products," says ethicist George Annas, who found himself unwillingly linked to this Web site. "In the name of individual liberty, are we are going to actually custom-make our kids the way we want them to be?"

There is, in fact, nothing to prevent it. Reproductive technology is the Wild West of the medical world. We can't legally sell sex. We can't sell organs. We can't sell babies. But there is nothing to prevent selling sperm or eggs. And there are no rules on the future sale of genes.

As Annas says, "We don't want to take Ron Harris seriously, but we do want to take genetic engineering seriously. We have a giant industry, the marriage of biotechnology and assisted fertility. It's all hype, and nobody is thinking about it seriously."

In the meantime, before you bid on a mother egg, think about this seriously. If beauty is the ultimate life advantage, how come angel Misty-Lee McFern described her life options as either egg sales or posing for Penthouse?

And, oh yes, a second genetics pop quiz. Are you buying the nature of the   20
DNA? Or the nurture of a collagen-enhanced, nose-bobbed, boob-jobbed, aer-
obicized, silicon-implanted and liposuctioned angel?

I have one wish for this Web site. In the words of the auctioneer: Going,
going, gone!

ANALYZING What the Writer Says

1. What fundamental change, according to Goodman, has occurred in infertile parents considering technology to help them conceive? What accounts for this change?
2. Why, primarily, is Goodman opposed to using genetic engineering to produce
   good-looking children?
3. Why does Goodman call "inevitable" Ron Harris's Web site auctioning off "the
   eggs of beautiful babes"?

ANALYZING How the Writer Says It

1. What words and phrases in the article reveal Goodman's attitude toward the issue?
2. Goodman begins and ends her piece with a tongue-in-cheek quiz. What is the effect
   of the questions she poses—and the language she uses—in the second pop quiz?

*"I told my parents that if grades were so important they
should have paid for a smarter egg donor."*

ANALYZING the Issue

1. Is it ethical for people to sell their DNA?

2. When people pay for a beautiful woman's eggs in the hopes of creating a beautiful child, what lesson do they teach that child?

ANALYZING Connections Between Texts

1. Nathaniel Hawthorne's "The Birthmark" (p. 417) moralizes about the ramifications of attempts to use science to improve on nature. To what extent does Goodman make the same argument? If the principals in Goodman's scenario appeared in "The Birthmark," who would be Aylmer? Georgiana? Aminadab?

2. What do you think Alice Walker ("Beauty: When the Other Dancer Is the Self," p. 250) would say about the kind of genetic manipulation Goodman discusses? What insights about the importance of beauty does Walker offer that Goodman's gene peddlers miss?

3. How does Donald Reilly's cartoon (p. 415) illustrate Goodman's essay?

The Birthmark

BY NATHANIEL HAWTHORNE

NATHANIEL HAWTHORNE
Much of the work of Nathaniel Hawthorne (1804–64) considers ethical questions and the nature of sin and morality in individuals. In the following story, published in 1846, a scientist obsessed with his wife's physical beauty pays a terrible price in the pursuit of perfection.

In the latter part of the last century there lived a man of science, an eminent proficient in every branch of natural philosophy, who not long before our story opens had made experience of a spiritual affinity more attractive than any chemical one. He had left his laboratory to the care of an assistant, cleared his fine countenance from the furnace smoke, washed the stain of acids from his fingers, and persuaded a beautiful woman to become his wife. In those days when the comparatively recent discovery of electricity and other kindred mysteries of Nature seemed to open paths into the region of miracle, it was not unusual for the love of science to rival the love of woman in its depth and absorbing energy. The higher intellect, the imagination, the spirit, and even the heart might all find their congenial aliment in pursuits which, as some of their ardent votaries believed, would ascend from one step of powerful intelligence to another, until the philosopher should lay his hand on the secret of creative force and perhaps make new worlds for himself. We know not whether Aylmer

In "The Birthmark" Hawthorne composed a small parable on the limits of earthly perfection, but the story also has affinities with the theme of intellectual arrogance explored in "Rappaccini's Daughter." "The Birthmark" was first published in *The Pioneer* for March, 1843, and was collected in *Mosses from an Old Manse* (1846). (Editor's note) possessed this degree of faith in man's ultimate control over Nature. He had devoted himself, however, too unreservedly to scientific studies ever to be weaned from them by any second passion. His love for his young wife might prove the stronger of the two; but it could only be by intertwining itself with his love of science, and uniting the strength of the latter to his own.

Such a union accordingly took place, and was attended with truly remarkable consequences and a deeply impressive moral. One day, very soon after their marriage, Aylmer sat gazing at his wife with a trouble in his countenance that grew stronger until he spoke.

"Georgiana," said he, "has it never occurred to you that the mark upon your cheek might be removed?"

"No, indeed," said she, smiling; but perceiving the seriousness of his manner, she blushed deeply. "To tell you the truth it has been so often called a charm that I was simple enough to imagine it might be so."

"Ah, upon another face perhaps it might," replied her husband; "but never on 5 yours. No, dearest Georgiana, you came so nearly perfect from the hand of Nature that this slightest possible defect, which we hesitate whether to term a defect or a beauty, shocks me, as being the visible mark of earthly imperfection."

"Shocks you, my husband!" cried Georgiana, deeply hurt; at first reddening with momentary anger, but then bursting into tears. "Then why did you take me from my mother's side? You cannot love what shocks you!"

To explain this conversation it must be mentioned that in the centre of Georgiana's left cheek there was a singular mark, deeply interwoven, as it were, with the texture and substance of her face. In the usual state of her complexion—a, healthy though delicate bloom—the mark wore a tint of deeper crimson, which imperfectly defined its shape amid the surrounding rosiness. When she blushed it gradually became more indistinct, and finally vanished amid the triumphant rush of blood that bathed the whole cheek with its brilliant glow. But if any shifting motion caused her to turn pale there was the mark again, a crimson stain upon the snow, in what Aylmer sometimes deemed an almost fearful distinctness. Its shape bore not a little similarity to the human hand, though of the smallest pygmy size. Georgiana's lovers were wont to say that some fairy at her birth hour had laid her tiny hand upon the infant's cheek, and left this impress there in token of the magic endowments that were to give her such sway over all hearts. Many a desperate swain would have risked life for the privilege of pressing his lips to the mysterious hand. It must not be concealed, however, that the impression wrought by this fairy sign manual varied exceedingly, according to the difference of temperament in the beholders. Some fastidious persons—but they were exclusively of her own sex—affirmed that the bloody hand, as they chose to call it, quite destroyed the effect of Georgiana's beauty, and rendered her countenance even hideous. But it would be as reasonable to say that one of those small blue stains which sometimes occur in the purest statuary marble would convert the Eve of

Powers[1] to a monster. Masculine observers, if the birthmark did not heighten their admiration, contented themselves with wishing it away, that the world might possess one living specimen of ideal loveliness without the semblance of a flaw. After his marriage,—for he thought little or nothing of the matter before,—Aylmer discovered that this was the case with himself.

Had she been less beautiful,—if Envy's self could have found aught else to sneer at,—he might have felt his affection heightened by the prettiness of this mimic hand, now vaguely portrayed, now lost, now stealing forth again and glimmering to and fro with every pulse of emotion that throbbed within her heart; but seeing her otherwise so perfect, he found this one defect grow more and more intolerable with every moment of their united lives. It was the fatal flaw of humanity which Nature, in one shape or another, stamps ineffaceably on all her productions, either to imply that they are temporary and finite, or that their perfection must be wrought by toil and pain. The crimson hand expressed the ineludible gripe in which mortality clutches the highest and purest of earthly mould, degrading them into kindred with the lowest, and even with the very brutes, like whom their visible frames return to dust. In this manner, selecting it as the symbol of his wife's liability to sin, sorrow, decay, and death, Aylmer's sombre imagination was not long in rendering the birthmark a frightful object, causing him more trouble and horror than ever Georgiana's beauty, whether of soul or sense, had given him delight.

At all the seasons which should have been their happiest, he invariably and without intending it, nay, in spite of a purpose to the contrary, reverted to this one disastrous topic. Trifling as it at first appeared, it so connected itself with innumerable trains of thought and modes of feeling that it became the central point of all. With the morning twilight Aylmer opened his eyes upon his wife's face and recognized the symbol of imperfection; and when they sat together at the evening hearth his eyes wandered stealthily to her cheek, and beheld, flickering with the blaze of the wood fire, the spectral hand that wrote mortality where he would fain have worshipped. Georgiana soon learned to shudder at his gaze. It needed but a glance with the peculiar expression that his face often wore to change the roses of her cheek into a deathlike paleness, amid which the crimson hand was brought strongly out, like a bas-relief of ruby on the whitest marble.

Late one night when the lights were growing dim, so as hardly to betray the stain on the poor wife's cheek, she herself, for the first time, voluntarily took up the subject.

"Do you remember, my dear Aylmer," said she, with a feeble attempt at a smile, "have you any recollection of a dream last night about this odious hand?"

---

[1]Hiram Powers (1805–1873), self-taught American sculptor. Hawthorne has reference to the first version of his "Eve Before the Fall." (Editor's note)

"None! none whatever!" replied Aylmer, starting but then he added, in a dry, cold tone, affected for the sake of concealing the real depth of his emotion, "I might well dream of it; for before I fell asleep it had taken a pretty firm hold of my fancy."

"And you did dream of it?" continued Georgiana, hastily; for she dreaded lest a gush of tears should interrupt what she had to say. "A terrible dream! I wonder that you can forget it. Is it possible to forget this one expression?—'It is in her heart now; we must have it out!' Reflect, my husband; for by all means I would have you recall that dream."

The mind is in a sad state when Sleep, the all-involving, cannot confine her spectres within the dim region of her sway, but suffers them to break forth, affrighting this actual life with secrets that perchance belong to a deeper one. Aylmer now remembered his dream. He had fancied himself with his servant Aminadab, attempting an operation for the removal of the birthmark; but the deeper went the knife, the deeper sank the hand, until at length its tiny grasp appeared to have caught hold of Georgiana's heart; whence, however, her husband was inexorably resolved to cut or wrench it away.

When the dream had shaped itself perfectly in his memory, Aylmer sat in his wife's presence with a guilty feeling. Truth often finds its way to the mind close muffled in robes of sleep, and then speaks with uncompromising directness, of matters in regard to which we practice an unconscious self-deception during our waking moments. Until now he had not been aware of the tyrannizing influence acquired by one idea over his mind, and of the lengths which he might find in his heart to go for the sake of giving himself peace.

"Aylmer," resumed Georgiana, solemnly, "I know not what may be the cost to both of us to rid me of this fatal birthmark. Perhaps its removal may cause cureless deformity; or it may be the stain goes as deep as life itself. Again: do we know that there is a possibility, on any terms, of unclasping the firm gripe of this little hand which was laid upon me before I came into the world?"

"Dearest Georgiana, I have spent much thought upon the subject." hastily interrupted Aylmer. "I am convinced of the perfect practicability of its removal."

"If there be the remotest possibility of it," continued Georgiana, "let the attempt be made at whatever risk. Danger is nothing to me; for life, while this hateful mark makes me the object of your horror and disgust,—life is a burden which I would fling down with joy. Either remove this dreadful hand, or take my wretched life! You have deep science. All the world bears witness of it. You have achieved great wonders. Cannot you remove this little, little mark, which I cover with the tips of two small fingers? Is this beyond your power, for the sake of your own peace, and to save your poor wife from madness?"

"Noblest, dearest, tenderest wife," cried Aylmer, rapturously, "doubt not my power. I have already given this matter the deepest thought—thought which might almost have enlightened me to create a being less perfect than yourself. Georgiana, you have led me deeper than ever into the heart of science. I feel myself fully competent to render this dear cheek as faultless as its fellow; and then, most beloved, what will be my triumph when I shall have corrected what Nature left imperfect in her fairest work! Even Pygmalion, when his sculptured woman assumed life, felt not greater ecstasy than mine will be."

"It is resolved, then." said Georgiana, faintly smiling. "And, Aylmer, spare   20
me not, though you should find the birthmark take refuge in my heart at last."

Her husband tenderly kissed her cheek—her right cheek—not that which bore the impress of the crimson hand.

The next day Aylmer apprised his wife of a plan that he had formed whereby he might have opportunity for the intense thought and constant watchfulness which the proposed operation would require; while Georgiana, likewise, would enjoy the perfect repose essential to its success. They were to seclude themselves in the extensive apartments occupied by Aylmer as a laboratory, and where, during his toilsome youth, he had made discoveries in the elemental powers of Nature that had roused the admiration of all the learned societies in Europe. Seated calmly in this laboratory, the pale philosopher had investigated the secrets of the highest cloud region and of the profoundest mines; he had satisfied himself of the causes that kindled and kept alive the fires of the volcano; and had explained the mystery of fountains, and how it is that they gush forth, some so bright and pure, and others with such rich medicinal virtues, from the dark bosom of the earth. Here, too, at an earlier period, he had studied the wonders of the human frame, and attempted to fathom the very process by which Nature assimilates all her precious influences from earth and air, and from the spiritual world, to create and foster man, her masterpiece. The latter pursuit, however, Aylmer had long laid aside in unwilling recognition of the truth—against which all seekers sooner or later stumble—that our great creative Mother, while she amuses us with apparently working in the broadest sunshine, is yet severely careful to keep her own secrets, and, in spite of her pretended openness, shows us nothing but results. She permits us, indeed, to mar, but seldom to mend, and, like a jealous patentee, on no account to make. Now, however, Aylmer resumed these half-forgotten investigations; not, of course, with such hopes or wishes as first suggested them; but because they involved much physiological truth and lay in the path of his proposed scheme for the treatment of Georgiana.

As he led her over the threshold of the laboratory, Georgiana was cold and tremulous. Aylmer looked cheerfully into her face, with intent to reassure her, but was so startled with the intense glow, of the birthmark upon the whiteness of her cheek that he could not restrain a strong convulsive shudder. His wife fainted.

"Aminadab! Aminadab!" shouted Aylmer, stamping violently on the floor.

Forthwith there issued from an inner apartment a man of low stature, but   25
bulky frame, with shaggy hair hanging about his visage, which was grimed with the vapors of the furnace. This personage had been Aylmer's underworker dur-

ing his whole scientific career, and was admirably fitted for that office by his great mechanical readiness, and the skill with which, while incapable of comprehending a single principle, he executed all the details of his master's experiments. With his vast strength, his shaggy hair, his smoky aspect, and the indescribable earthiness that incrusted him, he seemed to represent man's physical nature; while Aylmer's slender figure, and pale, intellectual face, were no less apt a type of the spiritual element.

"Throw open the door of the boudoir, Aminadab," said Aylmer, "and burn a pastil."

"Yes, master," answered Aminadab, looking intently at the lifeless form of Georgiana; and then he muttered to himself, "If she were my wife, I'd never part with that birthmark."

When Georgiana recovered consciousness she found herself breathing an atmosphere of penetrating fragrance, the gentle potency of which had recalled her from her deathlike faintness. The scene around her looked like enchantment. Aylmer had converted those smoky, dingy, sombre rooms, where he had spent his brightest years in recondite pursuits, into a series of beautiful apartments not unfit to be the secluded abode of a lovely woman. The walls were hung with gorgeous curtains which imparted the combination of grandeur and grace that no other species of adornment can achieve; and as they fell from the ceiling to the floor, their rich and ponderous folds, concealing all angles and straight lines, appeared to shut in the scene from infinite space. For aught Georgiana knew, it might be a pavilion among the clouds. And Aylmer, excluding the sunshine, which would have interfered with his chemical processes, had supplied its place with perfumed lamps, emitting flames of various hue, but all uniting in a soft, impurpled radiance. He now knelt by his wife's side, watching her earnestly, but without alarm, for he was confident in his science, and felt that he could draw a magic circle round her within which no evil might intrude.

"Where am I? Ah, I remember," said Georgiana, faintly; and she placed her hand over her cheek to hide the terrible mark from her husband's eyes.

"Fear not, dearest!" exclaimed he. "Do not shrink from me! Believe me, Georgiana. I even rejoice in this single imperfection, since it will be such a rapture to remove it." 30

"Oh. Spare me!" sadly replied his wife. "Pray do not look at it again. I can never forget that convulsive shudder."

In order to soothe Georgiana, and, as it were, to release her mind from the burden of actual things, Aylmer now put in practice some of the light and playful secrets which science had taught him among its profound lore. Airy figures, absolutely bodiless ideas, and forms of unsubstantial beauty came and danced before her, imprinting their momentary footsteps on beams of light. Though she had some indistinct idea of the method of these optical phenomena, still the illusion was almost perfect enough to warrant the belief that her husband possessed sway over the spiritual world. Then again, when she felt a wish to look forth from her seclusion, immediately, as if her thoughts were answered, the procession of external existence flitted across a screen. The scenery and the figures of actual life were perfectly represented, but with that bewitching, yet indescribable difference which always makes a picture, an image, or a shadow so much more attractive than the original. When wearied of this, Aylmer bade her cast her eyes upon a vessel containing a quantity of earth. She did so, with little interest at first; but was soon startled to perceive the germ of a plant shooting upward from the soil. Then came the slender stalk; the leaves gradually unfolded themselves; and amid them was a perfect and lovely flower.

"It is magical!" cried Georgiana. "I dare not touch it."

"Nay, pluck it," answered Aylmer,—"pluck it, and inhale its brief perfume while you may. The flower will wither in a few moments and leave nothing save its brown seed vessels; but thence may be perpetuated a race as ephemeral as itself."

But Georgiana had no sooner touched the flower than the whole plant suffered a blight, its leaves turning coal-black as if by the agency of fire.   35

"There was too powerful a stimulus," said Aylmer, thoughtfully.

To make up for this abortive experiment, he proposed to take her portrait by a scientific process of his own invention. It was to be effected by rays of light striking upon a polished plate of metal. Georgiana assented; but, on looking at the result, was affrighted to find the features of the portrait blurred and indefinable; while the minute figure of a hand appeared where the cheek should have been. Aylmer snatched the metallic plate and threw it into a jar of corrosive acid.

Soon, however, he forgot these mortifying failures. In the intervals of study and chemical experiment he came to her flushed and exhausted, but seemed invigorated by her presence, and spoke in glowing language of the resources of his art. He gave a history of the long dynasty of the alchemists, who spent so many ages in quest of the universal solvent by which the golden principle might be elicited from all things vile and base. Aylmer appeared to believe that, by the plainest scientific logic, it was altogether within the limits of possibility to discover this long-sought medium; "but," he added, "a philosopher who should go deep enough to acquire the power would attain too lofty a wisdom to stoop to the exercise of it." Not less singular were his opinions in regard to the elixir vitae. He more than intimated that it was at his option to concoct a liquid that should prolong life for years, perhaps interminably; but that it would produce a discord in Nature which all the world, and chiefly the quaffer of the immortal nostrum, would find cause to curse.

"Aylmer, are you in earnest?" asked Georgiana, looking at him with amazement and fear. "It is terrible to possess such power, or even to dream of possessing it."

"Oh, do not tremble, my love," said her husband. "I would not wrong either   40
you or myself by working such inharmonious effects upon our lives; but I

would have you consider how trifling, in comparison, is the skill requisite to remove this little hand."

At the mention of the birthmark, Georgiana, as usual, shrank as if a redhot iron had touched her cheek.

Again Aylmer applied himself to his labors. She could hear his voice in the distant furnace room giving directions to Aminadab, whose harsh, uncouth, misshapen tones were audible in response, more like the grunt or growl of a brute than human speech. After hours of absence, Aylmer reappeared and proposed that she should now examine his cabinet of chemical products and natural treasures of the earth. Among the former he showed her a small vial, in which, he remarked, was contained a gentle yet most powerful fragrance, capable of impregnating all the breezes that blow across a kingdom. They were of inestimable value, the contents of that little vial; and, as he said so, he threw some of the perfume into the air and filled the room with piercing and invigorating delight.

"And what is this?" asked Georgiana, pointing to a small crystal globe containing a gold-colored liquid. "It is so beautiful to the eye that I could imagine it the elixir of life."

"In one sense it is," replied Aylmer; "or, rather, the elixir of immortality. It is the most precious poison that ever was concocted in this world. By its aid I could apportion the lifetime of any mortal at whom you might point your finger. The strength of the dose would determine whether he were to linger out years, or drop dead in the midst of a breath. No king on his guarded throne could keep his life if I, in my private station, should deem that the welfare of millions justified me in depriving him of it."

"Why do you keep such a terrific drug?" inquired Georgiana in horror.   45

"Do not mistrust me, dearest," said her husband, smiling; "its virtuous potency is yet greater than its harmful one. But see! here is a powerful cosmetic. With a few drops of this in a vase of water, freckles may be washed away as easily as the hands are cleansed. A stronger infusion would take the blood out of the cheek, and leave the rosiest beauty a pale ghost."

"Is it with this lotion that you intend to bathe my cheek?" asked Georgiana, anxiously.

"Oh, no," hastily replied her husband; "this is merely superficial. Your case demands a remedy that shall go deeper."

In his interviews with Georgiana, Aylmer generally made minute inquiries as to her sensations and whether the confinement of the rooms and the temperature of the atmosphere agreed with her. These questions had such a particular drift that Georgiana began to conjecture that she was already subjected to certain physical influences, either breathed in with the fragrant air or taken with her food. She fancied likewise, but it might be altogether fancy, that there was a stirring up of her system—a strange, indefinite sensation, creeping through her veins, and tingling, half painfully, half pleasurably, at her heart. Still, whenever she dared to look into the mirror, there she beheld herself pale as a white rose and with the crimson birthmark stamped upon her cheek. Not even Aylmer now hated it so much as she.

To dispel the tedium of the hours which her husband found it necessary to 50 devote to the processes of combination and analysis, Georgiana turned over the volumes of his scientific library. In many dark old tomes she met with chapters full of romance and poetry. They were the works of the philosophers of the middle ages, such as Albertus Magnus, Cornelius Agrippa, Paracelsus, and the famous friar who created the prophetic Brazen Head. All these antique naturalists stood in advance of their centuries, yet were imbued with some of their credulity, and therefore were believed, and perhaps imagined themselves to have acquired from the investigation of Nature a power above Nature, and from physics a sway over the spiritual world. Hardly less curious and imaginative were the early volumes of the Transactions of the Royal Society, in which the members, knowing little of the limits of natural possibility, were continually recording wonders or proposing methods whereby wonders might be wrought.

But to Georgiana the most engrossing volume was a large folio from her husband's own hand, in which he had recorded every experiment of his scientific career, its original aim, the methods adopted for its development, and its final success or failure, with the circumstances to which either event was attributable. The book, in truth, was both the history and emblem of his ardent, ambitious, imaginative, yet practical and laborious life. He handled physical details as if there were nothing beyond them; yet spiritualized them all, and redeemed himself from materialism by his strong and eager aspiration towards the infinite. In his grasp the veriest clod of earth assumed a soul. Georgiana, as she read, reverenced Aylmer and loved him more profoundly than ever, but with a less entire dependence on his judgment than heretofore. Much as he had accomplished, she could not but observe that his most splendid successes were almost invariably failures, if compared with the ideal at which he aimed. His brightest diamonds were the merest pebbles, and felt to be so by himself, in comparison with the inestimable gems which lay hidden beyond his reach. The volume, rich with achievements that had won renown for its author, was yet as melancholy a record as ever mortal hand had penned. It was the sad confession and continual exemplification of the shortcomings of the composite man, the spirit burdened with clay and working in matter, and of the despair that assails the higher nature at finding itself so miserably thwarted by the earthly part. Perhaps every man of genius in whatever sphere might recognize the image of his own experience in Aylmer's journal.

So deeply did these reflections affect Georgiana that she laid her face upon the open volume and burst into tears. In this situation she was found by her husband.

"It is dangerous to read in a sorcerer's books," said he with a smile, though his countenance was uneasy and displeased. "Georgiana, there are pages in that volume which I can scarcely glance over and keep my senses. Take heed lest it prove as detrimental to you."

"It has made me worship you more than ever," said she.

"Ah, wait for this one success," rejoined he, "then worship me if you will. I 55 shall deem myself hardly unworthy of it. But come, I have sought you for the luxury of your voice. Sing to me, dearest."

So she poured out the liquid music of her voice to quench the thirst of his spirit. He then took his leave with a boyish exuberance of gayety, assuring her that her seclusion would endure but a little longer, and that the result was already certain. Scarcely had he departed when Georgiana felt irresistibly impelled to follow him. She had forgotten to inform Aylmer of a symptom which for two or three hours past had begun to excite her attention. It was a sensation in the fatal birthmark, not painful, but which induced a restlessness throughout her system. Hastening after her husband, she intruded for the first time into the laboratory.

The first thing that struck her eye was the furnace, that hot and feverish worker, with the intense glow of its fire, which by the quantities of soot clustered above it seemed to have been burning for ages. There was a distilling apparatus in full operation. Around the room were retorts, tubes, cylinders, crucibles, and other apparatus of chemical research. An electrical machine stood ready for immediate use. The atmosphere felt oppressively close, and was tainted with gaseous odors which had been tormented forth by the processes of science. The severe and homely simplicity of the apartment, with its naked walls and brick pavement, looked strange, accustomed as Georgiana had become to the fantastic elegance of her boudoir. But what chiefly, indeed almost solely, drew her attention, was the aspect of Aylmer himself.

He was pale as death, anxious and absorbed, and hung over the furnace as if it depended upon his utmost watchfulness whether the liquid which it was distilling should be the draught of immortal happiness or misery. How different from the sanguine and joyous mien that he had assumed for Georgiana's encouragement!

"Carefully now, Aminadab; carefully, thou human machine; carefully, thou man of clay!" muttered Aylmer, more to himself than his assistant. "Now, if there be a thought too much or too little, it is all over."

"Ho! ho!" mumbled Aminadab. "Look, master! look!"   60

Aylmer raised his eyes hastily, and at first reddened, then grew paler than ever, on beholding Georgiana. He rushed towards her and seized her arm with a grip that left the print of his fingers upon it.

"Why do you come hither? Have you no trust in your husband?" cried he, impetuously. "Would you throw the blight of that fatal birthmark over my labors? It is not well done. Go, prying woman, go!"

"Nay, Aylmer," said Georgiana with the firmness of which she possessed no stinted endowment, "it is not you that have a right to complain. You mistrust

your wife; you have concealed the anxiety with which you watch the development of this experiment. Think not so unworthily of me, my husband. Tell me
all the risk we run, and fear not that I shall shrink; for my share in it is far less
than your own."

"No, no, Georgiana!" said Aylmer, impatiently; "it must not be."

"I submit," replied she calmly. "And, Aylmer, I shall quaff whatever draught   65
you bring me; but it will be on the same principle that would induce me to take
a dose of poison if offered by your hand."

"My noble wife," said Aylmer, deeply moved, "I knew not the height and
depth of your nature until now. Nothing shall be concealed. Know, then, that
this crimson hand, superficial as it seems, has clutched its grasp into your being
with a strength of which I had no previous conception. I have already administered agents powerful enough to do aught except to change your entire physical
system. Only one thing remains to be tried. If that fail us we are ruined."

"Why did you hesitate to tell me this?" asked she.

"Because, Georgiana," said Aylmer, in a low voice, "there is danger."

"Danger? There is but one danger—that this horrible stigma shall be left
upon my cheek!" cried Georgiana. "Remove it, remove it, whatever be the cost,
or we shall both go mad!"

"Heaven knows your words are too true." said Aylmer sadly. "And now,   70
dearest, return to your boudoir. In a little while all will be tested."

He conducted her back and took leave of her with a solemn tenderness which
spoke far more than his words how much was now at stake. After his departure
Georgiana became rapt in musings. She considered the character of Aylmer, and
did it completer justice than at any previous moment. Her heart exulted, while it
trembled, at his honorable love—so pure and lofty that it would accept nothing
less than perfection nor miserably make itself contented with an earthlier nature
than he had dreamed of. She felt how much more precious was such a sentiment
than that meaner kind which would have borne with the imperfection for her
sake, and have been guilty of treason to holy love by degrading its perfect idea to
the level of the actual; and with her whole spirit she prayed that, for a single
moment, she might satisfy his highest and deepest conception. Longer than one
moment she well knew it could not be; for this spirit was ever on the march, ever
ascending, and each instant required something that was beyond the scope of the
instant before.

The sound of her husband's footsteps aroused her. He bore a crystal goblet
containing a liquor colorless as water, but bright enough to be the draught of
immortality. Aylmer was pale; but it seemed rather the consequence of a highly-
wrought state of mind and tension of spirit than of fear or doubt.

"The concoction of the draught has been perfect," said he, in answer to
Georgiana's look. "Unless all my science have deceived me it cannot fail."

"Save on your account, my dearest Aylmer," observed his wife, "I might
wish to put off this birthmark of mortality by relinquishing mortality itself in

preference to any other mode. Life is but a sad possession to those who have attained precisely the degree of moral advancement at which I stand. Were I weaker and blinder it might be happiness. Were I stronger, it might be endured hopefully. But, being where I find myself, methinks I am of all mortals the most fit to die."

"You are fit for heaven without tasting death!" replied her husband. "But why do we speak of dying? The draught cannot fail. Behold its effect upon this plant." 75

On the window seat there stood a geranium diseased with yellow blotches, which had overspread all its leaves. Aylmer poured a small quantity of the liquid upon the soil in which it grew. In a little time, when the roots of the plant had taken up the moisture, the unsightly blotches began to be extinguished in a living verdure.

"There needed no proof," said Georgiana, quietly. "Give me the goblet. I joyfully stake all upon your word."

"Drink, then, thou lofty creature!" exclaimed Aylmer, with fervid admiration. "There is no taint of imperfection on thy spirit. Thy sensible frame, too, shall soon be all perfect."

She quaffed the liquid and returned the goblet to his hand.

"It is grateful," said she with a placid smile. "Methinks it is like water from a heavenly fountain; for it contains I know not what of unobtrusive fragrance and deliciousness. It allays a feverish thirst that had parched me for many days. Now, dearest, let me sleep. My earthly senses are closing over my spirit like the leaves around the heart of a rose at sunset." 80

She spoke the last words with a gentle reluctance, as if it required almost more energy than she could command to pronounce the faint and lingering syllables. Scarcely had they loitered through her lips ere she was lost in slumber. Aylmer sat by her side, watching her aspect with the emotions proper to a man the whole value of whose existence was involved in the process now to be tested. Mingled with this mood, however, was the philosophic investigation characteristic of the man of science. Not the minutest symptom escaped him. A heightened flush of the cheek, a slight irregularity of breath, a quiver of the eyelid, a hardly perceptible tremor through the frame—such were the details which, as the moments passed, he wrote down in his folio volume. Intense thought had set its stamp upon every previous page of that volume, but the thoughts of years were all concentrated upon the last.

While thus employed, he failed not to gaze often at the fatal hand, and not without a shudder. Yet once, by a strange and unaccountable impulse, he pressed it with his lips. His spirit recoiled, however, in the very act; and Georgiana, out of the midst of her deep sleep, moved uneasily and murmured as if in remonstrance. Again Aylmer resumed his watch. Nor was it without avail. The crimson hand, which at first had been strongly visible upon the marble paleness of Georgiana's cheek, now grew more faintly outlined. She remained not less pale than ever; but the birthmark, with every breath that came and went, lost somewhat of its former distinctness. Its presence had been awful; its departure was more awful still. Watch the stain of the rainbow fading out of the sky, and you will know how that mysterious symbol passed away.

"By Heaven! it is well-nigh gone!" said Aylmer to himself, in almost irrepressible ecstasy. "I can scarcely trace it now. Success! success! And now it is like the faintest rose color. The lightest flush of blood across her cheek would overcome it. But she is so pale!"

He drew aside the window curtain and suffered the light of natural day to fall into the room and rest upon her cheek. At the same time he heard a gross, hoarse chuckle, which he had long known as his servant Aminadab's expression of delight.

"Ah, clod! ah, earthly mass!" cried Aylmer, laughing in a sort of frenzy, "you 85 have served me well! Matter and spirit—earth and heaven—have both done their part in this! Laugh, thing of the senses! You have earned the right to laugh."

These exclamations broke Georgiana's sleep. She slowly unclosed her eyes and gazed into the mirror which her husband had arranged for that purpose. A faint smile flitted over her lips when she recognized how barely perceptible was now that crimson hand which had once blazed forth with such disastrous brilliancy as to scare away all their happiness. But then her eyes sought Aylmer's face with a trouble and anxiety that he could by no means account for.

"My poor Aylmer!" murmured she.

"Poor? Nay, richest, happiest, most favored!" exclaimed he. "My peerless bride, it is successful! You are perfect!"

"My poor Aylmer," she repeated, with a more than human tenderness, "you have aimed loftily; you have done nobly. Do not repent that with so high and pure a feeling, you have rejected the best the earth could offer. Aylmer, dearest Aylmer, I am dying!"

Alas! it was too true! The fatal hand had grappled with the mystery of life, 90 and was the bond by which an angelic spirit kept itself in union with a mortal frame. As the last crimson tint of the birthmark—that sole token of human imperfection—faded from her cheek, the parting breath of the now perfect woman passed into the atmosphere, and her soul, lingering a moment near her husband, took its heavenward flight. Then a hoarse, chuckling laugh was heard again! Thus ever does the gross fatality of earth exult in its invariable triumph over the immortal essence which, in this dim sphere of half development, demands the completeness of a higher state. Yet, had Aylmer reached a profounder wisdom, he need not thus have flung away the happiness which would have woven his mortal life of the selfsame texture with the celestial. The momentary circumstance was too strong for him; he failed to look beyond the shadowy scope of time, and, living once for all in eternity, to find the perfect future in the present.

ANALYZING | What the Writer Says

1. What is the significance of the mark on Georgiana's cheek? Why do you think it is in the shape of a hand?

2. What is the relationship between Aylmer's love of science and his love of his wife?

3. What does the character Aminadab represent?

4. What does the story reveal about Hawthorne's attitude toward science?

ANALYZING | How the Writer Says It

1. Hawthorne writes using an omniscient point of view; that is, the story is not told from the perspective of a single character but from a narrator who moves freely from the thoughts of one character to those of another. How does the technique affect your interpretation of the story and your opinion of the characters? What if the story had been told strictly from Georgiana's point of view? Aylmer's?

2. Is the narrator completely objective? What is the point of the last line of the story?

ANALYZING | the Issue

1. Is surgery in the pursuit of some ideal of beauty ever justified?

2. How relevant today are the issues raised in this story, published over 150 years ago?

ANALYZING | Connections Between Texts

1. Compare the issues in Nancy Gibbs's "If We Have It, Do We Use It?" (p. 409) and Ellen Goodman's "Beauty on the DNA Auction Block" (p. 413). Considering that "The Birthmark" was published more than 150 years ago, do you think that Hawthorne was eerily prescient, or simply writing about a timeless and universal aspect of human nature?

2. Compare D. Keith Mano's "Plastic Surgery" (p. 238) to "The Birthmark": is the "moral" in Mano's piece explicit or implicit? Put the moral into your own words.

3. How does Hawthorne's story anticipate some of the issues raised in Max Aguilera-Hellweg's photograph "Reaching for Help" (p. 103)?

Joystick Jihad

The following are excerpts from reviews of KABOOM!, a video game released by newsgrounds.com in April 2002 (just seven months after the terrorist attacks on the World Trade Center). In the game, players move a suicide bomber around the streets of Israel. The piece was published in Harper's *in October the same year.*

REVIEWED BY: DirtyGerman
This is a great game, and i cant wait for the next release. the only thing i would like to see added is better sound effects. i wanna hear people screaming and crying. keep up the good work.

REVIEWED BY: Sick_In_The_Mind
EXCELLENT!!! This was amazing . . . only jealous that I didn't think of it first. Anyway, make another with old people in it as well.

REVIEWED BY: c_o_r_o_n_a_69
i thought it was funny how u run around blowing people up and i think that its not funny in real life unless the guy was gay or something.

REVIEWED BY: Ptarmigan
You should make a full version. Anyways, suicide bombings have been done in Sri Lanka a lot and in Japan during World War II. By the way, you should add people that no one likes. Also, you should add nuclear bombs. I think the conflict in Israel should end now. Ppl need to stop fighting and get a hobby or something.

REVIEWED BY: amf
decent. now i wanna see one where i can crush palestinian children with tanks and destroy their homes with bulldozers.

REVIEWED BY: Killdozer
It's funny Cuz it's true;)

REVIEWED BY: ice_cream528
what a great game! This game is an inspiration. I am gonna go buy some dynamite and become a martyr for Allah. Thank you for making this game.

5

REVIEWED BY: wilhous666
This is a VERY FUNNY game, considering the events that are going on in the world today! I found the game to be very amusing but, simple and only in one place! next version should be a little more interactive! And, more choises of locations (ie mall, movies, etc.) definately worth a checking out though!

REVIEWED BY: Mr_pink33
Kick ass. This game is amazing but its more fun to chase the children then blow up rather than killing adults

REVIEWED BY: deathman333
i live in canada so i dont really care about all this shit that is happening in the us but i would like to tell you something your fucking stupid men droped some bombs on some of canadas troops and after that you started booing at are national athem you are going to hell and im starting a war over the inter-net to fight for canadas rights and i dont say eh all the time you streotypeing bastards i dont even use eh it is not even a word so i will lead my army of can-dien troops all over newgrounds and every game and every toon i wacth i will keep you posted right about now i sent a few viruses to a power plant down in huston but it will be doing more i have other things to do like send a virus to whoever post something next on this good game and also im sending a few friends too ametica to plants some stink bombs all around huston because thats are main target now any way i will keep you posted about the cyber war canada vs usa any way nice game i enjoyed it

REVIEWED BY: Cky2k5Skater
Funny Good Shit. Fun game mocking the people in Pakistan and all them other crazy places, good job!

REVIEWED BY: Flea_420
I THOUGHT THE GAME SUCKED. BUT NOT NEARLY AS MUCH AS CANADA. IF THIS GUY COULD SPELL HE MIGHT BE INTIMIDATING.

REVIEWED BY: Fighter_PilotF35
Long Live the Intifada!!!!!! This was great. Finally, a game that praises the sui-cide bombers. These people are martyrs, and they deserve to be remembered and praised for their heroic actions. This is what the Jews deserve for stealing Palestinian terrority, and for the Israeli terrorism and occupation that has cripled the Palestinians.
    My record is 6 Jew kills and 1 Jew injury. Has anybody achieved more than 6 Jew kills? I can't wait for the full version when we can kill more Israeli Jews on buses and in resturants.

REVIEWED BY: Freako 100
Its OK but a little hard because in Isreal this happens every day. but put more people on te street and cars etc.

REVIEWED BY: NEFARIOUSRAE

<<**I'm a Heeb, and this game rocks! **> I can't wait until the final version comes out! keep up the great work. One problem . . . Where's the Israeli Army home demolition derby game though? I want to kill Palestinians in their own homes (with tanks) too, preferably while they're begging for their lives, HEHE-HE. Baawaaahaaa (maniacial laughter) Loveyouguys

REVIEWED BY: horseshoe7

There should be bombers with different capabilities, like car bombers, fast runners, women, fools who will get nervous and blow themselves up within 10 seconds, etc. . . . oh, and the women bombers should flash their tits just before they blow themselves up . . . you could even have tits rolling around on the ground, like the heads . . . oh, and while you are at it, the women walking on the street should be given BIGGER TITS . . . all the women in Isreal have BIG TITS . . . yes, yes—and they have nude sunbathing there too . . . the bomber could go down to the beach and check out all the chicks' asses before he takes himself out.

REVIEWED BY: Cardoso

God dammit. One of the best violent games i have ever played. I can't wait till you finish this thing. Please hurry. One of the funniest things is that if you really do enable multiple bombers, it'll look like "Lemmnings from the Middle East." Man, this would be great.

REVIEWED BY: Nostrant

I think this game would have been alot better if you were a smurf in the smurf village trying to kill other smurfs. Nobody likes smurfs but everyone likes people. Plus it's hard to enjoy this game after having seen pictures of an actual suicide bombing.

REVIEWED BY: eon_blue_apocalypse

Don't take this down! People are too sensitive. These are the same people who can't bear to watch the news when they talk about war in afganistan or hungry children in Somalia.

These are the same people who care more about what happens on FRIENDS then what is going on in the middle east. This is a FUCK YOU to the numb American public. God Bless you!

REVIEWED BY: Afroman_0002

This was a well rounded game. Loved the fact that you could kill men women AND children. Great Game!

REVIEWED BY: TastyArmageddon

Pretty innovative game making fun of the idiots back in the middle east. Also pretty addictive too. If you ever make another version, MAKE BETTER GRAPHICS! Killing random people just isn't as fun when they all look alike!

Oh, also, you ought to up the splash damage. It looks like the explosion only has a radius of like 20 feet, which is pretty unrealistic. =) Anyways, great game.

REVIEWED BY: Motech   25
As an Israeli I thought I'll be incredibly offended, but I wasn't. The author is right: this game is more anti-Arafat than anti-Israel (if it's at all anti-Israel). It shows the way the mind of a suicide bomber works: find the spot with most women and children in it. It's sick and utterly evil just like in real life.

REVIEWED BY: Elfer
I have some major issues with this game.
   You can only kill lots of people when they overlap. You should have a button that lets you reveal the bomb, but not blow it up to scare the people and herd them into one spot. But you could also have a thing like once you do that, you only have limited time before the cops come and sniper you to death.
   No ambient sound. You should get a sound for running and maybe a few bird calls in the background. Other than that, cool game!

REVIEWED BY: Hells_Angel69
I say fuck what the isral/palestine/jews think. they are the ones fucking blowing themselves up. i mean comon people its just a game what u idiots are doing is real.
   maybe if u stopped blowing yourselves and each other up this game would   30
have never been made, think of that.

REVIEWED BY: zeed_777
blowing up children never felt so good. I love this game, you can just sit back and blow people up for hours, which is exactly what I did.

ANALYZING What the Writer Says

1. What do the players who have tested the game particularly like about it?

2. What suggestions do they make to improve the game further?

3. How does the e-mail from "deathman333" (the Canadian player) mesh with the other comments?

4. Do you find it surprising that a player from Israel liked the game? Why or why not?

5. What do the comments by the testers of KABOOM! reveal about them?

ANALYZING How the Writer Says It

1. The editors at *Harper's* chose to publish the written review comments as is, grammar errors and all. How would the piece have been different had it been edited before publication?

2. Why do you think the editors of *Harper's* chose the title "Joystick Jihad" for this piece?

ANALYZING the Issue

Do video games such as KABOOM! glorify violence? Do they influence young people to regard violence as a viable solution to problems? Why or why not? Do you think violent video games should be controlled by law?

ANALYZING Connections Between Texts

1. Like the players in "Joystick Jihad," the young men Paul Keegan interviews in "Culture Quake" (p. 436) test video games for the companies that produce them. Keegan's respondents claim that violent video games do not influence them in any way, that playing has not inspired them toward violence in other areas of their lives. Consider their comments and compare them to those of the KABOOM! reviewers cited in "Joystick Jihad."

2. In "Bordering on Panic" (p. 555), Adnan R. Khan writes of the racial profiling Muslims have endured since the 9/11 terrorist attacks. Do you think video games such as KABOOM! exploit international conflicts and fan the fires of hatred? Why or why not?

3. Jay Ullal's photograph of the bridal couple in Beirut (p. 192) shows two people crossing the "green line," the boundary between enemy camps in bombed-out Beirut during Lebanon's civil war. How does the virtual world of KABOOM! compare to this picture from a real war zone? Do you think video games such as KABOOM! make it more difficult for real people to overcome political, racial, and cultural differences in their personal relationships? Explain.

WARMING UP: *Have you ever played video games like* Quake *or* Doom? *Do you think that playing these games could make a person more aggressive, possibly violent?*

Culture Quake

BY PAUL KEEGAN

And shall we just carelessly allow children to hear . . . tales which may be devised by casual persons, and to receive into their minds ideas for the most part the very opposite of those which we should wish them to have when they are grown up?

Plato, 374 B.C.

PAUL KEEGAN

Paul Keegan has written for the New York Times Magazine, *the* New England Monthly, Men's Journal, *and many others. In the following article, first published in* Mother Jones *in 1999, he analyzes the relationship between violent video games and increasingly violent behavior among teenagers, as evident in tragedies such as the one at Columbine.*

Walking down Figueroa Street toward the Los Angeles Convention Center earlier this year, it was impossible to miss the giant white face staring down from a billboard, the eyes glowing bright yellow-orange, the pupils twisted into black spirals. The promotion for the Sega Dreamcast, a new video-game console, was designed to psych up game fans for the zoned-out bliss awaiting them at E3—the Electronic Entertainment Exposition trade show—then getting under way.

But because it appeared just three weeks after the school shootings in Littleton, at a time when video and computer games were emerging as a favorite target of blame, the image suddenly took on new meaning. It succinctly posed the biggest question surrounding the mammoth, $6.3 billion electronic-games industry, now poised to blow past Hollywood in terms of both annual revenue and cultural impact: What's going on behind those eyes?

Images of evil that are destroying our children's minds, cried the critics immediately after it was reported that Eric Harris and Dylan Klebold were avid players of the popular shoot-'em-ups *Doom* and

Quake. CBS's "60 Minutes" broadcast a segment a few days later asking, "Are Video Games Turning Kids Into Killers?" Bills were introduced on Capitol Hill to ban the sale of violent video games to minors. In June, President Clinton ordered the surgeon general to study the effects of all violent media on children and young adults. He singled out video games in particular, pointing to research showing that half the electronic games a typical seventh-grader plays are violent. "What kind of values are we promoting," chimed in Hillary Clinton, "when a child can walk into a store and find video games where you win based on how many people you can kill or how many places you can blow up?"

The industry launched a counteroffensive, arguing that the vast majority of video games sold today are not violent, and emphasizing that no causal link has ever been established between aggressive behavior and prior exposure to violent media. "The entertainment software industry has no reason to run and hide," said Doug Lowenstein of the Interactive Digital Software Association (IDSA) at E3's opening press conference. He insisted that the simple reason the electronic-games industry is growing twice as fast as the movie business, and four times faster than the recording or book publishing industries, is that they "offer some of the most compelling, stimulating, and challenging entertainment available anywhere, in any form."

And so the E3 love-in carried on as usual this year, with 50,000 people 5 jammed into an enormous exhibition space to sample the hottest new games. But as I wandered through the booths amid a constant roar of car crashes, monster screams, gunfire, and deafening techno-pop soundtracks, I wondered how this industry could have become so wildly popular in some circles and so utterly vilified in others. Is it true, as game developers like to say, that future generations will look back at today's controversy with the kind of bemusement now reserved for those grainy black-and-white images of crew-cutted right-wingers denouncing comic books and rock 'n' roll back in the 1950s? Or do critics have a point in saying that today's media technology has become so powerful and ubiquitous that a laissez-faire attitude toward pop culture is naive and outdated, if not outright dangerous?

Clues to the answers lie within a peculiar subculture of young, white, American males who make up the industry's technological vanguard. But to get a sense of what's behind those swirling eyeballs, first you have to play some games.

According to industry ethos, the coolest electronic titles are not video games, which are played on dumbed-down console units made by Sony, Nintendo, and Sega, and account for nearly three-quarters of all game sales. Rather, the cutting edge is occupied by computer games—the other slice of the pie— because they run best on souped-up PCs that allow hardcore fans to customize a game by tinkering with its programming code.

Leaving the noisy main hall at E3, I enter a hushed room full of educational PC gaining titles and stop at the Mindscape Entertainment booth to check out the latest version of *Myst,* the best-selling PC title of all time. *Myst* earned its widespread popularity without benefit of rocket launchers or flying body parts. It's a role-playing game that takes place on a bucolic, forested island surrounded by clouds and ocean. The images are beautifully rendered: The forest mist is finely textured, and even the crevices on the tree bark are crisp and clear. The object of the game is to figure out why a team of scientists who were doing research on the island suddenly disappeared.

The game has a stately pace as you click through the foggy pathways and walkways, searching for clues. It's like looking at a series of pretty pictures. But if one thing is clear from spending time at E3, it's that this industry is driven largely by the pursuit of quite a different sensory experience: raw speed. That's true across the board, for the makers of PC games and video games alike. Sony, Nintendo, and Sega—all of which will introduce superpowerful, 128-bit game consoles to the market in the coming year—are not spending billions of dollars to create clever story lines. They are competing madly with one another to create the fastest video-game console ever, each boasting more horsepower than some of the most powerful supercomputers packed just 10 years ago.

Researchers and marketers have known for decades that when it comes to kids and their toys, speed sells. Give a child a choice between a storybook and a television set, and guess which one will grab his attention. " 'Sesame Street' learned in the '60s that it's best to change the scene often, move fast, keep the visual display constantly changing," says Professor John Murray, a child psychologist at Kansas State University who has studied the effects of television violence for 30 years. "Very often just the act of playing the game, regardless of content, is what is so engaging."

Myst is a storybook compared to the other games out in the main exhibition hall. There, I could lead a battalion of spaceships through the galaxy, make players dunk basketballs and hit home runs, and drive around a track in a race car. All of these games draw the player's attention because of that sense of moving through space; an appreciation of the rules and subtleties of gameplay come later.

But as thrilling as these games are, something's missing from all of them— something I can't quite put my finger on until I come upon an enormous poster of a guy who looks like an Aryan Nation thug: blond crew cut, open vest, a gun in each hand.

Duke Nukem is one of the bad-boy "first-person shooter" games that have brought such disrepute to the industry. Though shooters represent less than seven percent of overall sales, a recent *Time*/CNN poll showed that 50 percent of teenagers between 13 and 17 who have played video games have played them. Ten percent say they play regularly. A breakthrough game will fly off the shelves: Best-selling shooters *Doom* and *Quake* have had combined sales of 4.2 million. (*Myst* and its sequel, *Riven*, top the sales charts at 5.4 million.)

What makes these shooter games so compelling is the addition of freedom of movement to the sensation of speed. This is accomplished by the highly sophisticated underlying technology, called "real-time 3-D." Unlike the "pre-rendered" art of *Myst*—which limits your wanderings to predetermined paths—these images are not created in advance, but rather in "real time," on the fly, with the computer calculating at astronomical rates. Thus you get a euphoric sense of entering a fantastic new world and being able to roam about a breathtaking speeds. That freedom of movement is what's missing from the other games out on the floor at E3: The space game didn't let me go inside the ship, and the racing simulation wouldn't even let me get out of the car. Real-time 3-D gives you the illusion of maneuvering with no restrictions whatever.

Because real-time 3-D games and their fans stand firmly on the technology's   15
leading edge, they represent a new avant-garde in popular entertainment—in much the same way that innovative independent films have an impact on Hollywood far beyond what their grosses might suggest. In both cases, tastes and techniques formed in one subculture eventually migrate to the broader culture, with enormous impact.

One of the most remarkable new titles is *Quake III Arena,* on display at the id Software booth. The Dallas-based company has perhaps the most advance game software on the market. The detail in *Quake III Arena* is stunning—you believe you can reach out and touch the stone dungeon walls. Using the mouse, you can look around 360 degrees, which immediately makes you feel *inside* the gorgeous picture you're looking at. Able to go in any direction by pressing the arrow buttons on the keyboard, you instinctively start navigating this strange new universe, learning its laws of physics, mastering its peculiar rules and logic. When you jump from a launching pad located in outer space, it's exhilarating to hurtle through the airless void. This is virtual reality for the masses, on your home computer, without goggles or a trip to the arcade.

Calling these experiences "games" understates their significance. They are closer to acid trips, altering your sense of perception in a fundamental way. Your stomach churns with motion sickness even though you're sitting perfectly still. When you stop playing and stand up, objects in the room swim through space. The clock indicates you've been playing for an hour when you could swear it's been only 10 minutes. Later, driving down the highway, you feel like you are stopped in the middle of the road while cars around you slowly back up.

But *Quake III Arena,* like all shooters, gives you only a few seconds to enjoy the medium before you get the message, loud and clear. As you drop hundreds of feet through space, you notice other inhabitants milling about on the landing platform below. Being a friendly sort, you approach them.

Big mistake: They open fire. Reflexively, fearfully, you begin to shoot back. Heads and arms start exploding.

In this magical environment, only one form of social exchange is permitted. 20 The images this astonishing new technology is most often called upon to render so lovingly are rivers of blood and chunks of torn flesh.

In a middle-class neighborhood in suburban Dallas, five young guys in their 20s sit on two long, black leather couches. It's an ordinary living room except that the couches do not face each other. They are side-by-side, facing the altar: a video screen big enough to be a clubhouse they could all climb into.

These guys—"a bunch of kids who like to play games," says Steve Gibson, a skinny 23-year-old with long sideburns, in his soft, slightly embarrassed voice—are living out the fantasy of every hardcore gamer: earning a living making and playing 3-D action games. Steve runs a gaming website called shugashack.com; the rest work at companies that have sprouted up here after the runaway success of id Software's *Doom* and *Quake* in the mid-90s. As shooter fans, they belong to a largely hidden subculture whose members serve as the ultimate arbiters of cool within the larger electronic-games industry.

They go wild over shooter games not because they are inherently any more bloodthirsty than the average American male—they say they simply love the real-time 3-D programs and the sensations they stimulate. When it comes to "story," they care primarily about allowing the technology to fully express itself—which rules out peaceful adventure games like *Myst* that don't push the technological envelope or provide that crucial adrenaline rush.

Dan, Jack, Steve, Patrick, and Scott are nice guys—smart, courteous, some of them shy, others outgoing—and when they say that blowing away zillions of digital characters since they were kids hasn't made them the least bit aggressive in real life, you believe them.

"You're detached from the violence," explains Dan Hammans, a 19-year-old 25 who, playing under the name Rix, has won several major *Quake* tournaments.

"Yeah, saying you like computer games for violence is like saying you like baseball for running," Jack adds. "Violence is there to grab people, get them into it, and have them say, 'That looks cool.' But once you get into it, you don't even notice the violence. You don't go, 'Oh, cool, he blew up!'"

Their comments remind me of Marshall McLuhan's theory that all technology has a certain numbing effect, which he compared with Narcissus' rapture at lake's edge. Though every medium has this narcotic effect, McLuhan argued, modern technology is progressing so fast that we can finally see these changes as if for the first time, "like a growing plant in an enormously accelerated movie."

McLuhan uttered his famous dictum—"The medium is the message"—at a time when television was the miraculous new medium, and social scientists focused on the message, which was violence. Today's media experts say the last four decades of research (including a 1972 surgeon general's report) have shown a clear correlation between violence on television and the development and display of aggressive values and behavior by both children and adults.

So there's a statistical correlation. But is there direct proof of cause and effect? "Not only isn't there proof, but there may never be proof," says Kansas State's Murray. But, he continues, "At some point, you have to say that if exposure to violence is related to aggressive attitudes and values, and if [the latter] are related to shooting classmates or acting aggressively—all of which we know to be true—then it stands to reason that there is probably a link between exposure to violence and aggressive actions."

To substantiate this thesis, Murray is turning to physiology. He and a colleague are using functional magnetic resonance imaging to establish that certain areas of the brain controlling "fight-or-flight" impulses are stimulated in kids between the ages of 9 and 12 when they watch violent movies. More surprisingly, they have found, other parts of the brain are affected too—those involving memory and learning. Murray hopes these tests will eventually prove an elusive point: that repeated exposure to violent images is desensitizing, which he defines as having the effect of rendering a person "less sensitive to the pain and suffering of others, and more willing to tolerate ever-increasing levels of violence in our society." 30

"The issue people are worried about," Murray says, "is whether repeated rushes of stimulation cause the memory to store away ever-more-violent images, to be recalled later as a possible response to frustration. Are we producing hair-trigger responses and becoming so desensitized that we behave aggressively? Certainly that's what social-science work over the last 40 years has shown—that exposure to [media] violence changes our values, makes us more likely to act out aggressively. Not by viewing a particular program, but [after consuming] a steady diet of violence."

There hasn't been much research into the effects of video games, Murray says, and that's not only because they're so new. Many of the experts believe their point has already been proven, as much as humanly possible, with television. "It's a direct translation to video games," says Murray. "The only thing that's different and more worrisome is that the viewer or player is actively involved in constructing the violence."

According to other critics, playing games from the point of view of the killer is making some kids start thinking and acting like assassins. Lt. Col. Dave Grossman, a former West Point psychology professor, has been appearing on media outlets nationwide to plug his new book, *Stop Teaching Our Kids to Kill* (co-authored with Gloria DeGaetano), and to argue that children are getting the kind of sophisticated military training that until recently only the Pentagon could provide. "For the video game industry to claim that [research on] television and movie violence doesn't apply to them is like saying data on cigarettes doesn't apply to cigars," he says.

All these experts sound convincing until you find yourself in a Dallas living room chatting with five regular guys who play *Quake* long into the night, night after night. The fact that 99.99 percent of the kids who play violent games don't commit murder, they contend, disproves the experts' theories.

And in truth, not only do the games seem utterly harmless on this night, but these guys have so much fun playing together that it's hard to imagine the experience as anything but positive. Their camaraderie is as real as you'll find in any locker room. "It's how geeks get out their competitive spirit," says Steve, "because they're not athletic enough to play on the basketball team." 35

So benign is the mood here that I'm surprised by their reaction to a new game called *Kingpin: Life of Crime*. I fully expect them to draw the line here—for this is a game that goes way over the top with its graphic violence and racial stereotypes. Instead, they laugh and nod their approval at what a great game *Kingpin* is. *Kingpin* takes place in a ghetto. As the game starts, you're lying in an alley, having been beaten up by a rival gang. You want revenge, but don't know who to trust. You need guns and money to survive, and quickly learn that the easiest way to do that is to kill people. As you meet people on the street—like this tough, bare-midriffed chick with vaguely ethnic features coming toward you—you're encouraged to talk to them first in case they have any valuable information.

"Shit, man," she says, coming into view, filling up the whole screen.

Pressing letters on your keyboard produces either a positive or negative reply. You push the negative key: "Piss off."

"Hey, fuck you too!" she says, not missing a beat. "You a badass motherfucker."

Angry now, you push the negative key again: "You're not talking to me, are you?" 40

"Now that's it, motherfucker," she says.

"Turn the fuck around," you say. "You fuckin' piece of shit."

"Yeah, fuck you too," she says.

"You fuckin' want some of me?"

"I can get down with yo ass," she says. 45

"You can fuckin' kiss my ass," you say. "I will fuckin' bury you."

Conversations like this can go on indefinitely in this game until you either walk away or attack with your choice of a wide variety of weapons, including pipes, crowbars, pistols, shotguns, heavy rifles, tommy guns, flamethrowers, and rocket launchers. Not only can you blow off people's legs, arms, or heads, but *Kingpin*'s glossy magazine ads encourage you to do so. "Target specific body parts," the copy screams, "and actually see the damage done—including exit wounds."

Kingpin is rated "M" for mature audiences by the Entertainment Software Rating Board (the voluntary system created by the IDSA), but surveys show that parents don't follow these ratings, and stores don't enforce them. Even if they did, any clever eight-year-old could download a full-featured demo version of the game over the Internet and play all night.

Early reviews among hardcore gamers have been spectacular. "Good is an understatement for *Kingpin*," enthused the now-defunct website 4-Gamers.nu. "Amazing, stunning, and truly awe-inspiring are words which come closer to describing just how joyous this game is."

Separating the medium from the message is not easy when it comes to technologically advanced games like *Kingpin* because the two are so deeply intertwined—its dreamlike, three-dimensional world will vanish unless you learn to kill. 50

But regardless of whether you prefer McLuhan's theory about the numbing effect of the medium itself, or Murray's belief that desensitization flows from the constant message of mayhem, the result appears to be the same: a gradual increase in our cultural tolerance of violence, one we don't even notice until something shocking and new like *Kingpin* jolts us from our stupor.

Does that mean today's most gruesome games will eventually become so commonplace that they will elicit nothing more than a bored yawn? That's already happening among today's hardcore gamers, those taste makers who must give a computer game their blessing before it has much chance of migrating to the mainstream video-console market. Which makes hanging out with the Dallas shooter fans a bit like spending time in the future.

The main problem with *Kingpin*'s story is not the violence or the stereotypes, they say, but that it's too self-conscious. "It burned me because it seems like they *tried* to be shocking," says Jack Mathews, a baby-faced 22-year-old programmer. "Like, 'Look, we're saying "fuck" all the time.' But frankly, the whole game industry is not a very mature industry."

His last comment may reveal the most crucial point: that spending long periods of time absorbed in any medium, especially one as immersive as a video game, can keep you locked safely in a bubble, protected from the real world, in an extended state of arrested development. Growth, after all, seldom occurs without pain. Is the recent rash of school shootings being caused, at least in part, by the exponential increase in technology's ability to numb pain by drawing kids into an isolated world where violence and aggression have no consequences?

Eugene Provenzo thinks so. The professor of education at the University of 55 Miami, who is writing a book called *Children and Hyperreality: The Loss of the Real in Contemporary Childhood and Adolescence*, believes we're only at the beginning of an evolutionary process—one that has seen the gory comic book of the 1950s evolve first into the slasher movie and now into virtual nightmares like *Kingpin*. "I've been trying hard to make people realize we're going into a very different culture as a result of the introduction of new technologies," says Provenzo. "Video games are extremely powerful teaching machines, and we're still at a primitive level. We're on a trajectory toward increasing realism, or hyperreality, that makes people start thinking they can shoot someone and it doesn't hurt, that they can recover."

Cultural critics like Provenzo see evidence that the damaging effects of this phenomenon are hardly limited to a few crackpot shooters in remote places like Jonesboro and Paducah. And there is something chilling in the number of kids across the country who related deeply not only to the isolation and alienation of the Columbine killers, but to the way they vented their anger.

"My social studies teacher asked if we wanted to talk about Littleton," one high school kid in Illinois wrote in an e-mail posted recently on a website called Slashdot (its slogan: "News for nerds"). "I said I had some sense of how those two kids might have been driven crazy by cruel students, since it happens to me. I said I had thought of taking my father's gun to school when I was in the ninth grade and was so angry."

That was among thousands of e-mails received in the wake of Littleton by new-media columnist Jon Katz, now writing a book called *Geeks*. Katz wrote movingly on Slashdot about how self-described "geeks, nerds, dorks, and goths" were singled out for abuse by teachers and schoolmates after the Columbine massacre (the Illinois teenager who spoke so freely in class, in fact, came home to find three detectives going through his room); in follow-up postings they told horrible stories of being punched and kicked, tied up and beaten, and otherwise abused and humiliated. Pleas for help by these outcast kids instantly became part of the national dialogue, being entered into the Congressional Record, reprinted in the *New York Times* and *Los Angeles Times*, and read aloud on National Public Radio.

"The interesting thing about Littleton is that it was the first time the country realized there is this culture out there," says Provenzo. "It's not happening in the cities—it's an alienation we've created in suburbs and small towns, and it's being aggravated by a whole series of media formats. Our kids are losing their handle on reality because of everything from malls to video games. Each thing may be a drop in the bucket, but the bucket is full."

The computer-gamers gathered in the Dallas living room say they feel as 60 though they don't hear enough about the evils of other media—which, they point out, are far more politically powerful and entrenched than the electronic-games industry. "When people see stuff [like Littleton] happen, they say, 'Oh, these computer freaks! Look at them, they're freaks!" says Jack. "But when people see violence on TV, creatures exploding and people running around shooting with a shotgun, it's okay."

Dan acknowledges that what he loves about playing is that feeling of "being in another world with no consequences of your actions. You can jump off a ledge and smack on the ground and enjoy it." But there's a crystal-clear distinction in their minds between fantasy and real life, they add quickly, and for much of the evening they argue that spending so much time in their virtual worlds doesn't affect them at all.

At one point, though, Dan slips up.

"I've been walking around in a grocery store and swore I heard grenades bouncing around," he says. "Weird things like that—when you spend so much time doing it and [then] you hear a similar noise. . . ."

"Man!" cries Jack, interrupting him. "That's going to make it in the [magazine] now! 'These crazy game players!' 'Dan says he hears grenades while he walks around!'"

"No," Dan protests. "What I'm trying to say is there's no correlation between—" He stops. Some of their employers, afraid of being sued by the families of school-shooting victims, have instructed them not to discuss the issue of electronic games and its relationship to violent behavior.

Dan starts over. "It's so obvious to anybody who plays the game," he says. "You're running around in the game and you've got a shotgun, but it's a 3-D model being rendered by the game, and there's just no way I could see anybody not being able to tell the difference." Later, just to be sure the point is clear, Dan adds, "It doesn't transfer over to reality—that's the biggest thing."

But how could it not? If media doesn't affect real-world behavior, there would be no such thing as advertising, which at last count was a $25 billion international business. Exactly how it affects us depends on the person, of course, and the effect can be quite subtle. But arguing that these games have no effect at all is absurd, given that everybody in this room is devoting his life to developing increasingly powerful ways of fooling your mind and body into believing the game experience is really happening to you.

I have one last question for these guys. Isn't there anything else they would like to do in their miraculous virtual worlds besides killing people and blowing things up?

"It's more fun to blow up things than to build things," explains Dan.

Jack shrugs. "Violence sells."

It's years in the future. French terrorists have launched an attack on the Statue of Liberty, and you—a new agent in the United Nations Anti-Terrorist Coalition—have been sent to stop them. What you don't realize yet is that your employers are using you as a guinea pig in a nano-technology experiment. You are fully equipped with a range of weapons—everything from knives and pepper spray to rifles and rocket launchers. But here's the twist: You have to think twice before blowing people away.

"If you shoot somebody and anybody hears it, alarms are going to go off and the police are going to be all over you," says Warren Spector. The developer for Ion Storm, a Texas-based gaming software company, is standing in front of his booth at E3 excitedly describing the new game he's creating, called *Deus Ex,* due out next year. "People who would have talked to you before won't talk to you anymore. You'll still be able to win the game—I don't want to be disingenuous about this—but I want the player to be able to make a choice and then to really see the consequences of that choice. So suddenly we're in a medium that isn't just about adrenaline rushes."

Spector is part of a small band of game developers working in real-time 3-D who are quite literally trying to separate the medium from the message. He licensed the software program that runs a popular first-person shooter called *Unreal,* extracted most of the shooting gameplay, and is creating a new virtual universe that bears a closer resemblance to the real world, with some of its moral complexities and hard choices.

But Spector is the first to admit that his new game probably won't sell nearly as well as the gory shooters. And why should it? Who wants a fantasy that holds you responsible for your actions? Isn't that the whole point of American entertainment—to provide an escape from reality? Whether games like *Deus Ex* manage to succeed in the marketplace against the likes of *Quake* and *Kingpin* should provide some clues as to whether interactive entertainment is ready to take any tentative steps toward acknowledging what goes on in the real world.

The stakes are high, say social critics like Eugene Provenzo, who believes [75] that our embrace of electronic games represents nothing less than a massive renegotiation with reality, with profound implications for how kids, in particular, learn about and understand the world. As supercomputers and expanding band-width change passive television into an interactive medium that can draw us into the most astonishing simulated worlds, we are nearing a crossroads at least as important as the moment flickering television images began transforming the American cultural landscape in the '50s.

It was decades before the effects of television were broadly debated—by which time screen violence was something kids simply took for granted as a normal part of childhood. We have the chance to do things differently this time, but it may require discussions more imaginative than the usual free-market versus government-control polemics. Entertainers from Snoop Doggy Dogg to network-cop-show producers have eased up on the brutality lately, and consumers seem more open to the possibility that today's mass media may be creating public health problems as severe as those caused by our disruption of the natural environment during the last great technological revolution.

But a question remains: Now that the shock of Littleton has subsided, will we simply return to a fantasy world where we can pretend that the ways we choose to entertain ourselves have no consequences, like some kid zoned out in front of a computer game? If so, game's over.

ANALYZING What the Writer Says

1. Why are "shooter" games like *Duke Nukem* and *Quake* more attractive than games like *Myst*? What is the fundamental technological difference between the two types of games?

2. The third part of the essay focuses on the group of twenty-somethings who test games. How do they respond to questions about the violence in these games?

3. Marshall McLuhan was a Canadian who wrote on communications technology. What, according to Keegan, is McLuhan's theory? What do researchers say about the connection between media and violence?

4. How does Keegan connect video games and school violence in the fourth part of the article? What in the technology of these games could lead to tragedies such as the one at Columbine in 1999?

5. What is the take of the five game players on the connection between video games and violence? In what way is Dan's slip significant in this context?

6. In what way might the new game *Deus Ex* be different from the shooter games discussed in this article?

ANALYZING How the Writer Says It

1. Describe Keegan's introductory technique.

2. What effect does Keegan achieve by interspersing the testimony of young game players with comments and insights from researchers? How would his analysis have been different had he used only one or the other?

3. What is the significance of the essay's title?

ANALYZING the Issue

Does Keegan's evidence convince you that there is a connection between violent games and violent behavior? Why or why not?

ANALYZING | Connections Between Texts

1. How do you think "Joystick Jihad" (p. 431) proves or disproves Keegan's thesis?

2. Both Keegan and John Tierney ("Playing the Dozens," p. 527) describe adolescent boys playing games that offer outlets for their confrontational natures. Are there fundamental differences between trading verbal insults with actual people and blowing up virtual enemies? Explain.

3. In 1965, Boris Artzybasheff imagined the role the computer would play in society in his painting "The Computer in Society" (p. 104). How prophetic was his vision when it comes to the entertainment industry, such as the computer games Keegan writes about?

WARMING UP: *Go online and find an editorial about the issue of cloning—or find several, from a variety of different sources. What concerns do they voice? What do they tell us about cloning animals—or even humans?*

The Media and the Ethics of Cloning

By LEIGH TURNER

LEIGH TURNER

A professor of bioethics at the University of Toronto, Leigh Turner argues that scientists and ethicists need to understand each other's work so they can debate the issues intelligently. This essay first appeared in the Chronicle of Higher Education *in September 1997.*

If the contemporary debate on cloning has a patron saint, surely it is Andy Warhol.[1] Not only did Warhol assert that everyone would have 15 minutes of fame—witness the lawyers, philosophers, theologians, and bioethicists who found their expertise in hot demand on the nightly morality plays of network television following Ian Wilmut's cloning of the sheep Dolly—but he also placed "clones," multiple copies of the same phenomenon, at the heart of popular culture. Instead of multiple images of Marilyn Monroe and Campbell's soup cans, we now have cloned sheep. Regrettably, it is Warhol's capacity for hyperbole rather than his intelligence and ironic vision that permeates the current debate on cloning.

It would be unfair to judge hastily written op-ed pieces, popular talk shows, and late-night radio programs by the same standards that one would apply to a sustained piece of philosophical or legal analysis. But the popular media could do more to foster thoughtful public debate on the legal, moral, political, medical, and scientific dimensions of the cloning of humans and non-human animals.

---

[1]American artist (1928–1987) who mass-produced images by silkscreening. (Editor's note)

As did many of my colleagues at the Hastings Center,[2] I participated in several interviews with the media following Ian Wilmut's announcement in *Nature*[3] that he had succeeded in cloning Dolly from a mammary cell of an adult sheep. After clearly stating to one Los Angeles radio broadcaster before our interview that I was not a theologian and did not represent a religious organization, I was rather breathlessly asked during the taping what God's view on cloning is and whether cloning is "against creation." Predictably, the broadcaster didn't want to discuss how religious ethicists are contributing to the nascent public discourse about the ethics of cloning. Instead, he wanted me to provide a dramatic response that would get the radio station's phones ringing with calls from atheists, agnostics, and religious believers of all stripes.

In addition to inundating the public with hyperbolic sound bites and their print equivalents, the media have overwhelmingly emphasized the issues involved in cloning humans, paying almost no attention to the moral implications of cloning non-human animals. While the ethics of cloning humans clearly need to be debated, the cloning of non-human animals has already taken place and deserves to be treated as a meaningful moral concern.

Although I suspect that a compelling argument for the cloning of animals   5 can be made, we should not ignore the difference between actually formulating such arguments and merely presuming that non-human cloning is altogether unproblematic. Admittedly, humans already consider non-human animals as commodities in many ways, including as a source of food. Yet perhaps cloning animals with the intent of using them as "pharmaceutical factories," to produce insulin and other substances to treat human illnesses, should raise questions about how far such an attitude ought to extend. What moral obligations should extend to humans' use of other species? Do the potential medical benefits for humans outweigh the dangers of encouraging people to think of non-human animals as machines to be manipulated to fulfill human goals? These kinds of questions deserve to be part of the public discussion about cloning. Given some people's concerns about the use of traps to catch wild animals, the living conditions of farm animals, and the treatment of animals used in medical and pharmaceutical research, I find this gap in public discourse perplexing.

But perhaps the most significant problem with the media hyperbole concerning cloning is the easy assumption that humans simply are a product of their genes—a view usually called "genetic essentialism." Television hosts and radio personalities have asked whether it would be possible to stock an entire basketball team with clones of Michael Jordan. In response, philosophers, the-

---

[2]A nonprofit institute that supports research on ethical issues in medicine, health care, and science. (Editor's note)

[3]An important scientific journal published in Great Britain. (Editor's note)

ologians, and other experts have reiterated wearily that, although human behavior undeniably has a genetic component, a host of other factors—including uterine environment, family dynamics, social setting, diet, and other personal history—play important roles in an individual's development. Consequently, a clone produced from the DNA of an outstanding athlete might not even be interested in sports.

While this more-sophisticated message has received some media attention, we continue to see stories emphasizing that the wealthy might some day be able to produce copies of themselves, or that couples with a dying infant might create an identical copy of the child. The popular media seem to remain transfixed by what Dorothy Nelkin, the New York University sociologist of science, refers to as "DNA as destiny."

What's more, the cloning issue reveals the way in which the mass media foster attitudes of technological and scientific determinism by implying that scientific "progress" cannot be halted. Of course, many scientists share these attitudes, and, too often, they refuse to accept moral responsibility for their participation in research that may contribute to human suffering. But scientists should not merely ply their craft, leaving moral reasoning to others. They should participate in public debates about whether certain scientific projects are harmful and should not be allowed to continue because they have unjustifiable, dehumanizing implications. A good model is the outspoken criticism of nuclear weapons by many nuclear physicists, who have helped limit research intended to produce more effective nuclear devices.

Scientists are not riding a juggernaut capable of crushing everything in its path simply because mass cloning of animals, and possibly eventually humans, may be technically possible. There is no reason to think that scientific research has a mandate that somehow enables it to proceed outside the web of moral concerns that govern all other human endeavors; it does not exist above the law or outside the rest of society. To think otherwise is to succumb to a technological determinism that denies the responsibilities and obligations of citizenship.

Despite the media's oversimplifications, citizens have an obligation to scrutinize carefully all of the issues involved and, if necessary, to regulate cloning through laws, professional codes of behavior, and institutional policies. I want to suggest three ways that scholars, policy makers, and concerned citizens can, in fact, work to improve public debate about ethical issues related to new developments in science and technology.

First, scientists and ethicists need a fuller understanding of each other's work. Scientists must recognize the moral implications of their research and address those implications when they discuss the research in public. The formal education of most scientists does not encourage them to consider ethical issues. Whereas courses in bioethics are now found in most schools of medicine and nursing, graduate students in such disciplines as human genetics, biochemistry, and animal physiology are not encouraged to grapple with the ethical aspects of their research. Similarly, most ethicists have very little knowledge of science, although many of them feel perfectly entitled to comment on the moral issues of new scientific discoveries.

This gap in understanding fosters an inaccurate, unrealistic conception of what the most pressing ethical issues are. For example, the real challenges for researchers today involve the cloning of non-human animals for use in developing pharmaceutical products. Sustained study of non-human clones will be needed before researchers can even begin to seriously consider research involving human subjects. Rather than encouraging the media's interest in cloning humans, ethicists more knowledgeable about the science involved might have been able to shift the public debate toward the moral questions raised by cloning sheep, pigs, and other animals, questions that need immediate public debate.

Thus, we need to include more courses in various scientific departments on the ethics of contemporary scientific research; offer courses for ethicists on the basics of human genetics, anatomy, and physiology, and establish continuing-education courses and forums that bring together scientists and scholars in the humanities.

Second, ethicists need to do a better job of presenting their concerns in the popular media. Scientific journals written for a popular audience—such as *Scientific American, New Scientist, Discover,* and *The Sciences*—provide excellent popular accounts of scientific research and technological developments, but they rarely specifically address the moral implications of the discoveries they report. Regrettably, most of the academic journals that do address the ethical aspects of scientific topics—such as the *Hastings Center Report,* the *Journal of Medical Ethics,* and the *Cambridge Quarterly of Healthcare Ethics*—lack the broad readership of the popular-science magazines. Right now, perhaps the best "popular" source of sustained ethical analysis of science, medicine, and health care is *The New York Times Magazine.*

If ethicists hope to reach larger audiences with more than trivial sound bites, 15 they need to establish and promote appropriate outlets for their concerns. For example, Arthur Caplan, director of the Center for Bioethics at the University of Pennsylvania, wrote a regular weekly newspaper column for the *St. Paul Pioneer Press* when he directed a bioethics center at the University of Minnesota. His column addressed the ethical implications of medical and scientific research. Other scholars have yet to follow his example—perhaps, in part, because many academics feel that writing for the mass media is unworthy of their time. They are wrong.

One way of improving public debate on these important issues is for universities to encourage their faculty members to write for newspapers, popular magazines, and even community newsletters. Such forms of communication should be viewed as an important complement to other forms of published research. Leon Kass's writing on cloning in *The New Republic* and Michael Walzer's and Michael Sandel's writing on assisted suicide in the same publication should not be considered any less significant simply because the work appears in a magazine intended for a wide audience. After all, if universities are to retain their public support, they must consistently be seen as important players in society, and one easy way to do this is to encourage their faculty members to contribute regularly to public discussion.

Finally, we need to expand public debate about ethical issues in science beyond the mass media. To complement the activities of the National Bioethics Advisory Commission and the projects on ethics at universities and research centers, we should create forums at which academics and citizens from all walks of life could meet to debate the issues. Instead of merely providing a gathering place for scholars pursuing research projects, institutions such as the Hastings Center, Georgetown University's Kennedy Institute of Ethics, and the University of Pennsylvania's Center for Bioethics need to foster outreach programs and community-discussion groups that include nonspecialists. My experience suggests that members of civic organizations and community-health groups, such as the New York Citizens' Committee on Health Care Decisions, are quite eager to discuss the topic of cloning.

What we need are fewer commentaries by self-promoting experts on network television, and more intelligent discussions by scholars and citizens in local media including local public-television stations. We need creative alternatives to the onslaught of talking heads, all saying much the same thing (as though they themselves were clones) to docile, sheep-like audiences waiting for others to address the most pressing moral issues of the day.

ANALYZING What the Writer Says

1. What point does the anecdote of the radio interview illustrate?

2. What is "genetic essentialism," and what is Turner's stance on the matter?

3. Besides the presentation of "DNA as destiny," in what other ways is the popular media wrong in the way it presents the issue of cloning?

4. What are Turner's suggestions for "improv[ing] public debate about ethical issues related to new developments in science and technology"?

ANALYZING How the Writer Says It

1. Turner, a bioethicist, writes about a topic that may not interest a broad spectrum of readers. What techniques does she use to capture the attention of a nonscientific audience?

2. In her conclusion, Turner uses terms like "self-promoting experts" (to describe television commentators) and "sheep-like audiences." What is the effect of the emotionally charged language?

ANALYZING the Issue

Do you agree that the media have distorted the issue of cloning? What does your reading and research on the subject indicate?

ANALYZING Connections Between Texts

1. Both Ellen Goodman ("Beauty on the DNA Auction Block," p. 413) and Nancy Gibbs ("If We Have It, Do We Use It?," p. 409) write about genetic engineering. After reading Turner's argument about the media's treatment of the issue, do you think Goodman and Gibbs are guilty of the kind of distortion Turner addresses?

2. Katie Roiphe argues in "Profiles Encouraged" (p. 737) that the media tell basically one story about celebrity, ignoring any complexities or individual personalities. Although Turner's subject is weightier, how is her point about the media similar? What attitude toward the popular media do the writers share?

3. How does the Corbis image "Multiples" (p. 465) illustrate Turner's points?

WARMING UP: *Do you spend a lot of time on the Internet? Why or why not? What do you find attractive about it? What turns you off?*

The Museum of Me

BY ELLEN ULLMAN

ELLEN ULLMAN

A software engineer and the author of Close to the Machine: Technophilia and Its Discontents, *Ellen Ullman examines the danger of the Internet, which, for her, lies in the separation of cyberspace travelers from each other. Seen from this angle, the Internet is not a global connection but the antithesis to democracy and culture, which are, by definition, communal. Originally delivered as a lecture at the University of Vermont in 1999, the essay appeared in* Harper's *in May 2000.*

Years ago, before the Internet as we know it had come into existence—I think it was around Christmas, in 1990—I was at a friend's house, where her nine-year-old son and his friend were playing the video game that was the state of the art at the time, Sonic the Hedgehog. They jumped around in front of the TV and gave off the sort of rude noises boys tend to make when they're shooting at things in a video game, and after about half an hour they stopped and tried to talk about what they'd just been doing. The dialogue went something like this:

"I wiped out at that part with the ladders."

"Ladders? What ladders?"

"You know, after the rooms."

"Oh, you mean the stairs?"   5

"No, I think they were ladders. I remember, because I died there twice."

"I never killed you around any ladders. I killed you where you jump down off this wall."

"Wall? You mean by the gates of the city?"

"Are there gates around the city? I always called it the castle."

The boys muddled along for several more minutes,   10 making themselves more confused as they went. Finally they gave up trying to talk about their time with Sonic the Hedgehog. They just looked at each other and shrugged.

I didn't think about the two boys and Sonic again until I watched my clients try out the World Wide Web. By then it was 1995, the Internet as we know it was beginning to exist, but the two women who

worked for my client, whom I'd just helped get online, had never before connected to the Internet or surfed the Web. They took to it instantly, each disappearing into nearly an hour of obsessive clicking, after which they tried to talk
about it:

"It was great! I clicked that thing and went to this place. I don't remember
its name."

"Yeah. It was a link. I clicked here and went there."

"Oh, I'm not sure it was a link. The thing I clicked was a picture of the
library."

"Was it the library? I thought it was a picture of City Hall."

"Oh, no. I'm sure it was the library."

"No, City Hall. I'm sure because of the dome."

"Dome? Was there a dome?"

Right then I remembered Sonic and the two boys; my clients, like the two
boys, had experienced something pleasurable and engaging, and they very
much wanted to talk about it—talking being one of the primary ways human
beings augment their pleasure. But what had happened to them, each in her
own electronic world, resisted description. Like the boys, the two women fell
into verbal confusion. How could they speak coherently about a world full of
little wordless pictograms, about trails that led off in all directions, of idle visits to virtual places chosen on a whim-click?

Following hyperlinks on the Web is like the synaptic drift of dreams, a loos-
ening of intention, the mind associating freely, an experience that can be compelling or baffling or unsettling, or all of those things at once. And like
dreams, the experience of the Web is intensely private, charged with immanent meaning for the person inside the experience, but often confusing or
irrelevant to someone else.

At the time, I had my reservations about the Web, but not so much about
the private, dreamlike state it offered. Web surfing seemed to me not so much
antisocial as asocial, an adventure like a video game or pinball, entertaining,
sometimes interesting, sometimes a trivial waste of time; but in a social sense
it seemed harmless, since only the person engaged in the activity was affected.

Something changed, however, not in me but in the Internet and the Web and in
the world, and the change was written out in person-high letters on a billboard
on the corner of Howard and New Montgomery Streets in San Francisco. It was
the fall of 1998. I was walking toward Market Street one afternoon when I saw
it, a background of brilliant sky blue, with writing on it in airy white letters,
which said: *now the world really does revolve around you.* The letters were lower-
case, soft-edged, spaced irregularly, as if they'd been skywritten over a hot
August beach and were already drifting off into the air. The message they left
behind was a child's secret wish, the ultimate baby-world narcissism we are all
supposed to abandon when we grow up: the world really does revolve around me.

What was this billboard advertising? Perfume? A resort? There was nothing else on it but the airy, white letters, and I had to walk right up to it to see a URL written at the bottom; it was the name of a company that makes semiconductor equipment, machinery used by companies like Intel and AMD to manufacture integrated circuits. Oh, chips, I thought. Computers. Of course. What other subject produces such hyperbole? Who else but someone in the computer industry could make such a shameless appeal to individualism?

The billboard loomed over the corner for the next couple of weeks. Every time I passed it, its message irritated me more. It bothered me the way the "My Computer" icon bothers me on the Windows desktop, baby names like "My Yahoo" and "My Snap"; my, my, my; two-year-old talk; infantilizing and condescending.

But there was something more disturbing about this billboard, and I tried to figure out why, since it simply was doing what every other piece of advertising does: whispering in your ear that there is no one like you in the entire world, and what we are offering is for you, special you, and you alone. What came to me was this: Toyota, for example, sells the idea of a special, individual buyer ("It's not for everyone, just for you"), but chip makers, through the medium of the Internet and the World Wide Web, are creating the actual infrastructure of an individualized marketplace.

What had happened between 1995, when I could still think of the Internet as a private dream, and the appearance of that billboard in 1998 was the near-complete commercialization of the Web. And that commercialization had proceeded in a very particular and single-minded way: by attempting to isolate the individual within a sea of economic activity. Through a process known as "disintermediation," producers have worked to remove the expert intermediaries, agents, brokers, middlemen, who until now have influenced our interactions with the commercial world. What bothered me about the billboard, then, was that its message was not merely hype but the reflection of a process that was already under way: an attempt to convince the individual that a change currently being visited upon him or her is a good thing, the purest form of self, the equivalent of freedom. The world really does revolve around you.

In Silicon Valley, in Redmond, Washington, the home of Microsoft, and in the smaller silicon alleys of San Francisco and New York, "distintermediation" is a word so common that people shrug when you try to talk to them about it. Oh, disintermediation, that old thing. Everyone already knows about that. It has become accepted wisdom, a process considered inevitable, irrefutable, good.

I've long believed that the ideas embedded in technology have a way of percolating up and outward into the nontechnical world at large, and that technology is made by people with intentions and, as such, is not neutral. In the case of disintermediation, an explicit and purposeful change is being visited upon the structure of the global marketplace. And in a world so dominated by markets, I don't think I go too far in saying that this will affect the very structure of reality, for the Net is no longer simply a zone of personal freedoms, a pleasant diversion from what we used to call "real life"; it has become an actual marketplace that is changing the nature of real life itself.

Removal of the intermediary. All those who stand in the middle of a transaction, whether financial or intellectual: out! Brokers and agents and middlemen of every description: good-bye! Travel agents, real-estate agents, insurance agents, stockbrokers, mortgage brokers, consolidators, and jobbers, all the scrappy percentniks who troll the bywaters of capitalist exchange—who needs you? All those hard-striving immigrants climbing their way into the lower middle class through the penny-ante deals of capitalism, the transfer points too small for the big guys to worry about—find yourself some other way to make a living. Small retailers and store clerks, salespeople of every kind—a hindrance, idiots, not to be trusted. Even the professional handlers of intellectual goods, anyone who sifts through information, books, paintings, knowledge, selecting and summing up: librarians, book reviewers, curators, disc jockeys, teachers, editors, analysts—why trust anyone but yourself to make judgments about what is more or less interesting, valuable, authentic, or worthy of your attention? No one, no professional interloper, is supposed to come between you and your desires, which, according to this idea, are nuanced, difficult to communicate, irreducible, unique.

The Web did not cause disintermediation, but it is what we call an "enabling   30
technology": a technical breakthrough that takes a difficult task and makes it suddenly doable, easy; it opens the door to change, which then comes in an unconsidered, breathless rush.

We are living through an amazing experiment: an attempt to construct a capitalism without salespeople, to take a system founded upon the need to sell ever greater numbers of goods to ever growing numbers of people, and to do this without the aid of professional distribution channels—without buildings, sidewalks, shops, luncheonettes, street vendors, buses, trams, taxis, other women in the fitting room to tell you how you look in something and to help you make up your mind, without street people panhandling, Santas ringing bells at Christmas, shop women with their perfect makeup and elegant clothes, fashionable men and women strolling by to show you the latest look—in short, an attempt to do away with the city in all its messy stimulation, to abandon the agora for home and hearth, where it is safe and everything can be controlled.

The first task in this newly structured capitalism is to convince consumers that the services formerly performed by myriad intermediaries are useless or worse, that those commissioned brokers and agents are incompetent, out for themselves, dishonest. And the next task is to glorify the notion of self-service. Where companies once vied for your business by telling you about their courteous people and how well they would serve you—"Avis, We Try Harder"— their job now is to make you believe that only you can take care of yourself. The lure of personal service that was dangled before the middle classes, momentarily making us all feel almost as lucky as the rich, is being withdrawn. In the Internet age, under the pressure of globalized capitalism and its slimmed-down profit margins, only the very wealthy will be served by actual human beings. The rest of us must make do with Web pages, and feel happy about it.

One evening while I was watching television, I looked up to see a commercial that seemed to me to be the most explicit statement of the ideas implicit in the disintermediated universe. I gaped at it, because usually such ideas are kept implicit, hidden behind symbols. But this commercial was like the sky-blue billboard: a shameless and naked expression of the Web world, a glorification of the self, at home, alone.

It begins with a drone, a footstep in a puddle, then a ragged band pulling a dead car through the mud—road warriors with bandanas around their fore-heads carrying braziers. Now we see rafts of survivors floating before the ruins of a city, the sky dark, red-tinged, as if fires were burning all around us, just over the horizon. Next we are outside the dead city's library, where stone lions, now coated in gold and come to life, rear up in despair. Inside the library, red-coated Fascist guards encircle the readers at the table. A young girl turns a page, loudly, and the guard say, "Shush!" in time to their march-step. We see the title of the book the girl is reading: *Paradise Lost*. The bank, too, is a scene of ruin. A long line snakes outside it in a dreary rain. Inside, the teller is a man with a white, spectral face, who gazes upon the black spider that is slowly crawling up his window. A young woman's face ages right before us, and in response, in ridicule, the bank guard laughs. The camera now takes us up over the roofs of this post-apocalyptic city. Lightning crashes in the dark, red-tinged sky. On a telephone pole, where the insulators should be, are skulls.

Cut to a cartoon of emerald-green grass, hills, a Victorian house with a white   35
picket fence and no neighbors. A butterfly flaps above it. What a relief this house is after the dreary, dangerous, ruined city. The door to this charming house opens, and we go in to see a chair before a computer screen. Yes, we want to go sit in that chair, in that room with candy-orange walls. On the com-puter screen, running by in teasing succession, are pleasant virtual reflections of the world outside: written text, a bank check, a telephone pole, which now signifies our connection to the world. The camera pans back to show a win-dow, a curtain swinging in the breeze, and our sense of calm is complete. We hear the Intel-Inside jingle, which sounds almost like chimes. Cut to the leg-end: Packard Bell. Wouldn't you rather be at home?

In sixty seconds, this commercial communicates a worldview that reflects the ultimate suburbanization of existence: a retreat from the friction of the social space to the supposed idyll of private ease. It is a view that depends on the idea that desire is not social, not stimulated by what others want, but gen-erated internally, and that the satisfaction of desires is not dependent upon other persons, organizations, structures, or governments. It is a profoundly libertarian vision, and it is the message that underlies all the mythologizing about the Web: the idea that the civic space is dead, useless, dangerous. The only place of pleasure and satisfaction is your home. You, home, family; and beyond that, the world. From the intensely private to the global, with little in between but an Intel processor and a search engine.

In this sense, the ideal of the Internet represents the very opposite of democracy, which is a method for resolving differences in a relatively orderly manner through the mediation of unavoidable civil associations. Yet there can be no notion of resolving differences in a world where each person is entitled to get exactly what he or she wants. Here all needs and desires are equally valid and equally powerful. I'll get mine and you'll get yours; there is no need for compromise and discussion. I don't have to tolerate you, and you don't have to tolerate me. No need for messy debate and the whole rigmarole of government with all its creaky, bothersome structures. There's no need for any of this, because now that we have the World Wide Web the problem of the pursuit of happiness has been solved! We'll each click for our individual joys, and our only dispute may come if something doesn't get delivered on time. Wouldn't you really rather be at home?

But who can afford to stay at home? Only the very wealthy or a certain class of knowledge worker can stay home and click. On the other side of this ideal of work-anywhere freedom (if indeed it is freedom never to be away from work) is the reality that somebody had to make the thing you ordered with a click. Somebody had to put it in a box, do the paperwork, carry it to you. The reality is a world divided not only between the haves and have-nots but between the ones who get to stay home and everyone else, the ones who deliver the goods to them.

The Net ideal represents a retreat not only from political life but also from culture—from that tumultuous conversation in which we try to talk to one another about our shared experiences. As members of a culture, we see the same movie, read the same book, hear the same string quartet. Although it is difficult for us to agree on what we might have seen, read, or heard, it is out of that difficult conversation that real culture arises. Whether or not we come to an agreement or understanding, even if some decide that understanding and meaning are impossible, we are still sitting around the same campfire.

But the Web as it has evolved is based on the idea that we do not even want   40 a shared experience. The director of San Francisco's Museum of Modern Art once told an audience that we no longer need a building to house works of art; we don't need to get dressed, go downtown, walk from room to room among crowds of other people. Now that we have the Web, we can look at anything we want whenever we want, and we no longer need him or his curators. "You don't have to walk through *my* idea of what's interesting to look at," he said to a questioner in the audience named Bill. "On the Web," said the director, "you can create the museum of Bill."

And so, by implication, there can be the museums of George and Mary and Helene. What then will this group have to say to one another about art? Let's say the museum of Bill is featuring early Dutch masters, the museum of Mary is playing video art, and the museum of Helene is displaying French tapestries. In this privatized world, what sort of "cultural" conversation can there be? What can one of us possibly say to another about our experience except, "Today I visited the museum of me, and I liked it."

ANALYZING What the Writer Says

1. At the end of the first segment of her essay, Ullman says that, in the past, Web surfing struck her as "not so much antisocial but asocial." What precisely is the difference between the two terms? At the end of her essay, does Ullman conclude that the Internet is antisocial or asocial?

2. Why is Ullman disturbed by the billboard that says about the Internet, "Now the world really does revolve around you"?

3. According to Ullman, in what sense has online shopping changed the way in which we do business? What assumptions have changed fundamentally?

4. How does Ullman develop the idea that the Web suggests that "civic space is dead, useless, dangerous"? How is the Web's "profoundly libertarian vision" dangerous for our understanding of community and civic responsibility?

5. Ullman claims that the "Net ideal represents a retreat not only from political life but also from culture." What does she mean?

"User name and password?"

ANALYZING How the Writer Says It

1. Ullman starts her essay with two extended examples: children playing video games and adults surfing the Web. How do these two examples introduce her theme?

2. Ullman intersperses her discussion with vivid descriptions and passages of direct speech. What does she accomplish by mixing the concrete and the abstract?

3. Analyze the effect of Ullman's last sentence: "Today I visited the museum of me, and I liked it."

ANALYZING the Issue

Do you agree with Ullman's claim that ultimate freedom of the individual will weaken the community, which makes the Internet a fundamentally antisocial institution? Why or why not?

ANALYZING Connections Between Texts

1. How does Ullman's analysis reinforce the points Ian Frazier raises in "Dearly Disconnected" (p. 404)?

2. Michael Kinsley ("Orwell Got It Wrong, p. 559") argues that "high-tech devices . . . have *expanded* human freedom." While Ullman does not deny that, she sees another specter looming. What, would Ullman argue, does Kinsley overlook?

3. How does Arnie Levin's cartoon (p. 461) supply an ironic commentary on the issues Ullman raises in her essay?

YOUR TURN: **Suggestions for Writing About "Future Shock"**

1. The advantages of modern communication technology are obvious when it comes to speed and convenience. However, some writers have pointed out that cyberspace, while facilitating communication, also separates us from each other. Write an essay in which you analyze the paradox of the loss of a sense of community because of our abundant communication technology.

2. In the manner of Ian Frazier, write an essay about a new piece of technology that has changed the way we live our daily lives.

3. Using Gibbs's and Goodman's articles as sources, write an essay in which you analyze the advantages and disadvantages of genetically enhancing an unborn child's beauty or intelligence.

4. While Hawthorne's short story is over 150 years old, the themes are very topical. Write an essay in which you show how "The Birthmark" anticipates a current issue.

5. Do violent video games lead to violent behavior? Using "Culture Quake" and "Joystick Jihad" as sources, write an essay in which you try to answer this question.

6. Various readings in this unit analyze the benefits of developments in modern communication technology (for example, the Internet and cell phones) and question whether they are more blessing or threat. Choose one innovation in communication technology and argue for or against its ultimate merit.

7. Choose some emotionally charged medical or scientific issue that you think the media have distorted or oversimplified, and write an essay in which you set the record straight.

8. Analyze Boris Artzybasheff's 1965 "The Computer in Society" (p. 104), pointing out the ways in which the painting anticipates the current state of computer technology.

9. Look at the photos by John McGrail (p. 105) and Doug Menuez (p. 466). Then do some research on nuclear energy and/or alternative energy sources and write an essay in which you make a case for the most promising energy source.

IMAGE GALLERY 👁

MULTIPLES

This Image Source stock photo is a collage of frames all featuring the same head, albeit from different angles.

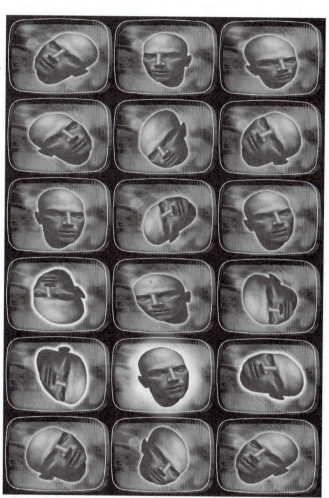

1. Although each of the multiple images shows the same face, how did the artist create subtle differences between the individual frames?

2. What effect does the artist achieve by distorting the model's head?

3. Is there significance in the artist's choice to frame each head in a rectangle with rounded corners?

4. What do you think the artist is saying with this image? How does this image fit with the readings in this chapter?

DOUG MENUEZ

Nuclear Lane

Doug Menuez took this picture in Richland, Washington, the home of Hanford Federal Nuclear Reservation, a gigantic nuclear power facility. The town is proud of its production of power and uranium; they have named streets and other landmarks after the plant, and the local high school cheerleaders cheer on the "Bombers" with chants of "Bomber Power!" The photo was published in A Day in the Life of America *in 1986.*

1. Describe the details in the picture.

2. How does the sky in the background reinforce the meaning of the photo?

3. How do light and contrast work in the picture?

4. What is the photographer suggesting about the town of Richland, Washington? Do you think the inhabitants of Richland share his views?

PORT AUTHORITY OF NEW YORK AND NEW JERSEY

World Trade Center

Although it is forever etched in the American consciousness as the site of the most devastating terrorist attack in history, the World Trade Center stands tall and proud in this photograph.

1. How does the photographer use line and shape in this picture?

2. What is the effect of the choice of black and white over color for this photograph?

3. What does the photo say about the World Trade Center and the people who built it?

14 TALK THE TALK

An all but forgotten nineteenth-century playwright and novelist, Edward George Bulwer-Lytton, is quoted often on the power of language, for it is he who wrote that "the pen is mightier than the sword." And while that may not always be the

"A word after a word/after a word is power."

—Margaret Atwood
"Spelling"

case, most of us understand the might of words, written or spoken. But we also understand that strong messages are often conveyed without words; we learn early to interpret other signs—signals, pictures, actions. Without uttering a word, a Ku Klux Klansman communicates loudly and clearly; in his language of hate, the hood is the word. Language, however it manifests itself, is power.

Whether considering the linguistic gamesmanship of teenage boys, as John Tierney does, or arguing, as Deborah Tannen does, that women are "marked" by the clothes they wear in ways that men are not, the writers represented here examine the many forms by which we communicate as well as the effect of how and what we speak, in word or deed. In a classic essay, George Orwell points to the political ramifications of vague language, and in a variation on that theme, Lewis H. Lapham looks at how post-9/11 rhetoric stymied useful debate and quashed alternate points of view. Following a similar line of reasoning, Jonathan Rauch deconstructs the meaning of "prejudice," arguing that "stamping out prejudice really means forcing everyone to share the same prejudice." Sharing her experience in a morning sing-along group with fundamentalist Christian students, Annie Dillard reflects on the power of labels to stereotype. Acknowledging the power of the *written* word, an AIDS activist photographed by Annie Leibovitz has painted them directly on to her body. Lending levity to this chapter, David Sedaris, with his usual wry wit, questions the effectiveness of one method of second-language instruction, while Amy Tan credits the fractured English she spoke in her family home for the authenticity of her writer's voice.

Language is both the first casualty—and the tool—of the oppressor. Totalitarian regimes recognize that those denied the chance to speak freely or to hear others speak freely are indeed powerless; they prop up themselves with propaganda, with programmed speech, controlling thought by controlling communication.

Talking the talk: it is the ultimate freedom—and the ultimate responsibility.

❈

WARMING UP: *What comes to your mind when you hear the term "fundamentalist Christians"? What expectations do you have of this group? If you are not a fundamentalist Christian yourself, what expectations do you have of this group?*

Singing with the Fundamentalists

BY ANNIE DILLARD

ANNIE DILLARD

Annie Dillard (b. 1945), noted especially for her philosophical musing in exquisitely detailed nature writing, teaches writing at Wesleyan University. In her Pulitzer Prize-winning Pilgrim at Tinker Creek, *Dillard argues that a certain naiveté is necessary for true sight. With such untainted vision, she considers fundamentalist Christians in "Singing with the Fundamentalists."*

It is early spring. I have a temporary office at a state university on the West Coast. The office is on the third floor. It looks down on the Square, the enormous open courtyard at the center of the campus. From my desk I see hundreds of people moving between classes. There is a large circular fountain in the Square's center.

Early one morning, on the first day of spring quarter, I hear singing. A pack of students has gathered at the fountain. They are singing something which, at this distance, and through the heavy window, sounds good.

I know who these singing students are: they are the Fundamentalists. This campus has a lot of them. Mornings they sing on the Square; it is their only perceptible activity. What are they singing? Whatever it is, I want to join them, for I like to sing; whatever it is, I want to take my stand with them, for I am drawn to their very absurdity, their innocent indifference to what people think. My colleagues and students here, and my friends everywhere, dislike and fear Christian fundamentalists. You may never have met such people, but you've heard what they do: they pile up money, vote in blocs, and elect right-wing crazies; they censor books; they carry handguns; they fight fluoride in the drinking water and evolution in the schools; probably they would lynch people if they could get away with it. I'm not sure my friends are correct. I close my pen and join the singers on the Square.

There is a clapping song in progress. I have to concentrate to follow it:

> Come on, rejoice,
> And let your heart sing,
> Come on, rejoice,
> Give praise to the king.
>
> Singing alleluia—
> He is the king of kings;
>
> Singing alleluia—
> He is the king of kings.

Two song leaders are standing on the broad rim of the fountain; the water is splashing just behind them. The boy is short, hardfaced, with a mustache. He bangs his guitar with the backs of his fingers. The blonde girl, who leads the clapping, is bouncy; she wears a bit of makeup. Both are wearing blue jeans.

The students beside me are wearing blue jeans too—and athletic jerseys, 5 parkas, football jackets, turtlenecks, and hiking shoes or jogging shoes. They all have canvas or nylon book bags. They look like any random batch of seventy or eighty students at this university. They are grubby or scrubbed, mostly scrubbed; they are tall, fair, or red-headed in large proportions. Their parents are white-collar workers, blue-collar workers, farmers, loggers, orchardists, merchants, fishermen; their names are, I'll bet, Olsen, Jensen, Seversen, Hansen, Klokker, Sigurdsen.

Despite the vigor of the clapping song, no one seems to be giving it much effort. And no one looks at anyone else; there are no sentimental glances and smiles, no glances even of recognition. These kids don't seem to know each other. We stand at the fountain's side, out on the broad, bricked Square in front of the science building, and sing the clapping song through three times.

It is quarter to nine in the morning. Hundreds of people are crossing the Square. These passersby—faculty, staff, students—pay very little attention to us; this morning singing has gone on for years. Most of them look at us directly, then ignore us, for there is nothing to see; no animal sacrifices, no lynchings, no collection plate for Jesse Helms, no seizures, snake handling, healing, or glossolalia. There is barely anything to hear. I suspect the people glance at us to learn if we are really singing: How could so many people make so little sound? My fellow singers, who ignore each other, certainly ignore passersby as well. Within a week, most of them will have their eyes closed anyway.

We move directly to another song, a slower one.

> He is my peace
> Who has broken down every wall;
> He is my peace,
> He is my peace.

> Cast all your cares on him,
> For he careth for you—oo—oo
> He is my peace
> He is my peace.

I am paying strict attention to the song leaders, for I am singing at the top of my lungs and I've never heard any of these songs before. They are not the old American low-church Protestant hymns; they are not the old European high-church Protestant hymns. These hymns seem to have been written just yesterday, apparently by the same people who put out lyrical Christian greeting cards and bookmarks.

"Where do these songs come from?" I ask a girl standing next to me. She seems appalled to be addressed at all, and startled by the question. "They're from the praise albums!" she explains, and moves away.

The songs' melodies run dominant, subdominant, dominant, tonic, dominant. The pace is slow, about the pace of "Tell Laura I Love Her," and with that song's quavering, long notes. The lyrics are simple and repetitive; there are very few of them to which a devout Jew or Mohammedan could not give wholehearted assent. These songs are similar to the things Catholics sing in church these days. I don't know if any studies have been done to correlate the introduction of contemporary songs into Catholic churches with those churches' decline in membership, or with the phenomenon of Catholic converts' applying to enter cloistered monasteries directly, without passing through parish churches.

> I'm set free to worship,
> I'm set free to praise him,
> I'm set free to dance before the Lord . . .

At nine o'clock sharp we quit and scatter. I hear a few quiet "see you's." Mostly the students leave quickly, as if they didn't want to be seen. The Square empties.

The next day we show up again, at twenty to nine. The same two leaders stand on the fountain's rim; the fountain is pouring down behind them.

After the first song, the boy with the mustache hollers, "Move on up! Some of you guys aren't paying attention back there! You're talking to each other. I want you to concentrate!" The students laugh, embarrassed for him. He sounds like a teacher. No one moves. The girl breaks into the next song, which we join at once:

> In my life, Lord,
> Be glorified, be glorified, be glorified;
> In my life, Lord.
> Be glorified, be glorified today.

At the end of this singularly monotonous verse, which is straining my tolerance for singing virtually anything, the boy with the mustache startles me by
shouting, "Classes!"

At once, without skipping a beat, we sing, "In my classes, Lord, be glorified,
be glorified . . ." I give fleet thought to the class I'm teaching this afternoon.
We're reading a little "Talk of the Town" piece called "Eggbag," about a cat in
a magic store on Eighth Avenue. "Relationships!" the boy calls. The students
seem to sing "In my relationships, Lord," more easily than they sang "classes."
They seemed embarrassed by "classes." In fact, to my fascination, they seemed
embarrassed by almost everything. Why are they here? I will sing with the
Fundamentalists every weekday morning all spring; I will decide, tentatively,
that they come pretty much for the same reasons I do: Each has a private relationship with "the Lord" and will put up with a lot of junk for it.

I have taught some Fundamentalist students here, and know a bit of what they
think. They are college students above all, worried about their love lives, their
grades, and finding jobs. Some support moderate Democrats; some support
moderate Republicans. Like their classmates, most support nuclear freeze,
ERA, and an end to the draft. I believe they are divided on abortion and bus-
ing. They are not particularly political. They read *Christianity Today* and
Campus Life and *Eternity*—moderate, sensible magazines, I think; they read a
lot of C. S. Lewis. (One such student, who seemed perfectly tolerant of me and
my shoddy Christianity, introduced me to C. S. Lewis's critical book on
Charles Williams.) They read the Bible. I think they all "believe in" organic
evolution. The main thing about them is this: There isn't any "them." Their
views vary. They don't know each other.

Their common Christianity puts them, if anywhere, to the left of their class-   15
mates. I believe they also tend to be more able than their classmates to think
well in the abstract, and also to recognize the complexity of moral issues. But
I may be wrong.

In 1980, the media were certainly wrong about television evangelists. Printed
estimates of Jerry Falwell's television audience ranged from 18 million to 30
million people. In fact, according to Arbitron's actual counts, fewer than 1.5
million people were watching Falwell. And, according to an Emory University
study, those who did watch television evangelists didn't necessarily vote with
them. Emory University sociologist G. Melton Mobley reports, "When that
message turns political, they cut it off." Analysis of the 1982 off-year election
turned up no Fundamentalist bloc voting. The media were wrong, but no one
printed retractions.

The media were wrong, too, in a tendency to identify all fundamentalist
Christians with Falwell and his ilk, and to attribute to them, across the board,
conservative views.

Someone has sent me two recent issues of *Eternity: The Evangelical Monthly*. One lead article criticizes a television preacher for saying that the United States had never used military might to take land from another nation. The same article censures Newspeak, saying that government rhetoric would have us believe in a "clean bomb," would have us believe that we "defend" America by invading foreign soil, and would have us believe that the dictatorships we support are "democracies." "When the President of the United States says that one reason to support defense spending is because it creates jobs," this lead article says, "a little bit of 1984 begins to surface." Another article criticizes a "heavy-handed" opinion of Jerry Falwell Ministries—in this case a broadside attack on artificial insemination, surrogate motherhood, and lesbian motherhood. Browsing through *Eternity*, I find a double crosstic. I find an intelligent, analytical, and enthusiastic review of the new London Philharmonic recording of Mahler's second symphony—a review which stresses the "glorious truth" of the Jewish composer's magnificent work, and cites its recent performance in Jerusalem to celebrate the recapture of the Western Wall following the Six Day War. Surely, the evangelical Christians who read this magazine are not bookburners. If by chance they vote with the magazine's editors, then it looks to me as if they vote with the American Civil Liberties Union and Americans for Democratic Action.

Every few years some bold and sincere Christian student at this university disagrees with a professor in class—usually about the professor's out-of-hand dismissal of Christianity. Members of the faculty, outraged, repeat the stories of these rare and uneven encounters for years on end, as if to prove that the crazies are everywhere, and gaining ground. The notion is, apparently, that these kids can't think for themselves. Or they wouldn't disagree.

Now again the mustached leader asks us to move up. There is no harangue, 20 so we move up. (This will be a theme all spring. The leaders want us closer together. Our instinct is to stand alone.) From behind the tall fountain comes a wind; on several gusts we get sprayed. No one seems to notice.

We have time for one more song. The leader, perhaps sensing that no one likes him, blunders on, "I want you to pray this one through," he says. "We have a lot of people here from a lot of different fellowships, but we're all one body. Amen?" They don't like it. He gets a few polite Amens. We sing:

> Bind us together, Lord,
> With a bond that can't be broken;
> Bind us together, Lord,
> With love.

Everyone seems to be in a remarkably foul mood today. We don't like this song. There is no one here under seventeen, and, I think, no one here who believes that love is a bond that can't be broken. We sing the song through three times; then it is time to go.

The leader calls after our retreating backs, "Hey, have a good day! Praise Him all day!" The kids around me roll up their eyes privately. Some groan; all flee.

The next morning is very cold. I am here early. Two girls are talking on the fountain's rim; one is part Italian. She says, "I've got the Old Testament, but I can't get the New. I screw up the New." She takes a breath and rattles off a long list, ending with "Jonah, Micah, Nahum, Habakkuk, Zephaniah, Haggai, Zechariah, Malachi." The other girl produces a slow, sarcastic applause. I ask one of the girls to help me with the words to a song. She is agreeable, but says, "I'm sorry, I can't. I just became a Christian this year, so I don't know all the words yet."

The others are coming; we stand and separate. The boy with the mustache   25 is gone, replaced by a big, serious fellow in a green down jacket. The bouncy girl is back with her guitar; she is wearing a skirt and wool knee socks. We begin without any preamble, by singing a song that has so few words that we actually stretch one syllable over eleven separate notes. Then we sing a song in which the men sing one phrase and the women echo it. Everyone seems to know just what to do. In the context of our vapid songs, the lyrics of this one are extraordinary:

> I was nothing before you found me.
> Heartache! Broken people! Ruined lives
> Is why you died on Calvary.

The last line rises in a regular series of half-notes. Now at last some people are actually singing; they throw some breath into the business. There is a seriousness and urgency to it: "Heartache! Broken people! Ruined lives . . . I was nothing."

We don't look like nothing. We look like a bunch of students of every stripe, ill-shaven or well-shaven, dressed up or down, but dressed warmly against the cold: jeans and parkas, jeans and heavy sweaters, jeans and scarves and blow-dried hair. We look ordinary. But I think, quite on my own, that we are here because we know this business of nothingness, brokenness, and ruination. We sing this song over and over.

Something catches my eye. Behind us, up in the science building, professors are standing alone at opened windows.

The long brick science building has three upper floors of faculty offices, thirty-two windows. At one window stands a bearded man, about forty; his opening his window is what caught my eye. He stands full in the open window, his hands on his hips, his head cocked down toward the fountain. He is drawn to look, as I was drawn to come. Up on the building's top floor, at the far right window, there is another: An Asian-American professor, wearing a white shirt, is sitting with one hip on his desk, looking out and down. In the middle of the row of windows, another one, an old professor in a checked shirt, stands sideways to the open window, stands stock-still, his long, old ear to the air. Now another window cranks open, another professor—or maybe a graduate student—leans out, his hands on the sill.

We are all singing, and I am watching these five still men, my colleagues, whose office doors are surely shut—for that is the custom here: five of them alone in their office in the science building who have opened their windows on this very cold morning, who motionless hear the Fundamentalists sing, utterly unknown to each other.

We sing another four songs, including the clapping song, and one which repeats, "This is the day which the Lord hath made; rejoice and be glad in it." All the professors but one stay by their open windows, figures in a frieze. When after ten minutes we break off and scatter, each cranks his window shut. Maybe they have nine o'clock classes too.

I miss a few sessions. One morning of the following week, I rejoin the Fundamentalists on the Square. The wind is blowing from the north; it is sunny and cold. There are several new developments.

Someone has blown up rubber gloves and floated them in the fountain. I saw them yesterday afternoon from my high office window, and couldn't quite make them out: I seemed to see hands in the fountain waving from side to side, like those hands wagging on springs which people stick in the back windows of their cars. I saw these many years ago in Quito and Guayaquil, where they were a great fad long before they showed up here. The cardboard hands said, on their palms, HOLA GENTE, hello people. Some of them just said HOLA, hello, with a little wave to the universe at large, in case anybody happened to be looking. It is like sending radio signals to planets in other galaxies: HOLA, if anyone is listening. Jolly folk, these Ecuadorians, I thought.

Now, waiting by the fountain for the singing, I see that these particular hands are long surgical gloves, yellow and white, ten of them tied off at the cuff. They floated upright and they wave, *hola, hola hola;* they mill around like a crowd, bobbing under the fountain's spray and back again to the pool's rim, *hola.* It is a good prank. It is far too cold for the university's maintenance crew to retrieve them without turning off the fountain and putting on rubber boots.

From all around the Square, people are gathering for the singing. There is no way I can guess which kids, from among the masses crossing the Square, will veer off to the fountain. When they get here, I never recognize anybody except the leaders.

The singing begins without ado as usual, but there is something different about it. The students are growing prayerful, and they show it this morning with a peculiar gesture. I'm glad they weren't like this when I first joined them, or I never would have stayed.

Last night there was an educational television special, part of "Middletown." It was a segment called "Community of Praise," and I watched it because it was about Fundamentalists. It showed a Jesus-loving family in the Midwest; the treatment was good and complex. This family attended the prayer meetings, healing sessions, and church services of an unnamed sect—a very low-church sect, whose doctrine and culture were much more low-church than those of the kids I sing with. When the members of this sect prayed, they held their arms over their heads and raised their palms, as if to feel or receive a blessing or energy from above.

Now today on the Square there is a new serious mood. The leaders are singing with their eyes shut. I am impressed that they can bang their guitars, keep their balance, and not fall into the pool. It is the same bouncy girl and earnest boy. Their eyeballs are rolled back a bit. I look around and see that almost everyone in this crowd of eighty or so has his eyes shut and is apparently praying the words of this song or praying some other prayer.

Now as the chorus rises, as it gets louder and higher and simpler in melody—

> I exalt thee,
> I exalt thee,
> I exalt thee,
> Thou art the Lord—

then, at this moment, hands start rising. All around me, hands are going up— that tall girl, that blond boy with his head back, the red-headed boy up front, the girl with the MacDonald's jacket. Their arms rise as if pulled on strings. Some few of them have raised their arms very high over their heads and are tilting back their palms. Many, many more of them, as inconspicuously as possible, have raised their hands to the level of their chins.

What is going on? Why are these students today raising their palms in this gesture, when nobody did it last week? Is it because the leaders have set a prayerful tone this morning? Is it because this gesture always accompanies this song, just as clapping, accompanies other songs? Or is it, as I suspect, that these kids watched the widely publicized documentary last night just as I did, and are adopting, or trying out, the gesture?

It is a sunny morning, and the sun is rising behind the leaders and the fountain, so those students have their heads tilted, eyes closed, and palms upraised toward the sun. I glance up at the science building and think my own prayer: Thank God no one is watching this.

The leaders cannot move around much on the fountain's rim. The girl has her eyes shut; the boy opens his eyes from time to time, glances at the neck of his guitar, and closes his eyes again.

When the song is over, the hands go down, and there is some desultory chatting in the crowd, as usual: Can I borrow your library card? And, as usual nobody looks at anybody.

All our songs today are serious. There is a feudal theme to them, or a feudal analogue:

> I will eat from abundance of your household.
> I will dream beside your streams of righteousness.
>
> You are my king.
>
> Enter his gates
> with thanksgiving in your heart;
> come before his courts with praise.
> He is the king of kings.
>
> Thou art the Lord.

All around me, eyes are closed and hands are raised. There is no social pressure to do this, or anything else. I've never known any group to be less cohesive, imposing fewer controls. Since no one looks at anyone, and since passersby no longer look, everyone out here is inconspicuous and free. Perhaps the palm-raising has begun because the kids realize by now that they are not on display; they're praying in their closets, right out here on the Square. Over the course of the next weeks, I will learn that the palm-raising is here to stay.

The sun is rising higher. We are singing our last song. We are praying. We are alone together.

> He is my peace
> Who has broken down every wall . . .

When the song is over, the hands go down. The heads lower, the eyes open and blink. We stay still a second before we break up. We have been standing in a broad current; now we have stepped aside. We have dismantled the radar cups; we have closed the telescope's vault. Students gather their book bags and go. The two leaders step down from the fountain's rim and pack away their guitars. Everyone scatters. I am in no hurry, so I stay after everyone is gone. It is after nine o'clock, and the Square is deserted. The fountain is playing to an empty house. In the pool the cheerful hands are waving over the water, bobbing under the fountain's veil and out again in the current, *hola*.

ANALYZING What the Writer Says

1. What stereotypes about Fundamentalists run through Annie Dillard's mind as she listens to the students sing? What makes her leave her office to join them?

2. What does Dillard notice about their group dynamics on her first day of singing with them? What does she mean when she says, "There isn't any 'them'"?

3. How have the media and popular opinion characterized Fundamentalist Christians? What examples does she give us?

4. What is Dillard's thesis? What does she want her audience to learn about Fundamentalists?

ANALYZING How the Writer Says It

1. Dillard's essay is divided into different sections. Each section presents a part of her insight. What partial insights does she present in each section? To what overall conclusion does she come?

2. What effect does Dillard achieve by alternating between personal narrative (her singing with the students) and analytical reflection about fundamentalist Christians?

3. How does the detail about the hands floating in the fountain tie in with the conclusions she reaches about the significance of her and the students' singing? What is the significance of the greeting "hola" she attributes to these hands? (Note that she ends the essay with it.)

ANALYZING the Issue

1. What did you learn from the essay about fundamentalist Christians? Did it change some of your assumptions?

2. Do you agree with Dillard's implied suggestion that to understand a group of people (and maybe to enhance one's tolerance for different ways of doing things), one should participate in some of their activities? In what ways is this sound advice? In what ways could this be dangerous?

ANALYZING Connections Between Texts

1. In "Playing the Dozens" (p. 527), John Tierney describes the ritual exchange of insults as a linguistic game played by African-American teenagers. Their participation in this "black tradition" marks them as a cultural group, a group whose linguistic games have attracted the attention of scholars. A scholar herself,

Annie Dillard confronts a religious group in her essay. What does she discover about the Fundamentalists and their group-forming routines as she joins their daily singing ritual for a few weeks?

2. In "Bordering on Panic" (p. 555), Adnan R. Khan describes the humiliation he and other Muslims were subjected to in the wake of the September 11 terrorist attacks. Can we read Annie Dillard's essay as a lesson about overcoming stereotypes? Explain. Does her message apply to the current political situation? Why or why not?

3. Compare both stereotypes of Fundamentalists as well as the conclusions Dillard draws about fundamentalist Christians to Dana Fineman's characterization of "Andy" Anderson, an anti-abortion activist (p. 535).

WARMING UP: *How do you feel about the way television has covered the aftermath of the attack on the World Trade Center?*

Audible Silence

BY LEWIS H. LAPHAM

> The limits of my language are the limits of my world.
> —*Ludwig Wittgenstein*

LEWIS H. LAPHAM

In ceremonies commemorating the September 11 attack on the World Trade Center, Lewis Lapham, editor of Harper's Magazine, *sees the transformation of public discourse from a democratic dialogue to a media spectacle in which truthful language gives way to empty rhetoric and a progression of emotional images. This essay appeared in the November 2002 edition of* Harper's.

On the morning of last September 11's requiem for America's lost innocence, the lead editorial in the New York *Daily News* spoke to the difficulty of the performance ("What can be said that hasn't been said? What can be written that hasn't been written? . . ."), but it wasn't until sometime around noon, while directing a confused bagpiper to the F train for Brooklyn, that I understood why, on what was billed as a day of reflection and remembrance, nobody was likely to say anything worth remembering. It wasn't that the city lacked for citizens capable of both high-end thought and eloquent speech, but so many people were staging so many shows of grief or patriotism that the vast cloud of inchoate emotion drifting through the streets and across the television screens suppressed, with the rhetorical equivalents of tear gas, even the most stubborn attempts to make sense of the festivities. So much was being said or seen that nothing could be heard.

The audible silence conformed with Mayor Michael R. Bloomberg's wish that everybody celebrating his or her status as a victim must be made to "feel comfortable." The city had gone to no small trouble or expense to mount a production comparable to an Academy Awards ceremony or a Super Bowl halftime show, and the municipal authorities had been careful to defend the speakers' platforms against any sudden outbreaks of meaning. The dignitaries invited to approach the microphones at ground zero came with the understanding that they were to say nothing controversial or insensitive, to bring no statements stained with vile political content, to let fall no offhand remarks that might be mistaken for tasteless irony or painful truth. In compliance with the security precautions, they confined their oratory to ritual incantation, reciting selected paragraphs from the Declaration of Independence, reading the names of those who perished in the ruin of the World Trade Center, declaiming the Gettysburg Address.

In place of words the events schedule presented images, multicultural and generic, expressive of anything and everything the spectators chose to see, wish for, or believe—moments of silence interspersed with the tolling of church bells, the Wiping Away Tears ritual performed by a troupe of Native Americans, Yo-Yo Ma playing Ave Maria on the cello, a groundbreaking for the Garden of Healing on Staten Island, numerous exhibits of melancholy photographs and inspirational quilts, the chanting of Buddhist monks cross-promoted with the murmuring of Catholic priests, firehouse chalkboards displayed at the Metropolitan Museum of Art, and the bookstores selling out their inventories of *Chicken Soup for the Soul of America*, a scattering of roses and the trembling of candlelight.

Citizens marooned in the suburbs could turn to a long day's festival of television programming, ninety hours of it as dedicated as Mayor Bloomberg to the proposition that every demographic division of the audience must feel comfortable in the warm baths of market-tested sentiment. Not wishing to be thought vulgar or exploitive, wealthy corporations (among them Coca-Cola, General Motors, and American Airlines) refrained from all forms of advertising between the hours of dawn and dusk; the network and cable broadcasts made such sparing use of "traumatic" or "assaultive" footage that the destruction of the World Trade Center was transported into the realm of delicate and remote metaphor, the damage merely hinted at with brief glimpses of a burning building or a falling man, with fragmentary wisps of smoke and fleeting, sidelong glances at the face of death or pain. Tom Brokaw on the verge of tears listened sympathetically to tales of loss and remembrance; Diane Sawyer dandled an orphan on her knee; a PBS documentary asked "Where was God on September 11?" and answered the question in words suitable for stitching on a throw pillow; from Ellis Island just after sunset, posed against the backdrop of the Statue of Liberty, President Bush called upon God to "see us through" and so preserve America as "the hope of all mankind" and the light that "shines in the darkness."

The day ended in an attitude of prayer, but it was by no means easy to know 5 to whom, or for what, the congregation prayed. So many symbols had been paraded through the streets or displayed in the show windows of the television screen that the significance of the spectacle remained open to interpretation. If a funeral service, who was the deceased—3,000 fellow citizens, a work of triumphalist architecture, or a flag? If an acceptance of paradise lost, was the news good or bad? A rite of passage or the tarot card for vain regret? If an offering of ritual sacrifice, was America the milk-white maiden or the Minotaur? If a tribute to the dark and terrible power of Osama bin Laden, why no prayers to Allah?

During the first months after the disappearance of the twin towers the newspapers burbled with predictions of America rising from its bed of moral and geopolitical stupor, forced to new ways of thinking not only about the world on the far side of the once-protective oceans but also about itself. The titles of the television anniversary programs promised reports of dramatic transformation ("The Day America Changed," "The Day That Changed America," "A New Day Dawning," etc.), but the subsequent footage, whether filmed, live, or digitally enhanced, failed to make good on the hyperbole of the opening montage. The New York skyline didn't look the way it once looked, but the on-air company of talking heads (anchors, learned scholars, distinguished statesmen) held fast to the doctrine of American exceptionalism, and the bland certainty of their belief in the country's innate goodness and invincible power argued for the conclusion that nothing had changed.

Although their assurance was unnerving, it didn't come as a surprise. The sophistication of our communications technology provides us with what Max Frisch recognized as "the knack of so arranging the world so that we don't have to experience it," and the substitution of a sensibility shaped by the electronic media for a sensibility formed by print results, as Marshall McLuhan long ago observed, in a vocabulary that reduces politics to gossip and history to the telling of fairy tales. The accelerated data streams of the omnipresent media carry us backward into a primitive past, eliminating the dimensions of space and time and eroding the presumption of cause and effect. In the lotus-land of the Eternal Now all the world's joy and suffering are always and everywhere present (if not on CNN or *Oprah*, then on the *Sunday Night Movie*, at www.whitehouse.gov, or with a 900 number answering to the name of Dominique). The more efficient and expensive the machinery, the poorer and smaller the meaning; the future comes and goes as quickly as yesterday's headline, before anybody has time to remember what it was supposed to be about, and the news appears as such a familiar montage—the same footage, the same words, the same official spokesmen—that we know that what was said last week will be said again this week, and then next week, and once again six weeks from now. Only the camera angles change, and the solo voices of uncomfortable thought sink into the chorus of a collective and corporate consciousness, which, as McLuhan well knew, doesn't "postulate consciousness of anything in particular."

Blessed with a system of knowledge that grants priority to the comfort of the inward feeling rather than to the strangeness of the observed circumstance or fact, we can listen to the words of the Gettysburg Address in the same way that we listen to elevator music. We don't hear what the words say or mean, but they evoke a pleasing mood, soft and elegiac, into which we can fit a memory of anything that comes easily to mind—the teacher's bright blue dress on the day when we first saw Abraham Lincoln's picture in a fourth-grade history book, leaves scattering across grandmother's porch in an autumn wind, the ice-cream man in the candy-striped coat on the lawn near the Washington Monument.

Who would want it otherwise, and why get off the couch? Here we all are living more or less happily ever after within the virtual reality provided by a news and entertainment media that can reconfigure death as a sales pitch for a weapons budget, an insurance policy, or a face cream. In the climate-controlled atmosphere under the dome of brightly packaged images floating over the stadium of the national consciousness, we can rely on the technical staff to repair any structural damage caused by low-flying aircraft or the weather—to plug the holes, fix the leaks, seal the cracks with quilts and Mozart's Requiem.

Fill up the dome with a sufficient volume of cultural product, and nobody 10
needs to find new words with which to tell a new story. A brave man on a hijacked plane says to his fellow passengers, "Let's roll," and within a matter of months the phrase shows up as a Neil Young song, a best-selling T-shirt, the motto of a president's speech to Congress, a college cheer for a Florida football team. The instant recognition of a familiar pattern stands as a synonym for wisdom (of being in the know, party to the joke), and the striking of a pose serves as a substitute for thought. We need only learn how to recycle last year's avalanche into next year's movie, when to put a new hat on an old play, how and where to shop for the future rather than go to the trouble of making it. To deepen character, add accessories.

Apply the fashion tip to the formulation of a foreign policy or the selling of a war, and we find Andrew Card, the White House chief of staff, saying to a *New York Times* reporter that President Bush chose to deliver his ultimatum to Saddam Hussein at a September meeting in the United Nations because, "from a marketing point of view, you don't introduce new products in August." Or, possibly more to the point, Secretary of Defense Donald Rumsfeld telling his deputy, Paul Wolfowitz, what to say at a press conference: "Here's how you deal with the media. Begin with an illogical premise and proceed perfectly logically to an illogical conclusion."

If the two remarks can be taken as indicative of the epistemology that governs the mechanism of the automatous media—i.e., the thing that sees but doesn't think, that says everything but hears nothing—I can make a kind of sense of the way in which both the print and broadcast press reported President Bush's militant speech to the United Nations on the day after his benign appearance in New York City's festival of mourning. At ground zero he presented himself as a humble man of God, comforting the faithful in their time of trouble, at the United Nations as an impatient and angry general shaking the fist of war at Saddam Hussein. In neither setting did it matter whether he, or anybody else, understood what he was saying. The congregation at ground zero didn't ask for words, and if the summons to a descent on Baghdad proceeded from premises both illogical and false (about Iraq's store of nuclear weapons and its stature as a great power) to an imbecile conclusion (that Iraq transform itself into the state of Connecticut or suffer the penalty of extinction), what difference did it make? The media were interested in mood and gesture, and so, on September 12 as on September 11, they directed their cameras and their questions to the presentation of an image rather than to the substance of an idea. Was the President acting presidential? When he hugged the widow, did he cry; when he threatened not only Saddam Hussein but also the United Nations (telling it to do what it was told to do or perish in the dungeon of irrelevance), did his petulance rise to the level of righteous wrath? Was the good shepherd well enough acquainted with the sorrows of his sheep; could the young Augustus bear the weight of empire? The foreign diplomats seated in the General Assembly didn't need to listen to the translations into Russian, French, or Arabic to know that they were confronted with a zealous true believer prepared to attack a poetic metaphor with a prosaic stick of bombs, but on the last point (the one about the fitting of a purple toga to the figure of the young Augustus), the American correspondents were so sensitive that they didn't follow up the President's speech with questions about the incoherence of his text. An important journalist on one of the important evening talk shows explained the courtesy by saying that the speech was so powerful—so strong and brave and presidential—that nobody wanted to spoil the effect by asking what it meant.

No law of nature holds that a society must come forward with works of the political or moral imagination. Through long periods of time the world has gotten along very well indeed without statesmen of enduring consequence. The Byzantine empire lasted for nearly 1,000 years, content with its genius for bureaucracy, dress design, church liturgy, and political assassination. But if it is no disgrace for any country at any particular time in its history to rest content among the relics of a lost language and an imaginary past, it is a matter of some interest in a country that possesses the power to poison the earth without possessing either the means or the desire to know itself.

ANALYZING What the Writer Says

1. "So much was being said or seen that nothing could be heard," Lapham says in his description of the services commemorating the September 11 terrorist attack. What does he mean by this statement?

2. What, according to Lapham, is wrong with the images shown on television at this event?

3. Why does "the significance of the spectacle [remain] open to interpretation" at the end of the day?

4. What convinces Lapham that "nothing has changed" a year after the terrorist attacks?

5. What role do the media and our communication technology play in creating the "virtual reality" we live in?

6. What consequences does this "virtual reality" have on political discourse?

ANALYZING How the Writer Says It

1. Lapham chooses a quote from Ludwig Wittgenstein, a German philosopher, as the epigraph for his essay. What is the relationship between the epigraph and Lapham's thesis?

2. Lapham's title—"Audible Silence"—is a paradox, a seeming contradiction. However, when looked at more closely, a paradox reveals an underlying truth about an issue. What is the truth underlying Lapham's paradox? How does the title summarize the essay?

ANALYZING the Issue

1. Do you agree with Lapham that "the virtual reality provided by a news and entertainment media" has succeeded in "arranging the world so that we don't have to experience it"? In other words, have we become speechless consumers, unable to detect and speak up against the political manipulation to which we are subject? Explain your reasons.

2. When the Dixie Chicks, a popular country-rock band, spoke out against the war in Iraq during one of their 2003 concerts, the media showed us enraged fans destroying the group's CDs. How does this event illustrate Lapham's argument?

ANALYZING Connections Between Texts

1. Both Lapham and George Orwell ("Politics and the English Language." p. 487) analyze the nature of political discourse. On what points do the two writers agree?

2. In "Spudding Out" (p. 700), Barbara Ehrenreich examines the impact television has on family life. Granted, Lapham's outlook on the media's influence on political consciousness is much less humorous, but he draws some similar conclusions. What are they?

3. The photograph "German Schoolboys Salute" (p. 401) shows how a totalitarian regime teaches appropriate political behavior even to small children. What do you think Lapham would say about this picture in connection with the current state of our democracy?

WARMING UP: *Have you ever noticed the slippery aspect of some political speech? Have you ever found yourself repeating similarly vague language to support your own positions?*

Politics and the English Language

BY GEORGE ORWELL

GEORGE ORWELL

George Orwell (1903–50), for whom writing was a means of addressing injustice, is best known for his novels Animal Farm *and* 1984. *His classic essay "Politics and the English Language" illustrates an abiding Orwellian truth— the moral-political responsibility of language.*

Most people who bother with the matter at all would admit that the English language is in a bad way, but it is generally assumed that we cannot by conscious action do anything about it. Our civilization is decadent and our language—so the argument runs— must inevitably share in the general collapse. It follows that any struggle against the abuse of language is a sentimental archaism, like preferring candles to electric light or hansom cabs to aeroplanes. Underneath this lies the half-conscious belief that language is a natural growth and not an instrument which we shape for our own purposes.

Now, it is clear that the decline of a language must ultimately have political and economic causes: it is not due simply to the bad influence of this or that individual writer. But an effect can become a cause, reinforcing the original cause and producing the same effect in an intensified form, and so on indefinitely. A man may take to drink because he feels himself to be a failure, and then fail all the more completely because he drinks. It is rather the same thing that is happening to the English language. It becomes ugly and inaccurate because our thoughts are foolish, but the slovenliness of our language makes it easier for us to have foolish thoughts. The point is that the process is reversible. Modern English, especially written English, is full of bad habits which spread by imitation and which can be avoided if one is willing to take the necessary trouble. If one gets rid of these habits one can think more clearly, and to think clearly is a necessary first step towards political regeneration: so that the fight against bad English is not frivolous and is not the exclusive concern of professional writers. I will come back to this presently, and I hope that by that time the meaning of what I have said here will have become clearer. Meanwhile, here are five specimens of the English language as it is now habitually written.

These five passages have not been picked out because they are especially bad—I could have quoted far worse if I had chosen—but because they illustrate various of the mental vices from which we now suffer. They are a little below the average, but are fairly representative samples. I number them so that I can refer to them when necessary:

(1) I am not, indeed, sure whether it is not true to say that the Milton who once seemed not unlike a seventeenth-century Shelley had not become, out of an experience ever more bitter in each year, more alien [*sic*] to the founder of that Jesuit sect which nothing could induce him to tolerate.

Professor Harold Laski (Essay in Freedom of Expression*)*

(2) Above all, we cannot play ducks and drakes with a native battery of idioms which prescribes such egregious collocations of vocables as the Basic *put up with* for *tolerate* or *put at a loss* for *bewilder.*

*Professor Lancelot Hogben (*Interglossa*)*

(3) On the one side we have the free personality: by definition it is not neurotic, for it has neither conflict nor dream. Its desires, such as they are, are transparent, for they are just what institutional approval keeps in the forefront of consciousness; another institutional pattern would alter their number and intensity; there is little in them that is natural, irreducible, or culturally dangerous. But *on the other side*, the social bond itself is nothing but the mutual reflection of these self-secure integrities. Recall the definition of love. Is not this the very picture of a small academic? Where is there a place in this hall of mirrors for either personality or fraternity?

Essay on psychology in Politics *(New York)*

(4) All the "best people" from the gentlemen's clubs, and all the frantic fascist captains, united in common hatred of Socialism and bestial horror of the rising tide of the mass revolutionary movement, have turned to acts of provocation, to foul incendiarism, to medieval legends of poisoned wells, to legalize their own destruction of proletarian organizations, and rouse the agitated petty-bourgeoisie to chauvinistic fervour on behalf of the fight against the revolutionary way out of the crisis.

Communist pamphlet

(5) If a new spirit *is* to be infused into this old country, there is one thorny and contentious reform which must be tackled, and that is the humanization and galvanization of the B.B.C. Timidity here will bespeak cancer and atrophy of the soul. The heart of Britain may be sound and of strong beat, for instance, but the British lion's roar at present is like that of Bottom in Shakespeare's *Midsummer Night's Dream*—as gentle as any sucking dove. A virile new Britain cannot continue indefinitely to be traduced in the eyes or rather ears, of the world by the effete languors of Langham Place, brazenly masquerading as "standard English." When the Voice of Britain is heard at nine o'clock, better far and infinitely less ludicrous to hear aitches honestly dropped than the present priggish, inflated, inhibited, schoolma'amish arch braying of blameless bashful mewing maidens!

Letter in Tribune

Each of these passages has faults of its own, but, quite apart from avoidable ugliness, two qualities are common to all of them. The first is staleness of imagery; the other is lack of precision. The writer either has a meaning and cannot express it, or he inadvertently says something else, or he is almost indifferent as to whether his words mean anything or not. This mixture of vagueness and sheer incompetence is the most marked characteristic of modern English prose, and especially of any kind of political writing. As soon as certain topics are raised, the concrete melts into the abstract and on one seems able to think of turns of speech that are not hackneyed: prose consists less and less of *words* chosen for the sake of their meaning, and more and more of *phrases* tacked together like the sections of a prefabricated henhouse. I list below, with notes and examples, various of the tricks by means of which the work of prose-construction is habitually dodged:

DYING METAPHORS

A newly invented metaphor assists thought by evoking a visual image, while on the other hand a metaphor which is technically "dead" (e.g. *iron resolution*) has in effect reverted to being an ordinary word and can generally be used without loss of vividness. But in between these two classes there is a huge dump of worn-out metaphors which have lost all evocative power and are merely used because they save people the trouble of inventing phrases for themselves. Examples are: *Ring the changes on, take up the cudgels for, toe the line, ride roughshod over, stand shoulder to shoulder with, play into the hands of, no axe to grind, grist to the mill, fishing in troubled waters, on the order of the day, Achilles' heel, swan song, hotbed.* Many of these are used without knowledge of their meaning (what is a "rift," for instance?), and incompatible metaphors are frequently mixed, a sure sign that the writer is not interested in what he is saying. Some metaphors now current have been twisted out of their original meaning without those who use them even being aware of the fact. For example, *toe the line* is sometimes written *tow the line*. Another example is the *hammer and the anvil*, now always used with the implication that the anvil gets the worst of it. In real life it is always the anvil that breaks the hammer, never the other way about: a writer who stopped to think what he was saying would be aware of this, and would avoid perverting the original phrase.

OPERATORS OR VERBAL FALSE LIMBS

These save the trouble of picking out appropriate verbs and nouns, and at the same time pad each sentence with extra syllables which give it an appearance of symmetry. Characteristic phrases are: *render inoperative, militate against, make contact with, be subjected to, give rise to, give grounds for, have the effect of, play a leading part (role) in, make itself felt, take effect, exhibit a tendency to, serve the purpose of, etc., etc.* The keynote is the elimination of simple verbs. Instead of being a single word, such as *break, stop, spoil, mend, kill*, a verb becomes a *phrase*, made up of a noun or adjective tacked on to some general-purposes verb such as *prove, serve, form, play, render*. In addition, the passive voice is wherever possible used in preference to the active, and noun constructions are used instead of gerunds (*by examination of* instead of *by examining*). The range of verbs is further cut down by means of the *-ize* and *de-* formations, and the banal statements are given an appearance of profundity by means of the *not un-* formation. Simple conjunctions and prepositions are replaced by such phrases as *with respect to, having regard to, the fact that, by dint of, in view of, in the interests of, on the hypothesis that;* and the ends of sentences are saved from anticlimax by such resounding commonplaces as *greatly to be desired, cannot be left out of account, a development to be expected in the near future, deserving of serious consideration, brought to a satisfactory conclusion*, and so on and so forth.

PRETENTIOUS DICTION

Words like *phenomenon, element, individual* (as noun), *objective, categorical, effective, virtual, basic, primary, promote, constitute, exhibit, exploit, utilize, eliminate, liquidate*, are used to dress up simple statements and give an air of scientific impartiality to biased judgments. Adjectives like *epoch-making, epic, historic, unforgettable, triumphant, age-old, inevitable, inexorable, veritable*, are used to dignify the sordid processes of international politics, while writing that aims at glorifying war usually takes on an archaic color, its characteristic words being: *realm, throne, chariot, mailed fist, trident, sword, shield, buckler, banner, jackboot, clarion*. Foreign words and expressions such as *cul de sac, ancien régime, deus ex machina, mutatis mutandis, status quo, gleichschaltung, weltanschauung*, are used to give an air of culture and elegance. Except for the useful abbreviations *i.e., e.g.,* and *etc.*, there is no real need for any of the hundreds of foreign phrases now current in English. Bad writers, and especially scientific, political and sociological writers, are nearly always haunted by the notion that Latin or Greek words are grander than Saxon ones, and unnecessary words like *expedite, ameliorate, predict, extraneous, deracinated, clandestine, subaqueous* and hundreds of others constantly gain ground from their Anglo-Saxon opposite numbers.[1] The jargon peculiar to Marxist writing (*hyena, hangman, cannibal, petty bourgeois, these gentry, lacquey, flunkey, mad dog, White Guard,* etc.) consists largely of words and phrases translated from Russian, German or French; but the normal way of coining a new word is to use a Latin or Greek root with the appropriate affix and, where necessary, the *-ize* formation. It is often easier to make up words of this kind (*deregionalize, impermissible, extra-marital, nonfragmentary* and so forth) than to think up the English words that will cover one's meaning. The result, in general, is an increase in slovenliness and vagueness.

MEANINGLESS WORDS

In certain kinds of writing, particularly in art criticism and literary criticism, it is normal to come across long passages which are almost completely lacking in meaning.[2] Words like *romantic, plastic, values, human, dead, sentimental, natural, vitality,* as used in art criticism, are strictly meaningless, in the sense that they not only do not point to any discoverable object, but are hardly ever expected to do so by the reader. When one critic writes, "The outstanding feature of Mr. X's work is its living quality," while another writes, "The immediately striking thing about Mr. X's work is its peculiar deadness," the reader accepts this as a simple difference of opinion. If words like *black* and *white* were involved, instead of the jargon words *dead* and *living,* he would see at once that language was being used in an improper way. Many political words are similarly abused. The word *Fascism* has now no meaning except in so far as it signifies "something not desirable." The words *democracy, socialism, freedom, patriotic, realistic, justice,* have each of them several different meanings which cannot be reconciled with one another. In the case of a word like *democracy,* not only is there no agreed definition, but the attempt to make one is

---

[1] An interesting illustration of this is the way in which the English flower names which were in use till very recently are being ousted by Greek ones, *snapdragon* becoming *antirrhinum, forget-me-not* becoming *myosotis,* etc. It is hard to see any practical reason for this change of fashion: it is probably due to an instinctive turning-away from the more homely word and a vague feeling that the Greek word is scientific [Orwell's note].

[2] Example: "Comfort's catholicity of perception and image, strangely Whitmanesque in range, almost the exact opposite in aesthetic compulsion, continues to evoke that trembling atmospheric accumulative hinting at a cruel, an inexorably serene timelessness. . . . Wrey Gardiner scores by aiming at simple bull's-eyes with precision. Only they are not so simple, and through this contented sadness runs more than the surface bittersweet of resignation" (*Poetry Quarterly*) [Orwell's note].

resisted from all sides. It is almost universally felt that when we call a country democratic we are praising it: consequently the defenders of every kind of régime claim that it is a democracy, and fear that they might have to stop using the word if it were tied down to any one meaning. Words of this kind are often used in a consciously dishonest way. That is, the person who uses them has his own private definition, but allows his hearer to think he means something quite different. Statements like *Marshal Pétain was a true patriot, The Soviet Press is the freest in the world, The Catholic Church is opposed to persecution*, are almost always made with intent to deceive. Other words used in variable meanings, in most cases more or less dishonestly, are: *class, totalitarian, science, progressive, reactionary, bourgeois, equality.*

Now that I have made this catalogue of swindles and perversions, let me give another example of the kind of writing that they lead to. This time it must of its nature be an imaginary one. I am going to translate a passage of good English into modern English of the worst sort. Here is a well-known verse from *Ecclesiastes:*

> I returned and saw under the sun, that the race is not to the swift, nor the battle to the strong, neither yet bread to the wise, nor yet riches to men of understanding, nor yet favour to men of skill; but time and chance happeneth to them all.

Here it is in modern English:

> Objective consideration of contemporary phenomena compels the conclusion that success or failure in competitive activities exhibits no tendency to be commensurate with innate capacity, but that a considerable element of the unpredictable must invariably be taken into account.

This is a parody, but not a very gross one. Exhibit (3), above, for instance, contains several patches of the same kind of English. It will be seen that I have not made a full translation. The beginning and ending of the sentence follow the original meaning fairly closely, but in the middle the concrete illustrations—race, battle, bread—dissolve into the vague phrase "success or failure in competitive activities." This had to be so, because no modern writer of the kind I am discussing—no one capable of using phrases like "objective consideration of contemporary phenomena"—would ever tabulate his thoughts in that precise and detailed way. The whole tendency of modern prose is away from concreteness. Now analyse these two sentences a little more closely. The first contains forty-nine words but only sixty syllables, and all its words are those of everyday life. The second contains thirty-eight words of ninety syllables: eighteen of its words are from Latin roots, and one from Greek. The first sentence contains six vivid images, and only one phrase ("time and chance") that could be called vague. The second contains not a single fresh, arresting phrase, and in spite of its ninety syllables it gives only a shortened version of the meaning contained in the first. Yet without a doubt it is the second kind of sentence that is gaining ground in modern English. I do not want to exaggerate. This kind of writing is not yet universal, and outcrops of simplicity will occur here and there in the worst-written page. Still, if you or I were told to write a few lines on the uncertainty of human fortunes, we should probably come much nearer to my imaginary sentence than to the one from *Ecclesiastes*.

As I have tried to show, modern writing at its worst does not consist in picking out words for the sake of their meaning and inventing images in order to make the meaning clearer. It consists in gumming together long strips of words which have already been set in order by someone else, and making the results presentable by sheer humbug. The attraction of this way of writing is that it is easy. It is easier—even quicker, once you have the habit—to say *In my opinion it is not an unjustifiable assumption that* than to say *I think*. If you use ready-made phrases, you not only don't have to hunt about for words; you also don't have to bother with the rhythms of your sentences, since these phrases are generally so arranged as to be more or less euphonious. When you are composing in a hurry—when you are dictating to a stenographer, for instance, or making a public speech—it is natural to fall into a pretentious, Latinized style. Tags like *a consideration which we should do well to bear in mind* or *a conclusion to which all of us would readily assent* will save many a sentence from coming down with a bump. By using stale metaphors, similes and idioms, you save much mental effort, at the cost of leaving your meaning vague, not only for your reader but for yourself. This is the significance of mixed metaphors. The sole aim of a metaphor is to call up a visual image. When these images clash—as in *The Fascist octopus has sung its swan song, the jackboot is thrown into the melting pot*—it can be taken as certain that the writer is not seeing a mental image of the objects he is naming; in other words he is not really thinking. Look again at the examples I gave at the beginning of this essay. Professor Laski (1) uses five negatives in fifty-three words. One of these is superfluous, making nonsense of the whole passage, and in addition there is the slip *alien* for *akin*, making further nonsense, and several avoidable pieces of clumsiness which increase the general vagueness. Professor Hogben (2) plays ducks and drakes with a battery which is able to write prescriptions, and, while disapproving of the everyday phrase *put up with*, is unwilling to look *egregious* up in the dictionary and see what it means. (3), if one takes an uncharitable attitude towards it, is simply meaningless: probably one could work out its intended meaning by reading the whole of the article in which it occurs. In (4), the writer knows more or less what he wants to say, but an accumulation of stale phrases chokes him like tea leaves blocking a sink. In (5), words and meaning have almost parted company. People who write in this manner usually have a general emotional meaning—they dislike one thing and want to express solidarity with another—but they are not interested in the detail of what they are saying. A scrupulous writer, in every sentence that he writes, will ask himself at least four questions, thus: What am I trying to say? What words will express it? What image or idiom will make it clear? Is this image fresh enough to have an effect? And he will probably ask himself two more: Could I put it more shortly? Have I said anything that is avoidably ugly? But you are not obliged to go to all this trouble. You can shirk it by simply throwing your mind open and letting the ready-made phrases come crowding in. They will construct your sentences for you—even think your thoughts for you, to a certain extent—and at need they will perform the important service of partially concealing your meaning even from yourself. It is at this point that the special connection between politics and the debasement of language becomes clear.

In our time it is broadly true that political writing is bad writing. Where it is not true, it will generally be found that the writer is some kind of rebel, expressing his private opinions and not a "party line." Orthodoxy, of whatever colour, seems to demand a lifeless, imitative style. The political dialects to be found in pamphlets, leading articles, manifestos, White Papers and the speeches of under-secretaries do, of course, vary from party to party, but they are all alike in that one almost never finds in them a fresh, vivid, home-made turn of speech. When one watches some tired hack on the platform mechanically repeating the familiar phrases—*bestial atrocities, iron heel, bloodstained tyranny, free peoples of the world, stand shoulder to shoulder*—one often has a curious feeling that one is not watching a live human being but some kind of dummy: a feeling which suddenly becomes stronger at moments when the light catches the speaker's spectacles and turns them into blank discs which seem to have no eyes behind them. And this is not altogether fanciful. A speaker who uses that kind of phraseology has gone some distance towards turning himself into a machine. The appropriate noises are coming out of his larynx, but his brain is not involved as it would be if he were choosing his words for himself. If the speech he is making is one that he is accustomed to make over and over again, he may be almost unconscious of what he is saying, as one is when one utters the responses in church. And this reduced state of consciousness, if not indispensable, is at any rate favourable to political conformity.

In our time, political speech and writing are largely the defence of the indefensible. Things like the continuance of British rule in India, the Russian purges and deportations, the dropping of the atom bombs on Japan, can indeed be defended, but only by arguments which are too brutal for most people to face, and which do not square with the professed aims of political parties. Thus political language has to consist largely of euphemism, question-begging and sheer cloudy vagueness. Defenceless villages are bombarded from the air, the inhabitants driven out into the countryside, the cattle machine-gunned, the huts set on fire with incendiary bullets: this is called *pacification.* Millions of peasants are robbed of their farms and sent trudging along the roads with no more than they can carry: this is called *transfer of population* or *rectification of frontiers.* People are imprisoned for years without trial, or shot in the back of the neck or sent to die of scurvy in Arctic lumber camps: this is called *elimination of unreliable elements.* Such phraseology is needed if one wants to name things without calling up mental pictures of them. Consider for instance some comfortable English professor defending Russian totalitarianism. He cannot say outright, "I believe in killing off your opponents when you can get good results by doing so." Probably, therefore, he will say something like this:

"While freely conceding that the Soviet régime exhibits certain features which the humanitarian may be inclined to deplore, we must, I think, agree that a certain curtailment of the right to political opposition is an unavoidable concomitant of transitional periods, and that the rigors which the Russian people have been called upon to undergo have been amply justified in the sphere of concrete achievement."

The inflated style is itself a kind of euphemism. A mass of Latin words falls upon the facts like soft snow, blurring the outlines and covering up all the details. The great enemy of clear language is insincerity. When there is a gap between one's real and one's declared aims, one turns as it were instinctively to long words and exhausted idioms, like a cuttlefish squirting out ink. In our age there is no such thing as "keeping out of politics." All issues are political issues, and politics itself is a mass of lies, evasions, folly, hatred and schizophrenia. When the general atmosphere is bad, language must suffer. I should expect to find—this is a guess which I have not sufficient knowledge to verify—that the German, Russian and Italian languages have all deteriorated in the last ten or fifteen years, as a result of dictatorship.

But if thought corrupts language, language can also corrupt thought. A bad usage can spread by tradition and imitation, even among people who should and do know better. The debased language that I have been discussing is in some ways very convenient. Phrases like *a not unjustifiable assumption, leaves much to be desired, would serve no good purpose, a consideration which we should do well to bear in mind,* are a continuous temptation, a packet of aspirins always at one's elbow. Look back through this essay, and for certain you will find that I have again and again committed the very faults I am protesting against. By this morning's post I have received a pamphlet dealing with conditions in Germany. The author tells me that he "felt impelled" to write it. I open it at random, and here is almost the first sentence that I see: "[The Allies] have an opportunity not only of achieving a radical transformation of Germany's social and political structure in such a way as to avoid a nationalistic reaction in Germany itself, but at the same time of laying the foundations of a co-operative and unified Europe." You see, he "feels impelled" to write—feels, presumably, that he has something new to say—and yet his words, like cavalry horses answering the bugle, group themselves automatically into the familiar dreary pattern. This invasion of one's mind by ready-made phrases (*lay the foundations, achieve a radical transformation*) can only be prevented if one is constantly on guard against them, and every such phrase anaesthetizes a portion of one's brain.

I said earlier that the decadence of our language is probably curable. Those who deny this would argue, if they produced an argument at all, that language merely reflects existing social conditions, and that we cannot influence its development by any direct tinkering with words and constructions. So far as the general tone or spirit of a language goes, this may be true, but it is not true in detail. Silly words and expressions have often disappeared, not through any evolutionary process but owing to the conscious action of a minority. Two recent examples were *explore every avenue* and *leave no stone unturned*, which were killed by the jeers of a few journalists. There is a long list of fly-blown metaphors which could similarly be got rid of if enough people would interest themselves in the job; and it should also be possible to laugh the *not un-* formation out of existence,[3] to re-duce the amount of Latin and Greek in the average sentence, to drive out foreign phrases and strayed scientific words, and, in general, to make pretentiousness unfashionable. But all these are minor points. The defence of the English language implies more than this, and perhaps it is best to start by saying what it does *not* imply.

To begin with, it has nothing to do with archaism, with the salvaging of obsolete words and turns of speech, or with the setting up of a "standard English" which must never be departed from. On the contrary, it is especially concerned with the scrapping of every word or idiom which has outworn its usefulness. It has nothing to do with correct grammar and syntax, which are of no importance so long as one makes one's meaning clear, or with the avoidance of Americanisms, or with having what is called a "good prose style." On the other hand it is not concerned with fake simplicity and the attempt to make written English colloquial. Nor does it even imply in every case preferring the Saxon word to the Latin one, though it does imply using the fewest and shortest words that will cover one's meaning. What is above all needed is to let the meaning choose the word, and not the other way about. In prose, the worst thing one can do with words is to surrender to them. When you think of a concrete object, you think wordlessly, and then, if you want to describe the thing you have been visualizing you probably hunt about till you find the exact words that seem to fit. When you think of something abstract you are more inclined to use words from the start, and unless you make a conscious effort to prevent it, the existing dialect will come rushing in and do the job for you, at the expense of blurring or even changing your meaning. Probably it is better to put off using words as

---

[3]One can cure oneself of the *not un-* formation by memorizing this sentence: *A not unblack dog was chasing a not unsmall rabbit across a not ungreen field* [Orwell's note].

long as possible and get one's meaning as clear as one can through pictures or sensations. Afterwards one can choose—not simply *accept*—the phrases that will best cover the meaning, and then switch round and decide what impression one's words are likely to make on another person. This last effort of the mind cuts out all stale or mixed images, all prefabricated phrases, needless repetitions, and humbug and vagueness generally. But one can often be in doubt about the effect of a word or a phrase, and one needs rules that one can rely on when instinct fails. I think the following rules will cover most cases:

(i) Never use a metaphor, simile, or other figure of speech which you are used to seeing in print.

(ii) Never use a long word where a short one will do.

(iii) If it is possible to cut a word out, always cut it out.

(iv) Never use the passive where you can use the active.

(v) Never use a foreign phrase, a scientific word or a jargon word if you can think of an everyday English equivalent.

(vi) Break any of these rules sooner than say anything outright barbarous.

These rules sound elementary, and so they are, but they demand a deep change of attitude in anyone who has grown used to writing in the style now fashionable. One could keep all of them and still write bad English, but one could not write the kind of stuff that I quoted in those five specimens at the beginning of this article.

I have not here been considering the literary use of language, but merely language as an instrument for expressing and not for concealing or preventing thought. Stuart Chase and others have come near to claiming that all abstract words are meaningless, and have used this as a pretext for advocating a kind of political quietism. Since you don't know what Fascism is, how can you struggle against Fascism? One need not swallow such absurdities as this, but one ought to recognize that the present political chaos is connected with the decay of language, and that one can probably bring about some improvement by starting at the verbal end. If you simplify your English, you are freed from the worst follies of orthodoxy. You cannot speak any of the necessary dialects, and when you make a stupid remark its stupidity will be obvious, even to yourself. Political language—and with variations this is true of all political parties, from Conservatives to Anarchists—is designed to make lies sound truthful and murder respectable, and to give an appearance of solidity to pure wind. One cannot change this all in a moment, but one can at least change one's own habits, and from time to time one can even, if one jeers loudly enough, send some worn-out and useless phrase—some *jackboot, Achilles' heel, hotbed, melting pot, acid test, veritable inferno* or other lump of verbal refuse—into the dustbin where it belongs.

ANALYZING What the Writer Says

1. Orwell establishes the purpose of his argument early in the essay. What is it?

2. Are Orwell's examples still relevant? Why or why not?

3. Orwell makes two essential points to complete his argument: In the first he supports using illustrations; in the second, reasoning. Point to a single sentence from different parts of the essay to summarize each point.

4. Why does Orwell briefly distinguish between political language and literary language at the end of his essay?

ANALYZING How the Writer Says It

1. Early in the essay, Orwell states that the passages he uses to illustrate typical language usage "have not been picked out because they are especially bad—[he] could have quoted far worse. . . ." What do you think the intended effect of this assertion is?

2. At several points Orwell uses long lists of examples to support his points. Is the number of examples per point necessary? Effective? Explain.

ANALYZING the Issue

1. Orwell's essay was originally published in 1946. Are his points relevant today? In what way? Can you cite recent examples of "political language" of the sort Orwell describes?

2. Apply Orwell's logic to the patriotic language of ordinary citizens.

3. Do you agree that debased political speech poses a real threat? Why or why not?

ANALYZING Connections Between Texts

1. How is Lewis H. Lapham's "Audible Silence" (p. 481) a variation on Orwell's theme?

2. Read Molly Ivins's "How 1984 and 2002 Add Up to Trouble" (p. 547). How do Ivins's concerns echo concerns Orwell raises?

3. Look at the WWII-era poster "He's Watching You" (p. 110). How does this poster illustrate some of Orwell's points, in both visual and linguistic terms?

WARMING UP: *In your own words, define "prejudice." How does prejudice make victims of people?*

In Defense of Prejudice

BY JONATHAN RAUCH

JONATHAN RAUCH

A long-time journalist and author of several books, Jonathan Rauch defends "intellectual pluralism" against what he calls "purism," the idea that "society cannot be just until the last traces of invidious prejudice have been scrubbed away." His essay first appeared in Harper's Magazine *in May 1995.*

The war on prejudice is now, in all likelihood, the most uncontroversial social movement in America. Opposition to "hate speech," formerly identified with the liberal left, has become a bipartisan piety. In the past year, groups and factions that agree on nothing else have agreed that the public expression of any and all prejudices must be forbidden. On the left, protesters and editorialists have insisted that Francis L. Lawrence resign as president of Rutgers University for describing blacks as "a disadvantaged population that doesn't have that genetic, hereditary background to have a higher average." On the other side of the ideological divide, Ralph Reed, the executive director of the Christian Coalition, responded to criticism of the religious right by calling a press conference to denounce a supposed outbreak of "name-calling, scapegoating, and religious bigotry." Craig Rogers, an evangelical Christian student at California State University, recently filed a $2.5 million sexual-harassment suit against a lesbian professor of psychology, claiming that anti-male bias in one of her lectures violated campus rules and left him feeling "raped and trapped."

In universities and on Capitol Hill, in workplaces and newsrooms, authorities are declaring that there is no place for racism, sexism, homophobia, Christian-bashing, and other forms of prejudice in public debate or even in private thought. "Only when racism and other forms of prejudice are expunged," say the crusaders for sweetness and light, "can minorities be safe and society be fair." So sweet, this dream of a world without prejudice. But the very last thing society should do is seek to utterly eradicate racism and other forms of prejudice.

I suppose I should say, in the customary I-hope-I-don't-sound-too-defensive tone, that I am not a racist and that this is not an article favoring racism or any other particular prejudice. It is an article favoring intellectual pluralism, which permits the expression of various forms of bigotry and always will. Although we like to hope that a time will come when no one will believe that people come in types and that each type belongs with its own kind, I doubt such a day will ever arrive. By all indications, *Homo sapiens* is a tribal species for whom "us versus them" comes naturally and must be continually pushed back. Where there is genuine freedom of expression, there will be racist expression. There will also be people who believe that homosexuals are sick or threaten children or—especially among teenagers—are rightful targets of manly savagery. Homosexuality will always be incomprehensible to most people, and what is incomprehensible is feared. As for anti-Semitism, it appears to be a hardier virus than influenza. If you want pluralism, then you get racism and sexism and homophobia, and communism and fascism and xenophobia and tribalism, and that is just for a start. If you want to believe in intellectual freedom and the progress of knowledge and the advancement of science and all those other good things, then you must swallow hard and accept this: for as thickheaded and wayward an animal as us, the realistic question is how to make the best of prejudice, not how to eradicate it.

Indeed, "eradicating prejudice" is so vague a proposition as to be meaningless. Distinguishing prejudice reliably and nonpolitically from nonprejudice, or even defining it crisply, is quite hopeless. We all feel we know prejudice when we see it. But do we? At the University of Michigan, a student said in a classroom discussion that he considered homosexuality a disease treatable with therapy. He was summoned to a formal disciplinary hearing for violating the school's policy against speech that "victimizes" people based on "sexual orientation." Now, the evidence is abundant that this particular hypothesis is wrong, and any American homosexual can attest to the harm that the student's hypothesis has inflicted on many real people. But was it a statement of prejudice or of misguided belief? Hate speech or hypothesis? Many Americans who do not regard themselves as bigots or haters believe that homosexuality is a treatable disease. They may be wrong, but are they all bigots? I am unwilling to say so, and if you are willing, beware. The line between a prejudiced belief and a merely controversial one is elusive, and the harder you look the more elusive it becomes. "God hates homosexuals" is a statement of fact, not of bias, to those who believe it; "American criminals are disproportionately black" is a statement of bias, not of fact, to those who disbelieve it.

Who is right? You may decide, and so may others, and there is no need to   5
agree. That is the great innovation of intellectual pluralism (which is to say, of
post-Enlightenment science, broadly defined). We cannot know in advance or
for sure which belief is prejudice and which is truth, but to advance knowledge
we don't need to know. The genius of intellectual pluralism lies not in doing
away with prejudices and dogmas but in channeling them—making them
socially productive by pitting prejudice against prejudice and dogma against
dogma, exposing all to withering public criticism. What survives at the end of
the day is our base of knowledge.

What they told us in high school about this process is very largely a lie. The
Enlightenment tradition taught us that science is orderly, antiseptic, rational,
the province of detached experimenters and high-minded logicians. In the popular view, science stands for reason against prejudice, openmindedness against
dogma, calm consideration against passionate attachment—all personified by
pop-science icons like the magisterially deductive Sherlock Holmes, the coolly
analytic Mr. Spock, the genially authoritative Mr. Science (from our junior-high
science films). Yet one of science's dirty secrets is that although science as a
whole is as unbiased as anything human can be, scientists are just as biased as
anyone else, sometimes more so. "One of the strengths of science," writes the
philosopher of science David L. Hull, "is that it does not require that scientists
be unbiased, only that different scientists have different biases." Another dirty
secret is that, no less than the rest of us, scientists can be dogmatic and pigheaded. "Although this pigheadedness often damages the careers of individual
scientists," says Hull, "it is beneficial for the manifest goal of science," which
relies on people to invest years in their ideas and defend them passionately.
And the dirtiest secret of all, if you believe in the antiseptic popular view of science, is that this most ostensibly rational of enterprises depends on the most
irrational of motives—ambition, narcissism, animus, even revenge. "Scientists
acknowledge that among their motivations are natural curiosity, the love of
truth, and the desire to help humanity, but other inducements exist as well, and
one of them is to 'get that son of a bitch,'" says Hull. "Time and again, scientists whom I interviewed described the powerful spur that 'showing that son of
a bitch' supplied to their own research."
Many people, I think, are bewildered by this unvarnished and all too human
view of science. They believe that for a system to be unprejudiced, the people
in it must also be unprejudiced. In fact, the opposite is true. Far from eradicating ugly or stupid ideas and coarse or unpleasant motives, intellectual pluralism relies upon them to excite intellectual passion and redouble scientific
effort. I know of no modern idea more ugly and stupid than that the Holocaust
never happened, nor any idea more viciously motivated. Yet the deniers'
claims that the Auschwitz gas chambers could not have worked led to closer

study and, in 1993, research showing, at last, how they actually did work. Thanks to prejudice and stupidity, another opening for doubt has been shut.

An enlightened and efficient intellectual regime lets a million prejudices bloom, including many that you or I may regard as hateful or grotesque. It avoids any attempt to stamp out prejudice, because stamping out prejudice really means forcing everyone to share the same prejudice, namely that of whoever is in authority. The great American philosopher Charles Sanders Peirce wrote in 1877: "When complete agreement could not otherwise be reached, a general massacre of all who have not thought in a certain way has proved a very effective means of settling opinion in a country." In speaking of "settling opinion," Peirce was writing about one of the two or three most fundamental problems that any human society must confront and solve. For most societies down through the centuries, this problem was dealt with in the manner he described: errors were identified by the authorities—priests, politburos, dictators—or by mass opinion, and then the error-makers were eliminated along with their putative mistakes. "Let all men who reject the established belief be terrified into silence," wrote Peirce, describing this system. "This method has, from the earliest times, been one of the chief means of upholding correct theological and political doctrines."

Intellectual pluralism substitutes a radically different doctrine: we kill our mistakes rather than each other. Here I draw on another great philosopher, the late Karl Popper, who pointed out that the critical method of science "consists in letting our hypotheses die in our stead." Those who are in error are not (or are not supposed to be) banished or excommunicated or forced to sign a renunciation or required to submit to "rehabilitation" or sent for psychological counseling. It is the error we punish, not the errant. By letting people make errors—even mischievous, spiteful errors (as, for instance, Galileo's insistence on Copernicanism was taken to be in 1633)—pluralism creates room to challenge orthodoxy, think imaginatively, experiment boldly. Brilliance and bigotry are empowered in the same stroke.

Pluralism is the principle that protects and makes a place in human company for that loneliest and most vulnerable of all minorities, the minority who is hounded and despised among blacks and white, gays and straights, who is suspect or criminal among every tribe and in every nation of the world, and yet on whom progress depends: the dissident. I am not saying that dissent is always or even usually enlightened. Most of the time, it is foolish and self-serving. No dissident has the right to be taken seriously, and the fact that Aryan Nation[1] racists or Nation of Islam[2] anti-Semites are unorthodox does not entitle them to respect. But what goes around comes around. As a supporter of gay marriage,   10

---

[1] A white separatist religious group in the United States. (Editor's note)

[2] An African American religious organization in the United States that combines some of the practices and beliefs of Islam with a philosophy of black separatism. (Editor's note)

for example, I reject the majority's view of family, and as a Jew I reject its view of God. I try to be civil, but the fact is that most Americans regard my views on marriage as a reckless assault on the most fundamental of all institutions, and many people are more than a little discomfited by the statement, "Jesus Christ was no more divine than anybody else" (which is why so few people ever say it). Trap the racists and anti-Semites, and you lay a trap for me too. Hunt for them with eradication in your mind, and you have brought dissent itself within your sights.

The new crusade against prejudice waves aside such warnings. Like earlier crusades against antisocial ideas, the mission is fueled by good (if cocksure) intentions and a genuine sense of urgency. Some kinds of error are held to be intolerable, like pollutants that even in small traces poison the water for a whole town. Some errors are so pernicious as to damage real people's lives, so wrongheaded that no person of right mind or goodwill could support them. Like their forebears of other stripe—the Church in its campaigns against heretics, the McCarthyites[3] in their campaigns against Communists—the modern anti-racist and anti-sexist and anti-homophobic campaigners are total-ists, demanding not that misguided ideas and ugly expressions be corrected or criticized but that they be eradicated. They make war not on errors but on error, and like other totalists they act in the name of public safety—the safety, especially, of minorities.

The sweeping implications of this challenge to pluralism are not, I think, well enough understood by the public at large. Indeed, the new brand of total-ism has yet even to be properly named. "Multiculturalism" for instance, is much too broad. "Political correctness" comes closer but is too trendy and snide. For lack of anything else, I will call the new anti-pluralism "purism," since its major tenet is that society cannot be just until the last traces of invid-ious prejudice have been scrubbed away. Whatever you call it, the purists' way of seeing things has spread through American intellectual life with remark-able speed, so much so that many people will blink at you uncomprehending-ly or even call you a racist (or sexist or homophobe, etc.) if you suggest that expressions of racism should be tolerated or that prejudice has its part to play.

The new purism sets out, to begin with, on a campaign against words, for words are the currency of prejudice, and if prejudice is hurtful then so must be prejudiced words. "We are not safe when these violent words are among us," wrote Mari Matsuda, then a UCLA law professor. Here one imagines gangs of racist words swinging chains and smashing heads in back alleys. To

---

[3]In the early 1950s, Senator Joseph McCarthy pursued suspected communists in the government and throughout the nation. Although his "Fight for America" did not result in a single conviction, he and his followers ruined the lives and careers of many they investigated. McCarthy was later condemned for "conduct contrary to Senatorial traditions." (Editor's note)

suppress bigoted language seems, at first blush, reasonable, but it quickly leads to a curious result. A peculiar kind of verbal shamanism takes root, as though certain expressions, like curses or magical incantations, carry in themselves the power to hurt or heal—as though words were bigoted rather than people. "Context is everything," people have always said. The use of the word "nigger" in *Huckleberry Finn*[4] does not make the book an "act" of hate speech—or does it? In the new view, this is no longer so clear. The very utterance of the word "nigger" (at least by a non-black) is a racist act. When a *Sacramento Bee* cartoonist put the word "nigger" mockingly in the mouth of a white supremacist, there were howls of protest and 1,400 canceled subscriptions and an editorial apology, even though the word was plainly being invoked against racists, not against blacks.

Faced with escalating demands of verbal absolutism, newspapers issue lists of forbidden words. The expressions "gyp" (derived from "Gypsy") and "Dutch treat" were among the dozens of terms stricken as "offensive" in a much-ridiculed (and later withdrawn) *Los Angeles Times* speech code. The University of Missouri journalism school issued a *Dictionary of Cautionary Words and Phrases*, which included "*Buxom:* Offensive reference to a woman's chest. Do not use. See 'Woman.' *Codger:* Offensive reference to a senior citizen."

As was bound to happen, purists soon discovered that chasing around after words like "gyp" or "buxom" hardly goes to the roots of the problem. As long as they remain bigoted, bigots will simply find other words. If they can't call you a kike then they will say Jewboy, Judas, or Hebe, and when all those are banned they will press words like "oven" and "lampshade" into their service. The vocabulary of hate is potentially as rich as your dictionary, and all you do by banning language used by cretins is to let them decide what the rest of us may say. The problem, some purists have concluded, must therefore go much deeper than laws: it must go to the deeper level of ideas. Racism, sexism, homophobia, and the rest must be built into the very structure of American society and American patterns of thought, so pervasive yet so insidious that, like water to a fish, they are both omnipresent and unseen. The mere existence of prejudice constructs a society whose very nature is prejudiced.

This line of thinking was pioneered by feminists, who argued that pornography, more than just being expressive, is an act by which men construct an oppressive society. Racial activists quickly picked up the argument. Racist expressions are themselves acts of oppression, they said, "All racist speech constructs the social reality that constrains the liberty of nonwhites because of their race," wrote Charles R. Lawrence III, then a law professor at Stanford. From the purist point of view, a society with even one racist is a racist society, because the idea itself threatens and demeans its targets. They cannot feel wholly safe or

15

---

[4]Mark Twain's 1889 novel includes coarse language, some of it now called racist. (Editor's note)

wholly welcome as long as racism is present. Pluralism says: There will always be some racists. Marginalize them, ignore them, exploit them, ridicule them, take pains to make their policies illegal, but otherwise leave them alone. Purists say: That's not enough. Society cannot be just until these pervasive and oppressive ideas are searched out and eradicated.

And so what is now under way is a growing drive to eliminate prejudice from every corner of society. I doubt that many people have noticed how far-reaching this anti-pluralist movement is becoming.

In universities: Dozens of universities have adopted codes proscribing speech or other expression that (this is from Stanford's policy, which is more or less representative) "is intended to insult or stigmatize an individual or a small number of individuals on the basis of their sex, race, color, handicap, religion, sexual orientation or national and ethnic origin." Some codes punish only persistent harassment of a targeted individual, but many, following the purist doctrine that even one racist is too many, go much further. At Penn, an administrator declared: "We at the University of Pennsylvania have guaranteed students and the community that they can live in a community free of sexism, racism, and homophobia." Here is the purism that gives "political correctness" its distinctive combination of puffy high-mindedness and authoritarian zeal.

In school curricula: "More fundamental than eliminating racial segregation has to be the removal of racist thinking, assumptions, symbols, and materials in the curriculum," writes theorist Molefi Kete Asante. In practice, the effort to "remove racist thinking" goes well beyond striking egregious references from textbooks. In many cases it becomes a kind of mental engineering in which students are encouraged to see prejudice.

Ah, but the task of scouring minds clean is Augean. "Nobody escapes," said [20] a Rutgers University report on campus prejudice. Bias and prejudice, it found, cross every conceivable line, from sex to race to politics. "No matter who you are, no matter what the color of your skin, no matter what your gender or sexual orientation, no matter what you believe, no matter how you behave, there is somebody out there who doesn't like people of your kind." Charles Lawrence writes: "Racism is ubiquitous. We are all racists." If he means that most of us think racist thoughts of some sort at one time or another, he is right. If we are going to "eliminate prejudices and biases from our society," then the work of the prejudice police is unending. They are doomed to hunt and hunt, scour and scour and scour.

What is especially dismaying is that the purists pursue prejudice in the name of protecting minorities. In order to protect people like me (homosexual), they must pursue people like me (dissident). In order to bolster minority self-esteem, they suppress minority opinion. There are, of course, all kinds of practical and legal problems with the purists' campaign: the incursions against the First Amendment; the inevitable abuses by prosecutors and activists who define as "hateful" or "violent" whatever speech they dislike or can score points off of; the lack of any evidence that repressing prejudice eliminates rather than inflames it. But minorities, of all people, ought to remember that by definition we cannot prevail by numbers, and we generally cannot prevail by force. Against the power of ignorant mass opinion and group prejudice and superstition, we have only our voices. If you doubt that minorities' voices are powerful weapons, think of the lengths to which Southern officials went to silence the Reverend Martin Luther King Jr. (recall that the city commissioner of Montgomery, Alabama, won a $500,000 libel suit, later overturned in *New York Times v. Sullivan* [1964], regarding an advertisement in the *Times* placed by civil-rights leaders who denounced the Montgomery police). Think of how much gay people have improved their lot over twenty-five years simply by refusing to remain silent. Recall the Michigan student who was prosecuted for saying that homosexuality is a treatable disease, and notice that he was black. Under that Michigan speech code, more than twenty blacks were charged with racist speech, while no instance of racist speech by whites was punished. In Florida, the hate-speech law was invoked against a black man who called a policeman a "white cracker"; not so surprisingly, in the first hate-crimes case to reach the Supreme Court, the victim was white and the defendant black.

In the escalating war against "prejudice," the right is already learning to play by the rules that were pioneered by the purist activists of the left. Last year leading Democrats, including the President, criticized the Republican Party for being increasingly in the thrall of the Christian right. Some of the rhetoric was harsh ("fire-breathing Christian radical right"), but it wasn't vicious or even clearly wrong. Never mind: when Democratic Representative Vic Fazio said Republicans were "being forced to the fringes by the aggressive political tactics of the religious right," the chairman of the Republican National Committee, Haley Barbour, said, "Christian-bashing" was "the left's preferred form of religious bigotry." Bigotry! Prejudice! "Christians active in politics are now on the receiving end of an extraordinary campaign of bias and prejudice," said the conservative leader William J. Bennett. One discerns, here, where the new purism leads. Eventually, any criticism of any group will be "prejudice."

Here is the ultimate irony of the new purism: words, which pluralists hope can be substituted for violence, are redefined by purists *as* violence. "The experience of being called 'nigger,' 'spic,' 'Jap,' or 'kike' is like receiving a slap in the face," Charles Lawrence wrote in 1990. "Psychic injury is no less an injury than being struck in the face, and it often is far more severe." This kind of talk is commonplace today. Epithets, insults, often even polite expressions of what's taken to be prejudice are called by purists "assaultive speech," "words that wound," "verbal violence." "To me, racial epithets are not speech," one University of Michigan law professor said. "They are bullets." In her speech accepting the 1993 Nobel Prize for Literature in Stockholm, Sweden, the author Toni Morrison[5] said this: "Oppressive language does more than represent violence; it is violence."

It is not violence. I am thinking back to a moment on the subway in
Washington, a little thing. I was riding home late one night and a squad of
noisy kids, maybe seventeen or eighteen years old, noisily piled into the car.
They yelled across the car and a girl said, "Where do we get off?"

A boy said, "Farragut North."   25

The girl: "*Faggot* North!"

The boy: "Yeah! Faggot North!"

General hilarity.

First, before the intellect resumes control, there is a moment of fear, an animal moment. Who are they? How many of them? How dangerous! Where is
the way out? All of these things are noted preverbally and assessed by the gut.
Then the brain begins an assessment: they are sober, this is probably too public a place for them to do it, there are more girls than boys, they were just talking, it is probably nothing.

They didn't notice me and there was no incident. The teenage babble flowed   30
on, leaving me to think. I became interested in my own reaction: the jump of
fear out of nowhere like an alert animal, the sense for a brief time that one is
naked and alone and should hide or run away. For a time, one ceases to be a
human being and becomes instead a faggot.

The fear engendered by these words is real. The remedy is as clear and as
imperfect as ever: protect citizens against violence. This, I grant, is something that American society has never done very well and now does quite
poorly. It is no solution to define words as violence or prejudice as oppression, and then by cracking down on words or thoughts pretend that we are
doing something about violence and oppression. No doubt it is easier to pass
a speech code or hate-crimes law and proclaim the streets safer than actually
to make the streets safer, but the one must never be confused with the other.
Every cop or prosecutor chasing words is one fewer chasing criminals. In a
world rife with real violence and oppression, full of Rwandas and Bosnias and
eleven-year-olds spraying bullets at children in Chicago and in turn being executed by gang lords, it is odious of Toni Morrison to say that words are
violence.

Indeed, equating "verbal violence" with physical violence is a treacherous,
mischievous business. Not long ago a writer was charged with viciously and
gratuitously wounding the feelings and dignity of millions of people. He was
charged, in effect, with exhibiting flagrant prejudice against Muslims and

---

[5]African American author (b. 1931). (Editor's note)

outrageously slandering their beliefs. "What is freedom of expression?" mused Salman Rushdie[6] a year after the ayatollahs sentenced him to death and put a price on his head. "Without the freedom to offend, it ceases to exist." I can think of nothing sadder than that minority activists, in their haste to make the world better, should be the ones to forget the lesson of Rushdie's plight: for minorities, pluralism, not purism, is the answer. The campaigns to eradicate prejudice—all of them, the speech codes and workplace restrictions and mandatory therapy for accused bigots and all the rest—should stop, now. The whole objective of eradicating prejudice, as opposed to correcting and criticizing it, should be repudiated as a fool's errand. Salman Rushdie is right, Toni Morrison wrong, and minorities belong at his side, not hers.

ANALYZING What the Writer Says

1. What is Rauch's main point about prejudice and its place in society?

2. How does Rauch define "intellectual pluralism"?

3. Why does Rauch say it is impossible to define "prejudice"? How does this impossibility constitute an argument in support of Rauch's thesis?

4. In what way is our view of unbiased science wrong? How does Rauch demonstrate that pluralism is more conducive to scientific pursuits than the banishment of prejudice?

5. What does Rauch mean when he says that "stamping out prejudice really means forcing everyone to share the same prejudice, namely that of whoever is in authority"?

6. What is Rauch's argument against purists' attempts to eliminate prejudice by eliminating offensive language? Does he deny the power of hate speech altogether? If not, why not?

7. What does Rauch mean when he says, "In order to protect people like me (homosexual), they must pursue people like me (dissident). In order to bolster minority self-esteem, they suppress minority opinion"?

---

[6]British novelist of Indian descent (b. 1947). Muslims condemned Rushdie's 1988 novel *The Satanic Verses* as an attack on the Islamic faith; in 1989, Iran's Ayatollah Khomeini declared that Rushdie and everyone involved in the book's publication should be put to death; the death sentence was lifted in 1998. (Editor's note)

ANALYZING   How the Writer Says It

1. How does Rauch structure his argument? What are his main points in defending his thesis, and how does he present them?

2. Rauch chooses a very provocative title for his piece. What would the effect of a less dramatic title have been on his essay?

3. Rauch tells his readers, in several places, that he is Jewish and homosexual. Why does he place so much emphasis on his biography?

ANALYZING   the Issue

1. Do you think it is possible, through laws and regulations, to eliminate prejudice? How?

2. Do you agree with Rauch's point that intellectual pluralism is a more efficient method to keep prejudice in check than the laws of political correctness although—or rather, because—it permits prejudiced acts of speech?

3. Rauch admits that "the fear engendered by [hate words] is real," but he disagrees with Toni Morrison's statement that "oppressive language does more than represent violence; it is violence." Do you find him convincing on this issue? Why or why not?

ANALYZING   Connections Between Texts

1. In "Politics and the English Language" (p. 487), George Orwell shows how political language can be used as a tool to manipulate people. In what way does Rauch's essay support Orwell's observations on language and power? In what way does it differ?

2. How would Adnan R. Khan ("Bordering on Panic," p. 555) respond to Rauch's argument?

3. What would Rauch say about the activities of the Ku Klux Klan, as pictured in Gerrit Fokkema's photograph (p. 536)?

WARMING UP: *Have you ever tried to learn a foreign language? If so, were you intimidated by the experience?*

Me Talk Pretty One Day

BY DAVID SEDARIS

DAVID SEDARIS

When writer and humorist David Sedaris (b. 1956) moved to Paris, he enrolled in a French language class—a somewhat harrowing experience that he recounts in the title essay from his collection Me Talk Pretty One Day. *Like most of his writing, as well as his commentary on National Public Radio, the essays in this book are characterized by a sharp ironic wit.*

At the age of forty-one, I am returning to school and have to think of myself as what my French textbook calls "a true debutant." After paying my tuition, I was issued a student ID, which allows me a discounted entry fee at movie theaters, puppet shows, and Festyland, a far-flung amusement park that advertises with billboards picturing a cartoon stegosaurus sitting in a canoe and eating what appears to be a ham sandwich.

I've moved to Paris with hopes of learning the language. My school is an easy ten-minute walk from my apartment, and on the first day of class I arrived early, watching as the returning students greeted one another in the school lobby. Vacations were recounted, and questions were raised concerning mutual friends with names like Kang and Vlatnya. Regardless of their nationalities, everyone spoke in what sounded to me like excellent French. Some accents were better than others, but the students exhibited an ease and confidence I found intimidating. As an added discomfort, they were all young, attractive, and well dressed, causing me to feel not unlike Pa Kettle trapped backstage after a fashion show.

The first day of class was nerve-racking because I knew I'd be expected to perform. That's the way they do it here—it's everybody into the language pool, sink or swim. The teacher marched in, deeply tanned from a recent vacation, and proceeded to rattle off a series of administrative announcements. I've spent quite a few summers in Normandy, and I took a monthlong French class before leaving New York. I'm not completely in the dark, yet I understood only half of what this woman was saying.

"If you have not *meimslsxp* or *lgpdmurct* by this time, then you should not be in this room. Has everyone *apzkiubjxow?* Everyone? Good, we shall begin." She spread out her lesson plan and sighed, saying, "All right, then, who knows the alphabet?"

It was startling because (a) I hadn't been asked that question in a while and   5 (b) I realized, while laughing, that I myself did *not* know the alphabet. They're the same letters, but in France they're pronounced differently. I know the shape of the alphabet but had no idea what it actually sounded like.

"Ahh." The teacher went to the board and sketched the letter *a*. "Do we have anyone in the room whose first name commences with an *ahh?*"

Two Polish Annas raised their hands, and the teacher instructed them to present themselves by stating their names, nationalities, occupations, and a brief list of things they liked and disliked in this world. The first Anna hailed from an industrial town outside of Warsaw and had front teeth the size of tombstones. She worked as a seamstress, enjoyed quiet times with friends, and hated the mosquito.

"Oh, really," the teacher said. "How very interesting. I thought that everyone loved the mosquito, but here, in front of all the world, you claim to detest him. How is it that we've been blessed with someone as unique and original as you? Tell us, please."

The seamstress did not understand what was being said but knew that this was an occasion for shame. Her rabbity mouth huffed for breath, and she stared down at her lap as though the appropriate comeback were stitched somewhere alongside the zipper of her slacks.

The second Anna learned from the first and claimed to love sunshine and   10 detest lies. It sounded like a translation of one of those Playmate of the Month data sheets, the answers always written in the same loopy handwriting: "Turn-ons: Mom's famous five-alarm chili! Turnoffs: insecurity and guys who come on too strong!!!!"

The two Polish Annas surely had clear notions of what they loved and hated, but like the rest of us, they were limited in terms of vocabulary, and this made them appear less than sophisticated. The teacher forged on, and we learned that Carlos, the Argentine bandonion player, loved wine, music, and, in his words, "making sex with the womens of the world." Next came a beautiful young Yugoslav who identified herself as an optimist, saying that she loved everything that life had to offer.

The teacher licked her lips, revealing a hint of the saucebox we would later come to know. She crouched low for her attack, placed her hands on the young woman's desk, and leaned close, saying, "Oh yeah? And do you love your little war?"

While the optimist struggled to defend herself, I scrambled to think of an answer to what had obviously become a trick question. How often is one asked what he loves in this world? More to the point, how often is one asked and then publicly ridiculed for his answer? I recalled my mother, flushed with wine, pounding the tabletop late one night, saying, "Love? I love a good steak cooked rare. I love my cat, and I love . . ." My sisters and I leaned forward, waiting to hear our names. "Tums," our mother said. "I love Tums."

The teacher killed some time accusing the Yugoslavian girl of masterminding a program of genocide, and I jotted frantic notes in the margins of my pad. While I can honestly say that I love leafing through medical textbooks devoted to severe dermatological conditions, the hobby is beyond the reach of my French vocabulary, and acting it out would only have invited controversy.

When called upon, I delivered an effortless list of things that I detest: blood   15
sausage, intestinal pâtés, brain pudding. I'd learned these words the hard way. Having given it some thought, I then declared my love for IBM typewriters, the French word for *bruise*, and my electric floor waxer. It was a short list, but still I managed to mispronounce *IBM* and assign the wrong gender to both the floor waxer and the typewriter. The teacher's reaction led me to believe that these mistakes were capital crimes in the country of France.

"Were you always this *palicmkrexis?*" she asked. "Even a *fiuscrzsa ticiwelmun* knows that a typewriter is feminine."

I absorbed as much of her abuse as I could understand, thinking—but not saying—that I find it ridiculous to assign a gender to an inanimate object incapable of disrobing and making an occasional fool of itself. Why refer to Lady Crack Pipe or Good Sir Dishrag when these things could never live up to all that their sex implied?

The teacher proceeded to belittle everyone from German Eva, who hated laziness, to Japanese Yukari, who loved paintbrushes and soap. Italian, Thai, Dutch, Korean, and Chinese—we all left class foolishly believing that the worst was over. She'd shaken us up a little, but surely that was just an act designed to weed out the deadweight. We didn't know it then, but the coming months would teach us what it was like to spend time in the presence of a wild animal, something completely unpredictable. Her temperament was not based on a series of good and bad days but, rather, good and bad moments. We soon learned to dodge chalk and protect our heads and stomachs whenever she approached us with a question. She hadn't yet punched anyone, but it seemed wise to protect ourselves against the inevitable.

Though we were forbidden to speak anything but French, the teacher would occasionally use us to practice any of her five fluent languages.

"I hate you," she said to me one afternoon. Her English was flawless. "I real-   20
ly, really hate you." Call me sensitive, but I couldn't help but take it personally.

After being singled out as a lazy *kfdtinvfm*, I took to spending four hours a night on my homework, putting in even more time whenever we were assigned an essay. I suppose I could have gotten by with less, but I was determined to create some sort of identity for myself: David the hard worker, David the cut-up. We'd have one of those "complete this sentence" exercises, and I'd fool with the thing for hours, invariably settling on something like "A quick run around the lake? I'd love to! Just give me a moment while I strap on my wooden leg." The teacher, through word and action, conveyed the message that if this was my idea of an identity, she wanted nothing to do with it.

My fear and discomfort crept beyond the borders of the classroom and accompanied me out onto the wide boulevards. Stopping for a coffee, asking directions, depositing money in my bank account: these things were out of the question, as they involved having to speak. Before beginning school, there'd been no shutting me up, but now I was convinced that everything I said was wrong. When the phone rang, I ignored it. If someone asked me a question, I pretended to be deaf. I knew my fear was getting the best of me when I started wondering why they don't sell cuts of meat in vending machines.

My only comfort was the knowledge that I was not alone. Huddled in the hallways and making the most of our pathetic French, my fellow students and I engaged in the sort of conversation commonly overheard in refugee camps.

"Sometime me cry alone at night."

"That be common for I, also, but be more strong, you. Much work and some- 25 day you talk pretty. People start love you soon. Maybe tomorrow, okay."

Unlike the French class I had taken in New York, here there was no sense of competition. When the teacher poked a shy Korean in the eyelid with a freshly sharpened pencil, we took no comfort in the fact that, unlike Hyeyoon Cho, we all knew the irregular past tense of the verb *to defeat*. In all fairness, the teacher hadn't meant to stab the girl, but neither did she spend much time apologizing, saying only, "Well, you should have been *vkkdyo* more *kdeynfulh*."

Over time it became impossible to believe that any of us would ever improve. Fall arrived and it rained every day, meaning we would now be scolded for the water dripping from our coats and umbrellas. It was mid-October when the teacher singled me out, saying, "Every day spent with you is like having a cesarean section." And it struck me that, for the first time since arriving in France, I could understand every word that someone was saying.

Understanding doesn't mean that you can suddenly speak the language. Far from it. It's a small step, nothing more, yet its rewards are intoxicating and deceptive. The teacher continued her diatribe and I settled back, bathing in the subtle beauty of each new curse and insult.

"You exhaust me with your foolishness and reward my efforts with nothing but pain, do you understand me?"

The world opened up, and it was with great joy that I responded, "I know the 30 thing that you speak exact now. Talk me more, you, plus, please, plus."

ANALYZING What the Writer Says

1. What is Sedaris's confidence level as he enters the language school?

2. How would you characterize Sedaris's instructor's teaching approach? Does it work?

3. How do the responses of the other students to the instructor identify and individualize them?

4. What is the significance of the verb that Hyeyoon Cho cannot conjugate? What is the significance of the fact that Sedaris and his classmates "took no comfort in the fact" that they could?

5. What has Sedaris gained by the time the essay closes?

ANALYZING How the Writer Says It

1. How does Sedaris temper what might be considered mockery of fellow students?

2. What is the effect of Sedaris's use of unintelligible groups of letters at various points in his essay? How does Sedaris compare and contrast his French literacy to his command of the English language?

3. Cite words and phrases that reveal Sedaris's attitude toward the instructor.

ANALYZING the Issue

1. Does the instructional method Sedaris recounts here have any particular benefit because it is used in a language class for non-native speakers? Explain.

2. Sedaris's experiences in his French class, while rendered humorously, are not entirely atypical: The French approach to education is teacher-centered and somewhat authoritarian by American standards. Yet the French education system is considered one of the best in the world. How does the more authoritarian French approach influence its success? Research the American system and the French system and comment on what Americans could learn from the French.

ANALYZING Connections Between Texts

1. Compare Sedaris's implicit criticism of the French instructional approach to the questions Amy Tan raises about American testing and labeling in "Mother Tongue" (p. 515). How are they similar?

2. How do you think Jacob Neusner (p. 375) would feel about Sedaris's experience in French language school? How would the students he describes fare in Sedaris's language class?

3. How does the photograph "German Schoolboys Salute"(p. 401) illustrate some of the experiences Sedaris recounts?

WARMING UP: *Do you speak differently at home—or among your friends—than you do at school or work?*

Mother Tongue

BY AMY TAN

AMY TAN

Amy Tan (b. 1952) con-siders "all the Englishes" of her Asian-American upbringing in "Mother Tongue," first published in Threepenny Review *in 1990. A successful novelist whose 1989* The Joy Luck Club *made it onto the big screen, she wonders if the "broken" English spoken in her home contributed to less-than-spectacular results on standardized tests in English—but con-cludes that the quirky rhythms of the family tongue have lent authen-ticity to her own literary voice.*

I am not a scholar of English or literature. I cannot give you much more than personal opinions on the English language and its variations in this country or others.

I am a writer. And by that definition, I am someone who has always loved language. I am fascinated by language in daily life. I spend a great deal of my time thinking about the power of language—the way it can evoke an emotion, a visual image, a complex idea, or a simple truth. Language is the tool of my trade. And I use them all—all the Englishes I grew up with.

Recently, I was made keenly aware of the different Englishes I do use. I was giving a talk to a large group of people, the same talk I had already given to half a dozen other groups. The nature of the talk was about my writing, my life, and my book, *The Joy Luck Club.* The talk was going along well enough, until I remem-bered one major difference that made the whole talk sound wrong. My mother was in the room. And it was perhaps the first time she had heard me give a lengthy speech, using the kind of English I have never used with her. I was saying things like, "The intersection of memory upon imagination" and "There is an aspect of my fiction that relates to thus-and-thus"—a speech filled with carefully wrought grammatical phrases, burdened, it suddenly seemed to me, with nominal-ized forms, past perfect tenses, conditional phrases, all the forms of standard English that I had learned in school and through books, the forms of English I did not use at home with my mother.

Just last week, I was walking down the street with my mother, and I again found myself conscious of the English I was using, and the English I do use with her. We were talking about the price of new and used furniture and I heard myself saying this: "Not waste money that way." My husband was with us as well, and he didn't notice any switch in my English. And then I realized why. It's because over the twenty years we've been together I've often used that same kind of English with him, and sometimes he even uses it with me. It has become our language of intimacy, a different sort of English that relates to family talk, the language I grew up with.

So you'll have some idea of what this family talk I heard sounds like, I'll   5 quote what my mother said during a recent conversation which I videotaped and then transcribed. During this conversation, my mother was talking about a political gangster in Shanghai who had the same last name as her family's, Du, and how the gangster in his early years wanted to be adopted by her family, which was rich by comparison. Later, the gangster became more powerful, far richer than my mother's family, and one day showed up at my mother's wedding to pay his respects. Here's what she said in part:

"Du Yusong having business like fruit stand. Like off the street kind. He is Du like Du Zong—but not Tsung-ming Island people. The local people call putong, the river east side, he belong to that side local people. That man want to ask Du Zong father take him in like become own family. Du Zong father wasn't look down on him, but didn't take seriously, until that man big like become a mafia. Now important person, very hard to inviting him. Chinese way, came only to show respect, don't stay for dinner. Respect for making big celebration, he shows up. Mean gives lots of respect. Chinese custom. Chinese social life that way. If too important won't have to stay too long. He come to my wedding. I didn't see, I heard it. I gone to boy's side, they have YMCA dinner. Chinese age I was nineteen."

You should know that my mother's expressive command of English belies how much she actually understands. She reads the *Forbes* report, listens to *Wall Street Week*, converses daily with her stockbroker, reads all of Shirley MacLaine's books with ease—all kinds of things I can't begin to understand. Yet some of my friends tell me they understand 50 percent of what my mother says. Some say they understand 80 to 90 percent. Some say they understand none of it, as if she were speaking pure Chinese. But to me, my mother's English is perfectly clear, perfectly natural. It's my mother tongue. Her language, as I hear it, is vivid, direct, full of observation and imagery. That was the language that helped shape the way I saw things, expressed things, made sense of the world.

Lately, I've been giving more thought to the kind of English my mother speaks. Like others, I have described it to people as "broken" or "fractured" English. But I wince when I say that. It has always bothered me that I can think of no way to describe it other than "broken," as if it were damaged and needed to be fixed, as if it lacked a certain wholeness and soundness. I've heard other terms used, "limited English," for example. But they seem just as bad, as if everything is limited, including people's perceptions of the limited English speaker.

I know this for a fact, because when I was growing up, my mother's "limited" English limited *my* perception of her. I was ashamed of her English. I believed that her English reflected the quality of what she had to say. That is, because she expressed them imperfectly her thoughts were imperfect. And I had plenty of empirical evidence to support me: the fact that people in department stores, at banks, and at restaurants did not take her seriously, did not give her good service, pretended not to understand her, or even acted as if they did not hear her.

My mother has long realized the limitations of her English as well. When I   10
was fifteen, she used to have me call people on the phone to pretend I was she. In this guise, I was forced to ask for information or even to complain and yell at people who had been rude to her. One time it was a call to her stockbroker in New York. She had cashed out her small portfolio and it just so happened we were going to go to New York the next week, our very first trip outside California. I had to get on the phone and say in an adolescent voice that was not very convincing, "This is Mrs. Tan."

And my mother was standing in the back whispering loudly, "Why he don't send me check, already two weeks late. So mad he lie to me, losing me money."

And then I said in perfect English, "Yes, I'm getting rather concerned. You had agreed to send the check two weeks ago, but it hasn't arrived."

Then she began to talk more loudly. "What he want, I come to New York tell him front of his boss, you cheating me?" And I was trying to calm her down, make her be quiet, while telling the stockbroker, "I can't tolerate any more excuses. If I don't receive the check immediately, I am going to have to speak to your manager when I'm in New York next week." And sure enough, the following week there we were in front of this astonished stockbroker, and I was sitting there red-faced and quiet, and my mother, the real Mrs. Tan, was shouting at his boss in her impeccable broken English.

We used a similar routine just five days ago, for a situation that was far less humorous. My mother had gone to the hospital for an appointment, to find out about a benign brain tumor a CAT scan had revealed a month ago. She said she had spoken very good English, her best English, no mistakes. Still, she said, the hospital did not apologize when they said they had lost the CAT scan and she had come for nothing. She said they did not seem to have any sympathy when she told them she was anxious to know the exact diagnosis, since her husband and son had both died of brain tumors. She said they would not give her any more information until the next time and she would have to make another appointment for that. So she said she would not leave until the doctor called her daughter. She wouldn't budge. And when the doctor finally called her daughter, me, who spoke in perfect English—lo and behold—we had assurances the CAT scan would be found, promises that a conference call on Monday would be held, and apologies for any suffering my mother had gone through for a most regrettable mistake.

I think my mother's English almost had an effect on limiting my possibili- 15 ties in life as well. Sociologists and linguists probably will tell you that a person's developing language skills are more influenced by peers. But I do think that the language spoken in the family, especially in immigrant families which are more insular, plays a large role in shaping the language of the child. And I believe that it affected my results on achievement tests, IQ tests, and the SAT. While my English skills were never judged as poor, compared to math, English could not be considered my strong suit. In grade school I did moderately well, getting perhaps B's, sometimes B-pluses, in English and scoring perhaps in the sixtieth or seventieth percentile on achievement tests. But those scores were not good enough to override the opinion that my true abilities lay in math and science, because in those areas I achieved A's and scored in the ninetieth percentile or higher.

This was understandable. Math is precise; there is only one correct answer. Whereas, for me at least, the answers on English tests were always a judgment call, a matter of opinion and personal experience. Those tests were constructed around items like fill-in-the-blank sentence completion, such as, "Even though Tom was _____, Mary thought he was _____." And the correct answer always seemed to be the most bland combinations of thoughts, for example, "Even though Tom was shy, Mary thought he was charming," with the grammatical structure "even though" limiting the correct answer to some sort of semantic opposites, so you wouldn't get answers like, "Even though Tom was foolish, Mary thought he was ridiculous." Well, according to my mother, there were very few limitations as to what Tom could have been and what Mary might have thought of him. So I never did well on tests like that.

The same was true with word analogies, pairs of words in which you were supposed to find some sort of logical, semantic relationship—for example, "*Sunset* is to *nightfall* as _____ is to _____." And here you would be presented with a list of four possible pairs, one of which showed the same kind of relationship: *red* is to *stoplight, bus* is to *arrival, chills* is to *fever, yawn* is to *boring.* Well, I could never think that way. I knew what the tests were asking, but I could not block out of my mind the images already created by the first pair, "*sunset* is to *nightfall*"—and I would see a burst of colors against a darkening sky, the moon rising, the lowering of a curtain of stars. And all the other pairs of words—red, bus, stoplight, boring—just threw up a mass of confusing images, making it impossible for me to sort out something as logical as saying: "A sunset precedes nightfall" is the same as "a chill precedes a fever." The only way I would have gotten that answer right would have been to imagine an associative situation, for example, my being disobedient and staying out past sunset, catching a chill at night, which turns into feverish pneumonia as punishment, which indeed did happen to me.

I have been thinking about all this lately, about my mother's English, about achievement tests. Because lately I've been asked, as a writer, why there are not more Asian Americans represented in American literature. Why are there few Asian Americans enrolled in creative writing programs? Why do so many Chinese students go into engineering? Well, these are broad sociological questions I can't begin to answer. But I have noticed in surveys—in fact, just last week—that Asian students, as a whole, always do significantly better on math achievement tests than in English. And this makes me think that there are other Asian-American students whose English spoken in the home might also be described as "broken" or "limited." And perhaps they also have teachers who are steering them away from writing and into math and science, which is what happened to me.

Fortunately, I happen to be rebellious in nature and enjoy the challenge of disproving assumptions made about me. I became an English major my first year in college, after being enrolled as pre-med. I started writing nonfiction as a freelancer the week after I was told by my former boss that writing was my worst skill and I should hone my talents toward account management.

But it wasn't until 1985 that I finally began to write fiction. And at first I 20 wrote using what I thought to be wittily crafted sentences, sentences that would finally prove I had mastery over the English language. Here's an example from the first draft of a story that later made its way into *The Joy Luck Club*, but without this line: "That was my mental quandary in its nascent state." A terrible line, which I can barely pronounce.

Fortunately, for reasons I won't get into today, I later decided I should envision a reader for the stories I would write. And the reader I decided upon was my mother, because these were stories about mothers. So with this reader in mind—and in fact she did read my early drafts—I began to write stories using all the Englishes I grew up with: the English I spoke to my mother, which for lack of a better term might be described as "simple"; the English she used with me, which for lack of a better term might be described as "broken"; my translation of her Chinese, which could certainly be described as "watered down"; and what I imagined to be her translation of her Chinese if she could speak in perfect English, her internal language, and for that I sought to preserve the essence, but neither an English nor a Chinese structure. I wanted to capture what language ability tests can never reveal: her intent, her passion, her imagery, the rhythms of her speech and the nature of her thoughts.

Apart from what any critic had to say about my writing, I knew I had succeeded where it counted when my mother finished reading my book and gave me her verdict: "So easy to read."

ANALYZING What the Writer Says

1. Why does Tan suddenly become self-conscious, as she speaks before a group about her novel, when she remembers that her mother is in the audience?

2. How do Tan's experiences belie the stereotype often applied to Asian Americans—which had been applied to Tan herself? How do they help explain the stereotype as well?

3. In what ways does Tan's decision to imagine her mother as an audience for her novels liberate her writing?

ANALYZING How the Writer Says It

1. Analyze the layers of meaning in Tan's title.

2. What is the effect of the final phrase of the essay, a quote from Tan's mother?

ANALYZING the Issue

1. Do you think standardized language tests measure a person's true grasp of a language? If not, what do you think they measure?

2. Do you think mastery of standard English is an essential component of American education? Should students have to master another language as well? Explain.

ANALYZING Connections Between Texts

1. In "Me Talk Pretty One Day" (p. 510), David Sedaris quotes his and his classmates' fractured French. Compare the mistakes he and his classmates make to those of Amy Tan's mother's fractured English. Why do you think the two writers quote the language "mistakes"?

2. Compare Amy Tan's experience to that of Caroline Hwang in "The Good Daughter" (p. 139).

3. How does Stephanie Maze's photograph "Lunch at Uncle Antonio's" (p. 99) illustrate concerns similar to those Tan writes about?

WARMING UP: *Do you find yourself making assumptions about women's characters or values based on their appearance, especially in the workplace? Do you do the same for men?*

Marked Women

By Deborah Tannen

DEBORAH TANNEN

Deborah Tannen (b. 1945), a Georgetown professor of linguistics and best-selling author of You Just Don't Understand *(1990) as well as several other books, has made a name for herself by bridging the gap between scholarship and popular reading, writing about the different ways in which women and men understand—and are understood. In "Marked Women," originally published in the* New York Times Magazine, *she points to the choices women are forced to make every day, choices that "mark" them.*

Some years ago I was at a small working conference of four women and eight men. Instead of concentrating on the discussion I found myself looking at the three other women at the table, thinking how each had a different style and how each style was coherent.

One woman had dark brown hair in a classic style, a cross between Cleopatra and Plain Jane. The severity of her straight hair was softened by wavy bangs and ends that turned under. Because she was beautiful, the effect was more Cleopatra than plain.

The second woman was older, full of dignity and composure. Her hair was cut in a fashionable style that left her with only one eye, thanks to a side part that let a curtain of hair fall across half her face. As she looked down to read her prepared paper, the hair robbed her of bifocal vision and created a barrier between her and the listeners.

The third woman's hair was wild, a frosted blond avalanche falling over and beyond her shoulders. When she spoke she frequently tossed her head, calling attention to her hair and away from her lecture.

Then there was makeup. The first woman wore facial cover that made her skin smooth and pale, a black line under each eye and mascara that darkened already dark lashes. The second wore only a light gloss on her lips and a hint of shadow on her eyes. The third had blue bands under her eyes, dark blue shadow, mascara, bright red lipstick and rouge; her fingernails flashed red.

I considered the clothes each woman had worn during the three days of the conference: In the first case, man-tailored suits in primary colors with solid-color

5

blouses. In the second, casual but stylish black T-shirts, a floppy collarless jacket and baggy slacks or a skirt in neutral colors. The third wore a sexy jump suit; tight sleeveless jersey and tight yellow slacks; a dress with gaping armholes and an indulged tendency to fall off one shoulder.

Shoes? No. 1 wore string sandals with medium heels; No. 2, sensible, comfortable walking shoes; No. 3, pumps with spike heels. You can fill in the jewelry, scarves, shawls, sweaters—or lack of them.

As I amused myself finding coherence in these styles, I suddenly wondered why I was scrutinizing only the women. I scanned the eight men at the table. And then I knew why I wasn't studying them. The men's styles were unmarked.

The term "marked" is a staple of linguistic theory. It refers to the way language alters the base meaning of a word by adding a linguistic particle that has no meaning on its own. The unmarked form of a word carried the meaning that goes without saying—what you think of when you're not thinking anything special.

The unmarked tense of verbs in English is the present—for example, *visit*.   10 To indicate past, you mark the verb by adding *ed* to yield *visited*. For future, you add a word: *will visit*. Nouns are presumed to be singular until marked for plural, typically by adding *s* or *es*, so *visit* becomes *visits* and *dish* becomes *dishes*.

The unmarked forms of most English words also convey "male." Being male is the unmarked case. Endings like *ess* and *ette* mark words as "female." Unfortunately, they also tend to mark them for frivolousness. Would you feel safe entrusting your life to a doctorette? Alfre Woodard, who was an Oscar nominee for best supporting actress, says she identifies herself as an actor because "actresses worry about eyelashes and cellulite, and women who are actors worry about the characters we are playing." Gender markers pick up extra meanings that reflect common associations with the female gender: not quite serious, often sexual.

Each of the women at the conference had to make decisions about hair, clothing, makeup and accessories, and each decision carried meaning. Every style available to us was marked. The men in our group had made decisions, too, but the range from which they chose was incomparably narrower. Men can choose styles that are marked, but they don't have to, and in this group none did. Unlike the women, they had the option of being unmarked.

Take the men's hair styles. There was no marine crew cut or oily longish hair falling into eyes, no asymmetrical, two-tiered construction to swirl over a bald top. One man was unabashedly bald; the others had hair of standard length, parted on one side, in natural shades of brown or gray or graying. Their hair obstructed no views, left little to toss or push back or run fingers through and, consequently, needed and attracted no attention. A few men had beards. In a business setting, beards might be marked. In this academic gathering, they weren't.

There could have been a cowboy shirt with string tie or a three-piece suit or a necklaced hippie in jeans. But there wasn't. All eight men wore brown or blue slacks and nondescript shirts of light colors. No man wore sandals or boots; their shoes were dark, closed, comfortable and flat. In short, unmarked.

Although no man wore makeup, you couldn't say the men didn't wear makeup in the sense that you could say a woman didn't wear makeup. For men, no makeup is unmarked.   15

I asked myself what style we women could have adopted that would have been unmarked, like the men's. The answer was none. There is no unmarked woman.

There is no woman's hair style that can be called standard, that says nothing about her. The range of women's hair styles is staggering, but a woman whose hair has no particular style is perceived as not caring about how she looks, which can disqualify her for many positions, and will subtly diminish her as a person in the eyes of some.

Women must choose between attractive shoes and comfortable shoes. When our group made an unexpected trek, the woman who wore flat, laced shoes arrived first. Last to arrive was the woman in spike heels, shoes in hand and a handful of men around her.

If a woman's clothing is tight or revealing (in other words, sexy), it sends a message—an intended one of wanting to be attractive, but also a possibly unintended one of availability. If her clothes are not sexy, that too sends a message, lent meaning by the knowledge that they could have been. There are thousands of cosmetic products from which women can choose and myriad ways of applying them. Yet no makeup at all is anything but unmarked. Some men see it as a hostile refusal to please them.

Women can't even fill out a form without telling stories about themselves.   20
Most forms give four titles to choose from. "Mr." carries no meaning other than that the respondent is male. But a woman who checks "Mrs." or "Miss" communicates not only whether she has been married but also whether she has conservative tastes in forms of address—and probably other conservative values as well. Checking "Ms." declines to let on about marriage (checking "Mr." declines nothing since nothing was asked), but it also marks her as either liberated or rebellious, depending on the observer's attitudes and assumptions.

I sometimes try to duck these variously marked choices by giving my title as "Dr."—and in so doing risk marking myself as either uppity (hence sarcastic responses like "*Excuse me!*") or an overachiever (hence reactions of congratulatory surprise like "Good for you!").

All married women's surnames are marked. If a woman takes her husband's name, she announces to the world that she is married and has traditional values. To some it will indicate that she is less herself, more identified by her husband's identity. If she does not take her husband's name, this too is marked, seen as worthy of comment: she has done something; she has "kept her own name." A man is never said to have "kept his own name" because it never occurs to anyone that he might have given it up. For him using his own name is unmarked.

A married woman who wants to have her cake and eat it too may use her surname plus his, with or without a hyphen. But this too announces her marital status and often results in a tongue-tying string. In a list (Harvey O'Donovan, Jonathan Feldman, Stephanie Woodbury McGillicutty), the woman's multiple name stands out. It is marked.

I have never been inclined toward biological explanations of gender differences in language, but I was intrigued to see Ralph Fasold bring biological phenomena to bear on the question of linguistic marking in his book "The Sociolinguistics of Language." Fasold stresses that language and culture are particularly unfair in treating women as the marked case because biologically it is the male that is marked. While two X chromosomes make a female, two Y chromosomes make nothing. Like the linguistic markers *s, es* or *ess*, the Y chromosome doesn't "mean" anything unless it is attached to a root form—an X chromosome.

Developing this idea elsewhere, Fasold points out that girls are born with fully female bodies, while boys are born with modified female bodies. He invites men who doubt this to lift up their shirts and contemplate why they have nipples. [25]

In his book, Fasold notes "a wide range of facts which demonstrates that female is the unmarked sex." For example, he observes that there are a few species that produce only females, like the whiptail lizard. Thanks to parthenogenesis, they have no trouble having as many daughters as they like. There are no species, however, that produce only males. This is no surprise, since any such species would become extinct in its first generation.

Fasold is also intrigued by species that produce individuals not involved in reproduction, like honeybees and leaf-cutter ants. Reproduction is handled by the queen and a relatively few males; the workers are sterile females. "Since they do not reproduce," Fasold says, "there is no reason for them to be one sex or the other, so they default, so to speak, to female."

Fasold ends his discussion of these matters by pointing out that if language reflected biology, grammar books would direct us to use "she" to include males and females and "he" only for specifically male referents. But they don't. They tell us that "he" means "he or she," and that "she" is used only if the referent is specifically female. This use of "he" as the sex-indefinite pronoun is an innovation introduced into English by grammarians in the 18th and 19th centuries, according to Peter Mühlhäusler and Rom Harré in "Pronouns and People." From at least about 1500, the correct sex-indefinite pronoun was "they," as it still is in casual spoken English. In other words, the female was declared by grammarians to be the marked case.

Writing this article may mark me not as a writer, not as a linguist, not as an analyst of human behavior, but as a feminist—which will have positive or negative, but in any case powerful, connotations for readers. Yet I doubt that anyone reading Ralph Fasold's book would put that label on him.

I discovered the markedness inherent in the very topic of gender after writing a book on differences in conversational style based on geographical region, ethnicity, class, age and gender. When I was interviewed, the vast majority of journalists wanted to talk about the differences between women and men. While I thought I was simply describing what I observed—something I had learned to do as a researcher—merely mentioning women and men marked me as a feminist for some. 30

When I wrote a book devoted to gender differences, in ways of speaking, I sent the manuscript to five male colleagues, asking them to alert me to any interpretation, phrasing or wording that might seem unfairly negative toward men. Even so, when the book came out, I encountered responses like that of the television talk show host who, after interviewing me, turned to the audience and asked if they thought I was male-bashing.

Leaping upon a poor fellow who affably nodded in agreement, she made him stand and asked, "Did what she said accurately describe you?" "Oh, yes," he answered. "That's me exactly." "And what she said about women—does that sound like your wife?" "Oh yes," he responded. "That's her exactly." "Then why do you think she's male-bashing?" He answered, with disarming honesty, "Because she's a woman and she's saying things about men."

To say anything about women and men without marking oneself as either feminist or anti-feminist, male-basher or apologist for men seems as impossible for a woman as trying to get dressed in the morning without inviting interpretations of her character.

Sitting at the conference table musing on these matters, I felt sad to think that we women didn't have the freedom to be unmarked that the men sitting next to us had. Some days you just want to get dressed and go about your business. But if you're a woman, you can't, because there is no unmarked woman.

ANALYZING What the Writer Says

1. What does Tannen's opening paragraph reveal about how deeply ingrained the concepts she explains in her article are?

2. What does Tannen mean by "marked" and "unmarked" as the terms apply to men and women? In what major way does marking affect men and women differently?

3. How, according to Tannen, does the very fact of her authoring this article mark her?

4. What, in Tannen's view, constitutes "male-bashing" by large segments of the population?

ANALYZING How the Writer Says It

1. A sociolinguist by profession, Tannen often writes for nonacademic audiences, as is the case here. Identify places in the text that indicate Tannen's audience awareness.

2. What is the effect of Tannen's inclusion of several paragraphs on the work of another sociolinguist, Ralph Fasold? Compare it to the anecdotal evidence with which she opens the piece.

ANALYZING the Issue

1. Do you agree with Tannen's argument? Are men able to escape being "marked" while women have no choice in the matter?

2. Does Tannen's essay indicate that she's a feminist? Why or why not?

ANALYZING Connections Between Texts

1. Using Tannen's explanation of marking, apply the concept to the students Annie Dillard writes about in "Singing with the Fundamentalists" (p. 470). How are they "marked"?

2. How, as a teenager, is Natalie Kusz ("Ring Leader," p. 223) "marked"? How, as an adult, does she mark herself? What is the difference? *Is* there a difference? Explain.

3. How is the young woman in Ruth Orkin's photograph "American Girl in Italy" (p. 537) "marked"?

WARMING UP: *When you were a child, did you ever play games that used language as a major tool? What kind of games were they?*

Playing the Dozens

BY JOHN TIERNEY

JOHN TIERNEY

A Yale graduate, the author of several books, and a journalist, John Tierney has contributed regularly to the New York Times, Atlantic Monthly, Discover, Newsweek, *and* Rolling Stone. *This piece was first published on May 15, 1994, in the* New York Times.

Alfred Wright, a 19-year-old whose manhood was at stake on Longwood Avenue in the South Bronx, looked fairly calm as another teen-ager called him Chicken Head and compared his mother to Shamu the whale.

He fingered the gold chain around his thin neck while listening to a detailed complaint about his sister's sexual abilities. Then he slowly took the toothpick out of his mouth; the jeering crowd of young men quieted as he pointed at his accuser.

"He was so ugly when he was born," Wright said, "the doctor smacked his mom instead of him."

Maybe it was the moment, or the way he said it, or the vagaries of adolescent sensibilities, but somehow it worked. The group hooted as Wright put the toothpick back in his mouth and crossed his arms triumphantly. Two nonadolescents observing the action also looked pleased.

"I like the energy," said Monteria Ivey, 35.

"There might be something we can use here," said Stephan Dweck, 33.

They were spending the afternoon on the streets of the Bronx and Harlem looking for duels of insults, scouting to catalogue an African-American oral tradition that developed among slaves and evolved in urban ghettos. The classic name for this verbal contest is playing the dozens; the current street name is snapping. "We played the dozens for recreation, like white folks play Scrabble," H. Rap Brown said of his youth in the 1950's, and the games are just as popular today, especially among young men. When Dweck walks along 125th Street in Harlem asking people

5

"Got any good snaps?" they all know what he wants. They oblige with something like, "Your mother is so old, she owes Jesus food stamps."

Before becoming professional collectors, Dweck and Ivey refined their own snapping techniques while growing up at the Frederick Douglass housing project on West 102nd Street. Ivey still likes to recall one formative moment when he sat watching Dweck in action. "It was a summer night and a guy named Al was snapping on Stephan. He was snapping on his whole family— his mother, his father, the car his father was driving, the hat his father was wearing. It got really bad. You could see the smoke coming out of Stephan's ears. Now Al was dark-skinned, and Stephan finally snapped on that. He said, 'Al, you so black, you sweat Bosco,'[1] and the whole bench fell out. And to this day, 15 years later, anybody who was there that night, every time we see Al, we all say, 'Bosco!' "

Another formative moment came last summer, by which time Dweck had become an entertainment lawyer and Ivey a comedian. One night at the Uptown Comedy Club in Harlem, after Ivey had spent five minutes on stage snapping on a white man in the audience ("You're so white, you think Malcolm X's name is Malcolm Ten"), Dweck explained to the victim that the attack was nothing personal, just a black tradition. The victim, James Percelay, a 37-year-old writer and television producer, responded by following a white tradition. Upon discovering an indigenous form of African-American culture, he realized: There's a bigger market for this.

He, Dweck and Ivey formed a company called Two Brothers and a White   10
Guy. They collected snaps on playgrounds and conducted speakerphone snapping sessions to get contributions from professionals, like the rapper Ice-T ("Your father is so old, he dreams reruns"). They catalogued snaps by traits (fatness, stupidity, smelliness) and subjects (your hair, your clothes, your house) to compile a Bartlett's of the dozens. Their book, "Snaps," was published by William Morrow in February, and suddenly an old oral tradition has gone multimedia. Already 75,000 books are in print, and the authors are taping two snapping specials for HBO, preparing an anti-violence campaign for MTV and developing a comic-book character called the Dark Snapper. They're also collecting snaps from around the country for a second book, and they've noticed certain trends according to geography and age.

"In L.A. the snaps are more soft and playful," Dweck said. "In Chicago you still get people doing the old-style rhyming—that's called signifying. New York is the meanest. In New York it's 10 quick one-liners in a row—very rough and raw, especially among the young guys. You can see the progression through the generations. The younger you go, the more vicious you get."

---

[1] A chocolate-flavored drink popular after the Second World War. (Editor's note)

The younger generation's snaps can be astonishingly crude—usually graphic versions of the old "your mother left her shoes under my bed" theme—and there are probably experts who see them as a worrisome sign of hostility in today's young urban males. But then, young males everywhere have always been crude and hostile. Testosterone does strange things to them, and snapping is one of the more benign outlets for their aggression. It's more egalitarian than status competitions based on money or clothes or sports ability. It takes more courage and imagination than the "Beavis and Butt-head"[2] brand of suburban anomie. And it takes a lot more intelligence than those grand old coming-of-age rituals, fighting and killing. In the news media, young African-American men always seem to be going at one another with razors and guns, but in the real world many more prefer to use similes and metaphors.

"If you touch your opponent or get mad, you lose," Ivey explained on Longwood Avenue as the teen-agers snapped. "That's an important lesson for these kids. If they can learn how to be patient and take it here, it helps them stay cool when their boss gets on them. This game isn't brain surgery, but it teaches them to vent without hurting someone."

After the young men had run out of snaps, Ivey stepped up and pointed to Dweck. "When he was growing up," Ivey said, "his family was so poor, they used to go to Kentucky Fried Chicken to lick other people's fingers."[3]

"I know his mother," Dweck said when the laughter died down. "His mother's so fat, her blood type is Ragu."[4] It was another hit with the teenagers, who issued a long, menacing "ooh" at Ivey.

"That might be true," Ivey replied. "That might be true. But let's talk about your father. Your father's so dumb, when you were born, he looked at the umbilical cord and said, 'Look, honey, it comes with cable.'"

That snap got the best reaction yet—applause—and Dweck had to wait a minute for the whoops and cheers to subside. He knew he needed a Bosco-quality snap to come back. "Your father's so stupid," Dweck said, "he put a ruler on the side of the bed to see how long he slept." The teen-agers groaned. Bowing to public opinion, Dweck surrendered. He managed to keep smiling as Ivey took on a new challenger. "This is one of those lessons in patience and restraint." Dweck explained. "Even when the momentum's shifted and you're out of creative bullets, you get points for being gracious in defeat. A great snapper always knows how to walk away."

---

[2]An animated MTV comedy that featured two teenage vandals (1992–1997). (Editor's note)

[3]From the Kentucky Fried Chicken advertising slogan, "Finger-lickin' good!" (Editor's note)

[4]A brand of tomato sauce. (Editor's note)

AN EXCERPT FROM

MEN ARE FROM BELGIUM, WOMEN ARE FROM NEW BRUNSWICK

When women and men say:

Guy: Is this meat loaf?

Gal: Of course it is, darling.

Guy: Mmm. It's _delicious!_

Gal: I'm so glad you're enjoying it.

Guy: Did you use a recipe?

Gal: To tell the truth, I was feeling kind of creative, so I made it up!

Guy: Next time, don't be shy about using a recipe, O.K.?

Gal: Okeydokey!

They actually mean:

Guy: This is meat loaf, isn't it?

Gal: Do you have a problem with that?

Guy: It's awful.

Gal: Isn't that a darn shame.

Guy: Did you just throw all this stuff together randomly, or what?

Gal: So what if I did. SO WHAT. _SO, SO, SO WHAT!!!_

Guy: It's completely inedible, _that's_ what!

Gal: Your criticism stems from your own feelings of inadequacy. You should seek professional help.

R. Chast

ANALYZING What the Writer Says

1. In your own words, describe "playing the dozens" and "snapping."

2. Who plays this game?

3. Why are men like Monteria Ivey, Stephan Dweck, and James Percelay interested in the game? What are the consequences of their interest?

4. What is John Tierney's opinion of this game? What does it teach its players? What does (or should) it teach the readers of his essay?

ANALYZING How the Writer Says It

Tierney weaves a generous sampling of snaps into his essay. Why does he do this?

ANALYZING the Issue

What kind of group behavior does snapping encourage in the players? Do you agree with Tierney that "snapping is one of the more benign outlets" for teenage aggression?

ANALYZING Connections Between Texts

1. Language—verbal and nonverbal—is an important factor in constituting groups: A person who "talks the talk" belongs; one who doesn't is an outsider. What do writers as unlike each other as Annie Dillard ("Singing with the Fundamentalists," p. 470), Amy Tan ("Mother Tongue," p. 515), and John Tierney say about the power of language (and linguistic rituals) to constitute groups?

2. In "The Inheritance That Got Away" (p. 163), Melanie Thernstrom admits that she could have inherited a valuable sculpture from her grandmother—if only she had asked for it. What kind of game went on between the writer and her grandmother? Does this personal game regulate power structures in any way similar to the ritual trading of insults Tierney describes in his essay?

3. How does Roz Chast's cartoon (p. 530) make fun of the different languages spoken by men and women?

YOUR TURN: Suggestions for Writing About "Talk the Talk"

1. Write an essay in which you argue for or against the suggestion that we can change people's attitudes and prejudices if we change (by law, if necessary) the language they use.
2. Using examples from your own experience and that of people you know, write an argument supporting or refuting Deborah Tannen's thesis in "Marked Women."
3. Get a copy of a recent political speech, and analyze it using Orwell's critical apparatus in "Politics and the English Language."
4. Write an essay in which you argue for or against Jonathan Rauch's thesis in "In Defense of Prejudice."
5. Write a letter to your campus newspaper in which you argue that your school needs a speech code to protect minorities from verbal assaults. If your school already has such a code, get a copy and defend it against its critics. Or write a letter to your campus newspaper arguing why your school doesn't need such a code, or why the existing code should be abolished. Use the points raised by Rauch and Orwell in support of your own arguments.

"What I don't, like, get is how she, like, figured out I was, like, having an affair with, like, the babysitter."

6. Using examples from your own experience and that of people you know, write an argument supporting Deborah Tannen's thesis in "Marked Women."

7. Get a copy of a recent political speech, and analyze it using Orwell's critical apparatus in "Politics and the English Language."

8. Having read David Sedaris's "Me Talk Pretty One Day," write an essay in which you point out the advantages of making foreign languages an integral part of the American elementary school curriculum.

9. Imagine you are a parent whose children habitually "play the dozens" with their friends at school. Write a letter to the school's principal arguing that he/she stop such ritual trading of insults between students. Alternately, write the principal's response in which he/she argues why these games should not be banned.

10. Annie Dillard describes how she and a group of Christians participate in a linguistic act—a daily singing ritual—that unites them as a group if only for a few minutes a day. Write an essay in which you describe some form of speech ritual that defines a group.

11. Write an essay in which you compare the way Andy Anderson, the subject of Dana Fineman's photograph, and the driver of the truck pictured in Inge Fink's "Talk the Talk" use slogans to make an argument. Alternately, analyze the reliance on slogans by special-interest groups to further their causes.

12. Lewis H. Lapham criticizes post-September 11 rhetoric, arguing that it privileges jingoism over political analysis. Find a political column or speech that engages the kind of rhetoric Lapham decries and write an essay analyzing it.

13. Listen to or read a political speech. Analyze it, looking for instances of doubletalk, generalizations, buzz words, fear-mongering, or other methods that seem designed to persuade the public without reason, facts, or evidence.

IMAGE GALLERY 👁

DANA FINEMAN

Abortion Activist

After studying at the Art Center College of Design in Pasadena, Dana Fineman worked as an assistant to celebrity photographer Douglas Kirkland for several years. Her work has appeared in Time, Newsweek, *and* New York Magazine.

1. What is Andy Anderson's religious denomination? How do you know?

2. What do Anderson's props say about his methods in fighting against abortion?

3. How does Fineman use composition effectively in her photograph?

4. Do you think people like Andy Anderson can effectively convince people that abortion is wrong? Why or why not?

GERRIT FOKKEMA

Ku Klux Klan

Even though their behavior breaks the law and embarrasses their fellow townspeople, the members of the Gainsville, Georgia, chapter of the Ku Klux Klan march through mostly black sections of town, allegedly to protest the sale of drugs and abortion clinics. When he took this photograph in 1986, Australian Gerrit Fokkema worked for the Sydney Morning Herald; *his work is included in the collection of the Australian National Gallery.*

1. How does Fokkema capture the rituals of the Ku Klux Klan? How does the Klan mark itself as a group?

2. How does this photograph use symbolism?

3. How does Fokkema use composition and light effects in this picture?

4. According to its mission statement, the Gainesville chapter of the Klan protests drugs and abortion with its rallies and marches through black neighborhoods. Do you believe them? Why or why not?

5. Do you think Fokkema takes a position about the Klan in his photograph, or does he merely objectively document one of its rallies?

RUTH ORKIN

American Girl in Italy

In her book A Photo Journal, *photographer Ruth Orkin tells the story of this picture, part of a 1951 photo essay about her travels in Europe: The idea had been incubating for some time when, in Florence, she met New Yorker Jinx Allen, who agreed to model for the picture.* Cosmopolitan *published the photograph as part of a five-page article titled "Don't Be Afraid to Travel Alone"—"the perfect accompaniment to my tongue-in-cheek photographs," says Orkin.*

1. Describe what the men in the picture are doing. What do their reactions to the young woman suggest?

2. What does the model's facial expression say about her reaction to the attention she is getting?

3. Although this picture is a snapshot (not a carefully styled studio picture), the photographer knows how to use line and composition. How does she use these two techniques for effect in this picture?

4. What does Orkin's title "American Girl in Italy" suggest about her opinion of her subject? Why would she call this photograph "tongue-in-cheek"?

15 BIG BROTHER

Few realized when *1984,* George Orwell's novel about totalitarianism, was published in 1949 that just over a half-century later the novel's famous slogan would resonate so deeply for so many. And few could have known on September 11, 2001, even as the twin towers of Manhattan's World Trade Center came crashing down in a cataclysm of fire and steel and concrete, claiming 3,000 lives, that within a year Orwell's chilling vision of a future where people are under con-

"Big Brother Is Watching You"

George Orwell
1984

stant surveillance, where language is controlled, where the only true patriot is the one who toes the party line, would be near—if not here. Who knew that signs in airport bathroom stalls would warn travelers to report any "suspicious" persons or activity? Who knew that we would need an Office of Homeland Security—or that the pyramid featured in the logo of the newly formed Office of Information Awareness would recall, so eerily, the architecture of the building housing Orwell's

Ministry of Truth? Who knew that the basic freedoms and civil rights we take for granted would be threatened by a Patriot Act?

Was George Orwell a prophet? Have we traded our civil liberties for national security? Or is calling up Orwell and other doomsday scenarios yet another form of hysteria? And have we been here before? After all, Dorothea Lange's photograph of Japanese-American children reciting the Pledge of Allegiance from their internment camps during WWII, predating Orwell's Big Brother, laments a disturbing distortion of democracy.

The selections in this unit offer several riffs on the themes of individual freedom and state control. In an excerpt from his multivolume *Discipline and Punish*, French philosopher Michel Foucault traces the development of surveillance as Western civilization's preferred method of discipline. And indeed we have lived with cameras in elevators and even department store dressing rooms for some time; we welcome them at cash machines and to monitor baby—and babysitter—but Farhad Manjoo raises the specter of cameras triggered by the goods we purchase. Anna Quindlen reminds us that our judicial system has long sanctioned spying on adults engaged in sexual activity through sodomy laws, laws Antonin Scalia supports. Deborah Sontag wonders if laws designed to protect families are too intrusive. In a pre-9/11 piece, Michael Kinsley dismisses Orwellian notions of techno-totalitarianism, embracing the essentially liberating function of technology.

But, to echo a standard refrain, 9/11 changed everything. Charles Krauthammer acknowledges that since 9/11, times *have* changed and makes a case for what he considers a commonsense security measure, profiling airline passengers, but a Canadian-Pakistani journalist, Adnan Khan, offers the perspective of one deemed suspicious by virtue of birthplace, chronicling the indignities he suffers at the U.S.–Canadian border. Lewis H. Lapham questions the wisdom of trading liberty for safety, and Molly Ivins invokes Orwell's spirit, arguing that our Big Brother is Big Business.

In a different time, Thomas Jefferson fretted over not a Big Brother but a tyrannical Father, laying out a case in "The Declaration of Independence" for the colonies wresting themselves from the grip of George III and the threats he posed to "life, liberty, and the pursuit of happiness." Could he have imagined the complicated democracy that evolved from those words? The untold freedom? Or its erosion—in the name of freedom? ✳

WARMING UP: *Imagine, for a second, that you are the mayor of your hometown. A terrible, contagious disease has broken out, a disease for which there is no known cure. How would you deal with it? What measures would you propose? What instructions (if any) would you give to the townspeople and the people who work for you?*

Panopticism

By Michel Foucault

MICHEL FOUCAULT

Michel Foucault (1926–1984) was a prominent French intellectual, philosopher, and university professor. The following excerpt from Discipline and Punish: The Birth of the Prison *(first published in 1975) traces the development of institutional punishment from the corporal punishment in the Middle Ages to modern prison systems, showing how we have substituted rigid surveillance for bloody retribution upon the criminal; we prefer to discipline than to punish.*

The following, according to an order published at the end of the seventeenth century, were the measures to be taken when the plague appeared in a town.

First, a strict spatial partitioning: the closing of the town and its outlying districts, a prohibition to leave the town on pain of death, the killing of all stray animals; the division of the town into distinct quarters, each governed by an intendant. Each street is placed under the authority of a syndic, who keeps it under surveillance; if he leaves the street, he will be condemned to death. On the appointed day, everyone is ordered to stay indoors: it is forbidden to leave on pain of death. The syndic himself comes to lock the door of each house from the outside; he takes the key with him and hands it over to the intendant of the quarter; the intendant keeps it until the end of the quarantine. Each family will have made its own provisions; but, for bread and wine, small wooden canals are set up between the street and the interior of the houses, thus allowing each person to receive his ration without communicating with the suppliers and other residents; meat, fish and herbs will be hoisted up into the houses with pulleys and baskets. If it is absolutely necessary to leave the house, it will be done in turn, avoiding any meeting. Only the intendants, syndics and guards will move about the streets and also, between the infected houses, from one corpse to another, the 'crows', who can be left to die: these are 'people of little substance who carry the sick, bury the dead, clean and do many vile and abject offices'. It is a segmented, immobile, frozen space. Each individual is fixed in his place. And, if he moves, he does so at the risk of his life, contagion or punishment.

Inspection functions ceaselessly. The gaze is alert everywhere: 'A considerable body of militia, commanded by good officers and men of substance', guards at the gates, at the town hall and in every quarter to ensure the prompt obedience of the people and the most absolute authority of the magistrates, 'as also to observe all disorder, theft and extortion'. At each of the town gates there will be an observation post; at the end of each street sentinels. Every day, the intendant visits the quarter in his charge, inquires whether the syndics have carried out their tasks, whether the inhabitants have anything to complain of; they 'observe their actions'. Every day, too, the syndic goes into the street for which he is responsible; stops before each house: gets all the inhabitants to appear at the windows (those who live overlooking the courtyard will be allocated a window looking onto the street at which no one but they may show themselves); he calls each of them by name; informs himself as to the state of each and every one of them—'in which respect the inhabitants will be compelled to speak the truth under pain of death'; if someone does not appear at the window, the syndic must ask why: 'In this way he will find out easily enough whether dead or sick are being concealed.' Everyone locked up in his cage, everyone at his window, answering to his name and showing himself when asked—it is the great review of the living and the dead.

This surveillance is based on a system of permanent registration: reports from the syndics to the intendants, from the intendants to the magistrates or mayor. At the beginning of the 'lock up', the role of each of the inhabitants present in the town is laid down, one by one; this document bears 'the name, age, sex of everyone, notwithstanding his condition': a copy is sent to the intendant of the quarter, another to the office of the town hall, another to enable the syndic to make his daily roll call. Everything that may be observed during the course of the visits—deaths, illnesses, complaints, irregularities—is noted down and transmitted to the intendants and magistrates. The magistrates have complete control over medical treatment; they have appointed a physician in charge; no other practitioner may treat, no apothecary prepare medicine, no confessor visit a sick person without having received from him a written note 'to prevent anyone from concealing and dealing with those sick of the contagion, unknown to the magistrates'. The registration of the pathological must be constantly centralized. The relation of each individual to his disease and to his death passes through the representatives of power, the registration they make of it, the decisions they take on it.

Five or six days after the beginning of the quarantine, the process of purify-5 ing the houses one by one is begun. All the inhabitants are made to leave; in each room 'the furniture and goods' are raised from the ground or suspended from the air; perfume is poured around the room; after carefully sealing the windows, doors and even the keyholes with wax, the perfume is set alight. Finally, the entire house is closed while the perfume is consumed; those who have carried out the work are searched, as they were on entry, 'in the presence of the residents of the house, to see that they did not have something on their persons as they left that they did not have on entering'. Four hours later, the residents are allowed to re-enter their homes.

This enclosed, segmented space, observed at every point, in which the individuals are inserted in a fixed place, in which the slightest movements are supervised, in which all events are recorded, in which an uninterrupted work of writing links the centre and periphery, in which power is exercised without division, according to a continuous hierarchical figure, in which each individual is constantly located, examined and distributed among the living beings, the sick and the dead—all this constitutes a compact model of the disciplinary mechanism. The plague is met by order; its function is to sort out every possible confusion: that of the disease, which is transmitted when bodies are mixed together; that of the evil, which is increased when fear and death overcome prohibitions. It lays down for each individual his place, his body, his disease and his death, his well-being, by means of an omnipresent and omniscient power that subdivides itself in a regular, uninterrupted way even to the ultimate determination of the individual, of what characterizes him, of what belongs to him, of what happens to him. Against the plague, which is a mixture, discipline brings into play its power, which is one of analysis. A whole literary fiction of the festival grew up around the plague: suspended laws, lifted prohibitions, the frenzy of passing time, bodies mingling together without respect, individuals unmasked, abandoning their statutory identity and the figure under which they had been recognized, allowing a quite different truth to appear. But there was also a political dream of the plague, which was exactly its reverse: not the collective festival, but strict divisions; not laws transgressed, but the penetration of regulation into even the smallest details of everyday life through the mediation of the complete hierarchy that assured the capillary functioning of power; not masks that were put on and taken off, but the assignment to each individual of his 'true' name, his 'true' place, his 'true' body, his 'true' disease. The plague as a form, at once real and imaginary, of disorder had as its medical and political correlative discipline. Behind the disciplinary mechanisms can be read the haunting memory of 'contagions', of the plague, of rebellions, crimes, vagabondage, desertions, people who appear and disappear, live and die in disorder.

If it is true that the leper gave rise to rituals of exclusion, which to a certain extent provided the model for and general form of the great Confinement, then the plague gave rise to disciplinary projects. Rather than the massive, binary division between one set of people and another, it called for multiple separations, individualizing distributions, an organization in depth of surveillance and control, an intensification and a ramification of power. The leper was caught up in a practice of rejection, of exile-enclosure; he was left to his doom in a mass among which it was useless to differentiate; those sick of the plague were caught up in a meticulous tactical partitioning in which individual differentiations were the constricting effects of a power that multiplied, articulated and subdivided itself; the great confinement on the one hand; the correct training on the other. The leper and his separation; the plague and its segmentations. The first is marked; the second analysed and distributed. The exile of the leper and the arrest of the plague do not bring with them the same political dream. The first is that of a pure community, the second that of a disciplined society. Two ways of exercising power over men, of controlling their relations, of separating out their dangerous mixtures. The plague-stricken town, traversed throughout with hierarchy, surveillance, observation, writing; the town immobilized by the functioning of an extensive power that bears in a distinct way over all individual bodies—this is the utopia of the perfectly governed city. The plague (envisaged as a possibility at least) is the trial in the course of which one may define ideally the exercise of disciplinary power. In order to make rights and laws function according to pure theory, the jurists place themselves in imagination in the state of nature; in order to see perfect disciplines functioning, rulers dreamt of the state of plague. Underlying disciplinary projects the image of the plague stands for all forms of confusion and disorder; just as the image of the leper, cut off from all human contact, underlies projects of exclusion.

They are different projects, then, but not incompatible ones. We see them coming slowly together, and it is the peculiarity of the nineteenth century that it applied to the space of exclusion of which the leper was the symbolic inhabitant (beggars, vagabonds, madmen and the disorderly formed the real population) the technique of power proper to disciplinary partitioning. Treat 'lepers' as 'plague victims', project the subtle segmentations of discipline onto the confused space of internment, combine it with the methods of analytical distribution proper to power, individualize the excluded, but use procedures of individualization to mark exclusion—this is what was operated regularly by disciplinary power from the beginning of the nineteenth century in the psychiatric asylum, the penitentiary, the reformatory, the approved school and, to some extent, the hospital. Generally speaking, all the authorities exercising individual control function according to a double mode; that of binary division and branding (mad/sane; dangerous/harmless; normal/abnormal); and that of coercive assignment, of differential distribution (who he is; where he must be; how he is to be characterized; how he is to be recognized; how a constant surveillance is to be exercised over him in an individual way, etc.). On the one hand, the lepers are treated as plague victims; the tactics of individualizing disciplines are imposed on the excluded; and, on the other hand, the universality of disciplinary controls makes it possible to brand the 'leper' and to bring into play against him the dualistic mechanisms of exclusion. The constant division between the normal and the abnormal, to which every individual is subjected, brings us back to our own time, by applying the binary branding and exile of the leper to quite different objects; the existence of a whole set of techniques and institutions for measuring, supervising and correcting the abnormal brings into play the disciplinary mechanisms to which the fear of the plague gave rise. All the mechanisms of power which, even today, are disposed around the abnormal individual, to brand him and to alter him, are composed of those two forms from which they distantly derive.

ANALYZING What the Writer Says

1. In your own words, summarize measures taken at the end of the seventeenth century to deal with the (Bubonic) plague. How did city magistrates expect this system to work?

2. What does Foucault mean when he says that this "surveillance is based on a system of permanent registration"?

3. In what way is a system of permanent registration different from earlier methods of dealing with incurable diseases such as leprosy?

4. How, according to Foucault, do discipline and exclusion fuse in the nineteenth century?

5. What does Foucault mean when he says that all "the authorities exercising individual control function according to a double mode, . . . binary division and . . . differential distribution"?

ANALYZING How the Writer Says It

How readable is Foucault's argument? What parts are most accessible? What passages are particularly difficult? Who is Foucault's intended audience? What makes you think so?

ANALYZING the Issue

1. The Bubonic plague in the seventeenth century had an impact on the population similar to that of the onset of the AIDS crisis in the 1980s. From what you know about the way authorities dealt with AIDS, do you think Foucault is right when he says that authorities use the double method of exclusion and surveillance? Explain.

2. Consider the "social disease" of crime in our society. Do our government officials deal with it the way Foucault says they do? Explain.

3. In order to combat the latest threat to our safety—terrorism—the Bush administration has established the Information Awareness Office, an organization whose task is to compile an enormous electronic database of information on all

citizens in an effort to detect and catch terrorists in their everyday movements. Information in this database may include documentation of our spending habits through credit card records, our movement through records of the tickets we purchase, our parking and speeding tickets, our entertainment preferences, the music or books we buy, our health records, and our marriages and divorces. Having read Foucault, do you think the Bush administration resembles the seventeenth-century city magistrates Foucault describes in any way? Why or why not?

ANALYZING Connections Between Texts

1. Michel Foucault and Lewis H. Lapham (p. 567) both write about tight systems of surveillance designed to control dangerous "diseases," whether a literal disease such as the Bubonic plague or a figurative one such as terrorism. Both writers emphasize the degree of power such surveillance gives to government representatives. Are such methods justified in the name of national health or security? Why or why not?

2. In "He's Still Ready for His Close-Up," (p. 794), Dennis Overbye alludes to the "1,500-page F.B.I. file" kept on Albert Einstein, evidence of the intense scrutiny and surveillance of one of history's undisputed geniuses and, arguably, one of American history's heroes. Using Overbye's information and Foucault's thesis, analyze the possible reasons for such close surveillance of Einstein.

MANKOFF

"Oh, <u>can't</u> complain."

3. In what way does Danny Lyon's photograph of the prisoner seen through the peephole in the door (p. 613) illustrate the concepts Michel Foucault tackles in "Panopiticism"? In what way does the picture illustrate the governmental surveillance techniques described by Lapham? Are the two systems—the prison system and a governmental strategy to fight terrorism through information—even comparable? Why or why not?

How 1984 and 2002 Add Up to Trouble

BY MOLLY IVINS

MOLLY IVINS

A Texas journalist, Molly Ivins often exposes the ridiculous side of American politics and culture with her trademark wit. In the following column, which appeared in Texas's Star-Telegram *on November 24, 2002, Ivins warns of the continuing erosion of our civil liberties—and our environment—in the government's response to September 11.*

Readin' the newspapers anymore is eerily reminiscent of all those bad novels warning of the advent of fascism in America. *It Can't Happen Here* by Sinclair Lewis was a bad book, and the genre shades off into right-wing paranoia about black helicopters, including the memorably awful *The Turner Diaries*. I don't use the f-word myself—in fact, for years, I've made fun of liberals who hear the approach of jackbooted fascism around every corner. But to quote a real authority on the subject, "Fascism should more properly be called corporatism, since it is the merger of state and corporate power"—Benito Mussolini.

New York Times columnist Paul Krugman recently quoted "the quite apolitical Web site Corporate Governance, which matter-of-factly remarks, 'Given the power of corporate lobbyists, government control often equates to de facto corporate control anyway.'" It's gettin' downright creepy out there.

The most hair-raising news du jour is about Total Information Awareness, a giant government computer spy system being set up to spy on Americans, run by none other than John Poindexter of Iran-contra fame.

Total Information Awareness will provide intelligence agencies and law enforcement with instant access to information from e-mail, telephone records, credit cards, banking transactions and travel records, all without a search warrant. It will, said Poindexter, "break down the stovepipes" that separate commercial and government databases. The just-passed Homeland

Security bill undermines the Privacy Act of 1974, which was intended to limit what government agencies can do with personal information.

And can we trust the government to keep all this information solely for the task of tracking terrorists? Funny you should ask. *The Wall Street Journal* reported last week that shortly after Sept. 11, the FBI circulated the names of hundreds of people it wanted to question to scores of corporations around the country, sharing the list with car rental companies, banks, travel firms, casinos, truckers, chemical companies and power plants.

"A year later, the list has taken on a life of its own, with multiplying—and error-filled—versions being passed around like bootleg music. Some companies fed a version of the list into their databases and now use it to screen job applicants and customers."

The list included people who were not suspects at all—just people whom the FBI wanted to talk to because they might have had some information. But, the *Journal* reports, a Venezuelan bank's security officer sent the list, headed "suspected terrorists sent by the FBI," to a Web site.

The great writer on the subject of totalitarianism was George Orwell, and *1984* is always worth rereading. Damned if GeeDubya Bush didn't pop up the other day to announce that we must fight a war "for the sake of peace." That's not vaguely Orwellian—it's a direct steal.

During another time of rampaging fear when civil liberties were considered a frivolous luxury—the late, unlamented McCarthy era—the American Civil Liberties Union chickened out on some big issues, and so an Emergency Civil Liberties Union had to be created to fight McCarthyism. The present ACLU, under Anthony Romero, is fighting hard, but I think we need a new coalition organization—civil libertarians, libertarians and principled conservatives—real patriots who believe in the Constitution. The blowhard right-wingers sometimes put down Barry Goldwater these days as "the liberals' favorite conservative," and so he was. But in your heart, you know Goldwater would have had a cow over all this.

Rep. Dick Armey has already announced that he will do consulting work with the ACLU on privacy issues (good of him). Rep. Ron Paul and columnist Bill Safire are stout on these matters, as are other unlikely suspects such as Rep. Bob Barr of Georgia.

For those who relish irony, there's a comical extent to which liberals are the new conservatives, exactly where the old principled Republicans used to be—reluctant to get involved in foreign wars, suspicious of foreign entanglements, harping on fiscal responsibility and worried about constitutional freedoms.

Personally, I still believe that internationalism makes more sense than isolationism because our major problems in the future—global warming, overpopulation and water shortage—are going to have to be dealt with on a global basis. This is an environmental struggle as well as a civil liberties struggle. I think it is inarguable that this is the most anti-environmental administration since before Teddy Roosevelt.

The corporatists in this administration, particularly those from the oil business, apparently have some grand imperialist schemes to keep us in cheap oil indefinitely.

As a matter of both foreign and environmental policy, it makes a lot more sense to lay rail, promote renewable energy and get serious about conserving oil. We subsidize the oil business with innumerable tax breaks, loopholes and support programs. For heaven's sake, why not support renewable energy instead? Why should we ask our military to die for cheap oil when the rest of us aren't even being asked to get better mileage?

ANALYZING What the Writer Says

1. In George Orwell's 1949 novel *1984*, "Big Brother," a mysterious, all-knowing, godlike power is a party construct who controls the population through intimidation and the vague, generalized threat that he is always watching. Who or what, according to Ivins, is our Big Brother?

2. What specific threats to our civil liberties does Ivins identify?

3. How does Ivins link the concept of Big Brother and her concerns about the environment?

4. What is Ivins's main point?

ANALYZING How the Writer Says It

1. Analyze the title of Ivins's piece.

2. What is the effect of Ivins's use of the slang word "bidness"?

3. Is Ivins's argument constructed fairly? Point to strengths and/or weaknesses.

ANALYZING the Issue

1. Should the government be free to investigate and share any aspects of our lives, in the name of our protection? Or are some areas off limits? Defend your answer.

2. Do you agree that government control equals corporate control equals environmental destruction? Why or why not?

ANALYZING Connections Between Texts

1. Compare Ivins's opinion of the government's "Total Information Awareness" project to Lewis H. Lapham's in "Regime Change" (p. 567). How are their concerns similar? How is the focus of each argument as it concerns "information awareness" different?

2. After suggesting that the Bush administration's imperialistic policies are rooted in a desire for inexpensive oil, Ivins asks at the end of her essay, "Why should we ask our military to die for cheap oil when the rest of us aren't even being asked to get better mileage?" How does Ivins's reasoning tie into the arguments of Jack Hitt in "The Hidden Life of SUVs" (p. 652) and Arianna Huffington in "The Coming SUV Wars" (p. 657)?

3. How does Trudeau's Doonesbury comic strip above illustrate some of Ivins's points about the Bush administration's Orwellian tactics?

The Declaration of Independence

By Thomas Jefferson

THOMAS JEFFERSON

Thomas Jefferson (1743–1826), third president of the United States, drafted the Declaration of Independence, a classic example of deductive reasoning, in 1776; it was one of the few accomplishments, he claimed, for which he wanted to be remembered.

When in the course of human events, it becomes necessary for one people to dissolve the political bands which have connected them with another, and to assume among the powers of the earth, the separate and equal station to which the Laws of Nature and of Nature's God entitle them, a decent respect to the opinions of mankind requires that they should declare the causes which impel them to the separation.

We hold these truths to be self-evident, that all men are created equal, that they are endowed by their Creator with certain inalienable rights, that among these are life, liberty, and the pursuit of happiness. That to secure these rights, governments are instituted among men, deriving their just powers from the consent of the governed. That whenever any form of government becomes destructive of these ends, it is the right of the people to alter or to abolish it, and to institute new government, laying its foundation on such principles and organizing its powers in such form, as to them shall seem most likely to effect their safety and happiness. Prudence, indeed, will dictate that governments long established should not be changed for light and transient causes; and accordingly all experience hath shown, that mankind are more disposed to suffer, while evils are sufferable, than to right themselves by abolishing the forms to which they are accustomed. But when a long train of abuses and usurpations, pursuing invariably the same object, evinces a design to reduce them under absolute despotism, it is their right, it is their duty, to throw off such government, and to provide new guards for their future security. Such has been the patient sufferance of these Colonies; and such is now the necessity which constrains them to alter their former systems of government. The history of the present King of Great Britain is a history of repeated injuries and usurpations, all having in direct object the establishment of an absolute tyranny over these States. To prove this, let facts be submitted to a candid world.

He has refused his assent to laws, the most wholesome and necessary for the public good.

He has forbidden his Governors to pass laws of immediate and pressing importance, unless suspended in their operation till his assent should be obtained; and when so suspended, he has utterly neglected to attend to them.

He has refused to pass other laws for the accommodation of large districts 5 of people, unless those people would relinquish the right of representation in the legislature, a right inestimable to them and formidable to tyrants only.

He has called together legislative bodies at places unusual, uncomfortable, and distant from the depository of their public records, for the sole purpose of fatiguing them into compliance with his measures.

He has dissolved representative houses repeatedly, for opposing with manly firmness his invasions on the rights of the people.

He has refused for a long time, after such dissolutions, to cause others to be elected; whereby the legislative powers, incapable of annihilation, have returned to the people at large for their exercise; the State remaining in the meantime exposed to all the dangers of invasion from without and convulsions within.

He has endeavoured to prevent the population of these States; for that purpose obstructing the laws for naturalization of foreigners; refusing to pass others to encourage their migration hither, and raising the conditions of new appropriations of lands.

He has obstructed the administration of justice, by refusing his assent to 10 laws for establishing judiciary powers.

He has made judges dependent on his will alone, for the tenure of their offices, and the amount and payment of their salaries.

He has erected a multitude of new offices, and sent hither swarms of officers to harass our people, and eat out their substance.

He has kept among us, in times of peace, standing armies without the consent of our legislatures.

He has affected to render the military independent of and superior to the civil power.

He has combined with others to subject us to a jurisdiction foreign of our 15 constitution, and unacknowledged by our laws; giving his assent to their acts of pretended legislation:

For quartering large bodies of armed troops among us:

For protecting them, by a mock trial, from punishment for any murders which they should commit on the inhabitants of these States:

For cutting off our trade with all parts of the world:

For imposing taxes on us without our consent:

For depriving us in many cases of the benefits of trial by jury: 20

For transporting us beyond seas to be tried for pretended offences:

For abolishing the free system of English laws in a neighboring Province, establishing therein an arbitrary government, and enlarging its boundaries so as to render it at once an example and fit instrument for introducing the same absolute rule into these Colonies:

For taking away our Charters, abolishing our most valuable laws, and altering fundamentally the forms of our governments:

For suspending our own legislatures, and declaring themselves invested with power to legislate for us in all cases whatsoever.

He has abdicated government here, by declaring us out of his protection, 25 and waging war against us.

He has plundered our seas, ravaged our coasts, burnt our towns, and destroyed the lives of our people.

He is at this time transporting large armies of foreign mercenaries to complete the works of death, desolation, and tyranny, already begun with circumstances of cruelty and perfidy scarcely paralleled in the most barbarous ages, and totally unworthy the head of a civilized nation.

He has constrained our fellow citizens taken captive on the high seas to bear arms against their country, to become the executioners of their friends and brethren, or to fall themselves by their hands.

He has excited domestic insurrections among us, and has endeavored to bring on the inhabitants of our frontiers, the merciless Indian savages, whose known rule of warfare, is an undistinguished destruction of all ages, sexes and conditions.

In every stage of these oppressions we have petitioned for redress in the 30 most humble terms: our repeated petitions have been answered only by repeated injury. A prince whose character is thus marked by every act which may define a tyrant is unfit to be the ruler of a free people.

Nor have we been wanting in attention to our British brethren. We have warned them from time to time of attempts by their legislature to extend an unwarrantable jurisdiction over us. We have reminded them of the circumstances of our emigration and settlement here. We have appealed to their native justice and magnanimity, and we have conjured them by the ties of our common kindred to disavow these usurpations, which would inevitably interrupt our connections and correspondence. They too have been deaf to the voice of justice and consanguinity. We must, therefore, acquiesce in the necessity which denounces our separation, and hold them, as we hold the rest of mankind, enemies in war, in peace friends.

We, therefore, the Representatives of the United States of America, in General Congress assembled, appealing to the Supreme Judge of the world for the rectitude of our intentions, do, in the name, and by authority of the good people of these Colonies, solemnly publish and declare, that these United Colonies are, and of right ought to be, Free and Independent States; that they are absolved from all allegiance to the British Crown, and that all political connection between them and the state of Great Britain, is and ought to be totally dissolved; and that as Free and Independent States, they have full power to levy war, conclude peace, contract alliances, establish commerce, and to do all other acts and things which Independent States may of right do. And for the support of this declaration, with a firm reliance on the protection of Divine Providence, we mutually pledge to each other our lives, our fortunes, and our sacred honor.

ANALYZING What the Writer Says

1. Summarize the logical premises of The Declaration of Independence.
2. Most of Jefferson's document is a list. What is enumerated in the list?

ANALYZING How the Writer Says It

Within Jefferson's argument is a long section of inductive reasoning—that is, using many specifics to arrive at a generalization. What argument must he establish, using facts, before proceeding to his conclusion? How adequate is the evidence?

ANALYZING the Issue

1. What do you think is the most important sentence in the Declaration? Why?
2. Jefferson's first draft of the Declaration of Independence contained both an antislavery statement and a specific attack upon the British people for tolerating George III's tyranny against the American colonists. How would America be different had either or both not been excised by the Congress?

ANALYZING Connections Between Texts

1. Compare the basic argument Jefferson makes about bad rulers to Anna Quindlen's (p. 583) about bad laws. What does each argument take for granted?
2. In what ways is Anndee Hochman's essay "Growing Pains: Beyond 'One Big Happy Family'" (p. 131) a personal declaration of independence? What aspects of her argument are analogous to Jefferson's?
3. Considering the context of Dorothea Lange's "Pledge of Allegiance" (p. 612)—a Japanese internment camp—how does the photo mock the principles of Jefferson's vision of American independence and the "inalienable rights" to "life, liberty, and the pursuit of happiness"?

WARMING UP: *If you have boarded a plane since the terrorist attack on the World Trade Center, have you caught yourself looking at the faces of your fellow passengers? Do you feel slightly uncomfortable when you see Middle Eastern-looking men among them?*

Bordering on Panic

By Adnan R. Khan

ADNAN R. KHAN

Adnan R. Khan, a Pakistani–Canadian free-lance photojournalist from Toronto, describes his encounter with immigration officials when he tried to cross the Canadian border into the United States shortly after the terrorist attack of September 11, 2001. In this article, which first appeared in Maclean's *on Nov. 25, 2002, he chronicles his resentment at being treated as a suspect because of his ethnic background and despite his Canadian passport.*

I'm getting accustomed to people asking me where I was born. Since 9/11, my brown skin's been a sort of blinking light to many curiosity seekers, my sleepy left eye a source of worry for the growing list of morphological profilers roaming the streets of North America. I usually respond offhandedly. "Pakistan," I say, and turn my attention elsewhere as if that should be enough. It never is. So when an American border official posed the same question to me on a recent trip to the U.S., I tried to sound as casual as if it were just another inebriated yokel slurring out a barely comprehensible, "Where you from?" It didn't work.

I know America has a right to defend its border, but Muslims are increasingly under suspicion these days, even comfortably hyphenated Canadian ones like myself. We should resign ourselves, I suppose, to the cold sterility of waiting rooms at American border crossings where towering models of the Statue of Liberty singe the ceilings and the depressingly happy faces of missing children stare out from dingy bulletin boards. It's our lot, I fatalistically think, to be subjected to overzealous immigration officials, grilling us to the point of near panic, ignoring language barriers, goading and prodding until we stumble over our words. That's more than enough to make us look suspicious, besides our place of birth, of course.

For the group of Muslims milling about for hours in the waiting room with me at the Lewiston-Queenston Bridge near Niagara Falls, the experience was enough to make them pull a Rohinton Mistry and refuse, as did the author, to enter the U.S. "I'm

never going back," one Pakistani father of four fumed after being fingerprint-
ed and photographed.

Another Middle Eastern man, after having his wallet unceremoniously emptied onto a counter before he was whisked away and locked in a back room,
only to be released an hour later and told to go back to Canada, refused to discuss his ordeal with me. Both men were Canadian citizens and neither could
understand why they were singled out. A few other visible minorities came in
and left within an hour, but for Muslims, it would not be so simple.

By the time my interrogation began, I'd lost all hope of making it into the   5
States before nightfall. The stock questions were asked by a droopy-eyed, uniformed immigration official who finally reached the inevitable one: "What
were you doing in Afghanistan?" I explained that I'm a freelance photojournalist and I was working for Maclean's at the time. I pointed out the "journalist" credentials clearly marked on the Afghan visa in my passport, which elicited an ambiguous "Hmmm" from my interlocutor. Every answer was recorded
on a sheet of foolscap. I asked why and he responded cryptically, "What's real
is unreal and what's unreal is real."

That could be the slogan for contemporary America—a fraying of reality in the
post-9/11 world. And when my car was searched by two white-gloved officials, I
felt as if I'd slipped into a David Lynch movie. They dissected my defenceless little Honda and its contents with a zeal that seemed utterly over the top. My notebook and personal organizer were confiscated and I worried whether I had any
cheesy love poetry scribbled into my notes (how embarrassing!) or if my friends'
phone numbers would be copied and filed away for future reference.

When the immigration official ushered me into a back room, drably furnished with a rectangular table and four chairs, my anxiety level skyrocketed.
Two casually dressed men entered the room, and introduced themselves as
members of the Joint Terrorism Task Force.

Now I was scared.

They pulled the chairs close together, crowding one corner of the table and
asked me to sit down between them. The Border Patrol agent and his New
York State trooper counterpart rifled through a set of prepared questions.
Their knowledge of Pakistani culture and geography seemed minimal, but I
thought this might be a ploy. (Was I becoming paranoid?) At one point, the
Border Patrol agent casually asked if I spoke Pakistani and I was tempted to
respond that while my Pakistani was a bit rough, I could speak Canadian flaw-
lessly. But I refrained. Why tempt fate, I thought, especially when fate's
accomplices had me cornered in a back office of a foreign country.

During the three-hour ordeal, I'd been made to feel like an unwanted out-   10
sider, as if I were guilty of some heinous crime and now it was my responsibility to prove my innocence. The alienation I felt was relatively minor for

someone with few ties to America, but for the thousands of Canadian-Muslims who have loved ones living south of the border, America's rejection of their kind wounds deeply.

When it was all over, I couldn't help but laugh as I drove back over the bridge, picturing my personal profile wasting kilobytes in an FBI database. I'd been grilled by three levels of American security and for what? Had America's national interest really been served?

Back at the Canadian border, a uniformed official inquired about how long I'd stayed in the U.S. Just a few hours, I responded, too ashamed to go into the details.

"And the value of goods you're bringing over?" he asked.

"Zero," I replied.

"Okay, go home." 15

Gladly.

ANALYZING What the Writer Says

1. Why is Khan detained at the U.S. border? How do the immigration officials react to his credentials (the visa in his passport, his description of what he is doing professionally)?

2. What does Khan mean when he says, "What's real is unreal and what's unreal is real . . . could be the slogan for contemporary America"?

3. What difference between the American and Canadian immigration officials does Khan notice when he returns to Canada after being denied entrance into the United States?

ANALYZING How the Writer Says It

1. What is ironic about Khan's description of the waiting room, "where towering models of the Statue of Liberty singe the ceiling"?

2. Analyze the title. How is it ironic?

3. What is the effect of the short, clipped statements that follow longer paragraphs, especially at the end of the essay?

ANALYZING the Issue

At the end of the essay, Khan asks, "Had America's national interest really been served?" Is the kind of racial profiling he describes justified in the name of national security? Explain.

ANALYZING Connections Between Texts

1. Compare Khan's argument to Charles Krauthammer's in "The Case for Profiling" (p. 563). How would Khan respond to Krauthammer's suggestion that not to profile is to ignore "probabilities"?

2. How is Khan's situation comparable to that of the speaker in Langston Hughes's "Theme for English B" (p. 372)? In what ways are the immigration officials like the instructor in Hughes's poem?

3. In different mediums, both Adnan R. Khan and Dorothea Lange (p. 612) argue that, in times of national crisis, American authorities tend to identify ethnic groups (such as Muslims and Japanese-Americans) as particularly dangerous and thus targets for suspicion and surveillance. Tactics used in the War Against Terrorism eerily resemble the methods used in World War II. Does ethnic profiling yield any results that justify its practice? Or is this type of "ethnic surveillance" largely a form of scapegoating, of creating easy targets to stand in the place of the real enemy who cannot be so easily defeated? Explain your answer in terms of the lessons from history.

WARMING UP: *Does the technology that most people take for granted now (faxes, e-mail, instant messaging) make you feel more—or less—free?*

Orwell Got It Wrong

BY MICHAEL KINSLEY

MICHAEL KINSLEY

In this 1997 piece, Michael Kinsley, the editor of Slate, *an online political magazine, argues that rather than restrict our personal freedom (as Orwell feared), modern computer technology has increased it. Kinsley acknowledges, however, that we pay a price for that freedom in the uncontrolled distribution of potentially dangerous material such as pornography.*

George Orwell's famous novel *1984* (written in 1948) opens with its hero, Winston Smith, returning to his squalid apartment. Attached to a wall is a "telescreen," described as "an oblong metal plaque like a dulled mirror." It is in essence a two-way television, which watches Smith's every movement while barking government propaganda at him. "Big Brother Is Watching You" is the state's slogan.

This was Orwell's vision of the future: technology would become the tool of totalitarian dictatorship. TV and computers would make Big Brother possible.

Fortunately, Orwell got it exactly wrong. The high-tech devices that have invaded our lives—home computers, fax machines, VCRs and now the Internet—have *expanded* human freedom.

On the Redmond, Wash. campus of the Microsoft Corporation, where I work these days, there is not much doubt that technology is a wonderful thing. It has made many of the software programmers, wandering the halls in jeans and T-shirts, rich men and women while still in their 20s or 30s.

But more than that: people in Cyberworld—short-hand for the culture of computers and telecommunications—passionately believe that today's technology revolution is also a revolutionary advance for human liberty. They're right. But most of them also don't remember a time when computers, especially, were thought to be a menace to freedom.

Orwell was far from the only doubter of the post–World War II period. During the 1950s and '60s many other seers worried that ever-bigger computers

5

would lead to centralization of information and power. The menace of giant computers was a major theme of popular culture.

Then around 1980, computers suddenly got small. The desktop personal computer (PC) came to market and gave enormous power to the individual. Tiny businesses could do what only large ones could before. Even within big businesses, employees had much more autonomy. A symbolic development was the arrival of inexpensive tax-preparation software. Today you can use your home PC to do your income tax quickly and accurately, while the Internal Revenue Service still can't get its own giant computers to work right.

INFORMATION POWER Even more important for political freedom was another development of the 1980s: the fax machine. It is no coincidence that communism collapsed in 1989 just as the fax machine was becoming wide-spread and fairly inexpensive. The fax made it impossible for the state to control the spread of information. News from outside couldn't be kept out, and information about conditions inside couldn't be kept in. Government lies were exposed, and the truth spread.

"Workers of the World, Fax!" was the headline of a *Washington Post* article in late 1990 during the waning days of the Cold War. The author, Michael Dobbs, reported that correspondents in the Soviet Union had gone from having too little information to too much. It was a "revolution by fax," he wrote, which "has made a mockery of attempts by Communist Party bureaucrats to control the flow of news."

Then in the 1990s, along came the Internet—and any government's ability   10
to control information was destroyed for good. At the same time, the Internet empowered individuals, compared with big corporations, even more dramatically than had the PC.

Now, there's nothing necessarily wrong with big corporations! I work at one. My job at Microsoft is publishing an on-line magazine called *Slate* (www.slate.com on the Internet). By publishing on-line, we have no paper costs, no printing costs, no postage costs. When we "go to press," our articles are instantly available to anyone with a computer and a modem anywhere in the world.

These same people can also use a computer and modem to publish on-line themselves. All it takes is a bit of software and $20 a month or so for Internet access.

The press critic A. J. Liebling once remarked sarcastically, "Freedom of the press is guaranteed only to those who own one." Today, thanks to the Internet, almost anyone can, in effect, own a printing press capable of reaching more people than William Randolph Hearst could in his heyday.

Meanwhile, the Internet mocks government efforts to control information. the *New York Times* reported last December that Serbian President Slobodan

Milosevic—no lover of freedom—was trying to shut down the independent press but was utterly thwarted by the Internet. Serbian journalists and dissidents set up their own Web sites to tell their story both to fellow Serbs and the outside world. And any Serb with Internet access can call up the Web sites of the *New York Times, Reader's Digest* or *Slate* almost as easily as citizens of the freest countries.

A government can try to restrict its citizens' access to the Internet, as China 15 is trying. But it will probably fail. For even if it could deny access to computers and modems, such a success would be too costly, since these tools are crucial to economic growth.

TOUGH TRADE-OFF It's true that the democracy of information can be a mixed blessing. Nothing about the Internet guarantees that the information it spreads so easily is true. In fact, the Internet is a caldron of implausible rumors and conspiracy theories, all zapping around the world at the speed of light.

More troubling, sexually explicit material can be disseminated on the Internet just as easily and widely as information about political oppression in Serbia. And many people want to stop that, mainly because of children.

This year the Supreme Court will rule on the constitutionality of the federal Communications Decency Act, which forbids disseminating "patently offensive" sexual material through computer networks. The dilemma is that laws which make smut harder for children to obtain make it harder for adults as well. Easing those laws increases freedom for adults but reduces protection for children.

To tip my own hand, I'm with those who think the decency law is unconstitutional censorship. But honesty requires admitting there's a cost.

On balance, most people would concede that the advantages of today's tech- 20 nologies, including the Internet, outweigh the disadvantages. Certainly our freedom has been enhanced on the everyday personal level. (Remember the time before VCRs when you had to watch a TV show or a movie when *they* wanted you to?)

On the more profound political level, is there anyone who thinks the world would be a freer place if computers, fax machines and the Internet didn't exist? This is one that Orwell really did get wrong.

ANALYZING What the Writer Says

1. Kinsley claims that modern communication technology has "expanded human freedom." What arguments does he use to support his point?

2. What, according to Kinsley, are the only drawbacks to freewheeling communication in cyberspace?

ANALYZING How the Writer Says It

In the section "Tough Trade-off," Kinsley points out possible dangers of unrestricted speech on the Internet. How does he refute this counterargument? What kind of evidence does he use to support his refutation?

ANALYZING the Issue

1. Kinsley doubts at the end of his essay that there is "anyone who thinks that the world would be a freer place if computers, fax machines and the Internet didn't exist." Do you agree with him? Why or why not?

2. Kinsley looks at the Internet as a safeguard of freedom of speech in the face of a totalitarian government, the kind Orwell describes in *1984*. In a democracy such as the United States, is freedom of speech really in danger? Why or why not? Does his essay address a real issue? If so, what is it?

ANALYZING Connections Between Texts

1. How would Kinsley respond to Molly Ivins's argument (p. 547) and to Lewis H. Lapham's (p. 567) that the government's use of the latest technology amounts to surveillance and thus inhibits civil liberties?

2. Michael Kinsley claims that modern technology has freed the individual from institutional control. Ellen Ullman ("The Museum of Me," p. 455) points out how the Internet promises its users that "the world will revolve around [them]," which she sees as an ultimate danger to our sense of community and thus our democracy. Looking at these two essays, discuss whether the Internet and other devices ultimately enhance or hinder our understanding of and our willingness to participate in a democratic community.

3. Consider the original Information Awareness Office logo and its slogan, "*Scientia est Potentia*" (Knowledge Is Power, p. 109). How do you think Kinsley would react to its message? Its purpose?

WARMING UP: *Do the random searches of "ordinary people" at airports make you feel safer about flying?*

The Case for Profiling

Why Random Searches of Airline Travelers Are a Useless Charade

BY CHARLES KRAUTHAMMER

CHARLES KRAUTHAMMER

In 1978 Charles Krauthammer (b. 1950) left a promising career in psychiatry to work in the Carter administration in Washington, D.C. In 1981 he began writing for the New Republic; *in 1985 he joined the* Washington Post. *The Pulitzer Prize–winning commentator currently writes a nationally syndicated column for the* Post *and contributes regularly to* Time *and other magazines.*

The latest airport-security scandal is the groping of female flight attendants and passengers during pat-downs. Not to worry. The Transportation Security Administration chief is right on it. "We're going to fix that right away," he said recently, announcing the appointment of an ombudsman.

A nice bureaucratic Band-Aid. No one, however, asks the obvious question: Why are we patting down flight attendants in the first place? Why, for that matter, are we conducting body searches of any female passengers?

Random passenger checks at airports are completely useless. We've all been there in the waiting lounge, rolling our eyes in disbelief as the 80-year-old Irish nun, the Hispanic mother of two, the Japanese-American businessman, the House committee chairman with the titanium hip are randomly chosen and subjected to head-to-toe searching for . . . what?

Not for security—these people are hardly candidates for suicide terrorism—but for political correctness. We are engaged in a daily and ostentatious rehearsal of the officially sanctioned proposition that suicide terrorists come from anywhere, without regard to gender, ethnicity, age or religious affiliation.

That is not true, and we know it. Random searches are a ridiculous charade, 5 a charade that not only gives a false sense of security but, in fact, diminishes security because it wastes so much time and effort on people who are obviously no threat.

Everyone now has his nail-clipper, tweezers or X-rayed-shoe story. Can-you-top-this tales of luggage and body searches have become a staple of cocktail chatter. Yet citizens would willingly subject themselves to delay, inconvenience and even indignity if they felt what they were undergoing was actually improving airport security. Since Sept. 11, subjecting oneself to security indignities has been a civic duty. But this has become a parody of civic duty. Random searches are being done purely to defend against the charge of racial profiling.

Imagine that Timothy McVeigh and Terry Nichols had not been acting alone but had instead been part of a vast right-wing, antigovernment, terrorist militia with an ideology, a network and a commitment to carrying out attacks throughout America. Would there have been any objection to singling out young white men for special scrutiny at airports and other public places? Of course not. And if instead, in response to the threat posed by the McVeigh Underground, airport security began pulling young black men or elderly Asian women out of airport lines for full-body searches, would we not all loudly say that this is an outrage and an absurdity?

As it happens, the suicide bombers who attacked us on Sept. 11 were not McVeigh Underground. They were al-Qaeda: young, Islamic, Arab and male. That is not a stereotype. That is a fact. And there is no hiding from it, as there is no hiding from the next al-Qaeda suicide bomber. He has to be found and stopped. And you don't find him by strip searching female flight attendants or 80-year-old Irish nuns.

This is not to say your plane could not be brought down by a suicide bomber of another sort. It could. It could also be brought down by a meteorite. Or by a Stinger missile fired by Vermont dairymen in armed rebellion. These are all possible. But because they are rather improbable, we do not alter our daily lives to defend against the possibility.

True, shoe bomber Richard Reid, while young and Islamic and male, was 10 not Arab. No system will catch everyone. But our current system is designed to catch no one because we are spending 90% of our time scrutinizing people everyone knows are no threat. Jesse Jackson once famously lamented how he felt when he would "walk down the street and hear footsteps and start thinking about robbery—then look around and see somebody white and feel relieved." Jackson is no racist. He was not passing judgment on his own ethnicity. He was simply reacting to probabilities. He would rather not. We all would rather not make any calculations based on ethnicity, religion, gender or physical characteristics—except that on airplanes our lives are at stake.

The pool of suicide bombers is not large. To pretend that it is universal is absurd. Airport security is not permitted to "racially" profile, but every passenger—white or black, male or female, Muslim or Christian—does. We scan the waiting room, scrutinizing other passengers not just for nervousness and shiftiness but also for the demographic characteristics of al-Qaeda. We do it privately. We do it quietly. But we do it. Airport officials, however, may not. This is crazy. So crazy that it is only a matter of time before the public finally demands that our first priority be real security, not political appearances—and puts an end to this charade.

ANALYZING What the Writer Says

1. Why, according to Krauthammer, do airport security officials conduct random searches?

2. What actual danger does Krauthammer argue that the practice poses?

ANALYZING How the Writer Says It

1. Krauthammer uses loaded language to draw readers' attention to the absurdity of random searches of airline passengers. Cite examples and comment on the effectiveness of his technique.

2. How do Krauthammer's descriptions of very particular types of people—"the 80-year-old Irish nun," "the Japanese-American businessman"—help convince you that his argument makes sense?

3. What pithy phrase does Krauthammer use to summarize his attitude about the effectiveness of random searches?

ANALYZING the Issue

1. Krauthammer makes a case for the controversial practice of ethnic or racial profiling. Is profiling an acceptable method of crime prevention? Why or why not?

2. Krauthammer's piece takes a swipe at "political correctness," the practice of sensitivity toward particular groups, suggesting that it is a flimsy excuse for ignoring "probabilities." How important is political correctness? In what areas is it less important than in others?

ANALYZING Connections Between Texts

1. How would Krauthammer respond to Adnan R. Khan's suggestion, in "Bordering on Panic" (p. 555), that "What's real is unreal and what's unreal is real . . . could be the slogan for contemporary America"?

2. Compare Krauthammer's ideas to those expressed by Jonathan Rauch in "In Defense of Prejudice" (p. 499).

3. Consider Krauthammer's views about profiling in light of Dorothea Lange's photographic statement about the singling out of a group of people for suspicion in "Pledge of Allegiance" (p. 612). Based on what he argues here, try to infer his opinion about the internment of Japanese–Americans during World War II.

WARMING UP: *Imagine that someone in your apartment building (or in your immediate neighborhood) is a suspected criminal, but the police are not sure who it is. They suggest tapping everybody's phone until they catch the guilty party. How would you feel about having your phone conversations recorded so police could find the offender?*

Regime Change

BY LEWIS H. LAPHAM

> They that can give up essential liberty to obtain a little temporary saftey deserve neither liberty nor safety.
>
> —*Benjamin Franklin*

LEWIS H. LAPHAM

Lewis H. Lapham, editor of Harper's Magazine, *claims that the Bush administration, in the wake of the 2001 terrorist attacks, has sacrificed the liberty of the American people for (the illusion of) national security. This essay appeared in the February 2003* Harper's.

Unrelenting in its search for Osama bin Laden and the roots of all the world's evil, the Defense Department some months ago established an Information Awareness Office that took for its letterhead emblem the all-seeing eye of God. Although still in the early stages of development and for the moment funded with an annual budget of only $200 million, the new medium of mass investigation seeks to "detect and classify" every prospective terrorist (foreign, hybrid, mutant, or native born) setting foot on American soil. No door or envelope unopened, no secret unexposed, no suspicious suitcase or Guatemalan allowed to descend unnoticed from a cruise ship or a bicycle.

To give weight and form to a paranoid dream of reason not unlike the one that sustained the sixteenth-century Spanish Inquisition, the government apparently means to recruit a synod of high-speed computers capable of sifting through "ultra-large" data warehouses stocked with every electronic proof of human movement in the wilderness of cyberspace—bank, medical, and divorce records, credit-card transactions, emails (interoffice and extraterritorial), college transcripts, surveillance photographs (from cameras in hospitals and shopping malls as well as from those in airports and hotel bars), driver's licenses and passport applications, bookstore purchases, website visits, and traffic violations. Connect all the names and places to all the dates and times, and once the systems become fully operational, in four years or maybe ten, the protectors of the public health and safety hope to reach beyond "truth maintenance" and "biologically inspired algorithms for agent control" to the construction of "FutureMap"—i.e., a set of indices programmed into the fiberoptic equivalent of a crystal ball that modifies "market-based techniques for avoiding surprise" in such a way that next week's nuclear explosion can be seen as clearly as last week's pornographic movie. In the meantime, while waiting for the technical upgrades with which to perform "entity extraction from natural language text," the clerks seated at the computer screens can look for inspiration to the mandala on their office stationery—an obverse of the Great Seal of the United States similar to the ornament on the back of the $1 bill, an Egyptian pyramid and mystic, Rosicrucian light buttressed by the rendering in Latin of the motto "Knowledge is power."

When reports of the IAO's existence belatedly appeared in the mainstream press in November of last year, nine months after the headquarters' staff began moving the first electronic robots into an air-conditioned basement in Virginia, the news didn't capture the attention of the Congress or excite the interest of the television networks. No politician uttered a discouraging word; no prominent historian entertained the risk of a possibly unpatriotic question. The talk-show gossip of the moment dwelled on the prospect of war in Iraq and the setting up of the Department of Homeland Security (soon to be equipped with its own domestic espionage service), and, except for an occasional lawyer associated with the American Civil Liberties Union, most of the people in New York to whom I mentioned the Pentagon's gift for totalitarian fantasy were inclined to think that intelligence gathering was somehow akin to weather forecasting—a routine and necessary precaution, annoying and possibly unconstitutional but entirely appropriate in a time of trouble.

William Safire entered an objection on the opinion page of the *New York Times* ("Orwellian scenario . . . sweeping theft of privacy rights . . . exploitation of fear"), but elsewhere in the large-circulation media protests were hard to find. The general opinion so clearly favored the Bush Administration's policies of forward deterrence and preemptive strike that I wasn't surprised by the absence of commentary, much less complaint, when it was announced in early December that the FBI had been jettisoning the baggage of due process while pursuing the rumor of an underwater terrorist attack against an unknown target somewhere along the 95,000 miles of the American coastline. From hundreds of dive-shop operators everywhere in the country the FBI demanded the names of the several million swimmers who had taken diving lessons over the course of the last three years. Only two citizens refused the request, the co-owners of Reef Seekers Dive Company in Beverly Hills, California. When word of their noncooperation showed up in a newspaper story, they were besieged by vindictive telephone calls expressing the hope that their shop prove to be the next locus of a terrorist bombing.

The incident speaks to the nervous temper of the times—hundreds of dive 5 shops, only one refusing to give up its client list; the voice of the people tuned to the pitch of an angry mob—and illustrates the lesson in obedience well and truly learned by a once free people during the second half of a century defined in the history books as America's own. I'm old enough to remember public speeches unfettered by the dogma of political correctness, a time when it was possible to apply for a job without submitting to a blood or urine test, when people construed their freedoms as a constitutional birthright, not as favors grudgingly bestowed by a sometimes benevolent government. I also can remember the days when people weren't afraid of tobacco smoke, sexual inter-course, and saturated fats; when irony was understood and money wasn't sacred; when even men in uniform could be trusted to recognize a joke.

The spacious and once familiar atmospheres of liberty (wisecracking and open-ended, tolerant, unkempt, experimental, and democratic) didn't survive the poisoning of Hiroshima or serve the purposes of the Cold War with the Russians. The easygoing, provincial republic of fifty years ago gradually assumed the character of a world-encircling nation-state, its plowshares beat-en into swords, borrowing from its enemies (first the nonexistent Communist empire, now the unseen terrorist jihad) the practice of restricting the freedom of its own citizens in the interest of what the increasingly oligarchic govern-ments in Washington proclaim to be "the national security." Begin the narra-tive almost anywhere in the late 1940s or early 1950s—with the National Security Act of 1947, the hearings before the House Un-American Activities Committee in 1951, President Harry Truman's decision to build the hydrogen bomb, the composition of the Hollywood Blacklist, or Senator Joe McCarthy's search for Marxists marching in the Rose Bowl Parade—and the plot develop-ment moves briskly forward in the direction of more fear and less courage, toward the substitution of White House intrigue for congressional debate and the professions of smiling loyalty preferred to the clumsy and impolitic fum-bling for the truth.

Bear in mind the conclusion of the Church committee hearings as long ago as 1976—"too many people have been spied upon by too many Government agencies and too much information has been collected"—and space permits only a brief acknowledgment of the various police powers seized by the gov-ernment under the rubric of the war on drugs (the use of anonymous inform-ants, the taking of property without conviction or arrest), of the illegal surveil-lance of American citizens by their own intelligence agencies (the CIA between

1953 and 1973 producing an index of 1.5 million suspicious American names, the FBI compiling a list of 26,000 individuals to be summarily rounded up in the event of "a national emergency"), of the Justice Department's long campaign against the civil rights granted by the First, Fourth, Fifth, Sixth, and Eighth amendments to the Constitution, and of a system of public education that offers its best-attended courses of instruction to the student populations in the army and the prisons. Add to the constant threat of nuclear extinction the sum of the wiretaps infiltrated into the American consciousness across the span of three generations, and it's no wonder that by the late 1990s, even in the midst of the reassuring prosperity allied with a buoyant stock market, and well before the destruction of the World Trade Center, the public-opinion polls found the bulk of the respondents willing to give up a generous percentage of their essential liberty in return for safer streets, secure suburbs, well-lighted parking garages, and risk-free cocktail waitresses.

Since the shock of September 11, 2001, the American public has quickened the pace of its retreat into the shelters of harmless speech and heavy law enforcement. If I were to measure the general level of submissiveness by my own encounters with the habit of self-censorship and the general concern with social hygiene—acquaintances reluctant to remark on the brutality of the Israeli army for fear of being thought anti-Semitic, public scolds who damn me as a terrorist for smoking a cigarette in Central Park, college students so worried about the grooming of their résumés that they avoid rock concerts on the off-chance that their faces might show up on a police department video-tape—I might be tempted to argue that American winning of the Cold War resulted in the loss of its soul. In place of the reckless and independent-minded individual once thought to embody the national stereotype (child of nature, descendant of Daniel Boone, hard-drinking and unorthodox) we now have a quorum of nervous careerists, psalm-singing and well-behaved, happy to oblige, eager to please, trained to hold up their hands and empty their pockets when passing through airport security or entering City Hall.

John Quincy Adams understood the terms of the bargain as long ago as 1821, speaking as the secretary of state against sending the U.S. Navy to rearrange Spain's colonial empire in Colombia and Chile. America, he said, "goes not abroad, in search of monsters to destroy." Were the country to embark on such a foolish adventure

she would involve herself beyond the power of extrication, in all the wars of interest and intrigue, of individual avarice, envy, and ambition, which assume the colors and usurp the standard of freedom. The fundamental maxim of her policy would insensibly change from *liberty* to *force*. . . . She might become the dictatress of the world. She would no longer be the ruler of her own spirit.

The Bush Administration equates the American spirit with power, not with $\quad$ 10
liberty. During the months since the fall of the twin towers it has assumed the
colors and usurped the standard of freedom to jury-rig the framework of an
autocratic state; bowing to the constituencies of fear and patriotic sentiment, a
servile Congress approves the requested legislation as eagerly as if it had been
called upon to save a sinking ship with the rapid slamming of steel doors. First
the USA Patriot Act (authorizing the government to arbitrarily decide who is
and who is not an un-American), then the president seeking the prerogative to
declare any citizen an "enemy combatant" (subject to being imprisoned, indefinitely, without charge or bail and forbidden access to a lawyer or a court
review), then the formation of the IAO and the several reconfigurations of
both the Justice Department and the FBI (always with the purpose of multiplying their pretexts for an arrest), and then, most recently, on November 25
of last year, the establishment of the Department of Homeland Security.

The supporting legislation runs to 484 pages, which Senator Robert C. Byrd
of West Virginia flung down on his desk with a gesture that reminded a *New
York Times* reporter of "the fury of Moses smashing the tablets." One of only
nine senators who voted against the bill, Byrd denounced it as a foolish and
unlawful seizure of power unlikely to do much harm to America's enemies but
certain to do a great deal of harm to the American people. "With a battle plan
like the Bush Administration is proposing," Byrd said, "instead of crossing the
Delaware River to capture the Hessian soldiers on Christmas day, George
Washington would have stayed on his side of the river and built a bureaucracy."

Not having read the small print in the Homeland Security Act, I can't guess
at the extent to which it will further subtract from the country's store of civil
liberty, but if I understand correctly its operative bias (170,000 functionaries
undefended by a labor union and serving at the pleasure and sole discretion of
the president of the United States) I all too easily can imagine a new department of bureaucratic control that incorporates the paranoid systems of
thought engendered by the Cold War with the dogmas of political correctness
meant to cure the habit of free speech, and deploys the surveillance techniques
made possible by the miracles of modern telecommunications technology.

I don't count myself a believer in the dystopian futures imagined in Aldous
Huxley's *Brave New World* or George Orwell's *1984*, but I think it would be a
mistake to regard the trend of events as somehow favorable to the cause of liberty. President Bush likes to present himself as the embodiment of the spirit of
1776, but to the directorship of the Pentagon's new Information Awareness
Office he appointed Vice Admiral John Poindexter, a royalist ideologue, a convicted felon, and a proven enemy of both the American Congress and the articles of the Constitution. As national security adviser to President Ronald
Reagan in 1985, the admiral supervised what came to be known as the Iran-
Contra swindle—the selling of missiles to the despotic ayatollahs in Iran in

return for money with which to fund, secretly and illegally, a thuggish junta in Nicaragua. After the scheme collapsed under the weight of its criminal stupidity, the admiral repeatedly lied to the congressional committee investigating the farce (thus his convictions on five felony counts), and when called upon to account for his false testimony he said that he considered it his "duty" to conceal information too sensitive to be entrusted to loud-mouthed politicians.

Not an honest or liberal-minded man, the admiral, but unfortunately representative of the arrogant corporatists currently in charge of the government in Washington. Glimpsed in the persons of Secretary of Defense Donald Rumsfeld, Vice President Dick Cheney, and Attorney General John Ashcroft, the senior managers of the Bush Administration make no secret of their contempt for the rules of democratic procedure (inefficient, wrong-headed, and slow), their distrust of the American people (indolent and immoral, corrupted by a debased popular culture, undeserving of the truth), and their disdain for the United Nations and the principle of international law (sophomoric idealisms popular with weak nations too poor to pay for a serious Air Force). I don't for a moment doubt the eager commitment to the great and noble project of "regime change," but on the evidence of the last eighteen months they've been doing their most effective work in the United States, not in Afghanistan, Saudi Arabia, or Iraq. Better understood as radical nationalists than as principled conservatives, they deploy the logic endorsed by the American military commanders in Vietnam (who found it necessary to destroy a village in order to save it), and they offer the American people a choice similar to the one presented by the officers of the Spanish Inquisition to independent-minded heretics—give up your liberty, and we will set you free.

ANALYZING What the Writer Says

1. What is the mission of the Information Awareness Office as Lapham describes it?

2. "I'm old enough to remember . . ." introduces Lapham's memory of the America of his youth. In what way was it different from the contemporary America he describes?

3. What does Lapham mean when he says that "America's winning of the Cold War resulted in the loss of its soul"?

ANALYZING How the Writer Says It

1. Lapham uses a Benjamin Franklin quote as the epigraph for his essay. How does the quote tie in with Lapham's thesis?

2. Cite instances of irony in the essay. What purpose does Lapham's use of irony serve?

ANALYZING the Issue

1. Consider the "Warming Up" question at the beginning of Lapham's essay. How does your response jibe with Lapham's ideas on the subject of individual liberties?

2. Do you agree with Lapham that the activities of the Information Awareness Office are an infringement on the liberties guaranteed in the American Constitution? Why or why not?

3. How do you interpret the motto that appeared in the Information Awareness Office's original logo, which translates to "Knowledge Is Power"? Why do you think the office uses the motto in Latin rather than English?

ANALYZING Connections Between Texts

1. Compare and contrast Lapham's ideas about the erosion of civil liberties to Charles Krauthammer's argument in favor of profiling (p. 563). How would Lapham respond to Krauthammer's contention that profiling is a commonsense safety measure?

2. Consider the other Lapham piece included in this book, "Audible Silence" (p. 481). How do the two pieces complement each other? How does Lapham build on ideas and themes he introduces in the earlier piece?

3. Look carefully at the original Information Awareness Office logo (p. 109). How do the details of the image illustrate Lapham's points?

WARMING UP: *Are you ever alarmed by the increasing sophistication of modern technology and the resulting decline in privacy?*

Everything Is Watching YOU

By Farhad Manjoo

FARHAD MANJOO

Farhad Manjoo, an Internet reporter who writes frequently about issues arising from the latest developments in technology, weighs the pros and cons of radio frequency identification (RFID), a technology that would tag consumer products electronically, allowing for easy collection of all kinds of data.

In the mid-1990s, David Brock and Sanjay Sarma, engineers at MIT, became preoccupied with a problem that has long vexed robotic scientists—how do you get a computer to understand what's happening in the physical world around it?

The standard approach is to have the machine emulate human beings; you build a robot with "eyes," with the crude ability to marshal rays of light into a "mental image" of its surroundings. But that is an enormously complex task, one that researchers have been working for decades to perfect, and Brock and Sarma wondered whether it might be possible to give the robot a little help. Instead of having the machine look around and guess what it could see, what if objects in the room simply identified themselves to the robot? Why couldn't a book carry some sort of electronic marker to alert the robot that there was a copy of Tolstoy nearby? Why couldn't a can of Coke "know" that it was a can of Coke, or a bar of soap know that it gets slippery when wet? "That way," says Sarma, "the robot could just ask the item what it was and then look up a database to see how to pick it up."

Life would certainly be much easier for robots if every item in the world—every book, every can of Coke, every bar of soap, every shirt, every shoe, every CD and DVD, everything you can think of, even pets and cattle—carried an electronic tag with a unique identifier. But it turns out that a world of electronically identifiable items would be beneficial to more than just machines. Many large retail firms—including Wal-Mart, Procter & Gamble, and Gillette—have embraced this vision; they say that it will do nothing less than revolutionize retail sales, and they're spending a lot of money to make the idea a reality.

But even as computer scientists wax lyrical over the prospects of a network where everything is broadcasting to everything else, and companies salivate at the chance to have total inventory control, privacy-concerned consumers are looking with alarm at a technology that promises levels of surveillance unprecedented in human history. It's bad enough, for some people, that a grocery store can assemble a database of your habits from everything that you've rung up on your credit card in the last year. But in a world where every product is embedded with identifying technology, the possibility would exist for companies to know what you're doing, in real time, in almost every aspect of life.

That world is on its way. In 1999, with the participation of several corpora- 5 tions, Brock and Sarma set up the *Auto-ID Center,* an MIT consortium whose goal is to create an inexpensive, industry-standard product-tagging system using a technology called radio frequency identification, or RFID. By 2006, Wal-Mart plans to use the center's RFID technology to track all shipments moving through its supply chain, the path from factory to store warehouse. Many firms, including the Gap and the U.K. supermarket chain Tesco, have tested systems that can track items as they move within individual stores, alerting employees if products are misplaced or are being stolen. Proponents of the technology say that RFID offers many benefits to consumers as well. Tagged items could enable quite extraordinary new consumer devices; you'd have smart shopping carts to calculate the nutritional value of the food you buy and to automatically check you out of a store, or smart washing machines to alert you if you're washing whites with colors.

But are such benefits worth the price? For the past couple of years, a small band of activists has been mounting a vociferous campaign against radio tags— they worry that tagged products will show up on store shelves without our knowledge, that we'll be tracked through stores and in the world without our consent, and that, in the worst case, brave-new-world-type scenarios will become an everyday reality. Katherine Albrecht, the head of a group called Consumers Against Supermarket Privacy Invasion and Numbering (*CASPIAN*) and RFID's loudest critic, often warns of the possibility of RFID getting into the hands of a dictatorial regime. What would a Saddam Hussein do with RFID?

Albrecht is tenacious, and her work has caused some embarrassment for the Auto-ID Center. She recently discovered an article in Smart Labels Analyst magazine, a subscription-only trade publication, that described an alarming RFID setup at a Tesco store in Cambridge, England. According to the Smart Labels Analyst article (which Albrecht read to Salon over the phone), a surveillance camera trained on Gillette razors was activated each time a customer removed a package of tagged razors from an RFID "smart shelf"; the system was apparently taking pictures of each razor-blade buyer (or browser) to prevent theft of the Gillette Mach 3 blades, the world's most-stolen retail product. Albrecht first alerted the (London) Guardian to the camera-enabled-shelf story; the newspaper reported the news on July 19, and within a few hours the story made its way to many blogs and discussion sites like Slashdot, where hundreds of readers railed against RFID.

For Albrecht, the Cambridge Tesco incident highlights the main concern of people fighting RFID—we won't know where these tagged products are, they say, and we won't know how they're being used.

Proponents of tagging say that the fears are easily assuaged. Kevin Ashton, the executive director of the Auto-ID Center, pledges that RFID technology will be used carefully: You'll be told that your items are tagged, you'll be given the choice to disable the tag when you leave a store, and your name will not be tied to the products you've purchased. If those guidelines are followed, what's so bad about RFID?

RFID, like cloning or genetically modified foods, promises to be one of those   10
technological advances that could remake, for the better, everything about how we live our daily lives. The technology is not just about making shopping cheaper and more pleasant—although, considering how much time Americans spend shopping, that would be good enough. But because RFID adds intelligence to the things around us, it would usher in an era of networked objects— an *"Internet of things,"* as the Auto-ID Center says—that would change the world dramatically: packages that know how to sort themselves for recycling, meat that alerts you when it's been recalled. So far, the debate surrounding its use has also echoed the debate around biotech. Opponents are long on speculation as to all the ways RFID could become disastrous, while proponents may be naive in their expectations that Americans will accept RFID without a fight. But what seems indisputable is the reality that this fully networked world is on its way, and we're going to have to learn how to live in it.

Radio frequency tagging is not exactly new technology. According to Bill Allen, a marketing executive at Texas Instruments, which makes key bits of RFID systems, radio tags were first used in the Second World War. "Each Allied aircraft was fitted with a transponder, which sends and receives signals," Allen says. "This was done to prevent friendly air battles—if you get a friendly signal from an aircraft, you do not shoot." Conceptually, the tags have not changed a great deal since then; the main difference between the tags of today and the tags of the 1940s is size. Today's tags are tiny—as big as a dime or as small as a grain of rice, though the size varies with the specific application.

Not only are radio tags not new, but they're also not very strange. Millions of people already use radio-tagged devices every day. RFID is found in electronic toll systems such as FasTrak and EZ Pass, and in gasoline quick-pay systems like Mobile's Speedpass; and millions of cars are equipped with *RFID immobi-*

lization, which prevents the engine from starting unless an RFID reader senses a radio tag embedded in the key.

Perhaps the largest application of RFID today is in agriculture. Cows all over the world have radio tags embedded in their shoulders or lodged in their second stomachs, and as they move through the various stages of their factory-farm lives, the radio tags let farmers know how they're doing. "You're recording data points," Allen says. "You record the cow's lineage, its shot records, feed lots that it may have visited." This sort of tracking becomes indispensable when problems arise. If you're trying to isolate a sick cow, or trying to determine which of your animals may have feasted on some mad-cow-infected rendered-protein feed, RFID will help.

It was only in the 1990s that businesses began thinking about using radio technology in retail sales. At the time, Kevin Ashton, the Auto-ID Center's director, was a brand management executive at Procter & Gamble. "We started to notice some fundamental problems in our business," he says. "It first manifested itself in products not being on the shelves. I would go to check the stores, and I noticed some of the best products, our beauty products, would be out of stock in four out of 10 stores at any one moment. That's a real moment of clarification. The average industry out-of-stock number is 10 percent, but what we actually found was that the extreme cases tended to be bigger, and that was usually the case for the products that we cared about the most. If the product is really good, that's going to drive it off the shelf."

He adds: "The root of the problem turned out to be information. There wasn't enough information about where things were to make good decisions." 15

All the apparent orderliness of a typical retail store, with a place for everything and everything in its place, is a bit of an illusion. Once a product gets out into the din of a busy store, it could go anywhere: Customers or employees may move it about, putting it in the wrong section, or they may steal it; or the employees might forget to restock the shelves, or they may make some other error. Keeping things orderly is very costly, and it's slow. In most stores, Bill Allen says, "an inventory is periodically taken where they have to shut down and pay people overtime. It can be very labor intensive and cost inefficient, and even then, the Gap says that any type of physical inventory they do, they guess it's only about 93 percent accurate."

The supply chain, the back-end machine of major retailers, is also prone to errors. Paul Fox, a spokesman for Gillette, one of the main sponsors of the Auto-ID Centers, explains: "Imagine I ship you 100 cases, but when you record it you put it down as 10. So now your inventory system has effectively lost 90 cases." This means that your computer will tell you that you've run out of the product long before you actually have, so you'll order more than you need—and your supplier will draw erroneous conclusions about the demand for the item in your store, giving a distorted picture of how the product is doing. Companies are loath to operate in this dark, data-less void; they'd do anything for more information, because any data they get could save them millions.

"At any given point in time, the Gap knows where 85 percent of their inventory is," Allen says. "You might think that's pretty good, but then you wonder what that 15 percent represents for a company as large as the Gap. What it multiplies out to is $1.7 billion of inventory that they don't know where it is. It could be stolen within the supply chain and they'd never know it, and on and on and on. What it means is they have to buy more inventory to make sure they have their supply stocked—and that is a cash-consuming type of situation."

At least for the next couple of years, most companies are looking at this back-end part of their businesses as a main target for RFID improvements. In the retail world, Wal-Mart's supply chain is regarded as by far the most advanced, and its decision to use radio tagging is likely to spur its rivals to do the same. Tom Williams, a company spokesman, says that Wal-Mart is convinced it can see huge savings by switching to this system. "We have 103 distribution centers throughout the U.S.," he says, "and many of them are over a million square feet. When products come into the center we track them—today, we primarily rely greatly on bar-coding, and as you know, bar code scanning is a step-by-step process. RFID is all at once, and for us that's really crucial for fast-moving merchandise."

The company—which has asked all its suppliers to put radio tags on pallets 20 and cases they ship to Wal-Mart within the next two years—will also track RFID-tagged merchandise as it moves on trucks around the country, which will allow it to more efficiently route stock to where it's needed most. In addition, Williams says, the mountains of data the firm gleans from all these tagged cases moving through its operations will "give us a lot of numbers to crunch, and we'll be able to spot trends we don't even know about."

But in Wal-Mart's case, for now, the tracking will stop in store warehouses. Individual products will not be tagged, and although the company has long been rumored to be working on plans to bring RFID into stores, Tom Williams, the spokesman, wouldn't confirm or deny anything. "I think the issue of item-level tagging is quite a ways down the road," he said. "Our immediate effort is with the supply chain."

Williams' reticence may be an indication of how nervous companies are about the prospect of bringing tagged products into stores. Although Bill Allen, at Texas Instruments, went into detail about the Gap's tests of the RFID at some of its stores, a Gap spokeswoman declined to divulge any specifics about its plans for the technology. She confirmed that the company had run some tests, but she would not say where or when they'd been done, or what the results were.

According to Allen, though, the Gap had tremendous success with RFID. "They did a study of four stores that fit the same demographics," he says. "One had RFID and the other three were a control. They looked at sales data in the stores from before, during and after the test, and what they saw was a 15 percent increase in sales in the store that had RFID. They determined that the main reason for the increase was because more of the merchandise was in the right place at the right time."

For retailers, this is the key promise of RFID—better control of inventory, leading to more efficiency, less waste, and higher profits.

But what will we, the customers, get out of this? Early in July, Katherine Albrecht, of CASPIAN, announced that she'd found *several "confidential" documents* lying in public view on the Auto-ID Center's Web site. Among these was a survey of consumer attitudes toward RFID that she thinks ought to give proponents of the technology a lot to think about. (The Auto-ID Center says the documents weren't confidential, just mislabeled.)

In focus groups the Auto-ID Center held in the United States, the United Kingdom, France, Germany and Japan, it found that many people saw no obvious benefits to RFID. "If consumers are made aware of any negatives (in the real world this could happen through negative press coverage) they have no benefits to balance their feelings against," wrote Helen Dulce, the Center's European director, in a research presentation. "For example, in Europe there is a large controversy over the health dangers of mobile phones, however mobile phone usage is on the up. This is because this technology has many benefits to consumers (convenience) and these benefits clearly over rule the very strong negatives. In the case of EPC network [the Auto-ID Center's name for its RFID technology] there are currently no clear benefits by which to balance even the mildest negative, so any negative press coverage, no matter how mild, would shift the neutral to a negative." . . .

But it's not true that we'll get nothing out of RFID. For one thing, even though Albrecht is dubious of the claim, radio tags seem certain to save us money. Wal-Mart, whose raison d'être is low prices, would not remake its back office for RFID if the technology couldn't cut costs. Activists say that even if the companies do save money by using RFID, the firms won't pass along the savings to us and will just keep bigger profits for themselves—but in the world of retail sales, lower prices are the key to winning market battles, and anything a company can do to cut costs will be reflected at the checkout counter.

The best argument critics of RFID have when presented with the idea that the technology will reduce prices is this one: It's not worth it. "To save 10 cents on a pack of Gillette I'm going to allow them to track me?" Albrecht asks incredulously. "I think many people will say, 'I think today I'll buy Schick.'"

The Auto-ID Center's numbers seem to support Albrecht's claim. In November 2001, Fleishman-Hillard, the center's public relations firm, conducted a small survey to gauge how people would respond to RFID the first time they heard about it. Of 317 people surveyed, more than 80 percent said that they grasped the technology and could see some benefits to it, but 78 percent also had privacy concerns. According to a presentation Albrecht found on the

Auto-ID Center's site, half the people said they were very worried about the implications of tagging; 15 people used the phrase "big brother," and telling people that the tags could be shut off was "not compelling." . . .

Why do people react this way to the idea of their products being tagged, even   30 if they're reassured that the tags will be shut off when they leave a store? One reason could be that people don't believe that the tags will actually be shut off. Kevin Ashton, the Auto-ID Center director, is insistent on that score: "The technology we built into this, called 'kill,' does exactly what it says. On receipt of that command, the tags will self-destruct," he says. "Now, they don't actually blow up, of course—but the tag will blow a tiny fuse and will be rendered physically incapable of receiving or sending any signals. It's as useful as a light bulb that's been blown."

The trouble is, you'll have to trust retailers about this. If you ask a store to kill the tags on everything you buy, you won't know that they've actually done it. And Albrecht, for one, does not trust that the stores will do what consumers want.

Ashton says that the market will take care of such problems. He recommends that every company using RFID agree to three broad principles—notification, choice and anonymity, he calls them. Items that are tagged will be stamped with a logo saying so. You'll have the choice to kill the tag when you leave the store. And the tag will never be associated with your name. If you buy a shirt from Wal-Mart using a credit card, for example, the card company will not record the tag of your shirt.

But depending on an industry to police itself is always a dicey proposition. The Gillette test at Tesco offers a case study in why there probably should be laws to police how RFID is used. According to the Guardian and Smart Labels Analyst, the shelf that activated a closed-circuit camera when Gillette razors were removed did not notify customers that it was set up that way. Why not? What happened to Ashton's policy of notification? That's not clear. When called for comment, Paul Fox, of Gillette, said it was not his place to talk about this specific test—"Those were Tesco's shelves," he said, characterizing the trial as a third-party affair that was completely out of Gillette's hands. The company, he said, had no interest at all in tracking goods within stores. "Our focus in establishing the feasibility of this technology is a very defined window," Fox said. "That window relates to the supply chain, and our only interest rests from the point of manufacture to the retail shelf. We have no interest in the application beyond that." (Tesco did not respond to Salon's requests for comment.)

When told about Gillette's response, Albrecht burst out laughing. She pointed out that Gillette is one of the main sponsors of the Auto-ID Center, whose explicit goal is to one day have most everything tagged. In many of the documents on the Auto-ID Center's site, Gillette razors are held up as an example of a good that could be better managed in stores with RFID. So for Gillette to say, now, that it only cares about the supply chain seems somewhat disingenuous.

When asked about the Tesco test, Ashton seemed to demur. "Ideally," he 35 said, such a shelf should tell people what it's doing. If it was me doing it, I would have had some sort of notice." But he said that in a test situation, a notice was not as important as in a full-scale rollout.

The more thorny ethical question is this one: If the shelf did tell you that it would record your picture if you removed a package of razors, would it then be OK? Albrecht says it would still be terrible. It's much worse than the ambient surveillance system that already pervades our stores, she says, because "this technology is presuming that every single Gillette customer is a criminal."

But don't all surveillance systems presume that you're a criminal? That's why they're watching you, right? Because you might do something naughty. And isn't this system, which focuses just on heavily stolen goods, actually better, since it's forgetting about all the other people in the store? That's the argument that Ashton makes. The system, he suggests, might be beneficial to all the razor shoppers who aren't stealing, as there would be some record of their innocence; such a shelf would prevent false accusations. And, Ashton notes, if such a shelf helps stop razor thefts, he won't apologize for that. "Stopping people from committing crimes is a good thing."

This is not an argument with which Ashton will change many people's minds, though. There is something viscerally disconcerting about a product triggering a camera to take your picture, however rational it may seem. And even if the tags on all your items have been killed when you go out the shop door, there'll be something disconcerting about knowing that, maybe, someone is tracking your new shoes.

Ashton recognizes that people will feel this way. He says he knows that people have concerns about RFID and that retail firms will face a huge battle in getting people to embrace it. But he has faith that people will come around. He doesn't have any real fears that—as happened with genetically modified foods, say—public concern will greatly slow down radio tagging, because he believes his industry will always be upfront about what it's doing. And, he says, "I think consumers are intelligent enough to see how good this will be."

ANALYZING What the Writer Says

1. What do manufacturers and retailers see as the main benefits of a radio frequency identification system?
2. What is the major drawback of RFID technology?
3. How might RFID benefit consumers?
4. RFID proponents assure consumers that the technology will be used fairly. Why do some people doubt that that can happen?

ANALYZING How the Writer Says It

1. Point to word choices that help reveal Manjoo's attitude toward proponents of RFID technology.

2. What techniques does Manjoo use to give a balanced view of RFID?

3. What is the effect of Manjoo's concluding comment by an RFID proponent: "I think consumers are intelligent enough to see how good this will be"?

ANALYZING the Issue

1. Are you willing to sacrifice some of your privacy for improved consumer services? For safety? Explain.

2. Are you in favor of laws that would prohibit businesses from collecting certain kinds of data from people using their products or services? Why or why not?

ANALYZING Connections Between Texts

1. How do you think Michael Kinsley ("Orwell Got It Wrong," p. 559) would respond to the arguments against RFID technology raised in Manjoo's piece?

2. Identify concerns Manjoo raises that are similar to those raised in Nancy Gibbs's "If We Have It, Do We Use It?" (p. 409).

3. How does the Information Awareness Office logo (p. 109) reinforce concerns raised by opponents of RFID technology in Manjoo's piece?

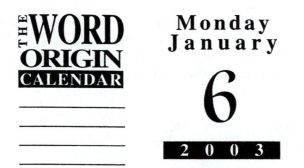

THE WORD ORIGIN CALENDAR

Monday January

6

2003

SCRUTINIZE • The root word here is the Latin noun *scruta*, meaning "trash," "rubbish," or "rags." This generated the verb *scrutari*, meaning "to search" or "to examine," roughly describing the action of ragpickers and refuse hunters.

WARMING UP: *Do you think the government is justified in spying on consenting adults engaged in private sexual activity?*

Getting Rid of the Sex Police

BY ANNA QUINDLEN

ANNA QUINDLEN

Pulitzer Prize-winning journalist, novelist, social critic, and children's book author Anna Quindlen (b. 1953) currently writes for Newsweek. *In the column that follows, she chastises the courts for upholding laws that sanction the invasion of the privacy of gays and lesbians. (In 2003, the Supreme Court struck down such laws in* Lawrence et al. v. Texas, *the case to which Quindlen refers.)*

Wedding announcements track American social history. Once they were the purview of the well-to-do, and the stereotypical division of roles was in the published details: the groom's work, the bride's gown. Point d'esprit, sweetheart neckline, Alençon lace: how quaint it all seems.

In the blink of an eye, historically speaking, the dress disappeared and in its place was a working woman, sometimes one who was keeping her own name. The idealized gave way to the real. A previous marriage had ended in divorce. The ring bearer was the 5-year-old son of the bride and groom. And couples of all classes, religions and races eventually smiled out from the pages of the daily papers.

So it said something about how the world works today when newspapers began to run announcements of the commitment ceremonies of gay men and lesbians. Although about 10 percent of America's dailies now do so, *The New York Times* got the most mileage from the decision because of its position as the industry gold standard. From the beginning it was just as the opponents feared: the same-sex announcements read so very much like the ones that surrounded them that they came close to simply blending in, the union of one well-educated documentary producer and psychotherapist reading very much like another.

That the *Times* as recently as 50 years ago referred to gay men as "deviants" in its pages and today is willing to report the joyous union of Daniel Gross and Steven Goldstein is a reflection of the ways of the world. Newspapers are essentially conservative in their internal decisions; they do not make social policy, only reflect it once it moves convincingly from the fringe into the mainstream.

The U.S. Supreme Court is not in the business of making social policy either. Nor is its job to reflect it, only to interpret the law intelligently without regard for popularity or prejudice. It conspicuously failed in this mission in 1986 when the justices were asked to rule on the constitutionality of state sodomy laws. From almost any legal promontory, their decision ought to have been clear. Hark back to *Griswold v. Connecticut* and the right to privacy in intimate affairs; use an equal-protection argument, given that law enforcement has traditionally granted heteros a free pass on conduct that is prosecuted among gay men and lesbians. But strike those statutes down.

Instead the court went the other way. As egregious as the decision was the lack of real jurisprudence in the pamphleteering of the majority opinion, which sounded as if it had been written by Cotton Mather during a particularly dirty-minded phase of adolescence. Years later, Justice Lewis Powell, who tipped the 5-4 balance, said he was sorry he had voted as he had.

So when the court announced recently that it would hear a Texas case that considered the same issue, the announcement suggested that the justices, too, saw the error of the earlier decision and might redress it. Every citizen who cares about what America is supposed to stand for should be rooting for that result. The sodomy laws are part of a dark tradition in this nation; they do not exist, and have never existed, to serve the public weal. They are meant only to demonize and marginalize a class of human beings. In this, their closest corollary is the now reviled Jim Crow laws, which excluded black Americans from hotels and restaurants and consigned them to separate schools and restrooms, not because it served any civic purpose but because it was a way to signal that black men and women were inferior. The sodomy laws may be the last laws standing that exist purely for the purpose of codifying and justifying bigotry.

The story of the Texas case the court is preparing to hear reveals just how such statutes turn a free country into a police state. Two consenting male adults were in the midst of a private act of sexual congress in the apartment of one when the police burst in. The men were arrested, jailed overnight and fined. The police showed up in the first place because of a tip by a neighbor of a "weapons disturbance." The neighbor himself was later jailed, convicted of filing a false report. He could be forgiven for thinking this result unfair, since in his behavior he seems to have been merely mimicking the government, monitoring private acts, targeting individuals on the basis of sexual orientation.

This is simply not supposed to be a country in which the law is a flimsy cover for punishing the unpopular. Nevertheless, America's history has been a history of doing just that, whether to immigrants, religious or racial groups, and then eventually having to admit remorse and self-disgust. (See "Trent Lott: The Apology Tour.") There is an irony in the fact that when newspapers in some states are printing the announcements of civil unions by gay men and lesbians, they are also printing the names of sexual desperadoes, breaking the law in the name of love. To resolve that peculiar dissonance does not require the high court to bow to culture change but instead to return to its own defining principles of fairness and freedom, to turn away from the prejudice that, last time out, substituted prurience for jurisprudence.

ANALYZING What the Writer Says

1. Quindlen points out that newspapers that run announcements of commitment ceremonies for gay and lesbian couples are also identifying "sexual desperadoes." What irony does she see in the situation?

2. What, according to Quindlen, is the difference between the conservatism of newspapers and the conservatism of judges?

ANALYZING How the Writer Says It

1. Upon first reading, Quindlen's opening sentence seems relatively benign, a simple observation about social customs. How does her later point about the double message of commitment ceremony announcements load the opening declaration with additional significance?

2. Point to word choices and phrases in Quindlen's piece that reveal her attitude toward American jurisprudence on the issue of sodomy laws. What is her attitude?

ANALYZING the Issue

1. Quindlen implies that sodomy laws remain on the books because of a judicial willingness to discriminate against lesbians and gays. Do you agree that such laws sanction discrimination against a particular class of people? Why or why not?

2. Most people who favor discrimination against homosexuals or support sodomy laws do so for moral or religious reasons. Are such beliefs valid as a basis of law? Why or why not? What other laws are you aware of that are based solely on religious or moral beliefs?

3. Can you think of any compelling reason to legislate the sexual practices of consenting adults? Explain.

ANALYZING Connections Between Texts

1. How does Quindlen's argument echo some of the concerns raised in Adnan R. Khan's "Bordering on Panic" (p. 555)?

2. Compare the kind of surveillance Quindlen derides to the study of the link between brain function and consumerism that Matthew Blakeslee writes about in "Madison Avenue and Your Brain" (p. 632). Is there any justification for the way that the information gathered—whether chronicling sexual habits or spending habits—is used?

3. Could the Office of Emergency Management poster serve (p. 110) also as an appropriate warning about sodomy laws? How so? Who would the figure in the poster represent?

WARMING UP: *Do you think same-sex partners should be prosecuted by the law if they have sex in the privacy of their home?*

From dissenting opinion

Lawrence et al. v. Texas

By Antonin Scalia

ANTONIN SCALIA

On June 26, 2003, the U.S. Supreme Court decided in Lawrence et al. v. Texas *that sodomy laws infringe upon the personal liberty of individuals as guaranteed by the United States Constitution. The following is an excerpt from the dissenting opinion of Justice Antonin Scalia, a devout Catholic and one of the court's most conservative members.*

Today's opinion is the product of a Court, which is the product of a law-profession culture, that has largely signed on to the so-called homosexual agenda, by which I mean the agenda promoted by some homosexual activists directed at eliminating the moral opprobrium that has traditionally attached to homosexual conduct. I noted in an earlier opinion the fact that the American Association of Law Schools (to which any reputable law school must seek to belong) excludes from membership any school that refuses to ban from its job-interview facilities a law firm (no matter how small) that does not wish to hire as a prospective partner a person who openly engages in homosexual conduct. See Romer, supra, at 653.

One of the most revealing statements in today's opinion is the Court's grim warning that the criminalization of homosexual conduct is "an invitation to subject homosexual persons to discrimination both in the public and in the private spheres." Ante, at 14. It is clear from this that the Court has taken sides in the culture war, departing from its role of assuring, as neutral observer, that the democratic rules of engagement are observed. Many Americans do not want persons who openly engage in homosexual conduct as partners in their business, as scoutmasters for their children, as teachers in their children's schools, or as boarders in their home. They view this as protecting themselves and their families from a lifestyle that they believe to be immoral and destructive. The Court views it as "discrimination" which it is the function of our judgments to deter. So imbued is the Court with the law profession's anti-anti-homosexual culture, that it is seemingly unaware that the attitudes of that culture are not obviously "mainstream"; that in most States what the Court calls "discrimination" against those who engage in homosexual acts is perfectly legal; that proposals to ban such "discrimination" under Title VII have repeatedly been rejected by Congress, see Employment Non-Discrimination Act of 1994, S. 2238, 103d Cong., 2d Sess. (1994); Civil Rights Amendments, H. R. 5452, 94th Cong., 1st Sess. (1975); that in some cases such "discrimination" is mandated by federal statute, see 10 U. S. C. §654(b)(1) (mandating discharge from the armed forces of any service member who engages in or intends to engage in homosexual acts); and that in some cases such "discrimination" is a constitutional right, see Boy Scouts of America v. Dale, 530 U. S. 640 (2000).

Let me be clear that I have nothing against homosexuals, or any other group, promoting their agenda through normal democratic means. Social perceptions of sexual and other morality change over time, and every group has the right to persuade its fellow citizens that its view of such matters is the best. That homosexuals have achieved some success in that enterprise is attested to by the fact that Texas is one of the few remaining States that criminalize private, consensual homosexual acts. But persuading one's fellow citizens is one thing, and imposing one's views in absence of democratic majority will is something else. I would no more require a State to criminalize homosexual acts—or, for that matter, display any moral disapprobation of them—than I would forbid it to do so. What Texas has chosen to do is well within the range of traditional democratic action, and its hand should not be stayed through the invention of a brand-new "constitutional right" by a Court that is impatient of democratic change. It is indeed true that "later generations can see that laws once thought necessary and proper in fact serve only to oppress," ante, at 18; and when that happens, later generations can repeal those laws. But it is the premise of our system that those judgments are to be made by the people, and not imposed by a governing caste that knows best.

One of the benefits of leaving regulation of this matter to the people rather than to the courts is that the people, unlike judges, need not carry things to their logical conclusion. The people may feel that their disapprobation of homosexual conduct is strong enough to disallow homosexual marriage, but not strong enough to criminalize private homosexual acts—and may legislate accordingly. The Court today pretends that it possesses a similar freedom of action, so that that we need not fear judicial imposition of homosexual marriage, as has recently occurred in Canada (in a decision that the Canadian Government has chosen not to appeal). See Halpern v. Toronto, 2003 WL 34950 (Ontario Ct. App.); Cohen, Dozens in Canada Follow Gay Couple's Lead, Washington Post, June 12, 2003, p. A25. At the end of its opinion—after having laid waste the foundations of our rational-basis jurisprudence—the Court says that the present case "does not involve whether the government must give formal recognition to any relationship that homosexual persons seek to enter." Ante, at 17. Do not believe it. More illuminating than this bald, unreasoned disclaimer is the progression of thought displayed by an earlier passage in the Court's opinion, which notes the constitutional protections afforded to "personal decisions relating to marriage, procreation, contraception, family relationships, child rearing, and education," and then declares that "[p]ersons in a homosexual relationship may seek autonomy for these purposes, just as heterosexual persons do." Ante, at 13 (emphasis added). Today's opinion dismantles the structure of constitutional law that has permitted a distinction to be made between heterosexual and homosexual unions, insofar as formal recognition in marriage is concerned. If moral disapprobation of homosexual conduct is "no legitimate state interest" for purposes of proscribing that conduct, ante, at 18; and if, as the Court coos (casting aside all pretense of neutrality), "[w]hen sexuality finds overt expression in intimate conduct with another person, the conduct can be but one element in a personal bond that is more enduring," ante, at 6; what justification could there possibly be for denying the benefits of marriage to homosexual couples exercising "[t]he liberty protected by the Constitution," ibid.? Surely not the encouragement of procreation, since the sterile and the elderly are allowed to marry. This case "does not involve" the issue of homosexual marriage only if one entertains the belief that principle and logic have nothing to do with the decisions of this Court. Many will hope that, as the Court comfortingly assures us, this is so.

The matters appropriate for this Court's resolution are only three: Texas's 5 prohibition of sodomy neither infringes a "fundamental right" (which the Court does not dispute), nor is unsupported by a rational relation to what the Constitution considers a legitimate state interest, nor denies the equal protection of the laws. I dissent.

ANALYZING What the Writer Says

1. What convinces Scalia that the American law profession has an "anti-anti-homosexual" bias?

2. Scalia maintains that the decision in *Lawrence et al. v. Texas* was made "in absence of democratic majority." What does he mean by this?

3. What consequences does Scalia fear this decision might have?

ANALYZING How the Writer Says It

1. How do you know that Scalia's text is a legal document? What kind of language characterizes these types of documents?

2. Where in the document does Scalia use language that one would not expect in such a text? What does he say? What is the effect of this use of language?

ANALYZING the Issue

1. Do you think there are compelling reasons to legislate the sexual practices of consenting adults? Explain.

2. Do you agree with Scalia that protecting the privacy of homosexuals will lead to the abolishment of "laws against adultery, fornication, and adult incest, and laws refusing to recognize homosexual marriage"? Why or why not?

ANALYZING Connections Between Texts

1. Adnan R. Khan ("Bordering on Panic," p. 555) and Charles Krauthammer ("The Case for Profiling," p. 563) demonstrate how the war against terrorism has led to close observation of individuals, measures the government defends in the name of national security. Although *Lawrence et al. v. Texas* concerns the private conduct of two consenting adults, Scalia argues that their behavior is just as corroding to our nation's moral fiber as terrorism is to our national security. Weigh his arguments against those made by Khan and Krauthammer to determine whether the government serves the public by watching certain individuals very closely.

2. In "Growing Pains" (p. 131), Anndee Hochman describes her mother's reaction to her coming out as a lesbian. Do you think the Supreme Court decision concerning the private behavior of same-sex couples will help or hinder the process of families' coming to terms with their sons' and daughters' sexual orientation? Explain.

3. In what way does Danny Lyon's "Against the Wall, Punishment, Ramsey" (p. 613) illustrate the ideas Scalia presents in his dissenting opinion?

WARMING UP: *Have you ever decided to give someone a second—or third—chance after being hurt very badly, despite warnings and advice from friends, family, and perhaps even professionals?*

Fierce Entanglements

By Deborah Sontag

DEBORAH SONTAG

A staff writer for the New York Times, *Deborah Sontag has written extensively on the Israeli-Palestinian conflict in the Middle East as well as on domestic politics and social issues. The following piece, offering an alternative, controversial perspective on the issue of family violence, first appeared in the* New York Times Magazine *on November 17, 2002.*

When Michael Wilkes left Sumter, S.C., two decades ago, he was trying to escape what he perceived to be his bloodstained fate. He was only 21, but he was already in trouble—in petty trouble with the law, in big trouble at home. He didn't want to end up like his father: a career criminal, a wife beater and dead by his wife's hand. So, baby-faced and jittery, Michael boarded a Greyhound for New York, fleeing an urge to exact vengeance on the stepmother who killed his father. He was running, too, from a failed, violence-ridden marriage of his own.

At first, things went well. Michael quickly found a job as a gofer for an art studio in Manhattan. He worked hard, the owner took him under his wing and within two years he had settled into a cozy basement apartment in Queens. That's where he met Sylvia.

Sylvia, the landlady's daughter, was voluptuous and dark-skinned, with fine features and twinkly eyes. She thought that Michael was "adorable and nice," and she was impressed by his cooking, especially his barbecue sauce. It was only a matter of time before they got involved. Michael's plans to recreate himself suddenly became more complicated.

Michael had succeeded in starting over as an industrious working man. But he thought that his hostility toward women was something he could not choose simply to rise above. He just felt it in him; if he got passionate about a woman, he was prepared to be betrayed, and his guard went up. And with Sylvia, the passion was intense. "I loved her to death," Michael says. It's a phrase that a man given to battering women probably shouldn't use.

Right from the start, Michael found himself falling into familiar patterns with   5 Sylvia. "The distrust of a woman—I had it deep," he says. "I physically abused my first wife—smacks punches, kicks. And then I turned around and did it again with Sylvia. The least little thing, I would fight her. I would hurt her. And she didn't deserve none of it." Speaking now as a sober-minded 41-year-old, after all he has been through and more precisely all he has put others through, Michael is trying hard to shoulder full responsibility for his actions.

Sylvia, however, argues that the dynamic was mutual all along. Michael wasn't the only one who had issues, she says. When they met, she had just escaped from a violent relationship that deteriorated to the point where the man was stalking her, armed with a knife. She was defensive and her fuse was short. "It's inaccurate to say only that Michael would beat me," Sylvia says, more forgiving of Michael than he is of himself. "He did. But we would beat each other. We would destroy the house. It became kind of dangerous for both of us. I didn't know who was going to kill who."

It was a complex situation, murkier than the black-and-white portrayal of domestic violence that currently guides public policy. In that view, there's a batterer and a victim; the batterer is an ogre molded—misshapen—by patriarchal society; the victim, a mouse made helpless by it. There is only one happy ending: the batterer is punished, the victim liberated.

But Sylvia did not see Michael as a monster. She saw him as the product of a lousy childhood. She also saw him as a good provider and, in time, as the father of their two daughters. Nor did she see herself as defenseless but rather as the beneficiary of a good upbringing, as a self-reliant working woman and as someone who stood her ground. She never wanted Michael locked up; she wanted him to change. She wanted to rehabilitate her family, not to break it up. And in that way, Sylvia—like so many other women who refuse to call themselves victims—is a formidable challenge to doctrinaire thinking about the nature of domestic violence and how to combat it.

Since the end of the 19th century, American courts have been denying husbands the right to "chastise" their wives, but abusive men were rarely arrested, much less prosecuted. The police didn't want to get involved in what was going on behind closed doors or usurp a man's authority in his home. In most cases, they didn't even have the legal authority to make domestic violence arrests unless they had personally witnessed an assault. When they were called into a domestic situation, officers would extricate the man for a walk around the block and then return to the job of fighting what they perceived as "real crime."

As the feminist movement grew in the 1970's, advocates for women began   10 to decry what they described as the government's collusion with batterers.

They struggled to build a network of shelters for battered women and to get domestic violence redefined as a serious crime. They lobbied for new state laws that would remove the police's discretion and mandate arrests for domestic violence. And they succeeded. Over the last two decades, and especially in the last 10 years, mandatory arrests have become a linchpin of the government's effort to address the issue; they are seen as a way to protect women, punish offenders, deter future violence and send a message that spousal abuse won't be tolerated.

Now, though, a growing number of professionals are questioning the effectiveness of the mandatory arrest policies that advocates fought so long and hard for. Making more arrests and ensnaring more couples in the criminal justice system has not yet proved itself as a policy of deterrence, they say. And arrests sometimes backfire, especially in inner-city neighborhoods, causing unintended problems for some of the women that society is trying to protect. It would seem, they argue, that we are ignoring human nature, putting principle above the lives involved and creating an unproductive antagonism between the system and some victims. Many battered women, for instance, don't want their men arrested or put away. The questioners, who include academics, crime experts, black feminists and social workers, are wondering aloud if we have come to rely too much on the law to solve a problem that defies easy solutions.

After all, the criminal justice system is a blunt club for a problem as psychologically dark, emotionally tangled and intimate as domestic violence. At the very least, it cannot address the abuse that is not criminal. Serious violence, physical and sexual, is only part of the problem, and many experts are equally concerned about the psychological and emotional abuse that warps so many lives.

Then, too, there is the vastness of the phenomenon. In New York, the police field at least 200,000 complaints of domestic abuse a year. Even under the new laws, only tens of thousands result in arrests, the vast majority for misdemeanor-level abuse. But that is still a significant number of offenders for the system to process, and in the end only a fraction of offenders get prison time. Thus, many men are cycled through the system to little avail, sometimes ending up angrier and back with their partners.

It is indisputable that many women are protected, educated and freed from misery by the courts and the counselors. But many others resist or resent the intrusion of the government into their intimate lives. Often, they are still deeply involved with their abusers and feel belittled by professionals who presume to know what's in their best interest. They don't want to be humiliated for choosing their partners, pressured into leaving them or blamed. They don't want to be "battered by the system," as a recent workshop given by survivors of domestic violence in New York was called.

"Crimes of an intimate nature make it much more difficult for people to come forward, and the volume of cases dictates that it can be an impersonal   15 and horrific experience," says Abena Darkeh, domestic violence coordinator for New York City's criminal courts. "I suspect that the majority of people working in the system would not choose to go through it" if they experienced domestic violence themselves.

Well-meaning professionals often find themselves in an uncomfortable and sometimes adversarial relationship with victims. Prosecutors, especially, become frustrated by the many women who balk at testifying against their husbands. Increasingly, social workers are pushing for an approach that is more clear-eyed and less judgmental.

As Ruth Schulder, a social worker in the Bronx, says: "Nobody has the right to say to a woman, 'You can't be with this guy.' So we have had to deal with the reality." And the reality is that abused women often make calculated decisions to stay with their partners. Sometimes a woman really has no choice; she's scared that leaving would make him more dangerous, or she doesn't think she can survive financially on her own. But other times she stays for the same reasons that people in other kinds of imperfect relationships do: because of the kids, because of her religion, because she doesn't want to be alone or simply because she loves him.

As they weigh the successes and inadequacies of the criminal-justice-dominated approach to domestic violence, a handful of experts are calling for a repeal of mandatory arrest laws altogether. Others, in larger numbers, are suggesting fine-tuning the criminal justice approach, making it both more humane and less central. They want more prevention and intervention on the community level. Still others, the therapeutically minded, are so bold as to suggest not only working more collaboratively with families but also doing so in a way that includes the men.

"If we don't work with the men, we can't change the world," Geraldine Abelson, a social worker, said at a recent conference in New York. Her comment underscores the idealism of many in the field. They don't just want to make women safer. They want to break the cycle of violence. They want to *change the world*. And that may well be too utopian a basis for any public policy.

Linda Mills took the podium at a New York City-sponsored domestic violence   20
conference this fall to give a keynote speech that she knew would rankle many. Her voice rang out with an accusation and a dare: "Mainstream feminism has maintained a stranglehold on our explanations of, and responses to, domestic violence, and it is time to take our voices back." Then Mills offered her credentials for making such a charge. Publicly, she is a legal scholar and social worker who is a vice provost at New York University. But, she told the crowd, she, too, is a feminist, and she, too, is a onetime victim of domestic violence— at the hands of a man she described as a violence-prevention expert.

"He was passionate about his work, passionate about me," Mills said. "I loved the attention he gave me; I started to love him. When he socked me in the arm the first time, I was surprised. I was hurt and I was angry. He shared with me his history: an abusive mother, an absent father. He was sure that's where his anger, his aggression, came from. I listened; I felt sad for him. I told him that if he ever hit me again, I would leave him. When he pushed me and later spat at me, I made the same threats."

Still, Mills said, her gaze defiant, even though the violence later escalated to include rape, she wouldn't have wanted the police to know. She would never have testified against him. "Doing so would have robbed me of the little dignity I had left." And, she said, the "system" needs to respect women who feel that way. The system, she said, patronizes victims by failing to listen to them, usurping their decision-making power and underestimating them—underestimating their ability to negotiate their own safety and underestimating their role in the abusive relationship. Domestic violence is construed as one-sided aggression, when often there is a warped dynamic of intimacy in which both the men and the women are players. It is dishonest, she went on, to stifle conversation about the ways in which women, too, are aggressive and violent.

Many in the audience shuddered. But Mills, who first created a stir when she published a 1999 Harvard Law Review article called "Killing Her Softly: Intimate Abuse and the Violence of State Intervention," was asking publicly questions that some in the field have been asking privately.

Some veteran advocates see Mills as an ivory-tower pontificator whose views are dangerous, capable of inspiring a backlash. They don't want to waste their energy engaging in an internal debate, not at a time when some government officials are asking them to justify the devotion of scarce resources to domestic violence. "Where's the bang for the buck in terms of public safety?" a senior New York police official asked advocates earlier this year.

These advocates find themselves in an uneasy position: first, relying on a male-dominated institution—the criminal justice system—then, defending it despite their own ambivalence about the arrest policies they encouraged. 25

Sylvia never thought the police belonged in her home. She didn't call them when Michael gave her black eyes. She didn't call them when he broke her nose in a fit of delusional jealousy, although she sat him down and pointed to her bloody, disfigured face and said, "What if someone did this to your daughter?" But she did call 911 one time and one time alone—about a decade ago, before New York passed its mandatory arrest law—when Michael threatened to leave and take their daughters. Two female officers showed up. Sylvia taunted him in front of them, playing on his chronic fear that she was cheating on him, a holdover from his bad first marriage. She told the officers that Michael couldn't take the children because the girls weren't his (a bald lie).

The officers then tried to rile him. "I wish a man would hurt me," one said, hand on the butt of her gun. "I would blow his brains out." But in the end, all they did was tell him to get lost. Michael camped out in his mother-in-law's basement, scared that this time Sylvia wouldn't take him back. After a few days, he returned with trepidation and apologies to the scene of the crime, his home. "After a man abuses a woman," he says, "his famous thing is, 'I'm sorry.'"

Sylvia stood firm. She said: "I'm goddamn sick of your sorries. You're just one sorry [expletive]." She shut him up and talked at him about his suspiciousness, his possessiveness, his temper and his violence. And a light went on for him, Michael says. A light went on, and it stayed on, because, he says, "she spoke the truth. For the first time, I was listening to a woman, and she made much more sense than I did."

As she was talking, though, Sylvia was questioning herself. "Lord, history is repeating itself," she was thinking. "I'm going back down this way with another guy." But she believed that Michael was different, that he had a good heart. "Being that he went through so much, he had a real problem," she said. "But we were determined to be with each other."

Sylvia understood to counsel Michael herself. "Sylvia's tongue-lashings," as Michael calls them, went on for years, always with the same bottom line. His actions had consequences. If he hit her again, she would leave. End of story. Unfortunately, though, it wasn't the end of the story. 30

The case of Tracey Thurman in Torrington, Conn., called national attention to just how dangerous—and costly to government—the old approach could be. In 1982, Thurman repeatedly and to no avail called the police to report brutal threats by her estranged husband. Then, in 1983, Thurman's husband, a short-order cook at a restaurant frequented by police officers, stabbed her repeatedly. When the police arrived, they didn't arrest him immediately; they stood by as he kicked his bleeding wife in the head twice. Thurman survived and won an approximately $2 million jury award against the local police department. Her story became a classic cautionary tale about police inaction in domestic violence cases.

An experiment in 1984 in Minneapolis played a defining role in reshaping the police approach. On the basis of 314 domestic violence cases, a study conducted by the criminologists Lawrence W. Sherman and Richard A. Berk concluded that arrests discouraged batterers from committing future acts of battery. The authors cautioned that the sample size was small and the findings preliminary, but their caution was not heeded. Citing their work, a federal task force recommended that arrest become the standard response to misdemeanor domestic violence cases. It did; most states now have mandatory arrest laws.

After his Minneapolis study, however, Sherman refined his thinking on the basis of further studies that revealed a far more complicated picture. He oversaw one such study in Milwaukee, which showed that arrest makes low-income men more violent than does a simple warning by the police. The low-income men in Milwaukee, most of whom happened to be black, were three times as likely to be arrested than employed white men were. Therefore, by his study's oddly precise calculations, mandatory arrest in Milwaukee prevented 2,504 acts of violence against primarily white women at the price of 5,409 additional acts of violence against primarily black women.

Although the results were expressed in racial terms, Sherman said the men's status in society was the determining factor. Arrests generally deterred employed offenders, the studies showed, but provoked unemployed offenders to commit up to twice as many more assaults. That is, if a goal of the arrest policy is to protect women, the policy seems to backfire when applied to the low-income population that is most likely to be arrested for domestic violence.

Sherman, now a University of Pennsylvania professor, began to argue that   35
laws mandating arrests for misdemeanor domestic violence offenses should be repealed. "Until you admit that mandatory arrest is a failure in our inner cities, you won't get anybody to spend a penny on looking for other alternatives," he told me. Defenders of pro-arrest tactics say that mandatory arrest laws work much better when they lead to prosecution and treatment. But Sherman and others counter that prosecution and treatment are problematic, too.

"It's because of O.J. that a lot of men are now catching the blunt end of it," Michael says. Indeed, some defenders of current policies like to cite the Simpson case to explain why mandatory arrest and no-drop prosecution policies are important, no matter what the studies show. During Simpson's trial, prosecutors played a 911 tape of a frightened Nicole Brown Simpson pleading with the police to rescue her from her husband. O.J. was never arrested because Nicole didn't want to press charges. If Los Angeles had had a mandatory intervention policy, Nicole Simpson's wishes wouldn't have mattered. The police could have built a case despite her. If prosecutors needed her testimony, they could have subpoenaed her, and if she refused to comply, a judge could have held her in contempt.

Cheryl Hanna, a Vermont Law School professor and former prosecutor, wrote in a 1996 Harvard Law Review article that it used to make her squeamish to use the state's powers to coerce a reluctant victim like Nicole Brown Simpson to cooperate. She preferred to dismiss or indefinitely postpone such cases rather than subject the women to revictimization by the state. She now says that she was wrong. She should have served the greater good by reaffirming the government's hard line against domestic violence.

Some cases are so unambiguous and gruesome that the government's instincts to override a victim's wishes seem entirely justified. In 1994 in New York City, Mario Russo stabbed his wife four times in the chest, missing her heart by just an inch. She was seriously injured, and Mario, then a new immigrant from Italy, told the police to arrest him. In the station house, he confessed to the stabbing in a torrent of broken English, saying his wife was mentally ill, that she "got out of line" and that he "went crazy." Yet, stunning prosecutors, Rosa Russo insisted on testifying in her husband's defense. She said she had been cooking, they got into an argument and she fell on her knife. On Valentine's Day in 1995, her husband was convicted of attempted murder and sent to prison. Nonetheless, at least for a while, the Russos kept up their relationship. He wrote to her, and she visited him. She even requested a conjugal visit, prosecutors said.

But then there are the cases in which the government seems overeager to take an unequivocal stance against spousal abuse. The case against Joseph P. Kirkner IV, in Chester County, Pa., for instance, was a simple assault case. Kellie Kirkner called 911 on July 4, 1999, to report that her husband had choked and shoved her. Kellie, however, decided that she didn't want to testify against her husband because she wanted to preserve her marriage. Prosecutors subpoenaed her; a judge quashed the subpoena. The prosecutors did not relent, appealing to the Pennsylvania Supreme Court and keeping the case open even as the Kirkners split up. In the end, the Supreme Court ruled that the judge's decision was inappropriate, and in October, three years after the incident, the case went to trial.

Kellie Kirkner requested immunity from prosecution—she, too, had hit and struck her spouse, she eventually testified. As the jury understood it, what transpired was more of a battle royal over credit-card spending than spousal abuse. Joseph Kirkner was acquitted. 40

One unforeseen consequence of the mandatory arrest laws has been that many women are getting arrested along with their boyfriends or husbands. Police arrive at a home, face accusations and counteraccusations and arrest both parties. Advocates for women see this as an unfortunate way in which the new laws, as interpreted by poorly trained police officers, have hurt women. In New York, legislators were persuaded to amend the law, requiring police officers to determine the "primary physical aggressor" and arrest only that person. Mills argues, however, that the proliferation of dual arrests might signal that there is more reciprocal abuse than people want to acknowledge.

Defenders of pro-arrest policies say that the legal system can and should learn to handle domestic violence cases both aggressively and with sensitivity. They often point to the way that domestic violence is addressed in a place like Brooklyn, which has a felony court dedicated to the issue. The court has an unusually low rate for dismissing cases while also assigning every victim an advocate who directs her to services. In preparing its cases, the D.A.'s office does far more social work than is traditionally done by prosecutors, says Wanda Lucibello, chief of the special victims division there.

"There's so much gray area in these cases," Lucibello says, with "land mines in every direction. It's a philosophical discussion, day in and day out."

As a result of some of those philosophical discussions, Galla Hendy, 33, is one former victim who says that the system was responsive enough to allow her to liberate herself from a dangerous relationship—eventually.

When I met Galla last summer, her ambivalence was right out there, prac- 45
tically sitting on the red plastic table of a Popeyes in Far Rockaway. Fingering
a gold hoop in her right ear, she talked wistfully about her ex-batterer and, as
of six months earlier, her ex-boyfriend, too. "I miss him," she said. "Yeah,
I do. I ain't going to lie. He's not so much of a bad person except for the
violence."

When Galla first met him in 1996, she was working two jobs to support her
three children. She was a home health aide by day, a stripper by night. One
evening, he came into the strip club, and she asked him if he wanted "a wall
dance or a lap dance." They ended up talking. She let him know she was dating
someone, and he said: "Forget about Mr. Wrong. Here is Mr. Right." And for
quite some time Galla agreed with him. They seemed to have so much in common—both health care workers, both immigrants (she from Guyana, he from
Jamaica), both parents.

They fell in love; four years ago they had a daughter. By Galla's account—all
of this is by her account; her ex-boyfriend could not be reached—he was frustrated because he wasn't working. He has sickle cell anemia, and he had gone
on disability after hip surgery. Galla tried to reassure him, to keep him from
beating up on himself. She didn't mean for him to start beating up on her. It
began on their daughter's first birthday. Galla's boyfriend was out of the apartment, and she left the baby in the care of her 11-year-old son to shop for a party.
When she bustled in with her packages, he was back, and she could see the fire
in his eyes. He was outraged by what he saw as her negligence; he struck her
with his cane. She calmed him down "by making myself available to him," but
things were never completely calm again.

After many unsettled months and one spectacular argument, she took their
daughter and went to stay with a friend. When she returned home, he was
angry, certain that she had been cheating on him. He hit her. She begged him
to stop. He even put on a pair of boxing gloves and started using her as a
punching bag. She felt as if she had nothing left in her to fight back with—
until he took out the rope. He encircled her neck, crazed to know if she was
somebody else's woman. The more she denied it, the more he tightened the
rope. "I actually thought I was a goner," she said. She lied, saying that she had
been cheating on him. He let her go, and he left the room. But he returned
with a gun, placing it under a pillow in front of her face. Eventually, the fight
drained out of him. "You see what you made me do?" he said.

At dawn, she said, he brought out a bottle of champagne, then forced her to
have anal sex. The kids woke up and absorbed the tension in the apartment.
Her son, then 12, got into an argument with her boyfriend, who ended up
throwing his gun at the boy and daring him to shoot. Galla sent her son outside and told him to call the police. They came quickly and just as quickly had
him on the ground in handcuffs as they searched for the weapon. Galla felt a
twinge of betrayal.

He was taken to jail. Galla went to the district attorney's office. She was   50
unsure if she should help prosecutors make a case against the father of her
daughter. But counselors there advised her to think about the possibility that
the violence could escalate and about the safety of her children. She listened.

When she went before the grand jury, though, she found it excruciating to
recount her story of physical and sexual abuse to a roomful of strangers, mostly men. She saw horror in some eyes, boredom in others. She felt as if she
were the one being judged.

He was indicted for assault, sodomy and child endangerment. Galla went to
visit him in jail. She was hurt and confused to see the man she loved behind bars.
"Why would I do this to him?" she asked herself. "Then again, why would he do
this to me?" He still didn't think he had done anything wrong, but Galla began
feeling sorry for him. It wasn't good for his health to be locked up. She herself
didn't want to go through a trial. Enough was enough. She wanted him freed and
she wanted him home.

So Galla went to the D.A.'s office and asked if some kind of deal could be
worked out. Her boyfriend needed help, she told them; he didn't need to be
locked up.

Lucibello's staff members arranged a plea deal; they eventually counted his
six months in jail as time served, and he accepted five years of intensive probation and assignment to a batterers' intervention group. And when he was
released from jail, the couple reunited.

But he came out of jail with a lot of animosity in him. He wanted to engage   55
Galla in relentless conversations about the incidents that led to his arrest. He
wanted her to agree that it was all her fault. He was angry about having to attend
a program. He kept his fists to himself, but he did grab her hard by the shoulders a few times. Their little daughter would hide the phone. "Don't call the
police on Daddy," she'd beg her mother. Earlier this year, after Galla refused to
let him use her new pearl white car for his newspaper delivery job, he moved out.

Still, a month later, Galla found herself calling him when she was lonely.
When she started dating someone else, he threatened to shoot the man, telling
Galla she would see her name in the papers. She called 911. There is now a full
order of protection that prohibits him from making any contact with her. Galla
doesn't miss him anymore, she told me in late October.

On a typical lackluster fall day, a parade of sad and angry men and women filed
before Judge John M. Leventhal in New York Supreme Court facing felony
charges of assaulting, kidnapping or murdering their wives, husbands and
same-sex partners. It was hard not to be struck by just how many of them there
were, dealing in such a public way with intimate lives gone awry, and to multiply it out across the country and queasily feel the vastness of the phenomenon.

It was also hard not to notice that while the judge and almost all the lawyers
were white, almost every defendant was black or Latino, either unemployed or

taking time off from jobs cleaning houses or stocking grocery shelves for their court appearances. Lisa C. Smith, a Brooklyn Law School professor and former prosecutor, told me that she doesn't think domestic violence really is a crime that cuts equally across all social classes. "In order to get people to care about the concept, it was painted that way, but it's not true," she said. "It's far more prevalent in the lower socioeconomic level."

Indeed, federal statistics show that low-income women are far more likely to be victims of domestic violence. But Judge Leventhal said he thought that the class composition of his courtroom reflected instead on under-reporting of domestic violence by more affluent people. Other experts echo this; the more affluent have the means to handle their domestic violence problems privately—using private physicians, therapists, hotels, divorce lawyers.

I asked the judge if it bothered him that the government was arresting more   60 poor people for crimes that he believed to be committed by all classes. "Sure it bothers me," he said, looking discomforted. A week later, he called me back to say he really didn't look at it that way: "Don't lower-income people deserve protection, too?"

Dr. John Aponte, a former police psychologist who counsels batterers, says that he hates that the vast number of men referred to him by the courts are on welfare, unemployed or have prior criminal records. "That says to me that the system is rounding up the usual suspects. The system is only getting those available for capture. And let me tell you, the men know it. When the men in my groups see only other poor people in the program, it makes them think, I'm just here because I got caught, so I have to learn how to not get caught."

The issue of race sometimes seems inescapable. One Tuesday this fall, I sat in on a batterers intervention group, a room full of black and Latino men mandated into a 26-week program. After one man denied that he had ever hit his wife, a man named James, playing the self-appointed role of lie-detector, burst out with: "Well, that's not what the white man say! Why do you think you're here, bro?"

Melinda Hunter, 30, a teacher in the Bronx, told me that her partner used to "play the race card" to stop her from calling the police and that it worked. She was a college-educated woman from Ohio who met her boyfriend when she arrived in New York in 1995. She was a tour guide at Radio City Music Hall, and he was building sets. Unaware of her own attractiveness, she was so flattered by his attention that she overlooked her qualms when she learned that he was in a work-release program. Having just finished "The Autobiography of Malcolm X," she told herself that most black men were going to pass through prison at some point.

Later, when her partner had grown abusive, he, by then the father of her children, restrained her from reporting him by saying: "They'll send me back to prison. Don't let the white man take me and break up another black family." Even when they finally did land in court, she covered up for him (encouraged by a police officer, she said, who told them, "These things happen"). The charges were dismissed, but her partner's probation officer made him move out. Hunter got herself into a support group, and when I met her last summer, she was adamantly liberated. Little by little, however, because he was familiar, because she is sentimental, because of the kids, she let her partner back into her life. She was embarrassed to tell me this, but, she said, they are going to church together, he is "reborn," and she is trying to have faith in the possible.

In the 1980's, Aponte moved from the police department to New York City's   65
victim services agency to help domestic violence advocates figure out how to deal with the men. At the time, he said, the thinking was (and remains): punishment. "There was a lot of anger in the feminist community. It was: 'They're lost. They're no good. They're beyond redeeming. To deal with the men is to consort with the enemy.'"

Aponte felt differently. Many men were first offenders, and he thought they were capable of learning and changing. Beyond that, it was undeniable that a majority of women returned to relationships involving abuse—"so it seemed kind of imperative to get the men into some kind of rehab."

Eventually, the system came to need comprehensive programs for men. Since only a small percentage of men arrested for domestic abuse get prison time, judges had to do something with the rest. Batterers intervention programs became a way of disposing of many cases, and they proliferated. Still, many judges view these programs skeptically, as do advocates for women, and New York State does not regulate them, so as to avoid giving them any stamp of approval.

"The jury is still out on whether they do any good," Judge Leventhal said, although he orders many into the programs as a condition of bail. "And there's a fear that they do some harm, that they give victims false hope that these men have been treated, so they welcome them back."

The very existence of the programs brings up the question of whether and how a batterer can be rehabilitated. Samuel Aymer, a psychotherapist in New York, says the belief that abusers can change is the guiding principle of his work. But he says that many of those running programs have doubts that limit or even poison the process. Indeed, many programs don't even try to be rehabilitative; they consist of didactic lectures based on feminist theory: domestic violence results not from individual personal or moral deficits but from an abuser's belief that he has the right to inflict his will on his partner. In these programs, needless to say, there is little sharing of personal histories; the circumstances and concerns of the men are not discussed.

"These men are not simply puppets of the patriarchal system who must   70
unlearn their pigheaded thinking," Aymer said. "The patriarchal system doesn't make all men abusers. So what is it about these guys? Let's help them

develop insights into their behavior. That does not mean excuse the abuse. Reject it. But don't reject him."

Aymer, who used to counsel battered women, was recruited into working with men by Aponte, who trains social workers to combine education and group treatment in 26-week programs that use a lot of role playing. One such program is run on Tuesday nights by Ruth Schulder and Carlos Scott at a Salvation Army office under an elevated subway line in the Bronx.

I attended the eighth and ninth weeks of the program this fall, before the men's resistance to being there had completely broken down. They sat in metal chairs in a semicircle, arms folded across their chests protectively, defiantly. Wearing hooded sweatshirts or jean jackets, they rocked backward on the institutional blue carpet, jiggling their legs. Many of the men asserted not only that they had never hit their wives but also that it was a matter of principle for them not to do so. I asked Schulder if I had come to the wrong class. "No," she said. "They're lying."

One, a chubby, talkative man said that everything was fine in his home except that his Maria was in a depression. Schulder, who has flaming red hair and a tough, jokey, compassionate manner, snorted and said out of the side of her mouth, "Oh, you can tell the new people."

Then she addressed the man, Alex, directly: "What was your act to get here?" He began, "Well, she——." Schulder cut him off. "Not she—you. You—what was the word you used? You shmushed her face, right?" Well, Alex said, after 12 years in a relationship, nobody's perfect. Twelve years and one thing, and suddenly you have the police at your door. That's when James, the self-appointed lie-detector, told him to get real.

Schulder played a horrific tape recording of a 6-year-old girl who calls 911 to 75 report that her mommy and daddy are having a fight. The girl is crying so hard that she is choking. Against the audible commotion in her home, she is screaming "Stop it!" and "Mommy!" and "No, don't take the baby!" The situation and her agitation escalate as her father apparently strikes her sister and tries to choke her mother. The call abruptly ends when, it seems, her mother discovers her on the phone and hangs it up.

"How does that make you feel?" Schulder asked the group. James jumped in first. "Like I want to kick somebody's butt." Several men said that they would never fight with their wives in front of their children, and Schulder pointed out that the parents of the girl on the tape didn't realize that she was there or on the phone. "Kids always see; kids always hear," she said. Schulder told the men that when she played the tape for women in her parenting classes, they all cried. "I was crying inside," one man said. Schulder asked why he held it in. "I am among men," he said.

At another point, Schulder asked the men if their partners respected them. "Every day I'm closer to asking my wife, 'Do you fear me?'" James said. A bulky man who wears a purple scarf over his plaited hair, James said that he doesn't think he has given her any reason to, but Schulder, letting that pass, asked if his present wife knows he was violent toward his ex. James explained how he dealt with his first wife: "To me it was like, you don't beat her, you can't get nothing from her. All her other babies' fathers, they punch her in the face and she act better. She did what she was supposed to do." Schulder asked what she was supposed to do, what was in her "contract." James said that she was supposed to look after the kids while he went to work. But when he came home from work, he used to find the kids alone in the apartment. So he would "smack her face." Schulder said that she fully understood why it upset him to find his children unattended. "But you don't have the right to hit her," she said. "What happens when you don't do your job at work, do you get smacked?"

At the end of one 26-week class, one of Aponte's men asked if he could hug him. Aponte was taken aback. He doesn't really do hugging. He asked the man why. The man told him that he had never before met a powerful man who wasn't abusive. Aponte hugged him.

After Sylvia laid down the law, Michael was intensely motivated to change. "I never really laid a hand on her again," he said. "I would want to, but I knew if I would do it, I'd lose this woman I really loved." But while he forced himself to stop hitting Sylvia, he couldn't rise up out of himself entirely. He didn't like any inkling that he was being disrespected in his home. He would feel overwhelmed by the need to assert his control. He would lose his temper and his palms would start sweating, and if not Sylvia then someone else was going to bear the brunt of it.

"I guess I kind of switched my pattern toward the kids," Michael mumbled, fingering his wisp of a mustache. He was embarrassed. He glanced over at Sylvia, who was asleep in the brass bed in the adjacent bedroom. Fully dressed, she was underneath a fluffy quilt blocking out all conversation, since she had just come home from work at a group home for disabled adults and was due to head out to a second shift, an all-nighter. Their daughters, 15 and 11, were in their rooms, giggling with friends.

"I would spank them," Michael said. "It started as spanking. But I overdid it."

One night a couple of years ago, his older daughter, then 12, crossed some kind of a line and angered him; Michael doesn't remember the precipitating incident. Her daughter really angered Michael, Sylvia told me later. "She was a big girl, too old to be spanked. But he spanked her anyway, and worse." Michael beat his daughter with a stick.

The girl, who is overweight and very sensitive, was hurt physically and devastated emotionally. When she went to school the next day, she showed her bruises to a teacher. The school called the child-welfare authorities. They took away the girls and put them in a foster home. Sylvia was furious and sad. Michael said he was disgusted with himself, the old familiar remorse that would sweep over him like a wave of nausea after he struck Sylvia.

Looking back, Sylvia draws from her bottomless supply of compassion for Michael, but it is hard-edged. "I don't think Michael intended to hurt the child," she said. "He never intended to hurt me either. But in the eyes of society today, abuse is abuse, and if you don't fix things in your own home, the system's going to fix it for you."

After a few weeks the girls returned home, and Michael left for several weeks on the court's order. He and Sylvia were made to take a parenting class. During the intake process, Michael acknowledged his history of domestic abuse. It was the first time Michael had ever identified himself to the authorities as a batterer. He was put on a waiting list for a batterers group.

Then, in the spring of 2001, while he was still waiting for a group to open up, Michael got into an argument with one of the housekeepers he supervised at a Manhattan hotel where he is facility manager. She wanted the weekend off, and he turned her down. He claims that she began swinging at him, he grabbed her hands and she kneed him. He then punched her "out of reflex," he said, breaking her eye socket. "When I saw the damage I inflicted on her. . . . She was a beautiful young lady, and after I struck her, it was like the beauty and the beast," Michael said. The police came. Michael was handcuffed, jailed for a night, charged and released. Despite his disgust with himself, it angered him that the police didn't arrest the housekeeper, too, because, he said, she had started it.

The system treated the case as a domestic assault, assuming that Michael and his subordinate were boyfriend and girlfriend and that Michael was the "primary physical aggressor." He pleaded guilty to a misdemeanor. His bosses at the hotel, where he has worked for 18 years, suspended him for two months and ordered him to go for counseling. Since the hotel was willing to pay for counseling, Michael was able to forget about the waiting list for a free class and enroll in a private program in Brooklyn.

Although Michael resisted at first, he came to see the group as his salvation. Schulder—"Miss Ruth" to Michael—led it along with "Mr. Q," Quentin Walcott. "I don't know what it was about Michael, but he was driven to be honest," Walcott says. "That really helped the group dynamic." Michael found it an exhilarating revelation to consider that his behavior was learned and could be unlearned. He was not crazy and he was not doomed. Battering was a choice.

Sylvia says the program started Michael soul-searching, which was alien to him. "They put everything in perspective for him, and he was amazed. He would talk to me about his past and how much it damaged him and how he could finally put it behind him." Still, Sylvia said, Michael did not undergo a miracle transformation. He continues to say things he shouldn't say and think in ways that undermine him. "When his job stresses him out, I tell him, 'Honey, your title means a lot,' Sylvia says. 'You are a professional. Act like a professional.'" Michael cools down by taking walks around the block. He takes a lot of walks around the block.

When I first met Michael, he struck me as a man who was tormented by the   90
consequences of his abusive behavior. He didn't like it that his daughter kept
reminding him that she had a lawyer's number in her pocket, that she had
rights, that he couldn't touch her. He didn't like it when his subordinates at
work teased him if he tried to discipline them. "Don't be thinking you can do
us like you did" that housekeeper, they'd say. Yet he was driven to be confessional, to hold himself accountable for his behavior.

He talks to himself every morning when he brushes his teeth, he told me,
trying to focus his energy on how it's in his best interest to keep his cool, to be
"a man in the new way I understand that word." It seems to me that a combination of forces over many years—Sylvia laying down the law, the city's taking
away his kids, his arrest at work and the subsequent treatment program—has
finally convinced him how much is at stake. "I don't want to lose my wife, I
don't want to lose my girls and I don't want to lose my job," he says. "I don't
want to hurt no one no more no way."

Whether his motivation will be sufficiently powerful to overcome a lifelong
pattern remains to be seen. For the moment, Michael and Sylvia are setting
their sights on a more concrete goal: a vacation in the Poconos.

ANALYZING What the Writer Says

1. What is the conventional wisdom on how to combat domestic violence?

2. Why are an increasing number of professionals now challenging that thinking?

3. Who, according to Sontag's article, benefits most from current laws regarding
   domestic abuse? Who is hurt most by them?

4. What are the arguments in favor of mandatory arrest laws?

ANALYZING How the Writer Says It

1. Sontag frames her article with stories from the complicated relationship of
   Sylvia and Michael. What does her use of this technique reveal about her attitude toward her subject?

2. Sontag cites six individual cases involving domestic violence, covering a range
   of attitudes on the parts of victims and a range of outcomes. Does the diversity,
   rather than the similarity, of the situations strengthen or weaken the article's
   main point?

ANALYZING the Issue

1. Look carefully at the case of Michael, as detailed in this article. Does he belong in his home, with Sylvia and their children?

2. Are mandatory arrest laws, however imperfect, the most effective way to deal with domestic violence? Why or why not?

3. Do you think law enforcement agencies are equipped to deal with domestic violence issues? Explain.

4. What dangers would keeping domestic violence out of the public arena pose?

5. Should victims of domestic violence have some input into what happens to the abusers? Why or why not?

ANALYZING Connections Between Texts

1. How are the points Anna Quindlen ("Getting Rid of the Sex Police," p. 583) makes about government involvement in private relationships relevant to questions Sontag raises?

2. In "Polygamy Now!" (p. 143) Elizabeth Joseph defends her decision to participate in a marriage that is widely misunderstood and conventionally understood to be especially detrimental to women and children. Compare the choices Sylvia makes, and the social condemnation of such choices, to Joseph's situation. Compare and contrast the rationales on the part of these wives and mothers. How do both women reject legal and governmental interference in the domestic arena?

3. For some people, being in a relationship with someone whose views are diametrically opposed to their own spells disaster. However, James Carville and Mary Matalin began their relationship during the heated 1992 Bush/Clinton presidential race, in which each was a high-profile political strategist—she for the Republicans, he for the Democrats. What does Richard Ellis's photograph (p. 93) of the couple (now married) say about the inexplicable dynamics of relationships? Is the mystery (of love) suggested by the photo of Carville and Matalin akin to what Sontag describes in her essay?

YOUR TURN: Suggestions for Writing About "Big Brother"

1. Write an essay in which you analyze the reasons behind ethnic profiling, the singling out of certain ethnic groups as suspects for crimes committed by individuals belonging to that group. You may use the current "war on terrorism" as your main example, but you are not limited to that subject. Or you may choose to research the internment of Japanese Americans during World War II or ethnic profiling of African American and Hispanic American groups in the ongoing "war" against crime in urban America.

2. Write a letter to the editor in which you argue for or against the establishment of a nationwide database designed to detect potential terrorists through surveillance of all citizens.

3. Write an essay in which you agree or disagree with Lewis H. Lapham's statement that the methods used by the U.S. government to fight the war on terrorism are "unlikely to do much harm to America's enemies but certain to do a great deal of harm to the American people."

4. Imagine Adnan R. Khan filing a grievance against the immigration officials that would not let him enter the United States because he *looked* like a potential terrorist. The case is heard in an American court, and the officials who harassed Khan have to explain their behavior to the judge. What would their defense sound like? Write it as a speech addressed to the court.

5. Do we live under the threat of a "Big Brother," as Molly Ivins argues? Write an essay in which you analyze the current national situation in Orwellian terms.

6. Thomas Jefferson argues in the Declaration of Independence that people have a moral obligation to abolish unjust laws or rulers; Anna Quindlen makes a similar argument when she says that sodomy laws, however legal, are just plain wrong. Write an argument describing the appropriate action of citizens when they believe laws are unjust.

7. Since September 11, many people have felt a renewed sense of patriotism, some to the point of criticizing anyone who does not agree with our government or our president. In times of tragedy or war, should citizens support government policy and refrain from criticizing government policies? Write an essay analyzing this issue.

8. Imagine you are a photographer who, like Dorothea Lange, wants to make her audience think critically about the way the U.S. government deals with the present crisis of terrorism. If you have the talent and the equipment, *create* the picture; if you can't do that, *invent* it. Then imagine yourself a critic who has to write an analysis of this picture for *Aperture*, an American photo magazine. Make sure to include a minute description (especially if the picture exists solely in your head) and to explain to your audience the artist's message and the techniques he/she uses to get this message across.

9. Research methods of punishment in the Colonial United States and write an essay in which you compare our present-day prison system to the punishment methods used by previous governments.

10. Compare two images published by the government: the WWII-era Office for Emergency Management poster "He's Watching You" (p. 110) and the more recent but quickly scrapped Information Awareness Office logo (p. 109), with its Latin phrase *Scientia est Potentia*, which translates to "Knowledge Is Power." Is there any irony in the comparison? Write an essay analyzing and comparing these images.

11. Since the 9/11 terrorist attacks, U.S. officials have implemented various methods to spot and stop potential terrorists before they can execute another attack. One of the methods is searching people who try to enter the country, especially people who look Middle Eastern, an experience Adnan R. Khan describes in "Bordering on Panic" (p. 555). Another method is to compile as much information as possible about every person living in America, in an attempt to identify terrorists by tracking their spending and travel habits. Both methods have attracted ample criticism: the first because it unfairly makes suspects of a particular ethnic group, the second because it makes suspects of everyone. Do you agree with these critics? Write an essay in which you attack or defend one (or both) of the above methods.

12. Write an essay in which you examine the costs, in terms of privacy or other civil liberties, of a particular technology or practice that may contribute to better business or improved medical knowledge or our safety.

IMAGE GALLERY

MICHELLE KASPRZAK

Surveillance Camera

An award-winning photographer and researcher, Kasprzak teaches at the Canadian Film Centre's new media program. Her work, which includes performance and collaboration, focuses on issues in the media. The photograph included here comes from a series entitled "Self Portraits in Surveillance Camera Monitors."

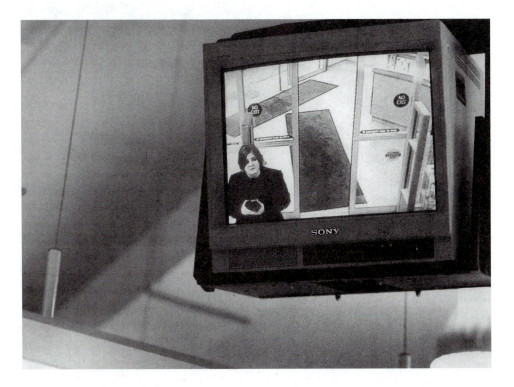

1. What does the photograph show?

2. How does the photographer use line in her composition?

3. How does she use value?

4. What do you think Kasprzak is trying to say with this picture?

DOROTHEA LANGE

Pledge of Allegiance

Dorothea Lange (1895–1965) is known for her portraits and her social documentation. In 1942, she photographed the internment of Japanese-Americans; "Pledge of Allegiance" was part of that project.

1. Describe the expressions on the faces of the girls as they recite the Pledge of Allegiance.

2. This picture was taken in 1942, at a time when, in the wake of the Japanese attack on Pearl Harbor, the U.S. government rounded up Japanese-Americans and sent them to internment camps because they suspected them of being secret allies of the Japanese enemy. What elements in the picture become very significant when you consider its historical background?

3. How does Lange structure her picture? How does she use light and shadow?

4. How does Lange's picture tie in with some of the other readings in this unit—Khan's, for instance?

DANIEL LYON

Against the Wall, Punishment, Ramsey

Born in 1942, Daniel Joseph Lyon is known for photographs and movies that express his strong sense of social commitment. In 1971 he published Conversations with the Dead: Photographs of Prison Life with the Letters and Drawings of Billy McCune, *from which this image is taken.*

1. Who are the two men in the picture? How do you know?

2. How does the picture reproduce the power relationship between the two men? How is the posture of the two men significant in this context?

3. How does Lyon use value and light effects in the picture?

4. What is the effect of the photographic perspective in the picture?

5. How does this image tie in with the overall topic of this unit, "Big Brother"?

16 TO MARKET, TO MARKET...

In more innocent—or more naive—times, your grandmother or great-grandmother might have invited the Avon Lady or the Fuller Brush Man in for a cup of coffee so she could look over the door-to-door ped-

> "Executive decision—
> a clinical precision
> Jumping from the
> windows—filled with
> indecision
> I get good advice—
> from the advertising
> world."
>
> —The Clash
> "Koka Kola"

dler's case full of lotions and creams or every conceivable kind of brush. Today, one needn't open the door for a sales pitch: we are inundated with ideas for separating us from our cash, from whole television networks devoted to home shopping to the ads that pop up without warning on our computer screens. We are saturated with offers to buy new cars, try new frozen dinners, refinance our houses, sell our old jewelry. In a culture where money talks, ads are aphrodisiac. But consumers are becoming more wary; angered by reports of corporate scandal and insider trading, they're fighting back. Consumer determination—and an act of Congress—have finally curbed the telemarketers.

The writers in this chapter cover business and advertising from a range of perspectives, from those of a marketing textbook author to a business reporter writing in the wake of the billion-dollar bilking by the Enron Corporation. John Caples instructs prospective marketers on the advertiser's most effective seduction techniques, while William Lutz deconstructs the language of advertising and G. Beate questions the practice of using advertising tactics to undermine advertisers. Matthew Blakeslee offers a scientific explanation of the buying impulse—which, Gloria Borger argues, Barbie helps to cultivate in young girls. In separate pieces, Jack Hitt and Arianna Huffington consider the feeding and the madness of the insatiable American appetite for sports utility vehicles. In an exposé on televised pharmaceutical advertising, Lisa Belkin shows how drug companies, by exaggerating their claims, create their markets. And Julie Schlosser's list of post-Enron course titles reveals the academic scramble to address business ethics.

Is the market economy an American phenomenon? Not any more. We are living, we are told, in a global marketplace. The tentacles of business and advertising reach far and wide, curling through our windows, from our computer screens, into our consciousness. Evading the capitalist clutch requires effort and vigilance. ✽

WARMING UP: *Are you influenced by advertising to make certain purchases? How do you know?*

Marketing
The Critics of Corporate Propaganda Co-Opt Its Best Weapon

BY G. BEATE

G. BEATE

Published in Mother Jones *in May 1999, the following article ponders the wisdom and effectiveness of "subvertising"— fighting advertising with its own weapons.*

Have you ever wondered how to "eliminate logos from your clothing without having to sacrifice good quality and funky-fresh styles"? A letter to the editor in the Winter 1999 issue of *Adbusters*, a Canadian magazine devoted to advertising criticism, contains a solution. All it takes to subvert corporate brands, writes Amira Eskenazi, is some electrical tape: The resourceful clotheshorse uses it to place large black X's over offending logos, which apparently do not exude the "funky-fresh style" that Eskenazi aspires to. And if some unenlightened logo serf should ridicule such rebellion? "You can then smilingly declare," Eskenazi writes, "What kind of moron would willingly be a walking billboard?"

As one who falls squarely in the moronic walking-billboard camp, I am perhaps uncharitably biased, but it seems to me that Eskenazi's fervor is simply the intellectual inverse of getting a tattoo of the Nike swoosh, minus the rash commitment that gives the latter act a sense of lunkheaded romanticism. Is this sort of knee-jerk logocide really the desired effect of the anti-advertising movement?

In fact, its goals are generally more ambitious and complex than that. "We've reached a point where people accept advertising as a natural part of the environment," says Larry Adelman, one of the founders of the Schmio Awards, an annual ceremony that parodies the advertising industry's Clio Awards by "honoring" dubious achievements such as enticing children to give out personal information over the Web. "The goal of the Schmios," he says, "is to make issues regarding advertising more visible, in the hope of starting a national debate: How much is too much? Should there be spaces that are free from advertising? What happens when advertising shapes our identities and our perceptions of the world to the extent that it does?"

Advertising criticism has been around for almost as long as advertising itself, though it's been markedly less successful. In 1905, *Collier's* magazine published an exposé of how snake-oil salesmen had "seduced [the press] into captivity" by making it so dependent on their advertising. In the early 1900s, Broadway shows such as *It Pays to Advertise* and *Nothing But Lies*, and magazines like *Ballyhoo*, lampooned advertising's penchant for deceit. Despite these efforts, advertising remains relatively underanalyzed—outside of industry trade magazines and academic circles, it rarely gets more than passing consideration.

"Our biggest challenge is showing people that advertising's not just a nuisance, and that if they ignore it, it will just get worse," says Carrie McLaren, editor of *Stay Free!*, a zine about commercialism and pop culture.   5

For an increasing number of advertising critics, the preferred method for getting people to think about advertising is that sexy, attention-getting, pathologically glib bane of contemporary discourse: advertising itself. *Adbusters*, which bills itself as the "Journal of the Mental Environment," has popularized the concept with slick parodies of popular print campaigns. Joe Camel becomes Joe Chemo; Tommy Hilfiger aficionados are depicted as sheep. And in such videos as *Dreamworlds* and *Advertising and the End of the World*, Sut Jhally, a professor of communication at the University of Massachusetts at Amherst, uses imagery from music videos and TV commercials to dramatize consumer culture's faults. He also uses commercials in his classes.

"When I show an ad in the lectures," he says, "people's attention is right there.

"It's like martial arts," explains Jhally, who is also the executive director of the Media Education Foundation. "The only language that operates in the modern world is the language of advertising culture. And if you want to fight, you've got to use that language. You've got to turn the power of your opponent back on itself."

The virtues of this approach—called variously "anti-advertising," "culture jamming," and "subvertising"—are obvious. "Ads talk about what people really want," Jhally says. "Love. Desire. Friendship. There's a reason why people like ads. They're the best things on television and in the media."

Adbusters editor Kalle Lasn has an even greater regard for the power of advertising. "We're not anti-advertising," he says. "We see ourselves as being part of   10 advertising. But we're not product marketers. We're social marketers who think that advertising has the power to set new agendas and create mass reversals of perspective."

In addition to its print ad parodies, *Adbusters* has produced a series of "uncommercials"—television spots that predict the "end of the automotive age" and publicize anticonsumerist events such as Buy Nothing Day. So far, however, Lasn has had little success in testing the power of these spots. All the major American networks, as well as the Canadian Broadcasting Corp., have declined to air them, under the shaky pretext that their policies prohibit any kind of advocacy advertising. In other words, an anti-automobile commercial is an example of advocacy advertising, but a pitch for the new Honda Accord, which implicitly advocates automobile usage, is just a good old-fashioned ad.

To Lasn, the networks' refusal broadcasts their fear of his message. He believes that if *Adbusters* and other advocacy advertisers had the same access to the airwaves as General Motors and Calvin Klein, product marketers would end up substantially reducing their own TV advertising. To validate his vision, Lasn refers to the showdown that occurred between antismoking ads and cigarette commercials in the late '60s after the FCC ordered broadcasters who aired cigarette commercials to run opposing viewpoints for free. "Those antismoking ads were so potent that, ultimately, the industry couldn't compete," recounts Lasn.

"Every time you were watching one of those pro-smoking ads, you just started snickering because they just didn't make sense anymore."

Actually, it was an act of Congress, rather than the antismoking ads, that forced cigarette commercials off television. And ultimately, that move did little to hinder the tobacco industry's efforts; it just spent more on other media. Ironically, cigarette sales increased dramatically in 1971, the first year of the cigarette-ad ban, probably because antismoking commercials, which had indeed caused a decline in cigarette consumption, could no longer be aired for free.

Still, if we are to learn anything from the cigarette-ad battle, it's that the most   15 likely industry response to uncommercials would be to simply air more commercials—in the realm of political advertising, has one attack ad ever failed to spawn a rebuttal? To be sure, escalation is a poor excuse for censorship; Lasn has as much a right to the airwaves as do his counterparts at Honda and GM. But how excited are we supposed to get about the notion that anticonsumerist arguments can be trivialized with the same smug, soundbitten language that graces Bud Light and Camel ads?

Lasn's paradigmatic cigarette ads are again a case in point. Taking for granted that kids start smoking because tobacco companies have convinced them that smoking is "cool," modern antismoking ads simply promote not smoking as being even *cooler*. What gets lost in the exchange is that being "cool" is a pretty flimsy reason to do anything.

In short, advertising may indeed be the operative language of the modern world, but it's a fairly limited idiom, designed to make you feel rather than think. For those whose message is simple—Buy me!—the language of advertising works beautifully. For those trying to express a more complicated idea, it's less effective.

Of course, parodies and publicity stunts (such as the soundbite-ready flack-tivism of Buy Nothing Day) are effective as bait-and-switch tactics:

You hook them with punch lines and eye candy, then educate them after you have their attention. But are the Absolut vodka ad collectors who call up *Adbusters* in search of its parodies of the well-known ad campaign sticking around for such schooling? And wouldn't it be just as effective if the funky-fresh brandinistas of the world simply applied black electrical tape to their eyes instead of their logos? In the end, is virtuous mindlessness better than materialistic mindlessness?

Tough question. When my copywriters hammer out a billboard-compatible   20
answer, I'll let you know.

ANALYZING What the Writer Says

1. What is the goal of the editors of *Adbusters* when they publish parodies of advertising campaigns?

2. What, according to *Adbusters* editor Kalle Lasn, is the difference between "product marketers" and "social marketers"?

3. Lasn points to the antismoking advertising campaign that ran concurrently with cigarette ads in the late sixties as an example of a successful subversion of advertising. What does Beate think of this example? Is he convinced by it? How do you know?

4. What is Beate's biggest concern with *Adbusters'* mission? What is the central question Beate leaves open at the end of the essay?

ANALYZING How the Writer Says It

1. In paragraph 2 Beate uses expressions like "lunkheaded romanticism" and "knee-jerk logocide," an interesting combination of slang and formal language. What other examples of this kind can you find in the essay? What does the author's choice of language and tone say about his intended audience?

2. Beate ends the essay with a question rather than a clear answer. What is the effect of this technique?

ANALYZING the Issue

1. Do you think that intelligent parodies of advertising campaigns can really make consumers think twice about the consumer culture they live in? Do you agree that the advertising industry will only be beaten with its own weapons? Explain.

2. Who is really to blame for the power of advertising—the advertising industry or unthinking consumers? Why?

ANALYZING Connections Between Texts

1. Matthew Blakeslee argues in "Madison Avenue and Your Brain" (p. 632) that the advertising industry aims at our instinctive cravings rather than our conscious minds. In the light of this evidence, can antiadvertising campaigns such as the ones Beate describes ever be successful? Why or why not?

2. In "Can Hollywood Kick the Habit?" (p. 273) Renee Graham accuses the film-making industry of glamorizing smoking. How does her essay reinforce Beate's pessimism about "subvertising" campaigns?

3. Choose any of the spoof ads in this chapter (p. 679) or in Chapter 10 (p. 263) and discuss their value as possible "antidotes" to our advertising culture. Do these spoofs make us think twice about our consumer habits? Why or why not?

WARMING UP: *Has a television commercial for a prescription drug ever made you wonder whether you might have a particular condition or disease?*

Prime-Time Pushers

By Lisa Belkin

LISA BELKIN

A veteran New York
Times *reporter, Lisa
Belkin often writes about
business and healthcare
issues. Her 1994 book*
First, Do No Harm *looks
at the healthcare industry
from the vantage point of
Houston's Hermann
Hospital and its ethics
committee. In "Prime-
Time Pushers," which first
appeared in* Mother Jones
*in 2001, Belkin argues that
televised ads for pharma-
ceutical drugs have spiked
a national hypochondria,
driving people to their doctors* en masse *for prescriptions for the latest "quick
fix"—just as the drug companies intended.*

Wherever you flip on the TV dial nowadays you will find commercials for medications that you cannot actually buy. Not without the permission of your doctor (or the aid of the Internet, but we'll talk more about that later). These are serious drugs, with potentially dangerous consequences, but the mood of the ads is upbeat and cheery. Cholesterol busters battle for market share. Antidepressants come with handy checklists of symptoms. Joan Lunden hawks Claritin. Newman from *Seinfeld* pitches an influenza drug. Pfizer spokesman Bob Dole promotes cures for erectile dysfunction.

No, you are not simply getting old and noticing this more. Television ads for prescription drugs, which were all but outlawed as recently as four years ago, are now taking over your TV set. To wit: pharmaceutical companies spent an estimated $1.7 billion on TV advertising in 2000, 50 percent more than what they spent in 1999, more than double the 1998 amount. In 1991, only one brand of prescription medication was marketed on network television by the route the industry calls "direct to consumer," or DTC. By the end of 1997, there were twelve drugs on that list, and by 2000, there were at least fifty.

The rush to the airwaves was triggered by the U.S. Food and Drug Administration, which, until four years ago, had required that manufacturers include nearly all of the consumer warning label in any pitch—something possible in a magazine advertisement but prohibitive in a thirty-second television spot. The sole exceptions were for so-called reminder and help-seeking ads—ones that named either the product or the condition being treated, but not both. The result was some very confusing ads.

For the better part of a decade, advertising agencies, pharmaceutical companies, and the major television networks lobbied for less restrictive rules, and, in August 1997, the FDA issued a "clarification" of its thirty-year-old regulations. Television commercials may now name both the product and the disease, as long as viewers are given information about "major" risks of the drug and directed to other sources of information—Web sites, magazine ads, toll-free numbers—for more detail. (And you thought those phone numbers were simply there to be helpful.)

Thus the United States became one of only two countries in the world (New Zealand being the other) where prescription drugs are hawked in prime time. Proponents of the FDA's policy shift say it creates a more informed patient because viewers see the ads, then have an intelligent give-and-take with a doctor. Critics say the shift creates more business for pharmaceutical companies by encouraging patients to seek out expensive, potentially dangerous drugs that they—and too often their doctors—know little about. "It was a sellout," says Larry D. Sasich, a pharmacist with Public Citizen's Health Research Group in Washington, D.C. "It's nothing more than a response to pressure from Madison Avenue."

Whatever the motivation, the shift has resulted in a quiet but dramatic transformation of the whole of our health care system. Gone is the time when doctors held complete power and prescription medicines were treated as a sacred and separate world. These ads mark the full dawning of an age when our very health is sold to us like soap. So turn on your TV set, relax, and take a pill. It's Prilosec time.

Before we talk about what is wrong (and unseemly and potentially dangerous about all of this), let's look at what's right. Seen through a certain lens, the explosion of DTC drug advertising is a continuation of the patients'-rights movement that began in force thirty years ago. Allowing such ads, says Nancy Ostrove, a branch chief within the FDA's Division of Drug Marketing, Advertising, and Communication, is not only a recognition of the unstoppable power of television but also the best way to inform consumers about available drugs. "There are certain real health benefits that can be achieved," she says.

Talk to any pharmaceutical company and they will tell you how thrilled they are to be educating the public. "From our point of view, one of the main purposes of direct-to-consumer advertising is education," says Emily Denney, a program manager in public affairs at AstraZeneca. Her company makes Prilosec, a drug that treats gastroesophageal reflux disease, a painful condition in which acid leaks from the stomach, causing chronic heartburn and even ulceration of the esophagus. Because of the $79.5 million the company spent on Prilosec ads in 1999, Denney says, "patients have been more easily able to diagnose symptoms that went ignored for many years. Our whole goal is just to encourage a conversation with your health care provider."

It is, to be sure, a self-interested, image-polishing argument, but the fact is that millions of us are sick and do not know it. According to the American Diabetes Association, more than 5 million diabetics in this country are unaware that they have the disease; one-third of Americans with major depression seek no treatment; and millions of Americans are ignorant of the fact that they have high blood pressure. Now consider this: in the two years since ads for Viagra first began to air, millions of men have visited their doctors specifically to get that drug—and thousands of them were diagnosed with serious underlying conditions. The Pharmaceutical Research and Manufacturers of America (PHRMA) estimates that for every million men who asked for the medicine, it was discovered that 30,000 had untreated diabetes, 140,000 had untreated high blood pressure, and 50,000 had untreated heart disease.

Let's face it, though; even the drug companies would agree that they are not   10
spending all this money just to be helpful. They are spending all this money to sell their products. "We don't invest in things we don't find valuable to the business," says AstraZeneca's Denney.

Direct-to-consumer advertising has paid off handsomely for the pharmaceutical companies—often turning solid earners into blockbuster drugs. After spending nearly $80 million on Prilosec advertising in 1999 (up from $50 million in 1998), AstraZeneca saw sales rise 27 percent, to $3.8 billion. Pfizer, in turn, upped consumer advertising for its cholesterol drug, Lipitor, by more than $45 million in 1999, and sales of the drug jumped too—56 percent, to $2.7 billion.

Some of the most dramatic ad-and-effect can be seen in the category of allergy drugs. Claritin maker Schering-Plough launched the televised assault against sneezing in 1998 when it spent $185 million on advertising and saw sales more than double to $2.1 billion. Following the leader, Pfizer spent $57 million to promote its drug Zyrtec in 1999 and saw a 32 percent increase in sales; that same year, Aventis spent $43 million to promote Allegra, and sales increased by 50 percent.

There is no reason to believe, however, that there was any increase in the number of allergy sufferers in the United States during this time, and no sudden outpouring of pollen either. There was just an increase in the sale of prescription allergy medications. According to Scott-Levin, a pharmaceutical consulting company in Pennsylvania, doctor visits by patients complaining of allergy symptoms were relatively stable between 1990 and 1998, at a rate of 13 to 14 million per year. In 1999, there were 18 million allergy visits. The cause of the spike, critics point out, is clearly the advertising.

The purpose of allergy ads in particular and pharmaceutical ads in general "is to drive patients into doctors' offices and ask for drugs by brand name," says

Sasich, of Public Citizen. And once they are in that office, patients often get what they want. "Physicians are more interested in pleasing their patients than you might think," says Steven D. Findlay, an analyst who is director of research and policy at the National Institute for Health Care Management. "It's a subtle interchange and exchange that happens between patient and doctor."

"Patients can be difficult to dissuade," says Dr. Jack Berger, an internist and [15] rheumatologist in private practice in White Plains, New York, and sometimes it is easier for doctors to give in. "It adds an extra source of confusion and frustration to the doctor/patient relationship when the patient starts directing the treatment based on what they learned on TV," he says.

Studies have shown that patients requesting specific drugs often get just what they ask for. A survey by the FDA of people who had recently been to their doctors, for instance, found that 72 percent had seen or heard an ad for prescription drugs in the previous three months, mostly on TV. Close to 25 percent of those respondents had also asked their doctors for the first time about a condition or illness. Of those who asked for a specific drug by name, nearly half were given a prescription for it; 21 percent were recommended a different drug.

"These ads have had a very large impact on a somewhat hypochondriacal public," says Findlay. The ads do, in fact, educate consumers, he says, but what they often teach is how to describe your symptoms so you will be given a certain medication. "The purpose of advertising is not to inform people," Findlay continues. "It never has been and it never will be. The purpose of advertising, as we all know, is to make people buy more product so the company can make more money. It makes you desire that new product, just like that new car or that new gizmo."

Yes, doctors still hold the prescription pad, but parents have long held the credit cards, and toys are advertised directly to kids. At a dinner recently, Findlay listened as two other guests "kept going on and on about Celebrex," a new arthritis drug from Pfizer/Pharmacia. "They were talking about it like you talk about PCs," he says, "and there was a pride in the fact that they both were taking Celebrex, because it's advertised, it's on TV."

Evolution in advertising favors the slick and jazzy, and so it is with DTC television spots. In the old days, when the ads could not mention both the disease and the cure, the industry argued that such rules led to confusion. In the words of the PHRMA, the restrictions "prompted companies to advertise on television in more oblique ways, which, while meeting legal requirements, may have been less helpful to consumers. Consumers were often left to guess what the medicine was for."

Now the rules have changed. What, then, are we to make of new ads like [20] those for Prilosec that feature a lithe woman in a flowing purple gown against the background of a clock with the uninformative slogan "It's Prilosec Time"? Is this a cure for depression? Irregularity? The ad itself gives no clue.

The original Prilosec ads, AstraZeneca's Denney says, described gastroesophageal reflux disease, or GERD, in some detail, showing cartoons of people in obvious distress and quizzing viewers about how often they experience heartburn. But GERD "is not the most pleasing-sounding word," Denney explains, and "you can't describe it perfectly in sixty seconds"—which may be why the company shifted to these more free-form reminder ads, which play up the fact that the pill itself is purple. And it's not just on television. The woman in the purple dress also appears in print ads, on the Web, and in subway stations plastered with purple pills. "The purpleness is a form of branding," Denney says. "People know Prilosec as 'the little purple pill.'"

One can't help but wonder, however, if such branding is having a far more troubling effect—whether occasional heartburn sufferers looking for a silver (or, in this case, purple) bullet might not be pressing their doctors for a powerful drug they don't really need. Americans tend to prefer the easy fix, and the ubiquitousness of direct-to-consumer ads, which dress medicine up in the same telegenic tinsel as perfume or sports cars, make our health seem as simple as we would like it to be. "The ads send a strong signal," says a report from the National Institute for Health Care Management, "that prescription drugs are just like any consumer product—soap, cereal, cars, snack food, et cetera."

Look more closely at a category of drugs known as statins—sold under such brand names as Lipitor, Pravachol, and Zocor—which have proved so effective at lowering cholesterol that some doctors see advertising them as a public service. "There are countless people who would be better served if they knew these drugs were available," says Dr. Ira S. Nash, associate director of the cardiovascular institute at the Mount Sinai School of Medicine in New York City. Yet other doctors worry about the side effect of those same ads. Statins can cause dangerous liver complications and their use needs to be carefully monitored by a doctor. In most cases, statins should be prescribed only to patients who have tried the lines of first defense—namely, diet and exercise—and who have failed to lower their cholesterol in spite of these lifestyle changes. If the ads make fighting cholesterol look too easy, patients may insist on skipping the hard part and going straight for the pill. "It takes time to speak to a patient about exercise, weight control, and diet. It takes less time to just write a prescription," says Dr. Berger, the private practitioner, and there is a danger that doctors will choose the easier course.

Cholesterol, at least, is a problem that can be measured. What about conditions whose symptoms are far more difficult to evaluate? Last year's ads for Paxil fall into this category. Paxil is an antidepressant approved by the FDA for the secondary purpose of treating social anxiety disorder, which GlaxoSmithKline's ads describe as "an intense, persistent fear and avoidance of social situations." In its true, clinical form, it is a real and debilitating condition, but by reducing it to an ad—in which the subject experiences dread while giving an office presentation—Paxil can too easily sound like a pill for shyness.

One television ad that I find particularly egregious, bordering on offensive, is for a relatively new drug called Sarafem. The chemical composition of the pill is identical to that of Prozac, but last summer manufacturer Eli Lilly and Company received FDA permission to market it simultaneously for treatment of premenstrual disphoric disorder, or PMDD. The condition differs from PMS in that its symptoms are more emotional than physical and include depression, anxiety, and bursts of anger. And yet a television spot for the drug shows a frustrated woman struggling with a shopping cart in front of a supermarket, and makes Sarafem look like an easy fix for your average bad day.

"They're making everything into a disease," adds Dr. Nash, "and not only is it a disease, but it's a disease that society has a pill for."

Because more is at stake, viewers should bring a higher level of skepticism to pharmaceutical ads. Instead, there is reason to believe they are bringing less. A recent study in the *Journal of General Internal Medicine* found that nearly half of respondents believed that drug ads are prescreened and somehow sanctioned by the FDA. In fact, quite the opposite is true. The FDA's Ostrove explains that the agency is "forbidden by law from requiring preclearance." Although some pharmaceutical companies choose to submit their ads in advance, she says, they do so at their own discretion. All the FDA can require is that a copy of an ad be sent to its office when the ad begins to air.

Once the commercial arrives at the agency's Rockville, Maryland, headquarters, it is reviewed by one of the fourteen employees who screen 30,000 pieces of promotional material each year. "We allow a certain degree of puffery," Ostrove says, "but we don't allow overstatement of effectiveness or minimization of the risks." Even with such allowances, the FDA found that for the first thirty-seven drugs marketed directly to consumers on television, twenty ads failed to comply with federal regulations, including those requiring "fair balance" and the disclosure of side effects.

Of the estimated 200 television drug spots aired since the 1997 FDA rule change, the agency has cited thirty-two for noncompliance and has asked the companies to change all or part of the ads. The FDA told Pfizer/Pharmacia, for instance, that an advertisement for the arthritis drug Celebrex was misleading because "various multiple physical activities portrayed by arthritis patients (such as rowing a boat and riding a scooter)," along with "the audio statement 'Powerful twenty-four-hour relief from osteoarthritis pain and stiffness,'" collectively suggest that Celebrex is more effective than has been demonstrated by substantial evidence." In other words, the product does not work as advertised. Judith Glova, a spokeswoman for the company, says the ad was pulled and modified slightly—a statement was added, for example, noting that "individual results may vary"—and put back on television.

Similarly, Eli Lilly and Company was told that an ad for the osteoporosis drug Evista was misleading because "it mischaracterizes the nature of osteoporosis, resulting in an overstatement of Evista's benefits." Specifically, the agency said, the ad's description of osteoporosis as "a disease of thin, weak bones that can fracture and take away your independence" exaggerated both the risk and the consequence of a fracture. Eli Lilly spokesman David Marbaugh says the ad has been "suspended" while the company works with the FDA to revise it.

Most recently, I was pleased to learn, the FDA sent a letter to Eli Lilly about the ads for Sarafem—the very spots showing a woman struggling with a shopping cart. The ad does not define the condition it is designed to treat, the agency said, and as a result "trivializes the seriousness of PMDD." The company was asked to "immediately cease using this broadcast advertisement."

Eli Lilly decided to honor the agency's request, but, legally, the company could have kept running the ads indefinitely. As Findlay, the health care analyst, notes, "Everybody thinks the agency [the FDA] is this big nine-hundred-pound gorilla, but their actual power is limited." Essentially, all the agency can do is request compliance. If a company refuses, the FDA cannot impose fines or other punishments but must instead go through the courts for an injunction. "As a matter of course, most companies do change their ads," Findlay says, "but that is because they are concerned about the public relations implications. The heaviest hammer the FDA has in this department is embarrassing manufacturers."

The guiding rule of medicine is, "First, do no harm." What, then is the harm of pharmaceutical ads? Yes, they may be misleading, but it can be argued that most consumer ads are misleading. Why should we care? Who is this hurting? The most measurable harm is economic. "There is very strong circumstantial evidence," says Public Citizen's Sasich, "that some patients are getting drugs that may be stronger than they need. A less expensive, more easily obtained drug may be more appropriate."

Celebrex, says Findlay, is one example of potential pharmaceutical overkill. With first-year sales of $1.3 billion in 1999, it was the most successful drug launch in history. Celebrex and similar new arthritis drugs, such as Vioxx, represent an advance because they do not cause the level of gastrointestinal distress that alternative treatments, such as over-the-counter ibuprofen tablets, can. However, Findlay says that "the proportion of people with arthritis at high risk for that side effect is between 10 and 20 percent." But if you extrapolate from the number of prescriptions written for the drug, he says, then Celebrex and similar medications are "being taken by potentially 40 percent of arthritis patients. These medicines are going to people who have no clinically defined need."

A one-year dosage of Celebrex costs $900, says William Pierce, a spokes- 35 man for the Blue Cross and Blue Shield Association (BCBSA), while a one-year dosage of generic ibuprofen costs $24. Numbers like these are the major reason why BCBSA expects prescription drug costs to rise at least 15 percent each year through 2004.

"In some plans we are spending more on prescription drugs than on in-patient hospitalization, and one of the major reasons is direct-to-consumer advertising," says Christine Simmon, also of BCBSA, who notes that another reason is the aging of the population. Last year alone, BCBSA saw an estimated "25 percent increase in the cost of prescription drugs compared with 6 to 8 percent for physician and hospital services," she says.

In an effort to curb demand for expensive prescriptions, BCBSA has gone so far as to launch a new corporation, called RxIntelligence, which will attempt to inform the public about why they may not need the newest, flashiest drugs on the market. RxIntelligence, says Simmon, will study such things as the "cost benefit and risk of the drug and whether the existing treatment is just as good"—the sort of information that does not appear in pharmaceutical ads.

The PHRMA argues that the increase in prescription drug use "reflects the extraordinary value that medicines provide, to patients and the health care system. Increased utilization of medicines is a good thing—it helps many patients get well quicker." But Findlay reminds us that what we allocate to one slice of the health care pie must be taken from another. "Is this how we want to be spending our money?" he asks. "Do we want to be spending 25 percent of health care dollars on medication at the expense of home care or PET scans?"

A second harm of rampant pharmaceutical advertising, a harm that is harder to quantify but far more frightening, is to our health. The entire system of direct-to-consumer advertising relies on the assumption that there is an intermediary between the patient and the potentially harmful drug. "While DTC ads prompt patients to consult their doctors about available medicines," says a recent PHRMA report, "the doctor still holds the prescribing pen. Patients cannot get prescription medicines unless their physicians find that the medicines are necessary and appropriate."

But the world is changing in ways that make this statement untrue. Patients   40 are increasingly hearing about new drugs before their doctors do. A recent poll by the American Association of Retired Persons found that 21 percent of consumers had asked their doctors for prescription drugs that the doctors knew little or nothing about. Dr. Berger tells me he knows of doctors who began to prescribe Celebrex before the clinical trials were even published, because patients were asking for it and because initial reports in the press indicated it was effective. Indeed, sales of Celebrex reached $1 billion before the final clinical-trial results were published in a peer-reviewed journal. Many doctors apparently didn't read Celebrex's package insert either. The drug contains sulfa, which can cause an allergic reaction in some patients. "People came in itching with hives," says Berger.

Even when all the known facts about a drug are published, there is no guarantee that new facts might not emerge, especially when the drug is new. One example is the ongoing controversy over the GlaxoSK drug Relenza. Approved in 1999, Relenza is an inhalable powder designed to treat common flu symptoms, reducing the illness's length by about a day. It was introduced with a cheeky television campaign featuring the character Newman from *Seinfeld*. The campaign received awards within the advertising industry, but the FDA was not amused. It described the ads as "misleading because they . . . suggest that Relenza is more effective" than has been "demonstrated by substantial evidence."

Soon after Relenza hit the market in October 1999, seven patients using it died. In part because Relenza had been so heavily promoted, the FDA then issued a "public health advisory" saying that while the exact involvement of the drug was unclear, there had been "several reports of deterioration of respiratory function following inhalation of Relenza" in patients with underlying breathing problems. By June 2000, use of Relenza had been linked to twenty-two deaths; in July, GlaxoSK announced a strengthened warning label for the drug. The FDA has since reaffirmed the safety of Relenza, when it is used as directed, and attributes many of the deaths to its use by patients to whom it should never have been prescribed. Relenza remains on the market, says GlaxoSK spokeswoman Laura Sutton, but the ads are not longer on the air.

It is still possible to buy Relenza over the Internet, however, which adds another variable to consumer access to prescription drugs. In March 1999, fifty-two-year-old Robert McCutcheon, of Lisle, Illinois, died of a heart attack that may have been triggered by Viagra, although there is no definitive way to know. Despite a family history of heart problems, which would have meant he was a poor candidate for the drug, McCutcheon had ordered Viagra on-line, at one of the growing number of Web sites that sell prescription medications without a doctor visit.

Viagra is hardly the only drug being sold this way. As part of my research for this article, I spent less than five minutes on-line and purchased a month's supply of Xenical, the Hoffmann–La Roche product for weight loss. It is intended only for patients who are clinically obese, but since no doctor ever saw me, I lied and said I weighed 300 pounds. The site even provided a handy chart telling me the exact weight cutoff for any given height in order to qualify. The pills arrived, as promised, within five business days, charged to my credit card.

Pharmaceutical companies, it should be said, are distressed by this phe-   45
nomenon. Pfizer, which manufactures Viagra, recently reminded physicians that it is "improper" (though not actually illegal) to prescribe the drug without first examining the patient. And Ostrove calls the availability of drugs on-line "a separate but serious issue." When the FDA announced in 1997 that it was "clarifying" its regulations to favor television ads, it also announced that it would review the new approach this coming summer. "If we have reason to believe that our policies are creating a public health problem," Ostrove says, "we will reevaluate."

In the meantime, I have this bottle of Xenical sitting on my desk. While I'm not obese, there are those "few extra pounds" I put on over the holidays. What could be the harm? After all, the ads say that this stuff really works.

ANALYZING What the Writer Says

1. What are some of the benefits of the recent wave of television ads touting prescription medications? What does Belkin see as a potentially more serious detriment?

2. Why, according to Belkin, are so many doctors inclined to let their patients dictate their own medication program?

3. Why should ads for pharmaceutical drugs be met with more skepticism than ads for cereal or perfume?

4. What does Belkin view as the most *measurable* harm of aggressive advertising of prescription drugs?

ANALYZING How the Writer Says It

1. Analyze Belkin's title. What does it reveal about her attitude toward her subject?

2. Look at the conclusions of each of the five sections of her article. Identify Belkin's techniques and comment upon their effectiveness.

3. What is the purpose of the many statistics Belkin cites in the second section of her article?

4. Belkin quotes various authorities on both sides of the prescription drug advertising issue to set up her argument. Comment on the effectiveness of this technique.

ANALYZING the Issue

1. Should advertising for prescription medications be subject to restrictions that other product advertising is not? Why or why not?

2. Do the benefits of television advertising of pharmaceuticals—education and awareness—outweigh the negative implications? Explain.

ANALYZING Connections Between Texts

1. One of the points in Matthew Blakeslee's "Madison Avenue and Your Brain" (p. 632) is that marketers are constantly creating new products and new markets. How does this explanation jibe with Belkin's complaint about drug advertising?

2. In "Running Scared" (p. 279), Stanton Peele contends that Americans are obsessed with finding biological explanations and medical cures for psychic ills, turning them into "diseases." How does Peele's analysis inform Belkin's argument?

3. Eugene Richards's photograph "Crack for Sale" (p. 328) depicts a transaction in the underground drug trade. Belkin's title, "Prime-Time Pushers," suggests that, in some ways, pharmaceutical companies are not that much different from drug dealers on the street. What do you see as the main differences?

Madison Avenue and Your Brain

BY MATTHEW BLAKESLEE

MATTHEW BLAKESLEE

A Los Angeles-based free-lance writer, Matthew Blakeslee focuses on science issues. In the following salon.com *piece, he looks at the neurological explanations for consumer behavior.*

Pity the poor overstuffed couch potato, little suspecting that his latest turn of appetite is not the true call of hunger but a hijacking of his brain's circuitry from afar. While he waits for his favorite rerun to air, a fast-food commercial shows him images of moist, steaming meat; crisp, glistening vegetables; and taut strands of melted cheese. A cascade of neurotransmitters is set off in an ancient part of his brain, and his food cravings reawaken.

Several decades into the era of consumer capitalism, the whiz kids on Madison Avenue have learned fairly well how to attach psychic puppet strings to our minds, but they have never really known why (or often whether) their tricks worked. Enter the age of neuroscience. As investigators plumb ever deeper into the strange dynamics of the brain, they are shedding new light on many domains of human behavior, including mental illness, violence, cooperation, addiction, eating and even aesthetics.

Stock assertions like "People buy designer clothes because it makes them happy" or "Americans are overweight because they're weak-willed" are not real explanations. There are deeper reasons why comely pop stars make us desire a certain brand of fill-in-the-blank, or why billboards coax us off the expressway and into a drive-through.

"The mainstream economic theory behind advertising is just horrible," says Caltech behavioral economist Colin Camerer. "For some reason economists are reluctant to accept the idea that advertising makes you want to buy something you didn't necessarily want before. . . . Some of this new evidence from neuroscience could be very powerful in overturning that kind of silly, narrow conception."

Take the case of the hunger-struck couch potato. A recent brain-imaging study sheds light on the mechanism that makes the mere presence of food alluring. When people were allowed to see and smell their favorite chow, a deep-lying brain structure called the dorsal striatum was activated and the subjects reported feeling hungrier. Notably, this neural circuit was different from the pleasure pathways that are tickled when people actually get to eat.

"The *dorsal striatum* is being linked to addiction formation and to things that you learn and do almost uncontrollably," says Nora Volkow, the neuroscientist at the Brookhaven National Laboratory who led the study. "When it's active, it creates a very strong drive to consume food. This is a reason why [fast food] advertisements are so compelling, and why we are having an epidemic of obesity in this country."

The job of the *dorsal striatum* is to enhance the desirability of food automatically, says Volkow. Though it sits right next door to one of the brain's most important pleasure centers, it is not itself a generator of warm, fuzzy feelings. Indeed, being hungry in the presence of forbidden food is distinctly unpleasurable.

What this and similar research implies is that, contrary to how it may feel, the reward of eating is not the sole, perhaps not even the primary, thing motivating us to stuff our faces. The *dorsal striatum* draws us to food (and other objects of our addiction) in the first place, says Volkow, even when we are not hungry.

"This system was once very important for survival," she says. "It was important to want food whenever you could get it, because you never knew when it was going to be around.

"But now with refrigerators and 7-Elevens all over the place it doesn't serve any purpose anymore. Individuals are being constantly exposed to food stimulus. In an almost reflexive way, people's brains are responding to these signals, generating a biochemical change and a motivation to eat."

The *dorsal striatum* is not the only avenue into a consumer's brain. A structure right beneath it, called the *nucleus accumbens*, is another. Like the *dorsal striatum*, it is rich in the neurotransmitter dopamine, a brain chemical associated with feelings of satisfaction and reward. But unlike its upstairs partner, the *nucleus accumbens* is a *bona fide* pleasure center. It is activated by food, sex, drugs, money, victory, just about anything that feels rewarding. It helps animals to form pleasure-related mental associations and to stay motivated in the pursuit and repetition of positive experience.

The *nucleus accumbens* also turns out to be crucial to our taste for novelty—which, as any marketer will avow, is a tried-and-true road to healthy (if not always healthful) sales.

"It is very deeply ingrained for us to associate potential reward with things that are new and unexpected," says Gregory Berns, an Emory University neuroscientist who studies how the brain responds to novelty. "New things grab the brain's attention by tapping directly into these reward pathways."

New information elicits activity in a neighborhood of brain structures often referred to as the limbic system, Berns says, which includes the *nucleus accumbens* and the *striatum*. Tying perceptions of novelty into the reward system makes good evolutionary sense, he explains, as it's an excellent way to keep animals attuned to changes in their environment. Nowadays, it probably also helps to make us indefatigable consumers.

"Are marketers tapping into this system unknowingly? I'd venture to say yes," says Berns. "They have this notion that they need to keep creating new things, new products, new versions of products.   15

"Why do people want to get new cars when their old ones work fine? It isn't just 'because it makes them happy.' A deeper explanation is that the brain is constantly seeking out new information and gets rewarded through these specific neural circuits when it finds it."

It is not only food and novelty that give an extra-hard tug on the brain's attentional resources. Just about anything a person finds especially pleasant to observe is reaching in and twisting the dopamine spigot.

One recent brain-imaging study found that the *nuclei accumbentes* (to use the proper plural) of young heterosexual males were activated by beautiful female faces. Plain female faces and male faces that the subjects rated as extremely good-looking had no effect. The experiment aimed to control for gender and for "pure" aesthetic judgment, and was left, it would seem, with that most marketable of blatancies, sex appeal.

Neuroscientists have made good headway in recent years figuring out why emotionally charged experiences get turned into stronger, more vivid memories than do humdrum and routine events. The key player is another limbic system structure called the *amygdala*. When revved up by a potent emotion—which a good thrumming in the *nucleus accumbens* will generate—the *amygdala* stamps the engendering event firmly into memory.

"Memories stored by the *amygdala* are extremely powerful," says Volkow,   20
"because from then on, whenever you re-encounter that stimulus you will immediately associate it with the pleasure [or aversion] you first experienced."

Presumably this is one of the reasons it pays to place shapely young women on-screen mugging next to anything from flashy gizmos to fizzy sugar water. The pairing is arbitrary, but it engages a set of brain mechanisms that evolved originally to select mates, learn from serendipity, and remember intense experiences on which future survival might hinge.

Just as early mariners were clueless about the Coriolis forces that drove the trade winds, so have advertisers honed their craft without understanding the neural underpinnings of the desires and perceptions on which they seek to capitalize. And just as understanding the physics of trade winds had little practical effect on maritime navigation, so, too, will the march of cognitive science be unlikely to spin off a scientific field of neuroadvertising.

"For about 50 years there have been people who looked at physiological or neurological responses to marketing stimuli," says David Stewart, a marketing expert at the University of Southern California. "[But] they have not had much real impact on the way advertising is created or assessed. The reality is that it's almost always easier to just directly ask people what they liked about an ad," or follow their behavior afterward to gauge its effectiveness.

From this point of view, neuroscience will probably not soon be adding any tools to the marketing industry's bag of tricks. But as these examples show, it will at least help explain how the current tools work. Indeed, as cognitive science emerges from its own Bronze Age, it is holding up the hope (or for some onlookers, the horror) of a new set of concepts for charting the lay of human nature.

How deep these new ideas will penetrate into civic policy and individual self-   25
conception (as, for example, the psychoanalytic revolution did a century ago) will be interesting to watch. It will be interesting to see, for instance, whether the activist-planned lawsuits to hold the fast-food industry *accountable* for supersizing America's collective waistline (and medical bill) will prevail. While neuroscience provides a plausible foundation for the case that the industry's marketing practices will inevitably net consumers en masse into excess consumption, society may never be ready to let individuals off the hook for taking the bait. Or, as it did in the suits against Big Tobacco—where the science of addiction was a central issue—it might.

Each side in the debate should prepare to be surprised over the next few decades. The lines between manipulation, free choice and manufactured vs. true desire could turn out to lie quite differently from how they feel.

Meanwhile, other areas of marketing and consumerism will come into better focus as well. Scientists who study music and memory will figure out why melodies and jingles lodge so firmly in the mind's ear. Researchers who study social cognition will continue to zero in on the circuitry that drives us, broadly speaking, to keep up with the Joneses. And psychologists who study people's sense of happiness may some day be able to approach directly the central, yet seldom stated, question of consumer capitalism: Do we really increase our long-term happiness by buying as voraciously as we do? Or does that sense, like many other aspects of our intuitive self-knowledge, turn out to be steeped in illusion?

ANALYZING What the Writer Says

1. What does current research in neuroscience contribute to the study of how advertising affects consumers' brains?

2. What is the difference between the *dorsal striatum* and the *nucleus accumbens*? What is the significance of the *dorsal striatum*?

3. Why are memories stored by the *amygdala* more potent than other memories?

4. Why, according to one marketing expert cited by Blakeslee, are findings in neuroscience not likely to spawn a field of "neuroadvertising"?

5. What are the social/political implications of neuroscience?

ANALYZING How the Writer Says It

1. What techniques does Blakeslee use to support the essentially scientific nature of his piece?

2. What techniques help soften the hard edge of science and demystify the complexities of neuroscience?

3. Analyze the title. Does it raise expectations about the content of the article that are thwarted upon reading? Explain.

ANALYZING the Issue

If marketers can control the "psychic puppet strings" of consumers, should they be held responsible for the negative consequences of the habits developed or intensified in product users?

ANALYZING Connections Between Texts

1. How do Blakeslee's points support G. Beate's skepticism about the wisdom and effectiveness of "subvertising" ("Marketing: The Critics of Corporate Propaganda Co-Opt Its Best Weapon," p. 616)?

2. Do the children in Toni Cade Bambara's "The Lesson" (p. 332) support the theories about which Blakeslee writes?

3. How does Ruth Orkin's photograph "Lady Buys Tomatoes" (p. 678) illustrate Blakeslee's points?

WARMING UP: *When you were a child, did you play with Barbies or action figures, dolls whose bodies are radically out of proportion with those of real men and women? Did you hope that when you grew up your body would resemble those of the dolls?*

Barbie's Newest Values

By Gloria Borger

GLORIA BORGER

Gloria Borger, currently a contributing editor at U.S. News & World Report *and co-host of CNBC's* Capital Report, *criticizes Barbie not only for her outlandish figure and the dangers such a freakish ideal poses to the self-perception of little girls but also for the unabashed consumerism she repre-sents. "Barbie's Newest Values" appeared in* U.S. News & World Report *on December 1, 1997.*

I was all set to write something nasty about Iraq when a headline on the front page of the *Wall Street Journal* trumpeted some news not to be disregarded: "Top-Heavy Barbie Is Getting Body Work." And more. The headline also reveals this new line of Barbie dolls will have a new face, too. "When Plastic Surgery Is Done, She Will Be 'Really Rad,'" which happens to be her new name, as in "radical." All told, Barbie is getting new breasts (smaller), a new waist (wider), and a dif-ferent mouth (closed). The folks at Mattel Inc. hope that little girls will (a) find this makeover awesome and (b) be struck with a sudden urge to replenish their collections.

Enough already. Every time Mattel tries to update Barbie, it turns into a PC nightmare. Remember the Teen Talk Barbie who said, "Math class is tough"? Feminists revolted. The wheelchair of Barbie's recently invented disabled friend, Share a Smile Becky, didn't fit inside Barbie's two-story pink man-sion. Advocates for the disabled protested. And now the toy maker is changing Barbie's buxom, leggy fig-ure partly out of "sensitivity" to those who say that girls grow up wanting to look like Barbie, whose measurements would make it impossible for her to stand upright in real life. The other (real) reason is so Barbie can look good in her new hip-huggers.

Don't get me wrong: I'm no Barbie hater. I once owned one, or 10. I believe it's a good thing that

Barbie is now available in an assortment of races, hair colors, and professions. And maybe Barbie's upcoming effort at physical correctness will inspire a whole generation of female plastic surgeons. Or patients.

Baby Boom Barbie. But Barbie's bosom aside, let's be clear about something: Six-year-olds are not protesting that Barbie is too glamorous or too tacky. It's the self-indulgent gen X-ers who complain that Barbie has hurt their self-image. (Thereby forcing them into their nose-ring phase?) And it's the narcissistic (and aging) baby boomers who still believe they determine every fashion and cultural trend—even Barbie's style. (What's next? Barbie in Birkenstocks? Totally Cellulite Barbie?)

All of this, however, misses a more important point: It's not Barbie's figure   5 that's the big problem. It's her values. Whatever size blouse Barbie wears, she lately seems to be ordering most of her clothes from the likes of Ralph Lauren, Bill Blass, Bob Mackie, and Christian Dior. These designers are a part of a line of Barbie collectibles that are groomed to appeal to those upwardly mobile baby boomer moms who thought Barbie looked too cheap for their children. "When I grew up, I thought Barbie was middle class," says Democratic pollster Celinda Lake. "I thought she was like us." No more. Now Barbie is into labels, and she's not shopping at outlet malls.

Alas, Barbie has become a snob. While she was mod in the '60s and disco in the '70s, by 1980, "she had the taste of a lottery winner," says M. G. Lord, author of *Forever Barbie*. "At the core of this change is class." Mattel spokeswoman Lisa McKendall says this is rubbish, since these upwardly mobile dolls—which start at about $65 a pop—are designed for grown-ups to play with. Please. What about a recent ad for Bloomingdale's Ralph Lauren Barbie, which claims to be "the most sophisticated Barbie ever"? What adult is this aimed at? Barbie's makers also say they want more realism in their dolls, and maybe that's what we're getting: You're never too young to become an elitist.

As the mother of young sons, I've never had lengthy wardrobe discussions. Boys into Power Rangers do not feel the need to find shoes to match their laser guns. But wait. Like those girls begging for Barbie's glen plaid Ralph Lauren handbag, my boys have shown an increasing fondness for Nike-brand items— shorts, shirts, and sneakers. Getting hooked early is what it's about, and we make it easy. After all, insecure baby boomers teach their kids to constantly strive upward. Class warfare, once a Democratic party line, is definitely not a boomer gig. Class coding is. And the marketers know it.

Of course, it's easy to overstate the impact of Barbie. She's a fantasy doll for girls, not a real role model for women. (Some of us, however, await the Madeleine Albright diplomatic collection, featuring a secretary of state who finally knows how to accessorize.) As for the controversy over Barbie's new body, there's one more hidden lesson for little girls who want to be big girls: No matter how her measurements evolve, Barbie will always be a smallish size—as long as she's wearing expensive clothes. In real life, designers reduce sizes all the time, making size-8 baby boomers feel like a young size 6 again. Surely they'll do it for Barbie, too.

ANALYZING What the Writer Says

1. Why is Borger apprehensive about Mattel's plans to issue a Barbie doll whose measurements more closely resemble those of real women?

2. According to Borger, who really cares about Barbie's figure?

3. What does Borger believe is Barbie's *real* problem?

ANALYZING How the Writer Says It

1. "Don't get me wrong: I'm no Barbie hater," Borger states in her third paragraph. "Of course, it's easy to overstate the impact of Barbie," she says in her last. Why would she include these statements in her essay, the acknowledgments that she might, after all, be wrong? Is this a sign of the writer's insecurity or does she have a larger rhetorical purpose? Explain.

2. Throughout the essay Borger adds comments in parentheses. What is the purpose of these asides?

ANALYZING the Issue

Whereas many critics have complained about Barbie's unnatural body, Borger claims that much more dangerous to children is the materialism the doll represents. Do you agree with her? Why or why not?

ANALYZING Connections Between Texts

1. How would Matthew Blakeslee ("Madison Avenue and Your Brain," p. 632) answer Borger's arguments about Barbie's consumerism?

2. Toni Cade Bambara ("The Lesson," p. 332) writes of a painful social lesson learned by underprivileged kids when they visit an upscale toy store. How do Borger's points about Barbie's consumerism compare to Bambara's themes?

3. How does Jim Arbogast's photograph "Shopping Spree," (p. 327) reinforce Borger's points?

WARMING UP: *When a magazine ad pulls you in, what about it grabs your attention? To what colors, words, kinds of pictures are you drawn?*

Layouts and Illustrations that Attract the Most Readers

BY JOHN CAPLES

JOHN CAPLES

In a chapter from a popular marketing textbook, the author spells out the basics of successful print ad design.

It has been said that the greatest crime an advertisement can commit is to remain unnoticed. Getting advertisements to be noticed is the job of the layout artist and the art director. But just as the copywriters who hope to write the Great American Novel must put away "fine writing" when they are writing copy, so must the art directors put away "fine art" when they are producing an advertisement. At least, fine art must be made a secondary consideration. The principal job of an advertisement is to sell goods. Therefore, you should use layouts and illustrations in which salesmanship comes first and art second.

An art director described the mental development she went through in trying to produce advertisements that sold goods. When she first started in the advertising business, she tried to apply the things she learned in art school. Her first consideration in making an ad layout was good taste and good design. Her first consideration in selecting an illustration was that it should be as similar as possible to the painting of the old masters. The result was that her advertisements brought "Ooo's!" and "Ah's!" of delight from other art directors. Her advertisements were the kind that won prizes at commercial art exhibitions.

Being practical and knowing that the principal job of an advertisement is to sell merchandise to a mass audience, this art director showed her creations to taxi drivers, stenographers, clerks, and others not directly interested in art. She showed each of these people a group of advertisements and asked which attracted them the most. When the first man showed preference for the most inartistic advertisement, the art director laughed the matter off. When a female clerk did the same thing, it seemed like a coincidence.

But when dozens of people passed over the artistic creations and selected something that looked like a typical Sears Roebuck ad, the art director began to see a great light. Since then she has conducted hundreds of tests. She has found that the artistic qualities of an advertisement are not nearly as important as the ability of the advertisement to get attention and to drive home a selling point. Sometimes the rules of fine art must be completely reversed in producing an effective advertisement.

FINE ART VERSUS COMMERCIAL ART

Many advertising artists are still in the mental stage that this art director was in before she started showing advertisements to average people. The trouble with applying the rules of fine art to advertising is that fine art seeks to please the senses and to tone in with surroundings. Why are park benches usually painted green instead of orange? Because green is more artistic. Because green tones in with the surroundings. But do advertisers want to tone in with their surroundings? Do manufacturers want to pay $40,000 for a color page in a magazine just to soothe the artistic senses of the readers? No. They want to jar the readers and stop them on the spot—to rouse them and stir them to action.

HOW TO MAKE TYPE WORK FOR YOU

The principal consideration in selecting the style of type for your headline is that it should be big enough and powerful enough to seize the attention of the reader.

The principal consideration in selecting type for your copy is that it should be easy to read. The easiest type for people to read is the type they read most often. Therefore, set your copy in the customary, everyday styles of type used in newspaper articles and magazine articles. Avoid fancy type. Avoid script. Avoid too many italics. Avoid type that is too faint or too bold. Avoid any style of type that calls attention to the type itself rather than to the message. Do not try to create atmosphere with type.

Some art directors use type merely as a decoration. They force the type into neat squares or oblongs or other shapes. They arrange it so that all the lines will come out to equal length, like the inscription on a memorial tablet. Sometimes they use an unusually light (thin)-face type or a script so that the block of copy will not interfere with the illustration. Sometimes they use the type as part of the design by setting it in long, hard-to-read lines of fancy type with wide white spaces between the lines. Devices of this kind may make an advertisement more artistic, but they do not invite the eye to read. Remember that people buy magazines and newspapers to read stories and articles. Therefore, if you want your copy to be read, set the text like a story or an article.

In selecting type for your advertisements, you would do well to take a look at the typical mail-order ads. Note the strong, black, readable type in which the headlines are set. Note the clear-cut type in which the copy is set. If you do not know the names of the various styles of type, you will not go wrong if you tear a good mail-order ad out of a magazine or newspaper and say to your typesetter: "Please set my ad like this."

In preparing your ad layout, make your headline large enough and bold enough so that even the most careless glancer cannot help but catch your message. If your headline is a long one, set some of the more important words in capitals or extra-large type, or both.

Large type in a headline has strong attention value. It also gives force to your message. Consider this headline in ordinary size type:

ANNOUNCING NEW MODELS

Now see how much more emphatic the headline looks in larger type:

ANNOUNCING NEW MODELS

The big type adds strength and force to your announcement. It makes big news out of it instead of little news. It gives the impression that you are speaking in a strong voice instead of in a whisper. An announcement in small type suggests that you yourself do not think that the announcement is important.

Even when you have no news—no announcement to make—you can give your headline a news flavor by putting it in big type. Consider this headline in ordinary size type:

TO MEN AND WOMEN WHO WANT TO GET AHEAD

This is an interesting headline, but consider how much more important it becomes when it is spread clear across the page in large type:

TO MEN AND WOMEN WHO WANT TO GET AHEAD

The big type seems to add an announcement quality, a news quality, even though the headline contains no news at all. Do not, however, use capitals for more than six or seven words in a row. For almost all adults, "All-Caps" becomes harder to read easily beyond that point. Set the above headline as:

To men and women
who want to get ahead

FEATURING IMPORTANT WORDS IN HEADLINES

When you are dealing with a lengthy headline, you may not have room to set all the words in large type. In that case, you can set part of the headline in large type. For example, here is a long headline in which none of the words have been featured:

YOU CAN LAUGH AT MONEY WORRIES
IF YOU FOLLOW THIS SIMPLE FINANCIAL PLAN

Here is the same headline with certain words featured in large type. In setting up an ad, these featured words can be made to stand out on the page and stop readers. Note that the featured words convey a complete message in themselves. This is important. Do not feature words that are meaningless by themselves.

YOU CAN LAUGH
AT MONEY WORRIES
if you follow this simple
financial plan

Here are four more headlines that have been given the same treatment. In the first version of each, no words have been featured. In the second version certain meaningful words have been set in large type:

(1) To men and women who want
    to quit work some day

(2) To men and women who want
    to QUIT WORK some day

(1) Break up a cold
    this quick way

(2) BREAK UP A COLD
    this quick way

(1) Thousands now play
    who never thought they could

(2) THOUSANDS NOW PLAY
     who never thought they could

(1) Who else wants a whiter wash
     with no hard work

(2) WHO ELSE WANTS A WHITER WASH
     with no hard work

When you hand your ad copy to your layout artist or to your art director, they will appreciate it if you will indicate which, if any, important words in your headline should be emphasized or set in larger type than the rest of the headline.

If you write a long headline, it is wise to include a meaningful phrase that can be set in extra bold or extra-large type. If you can do so, it is especially good to arrange your thoughts so that the meaningful phrase occurs at the beginning of your headline. This arrangement is used in three out of four of the headlines listed above. It is not used in the headline "To men and women who want to QUIT WORK some day."

PICTURES THAT GET ATTENTION

Hundreds of readership surveys have been conducted in which people have been asked which ads they noticed in various publications. As a result, it is possible to list certain types of pictures that are especially effective in getting attention. For example:

- Pictures of brides
- Pictures of babies
- Pictures of animals
- Pictures of famous people
- Pictures of people in odd costumes, such as might be worn at a masquerade
- Pictures of people in odd situations, such as a man wearing an eye patch
- Pictures that tell a story, such as a little girl trying on her mother's hat
- Romantic pictures, such as a man carrying a girl across a rushing brook
- Catastrophe pictures, such as car accidents
- News pictures, such as the launching of a space vehicle
- Timely pictures, such as pictures of Santa Claus at Christmas time and pictures of Abraham Lincoln on Lincoln's birthday

One interesting observation that has come out of readership surveys is, for most products, men tend to look at ads containing pictures of men and that women tend to look at ads containing pictures of women. Apparently, the pictures act as labels. A man figures that an ad containing a picture of a man is likely to be an ad for a man's product and that an ad containing a picture of a woman is likely to be an ad for a woman's product.

Before the widespread use of readership surveys, some advertisers believed that the way to stop a male reader was to show a picture of a bathing beauty. Apparently this technique stops the wrong readers or it stops them in the wrong mood. This type of picture may create desire for the girl, but it does not seem to create desire for the product being advertised. There was a story from the early days of direct mail about the man who sent $29.95 in response to a mail-order catalog ad for a woman's dress. When the dress was delivered, the man complained. For $29.95 he had expected to get the woman model who had been shown wearing the dress in the catalog illustration!

PICTURES THAT SELL

In using information gained from readership surveys, it is wise to remember that the high attention value of a picture does not necessarily mean high sales value. In order to have sales value, the picture should be related to the product.

Some advertisers have wrongly used readership survey results by illustrating ads with pictures of high attention value but without relation to the product. For example, if you use a picture of a bride or a baby in order to get high attention value for an automobile ad, you will stop the wrong people in the wrong mood. On the other hand, a picture of a bride is fine for selling wedding gifts such as silverware. And a picture of a baby is fine for selling baby powder.

Based on sales tests of advertisements, following are typical examples of pictures that have sales value:

1. Picture of the product. For example, in an automobile ad, show a picture of the automobile.

2. Picture of product in use. For example, a woman using a new garden tool she just bought.

3. Picture of reward of using the product. For example, a woman admiring a cake she baked, or eating a pudding she prepared, or wearing the better coat she's always wanted.

4. Picture of attainment of ambition. For example, a boy receiving a diploma. Another example: A correspondence school ad showing a smiling man handing his wife some money. Headline: "Here's an extra $50, Grace—I'm making real money now."

5. Picture of an enlarged detail. For example, a magnifying glass showing an enlargement of a new kind of pen point.

6. Dramatic pictures. For example, an ad for a memory course showed a picture of a blindfolded man. Headline: "A startling memory feat you can do."

An error to avoid in the choice of pictures is the use of pictures that are too far-fetched or too clever. Here is what sometimes happens. An agency works for years preparing ads for seagoing cruises. They get tired of pictures of happy people embarking on a ship or pictures of joyful groups playing shuffleboard on the deck of a ship. They crave something different. And so they prepare a cruise ad that features a picture of a ship's compass or a picture of a ship captain's hat. This is clever, but too far-fetched. This agency has forgotten two important truths, namely:

1. To the average person who is glancing rapidly through a publication, a picture of a compass is an ad for a compass. A picture of a hat is an ad for a hat.

2. The persons who have finally saved up enough money to take a cruise are delighted with pictures of people embarking or pictures of groups playing games aboard ship. Thus is just what they are looking for. So don't lose them or confuse them with pictures of hats or compasses.

When you are looking for an idea for an ad illustration, you will often find that a picture of the product will produce the most sales. For example, the Book-of-the-Month Club shows pictures of books. If you look through a mail order catalogue you will find the following:

- Pictures of sewing machines in sewing machine ads.
- Pictures of vacuum cleaners in vacuum cleaner ads.
- Pictures of dresses in ads for dresses.
- Pictures of shoes in ads for shoes.

The preceding examples are not intended to rule out the use of dramatic and exciting illustrations. Exciting pictures are fine if you can think up a picture in which the excitement in the picture is related to the product.

WHY PHOTOGRAPHS MAKE GOOD ILLUSTRATIONS

After you have selected the subject matter for your illustration, it is usually better to use a photograph of a subject instead of a drawing. For believability, there is nothing as effective as a photograph. If you do use a drawing or a painting, let your drawing be as lifelike as possible—as photographic in style as possible.

The effectiveness of photographs can be illustrated by a few personal experiences. A woman friend of mine spent half an hour telling me about her little nephew, whom she adored. I didn't learn much about the child from what she said. Her description was too idealized. Then she showed me a large crayon portrait of a beautiful boy. I looked at the drawing, but there wasn't enough reality in it for me to tell what he was really like. Finally, she showed me a snapshot of the youngster on roller skates. This tiny photograph told me what the boy was really like. He looked like a real boy with a character of his own and a nice smile. I could have recognized him. But I could never have recognized him from the crayon portrait. The portrait was unreal and unconvincing.

Another time, I was looking through a summer resort catalog. The advertisements of two resorts attracted me. But one advertisement had a distinct advantage over the other. It showed photographs of the resort and the surrounding country. These photographs told me exactly what the resort was like. They offered the next best thing to an actual visit of inspection. The other advertisement showed an idealized drawing of the hotel and surrounding grounds. It pictured flags flying, fountains playing, and artistic sailboats on the lake nearby. The drawing didn't prove a thing. It gave no real information. It failed to convince. It was plainly just an artist's ideal conception of a summer hotel.

At another time, I wanted to buy airplane luggage. I searched through newspapers and magazines for advertisements. Some of the ads showed drawings of luggage, some showed paintings, others showed photographs. The ads with the photographs interested me most. I knew that if I went to look at that luggage, I would not be disappointed. The actual luggage would look like the photographs. On the other hand, if I went looking for luggage of which I had seen only a drawing or an idealized painting, I might be disappointed. The actual article might not look anything like its portrait.

A photograph adds real information to an advertisement. Photographs convince. Photographs are proof. Everybody knows that when you look at a photograph of a person or a piece of merchandise or a summer resort, you are looking at a real likeness. There are little details in photographs that tell so much—little details of expression or surrounding atmosphere. A glance at a photograph is the next best thing to seeing the actual object.

An old Chinese proverb, often misquoted, says, "A *good* picture is worth a thousand words." If this is true, then a good photograph is worth two thousand words.

USING HEADS OF PEOPLE IN ADVERTISEMENTS

Why do mail-order advertisers so often use men's heads and women's heads as illustrations for advertisements? The answer is that this type of illustration often brings more sales than other types.

Pictures of people's heads are good attention-getters. This is especially true when the model is looking directly at you and is related to the product or service, for example, a photo of a user of the product or a graduate of a mail order correspondence course. A photograph of a person looking you square in the eye will stop you quicker than a picture of a cake of soap or a landscape.

Pictures of people's heads are economical in the matter of space. All you need to show is the face. This means that if you have a large space reserved for your illustration, you can enlarge the face until it fills the space, thus making an illustration that simply cannot be missed.

If you are using long copy and have only a small space left for the illustration, there is nothing you can put in that space that is more eye-catching than a person's head. Many 60-line mail-order advertisements are so crowded with copy that the space left for the illustration is no larger than a postage stamp. Yet this small space is big enough to carry an effective picture of a man's or woman's head.

What are the other types of illustrations used in advertisements? Outdoor 40 scenes, groups of people, office scenes, home scenes, and landscapes are some. Illustrations of this kind are all right if you have plenty of space in which to put them. But they cannot be used to good advantage where you are using quarter-pages or where your copy is long.

Take the case of the landscape picture. You cannot crowd an effective landscape into a small space. If you show a miniature of the entire landscape, the details of the picture become unrecognizable. If you try to cut off parts of the landscape, you are likely to spoil it.

But suppose you are using a man's head. You can omit his shoulders and his collar. You can even cut off the top of his head, leaving only his face, and still have a good illustration. A person's head, especially if he is looking at you, is one of the most effective illustrations you can use in small space. It is also extremely effective when enlarged to fill a larger space.

There are other strong reasons for using people's heads as advertising illustrations. Take the case of a testimonial advertisement. If you show a photograph of the person who wrote the testimonial, the readers will feel more confidence in the message. They will feel that it must be true, or else the testimonial givers would not dare to allow their photograph to be used. Furthermore, as the readers read the testimonial, they can glance every now and then at the person who wrote it. They can see what that person looks like. This increases reader interest and gives a more intimate touch to the message.

THE ADVERTISER'S LOGOTYPE

An important part of many advertisements is the advertiser's logotype or name of the advertiser, which is featured in large type, usually at the bottom of the ad.

Sometimes the logotype is the name of the manufacturer and sometimes it   45
is the name of the product. For example, here are some manufacturers' names
that are often used as logotypes:

- General Electric
- General Motors
- IBM
- Kodak

Here are some product names that have frequently been used as logotypes:

- Tide
- Nike
- Chanel
- Cadillac

The manufacturer repeats the logotype over and over again in the hope that
you will remember it and be favorably inclined toward that brand when you
buy. This is long-haul advertising as distinguished from short-haul advertising
for immediate sales.

In radio advertising, the manufacturers cannot feature a logotype in big print
and so they often compensate for this by repeating the name or the name of the
product over and over again. For example, in a one-minute radio commercial
for Colgate Toothpaste, the name Colgate may be repeated many times.

In TV advertising, the manufacturers can get name publicity in two ways if
they desire, namely, by flashing the product name in big print on the screen and
by having the name frequently repeated by the announcer.

The effect of the logotype on the consumer is difficult to measure because it   50
takes months and sometimes years to produce a measurable result. Yet the
effect is known to exist because tests have shown that people will buy a familiar product in preference to one that is unfamiliar. They will buy from a known
manufacturer more readily than from an unknown manufacturer. Therefore,
the advertiser's logotype should not be omitted from an ad except under special conditions such as the following:

1. If the name of the product is mentioned in the headline of an ad, it
   need not be mentioned again in the logotype.

2. Sometimes a picture of the product with the name printed on the
   package takes the place of the logotype.

3. Some mail order advertisers omit the logotype because they are selling an item or service that is bought only once in a lifetime, for
   example, a book or a correspondence course. These advertisers are
   advertising for an immediate sale instead of building up name

publicity over the years. By omitting the logotype, these concerns reduce their space cost.

4. Readership surveys are mixed about whether editorial items get higher reading than ads. Much, obviously, depends on the specific headline or illustration for each. Nevertheless, some advertisers omit the logotype in order to produce ads that don't look like ads, for example, ads that look like cartoons, or ads that look like news items, articles, or stories. These ads sacrifice the advantage of a logotype in order to gain the advantage of increased readership of their complete text set in small print.

ADS WITHOUT PICTURES

Some of the best pulling mail order ads have been all-type ads with no pictures. For example, the ad for the Roth Memory Course with the headline: "How I Improved My Memory in One Evening." This ad pulled so well that it ran for years. An all-type ad for Tecla Pearls was also run for years and became famous.

An all-type ad selling subscriptions to a well-known newspaper was the best puller of a number of ads tested, some with illustrations, some without illustrations. The headline of this ad was: "How to Get the *Times* Delivered to Your Home." At the present writing, this ad has been running for 14 years. No other ad has equalled it in pulling power.

These examples are not intended to sell you off the idea of using pictures, but to point out that a picture is not a must in every ad. Pictures cost money, and the space they occupy costs money. Every illustration should be tested with this question: Does it add sufficient sales value to warrant its cost?

SUMMING UP

In choosing illustrations for your ads, you will usually get more sales if you cash in on the experience of mail-order advertisers and department stores whose existence depends on ads that produce direct, traceable sales.

Avoid weird, outlandish, or far-fetched pictures that have nothing to do with the product or service you are selling. Use pictures that attract buyers, not curiosity seekers. Here are some safe bets: 55

1. Pictures of the product.

2. Pictures of the product in use.

3. Pictures of people who use the product.

4. Pictures showing the reward of using the product.

American standard of living is due in no small measure to the imaginative genius of advertising, which not only creates and sharpens demand, but also, by its impact upon the competitive process, stimulates the never-ceasing quest of improvement in quality of the product.

—Adlai E. Stevenson

ANALYZING What the Writer Says

1. What is the most important consideration in creating a successful ad?
2. What is the main difference between fine art and commercial art?
3. Is the attention value of a picture the most important aspect when creating an ad?
4. Who tends to look at ads containing pictures of women? Why?
5. Why are photographs more effective than other illustrations in ads?
6. What does Caples tell us about the consuming public?

ANALYZING How the Writer Says It

1. Caples's presentation of effective advertising layout methods is a chapter from a textbook. How does he avoid dry textbooklike discussion of a potentially dry subject?
2. How does Caples employ some of his techniques for effective ads in his textbook presentation?

ANALYZING the Issue

Considering the manipulative techniques advertisers use to sell products, do you think advertising can be considered a basically ethical practice?

ANALYZING Connections Between Texts

1. What types of advertising techniques cited by Caples do Jack Hitt ("The Hidden Life of SUVs," p. 652) and William Lutz ("Weasel Words," p. 661) pinpoint in their essays?
2. Which techniques of advertising layout cited by Caples does the writer of the ad for Phoenix Wealth Management, "Money: It's Not What It Used to Be" (p. 114), identify?
3. Analyze how Adbusters ("Absolute on Ice," "Hitler Wore Khakis," both p. 679, "Reality for Men," "Obsession for Women," both p. 263) uses the kinds of advertising techniques Caples discusses to make us aware of the advertising "game."

WARMING UP: *If you had to choose between a sports utility vehicle or another vehicle of comparable value, which one would you choose? Why?*

The Hidden Life of SUVs

By Jack Hitt

JACK HITT

A contributing writer for Harper's Magazine *and the* New York Times, *Jack Hitt analyzes some of the marketing strategies at work in the SUV industry. His essay first appeared in the July/ August 1999 issue of* Mother Jones.

What's in a name? What do you make of a passenger vehicle called a Bronco?

Or one dubbed a Cherokee? How about a Wrangler? Are they just chrome-plated expressions of sublimated testosterone flooding the highways? Check out the herd that grazes the average car lot these days: Blazer, Tracker, Yukon, Navigator, Tahoe, Range Rover, Explorer, Mountaineer, Denali, Expedition, Discovery, Bravada. Besides signaling that we're not Civic or Galant, they indicate there's something else going on here.

These are, of course, all names of sport utility vehicles, the miracle that has resurrected Motown. Think back to the dark days of the previous decade when the Japanese auto industry had nearly buried Detroit. In 1981, only a relative handful of four-wheel-drives traveled the road, and the phrase "sport utility vehicle" hadn't entered the language. Today, they number more than 14 million, and that figure is growing fast. If you include pickups and vans, then quasi trucks now constitute about half of all the vehicles sold in America. Half. They're rapidly displacing cars on the highways of our new unbraking economy.

Go to any car lot and jawbone with a salesman, and you'll find that big is once again better. Any savvy dealer (clutching his copy of Zig Ziglar's *Ziglar on Selling*) will try to talk you up to one of the latest behemoths, which have bloated to such Brobdingnagian[1] dimensions as to have entered the realm of the absurd.

Ford, in fact, has unveiled a new monster, the Excursion, due to hit the show-   5
rooms before the millennium. With a corporate straight face, its literature touts as selling points that the Excursion is "less than 7 feet tall . . . and less than 20 feet long" and is "more fuel efficient . . . than two average full-size sedans."

These Big Berthas have even spawned new vocabulary words. The biggest of the big, for instance, can no longer fit comfortably in a standard-size garage or the average parking space. So salesmen will often sell you on one of the "small-er" SUVs by praising its "garage-ability."

What, then, explains the inexorable advance of these giant SUVs into our lives? Why do we want cars that are, in fact, high-clearance trucks with four-wheel drive, an optional winch, and what amounts to a cowcatcher?

The answer, in part, lies in the vehicles themselves. Cars are not fickle fash-ions. They are the most expensive and visible purchases in an economy drenched in matters of status and tricked out with hidden meanings.

Some people will tell you that the shift from car to truck can be explained simply: We Americans are getting, um, bigger in the beam. We aren't com-fortable in those Camrys, so we trade up to a vehicle we can sit in without feel-ing scrunched. Here's a new buzzword for Ziglar disciples: fatassability.

But I think the key is found not so much in their size or expense (although   10
both keep ballooning) but in those ersatz Western names. The other day, I saw an acquaintance of mine in a boxy steed called a Durango. Say it out loud for me: "Durango." Can you get the syllables off your tongue without irony? In the post-*Seinfeld* era, can anyone say Durango without giving it an Elaine Benes enunciation at every syllable? Doo-RANG-Go.

The true irony comes from the fact that this thoroughly market-researched word no longer has any core meaning. No one comprehends its denotation (Colorado town) but only its vague connotations (rugged individualism, mas-tery over the wilderness, cowboy endurance). The word does not pin down meaning so much as conjure up images.

These names are only the end product of the intense buyer-profiling that the car companies and the marketing firms continuously carry out. By the time they make it to the lot, these cars are streamlined Frankensteinian con-coctions of our private anxieties and desires. We consumers don't so much shop for one of these SUVs as they shop for us.

A typical focus-group study might be one like the "cluster analysis" con-ducted by college students for Washington, D.C.–area car dealers in 1994 and reported in *Marketing Tools*. The analysts coordinated numerous databases, mail surveys, and census information to profile the typical "Bill and Barb

---

[1] *Brobdingnagian:* Gigantic; the term derives from *Brobdingnag,* the land of giants in Jonathan Swift's *Gulliver's Travels* (1726). (Editor's note)

Blazers," whose consumer apprehensions can shift from block to block, but can be pinpointed down to the four-digit appendix on the old zip code.

Each Bill and Barb then got tagged as "Young Suburbia" or "Blue-Collar Nursery" or "Urban Gentry." Translation, respectively: "college-educated, upwardly mobile white" or "middle-class, small-town" or "educated black" people. The students next identified what images spoke to the underlying appeal of an SUV for each group (prestige, child space, weekend leisure). Then they developed targeted ads to run in the media most favored by each group: the *Wall Street Journal, National Geographic,* Black Entertainment Television.

Many of the ads they developed were directed at women. For example, the one meant for upscale homeowners depicted a "woman architect standing next to her four-door [Blazer] at a Washington-area construction site" and "conveyed her professional leadership in a city with one of the highest rates of labor force participation for women." 15

Sport utility vehicles are quickly becoming women's cars. In fact, current statistics show that 40 percent of all SUV sales are to women, and the proportion is growing. (More men, on the other hand, are buying bigger, tougher pickup trucks.) But one wonders what's going on in the mind of that female architect or that soccer mom, high above the world in her soundproof, tinted-glass SUV, chatting on her cellular phone as she steers her mobile fortress down the street.

When GMC decided to launch the Denali (an SUV named for the Alaskan mountain), the auto-trade papers discussed the subtleties of that outdoorsy name: Even though most buyers "will never venture into territory any less trampled than the local country club parking lot," wrote Ward's *Auto World,* "the important goal of the Denali marketing hype is to plant the image in customers' minds that they can conquer rugged terrain. The metaphor of Alaska is particularly apt because SUVs, especially the larger of the species, depend on the myth that we have new frontiers yet to pave. Perhaps we're trying to tame a different kind of wilderness. Indeed, in an age of gated communities the SUV is the perfect transportation shelter to protect us from fears both real and imagined."

In one focus group, female drivers confessed they hesitated even to exit the interstate "because they are afraid of what they are going to find on some surface streets."

G. Clotaire Rapaille, a French medical anthropologist and student of the consumer mind, practices a more advanced marketing technique called "archetype research." In one session he has consumers lie on the floor and lulls them into a relaxed alpha state with soothing music. Then he asks them to free-associate from images of different vehicle designs and write stories about what they hoped the design would become. Overwhelmingly, Rapaille told the *Wall Street Journal,* his participants had the same reaction: "It's a jungle out there. It's Mad Max. People want to kill me, rape me. Give me a big thing like a tank."

More and more, SUVs give us that tanklike security, and part of the feeling 20
derives from their literal altitude. Down there is the old working class, the new
peasants who haven't figured out how to snatch a six-figure income out of our
roaring economy—the little people who don't own a single Fidelity fund.
There's a brutal Darwinian selection at work: They huddle down in their
wretched Escorts and their Metros—not merely because they are poor but
because they deserve to be.

These are the new savages: people who drive cars. They scrape and fetch
about in their tiny compacts, scuttling along on surface streets. But above it all,
in their gleaming, skyscraping vehicles, is the new high society—the ambitious, the exurban pioneers, the downtown frontiersmen.

It's been said that the most distinctive feature of the American character is
that we continually define ourselves as pilgrims facing a new frontier. In their
darkest hearts, the members of the new-money bourgeoisie have convinced
themselves that we live in an unforgiving wilderness of marauders and brutes.
The hidden meaning of our new conveyances can be found right on the surface. Once upon a time, Trailblazers, Explorers, and Trackers tamed the Wild
West. Now, through the sorcery of focus groups, the bull-market gentry have
brought the Pathfinders and Mountaineers back into their lives in the belief
that they need to conquer the savage land one more time.

ANALYZING What the Writer Says

1. What, according to Hitt, is the most obvious reason people are increasingly buying SUVs?

2. What is the hidden reason that might explain why SUVs are so popular in the
   United States?

3. What audience do SUV marketing campaigns target?

4. What did the focus group studies conducted by the auto industry discover about
   what people want in their cars?

5. In what way have SUVs become a new status symbol?

ANALYZING How the Writer Says It

1. What is Hitt suggesting in the expression "the herd that grazes the average car
   lot"? What else in his essay ties in with this metaphor?

2. What words reveal Hitt's attitude toward SUVs? Look at emotionally charged
   words besides the names he uses for the vehicles.

3. Where does Hitt use humor in his essay? How would his essay have been different if he had written it without humor?

ANALYZING the Issue

1. Consider your responses to the "Warming Up" question. Do your reasons for wanting (or not wanting) an SUV support or contradict Hitt's analysis? Do people really buy these cars because of their wilderness appeal and their social status? Explain.

2. Many people believe that it is unethical for the Detroit car industry to continue to market SUVs aggressively even though it is well known that they are much less gas-efficient and emit much more pollution into the atmosphere than compact cars do. Do you agree? Why or why not? Is the economic edge over the Japanese car manufacturers worth the environmental sacrifice? Explain.

ANALYZING Connections Between Texts

1. Compare Hitt's essay to Arianna Huffington's "The Coming SUV Wars" (p. 652). What similar points do the authors make? Where do they differ?

2. G. Clotaire Rapaille, "a French medical anthropologist and student of the consumer mind" that Hitt cites, discovered that many consumers want big cars because they are afraid that the world outside is "a jungle" that can only be conquered with "a big thing like a tank." Ellen Ullman, in "The Museum of Me" (p. 455) and Barbara Ehrenreich, in "Spudding Out" (p. 700), observe that many people prefer to interact with the world through computers and TV sets rather than participate actively. How do these opinions reinforce Hitt's argument?

"Oh, just give me a pack of whatever the guys in marketing are targeting for jerks like me."

3. How does Robert Mankoff's cartoon above satirize the practice of advertising to target groups?

WARMING UP: *Do you consider gas mileage and general environmental friendliness important factors in car selection?*

The Coming SUV Wars

BY ARIANNA HUFFINGTON

ARIANNA HUFFINGTON

A nationally syndicated columnist and the author of nine books, Huffington lambasts sports utility vehicles—"gas-guzzling, pollution-spewing, down-right dangerous behe-moths"—hoping that people will soon wake up and stop buying these cars.

Once again, America is a nation divided.

I'm not talking about the irreparable, brother-against-brother split between those who think the Bachelor should have proposed to Brooke instead of Helene. I'm talking about a contentious clash that is just beginning to rage. Call it the SUV war. As you read this, the opposing camps are staking out their turf.

On one side sales of the gas-guzzling, pollution-spewing, downright dangerous behemoths continue to soar. And apparently, the more fuel-inefficient the better: Dealers are having a hard time keeping up with the demand for the Hummer H2, GM's new $50,000 barely domesticated spinoff of the Gulf War darling, which struggles to cover 10 miles for every gallon of gas it burns. The symbolism of these impractical machines' military roots is too delicious to ignore. We go to war to protect our supply of cheap oil in vehicles that would be prohibitively expensive to operate without it.

There seems to be no shortage of Americans who think that consuming 25 percent of the world's oil just isn't enough. Maybe the next model, the H3, will need to be connected to an intravenous gas-pump hose all the time. And there would still be people eager to buy it.

These are the same folks who don't give a whit (this being a family newspaper) that at an OPEC meeting last month, the oily group's secretary general

5

announced that one of the few bright spots in an otherwise gloomy world was the U.S.'s seemingly unslakable thirst for its product. How nice it must feel for SUV owners, knowing that their swaggering imprudence is helping the world's anti-democratic oil sheiks sleep just a little better at night. Call this camp the Bigger Is Better crowd. Their motto: "Burn, baby, burn . . . 30 percent more carbon monoxide and hydrocarbons and 75 percent more nitrogen oxides than passenger cars." How about this for a bumper sticker: "Honk if you hate the ozone layer!"

Lining up on the other side of the SUV DMZ are a disparate collection of groups and individuals whose aim is to win the hearts and minds—and change the driving habits—of the American public.

These include the Evangelical Environmental Network, which is promoting greater fuel efficiency through a provocative TV ad campaign that asks: "What would Jesus drive?" Hint: I don't think the answer is a Hummer. (Turning water into oil wasn't really his thing.) This comes at the same time that Americans for Fuel Efficient Cars, a group I co-founded with film producer Lawrence Bender, environmental activist Laurie David, and movie and TV agent Ari Emanuel, is producing ads parodying the drugs-equal-terror ads the administration is running. In this case, we're linking driving SUVs to our national security. When Hollywood progressives and the "WWJD?" crowd independently hit on the same idea, you know that something is up.

Even as SUVs continue to roll off the assembly line and out of car dealers' showrooms at a record pace, there is a growing sense that the tide of public opinion is turning against these metal monstrosities. A tipping point in the push to wean ourselves from foreign oil has finally been reached. The SUV makers have won a few battles, but they may be about to lose the war.

The new mood is very similar to the consciousness-raising that followed the efforts of Mothers Against Drunk Driving and the Designated Driver campaign. Before that, the prevailing attitude was, "Hey, what's the big deal?" The campaign hammered home a very compelling answer to that question, and the public's perception of drinking and driving was changed forever. Getting loaded and getting behind the wheel went from being cool to being antisocial. With luck, getting behind the wheel of a loaded gas-guzzler is about to undergo the same transformation.

To see how the SUV fight is going, take a look at the media, usually an excel- 10 lent weather vane when it comes to these kinds of societal shifts. In the last week alone there has been an explosion in the amount of positive coverage given to the anti-SUV movement, including segments on all the networks' nightly news shows. This is no small thing when you consider the megamillions in advertising dollars the auto industry represents.

And in Washington, after steadfastly opposing any raise in fuel efficiency standards, the Bush administration let it be known last week that it is considering a proposal to increase the standard for light trucks and SUVs by 1.5 miles per gallon by 2007.

While Team Bush hailed the proposed boost as a major victory in the battle for energy independence, Sen. John Kerry, who along with Sen. John McCain last spring proposed raising the SUV standard by 50 percent, called the 7 percent increase "window dressing." Others labeled it "political theater" and "almost an insult in its modesty." A thousand dittos.

It does seem woefully inadequate—especially when you consider how many loopholes have already been driven through by light trucks and SUVs, which are currently allowed to average 7 miles per gallon less than regular cars. And the ultimate absurdity is that if an SUV is massive enough, it is entirely exempt from federal fuel economy standards. That's right, build one with a gross vehicle weight of over 8,500 pounds—like the Ford Excursion or the new Hummer—and the leviathan's lousy gas mileage doesn't even have to be reported to the government.

Chew on that one and see if it doesn't rev your engine: Automakers are rewarded for being particularly inefficient. There's the Bush Free Market for you.

Even the muckety-mucks in Detroit are starting to get the message. Ford, for 15 instance, whose executives met last week with representatives from the "What Would Jesus Drive?" campaign, has pledged to boost the overall fuel efficiency of its SUVs by 25 percent over the next three years, and plans to introduce a hybrid gas-electric model that will get around 40 mpg.

Of course, much of the industry's "we care" message is little more than a desperate attempt to forestall the inevitable and put a pretty P.R. bow on a very ugly reality. Their real message is: "We care about making money, and if doing that now means we have to make it seem like we care about the environment, then so be it." Take, for example, this "faux" socially conscious reminder offered in the new Hummer brochure: "With the power to cross any terrain comes the responsibility to protect that terrain and its potentially fragile ecosystems."

The war's not going the SUV makers' way, and they know it. So now they want to make it look like we're all on the same side. At the moment, they're trying to figure out just how far they have to go to quell the uprising. It's in all of our interests to let them know that a 1.5 mpg improvement is not enough. The consequences of our addiction to foreign oil are no longer an abstraction.

ANALYZING What the Writer Says

1. Who are the "opposing camps . . . staking out their turf" that Huffington writes about?

2. What does Huffington find ironic about the United States going to war "to protect our supply of cheap oil"?

3. What suggests to Huffington that "the tide of public opinion is turning" against SUVs?

4. In what ways is the Bush administration "woefully inadequate" in its thinking about SUVs and their gas consumption?

ANALYZING How the Writer Says It

1. Identify examples of Huffington's emotionally charged language. What is the effect she achieves by using this language? Do you think her essay would have been more effective without it? Why or why not?

2. "The war's not going the SUV makers' way, and they know it," says Huffington in the last paragraph of her essay. Does she offer convincing evidence that her statement is correct?

ANALYZING the Issue

1. Huffington expresses hope that public opinion will turn anti-SUV before long. Do you agree with her? Have you observed any trends in this direction in your immediate social environment?

2. If SUVs are so dangerous and energy-inefficient, why do people continue to buy them? What makes these cars so attractive to the consumer?

ANALYZING Connections Between Texts

1. Look at Jack Hitt's analysis of why people buy SUVs in "The Hidden Life of SUVs" (p. 652). Do his reasons explain the market trend? If so, do Hitt's observations contradict Huffington's belief that public opinion will soon turn against SUVs?

2. Eric Schlosser's *Fast Food Nation* (excerpted in Chapter 11, "Appetites and Addictions," p. 307) analyzes the industry that drives America's infatuation with fast food. Compare Schlosser's points to Huffington's.

3. Despite working in different media, Huffington and Doug Menuez ("Nuclear Lane," p. 466) aim for a similar effect on their audiences. How are their techniques similar?

WARMING UP: *Have you ever bought a product only to find out that it did not live up to its advertising claims? How did the ad mislead you into believing that the product was really worth your money?*

Weasel Words

By William Lutz

WILLIAM LUTZ

William Lutz is known for his analyses of "double-speak," exposing the way public officials use language to manipulate their audiences. The following essay is an excerpt from his 1980 Doublespeak: From Revenue Enhancement to Terminal Living.

One problem advertisers have when they try to convince you that the product they are pushing is really different from other, similar products is that their claims are subject to some laws. Not a lot of laws, but there are some designed to prevent fraudulent or untruthful claims in advertising. Even during the happy years of nonregulation under President Ronald Reagan, the FTC did crack down on the more blatant abuses in advertising claims. Generally speaking, advertisers have to be careful in what they say in their ads, in the claims they make for the products they advertise. Parity claims are safe because they are legal and supported by a number of court decisions. But beyond parity claims there are weasel words.

Advertisers use weasel words to appear to be making a claim for a product when in fact they are making no claim at all. Weasel words get their name from the way weasels eat the eggs they find in the nests of other animals. A weasel will make a small hole in the egg, suck out the insides, then place the egg back in the nest. Only when the egg is examined closely is it found to be hollow. That's the way it is with weasel words in advertising: Examine weasel words closely and you'll find that they're as hollow as any egg sucked by a weasel. Weasel words appear to say one thing which in fact they say the opposite, or nothing at all.

"HELP"—THE NUMBER ONE WEASEL WORD

The biggest weasel word used in advertising doublespeak is "help." Now "help" only means to aid or assist, nothing more. It does not mean to conquer, stop, eliminate, end, solve, heal, cure, or anything else. But once the ad says "help," it can say just about anything after that because "help" qualifies everything coming after it. The trick is that the claim that comes after the weasel word is usually so strong and so dramatic that you forget the word "help" and concentrate only on the dramatic claim. You read into the ad a message that the ad does not contain. More importantly, the advertiser is not responsible for the claim that you read into the ad, even though the advertiser wrote the ad so you would read that claim into it.

The next time you see an ad for a cold medicine that promises that it "helps relieve cold symptoms fast," don't rush out to buy it. Ask yourself what this claim is really saying. Remember, "helps" means only that the medicine will aid or assist. What will it aid or assist in doing? Why, "relieve" your cold "symptoms." "Relieve" only means to ease, alleviate, or mitigate, not to stop, end, or cure. Nor does the claim say how much relieving this medicine will do. Nowhere does this ad claim it will cure anything. In fact, the ad doesn't even claim it will *do* anything at all. The ad only claims that it will aid in relieving (not curing) your cold symptoms, which are probably a runny nose, watery eyes, and a headache. In other words, this medicine probably contains a standard decongestant and some aspirin. By the way, what does "fast" mean? Ten minutes, one hour, one day? What is fast to one person can be very slow to another. Fast is another weasel word.

Ad claims using "help" are among the most popular ads. One says, "Helps keep you young looking," but then a lot of things will help keep you young looking, including exercise, rest, good nutrition, and a facelift. More importantly, this ad doesn't say the product will keep you young, only "young *looking.*" Someone may look young to one person and old to another.

A toothpaste ad says, "Helps prevent cavities," but it doesn't say it will actually prevent cavities. Brushing your teeth regularly, avoiding sugars in food, and flossing daily will also help prevent cavities. A liquid cleaner ad says, "Helps keep your home germ free," but it doesn't say it actually kills germs, nor does it even specify which germs it might kill.

"Help" is such a useful weasel word that it is often combined with other action-verb weasel words such as "fight" and "control." Consider the claim, "Helps control dandruff symptoms with regular use." What does it really say? It will assist in controlling (not eliminating, stopping, ending, or curing) the *symptoms* of dandruff, not the cause of dandruff nor the dandruff itself. What are the symptoms of dandruff? The ad deliberately leaves that undefined, but assume that the symptoms referred to in the ad are the flaking and itching commonly associated with dandruff. But just shampooing with *any* shampoo will temporarily eliminate these symptoms, so this shampoo isn't any different from any other. Finally, in order to benefit from this product, you must use it regularly. What is "regular use"—daily, weekly, hourly? Using another shampoo "regularly" will have the same effect. Nowhere does this advertising claim say this particular shampoo stops, eliminates, or cures dandruff. In fact, this claim says nothing at all, thanks to all the weasel words.

Look at ads in magazines and newspapers, listen to ads on radio and television, and you'll find the word "help" in ads for all kinds of products. How often do you read or hear such phrases as "helps stop . . . ," "helps overcome . . . ," "helps eliminate . . . ," "helps you feel . . . ," or "helps you look . . . ,"? If you start looking for this weasel word in advertising, you'll be amazed at how often it occurs. Analyze the claims in the ads using "help," and you will discover that these ads are really saying nothing.

There are plenty of other weasel words used in advertising. In fact, there are so many that to list them all would fill the rest of this book. But, in order to identify the doublespeak of advertising and understand the real meaning of an ad, you have to be aware of the most popular weasel words in advertising today.

VIRTUALLY SPOTLESS

One of the most powerful weasel words is "virtually," a word so innocent that   10
most people don't pay any attention to it when it is used in an advertising claim. But watch out. "Virtually" is used in advertising claims that appear to make specific, definite promises when there is no promise. After all, what does "virtually" mean? It means "in essence or effect, although not in fact." Look at that definition again. "Virtually" means *not in fact*. It does *not* mean "almost" or "just about the same as," or anything else. And before you dismiss all this concern over such a small word, remember that small words can have big consequences.

In 1971 a federal court rendered its decision on a case brought by a woman who became pregnant while taking birth control pills. She sued the manufacturer, Eli Lilly and Company, for breach of warranty. The woman lost her case. Basing its ruling on a statement in the pamphlet accompanying the pills, which stated that, "When taken as directed, the tablets offer virtually 100% protection," the court ruled that there was no warranty, expressed or implied, that the pills were absolutely effective. In its ruling, the court pointed out that, according to *Webster's Third New International Dictionary*, "virtually" means "almost entirely" and clearly does not mean "absolute" (*Whittington* v. *Eli Lilly and Company*. 333 F. Supp. 98). In other words, the Eli Lilly company was really saying that its birth control pill, even when taken as directed, *did not in fact* provide 100 percent protection against pregnancy. But Eli Lilly didn't want to put it that way because then many women might not have bought Lilly's birth control pills.

The next time you see the ad that says that this dishwasher detergent "leaves dishes virtually spotless," just remember how advertisers twist the meaning of the weasel word "virtually." You can have lots of spots on your dishes after using this detergent and the ad claim will still be true, because what this claim really means is that this detergent does not *in fact* leave your dishes spotless. Whenever you see or hear an ad claim that uses the word "virtually," just translate that claim into its real meaning. So the television set that is "virtually trouble free" becomes the television set that is not in fact trouble free, the "virtually foolproof operation" of any appliance becomes an operation that is in fact not foolproof, and the product that "virtually never needs service" becomes the product that is not in fact service free.

NEW AND IMPROVED

If "new" is the most frequently used word on a product package, "improved" is the second most frequent. In fact, the two words are almost always used together. It seems just about everything sold these days is "new and improved." The next time you're in the supermarket, try counting the number of times you see these words on products. But you'd better do it while you're walking down just one aisle, otherwise you'll need a calculator to keep track of your counting.

Just what do these words mean? The use of the word "new" is restricted by regulations, so an advertiser can't just use the word on a product or in an ad without meeting certain requirements. For example, a product is considered new for about six months during a national advertising campaign. If the product is being advertised only in a limited test market area, the word can be used longer, and in some instances has been used for as long as two years.

What makes a product "new"? Some products have been around for a long time, yet every once in a while you discover that they are being advertised as "new." Well, an advertiser can call a product new if there has been "a material functional change" in the product. What is "a material functional change," you ask? Good question. In fact it's such a good question it's being asked all the time. It's up to the manufacturer to prove that the product has undergone such a change. And if the manufacturer isn't challenged on the claim, then there's no one to stop it. Moreover, the change does not have to be an improvement in the product. One manufacturer added an artificial lemon scent to a cleaning product and called it "new and improved," even though the product did not clean any better than without the lemon scent. The manufacturer defended the use of the word "new" on the grounds that the artificial scent changed the chemical formula of the product and therefore constituted "a material functional change."

Which brings up the word "improved." When used in advertising, "improved" does not mean "made better." It only means "changed" or "different from before." So, if the detergent maker puts a plastic pour spout on the box of detergent, the product has been "improved," and away we go with a whole new advertising campaign. Or, if the cereal maker adds more fruit or a different kind of fruit to the cereal, there's an improved product. Now you know why manufacturers are constantly making little changes in their products. Whole new advertising campaigns, designed to convince you that the product has been changed for the better, are based on small changes in superficial aspects of a product. The next time you see an ad for an "improved" product, ask yourself what was wrong with the old one. Ask yourself just how "improved" the product is. Finally, you might check to see whether the "improved" version costs more than the unimproved one. After all, someone has to pay for the millions of dollars spent advertising the improved product.

Of course, advertisers really like to run ads that claim a product is "new and improved." While what constitutes a "new" product may be subject to some regulation, "improved" is a subjective judgment. A manufacturer changes the shape of its stick deodorant, but the shape doesn't improve the function of the deodorant. That is, changing the shape doesn't affect the deodorizing ability of the deodorant, so the manufacturer calls it "improved." Another manufacturer adds ammonia to its liquid cleaner and calls it "new and improved." Since adding ammonia does affect the cleaning ability of the product, there has been a "material functional change" in the product, and the manufacturer can now call its cleaner "new," and "improved" as well. Now the weasel words "new and improved" are plastered all over the package and are the basis for a multimillion-dollar ad campaign. But after six months the word "new" will have to go, until someone can dream up another change in the product. Perhaps it will be adding color to the liquid, or changing the shape of the package, or maybe adding a new dripless pour spout, or perhaps a ____. The "improvements" are endless, and so are the new advertising claims and campaigns.

"New" is just too useful and powerful a word in advertising for advertisers to pass it up easily. So they use weasel words that say "new" without really saying it. One of their favorites is "introducing," as in, "Introducing improved Tide," or "Introducing the stain remover." The first is simply saying, here's our improved soap; the second, here's our new advertising campaign for our detergent. Another favorite is "now," as in, "Now there is Sinex." which simply means that Sinex is available. Then there are phrases like "Today's Chevrolet," "Presenting Dristan," and "A fresh way to start the day." The list is really endless because advertisers are always finding new ways to say "new" without really saying it. If there is a second edition of [my] book, I'll just call it the "new and improved" edition. Wouldn't you really rather have a "new and improved" edition of [my] book rather than a "second" edition?

ACTS FAST

"Acts" and "works" are two popular weasel words in advertising because they bring action to the product and to the advertising claim. When you see the ad for the cough syrup that "Acts on the cough control center," ask yourself what this cough syrup is claiming to do. Well, it's just claiming to "act," to do something, to perform an action. What is it that the cough syrup does? The ad doesn't say. It only claims to perform an action or do something on your "cough control center." By the way, what and where is your "cough control center"? I don't remember learning about that part of the body in human biology class.

Ads that use such phrases as "acts fast," "acts against," "acts to prevent," and the like are saying essentially nothing, because "act" is a word empty of any specific meaning. The ads are always careful not to specify exactly what "act" the product performs. Just because a brand of aspirin claims to "act fast" for headache relief doesn't mean this aspirin is any better than any other aspirin. What is the "act" that this aspirin performs? You're never told. Maybe it just dissolves quickly. Since aspirin is a parity product, all aspirin is the same and therefore functions the same. [20]

WORKS LIKE ANYTHING ELSE

If you don't find the word "acts" in an ad, you will probably find the weasel word "works." In fact, the two words are almost interchangeable in advertising. Watch out for ads that say a product "works against," "works like," "works for," or "works longer." As with "acts," "works" is the same meaningless verb used to make you think that this product really does something, and maybe even something special or unique. But "works," like "acts," is basically a word empty of any specific meaning.

LIKE MAGIC

Whenever advertisers want you to stop thinking about the product and to start thinking about something bigger, better, or more attractive than the product, they use that very popular weasel word "like." The word "like" is the advertiser's equivalent of a magician's use of misdirection. "Like" gets you to ignore the product and concentrate on the claim the advertiser is making about it. "For skin like peaches and cream" claims the ad for a skin cream. What is this ad really claiming? It doesn't say this cream will give you peaches-and-cream skin. There is no verb in this claim, so it doesn't even mention using the product. How is skin ever like "peaches and cream"? Remember, ads must be read literally and exactly, according to the dictionary definition of words. (Remember "virtually" in the Eli Lilly case.) The ad is making absolutely no promise or claim whatsoever for this skin cream. If you think this cream will give you soft, smooth, youthful-looking skin, you are the one who has read that meaning into the ad.

The wine that claims "It's like taking a trip to France" wants you to think about a romantic evening in Paris as you walk along the boulevard after a wonderful meal in an intimate little bistro. Of course, you don't really believe that a wine can take you to France, but the goal of the ad is to get you to think pleasant, romantic thoughts about France and not about how the wine tastes or how expensive it may be. That little word "like" has taken you away from crushed grapes into a world of your own imaginative making. Who knows, maybe the next time you buy wine, you'll think those pleasant thoughts when you see this brand of wine, and you'll buy it. Or, maybe you weren't even thinking about buying wine at all, but now you just might pick up a bottle the next time you're shopping. Ah, the power of "like" in advertising.

How about the most famous "like" claim of all, "Winston tastes good like a cigarette should"? Ignoring the grammatical error here, you might want to know what this claim is saying. Whether a cigarette tastes good or bad is a subjective judgment because what tastes good to one person may well taste horrible to another. Not everyone likes fried snails, even if they are called escargot. (*De gustibus non est disputandum,* which was probably the Roman rule for advertising as well as for defending the games in the Colosseum.) There are many people who say all cigarettes taste terrible, other people who say only some cigarettes taste all right, and still others who say all cigarettes taste good. Who's right? Everyone, because taste is a matter of personal judgment.

Moreover, note the use of the conditional, "should." The complete claim is, 25 "Winston tastes good like a cigarette should taste." But should cigarettes taste good? Again, this is a matter of personal judgment and probably depends most on one's experiences with smoking. So, the Winston ad is simply saying that Winston cigarettes are just like any other cigarette: Some people like them and some people don't. On that statement R. J. Reynolds conducted a very successful multimillion-dollar advertising campaign that helped keep Winston the number-two-selling cigarette in the United States, close behind number one, Marlboro.

CAN IT BE UP TO THE CLAIM?

Analyzing ads for doublespeak requires that you pay attention to every word in the ad and determine what each word really means. Advertisers try to wrap their claims in language that sounds concrete, specific, and objective, when in fact the language of advertising is anything but. Your job is to read carefully and listen critically so that when the announcer says that "Crest can be of significant value . . ." you know immediately that this claim says absolutely nothing. Where is the doublespeak in this ad? Start with the second word.

Once again, you have to look at what words really mean, not what you think they mean or what the advertiser wants you to think they mean. The ad for Crest only says that using Crest "can be" of "significant value." What really throws you off in this ad is the brilliant use of "significant." It draws your attention to the word "value" and makes you forget that the ad only claims that Crest "can be." The ad doesn't say that Crest *is* of value, only that it is "able" or "possible" to be of value, because that's all that "can" means.

It's so easy to miss the importance of those little words, "can be." Almost as easy as missing the importance of the words "up to" in an ad. These words are very popular in sale ads. You know, the ones that say, "Up to 50% Off!" Now, what does that claim mean? Not much, because the store or manufacturer has to reduce the price of only a few items by 50 percent. Everything else can be reduced a lot less, or not even reduced. Moreover, don't you want to know 50 percent off of what? Is it 50 percent off the "manufacturer's suggested list price," which is the highest possible price? Was the price artificially inflated and then reduced? In other ads, "up to" expresses an ideal situation. The medicine that works "up to ten times faster," the battery that lasts "up to twice as long," and the soap that gets you "up to twice as clean" all are based on ideal situations using those products, situations in which you can be sure you will never find yourself.

UNFINISHED WORDS

Unfinished words are a kind of "up to" claim in advertising. The claim that a battery lasts "up to twice as long" usually doesn't finish the comparison—twice as long as what? A birthday candle? A tank of gas? A cheap battery made in a country not noted for its technological achievements? The implication is that the battery lasts twice as long as batteries made by other battery makers, or twice as long as earlier model batteries made by the advertiser, but the ad doesn't really make these claims. You read these claims into the ad, aided by the visual images the advertiser so carefully provides.

Unfinished words depend on you to finish them, to provide the words the advertisers so thoughtfully left out of the ad. Pall Mall cigarettes were once advertised as "A longer finer and milder smoke." The question is, longer, finer, and milder than what? The aspirin that claims it contains "Twice as much of the pain reliever doctors recommend most" doesn't tell you what pain reliever it contains twice as much of. (By the way, it's aspirin. That's right; it just contains twice the amount of aspirin. And how much is twice the amount? Twice of what amount?) Panadol boasts that "nobody reduces fever faster," but, since Panadol is a parity product, this claim simply means that Panadol isn't any better than any other product in its parity class. "You can be sure if it's Westinghouse," you're told, but just exactly what it is you can be sure of is never mentioned. "Magnavox gives you more" doesn't tell you what you get more of. More value? More television? More than they gave you before? It sounds nice, but it means nothing, until you fill in the claim with your own words, the words the advertiser didn't use. Since each of us fills in the claim differently, the ad and the product can become all things to all people, and not promise a single thing.

Unfinished words abound in advertising because they appear to promise so much. More importantly, they can be joined with powerful visual images on television to appear to be making significant promises about a product's effectiveness without really making any promises. In a television ad, the aspirin product that claims fast relief can show a person with a headache taking the product and then, in what appears to be a matter of minutes, claiming complete relief. This visual image is far more powerful than any claim made in unfinished words. Indeed, the visual image completes the unfinished words for you, filling in with pictures what the words leave out. And you thought that ads didn't affect you. What brand of aspirin do you use?

Some years ago, Ford's advertisements proclaimed "Ford LTD—700% quieter." Now, what do you think Ford was claiming with these unfinished words? What was the Ford LTD quieter than? A Cadillac? A Mercedes Benz? A BMW? Well, when the FTC asked Ford to substantiate this unfinished claim, Ford replied that it meant that the inside of the LTD was 700% quieter than the outside. How did you finish those unfinished words when you first read them? Did you even come close to Ford's meaning?

COMBINING WEASEL WORDS

A lot of ads don't fall neatly into one category or another because they use a variety of different devices and words. Different weasel words are often combined to make an ad claim. The claim, "Coffee-Mate gives coffee more body, more flavor," uses Unfinished Words ("more" than what?) and also uses words that have no specific meaning ("body" and "flavor"). Along with "taste" (remember the Winston ad and its claim to taste good), "body" and "flavor" mean nothing because their meaning is entirely subjective. To you, "body" in coffee might mean thick, black, almost bitter coffee, while I might take it to mean a light brown, delicate coffee. Now, if you think you understood that last sentence, read it again, because it said nothing of objective value; it was filled with weasel words of no specific meaning: "thick," "black," "bitter," "light brown," and "delicate." Each of those words has no specific, objective meaning, because each of us can interpret them differently.

Try this slogan: "Looks, smells, tastes like ground-roast coffee." So, are you now going to buy Taster's Choice instant coffee because of this ad? "Looks," "smells," and "tastes" are all words with no specific meaning and depend on your interpretation of them for any meaning. Then there's that great weasel word "like," which simply suggests a comparison but does not make the actual connection between the product and the quality. Besides, do you know what "ground-roast" coffee is? I don't, but it sure sounds good. So, out of seven words in this ad, four are definite weasel words, two are quite meaningless, and only one has any clear meaning.

Remember the Anacin ad—"Twice as much of the pain reliever doctors rec- [35] ommend most"? There's a whole lot of weaseling going on in this ad. First, what's the pain reliever they're talking about in this ad? Aspirin, of course. In fact, any time you see or hear an ad using those words "pain reliever," you can automatically substitute the word "aspirin" for them. (Makers of acetaminophen and ibuprofen pain relievers are careful in their advertising to identify their products as nonaspirin products.) So, now we know that Anacin has aspirin in it. Moreover, we know that Anacin has twice as much aspirin in it, but we don't know twice as much as what. Does it have twice as much aspirin as an ordinary aspirin tablet? If so, what is an ordinary aspirin tablet, and how much aspirin does it contain? Twice as much as Excedrin or Bufferin? Twice as much as a chocolate chip cookie? Remember those Unfinished Words and how they lead you on without saying anything.

Finally, what about those doctors who are doing all that recommending? Who are they? How many of them are there? What kind of doctors are they? What are their qualifications? Who asked them about recommending pain relievers? What other pain relievers did they recommend? And there are a whole lot more questions about this "poll" of doctors to which I'd like to know the answers, but you get the point. Sometimes, when I call my doctor, she tells me to take two aspirin and call her office in the morning. Is that where Anacin got this ad?

ANALYZING What the Writer Says

1. How do you define the term "weasel word"? Explain how it got its name.

2. Make a list of the types of weasel words Lutz discusses in his essay and give one or two examples of each. Do some field research (by looking through newspapers and magazines or by looking at the packages of various products) and find some more examples for each category.

3. Why do advertisers use weasel words?

ANALYZING How the Writer Says It

Who is Lutz's audience? What is his argument? How does his use of language and examples help him convince his audience?

ANALYZING the Issue

1. Were you aware of "weasel words" before you read this essay? If not, does it surprise you to hear about them? Do you think the practice is unethical? Explain.

2. Look at the collection of examples you have gathered from your field research; are there any examples of weasel words that do *not* work for you? Why not?

ANALYZING Connections Between Texts

1. What's in a name? In his essay "The Hidden Life of SUVs" (p. 652), Jack Hitt investigates the evocative power of product names. How is the technique of naming products related to Lutz's discussion of weasel words?

2. In "Politics and the English Language" (p. 487), George Orwell examines the relationship between language, thinking, and propaganda. Compare Lutz's points to Orwell's.

"I like it. It's dumb without trying to be clever."

3. How does Warren Miller's cartoon (above) make fun of the kinds of advertising techniques Lutz (and others) describe in this unit?

WARMING UP: *Are you aware of any courses inspired by the business scandals of 2002 that are currently taught at your college or university?*

Scandal 101: Lessons from Ken Lay

BY JULIE SCHLOSSER

JULIE SCHLOSSER
In this brief piece published in Fortune *magazine in the aftermath of the 2002 collapse of Houston-based Enron Corporation, Julie Schlosser, a business reporter, shows how the academy keeps up with current events.*

ETHICS AND MANAGEMENT COURSES FALL 2002[1]

CASE WESTERN RESERVE UNIVERSITY Business Ethics Part 1: The Short Road From Unbelievable Success to Unmitigated Disaster Part 2: Enron 101 "The class features a discussion of how Ken Lay became addicted to success. Students must write an ethical analysis of what went wrong at Enron using either an Aristotelian or a Kantian framework."

UNIVERSITY OF PENNSYLVANIA Ethics and Management "[The class] does not attempt to convert sinners to saints, preach absolute truths, or deter the morally vulnerable."

NEW YORK UNIVERSITY Professional Responsibility From a session called "Truth and Disclosure": "Exaggeration and bluffing are . . . part of the business game, but how much is too much?"

---

[1]All of these are actual business school course excerpts and class highlights.

UNIVERSITY OF CALIFORNIA AT IRVINE The Enron Case "One of the classes will be a lecture by [Sherron Watkins]." The alumni network will be funding an overflow room.

NORTHEASTERN UNIVERSITY Fraud: The Dark Side of Business "Topics   5 include legal aspects of fraud, Ponzi and pyramid schemes."

PEPPERDINE UNIVERSITY Ethics and Law for Executives "For the past ten years, 2% of students attending the three-day course have quit their jobs within seven days, citing ethical reasons."

HARVARD UNIVERSITY The Moral Leader "This course relies heavily on works of fiction, including Macbeth, The Secret Sharer, The Last Tycoon, Remains of the Day, and I Come as a Thief, to examine in-depth the practical moral issues that managers face."

UNIVERSITY OF TEXAS AT AUSTIN Management of Auditing and Control One session has been titled "Executive Compensation: Is Jail Time Necessary?" Another session delves into Anatomy of Greed: The Unshredded Truth From an Enron Insider, which was penned by a University of Texas alum.

UNIVERSITY OF MARYLAND Business Ethics (Spring 2003) "A visit to a federal prison provides a unique opportunity to speak with former-executives-turned-inmates about the serious consequences of compromising ethical standards."

ANALYZING What the Writer Says

1. What does Schlosser's list of courses suggest about the academic response to the Enron debacle?
2. How does Schlosser's list address the seriousness of the Enron scandal?
3. What is the difference between the approaches of Case Western Reserve, the University of Pennsylvania, and Harvard?

ANALYZING How the Writer Says It

1. Schlosser chooses to simply list, without comment, nine excerpts from course descriptions at a variety of major universities. How effective is this technique?
2. Analyze Schlosser's title. How does it affect how you read the list?

ANALYZING the Issue

1. The line between ethics and legality can be a fine one. Some would argue that hyping ethics in the cutthroat world of competitive business, in a free market economy, is hypocritical. How important are business ethics? As long as companies operate within the law, should business ethics be a primary concern? Explain.

2. Has Kenneth Lay been unfairly scapegoated? Did he simply engage in common practices in big business—manipulating data, spinning quarterly reports advantageously, taking advantage of tax loopholes? Explain.

3. What does Schlosser's list suggest about trends in higher education? Do you think she is mocking the academy in any way?

ANALYZING Connections Between Texts

1. In "Marketing: The Critics of Corporate Propaganda Co-Opt Its Best Weapon" (p. 616), G. Beate discusses "subvertising" techniques. Apply parody, a favorite technique of Adbusters, to some of the course descriptions in Schlosser's list. Alternatively, point to elements of parody in the course descriptions as they exist.

2. Compare the *Harper's* list "Passed by a Hair" (p. 276) to Schlosser's. Why are these formats effective? What do their respective titles contribute to the overall impact of the pieces?

3. Look at the University of Louisville photograph "Golden Rules" (p. 400), which illustrates the importance of cleanliness to an early twentieth-century child's education. In what ways do the university courses Schlosser lists suggest that business schools are reviving the ethos, metaphorically speaking, of earlier values?

> ## YOUR TURN: Suggestions for Writing About "To Market, To Market . . ."

1. In "Prime-Time Pushers," Lisa Belkin quotes a doctor who complains about marketers "making everything into a disease." Write an essay in which you examine the trend toward making diseases of conditions, habits, or even personality traits—whether moodiness, smoking, or hyperactivity. Or if you prefer, focus on one example of a condition that has been "diseased" through marketing and advertising and write an in-depth analysis of it.

2. Use satire to argue for disease status of a habit or condition that has so far escaped the scrutiny of marketers and advertisers.

3. Although laws prohibit advertisers from making fraudulent claims about their products, in what ways do commercials and advertisements circumvent these laws? In an essay, analyze the methods advertisers use to make us believe that their product is better than the competition's without actually saying it.

4. Given that it is very difficult for government agencies to control truth in advertising, should we simply abandon any rules and go back to the old system of *caveat emptor*—"let the buyer beware"? Write an essay in which you investigate the advantages and disadvantages of putting the responsibility for evaluating products on the consumer rather than the producer or the government. End your essay with your recommendations.

5. Using a single ad or commercial (or several ads/commercials that constitute an advertising campaign), point to the techniques discussed by John Caples, William Lutz, and others.

6. Design a spoof ad that parodies (and undermines) the original ad for a cigarette, an alcoholic beverage, or certified "unhealthy" food. Write an essay in which you describe your spoof ad, and explain how its features are designed to make consumers aware of the dangers of the product.

7. Imagine that you are an environmentalist addressing an audience of Detroit car manufacturers. In your speech, try to convince them to market vehicles that are more environmentally friendly than SUVs. Research the issue for facts to support your arguments.

8. Imagine that you are an economist addressing an audience of environmentally concerned citizens. In your speech, point out how economic concerns such as a healthy car industry are just as important as (if not more so than) their environmental concerns. Research the issue for facts and figures to support your arguments.

9. Do some research on alternative vehicles (electric or hydrogen-powered cars, for example) or on methods we could use to reduce our oil consumption and thereby help save the environment. Based on your research, write an essay in which you point out the most sensible and economically feasible way to accomplish these goals.

10. Write an essay in which you take a position on whether or not it is good business ethics to promote products proven to be environmentally unfriendly and wasteful of natural resources.

IMAGE GALLERY 👁

FRANCIS MILLER

Bringing Home the Bacon

Miller's photograph shows 54 children on a shopping spree in a supermarket, an experiment sponsored by the Kroger Food Foundation in 1954. Sociologists and marketing experts were sure the young shoppers would go straight for the candy and the comic books, but to their amazement, the youngsters bought basic groceries, which led researchers to believe that they had been coached by their parents.

1. When you first look at the picture, do you find it surprising? Why or why not?

2. What are the adults doing in this picture? What are the children doing? What do their facial expressions say about their attitudes toward this shopping experiment?

3. How does the photographer create a sense of movement in this picture?

4. The picture was included in the 2000 collection *Life: Century of Change,* so the editors must have considered it significant in the context of the twentieth century. What do you think makes it significant?

5. Do you agree that the children were coached by their parents? If not, how would you explain their grocery choices?

RUTH ORKIN

Lady Buys Tomatoes

Ruth Orkin (1921–85), who became a photojournalist in the 1930s, photographed many celebrities in her time, but, as she says in her 1981 book A Photo Journal, *she "was always looking and waiting for those moments that are 'true to life.'" This 1948 shot of a lady studying the display of tomatoes must have been one of these.*

1. What assumptions can you make about the woman based on her clothes and her facial expression?

2. How does the photograph attest to Orkin's eye for effective composition?

3. How is texture important in this picture?

4. What does this picture say about the power of advertising?

ADBUSTERS

Spoof ads

Adbusters, an organization dedicated to making consumers aware of the power of advertising, designed these two spoof ads in response to wildly successful advertising campaigns for Absolut and Gap.

1. What does the picture in the Absolut spoof ad depict?

2. Locate a real ad for Absolut Vodka. What elements from the ad campaign does the spoof ad borrow?

3. What is ironic about the slogan "ABSOLUTE ON ICE"? What is the purpose of this spoof ad?

4. What very common advertising technique does the Gap spoof ad skewer?

5. Has analyzing these spoof ads made you less susceptible to common advertising ploys? Why or why not?

17

SPECTACLES AND SPECTATORS

Although she fancies herself an actress in a theatrical performance at the park she sits in each Sunday, Miss Brill, the protagonist in Katherine Mansfield's short story, is truly a spectator to life's drama. The irony in her situation is that

> "And I'll be on the sidelines, with my hands tied, watching the show . . ."
>
> —*Aimee Mann*
> *"Red Vines"*

she finds meaning for her life by fantasizing that she has an *acting* role and that by virtue of that "role" she is somehow connected to the strangers she observes. But as the reader becomes painfully aware, she is merely sitting on the sidelines; she has no part in the spectacle she conjures.

The role of spectator is safe, comfortable, and familiar. Millions of Americans are sidelined in their own homes by television, arguably the most transforming development of the twentieth century. People tune in—and tune out their family members, their realities, their thoughts. Ironically, Barbara Ehrenreich argues, they are transfixed by television families because those families exist in a world without television. Recently, the popularity of the familiar family sitcom has been eclipsed by that of reality TV, which Steven Reiss and James Wiltz attribute to the viewing audience's desire to witness the foibles of ordinary folks milking their fifteen minutes of fame. Jonah Goldberg reads the foibles of the not-so-ordinary Osbournes as a morality tale, a warning against the ravages of drugs. Drawing on the principles of ecopsychology, Jeremiah Creedon attempts a diagnosis of cable television's wildly popular, anxiety-plagued crime boss, Tony Soprano.

Sports events, live or televised, have always captivated audiences, and Roland Barthes explains why, comparing the modern wrestling match to the theatrical spectacles of classical antiquity. Terry Golway warns that the spectacle in women's sports is unfortunately not yet the sport itself. Sizing up basketball giant Shaquille O'Neal, Rebecca Mead suggests that O'Neal's super-celebrity has arrested his development.

For some of those people who can't *be* celebrities, watching and reading about celebrities, tracking their every move, is a favorite pastime; Katie Roiphe analyzes the peculiar genre of the celebrity profile, revealing the formula that keeps audiences reading.

In a society that celebrates celebrity, it is not surprising that so many people yearn for the spotlight—or at least a backstage pass. To be part of the spectacle and not merely a watcher is a human impulse that dies hard. But the reality for most people is that of spectator, often to the point of numbness. Why do people *watch* so much, whether sports, reality shows, films, their computer screens?

The answer may lie in the complexity—or the emptiness—of our lives. The nature of spectacle is distraction, and distraction is easier than reality. ✳

WARMING UP: *Have you ever watched professional wrestling? If not, do you know some-one who loves it? Why are wrestling fans fascinated with the sport?*

The World of Wrestling

BY ROLAND BARTHES

> The grandiloquent truth of gestures on life's great occasions.
>
> *Baudelaire*

ROLAND BARTHES

*Roland Barthes
(1915–80), a French
social and literary critic,
spent his life teaching and
researching language and
culture. In* Mythologies,
*a collection from which
this essay was taken,
Barthes, in the manner of
the structuralists, exam-
ines individual "signs" of
everyday life and establishes their meaning in the
larger context of French
culture.*

The virtue of all-in wrestling is that it is the spectacle of excess. Here we find a grandiloquence which must have been that of ancient theatres. And in fact wrestling is an open-air spectacle, for what makes the circus or the arena what they are is not the sky (a romantic value suited rather to fashionable occasions), it is the drenching and vertical quality of the flood of light. Even hidden in the most squalid Parisian halls, wrestling partakes of the nature of the great solar spectacles, Greek drama and bullfights: in both, a light without shadow generates an emotion without reserve.

There are people who think that wrestling is an ignoble sport. Wrestling is not a sport, it is a specta-cle, and it is no more ignoble to attend a wrestled per-formance of Suffering than a performance of the sor-rows of Arnolphe or Andromaque.[1] Of course, there exists a false wrestling, in which the participants unnecessarily go to great lengths to make a show of a fair fight; this is of no interest. True wrestling, wrongly called amateur wrestling, is performed in second-rate halls, where the public spontaneously

_____

[1] In Molière's *L'École des Femmes* and Racine's *Andromaque*.

attunes itself to the spectacular nature of the contest, like the audience at a suburban cinema. Then these same people wax indignant because wrestling is a stage-managed sport (which ought, by the way, to mitigate its ignominy). The public is completely uninterested in knowing whether the contest is rigged or not, and rightly so; it abandons itself to the primary virtue of the spectacle, which is to abolish all motives and all consequences: what matters is not what it thinks but what it sees.

This public knows very well the distinction between wrestling and boxing; it knows that boxing is a Jansenist sport, based on a demonstration of excellence. One can bet on the outcome of a boxing-match: with wrestling, it would make no sense. A boxing-match is a story which is constructed before the eyes of the spectator; in wrestling, on the contrary, it is each moment which is intelligible, not the passage of time. The spectator is not interested in the rise and fall of fortunes; he expects the transient image of certain passions. Wrestling therefore demands an immediate reading of the juxtaposed meanings, so that there is no need to connect them. The logical conclusion of the contest does not interest the wrestling-fan, while on the contrary a boxing-match always implies a science of the future. In other words, wrestling is a sum of spectacles, of which no single one is a function: each moment imposes the total knowledge of a passion which rises erect and alone, without ever extending to the crowning moment of a result.

Thus the function of the wrestler is not to win; it is to go exactly through the motions which are expected of him. It is said that judo contains a hidden symbolic aspect; even in the midst of efficiency, its gestures are measured, precise but restricted, drawn accurately but by a stroke without volume. Wrestling, on the contrary, offers excessive gestures, exploited to the limit of their meaning. In judo, a man who is down is hardly down at all, he rolls over, he draws back, he eludes defeat, or, if the latter is obvious, he immediately disappears; in wrestling, a man who is down is exaggeratedly so, and completely fills the eyes of the spectators with the intolerable spectacle of his powerlessness.

This function of grandiloquence is indeed the same as that of ancient the- 5 atre, whose principle, language and props (masks and buskins) concurred in the exaggeratedly visible explanation of a Necessity. The gesture of the vanquished wrestler signifying to the world a defeat which, far from disguising, he emphasizes and holds like a pause in music, corresponds to the mask of antiquity meant to signify the tragic mode of the spectacle. In wrestling, as on the stage in antiquity, one is not ashamed of one's suffering, one knows how to cry, one has a liking for tears.

Each sign in wrestling is therefore endowed with an absolute clarity, since one must always understand everything on the spot. As soon as the adversaries are in the ring, the public is overwhelmed with the obviousness of the roles. As in the theatre, each physical type expresses to excess the part which has been assigned to the contestant. Thauvin, a fifty-year-old with an obese and sagging body, whose type of asexual hideousness always inspires feminine nicknames, displays in his flesh the characters of baseness, for his part is to represent what, in the classical concept of the *salaud*, the 'bastard' (the key-concept of any wrestling-match), appears as organically repugnant. The nausea voluntarily provoked by Thauvin shows therefore a very extended use of signs: not only is ugliness used here in order to signify baseness, but in addition ugliness is wholly gathered into a particularly repulsive quality of matter: the pallid collapse of dead flesh (the public calls Thauvin *la barbaque*, 'stinking meat'), so that the passionate condemnation of the crowd no longer stems from its judgment, but instead from the very depth of its humours. It will thereafter let itself be frenetically embroiled in an idea of Thauvin which will conform entirely with this physical origin: his actions will perfectly correspond to the essential viscosity of his personage.

It is therefore in the body of the wrestler that we find the first key to the contest. I know from the start that all of Thauvin's actions, his treacheries, cruelties and acts of cowardice, will not fail to measure up to the first image of ignobility he gave me; I can trust him to carry out intelligently and to the last detail all the gestures of a kind of amorphous baseness, and thus fill to the brim the image of the most repugnant bastard there is: the bastard-octopus. Wrestlers therefore have a physique as peremptory as those of the characters of the *Commedia dell' Arte*, who display in advance, in their costumes and attitudes, the future contents of their parts; just as Pantaloon can never be anything but a ridiculous cuckold, Harlequin an astute servant and the Doctor a stupid pedant, in the same way Thauvin will never be anything but an ignoble traitor, Reinières (a tall blond fellow with a limp body and unkempt hair) the moving image of passivity, Mazaud (short and arrogant like a cock) that of grotesque conceit, and Orsano (an effeminate teddy-boy first seen in a blue-and-pink dressing gown) that, doubly humorous, of a vindictive *salope*, or bitch (for I do not think that the public of the Elysée-Montmartre, like Littré, believes the word *salope* to be a masculine).

The physique of the wrestlers therefore constitutes a basic sign, which like a seed contains the whole fight. But this seed proliferates, for it is at every turn during the fight, in each new situation, that the body of the wrestler casts to the public the magical entertainment of a temperament which finds its natural expression in a gesture. The different strata of meaning throw light on each other, and form the most intelligible of spectacles. Wrestling is like a diacritic writing: above the fundamental meaning of his body, the wrestler arranges comments which are episodic but always opportune, and constantly help the reading of the fight by means of gestures, attitudes and mimicry which make the intention utterly obvious. Sometimes the wrestler triumphs with a repulsive sneer while kneeling on the good sportsman; sometimes he gives the crowd a conceited smile which forebodes an early revenge; sometimes, pinned to the ground, he hits the floor ostentatiously to make evident to all the intolerable nature of his situation; and sometimes he erects a complicated set of signs meant to make the public understand that he legitimately personifies the ever-entertaining image of the grumbler, endlessly confabulating about his displeasure.

We are therefore dealing with a real Human Comedy, where the most socially-inspired nuances of passion (conceit, rightfulness, refined cruelty, a sense of 'paying one's debts') always felicitously find the clearest sign which can receive them, express them and triumphantly carry them to the confines of the hall. It is obvious that at such a pitch, it no longer matters whether the passion is genuine or not. What the public wants is the image of passion, not passion itself. There is no more problem of truth in wrestling than in the theatre. In both, what is expected is the intelligible representation of moral situations which are usually private. This emptying out of interiority to the benefit of its exterior signs, this exhaustion of the content by the form, is the very principle of triumphant classical art. Wrestling is an immediate pantomime, infinitely more efficient than the dramatic pantomime, for the wrestler's gesture needs no anecdote, no decor, in short no transference in order to appear true.

Each moment in wrestling is therefore like an algebra which instantaneous- 10
ly unveils the relationship between a cause and its represented effect. Wrestling fans certainly experience a kind of intellectual pleasure in *seeing* the moral mechanism function so perfectly. Some wrestlers, who are great comedians, entertain as much as a Molière character, because they succeed in imposing an immediate reading of their inner nature: Armand Mazaud, a wrestler of an arrogant and ridiculous character (as one says that Harpagon[2] is a character), always delights the audience by the mathematical rigour of his transcriptions, carrying the form of his gestures to the furthest reaches of their meaning, and giving to his manner of fighting the kind of vehemence and precision found in a great scholastic disputation, in which what is at stake is at once the triumph of pride and the formal concern with truth.

What is thus displayed for the public is the great spectacle of Suffering, Defeat, and Justice. Wrestling presents man's suffering with all the amplification of tragic masks. The wrestler who suffers in a hold which is reputedly cruel (an arm-lock, a twisted leg) offers an excessive portrayal of Suffering; like a primitive Pietà, he exhibits for all to see his face, exaggeratedly contorted by an intolerable affliction. It is obvious, of course, that in wrestling reserve would be out of place, since it is opposed to the voluntary ostentation of the spectacle, to this Exhibition of Suffering which is the very aim of the fight. This is why all the actions which produce suffering are particularly spectacular, like the gesture of a conjuror who holds out his cards clearly to the public. Suffering which appeared without intelligible cause would not be understood;

---

[2]In Molière's *L'Avare*.

a concealed action that was actually cruel would transgress the unwritten rules of wrestling and would have no more sociological efficacy than a mad or parasitic gesture. On the contrary suffering appears as inflicted with emphasis and conviction, for everyone must not only see that the man suffers, but also and above all understand why he suffers. What wrestlers call a hold, that is, any figure which allows one to immobilize the adversary indefinitely and to have him at one's mercy, has precisely the function of preparing in a conventional, therefore intelligible, fashion the spectacle of suffering, of methodically establishing the conditions of suffering. The inertia of the vanquished allows the (temporary) victor to settle in his cruelty and to convey to the public this terrifying slowness of the torturer who is certain about the outcome of his actions; to grind the face of one's powerless adversary or to scrape his spine with one's fist with a deep and regular movement, or at least to produce the superficial appearance of such gestures: wrestling is the only sport which gives such an externalized image of torture. But here again, only the image is involved in the game, and the spectator does not wish for the actual suffering of the contestant; he only enjoys the perfection of an iconography. It is not true that wrestling is a sadistic spectacle; it is only an intelligible spectacle.

There is another figure, more spectacular still than a hold; it is the forearm smash, this loud slap of the forearm, this embryonic punch with which one clouts the chest of one's adversary, and which is accompanied by a dull noise and the exaggerated sagging of a vanquished body. In the forearm smash, catastrophe is brought to the point of maximum obviousness, so much so that ultimately the gesture appears as no more than a symbol; this is going too far, this is transgressing the moral rules of wrestling, where all signs must be excessively clear, but must not let the intention of clarity be seen. The public then shouts 'He's laying it on!', not because it regrets the absence of real suffering, but because it condemns artifice: as in the theatre, one fails to put the part across as much by an excess of sincerity as by an excess of formalism.

We have already seen to what extent wrestlers exploit the resources of a given physical style, developed and put to use in order to unfold before the eyes of the public a total image of Defeat. The flaccidity of tall white bodies which collapse with one blow or crash into the ropes with arms flailing, the inertia of massive wrestlers rebounding pitiably off all the elastic surfaces of the ring, nothing can signify more clearly and more passionately the exemplary abasement of the vanquished. Deprived of all resilience, the wrestler's flesh is no longer anything but an unspeakable heap spread out on the floor, where it solicits relentless reviling and jubilation. There is here a paroxysm of meaning in the style of antiquity, which can only recall the heavily underlined intentions in Roman triumphs. At other times, there is another ancient posture which appears in the coupling of the wrestlers, that of the suppliant who, at the mercy of his opponent, on bended knees, his arms raised above his head, is slowly brought down by the vertical pressure of the victor. In wrestling, unlike judo, Defeat is not a conventional sign, abandoned as soon as it is understood; it is not an outcome, but quite the contrary, it is a duration, a display, it takes up the ancient myths of public Suffering and Humiliation: the cross and the pillory. It is as if the wrestler is crucified in broad daylight and in the sight of all. I have heard it said of a wrestler stretch on the ground: 'He is dead, little Jesus, there, on the cross,' and these ironic words revealed the hidden roots of a spectacle which enacts the exact gestures of the most ancient purifications.

But what wrestling is above all meant to portray is a purely moral concept: that of justice. The idea of 'paying' is essential to wrestling, and the crowd's 'Give it to him' means above all else 'Make him pay'. This is therefore, needless to say, an immanent justice. The baser the action of the 'bastard', the more delighted the public is by the blow which he justly receives in return. If the villain—who is of course a coward—takes refuge behind the ropes, claiming unfairly to have a right to do so by a brazen mimicry, he is inexorably pursued there and caught, and the crowd is jubilant at seeing the rules broken for the sake of a deserved punishment. Wrestlers know very well how to play up to the capacity for indignation of the public by presenting the very limit of the concept of Justice, this outermost zone of confrontation where it is enough to infringe the rules a little more to open the gates of a world without restraints. For a wrestling-fan, nothing is finer than the revengeful fury of a betrayed fighter who throws himself vehemently not on a successful opponent but on the smarting image of foul play. Naturally, it is the pattern of Justice which matters here, much more than its content: wrestling is above all a quantitative sequence of compensations (an eye for an eye, a tooth for a tooth). This explains why sudden changes of circumstances have in the eyes of wrestling habitués a sort of moral beauty: they enjoy them as they would enjoy an inspired episode in a novel, and the greater the contrast between the success of a move and the reversal of fortune, the nearer the good luck of a contestant to his downfall, the more satisfying the dramatic mime is felt to be. Justice is therefore the embodiment of a possible transgression; it is from the fact that there is a Law that the spectacle of the passions which infringe it derives its value.

It is therefore easy to understand why out of five wrestling-matches, only about one is fair. One must realize, let it be repeated, that 'fairness' here is a role or a genre, as in the theatre: the rules do not at all constitute a real constraint; they are the conventional appearance of fairness. So that in actual fact a fair fight is nothing but an exaggeratedly polite one: the contestants confront each other with zeal, not rage; they can remain in control of their passions, they do not punish their beaten opponent relentlessly, they stop fighting as soon as they are ordered to do so, and congratulate each other at the end of a particularly arduous episode, during which, however, they have not ceased to be fair. One must of course understand here that all these polite actions are brought to the notice of the public by the most conventional gestures of fairness: shaking hands, raising the arms, ostensibly avoiding a fruitless hold which would detract from the perfection of the contest.

Conversely, foul play exists only in its excessive signs: administering a big kick to one's beaten opponent, taking refuge behind the ropes while ostensibly invoking a purely formal right, refusing to shake hands with one's opponent before or after the fight, taking advantage of the end of the round to rush treacherously at the adversary from behind, fouling him while the referee is not looking (a move which obviously only has any value or function because in fact half the audience can see it and get indignant about it). Since Evil is the natural climate of wrestling, a fair fight has chiefly the value of being an exception. It surprises the aficionado, who greets it when he sees it as an anachronism and a rather sentimental throwback to the sporting tradition ('Aren't they playing fair, those two'); he feels suddenly moved at the sight of the general kindness of the world, but would probably die of boredom and indifference if wrestlers did not quickly return to the orgy of evil which alone makes good wrestling.

Extrapolated, fair wrestling could lead only to boxing or judo, whereas true wrestling derives its originality from all the excesses which make it a spectacle and not a sport. The ending of a boxing-match or a judo-contest is abrupt, like the full-stop which closes a demonstration. The rhythm of wrestling is quite different, for its natural meaning is that of rhetorical amplification: the emotional magniloquence, the repeated paroxysms, the exasperation of the retorts can only find their natural outcome in the most baroque confusion. Some fights, among the most successful kind, are crowned by a final charivari, a sort of unrestrained fantasia where the rules, the laws of the genre, the referee's censuring and the limits of the ring are abolished, swept away by a triumphant disorder which overflows into the hall and carries off pell-mell wrestlers, seconds, referee and spectators.

It has already been noted that in America wrestling represents a sort of mythological fight between Good and Evil (of a quasipolitical nature, the 'bad' wrestler always being supposed to be a Red). The process of creating heroes in French wrestling is very different, being based on ethics and not on politics. What the public is looking for here is the gradual construction of a highly moral image: that of the perfect 'bastard'. One comes to wrestling in order to attend the continuing adventures of a single major leading character, permanent and multiform like Punch or Scapino, inventive in unexpected figures and yet always faithful to his role. The 'bastard' is here revealed as a Molière character or a 'portrait' by La Bruyère, that is to say as a classical entity, an essence, whose acts are only significant epiphenomena arranged in time. This stylized character does not belong to any particular nation or party, and whether the wrestler is called Kuzchenko (nicknamed Moustache after Stalin), Yerpazian, Gaspardi, Jo Vignola or Nollières, the aficionado does not attribute to him any country except 'fairness'—observing the rules.

What then is a 'bastard' for this audience composed in part, we are told, of people who are themselves outside the rules of society? Essentially someone unstable, who accepts the rules only when they are useful to him and transgresses the formal community of attitudes. He is unpredictable, therefore asocial. He takes refuge behind the law when he considers that it is in his favour, and breaks it when he finds it useful to do so. Sometimes he rejects the formal boundaries of the ring and goes on hitting an adversary legally protected by the ropes, sometimes he reestablishes these boundaries and claims the protection of what he did not respect a few minutes earlier. This inconsistency, far more than treachery or cruelty, sends the audience beside itself with rage: offended not in its morality but in its logic, it considers the contradiction of arguments as the basest of crimes. The forbidden move becomes dirty only when it destroys a quantitative equilibrium and disturbs the rigorous reckoning of compensations; what is condemned by the audience is not at all the transgression of insipid official rules, it is the lack of revenge, the absence of a punishment. So that there is nothing more exciting for a crowd than the grandiloquent kick given to a vanquished 'bastard'; the joy of punishing is at its climax when it is supported by a mathematical justification; contempt is then unrestrained. One is no longer dealing with a *salaud* but with a *salope*—the verbal gesture of the ultimate degradation.

Such a precise finality demands that wrestling should be exactly what the public expects of it. Wrestlers, who are very experienced, know perfectly how to direct the spontaneous episodes of the fight so as to make them conform to the image which the public has of the great legendary themes of its mythology. A wrestler can irritate or disgust, he never disappoints, for he always accomplishes completely, by a progressive solidification of signs, what the public expects of him. In wrestling, nothing exists except in the absolute, there is no symbol, no allusion, everything is presented exhaustively. Leaving nothing in the shade, each action discards all parasitic meanings and ceremonially offers to the public a pure and full signification, rounded like Nature. This grandiloquence is nothing but the popular and age-old image of the perfect intelligibility of reality. What is portrayed by wrestling is therefore an ideal understanding of things; it is the euphoria of men raised for a while above the constitutive ambiguity of everyday situations and placed before the panoramic view of a univocal Nature, in which signs at last correspond to causes, without obstacle, without evasion, without contradiction.

When the hero or the villain of the drama, the man who was seen a few minutes earlier possessed by moral rage, magnified into a sort of metaphysical sign, leaves the wrestling hall, impassive, anonymous, carrying a small suitcase and arm-in-arm with his wife, no one can doubt that wrestling holds that power of transmutation which is common to the Spectacle and to Religious Worship. In the ring, and even in the depths of their voluntary ignominy, wrestlers remain gods because they are, for a few moments, the key which opens Nature, the pure gesture which separates Good from Evil, and unveils the form of a Justice which is at last intelligible.

ANALYZING What the Writer Says

1. "Wrestling is not a sport, it's a spectacle," says Barthes. How does he distinguish between the two? What, for him, is the difference between a "sport" like boxing or judo and a "spectacle" like wrestling?

2. How does Barthes support his point that wrestling is more like theater than athletics?

3. What is the meaning of the wrestler's body and the gestures he performs? In what ways do body and gesture connect wrestling with theater?

4. Wrestling, says Barthes, displays "for the public . . . the great spectacle of Suffering, Defeat, and Justice." How does he support his claim? In what ways do wrestlers display suffering, defeat, and justice for the audience?

5. Why, according to Barthes, is wrestling seldom "fair"?

6. What is Barthes's definition of the "perfect bastard," and why do wrestling audiences find the "perfect bastard" so fascinating?

ANALYZING How the Writer Says It

In order to support his point, Barthes makes numerous references to French and classical theater. What does this technique say about Barthes's intended audience?

ANALYZING the Issue

1. Whereas some people might claim that wrestling is barbaric entertainment, Barthes sees it as a modern equivalent of the theatrical spectacles of classical antiquity. Do you think his analogy is justified? Explain.

2. Barthes says that "in America wrestling represents a sort of mythological fight between Good and Evil." If you have ever watched a wrestling match or seen highlights on the news, do you find this to be true? Why or why not? If you have never seen even a brief highlight of wrestling, is Barthes's claim partly the reason? Explain.

ANALYZING Connections Between Texts

1. How, in Rebecca Mead's "A Man-Child in Lotusland" (p. 717), is Shaquille O'Neal's fans' perception of him—and his perception of himself—related to the ancient spectacle Barthes describes on the wrestling stage? Is it possible that we think of *all* our star athletes as super-heroes? Explain.

2. Compare Barthes's view of wrestling with the account Gary Smith ("The Chosen One," p. 811) gives us of Tiger Woods and his father's admiration for his son. Is Tiger Woods (at least in his father's eyes) some kind of mythic super-hero? Explain.

3. How does Neil Leifer's famous picture of Cassius Clay beating Sonny Liston (p. 116) illustrate Barthes's observations about the spectacle (even though Barthes sees boxing as a "fair" sport, a sport that does not follow the rules of ancient spectacle)?

WARMING UP: *How close a connection to nature do you feel? Have you ever craved a deeper connection?*

The Greening of Tony Soprano

BY JEREMIAH CREEDON

JEREMIAH CREEDON

A senior editor at Utne, *Jeremiah Creedon tries to get to the root of the psychic distress of Tony Soprano, the main character in the popular and critically acclaimed television series* The Sopranos, *about a suburban family not so different from those many of us grew up in— except perhaps for its mob connections.*

Dimpled chads, crashing stocks, anthrax, smallpox, and Saddam. All that and we're still wondering what's wrong with Tony Soprano. As the fans of the hit HBO series will tell you, *The Sopranos* began in 1999 with Tony, a mob boss, blacked out beside his swimming pool in suburban New Jersey. He promptly hired a therapist to help him deal with a set of psychological issues, including the panic attacks that now and then dropped him like a stone. Four years and 52 episodes later, Dr. Jennifer Melfi has dredged up all there is to know about her thuggish but complicated client, his wife and kids, and his dealings in what he likes to call "waste management." The only mystery left is what's ailing him.

Melfi's real-life peers have called her sessions with Tony the best portrayal of psychotherapy ever seen in the popular media, and the show has apparently led a lot of men to try it. Among therapists, there's been no end to the discussion about the series, in print and online. When they bring up Melfi's failure to get at the root of Tony's problems, they blame everything from her short skirts to her various missteps (which nicely complicate the story) to the chance that her client is a psychopath who *can't* be cured. Very few have suggested that the problem may be a blind spot shared by her entire profession.

Tony fired his psychiatrist at the end of last season, but she's almost certain to return for the fifth and perhaps last chapter in the Soprano saga. Their exchange goes back to the first episode, when Tony tells Melfi that his attacks began when the ducks that were living in his yard decided to fly away. He explains how happy he was when "wild creatures" came to his pool and had their babies. "I was sad to see them go," he adds, and "I'm afraid I'm going to lose my family." Week after week, Melfi explores every possible thing those birds could symbolize, from issues with Mom and Dad to his own teenage children leaving home. She consults the *Diagnostic and Statistical Manual of Mental Disorders*—the *DSM*—and even recites from the profession's handbook in the dogmatic drone of the true believer. She never considers that sometimes a duck is just a duck.

In the volumes that have been written about *The Sopranos*, there's hardly a word about how its natural backdrop, the duck's world, or what remains of it today, is such a mess. Nevertheless, a case can be made that our troubled relationship with nature is one of the show's ongoing themes. Creator David Chase and his colleagues usually touch on the subject in a fleeting and witty way, with a character's offhand remark or the camera's deadpan stare at some ugly urban artifact; but it's often there, and has been from the start. That all of us seem to look right past it says a lot about how conditioned we are to take the degraded state of the natural world for granted.

In recent books like *The Psychology of The Sopranos* and *A Sitdown with The Sopranos*, Tony's id, ego, and Italian heritage are studied in depth. Both are good reads that examine Tony's character through today's standard therapeutic lenses: ethnicity, family, and the Freudian gaze on early childhood. But what if his ills are tied to issues that modern therapy never explores? Well, it might help to widen the frame and look at the "ecopsychology" of *The Sopranos*.

Eco *what?* You can almost see Carmela Soprano's face as her daughter, Meadow, blurts out the latest new idea she's caught like a cold at Columbia University. Over the last decade, ecopsychology has emerged as an alternative view of mental health that's been shaped by influences as far afield as Darwinian biology, Gaia theory, Buddhism, and the work of various philosophers. An ecopsychologist might say that Dr. Melfi will never understand the true nature of Tony's disease without factoring in the diseased state of nature. In other words, the Sopranos live in a world that is sick, and that world in turn is sickening them. What's more, they don't fully realize what's making them ill because the illness leaves them numb to its cause.

Ecopsychology today is less a formal discipline than an ethic of lament shared by people in many fields. If it has a core belief, it's that our broken ties to the nonhuman world are the cause of both the modern ecological crisis and a related epidemic of alienation and distress. Ecopsychology offers some curious insights into what's eating at Tony Soprano and everyone in his orbit, including his would-be healers. That said, the show's vivid gallery of American types, all on the make and all capable of stunning self-deception, might hold a few lessons for the ecopsychologists as well.

*   *   *

Each episode of *The Sopranos* begins with Tony driving his SUV out of Manhattan onto the New Jersey Turnpike. Alone with his cigar, bound for his big suburban home, he first passes over the Meadowlands, a former lush Eden of tidal marshes that for thousands of years has been a haven for migrating birds. What Tony sees (or doesn't see) is a blasted vista of smokestacks, tank farms, and other industrial detritus rising from a polluted swamp. Some observers have noted that Tony's trip is a jump-cut history of America's march to the suburbs packed into a rock video. It's also a visual record of the price we've paid, in terms of environmental damage, to enclose a parcel of lost Eden in our own backyards.

Tony and Carmela Soprano ruthlessly strive to secure the standard American good life for their kids, even as they try to suppress the truth that they owe it all to violent crime. Meanwhile, their private pursuit of happiness, multiplied across the culture, is creating its own sort of havoc. Cancer seems to whack as many people on the series as wise guys do with guns. Almost everyone relies on a drug or two (or three), from chemo, coke, and heroin to the many legal nostrums for depression and stress. Tony pops Prozac and lithium like mixed nuts. Melfi goes for tranquilizers and vodka. Meadow's freshman roommate from Oklahoma quickly unravels under the sensory assault of the big city. "I think I miss my ferrets," she says, but anti-anxiety pills will have to do.

In much of America today, this psychologically abrasive milieu is now often 10 taken to be the norm. More than a decade ago, the growing acceptance of such conditions began to fascinate cultural critic Theodore Roszak. Back in the late 1960s, Roszak coined the term *counterculture* to describe those who were trying to live outside industrial society and its values. In *Voice of the Earth*, first published in 1992, he examined the aftermath of a social revolution that may or may not have failed, but clearly had stalled. The result was an emerging perspective he called "ecopsychology."

As he notes in a recent new edition of the book, Roszak couldn't figure out why so many people were willing to damage the planet—and why environmentalists usually failed in getting them to change their ways. Then he began to view our runaway spending and driving patterns as compulsive self-medication. Most people know such behavior hurts the natural world, he says, and may actually feel bad about the damage, but they're too hooked on the little relief it brings to stop.

To understand this syndrome, Roszak turned to Paul Shepard (1925–1996), whom he calls "the first ecopsychologist." In *Nature and Madness* and other books, Shepard argues that our disregard for the earth deepens into a kind of insanity as we lose touch with the other animals that have played an age-old role in shaping the human mind. Worse yet, in Shepard's view, this growing estrangement from our natural family has profoundly altered the way we raise and educate children, especially boys. For complex reasons, the result is a culture whose men often claim both the right and the *need* to destroy other living things, in response to their own insecurities. Roszak agrees: "I have also come to believe that, at its deepest level, the environmental crisis traces to the twisted dynamics of male gender identity."

Roszak found that mainstream psychologists weren't much help with these issues. Their models of mental health were usually limited to a realm defined by the bedroom and the job. In Roszak's view, it's a bias shared by the profession's big book, the *DSM*, which "never asks about the quality of people's relationship with the natural world in which our species spent 99 percent of its evolutionary history." The oversight is all the more odd in light of ample research that shows time in the wild can be deeply therapeutic, especially for the young. (Melfi confides in *her* shrink how ashamed she is when her son considers dropping out of college to join the forestry service.) The underlying problem is that most therapists are as deeply invested in our industrial culture as the rest of us. They don't have much incentive to look into the deeper social disease when, in Roszak's words, they "earn from urban angst."

Roszak would like to see mainstream psychology repair itself by adopting a more ecological perspective. But Canadian psychotherapist Andy Fisher says, in effect, don't bother. In his recent book, *Radical Ecopsychology*, he warns his peers to keep their distance from mental health care institutions that ultimately serve "the dominant power-interests of our society." Fisher is convinced we'll never be well until we dismantle a social machine that keeps us in a state of war with nature. Because standard therapy may be propping up this system on some deep level, he urges his colleagues to explore new methods, including the therapeutic power that earlier peoples found (or summoned) in rites and rituals. Once therapists have become social critics as well as healers, they can help to create a new culture that doesn't so brutally sever us from the ancient needs and rhythms of human life.

Ironically, Tony believes that he, too, is living out a revolt against modern   15
society. As he tells Dr. Melfi, he was determined not to end up like the "worker bees" that the earliest industrialists exploited "to build their cities and dig their subways and make them richer." In one of the essays on Italian American life in *A Sitdown with The Sopranos*, E. Anthony Rotundo, author of a book on modern American masculinity, looks at the standards of manhood inside Tony's band of thieves. "Whatever else organized crime may be," he notes, "it is a vehicle for recreating an Italian village in a New World." The show's creator, David Chase, puts it more universally: "People are basically tribal." Tribalism is alive and well in Soprano country, not only in Tony's crew, but also in street gangs, police forces, unions, schools, and churches. All provide the status systems that we as primates seem to crave—and that society at large has gotten too large and complicated to provide for us.

And yet, could our tribal impulses be part of the problem? Tony's own revival of traditional culture in the form of the Mob, complete with initiation rites and a ferociously rigid code of male behavior, makes you wonder. In fact, it's hard to watch this dark comedy of American manners (or read about ecopsychology) without musing over the old question about just what kind of animal we really are. Back in the 18th century, the French moralist Jean Jacques Rousseau argued that we're basically peaceful creatures trapped in a society that corrupts us. The 19th-century English romantics shared his anti-urban vision, as do most ecopsychologists today. An opposing view, expressed by Freud and the songwriter Nick Lowe among many others, is that a beast lurks inside us "caged by frail and fragile bands." (Lowe's bare-bones classic, "The Beast in Me," fittingly closes the first *Sopranos* episode.) The Russian novelist Fyodor Dostoyevsky was just as pessimistic. Evil was destined to poison every society, he wrote, because it rises from "man's soul alone."

In season three, Carmela visits an elderly psychiatrist who has become a harsh critic of his profession. He bluntly tells her that Tony's only hope of being cured is to spend seven years in jail reflecting on his misdeeds and reading Dostoyevsky's *Crime and Punishment*. Calling Carmela an "accomplice" to her husband's violence, he advises her to leave Tony and take the kids, "or what's left of them" after growing up in a family riddled with deceit. Though she knows he's right, she eventually seeks out a second opinion from a Catholic priest who is studying to be a psychologist. His subtle argument against divorce gives her the excuse she needs to put off the painful decision to leave her husband (and his money).

From a radical perspective like Andy Fisher's, the priest appears to be confusing Carmela's best interests with those of the social institution he ultimately serves. But you also have to acknowledge her willingness to play along. Carmela is tempting fate, and so are we, given our complicity in no less violent crimes against nature.

Fisher says that "ecopsychology has emerged largely from a sense of loss," and one of its goals is simply to articulate such sorrow, which many people might feel today but have no way to express. Only then will anyone be able to realize that the "family" an animal lover like Tony fears losing may extend beyond his wife and children.

This deep sense of grief underlies one of the most troubling (and perhaps problematic) themes in ecopsychology. It's the belief that most of us suffer from "psychic numbing," a term first used by psychiatrist Robert Jay Lifton to describe a state he found among atomic bomb survivors in Japan. Many insist that environmental damage is having the same effect on a vastly wider scale. Activist and teacher Joanna Macy calls it our "dulled human response to our world," born in the effort to repress an "anguish beyond naming." For the perceptual psychologist Laura Sewall, it's "a form of denial that shields us from fully experiencing the latest reports on ozone depletion, increasing pollution, toxicity, poverty, illness, and the death of species." Roszak, Fisher, and many others would agree. [20]

Accepting for now that we *are* living in a trance, how are we to deal with the pain of waking up? Both Macy and Fisher find some guidance in the noble truths of Buddhism. Tony agrees, or so it would seem, given his comment to Dr. Melfi at one of his sessions: "You have to joyfully participate in the suffering of the world." Explaining his rare good mood, he tells her he's been to the zoo, where it felt "good to be in nature." Actually, he was getting it on in the reptile house with his latest girlfriend, a Buddhist Mercedes saleswoman. She's also one of Melfi's clients, though the doctor has no idea that the two have gotten together until Tony's bit of advice gives them away. When Melfi suspiciously notes that his "thoughts have a kind of Eastern flavor to them," Tony shrugs. "Well," he says, "I've lived in Jersey my whole life."

In the course of that life, the Sopranos encounter all sorts of characters, from vain surgeons and lawyers to cynical federal agents, media-savvy Indian activists, crack addicts, crooked ministers, and shrewd Russian thugs. One of the show's pleasures is how well these bit players in the modern human comedy are drawn and acted, perfect down to the clothes they wear—and the fashionable ideas that drape them just as lightly. Viewers are constantly reminded how ready we are to turn the pop philosophies of the day, or what Tony calls "California bullshit," into self-deceiving excuses for doing exactly what we want to do.

It's this portrait of a flawed and spiritually needy creature, often kind but no stranger to aggression—and deeply committed to its own best interests—that the ecopsychologists might want to take a closer look at. In the show's many character studies, we see our capacity not only to *be* both good and evil, but also in certain cases to *enjoy* both. Though we often do destructive things in the quest to dull our pain, we're driven by other motives as well, including the hunger for honor, riches, and sensual excess. This view of human nature doesn't contradict the critique that the larger society may be ill, and that many of us are deeply saddened by what we're doing to the natural world. But the individual is given a more complex and active role in spreading (and perhaps curing) the disease, as life inside the Soprano household constantly reminds us.

It's a nice touch that Tony and Carmela have given their daughter a pagan name, Meadow, as if to say she's the only one whose destiny isn't bound to the patron saints (and sinners) of their Italian ethnic past. If there ever is to be another Meadowlands rising from the toxic broth, a place that is more than a body dump for local gangsters, the suggestion is that it might have to be the handiwork of young women. As for Meadow's younger brother, Anthony Jr., the burden of his father's name may say it all. Paul Shepard and Theodore Roszak might argue that he's doomed to have the same cauterized self that awaits most grown men. Like Tony, he'll go on exploiting nature despite his clumsy love for it.

Though Shepherd and Roszak are certainly right to a point, it's worth noting that women play a powerful role in shaping male gender identity. Tony's mother has surely helped to steer him into his criminal life, and Carmela is more than a little guilty of keeping him there. It's been fascinating to watch Meadow approach the age where these issues now loom before her. While always aware of the cruel machinery beneath the family lie, she soon will have to choose, like her mother, whether to assume a part in keeping it hidden.

Given our deep loyalties to tradition and kin, such decisions are terribly hard, and it isn't clear what she'll do; but there can be no doubt that it will be a *choice*. That is the one real luxury that her affluence has given her (and a lot of the rest of us). If in 10 years time she finds herself numb to the world, there will be no mystery why. It won't be a case of repression following traumatic shock. It will be a conscious act.

"I'm tired of telling people that you help with *environmental cleanup!*" she finally shouts at her father. (If only former New Jersey governor Christie Whitman, now head of the EPA, would say the same to her boss.) When it comes to our destruction of the wild, the lies and self-deception that are eating away at the House of Soprano in fact pervade the entire culture. Psychiatrists have said that Tony's problem is a "vertical split" that allows his good and bad sides to operate in full awareness of each other, thanks to a hefty dose of denial. An ecopsychologist might say the larger society is likewise divided in our love-hate relationship with nature. With or without the help of our healers, the next step will be harder. We have to admit we're pretty much all accomplices in the most dangerous form of organized crime today—our ruthless shakedown of the planet.

ANALYZING What the Writer Says

1. What, according to Creedon, *is* wrong with Tony Soprano?

2. How does the camera on the Soprano family provide a lens through which we might view our broader culture?

3. What is ecopsychology? How does *The Sopranos* explore the connection between nature and psychology?

4. Why does Creedon think most coverage of *The Sopranos* has missed what he sees as the show's ongoing theme?

5. What significance does Creedon attach to the Soprano children's given names?

ANALYZING How the Writer Says It

1. Creedon's article makes very serious points about the widening gulf between nature and society, about the growing indifference of humans toward their planet, but the writer uses an extended example of a popular, darkly humorous television show to make those points. Does the technique trivialize his argument or render it more potent? Explain.

2. Operating on the premise that Creedon's article is not just another fluff piece about a television show and its stars, analyze its structure and style. What techniques does Creedon employ that add heft to the piece or provide a larger context?

ANALYZING the Issue

1. Do you agree with Creedon that what's wrong with society is that we are destroying our environment and losing any connection to nature? Why or why not?

2. Do you agree that urbanization drives the field of psychology and encourages therapies that ignore the root of our societal and psychological woes? Why or why not?

ANALYZING Connections Between Texts

1. After reading Jonah Goldberg's "Ozzy Without Harriet: What *The Osbournes* Tells Us About Drugs" (p. 704), compare Goldberg's analysis of *The Osbournes* to Creedon's analysis of *The Sopranos*. What is common to both pieces?

2. Scott Russell Sanders ("Under the Influence," p. 295) explains how a family finds ways to function around a family secret, to ignore, as it were, the elephant in the living room. In what ways, according to Creedon, does the Soprano family do the same?

3. How does Doug Menuez's photo "Nuclear Lane" (p. 466) capture symbolically what Creedon sees as the root of Tony Soprano's psychic alienation?

WARMING UP: *Approximately how much of your free time do you spend watching TV? What is the advantage of TV over other forms of recreation—or vice versa?*

Spudding Out

BY BARBARA EHRENREICH

BARBARA EHRENREICH

Barbara Ehrenreich, who has written for Time *and other magazines and authored several books, often uses humor as a means of making people see what she has to show them. "Spudding Out," from her 1990 collection* The Worst Years of Our Lives, *argues that couch potatoes "love television because television brings us a world in which television does not exist."*

Someone has to speak for them, because they have, to a person, lost the power to speak for themselves. I am referring to that great mass of Americans who were once known as the "salt of the earth," then as "the silent majority," more recently as "the viewing public," and now, alas, as "couch potatoes." What drives them—or rather, leaves them sapped and spineless on their reclining chairs? What are they seeking—beyond such obvious goals as a tastefully colorized version of *The Maltese Falcon?*

My husband was the first in the family to "spud out," as the expression now goes. Soon everyone wanted one of those zip-up "Couch Potato Bags," to keep warm in during David Letterman. The youngest, and most thoroughly immobilized, member of the family relies on a remote that controls his TV, stereo, and VCR, and can also shut down the neighbor's pacemaker at fifteen yards.

But we never see the neighbors anymore, nor they us. This saddens me, because Americans used to be a great and restless people, fond of the outdoors in all of its manifestations, from Disney World to miniature golf. Some experts say there are virtues in mass agoraphobia, that it strengthens the family and reduces highway deaths. But I would point out that there are still a few things that cannot be done in the den, especially by someone zipped into a body bag. These include racquetball, voting, and meeting strange people in bars.

Most psychologists interpret the couch potato trend as a negative reaction to the outside world. Indeed, the list of reasons to stay tucked indoors lengthens yearly. First there was crime, then AIDS, then side-stream smoke. To this list should be added "fear of the infra-structure," for we all know someone who rashly stepped outside only to be buried in a pothole, hurled from a collapsing bridge, or struck by a falling airplane.

But it is not just the outside world that has let us down. Let's face it, despite   5 a decade-long campaign by the "profamily" movement, the family has been a disappointment. The reason lies in an odd circular dynamic: we watch televi-sion to escape from our families because television shows us how dull our families really are.

Compare your own family to, for example, the Huxtables, the Keatons, or the peppy young people on *thirtysomething*. In those families, even the three-year-olds are stand-up comics, and the most insipid remark is hailed with hearten-ing outbursts of canned laughter. When television families aren't gathered around the kitchen table exchanging wisecracks, they are experiencing brief but moving dilemmas, which are handily solved by the youngest child or by some cute extraterrestrial house-guest. Emerging from *Family Ties* or *My Two Dads*, we are forced to acknowledge that our own families are made up of slow-witted, emotionally crippled people who would be lucky to qualify for seats in the studio audience of *Jeopardy!*

But gradually I have come to see that there is something besides fear of the outside and disgust with our families that drives us to spudhood—some posi-tive attraction, some deep cathexis to television itself. For a long time it elud-ed me. When I watched television, mainly as a way of getting to know my hus-band and children, I found that my mind wandered to more interesting things, like whether to get up and make ice cubes.

Only after many months of viewing did I begin to understand the force that has transformed the American people into root vegetables. If you watch TV for a very long time, day in, day out, you will begin to notice something eerie and unnatural about the world portrayed therein. I don't mean that it is two-dimensional or lacks a well-developed critique of the capitalist consumer cul-ture or something superficial like that. I mean something so deeply obvious that it's almost scary: when you watch television, you will see people doing many things—chasing fast cars, drinking lite beer, shooting each other at close range, etc. But you will never see people *watching television*. Well, maybe for a second, before the phone rings or a brand-new, multiracial adopted child walks into the house. But never *really watching*, hour after hour, the way *real* people do.

Way back in the beginning of the television era, this was not so strange, because real people actually did many of the things people do on TV, even if it was only bickering with their mothers-in-law about which toilet paper buy. But modern people, i.e., couch potatoes, do nothing that is ever shown on televi-sion (because it is either dangerous or would involve getting up from the couch). And what they do do—watch television—is far too boring to be televised for more than a fraction of a second, not even by Andy Warhol, bless his boredom-proof little heart.[1]

So why do we keep on watching? The answer, by now, should be perfectly 10
obvious: we love television because television brings us a world in which television does not exist. In fact, deep in their hearts, this is what the spuds crave most: a rich, new, participatory life, in which family members look each other in the eye, in which people walk outside and banter with the neighbors, where there is adventure, possibility, danger, feeling, all in natural color, stereophonic sound, and three dimensions, without commercial interruptions, and starring . . . us.

"You mean some new kind of computerized interactive medium?" the children asked hopefully, pert as the progeny on a Tuesday night sitcom. But before I could expand on this concept—known to our ancestors as "real life"—they were back at the box, which may be, after all, the only place left to hide.

ANALYZING What the Writer Says

1. What is the "agoraphobia" Ehrenreich talks about? What has caused the phenomenon?

2. What is Ehrenreich's thesis?

ANALYZING How the Writer Says It

1. How does Ehrenreich use the metaphor in the title throughout the essay?

2. Point out the instances in Ehrenreich's essay that are funny. How does she use humor to drive home a point that is not terribly funny when looked at closely?

ANALYZING the Issue

Do you think Ehrenreich's essay accurately describes American family life, or do you think she exaggerates the degree of "spudhood" we have achieved? Back up your answer with personal examples.

---

[1] Artist and filmmaker Andy Warhol (1928–1987) became well-known for his use of popular culture for high art. Warhol's intentional repetitions of images and deliberately boring recording of mundane activities—such as *Empire*, which filmed The Empire State Building for 24 hours from a position across the street—led one critic to announce that "not one ounce of sentiment disturbs the numb silence of these images." (Editor's note)

ANALYZING Connections Between Texts

1. Compare Ehrenreich's conclusions about why we watch TV to Steven
   Reiss's and James Wiltz's analysis in "Why America Loves Reality TV"
   (p. 734). In what ways do the two writers come to similar conclusions?

2. Ehrenreich argues that television has isolated people from each other,
   substituting a virtual reality for the thrills (and dangers) of real life. To
   what degree would Ellen Ullman ("The Museum of Me," p. 455) agree
   with Ehrenreich's points?

3. How does Ralph Morse's photograph "Transfixing Experience" (p. 751)
   illustrate the points Ehrenreich makes in her essay?

WARMING UP: *What is your opinion of "reality shows" on television? If you've seen any episodes of* The Osbournes, *what do you think of the show?*

Ozzy Without Harriet

What *The Osbournes* Tells Us About Drugs

BY JONAH GOLDBERG

JONAH GOLDBERG

Jonah Goldberg's career took off during the Clinton-Lewinsky scandal, when he was a much-sought-after guest on talk shows because of his close connections to the Linda Tripp tapes. Since then, conservative Gen X-er Goldberg has appeared on various television shows and written for a wide variety of publications, ranging from the New Yorker *to* Vanity Fair. *He is currently editor-at-large of* National Review Online.

Toward the end of the Clinton administration, pundits got themselves into a tizzy over the fact that the U.S. government was giving what amounted to tax write-offs to television networks for incorporating anti-drug messages into their programming. The policy died at the hands of the hypocritical media establishment, which has no problem with the government forcing tobacco companies to fund multimillion-dollar ad campaigns against their own legal products, but sees, in the words of the New York Times, "the possibility of censorship and state-sponsored propaganda" in an anti-drug scene in a drama about an emergency room.

Such absurdity only highlights the bizarre state of the drug war. Whether you are for or against drug legalization, it's impossible to dispute that the public debate is deadlocked. On one side, zero-tolerance drug warriors like drug czar John P. Walters insist that even marijuana is a "pernicious" drug closely associated with violence, addiction, and death. On the other side is a fractious coalition including drug boosters, libertarians, conservatives, and people who have simply had enough of the drug war's excesses. It's difficult to see how this impasse can be broken.

One man may have shown us the way: Ozzy Osbourne.

The Osbournes, the reality-TV show about the 53-year-old former lead singer of the metal band Black Sabbath and his dysfunctional family, is an unprecedented hit. It receives the highest ratings in MTV's history. More people watch it than Meet the Press or the Sopranos.

If the policy of tax write-offs for anti-drug messages were still in effect, MTV   5
would be in the black for the year thanks to *The Osbournes*. Never in history has television delivered such a relentlessly compelling anti-drug message week after week. Ozzy, who spent much of his life on drugs and alcohol, is a complete and total mess. Without changing a single thing about himself, he could ease into the crowds of homeless wastoids on any Skid Row in America and ask passersby for a quarter. He can barely speak. Virtually every sentence comes out of him as if he'd been shot up with Novocaine. Indeed, he's so unintelligible that various reviews of the show quote the same lines of Osbourne's dialogue differently; not even journalists with a videotape can quite make out what the hell he's saying.

The Osbourne house, a stunningly beautiful manse in Beverly Hills, is a train wreck. With six dogs, a few cats, and a steady traffic of his kids' ne'er-do-well friends, Ozzy's life is near-total chaos. An entire episode of *The Osbournes* was dedicated to the family's collective inability to housetrain its dogs: The house is drenched in dog urine, and the Persian rugs are minefields of canine droppings.

Ozzy and his wife Sharon are only moderately more successful in house-training the plump, self-absorbed kids, who, like Dad, can't go a sentence without cussing (and thus getting bleeped, by MTV). Only two of the three Osbourne kids, Kelly and Jack, appear on camera. The oldest daughter is reportedly mortified and is living in the guesthouse for the duration of the series.

It's not hard to see why. All teenagers are embarrassed about their parents at some point, but *The Osbournes* takes it to the limit: When Kelly sees her mom urinating in a bottle to send a message about drinking in the house, she screams: "She's pissing in the bottle just like she s**t in Dad's bag of weed in Hawaii."

To be sure, part of the appeal of the show is how much it exaggerates the run-of-the-mill conflicts in normal families. Dad tries to lay down the law and the world ignores him. "I feel like I'm invisible here," he complains over breakfast, to which his wife replies, "Oh, shut up!" Osbourne loves his kids unconditionally but finds them incomprehensible. "I love you all," he tells his son. "I love you more than life itself, but you're all [bleeping] mad." Ozzy can't even figure out the remote control. "What the [bleep] am I doing? Can't get this [bleeping] television to work! I'm [bleeping] stuck on the Weather Channel!" Panicked, he yells, "I press this one button and the [bleeping] shower starts. Where the [bleep] am I? It's a [bleeping] nightmare! Nightmare in Beverly Hills!"

Ultimately, the man who famously bit the head off a live bat and urinated on   10
the Alamo just wants a normal, peaceful life, but he's at a loss about how to

get one. When the neighbors make too much noise, his wife chucks a rotten ham into their yard and Ozzy follows suit with a log. Afterwards, Mr. and Mrs. Osbourne wax nostalgic about their former (and favorite) neighbor, Pat Boone. "He was just the best person ever to live next door to," says the Missus. "He was such a lovely man."

But the reason the show has such a cartoonish hilarity to it (more than a few commentators have called it a real-world Simpsons) is that Osbourne is such a physical and psychological mess. During a recent interview for the British magazine *Loaded*, Osbourne was asked about reports that he'd broken his leg recently but didn't notice. "The truth of the matter is," Osbourne replied, "I'm f***ing crazy. Seriously. I'm mentally unbalanced. I've done so many drugs that I've f***ed up my brain somewhere." Asked if he feels lucky to be alive, Osbourne replied, "Lucky? Well, I ain't f***ing clever, that's for sure. Everybody says: 'Ozzy, you're a legend.' But behind the facade is a sad, lonely, wet fart of a person."

This comes through in every episode: His debauchery makes him pathetic, though endearingly so. "I don't think his fans have any illusions," Doc Coyle, lead guitarist of the metal band God Forbid, explained to the New York Times. "Everybody knows his brain is fried." In a sense, MTV is paying some small penance for the damage it has done to the culture. For years the network glorified the rocker lifestyle without paying much heed to its consequence. For example, Madonna's sluttiness was celebrated as if there were no downside to it. While the lady has the financial resources to compensate for her lifestyle (she brags, for instance, that she's never changed her children's diapers), no amount of money can unscramble your brain. Ozzy may be a sympathetic figure, but even a would-be rock star would hesitate to be in his shoes.

But while Ozzy is a useful cautionary tale against drug abuse, the success of *The Osbournes* should also teach a thing or two to the drug warriors. Drugs, like it or not, are part of the culture; law enforcement alone is inadequate to either their regulation or their eradication. Yes, cigarette smoking is on the wane, in part because of some draconian measures taken by an overzealous government. But smoking's real defeat has come at the hands of a cultural transformation. Similarly, laughing at, and hence ridiculing, drug use is far more useful than one more Eliot Ness lecture about, say, the connection of pot to the war on terrorism.

The same lesson was on view in last summer's surprise hit song, "Because I Got High," by a fellow named Afroman. The whole song was a hilarious send-up of pot-heads: "I was gonna go to court before I got high, I was gonna pay my child support but then I got high, they took my whole paycheck and I know why—'cause I got high, 'cause I got high, 'cause I got high. I messed up my entire life because I got high, I lost my kids and wife because I got high, now I'm sleeping on the sidewalk and I know why—'cause I got high, 'cause I got high."

Unfortunately, some folks who think drugs are never a laughing matter didn't   15
think the song was so funny. When MTV initially refused to show the song's
video, because it depicted people smoking marijuana, The Weekly Standard—
a zealous supporter of John Walters—noted in an earnest finger-wag: "It's a pity
that the most humorous pop song in recent years is about getting high, but [we
are] pleased to find MTV for once on the right side of the culture war."

Actually, it was great news that the most humorous pop song in recent
memory was about how stupid it is to get high, or at least too high. Similarly,
it's even better news that the most popular show in MTV history makes fun of
drug use and, finally, puts MTV on the right side of the culture war.

ANALYZING What the Writer Says

1. How is Ozzy Osbourne "a useful cautionary tale against drug abuse"?
2. What two camps in the current drug war does Goldberg identify? What is
   notable, according to Goldberg, about those who support drug legalization?
3. How might Ozzy Osbourne be able to break down the "impasse" of the two sides?
4. What do you think Goldberg's views are toward drugs and U.S. drug policy?
5. What does Goldberg see as a more useful approach to the drug war than the
   current one?

ANALYZING How the Writer Says It

1. What is the effect of Goldberg's third paragraph?
2. Identify instances of irony in Goldberg's piece. How does the irony contribute
   to the argument he's making?
3. Goldberg quotes extensively from The Osbournes, including several bleeped-out
   obscenities. Why does Goldberg use so many quotes, and what is the effect of
   seeing (the representation of) so many bleeped-out words and phrases?

ANALYZING the Issue

1. Do you agree with the zero-tolerance approach to drugs? Why or why not?
2. Consider the pros and cons of legalizing drugs. Why is or isn't MTV an effective venue for getting across messages about drugs?

ANALYZING Connections Between Texts

1. How would Steven Reiss and James Wiltz ("Why America Loves Reality TV,"
   p. 734) explain America's fascination with the reality series The Osbournes? How
   would it differ from Goldberg's explanation?

2. Scott Russell Sanders's "Under the Influence" (p. 295) shows the debilitating consequences of substance abuse. In what way does *The Osbournes* (according to Goldberg) deliver the same message? Or does it?

3. Consider Eugene Richards's "Crack for Sale" (p. 328) and Goldberg's example of *The Osbournes*. Which do you consider a better "cautionary tale against drug abuse"? Why?

WARMING UP: *Think about a female athlete who has recently made headlines. Have you noticed a difference in the way the sports media covers women and men?*

Life in the 90's

BY TERRY GOLWAY

TERRY GOLWAY

In the wake of the U.S. women's soccer team's 1999 World Cup championship, Terry Golway analyzes the status of women in sports. "As long as the media call women athletes sweethearts," she muses, "we'll still be stuck in the past."

The memorable victory of the U.S. women's soccer team in this year's World Cup inspired lots of celebratory assertions that women athletes finally have taken their rightful place in the world of sports. The data by which success is measured certainly spoke of high achievement: More than 90,000 people were on hand in the Rose Bowl for the championship game; millions more Americans, more than watched the men's World Cup final in 1996, caught the game on national television.

An astounding success, no? A sure sign that America accepts the notion of fit, muscled women engaging in sports previously thought of as bastions of masculinity, right?

So it seemed, at least at first. But as soon as the media started referring to the team as "America's sweethearts," it was clear that women athletes still have long way to go.

The grouchy dogma of the politically correct has spoiled a fair amount of plain old fun in recent years. So perhaps some will find it tiresome when spoilsports point out that for all the superficial celebration of America's newest sport stars, the media still can't avoid falling back into sexist stereotypes. Tiresome or not, the fact remains. Apparently editors can't help themselves.

Successful male athletes are lauded as heroes. 5 Remember those scrappy, over-achieving ice hockey players at the 1980 Winter Olympics? Successful female athletes, on the other hand, are patronized as sweethearts. This was to be expected back in the less enlightened days when Peggy Fleming won her gold medal in figure skating or when Cathy Rigby ruled the world of gymnastics. Women athletes were still something of a novelty as recently as a quarter-century ago. Sure, they could be figure skaters and gymnasts and tennis players, but basketball players? Softball players? Soccer players? Only if they attended forward-thinking Catholic schools (Immaculata College comes to mind) that were the incubators of modern women's sports.

Nowadays, of course, women are playing basketball, soccer, baseball and ice hockey. And, in a sign that not all change is for the better, there are even some women boxers (perhaps they couldn't quite master the art of the slapshot and turned to the next best thing). They have wonderful skills, great energy, and are marvels of physical fitness, with arms that would put many a male weekend warrior to shame.

Sweethearts? Please. Meanwhile, the cover of one national news magazine marked the women's victory with a headline that read: "Girls rule!" The magazine's editors must have been watching another game, for there were no girls running up and down the Rose Bowl playing field. They were women. At least one was a mother. They deserve to be taken seriously as athletes, as adults and, yes, as women.

No doubt some will argue that such complaints not only sound like a petition from a bunch of gender-studies majors, but also show little knowledge of the sport world's casual lingo. The sports pages are populated with young adults playing kids' games, and those adults always have been referred to as if they were children. Thanks to author Roger Kahn, the Brooklyn Dodgers of the 1950's are known as the boys of summer. So, in such parlance, it is no sign of a double standard to refer to the young women on the U.S. soccer team as girls.

That's all true. But still, the "sweetheart" business is a bit too much, and it suggests that female athletes and women in general have their work cut out for them in the coming century. They still are measured in terms of their sexual desirability—otherwise, why not simply call them heroes, or heroines, if you prefer, just like the young men who win our admiration with their skill and determination?

To some extent, the women soccer players have themselves to blame for some of the sexism that seeped into coverage of their victories. They knew they were a photogenic group, which is the politest way I can find of acknowledging that they were a group of very attractive young women. And they were not shy about playing that angle, particularly when David Letterman announced that he was in love with all of them. They sent him a team picture in which they seemed to be wearing only long "Late Night" T-shirts.

That was fun, and perfectly understandable. After all, these women shared with their male counterparts a love for a game that few Americans care about. Any publicity, then, was good publicity. So only a dour cultural critic would have objected to any late-night gimmicks designed to make soccer more popular with those millions of kids who play the game until they're teen-agers and then give it up when they reach adulthood. (The red-blooded American in me wishes to point out that another good way to make soccer more popular would be for players to score a goal every now and again, just to keep fans guessing.)

I'm old enough to remember when public high schools and colleges were just starting to recognize the importance of women's sports. Back then, in the early 1970's, I spent several years covering women's sports because nobody else at my newspaper wanted the assignment. A great deal has changed since those days. Women win athletic scholarships to college now. They can aspire to play professionally or to have careers as coaches, referees and trainers. Women sportswriters were rare 25 years ago; today, they're common, as are women sportscasters. In New York, in fact, a woman is part of the announcing team that covers the Yankees.

That's progress, all right. But as long as the media call women sweethearts, we'll still be stuck in the past.

ANALYZING What the Writer Says

1. Why is Golway upset that the media called the victorious U.S. women's soccer team "America's sweethearts"?
2. What, rather than athletic prowess, is the true measure of success for female athletes, according to Golway?

ANALYZING How the Writer Says It

1. Give examples of where Golway anticipates the arguments of those who would dismiss her point.
2. What does Golway use as an introductory hook?

ANALYZING the Issue

Do you agree with Golway that women athletes are treated differently from their male counterparts by the sports media? Explain.

ANALYZING Connections Between Texts

1. Does Rebecca Mead's treatment of Shaquille O'Neal in "A Man-Child in Lotusland" (p. 717) support or refute Golway's points about the way sports writers report on male and female athletes?
2. In "Everywoman.com" (p. 754), Joan Didion analyzes Martha Stewart's rise to fame and fortune. Do you think Martha Stewart did in business what the women's soccer team did in sports—show that women can compete as equals in a man's world? Are successful businesswomen treated similarly to successful women athletes?
3. How does Annie Leibovitz's photo "Lenda Murray, Ms. Olympia 1990–95" (p. 97) depart from the standard treatment, according to Golway, of female athletic champions? Or does it? Explain.

Miss Brill

BY KATHERINE MANSFIELD

KATHERINE MANSFIELD

Born in New Zealand and raised in a comfortable middle-class family, Katherine Mansfield (1888–1923) often depicts seemingly trivial events in her stories, using them as the landscape against which characters experience extraordinary though subtle moments of transformation.

Although it was so brilliantly fine—the blue sky powdered with gold and great spots of light like white wine splashed over the Jardins Publiques—Miss Brill was glad that she had decided on her fur. The air was motionless, but when you opened your mouth there was just a faint chill, like a chill from a glass of iced water before you sip, and now and again a leaf came drifting—from nowhere, from the sky. Miss Brill put up her hand and touched her fur. Dear little thing! It was nice to feel it again. She had taken it out of its box that afternoon, shaken out the moth-powder, given it a good brush, and rubbed the life back into the dim little eyes. "What has been happening to me?" said the sad little eyes. Oh, how sweet it was to see them snap at her again from the red eiderdown! . . . But the nose, which was of some black composition, wasn't at all firm. It must have had a knock, somehow. Never mind—a little dab of black sealing-wax when the time came—when it was absolutely necessary. . . . Little rogue! Yes, she really felt like that about it. Little rogue biting its tail just by her left ear. She could have taken it off and laid it on her lap and stroked it. She felt a tingling in her hands and arms, but that came from walking, she supposed. And when she breathed, something light and sad—no, not sad, exactly—something gentle seemed to move in her bosom.

There were a number of people out this afternoon, far more than last Sunday. And the band sounded louder and gayer. That was because the Season had begun. For although the band played all the year round on Sundays, out of season it was never the same. It was like some one playing with only the family to listen; it didn't care how it played if there weren't any strangers present. Wasn't the conductor wearing a new coat, too? She was sure it was new. He scraped with his foot and flapped his arms like a rooster about to crow, and the bandsmen sitting in the green rotunda blew out their cheeks and glared at the music. Now there came a little "flutey" bit—very pretty!—a little chain of bright drops. She was sure it would be repeated. It was; she lifted her head and smiled.

Only two people shared her "special" seat: a fine old man in a velvet coat, his hands clasped over a huge carved walking-stick, and a big old woman, sitting upright, with a roll of knitting on her embroidered apron. They did not speak. This was disappointing, for Miss Brill always looked forward to the conversation. She had become really quite expert, she thought, at listening as though she didn't listen, at sitting in other people's lives just for a minute while they talked around her.

She glanced, sideways, at the old couple. Perhaps they would go soon. Last Sunday, too, hadn't been as interesting as usual. An Englishman and his wife, he wearing a dreadful Panama hat and she button boots. And she'd gone on the whole time about how she ought to wear spectacles; she knew she needed them; but that it was no good getting any; they'd be sure to break and they'd never keep on. And he'd been so patient. He'd suggested everything—gold rims, the kind that curved round your ears, little pads inside the bridge. No, nothing would please her. "They'll always be sliding down my nose!" Miss Brill had wanted to shake her.

The old people sat on the bench, still as statues. Never mind, there was 5 always the crowd to watch. To and fro, in front of the flower-beds and the band rotunda, the couples and groups paraded, stopped to talk, to greet, to buy a handful of flowers from the old beggar who had his tray fixed to the railings. Little children ran among them, swooping and laughing; little boys with big white silk bows under their chins, little girls, little French dolls, dressed up in velvet and lace. And sometimes a tiny staggerer came suddenly rocking into the open from under the trees, stopped, stared, as suddenly sat down "flop," until its small high-stepping mother, like a young hen, rushed scolding to its rescue. Other people sat on the benches and green chairs, but they were nearly always the same, Sunday after Sunday, and—Miss Brill had often noticed—there was something funny about nearly all of them. They were odd, silent, nearly all old, and from the way they stared they looked as though they'd just come from dark little rooms or even—even cupboards!

Behind the rotunda the slender trees with yellow leaves down drooping, and through them just a line of sea, and beyond the blue sky with gold-veined clouds.

Tum-tum-tum tiddle-um! tiddle-um! tum tiddley-um tum ta! blew the band.

Two young girls in red came by and two young soldiers in blue met them, and they laughed and paired and went off arm-in-arm. Two peasant women with funny straw hats passed, gravely, leading beautiful smoke-colored donkeys. A cold, pale nun hurried by. A beautiful woman came along and dropped her bunch of violets, and a little boy ran after to hand them to her, and she took them and threw them away as if they'd been poisoned. Dear me! Miss Brill didn't know whether to admire that or not! And now an ermine toque and a gentleman in grey met just in front of her. He was tall, stiff, dignified, and she was wearing the ermine toque she'd bought when her hair was yellow. Now everything, her hair, her face, even her eyes, was the same color as the shabby ermine, and her hand, in its cleaned glove, lifted to dab her lips, was a tiny yellowish paw. Oh, she was so pleased to see him—delighted! She rather thought they were going to meet that afternoon. She described where she'd been—everywhere, here, there, along by the sea. The day was so charming—didn't he agree? And wouldn't he, perhaps? . . . But he shook his head, lighted a cigarette, slowly breathed a great deep puff into her face, and, even while she was still talking and laughing, flicked the match away and walked on. The ermine toque was alone; she smiled more brightly than ever. But even the band seemed to know what she was feeling and played more softly, played tenderly, and the drum beat, "The Brute! The Brute!" over and over. What would she do? What was going to happen now? But as Miss Brill wondered, the ermine toque turned, raised her hand as though she'd seen some one else, much nicer, just over there, and pattered away. And the band changed again and played more quickly, more gaily than ever, and the old couple on Miss Brill's seat got up and marched away, and such a funny old man with long whiskers hobbled along in time to the music and was nearly knocked over by four girls walking abreast.

Oh, how fascinating it was! How she enjoyed it! How she loved sitting here, watching it all! It was like a play. It was exactly like a play. Who could believe the sky at the back wasn't painted? But it wasn't till a little brown dog trotted on solemn and then slowly trotted off, like a little "theatre" dog, a little dog that had been drugged, that Miss Brill discovered what it was that made it so exciting. They were all on the stage. They weren't only the audience, not only looking on; they were acting. Even she had a part and came every Sunday. No doubt somebody would have noticed if she hadn't been there; she was part of the performance after all. How strange she'd never thought of it like that before! And yet it explained why she made such a point of starting from home at just the same time each week—so as not to be late for the performance—and it also explained why she had quite a queer, shy feeling at telling her English pupils how she spent her Sunday afternoons. No wonder! Miss Brill nearly laughed out loud. She was on the stage. She thought of the old invalid gentleman to whom she read the newspaper four afternoons a week while he slept in the garden. She had got quite used to the frail head on the cotton pillow, the hollowed eyes, the open mouth, and the high pinched nose. If he'd been dead she mightn't have noticed for weeks; she wouldn't have minded.

But suddenly he knew he was having the paper read to him by an actress! "An actress!" The old head lifted; two points of light quivered in the old eyes. "An actress—are ye?" And Miss Brill smoothed the newspaper as though it were the manuscript of her part and said gently: "Yes, I have been an actress for a long time."

The band had been having a rest. Now they started again. And what they played was warm, sunny, yet there was just a faint chill—a something, what was it?—not sadness—no, not sadness—a something that made you want to sing. The tune lifted, the light shone; and it seemed to Miss Brill that in another moment all of them, all the whole company, would begin singing. The young ones, the laughing ones who were moving together, they would begin, and the men's voices, very resolute and brave, would join them. And then she too, she too, and the others on the benches—they would come in with a kind of accompaniment—something low, that scarcely rose or fell, something so beautiful—moving. . . . And Miss Brill's eyes filled with tears and she looked smiling at all the other members of the company. Yes, we understand, we understand, she thought—though what they understood she didn't know.

Just at that moment a boy and a girl came and sat down where the old couple had been. They were beautifully dressed; they were in love. The hero and heroine, of course, just arrived from his father's yacht. And still soundlessly singing, still with that trembling smile, Miss Brill prepared to listen.

"No, not now," said the girl. "Not here, I can't."

"But why? Because of that stupid old thing at the end there?" asked the boy. "Why does she come here at all—who wants her? Why doesn't she keep her silly old mug at home?"

"It's her fu-fur which is so funny," giggled the girl. "It's exactly like a fried whiting."

"Ah, be off with you!" said the boy in an angry whisper. Then: "Tell me, ma petite chère——"

"No, not here," said the girl. "Not *yet*."

On her way home she usually bought a slice of honey-cake at the baker's. It was her Sunday treat. Sometimes there was an almond in her slice, sometimes not. It made a great difference. If there was an almond it was like carrying home a tiny present—a surprise—something that might very well not have been there. She hurried on the almond Sundays and struck the match for the kettle in quite a dashing way.

But today she passed the baker's by, climbed the stairs, went into the little dark room—her room like a cupboard—and sat down on the red eiderdown. She sat there for a long time. The box that the fur came out of was on the bed. She unclasped the necklet quickly; quickly, without looking, laid it aside. But when she put the lid on she thought she heard something crying.

ANALYZING What the Writer Says

1. Describe the central character, looking carefully at her attitudes and her motivations.

2. Describe Miss Brill's fur. What is its function in the story?

3. How does Miss Brill relate to the other characters in the story? Why are they important to her?

4. Why is the idea of being an actress appealing to Miss Brill? Is her revelation ironic? Explain.

5. Discuss Miss Brill as both spectator and spectacle.

6. What makes the comments and actions of the young couple that come and sit beside Miss Brill particularly poignant?

ANALYZING How the Writer Says It

1. The "faint chill" mentioned in the story's opening paragraph is repeated later in the story. What is the significance of the detail as it is used in the story?

2. Point to as many instances of irony as you can find in this story.

ANALYZING the Issue

1. Is Mansfield's Miss Brill a sympathetic character, one to be commended for constructing a life for herself that defies loneliness? Is she a self-actualized figure? Or is she merely a spectator, a figure sidelined by her lack of self-awareness? Explain your answer.

2. Who is to blame for the deflation of Miss Brill's ego?

ANALYZING Connections Between Texts

1. What does Miss Brill have in common with the audiences Steven Reiss and James Wiltz analyze in "Why America Loves Reality TV" (p. 734)?

2. What is the difference between Annie Dillard's description of her experience as outsider and participant in "Singing with the Fundamentalists" (p. 470) and the main character's experience in "Miss Brill."

3. How does Elliott Erwitt's photo "Spectator" (p. 750) echo the central theme in "Miss Brill"?

WARMING UP: *Who is your favorite athlete? What personality traits are particularly appealing to you?*

A Man-Child in Lotusland

BY REBECCA MEAD

REBECCA MEAD

In a profile of basketball superstar Shaquille O'Neal, Rebecca Mead, a staff writer at the New Yorker, *reveals the child inside the giant. The essay appeared in the* New Yorker *on May 20, 2002.*

Shaquille O'Neal, the Los Angeles Lakers center, lives, during the basketball season, in a large cream-colored mansion at the end of a leafy cul-de-sac in Beverly Hills. The exterior of O'Neal's house is discreetly opulent, and it is not until you approach the double front doors that you notice, etched in the glass, two large Superman symbols. The first superhero that O'Neal ever felt an affinity with was the Incredible Hulk, because, as he told me recently, "he was big and green." The young O'Neal knew what it was to be a physical oddity; when he was five years old, his mother was obliged to carry her son's birth certificate with her around their home town of Newark, New Jersey, to prove to bus drivers that he was not eight or nine. Somewhere around the age of seven, O'Neal switched over to Superman, and now, at the age of thirty, his allegiance is steady.

Today, O'Neal, who is seven feet one, has a Superman "S" tattooed on his left biceps, and when he slams the ball into the basket with a particularly incontrovertible defiance at the Staples Center, the Lakers' home court, the Superman theme is played over the loudspeakers. The Superman logo is engraved in the headlights of his silver Mercedes, one of about fifteen cars and trucks he owns. More than five hundred framed Superman comic-book covers hang on the wall of a corridor in his off-season house, in Orlando, where he also has a vintage Superman pinball machine. For a while, he had a Superman bedspread on his bed. O'Neal considers it lucky that he shares a first initial with Superman. "The only reason I call myself Superman is that it starts with 'S,'" he says. "If my name was Tim, I couldn't be Superman. It wouldn't look right."

One of O'Neal's grandmothers died recently, and at her funeral he contemplated the design of his own final resting place. "I started to think about what my mausoleum would look like, and I thought it should be all marble, with Superman logos everywhere," he told me. "There would be stadium seating, and only my family would have the key, and they would be able to go in there and sit down, like in a little apartment. My grave would be right there, and there would be a TV showing, like, an hour-long video of who I was."

O'Neal considers himself to have a dual nature. "Shaquille is corporate, nice-looking, soft-spoken, wears suits, and is very cordial to people, whereas Shaq is the dominant athlete who is the two-time champion," he told me. "They are the same person, but it's kind of like Clark Kent and Superman. During the day, I am Shaquille, and at night I am Shaq." O'Neal also has a nemesis, an evil twin, whom he calls Elliuqahs Laeno. "That's my name spelled backward," he said. "That's the person that I am not allowed to be because of my status. He does what a normal young rich guy would do—party, hang out, use bad language. He stays out all night, tries to practice the next day, isn't focussed. That is him. He's dead, though. I killed him off."

We were talking in a back office at the Lakers' training facility, in El Segundo, a suburb of Los Angeles, after O'Neal had come off the court from an afternoon practice. His skin was tide-marked with drying sweat, and he sat with his legs spread wide, like those riders on the New York subway who laugh in the face of the one-man-one-seat convention. O'Neal, who weighs somewhere around three hundred and forty pounds, would need at least three seats, and perhaps four. His identification with Superman is based on his sense of himself as a crusading force for good—good being, for the moment, the continued success of the Los Angeles Lakers, who are currently in the N.B.A. play-offs—but it is also grounded in a sense of physical supremacy.

O'Neal is one of the largest men alive. He wears size-22 basketball shoes, which are made for him by a company called Starter; they are all white and finished with a shiny gloss, reminiscent, in their sheen and size, of the hull of a luxury yacht. (When the Lakers' equipment manager, a rotund man in the mid-five-foot range named Rudy Garciduenas, carries the shoes into the locker room before a game, he cradles them in gentle arms, as if he were the nursemaid of Otus and Ephialtes, the twin giant sons of Poseidon.) O'Neal's cars must have their interiors ripped out and their seats moved back ten inches before he is able to drive them. (His most recent acquisition is a Ferrari Spider convertible, a birthday gift from his father that was, as he pointed out to reporters in the Lakers' locker room one night, bought with his own earnings. O'Neal's Spider has its top down permanently, since he's too big for the convertible to convert.) O'Neal's pants have an outside seam of four feet six and a half inches. He has never encountered a hotel-room showerhead that was high enough for him to stand under, an inconvenience for a man who spends months at a time on the road. When he speaks on a cell phone, he holds it in front of his mouth and talks into it as if it were a walkie-talkie, and then swivels it up to his ear to listen, as if the phone were a tiny planet making a quarter orbit around the sun of his enormous head.

O'Neal isn't the tallest player in the N.B.A.—that's Shawn Bradley, of the Dallas Mavericks, who is seven feet six—and many teams have at least one seven-footer. But Shawn Bradley is seventy-odd pounds lighter than O'Neal, and when they are on the court together it looks as if Bradley would be well advised to abandon basketball and return to his former calling, as a Mormon missionary. O'Neal is daunting even to the most accomplished of seven-footers, like Dikembe Mutombo, of the Philadelphia 76ers, who is an inch taller than O'Neal but, at two hundred and sixty-five pounds, a bantamweight by comparison. When the 76ers met the Lakers in last year's N.B.A. Finals, Mutombo and O'Neal clashed repeatedly under the boards, with Mutombo bouncing off O'Neal's body—the hulking, barging shoulder, the prodigious posterior backing into implacable reverse.

Many centers move like articulated trucks on a highway filled with Mercedes SLs—they can't weave from lane to lane or make sharp turns or suddenly accelerate. But O'Neal's physical power is augmented by an unlikely agility: he is able to jump and loft his massive body above the rim, and his recovery when he hits the ground is such that should he miss the basket on the first try he can go up again, just as high and just as quickly, grab the ball, feint to fool the three defenders leaping around him, and hit his mark. On the official play-by-play reports that are given to reporters covering the game, O'Neal's performance is condensed into a code: "MISS O'Neal Lay-up/O'Neal REBOUND/ MISS O'Neal Lay-up/O'Neal REBOUND/O'Neal Slam Dunk"—all happening within the space of seven seconds. O'Neal was the second-best scorer in the league this season, with 27.2 points per game, after Philadelphia's Allen Iverson, who scored an average of 31.4. And he has been the N.B.A. Finals' Most Valuable Player for the past two years.

O'Neal's body isn't as cut as he'd like it to be, and friends say that what he really wants is a six-pack stomach, but he takes pride in his solid muscularity. At one point while we were talking, he rose from his chair, hoisted up his yellow No. 34 jersey, and invited me to pinch his fat. A brief investigation revealed that there wasn't any fat to pinch—though there was an acreage of belly, tattooed just above the navel with "LIL Warrior"; and, glinting on the higher reaches of his torso, a gold bar piercing a nipple. "Sixteen per cent body fat, baby," O'Neal said.

* * *

It is perhaps inevitable that O'Neal is routinely described as having a huge per-   10
sonality, although his personality is probably the most ordinary-sized thing
about him. Even when he is silent in the presence of reporters, which he often
is, or when his public comments are restricted to mumbles, his importance on
the court means that his pronouncements are invested with extra significance.
When O'Neal does talk to reporters, after a game, they swarm around him,
pointing miniature tape recorders up over their heads, toward his mouth. His
voice can be so low that you don't know what he's said until you bring the tape
recorder back down to earth and play the tape.

O'Neal's on-court persona is ferocious, and his comments about his opponents are usually of the standard aggressive-athlete variety. "They ought to
make those lazy-ass millionaires play some defense," he told me one day.
O'Neal aspires to a career in law enforcement after he retires from basketball,
and his profile as a player is that of a crushing, point-scoring bad cop, with no
good cops in sight. "He likes to enforce things," Herb More, one of O'Neal's
high-school coaches, says. But his disposition is fundamentally sunny, and if
his sense of humor runs to the excruciatingly broad—he derives great pleasure from picking up a defenseless member of the Lakers' staff, or a reporter,
and manhandling him like a burly father with a squealing three-year-old—it is
deeply felt.

These characteristics, along with his enthusiastic if less than triumphant
excursions into the territories of rap music and movie acting, have made him
a central figure in the popular culture. His affability is currently being har-
nessed to promote Burger King, Nestlé Crunch, and Swatch; and his endorsements have been estimated to earn him between eight and ten million dollars
a year. He offers a combination of cartoonish playfulness and wholesome values. He has never taken drugs, unless you count a brief dalliance with creatine
and androstenedione, the legal bodybuilding supplements. He never drinks in
public, unless it's a soda he's endorsing. He is well known for his rapport with
children, and he does a lot of charity work with them. Every Christmas, he
dresses up in a Santa suit and hands out gifts in an event known as Shaq-A-
Claus, and he has granted twelve wishes through the Make-A-Wish Foundation over the past two years. He's not the kind of player you'd expect to see
slapped with a paternity suit. (O'Neal has four children: two with his girlfriend
of three years, Shaunie Nelson, one daughter from a previous relationship,
and a son of Shaunie's whom O'Neal considers his own.) Nor is he likely to
participate in any of those activities that advertisers most fear, and be charged
with D.U.I., like Rod Strickland, who plays for the Miami Heat, or, like the former New Jersey Net Jayson Williams, have a chauffeur found shot to death in
his bedroom.

O'Neal has had some misadventures in marketing, largely because he and
his former agent Leonard Armato tried in the late nineties to sell Shaq as an

independent brand, something that had never been done by a basketball player. They launched an online clothing-and-shoe company, Dunk.net, which
never took off and went bust after the dot-com crash; another clothing line,
called TWIsM.—"The world is mine," O'Neal's personal motto—was similarly unsuccessful. O'Neal and Armato parted ways last year, and O'Neal replaced
him with Perry Rogers, a sports marketer who built his career on selling Andre
Agassi; Mike Parris, O'Neal's uncle and a former cop, has become O'Neal's
manager. "Shaq is a brand, and we are trying to match him up with companies
that match his personality and calibre as an athlete," Parris explained to me.
(This realignment has yet to be entirely accomplished—O'Neal has until
recently been associated with a health-club company called ZNetix, whose
founder was accused of bilking investors of millions of dollars.)

Apart from Michael Jordan, who has made more than four hundred and
twenty-five million dollars from the likes of Nike and Gatorade during the
course of his career, the only other player whose advertising deals rival
O'Neal's is Kobe Bryant, his Lakers teammate. Unlike some Lakers before
him, such as Kareem Abdul-Jabbar, O'Neal thoroughly enjoys being a celebrity. He considers it his duty to present a friendly face in public, even on occasions when he would prefer not to be badgered by autograph hunters, and he
accepts the inevitability of being recognized. O'Neal was startled to discover,
after being stranded on September 11th in Baton Rouge for several days, that
he was expected to show ID when boarding the charter plane he'd hired. "I'm
not prejudiced, but those pilots had better have some ID," he told a friend.

O'Neal's public persona could not be more different from that of Jordan,   15
who was the dominant force in basketball throughout most of the late eighties
and the nineties, and is still the world's best-known athlete. Jordan, like the
style of basketball he perfected, was transcendent. His athleticism resembled
aeronautics, and he regularly evoked celestial comparisons: Larry Bird once
described him as "God disguised as Michael Jordan." O'Neal, by contrast, is
solidly earth-bound. (On the court, Kobe Bryant is Ariel to O'Neal's Caliban.)
Michael Jordan was a wise figure who invited aspiration: the elegant Nike
commercials that urged fans to Be Like Mike encouraged an identification
with his prowess, even as they celebrated his superlative capacities.

Being Like Shaq is demonstrably impossible, and more or less unimaginable. Instead, O'Neal with his taste for souped-up cars, and his appetite
for dumb jokes, and his tendency toward braggadocio, looks like a regular
American guy, albeit a drastically oversized one. Shaq appears to want to Be
Like Us.

The growth of professional basketball over the past twenty-odd years from a relatively minor spectator sport to a mass-cultural phenomenon is an example of
the way in which all of American culture is increasingly geared to the tastes of
teen-age boys. Marketers hold that adolescent boys, with their swiftly changing

appetites and their enormous buying power, are the most difficult and most critical consumers to reach. Basketball is a perfect game for teen-agers: it's fast, it's energetic, it requires little equipment, and it can be practiced in driveways and on the playground without so much as an opponent; and it has been appropriated by products that have nothing to do with sports—Coke, milk—as an excellent way to reach that desired demographic. Teen boys function, in turn, as cultural emissaries to the global population: Nikes aren't cool all over the world because Vince Carter wears them but because cool American teen-agers wear them.

Basketball itself is marketed with teen tastes in mind. The theatre of a Lakers game has an adolescent-boy aesthetic: goofy and overheated. There are the whirling spotlights when the players emerge from the locker room, high-fiving; the snippets of roaring rap music and of the teen-boy anthem "We Will Rock You," by Queen; the absurd contests held between quarters, in which competitors do things like play musical chairs on a set of huge inflatable seats. Should all this hilarity be inadequate to the task of holding a young man's interest, there is always the Laker Girls.

The prevalence of teen-boy tastes in American culture is something that suits Shaquille O'Neal since those are also his tastes. There are, of course, certain adult dimensions to his life. He talks of marrying Shaunie—she wears a big diamond engagement ring—although he says he's not quite ready yet. And he speaks often of his responsibilities and the fact that he doesn't go clubbing the way he used to. "When I was by myself, the only people I had to take care of were my parents," he says. "But then I had my first child and I had to slow down; and now I've got four." But in many ways his life style is a thirteen-year-old's fantasy existence. O'Neal has surrounded himself with cousins from Newark and old friends from high school, who share his interests in goofing off, breaking stuff, making noise, shooting guns, and driving a wide range of motorized vehicles, which include customized Harley-Davidsons and, on the lake at his house in Orlando, a fleet of Jet Skis.

O'Neal has installed one of his high-school buddies, Joe Cavallero, to look after the Orlando house, which also appears to mean wreaking measured destruction. "We have food fights, where Thomas, the chef, will come in from the grocery store with all these things, and Shaquille will break a whole water-melon over my head, and I'll hit him with a pudding cake," Cavallero told me. "Shaquille doesn't really have many books, but he has got a big video collection: the whole Little Rascals series, and every kung-fu thing you can think of, and sometimes we play-fight like that, too. And every night he'll get on his d.j. deck and play for a couple of hours, and he'll turn that thing up as loud as it will go, and everything in his house is marble, so it echoes through the whole house. And Shaquille likes to wake me up with a pillow smash to the face. You know how you get to being sound asleep, and someone smashes you in the face with a pillow? It is so funny."

The house in Los Angeles is home not only to Shaunie and the children but to Thomas Gosney, Shaq's chef, factotum, and close friend, whose loyalty is such that he responds to questions about O'Neal in the first-person plural: when I asked Gosney whether O'Neal was ever going to get around to marrying Shaunie, he said, "I think we will, but I think we need to get out of the N.B.A. first." In addition to feeding O'Neal lots of fruits and vegetables and preventing him from indulging his particular culinary vice of eating sandwiches late at night, Gosney provides round-the-clock companionship if necessary. "The night before that first championship that we won, O'Neal was up all night," Gosney said. "He was stressing out, and I knew he needed a release. He came in and found me and said, 'Are you sleeping?' So we got up, and we rode go-carts, and then we rode motorcycles. He needed to get up and do these things in the middle of the night." O'Neal depends on his friends not just for entertainment but for home management, and Gosney told me, "Before Shaunie came and lived with us, I would say that I was his wife, except for the sex. Shaquille has said to me, 'If you were a girl, I don't know what I would do.'"

O'Neal's size gives him a storybook quality that also exaggerates the childish aspect of his nature. In myth, giants are primordial creatures, who are often beloved for their lumbering doltishness. O'Neal is much sharper than the typical fairy-tale giant, but the simplicity of his tastes and of his manner of expression has currency in a popular culture where childishness is valued above adult sophistication. "Kids like me because they see themselves in me," he said. "I don't speak with a Harvard-type vocabulary. I only wear suits when I need to. I don't talk about stuff I haven't gone through. I am just me. They like rims; I like rims. They like rap music; I like rap music. They like platinum; I like platinum."

A few years ago, O'Neal took up hunting, and one of his favorite activities is disappearing for the day into a game preserve in Florida with a few friends and a few guns. He is a bit defensive about this hobby. "It's not like I'm just sneaking around and killing animals. I am a law-abiding citizen," he told me. "What I like about it, first, is looking at the animals, and then I like getting the big ones. You can be out there all day, walking around, looking at leaves, looking at grass, looking at footprints." Off the marble entrance hall of O'Neal's house in Beverly Hills, there is a carpeted room, filled with his hunting trophies: mounted heads of antlered creatures cover the walls and, because the walls are filled, cover the floor, too, their noses pointing quirkily up at the high ceiling. There are a few animals that O'Neal bought already stuffed: a polar bear, and a taxidermic tableau of a lion attacking a zebra. The scent of the room is a pungent mixture of the chemical and the irredeemably organic, and the door is usually kept closed, like Bluebeard's bloody chamber.

A few days after O'Neal turned thirty, in March, he threw a party for himself at his house for a couple of hundred friends, family members, and business associates. An archway of red balloons had been set up at the foot of the drive-way, which was covered with a red carpet upon which Superman logos were projected in spinning light. The red carpet led into a large tent behind the house, above the tennis court, which was decorated with long tubular balloons in red and yellow and blue, twisted together like something from a medical diagram of the lymphatic system.

Large Superman logos hung from the tent's ceiling, and on either side of a d.j. deck were two telephone booths with Superman logos on them. There were buffet tables piled with food: steaming lobster tails and a pyramid of shrimp; a birthday cake featuring a cardboard image of O'Neal in full Superman attire, swooping up through a basketball hoop. Guests could help themselves to Häagen-Dazs from a refrigerated cart, and order drinks from bars sponsored by Red Bull and E & J cognac. A cigar company had set up a table arrayed with different kinds of cigars, each of them bearing a paper ring printed with the words "Happy 30th Shaq." 25

O'Neal, who had a cigar clamped in his mouth, wore a gray leather suit with a three-quarter-length jacket. (The suit required a hundred and fifty square feet of leather, the skins of about eighteen lambs.) He greeted his guests—his Lakers teammate Rick Fox and Fox's wife, the actress Vanessa Williams; Ray Lewis, the Baltimore Ravens linebacker; the actor Tom Arnold, who lives across the street; the rap musicians Lord Tariq and Peter Gunz; and any number of Shaq service-industry members, including his masseur and the guy who installed the audio and video equipment in his house—with unflagging enthusiasm, hugging the men, bending down low to kiss the women's cheeks. Guests wandered in and out of the house, past a triangular swimming pool on the patio, in which a surfboard decorated with an image of O'Neal's Lakers jersey floated, and into the kitchen, which was filled with gifts that he'd received: sugar cookies, a big toy truck, a box from the Sharper Image. On the walls of the marble hallway leading out of the kitchen, there was bad basketball art—a painting of tall figures leaping around a basket, and another of an athlete's back as he holds a basketball on his shoulders, Atlas-like. There were photographs of O'Neal's children, and a framed clipping from the Star bearing the headline "CAUGHT! SHAQ DATING UP A STORM WITH HALLE BERRY."

The living room, which has a view of the San Fernando Valley, is flanked by two fish tanks made from curving glass. The tanks are filled with brightly colored exotic fish, swimming flickeringly, and at one point in the evening O'Neal, coming into the house, found a few guests standing mesmerized in front of the tanks. He went behind a staircase that led off the hallway, where, hidden from view was a smaller tank, filled with goldfish. He scooped into the goldfish tank with a net and filled a glass with slippery orange bodies. Then he climbed up a stepladder that was set along side one of the big tanks, lifted its lid, and dumped in the goldfish. The angel fish and clown fish and puffer fish went wild, darting to swallow the flailing goldfish whole. A ruthless-looking

barracuda snapped one up, and then went for the rebound and snared another. O'Neal looked extremely satisfied with the whole scene. "I love the sport of
hunting," he said.

The host spent most of the night bopping among a crowd of his friends in
the middle of the dance floor, head and shoulders and most of a torso above
everyone around him. Halfway through the evening, the music was turned
down, and O'Neal was summoned to the stage, where he sat in a chair and,
along with everyone else, watched a video tribute devoted to the greatness of
Shaq. There was O'Neal playing basketball at Louisiana State University, a
spindly version of himself, breaking the hoop from the backboard. There was
home-video footage of him on a beach, and playing with his kids, and dancing—to one Dr. Dre tune, he dropped to his knees, kicked his legs in the air
behind him, and humped the carpet. There were also innumerable shots of
him mooning the camera. The final image was of O'Neal, shirtless and sweaty,
at the turntables; he unzipped his pants, shifted them gradually down his
ample hips, hoisted his underwear up above his waist, and finally turned
around and dropped his pants to show the camera his glistening rear. After the
show was over, O'Neal stood up, unzipped his fly, zipped it up again, and said,
"I never knew I had such a good ass until I saw that film. Damn, I'm sexy."

The reason O'Neal dedicated himself to the pursuit of excellence in basketball,
he says, was to impress girls. "I was always the class clown, and always wanted everybody to like me," he told me recently. "Everyone else had a girlfriend,
and how come I couldn't have a girlfriend?" We were at the Mondrian Hotel,
in Los Angeles, where he was being photographed by ESPN while perched on
top of a six-foot-tall flowerpot, a design feature of the hotel's pool area. When
we sat down at a table to talk, O'Neal smashed his head against the light fix-
ture hanging overhead. "I had to learn around age fifteen to accept my size,"
he said. "My father told me, 'You are going to be someone. Just keep playing
and you are going to be a football player, a basketball player, or even a baseball
player.' Around the age of thirteen, I got my name in the papers for basketball
and the girls started liking me, and ever since then it's been nothing but up."

O'Neal get his height from his mother's side of the family. Lucille O'Neal ³⁰
Harrison is six feet two inches tall, and her grandfather, who was a farmer in
Georgia, was about six-ten. O'Neal met his great-grandfather once before he
died, and says he is one of the people from history he'd most like to know. The
others are Walter Matthau, because of the movie "The Bad News Bears" ("He
was a drunk coach who got a bunch of misfit kids together—black kids, Chinese
kids, girls—and they played baseball and won the championship"), and Redd
Foxx, "because I used to watch 'Sanford and Son' all the time, and laughter is
the best stress reliever."

He credits Phil Harrison, his stepfather, actually, with having given him
the emotional impetus to succeed in basketball. (Harrison married O'Neal's

mother when Shaq was two. His biological father is Joe Toney, who, in 1994, appeared in the *National Enquirer* claiming paternity and thereafter did the talk-show rounds. O'Neal's response was to write a rap song called "Biological Didn't Bother.") Harrison, who was a sergeant in the Army, was a disciplinarian, the kind of father who wouldn't let O'Neal keep trophies in the house for fear that he would become conceited. O'Neal still gives all his trophies to Harrison, and he tends to treat older men with the utmost respect.

O'Neal's earliest years were spent in Newark, but when he was in the sixth grade the family was transferred to an Army base in Wildflecken, Germany. There O'Neal started to play basketball seriously, and though he was not a prodigious talent, he worked hard and was unfeasibly tall. As O'Neal recounts in his autobiography, "Shaq Talks Back," he was scouted by Dale Brown, the coach of L.S.U., who had come to Germany to give a basketball clinic. Brown asked how long the six-foot-nine-inch O'Neal had been in the Army; O'Neal replied that he was fourteen. By the middle of O'Neal's sophomore year in high school, when he was six-eleven, the family had moved back to the United States, to San Antonio, where he was on his school's basketball team. From San Antonio, O'Neal went to L.S.U., and after three years there he opted for the N.B.A. draft and signed, in 1992, with the Orlando Magic for forty million dollars over seven years, which was then the most lucrative contract in N.B.A. history. O'Neal spent four years in Orlando, long enough to earn a reputation as a weak playoff player and to endure an ugly falling-out with his teammate Penny Hardaway. And yet there was no doubt that he had the potential to be one of the most formidable centers to play the game since Abdul-Jabbar, and even Bill Russell and Wilt Chamberlain. In 1996, Jerry Buss, the owner of the Lakers, and his general manager, Jerry West, lured O'Neal to Los Angeles, at a salary of a hundred and twenty million dollars over seven years—the biggest contract in the game.

By the time, O'Neal had started to make rap records for Jive—for example, "Shaq Diesel," which included songs with titles such as "Shoot Pass Slam" and "(I Know I Got) Skillz"—and had played a genie in the movie "Kazaam," one of a handful of films in which he demonstrated the limitations of his acting ability. He had not, however, helped Orlando win an N.B.A. championship, and critics suggested that his proximity to Hollywood would lead to similar results for the Lakers. But O'Neal's performing career failed to take off; and his game improved when, in 1999, Phil Jackson, the former coach of the Chicago Bulls, took over the job of coaching the Lakers. Under Jackson, O'Neal started to play more of a team game, passing to other players rather than bullying his way to the hoop. In 2000, the team won its first championship since 1988, the era of Magic Johnson and Abdul-Jabbar.

Jackson is well known for applying the principles of Zen to the game of basketball, and O'Neal says that Jackson's methods meshed with his own strategies for victory. "I control my dreams," O'Neal told me. "So-called educated people call it meditation, but I don't. I call it 'dreamful attraction.' The mind controls everything, so you just close your eyes and see yourself dribbling, see yourself shooting." Contrary to some reports, O'Neal says that Jackson has not induced the team to practice yoga. "We tried Tai Chi one year, but the guys didn't like it, because, even though it was stretching, it would make us tight," he said. "Anyway, I don't stretch. I just play."

O'Neal is regularly described as the league's most dominant player: there is no   35 other single player who can match him physically, and there is no defensive strategy that another team can devise which will decisively shut him down. Jerry West told me, "If you could construct a basketball player physically, Shaq would be the model. He has this great size and incredible strength, but on top of that he has unbelievable balance, incredible footwork, and a great sense of where he is on the court." Most dominant isn't synonymous with best, how-ever; the players who usually win that accolade are smaller, faster men like Kobe Bryant or Jason Kidd of the New Jersey Nets. And O'Neal's weaknesses, for all his power, are transparently evident. His free-throw average has been only around fifty per cent for most of his career.

His detractors say that he is dominant only because of his size. Whenever *Slam*, whose readers are the young fans upon whom the game depends, puts O'Neal on the cover, the editors receive letters complaining that Shaq is just big and fat and boring. O'Neal's weight is given in the official statistics about the team as an implausible three hundred and fifteen pounds. (People close to Shaq claim that he sometimes hits three hundred and fifty.) When, in mid-March, I asked O'Neal what he weighed, he told me three hundred and thirty-eight pounds, though he said it in the slightly hesitant tone of a kid asserting that he has done his homework. "I'm just a big-boned guy," he said. "Muscle weighs more than fat, and a big guy has big muscles. People look at me and see this big guy and they think it's fat. How can I be fat and out of shape and do what I do? You could put me up against any athlete in the world, you could put them on a computerized diet, and on a treadmill and all that, and I will bust their ass."

Being called the most dominant rather than the best is fine with O'Neal. "They've changed the game because of me; other organizations whine and cry because of me," he said. "Being the best is too easy for me." His free-throw failings are spurs to his ambition, he says. "If I played the game I play and shot eighty-eight per cent from the line, it would take away from my mental focus, because I would know how good I was and I wouldn't work so hard." (In fact, O'Neal has been making about sixty-five percent of his free throws during the current playoffs.) "I'm not allowed to be as dominant as I want to be," he told me. "I would probably average fifty points a game, twenty rebounds, and the opponents would foul out in the first or second quarter." O'Neal suspects that his game is being reined in by the N.B.A. referees. "I guess they have to keep it even so that the viewers won't get bored," he said. David Stern, the N.B.A.

commissioner, recently acknowledged to the Los Angeles *Daily News* that it is difficult to know when to call a foul on Shaq, and said, "We used to get the same calls on Kareem and every other big man that's been as great as Shaq is."

N.B.A. viewing figures are well down since their peak of 6.6 million at the height of Jordan's career. Last year, an average of four million people watched the regular season games on NBC. But a game in which O'Neal plays can sometimes make for dull viewing. His strengths aren't as thrilling to watch as those of a player who flies and leaps, and the defenses used against him slow everything down so much that a viewer's attention can dwindle. The most notorious of these is the Hack-a-Shaq, in which opposing players make repeated fouls on O'Neal by throwing their arms around his waist, hoping to regain possession of the ball at little cost by sending him to the free-throw line. Phil Jackson agrees that O'Neal is expected to play by different rules from everyone else. "It's totally unfair, but the referees have to be," Jackson told me. "Everybody fouls Shaq all the time, because they know the referees can't call every foul that is created against him. There isn't a shot in which he's not fouled except maybe twice a game. There are guys hitting him on the way up, hitting him at the top, knocking him around." O'Neal says, "The beating that I take is like wrestling. It ain't even basketball sometimes. I'm the N.B.A.'s best W.W.F. wrestler, and I'm the W.W.F.'s best N.B.A. player."

O'Neal has a tattoo on his right arm that says "Against the Law," and, since he's famously supportive of the uniformed services, I asked him what he meant by it. "It's against the law to be this talented, this beautiful, this smart, this sexy," he said. "I don't mean penal-code law. I mean laws of nature."

Like a Hollywood movie or a mass-market paperback, every sports season 40 needs a narrative of conflict and resolution, and in the 2000–01 season the story was the rivalry and animosity between O'Neal and Kobe Bryant. The narrative is crafted by the Lakers' beat reporters, who attend around a hundred games a season—hanging out in the locker rooms for their appointed forty-five minutes before the game—and show up at countless closed practice sessions. The structure of team coverage creates what a therapist would diagnose as a cycle of dependency and resentment on the part of the reporters, who are a group of mostly smallish men obliged to wait around grudgingly for a bunch of mostly huge men to stoop and speak to them. The reporters exercise their own power, of course, in making a drama out of the daily shifts in locker-room mood, which in turn earns them the occasional enmity of the players. O'Neal barely talks to the press for weeks at a time, or does what he calls "SHAM-ming them"—giving them the Short Answer Method. "They're yellow journalists," he said to me one day. "Don't focus on whether Shaq is having problems with Phil, or whether Shaq is liking Kobe or not, or what Rick and Vanessa are doing—if we're a great team, say we're a great team. I think they get so bored with us winning all the time, they focus on that other stuff."

But the Shaq-Kobe feud was genuine, and it provided excellent copy. O'Neal and Bryant had never got along. Bryant, who came to the league a polished eighteen-year-old from a wealthy family, seemed to find O'Neal's antic goofiness distasteful; O'Neal thought Bryant was a selfish player who was interested only in demonstrating his own virtuosity and was insufficiently deferential. O'Neal would say ominous things like "If the big dog don't get fed, the house won't get guarded," after nights of what he saw as Kobe hogging the ball, and Kobe would say to reporters, "Turn my game down? I need to turn it up." The whole affair culminated, happily enough for the team and its chroniclers, in a reconciliation sentimental enough for the most golden-hued of Hollywood drama, with Bryant shucking off his natural aloofness both on and off the court—he started to laugh at teammates' jokes on the bus instead of listening to his Walkman—and with O'Neal referring to the quicksilver Bryant as "my idol." (The saga forms the basis of a new book, "Ain't No Tomorrow: Kobe, Shaq and the Making of a Lakers Dynasty," by Elizabeth Kaye.) This season, Bryant and O'Neal have been coexisting quite chummily. O'Neal took a few shots at Bryant while delivering an impromptu rap to the crowd at his birthday party, castigating him for not showing up ("Kobe, if you hear me, I'm talking about your ass," and so on), but the razzing seemed good-natured.

This season's master narrative has been Shaq vs. Shaq—O'Neal's battle with his own body and its ailments. Chronic pain in an arthritic toe and other injuries that have cropped up have been endlessly inquired after by the beat reporters. "We started out with the small toe on his left foot—that was getting to him early—and at some point in the season we all made the transition to the right big toe," Tim Brown, who covers the team for the Los Angeles *Times*, explained. The paper has been running headlines like "LAKERS' BIG HOPES REST IN SHAQ'S BIG TOE," and reams of newsprint have been devoted to the orthotics that have been devised by O'Neal's podiatrist, Robert Mohr, to alleviate the strain on the big toe. Last week, the papers reported that not only had O'Neal cut his finger while playing against the San Antonio Spurs in the first game of the Western Conference semifinals but he had also required stitches to mend a cut sustained earlier that day at home while he was pretending to be Spider-Man.

This season, O'Neal has thought a lot about the toll the game is taking on his body. "I feel beat up," he told me a few days after his birthday. "I'm probably one of the only guys in history who has taken a pounding night in and night out." He was sitting on a massage bench after a practice session, and he rubbed his arms and slapped his biceps as if he were looking over a recalcitrant piece of machinery. "With the last two championships, afterward I just had to sit down for a week and do nothing, like this"—and he struck a catatonic pose, stiff-limbed and staring into space—"and let all the injuries go away. And then there's another week to do this"—he stretched his thick, muscled arms above his head, exposing the spacious geography of his armpits—"and then, by the time my shit is all gone, we've only got another week until training camp." He worried, too, about the effects of the anti-inflammatory drugs he was taking. "They are the same drugs they say might have messed up Alonzo Mourning's kidneys," he said, referring to the Miami center who missed most of last season as a result of kidney disease.

Rick Fox, O'Neal's teammate, coming off the court after a practice in New Jersey a few weeks ago, said, "Shaq is dealing with injuries that he never thought he'd have to deal with. This is new to him. Even Superman had his kryptonite, but after ten years there are only so many hits of kryptonite you can take." One day, O'Neal told me, mournfully, "When I was Kobe's age, I could play a magnificent game and stay out all night, but now I am old, and my toe is killing me." O'Neal, whose contract expires in 2006, has started to say that he may have only two more years in the game, though in 1999 he told *Slam* that he thought he might be out by the time he reached thirty.

O'Neal will be under pressure to keep playing. Jerry West told me, "If I ever   45 see him retire early, I'll kill him. You play until you can't play. This is a tough guy, and he can play through things that mortal people wouldn't want to." Sometimes O'Neal talks about himself this way, too. Toward the end of this year's regular season, he was out for two games, with a sprained wrist, causing the reporters to shift their focus from foot to arm. The Lakers lost both games, and just before the next game, in which O'Neal was to return, against Miami, I asked him whether he felt responsible for being hurt or whether he felt as if his body were betraying him as well as the team.

He rejected the premise of the question. "I don't get hurt—I get taken out," he said. "My wrist is hurting for a reason—it's not hurting because I fell on it. My stomach is hurting for a reason. My knee is hurting for a reason. I don't get hurt, baby, I get taken out. You can't hurt this"—and, with that, he flexed his left biceps, like a bodybuilder, and, with one huge fist, banged on his Superman tattoo. Then he went out and scored forty points against Miami, leading the Lakers to victory.

In other moods, though, O'Neal admits to his own mortality. "Everything hurts," he told me. "A pinch is a pinch. If you pinch an elephant, it will hurt him. Pain is pain, and pain doesn't care how big you are or how strong you are." One day, he said, "You know who my favorite basketball player is? People might be surprised when they hear this. It's Dave Bing." I said I didn't know who Dave Bing was. "I don't know who he is, either," said O'Neal. "Who did he play for? Detroit? He's retired now, and he owns a big steel factory in Detroit." Bing left the game in 1978, and subsequently became a Hall of Famer, and the winner, in 1984, of the National Minority Small Business Person of the Year and the National Minority Supplier of the Year awards.

O'Neal says he's starting to develop business interests that have nothing to do with basketball: he told me he'd bought a couple of car washes and strip malls, and had just signed a deal for some Burger King franchises. "Basketball is cool, but we can't do it forever. After basketball, Dave Bing is my guy," he said. "Those players who are smart enough save their money, so that after you stop playing you can keep it going—that is what I plan on doing, like the Kennedy money." I asked O'Neal whether he saw himself as Joe Kennedy, a patriarch establishing a dynasty. "No, I'm the one who passed away in a plane crash—what's his name?" he said. "The good-looking one. That's who I am: good-looking, educated."

On those few evenings and afternoons when O'Neal is not playing basketball or filming a commercial or visiting the children's ward of a hospital or otherwise engaging in the various duties of an N.B.A. superstar, he is often in a classroom, studying penal-code law. O'Neal has always been fascinated by the police—both Mike Parris, his business manager, and Jerome Crawford, who serves as his bodyguard, are retired police officers—and some years ago O'Neal decided that he wanted to train as a cop himself, with the intention of pursuing a law-enforcement career after he leaves basketball, along with developing his business interests. He is already an honorary deputy for the Orange County sheriff's office in Orlando, where he once surprised an international group of swat-team officers who were performing a practice exercise of freeing a hostage from a bus by playing the hostage.

In Los Angeles, he is training to become an auxiliary member of the Port of Los Angeles Police, and he drives around with a senior officer, learning about how the law works. O'Neal frequently practices his law-enforcement techniques on his teammates and the Lakers' staff: Mark Madsen, a six-foot-nine-inch, two-hundred-and-thirty-six-pound twenty-six-year-old, who has become a close friend of O'Neal's since joining the Lakers, last season, told me, "He will come up to me and put me in all these police grips. He'll say, 'Which wrist did you have surgery on?' and then he'll do it on the other wrist. If I put up any sort of fight, I'm on the ground, quick."

O'Neal hasn't arrested anyone yet, but he does horse around by threatening to make citizen's arrests on Lakers employees, and regularly orders members of the team's support staff to stand against the wall with their legs spread. It's unlikely that he will ever be a beat cop, since what he really wants to do is be a chief of police or run for sheriff, either in Louisiana or in Orlando: "Sheriff is an elective position, and I don't just want to be a figurehead. And I don't want to win because I'm Shaq, but because I have the knowledge and understand what is going on." O'Neal generally avoids politics (though he recently went to a Nation of Islam meeting to hear Louis Farrakhan speak, and says that he is a friend of the Farrakhan family). He says that he wouldn't run for sheriff on either a Republican or a Democratic ticket, but as an Independent, "like Ross Perot." He told me, "Of course, I am not going to stop crime, make it zero per cent, but I would try."

＊   ＊   ＊

When O'Neal returns to Orlando this summer, with or without a third championship ring, there will be plenty to do. He may undergo surgery on his foot,
which would put him out of action for six to eight weeks. "Without any surgery,
nothing is going to change," Robert Mohr, the podiatrist, says. "For ordinary
motion, you need about sixty degrees of pain-free movement in your toe. For
jumping or running, you need close to ninety degrees. He has maybe twenty to
thirty degrees. You imagine a three-hundred-and-fifty-pound body coming
down on that joint."

Fortunately, if O'Neal is recovering from surgery he will have the solace of
various home improvements that are under way in Orlando, where his house
measures thirty-six thousand square feet, and faces four hundred yards of
waterfront. He has already added an eight-thousand-square-foot gym and a
regulation-size basketball court, and contractors have started on the other side
of the house, adding a new swimming pool and another nine thousand square
feet of living space, including seven new bedrooms (O'Neal already has a master bedroom with a circular bed measuring twenty feet across), a recreation
room, a cigar room, a movie theatre, and a private dance club with a state-of-
the-art d.j. booth.

Injuries permitting, O'Neal will also be able to engage in one of his favorite
activities—going on the Skycoaster, and amusement-park ride in Orlando,
which combines the sensations of hang gliding, bungee jumping, and skydiv-
ing. Riders are strapped into harnesses and hoisted to the top of a hundred-
foot tower, where they pull a release cord that puts them into a pendulum
swing, above an expanse that is the size of a football field, at about sixty miles
an hour. The sensation is as close to flying as anyone who is not Superman or
Michael Jordan is likely to experience, and O'Neal is fanatical about it.

"It's like a roller coaster, and it is dangerous—if that cord breaks, you can ⁵⁵
die," O'Neal told me. "It's scary. It feels like you're actually flying. It's like you
are falling from the top of a building, and someone grabs you and says, 'O.K.,
I ain't going to let you die.' And then they swing you—*whoosh*. I go on it all the
time." One evening, he flew for two hours, in his customized harness; and
when other would-be Skycoasters asked for his autograph he offered instead to
take them on a ride with him. So all evening astonished patrons stood in line
to fly with Shaq, waiting for their chance to swoop through the air, the kind of
thing that happens in dreams.

ANALYZING What the Writer Says

1. Why does O'Neal compare himself to Superman? What other personas does he acknowledge?

2. What is the major difference between the public personas of stars like Michael Jordan and Shaquille O'Neal?

3. "Basketball itself is marketed with teen tastes in mind," says Mead. In what way does O'Neal fit this image?

4. What battles does he fight every day?

5. What are his plans for the future?

ANALYZING How the Writer Says It

1. Mead starts the essay noting O'Neal's enthusiasm for Superman. How is the image of the caped crusader a fitting beginning for her essay?

2. The fifth segment of the essay provides a glimpse of O'Neal's biography. How is this information useful to understanding the athlete's personality?

3. The piece ends with an image of O'Neal swinging on the Skycoaster, a ride in an Orlando amusement park. How does this image tie in with the rest of the essay? How does it tie in with the introduction?

4. What is the meaning of the essay's title?

ANALYZING the Issue

Do you think that pro sports and the money invested in them inhibit young star athletes from growing into mature, responsible adults?

ANALYZING Connections Between Texts

1. Does Rebecca Mead's essay fall into the category of celebrity profile Katie Roiphe talks about in "Profiles Encouraged" (p. 737)?

2. Compare O'Neal's personality to that of Tiger Woods as it emerges in Gary Smith's "The Chosen One" (p. 811).

3. In what way does Walter Iooss's portrait of Michael Jordan (p. 121) echo points Mead makes about superstar athletes?

WARMING UP: *Watch one episode of a reality TV show (such as* Survivor, The Real World, *or* The Osbournes*) and come up with reasons people watch week after week. If you are a fan of one particular reality TV show, write down what you like about it and why you watch it regularly.*

Why America Loves Reality TV

BY STEVEN REISS AND JAMES WILTZ

STEVEN REISS AND JAMES WILTZ

Steven Reiss, a professor at Ohio State University, and James Wiltz, a Ph.D. candidate at the same institution, describe the results of a survey they conducted about why people watch reality TV.

Even if you don't watch reality television, it's becoming increasingly hard to avoid. The salacious Temptation Island was featured on the cover of *People* magazine. Big Brother aired five days a week and could be viewed on the Web 24 hours a day. And the Survivor finale dominated the front page of the *New York Post* after gaining ratings that rivaled those of the Super Bowl.

Is the popularity of shows such as Survivor, Big Brother and Temptation Island a sign that the country has degenerated into a nation of voyeurs? Americans seem hooked on so-called reality television—programs in which ordinary people compete in week-long contests while being filmed 24 hours a day. Some commentators contend the shows peddle blatant voyeurism, with shame-less exhibitionists as contestants. Others believe that the show's secret to ratings success may be as simple and harmless as the desire to seem part of the in crowd.

Rather than just debate the point, we wanted to get some answers. So we conducted a detailed survey of 239 people, asking them about not only their television viewing habits but also their values and desires through the Reiss Profile, a standardized test of 16 basic desires and values. We found that the self-appointed experts were often wrong about why people watch reality TV.

Two of the most commonly repeated "truths" about reality TV viewers are that they watch in order to talk to friends and coworkers about the show, and that they are not as smart as other viewers. But our survey results show that both of these ideas are incorrect. Although some people may watch because it helps them participate in the next day's office chat, fans and nonfans score almost equally when tested on their sociability. And people who say they enjoy intellectual activities are no less likely to watch reality TV than are those who say they dislike intellectual activities.

Another common misconception about Temptation Island, a reality program in which couples were enticed to cheat on their partners, is that the audience was watching to see scenes of illicit sex. Some critics were surprised that the show remained popular when it turned out to be much tamer than advertised. In fact, our survey suggests that one of the main differences between fans of the show and everyone else is not an interest in sex but a lack of interest in personal honor—they value expedience, not morality. What made Temptation Island popular was not the possibility of watching adultery, but the ethical slips that lead to adultery.

One aspect that all of the reality TV shows had in common was their competitive nature: contestants were vying with one another for a cash prize and were engaged in building alliances and betraying allies. The first Survivor series climaxed with one contestant, Susan Hawk, launching into a vengeful tirade against a one-time friend and ally before casting the vote that deprived her of the million-dollar prize. It makes sense, then, that fans of both Survivor and Temptation Island tend to be competitive—and that they are more likely to place a very high value on revenge than are other people. The Survivor formula of challenges and voting would seem to embody both of these desired qualities: the spirit of competition paired with the opportunity for payback.

But the attitude that best separated the regular viewers of reality television from everyone else is the desire for status. Fans of the shows are much more likely to agree with statements such as, "Prestige is important to me" and "I am impressed with designer clothes" than are other people. We have studied similar phenomena before and found that the desire for status is just a means to get attention. And more attention increases one's sense of importance: We think we are important if others pay attention to us and unimportant if ignored.

Reality TV allows Americans to fantasize about gaining status through automatic fame. Ordinary people can watch the shows, see people like themselves and imagine that they too could become celebrities by being on television. It does not matter as much that the contestants often are shown in unfavorable light; the fact that millions of Americans are paying attention means that the contestants are important.

And, in fact, some of the contestants have capitalized on their short-term celebrity: Colleen Haskell, from the first Survivor series, has a major role in

the movie The Animal, and Richard Hatch, the scheming contestant who won
the game, has been hired to host his own game show. If these former nobod-
ies can become stars, then who couldn't?

The message of reality television is that ordinary people can become so   10
important that millions will watch them. And the secret thrill of many of those
viewers is the thought that perhaps next time, the new celebrities might be
them.

ANALYZING What the Writer Says

1. Do people watch shows like "Temptation Island" because they expect to witness
   adultery? What are they really interested in seeing, according to Reiss and
   Wiltz?

2. What do Reiss and Wiltz find is the most significant difference between people
   who watch reality TV and those who don't?

3. Identify the article's thesis.

ANALYZING How the Writer Says It

1. Reiss and Wiltz are academics. Does their writing style indicate an academic
   audience? Cite examples to support your answer.

2. Why do you think this piece has such a straightforward title, with no humorous
   or ironic hook?

ANALYZING the Issue

Do you agree with Reiss and Wiltz's conclusions? Or do they leave out important reasons why some people like reality TV? Explain.

ANALYZING Connections Between Texts

1. Compare Barbara Ehrenreich's analysis of why people watch family sitcoms
   (p. 700) to what Reiss and Wiltz say about people watching reality TV. Do the
   writers make similar points about their subjects? Where do they differ?

2. In what way is reality television, as described by Reiss and Wiltz, an extension
   of the phenomenon Farhad Manjoo analyzes in "Everything Is Watching YOU"
   (p. 574)?

3. What does the woman in Elliott Erwitt's photograph "Spectator" (p. 750) have in
   common with the television audience Reiss and Wiltz write about?

Profiles Encouraged

BY KATIE ROIPHE

KATIE ROIPHE

Second-generation feminist Katie Roiphe writes about social issues and pop culture, casting a young, critical eye on the way the values of the previous generation, particularly what she views as the hypocrisy of an earlier feminist culture, have shaped attitudes and social policy. Educated at Harvard and Princeton, she is the author of The Morning After: Sex, Fear and Feminism on Campus *(1993), which ignited widespread debate about sexual mores and the role of feminism. Here she turns her attention to a different subject, the subgenre of celebrity journalism.*

In May, a freelance writer named Tom Kummer was caught fabricating movie-star profiles for one of Germany's most respected newspapers, *Süddeutsche Zeitung*. He wrote graceful articles about stars he had never met. He had been doing it for years. *The Times* of London reported that his interviews were so good that *Marie Claire* interviewed him about "the secrets of his success," which he ironically said was demanding at least 45 minutes with his subjects. What eventually betrayed him was his inability to be banal, his desire to put ideas into people's mouths that they would never actually utter. In other words, his fatal mistake was to make the celebrity profile interesting. *The Times* of London also reported that he had Sharon Stone saying she is trying "to irritate men from wholly different classes of society," and Courtney Love saying she felt: "Empty, depressed, rather dumb." The fact that he was able to carry on for so long tells us less about Kummer than it does about the genre itself. The style of celebrity profiles has become so rigid, so absolutely predictable, that the substance, the poor ephemeral star herself, is wholly superfluous. That was the piece of information Tom Kummer passed along, the valuable contribution he made to the journalistic community, the point he dramatized as no one had before: *All movie-star profiles are the same.*

Our celebrity culture has become so greedy and wild that it overwhelms and consumes the writer's individual voice. It feels, sometimes, like the writer gives up, thinks of the rent bill, and types on a kind of automatic pilot, giving the magazine or the reader or the movie publicists what they want—and nothing more. Our appetite for the same photograph of a movie star in a spaghetti-strap dress is insatiable, and so, it seems, is our appetite for the same article. But why do we continue to read it over and over, why are we interested in it when we could generate it from thin air as easily as Tom Kummer? It may be because the celebrity profile is not about information, it is not about journalism, it is not about words; it is a ritual.

No matter who the celebrity is, the pieces follow the same narrative arc. There is the moment when the movie star reveals himself to be just like us. (In *Vanity Fair*, "Pitt, then, turns out to be that most surprising of celebrities—a modest man" and "Paltrow jumps up to clear the table, and has to be told almost sternly not to do the dishes.") There is the moment when the movie star is not mortal after all. (In *Entertainment Weekly*, Julia Roberts has "a long, unbound mass of chocolate-brown curls—just the kind of Julia Roberts waterfall tangle of tresses that makes America think of bumper crops and Wall Street rallies and $100 million at the box office.") There is the fact that the movie star was funny-looking and gawky as a child ("'I had braces, and I was skinny.'" says Gwyneth Paltrow in *People*. Winona Ryder told *Life* she was taken "'for an effeminate boy'"). There is the J. D. Salinger book the movie star is reading (*Entertainment Weekly* reports that Julia Roberts "has a book of J. D. Salinger stories . . . on the coffee table," and Winona Ryder tells *In Style*, "'I have every edition, every paperback, every translation of *The Catcher in the Rye*'"). And then there is the moment when the author of the piece wryly acknowledges the artificiality of the situation. ("I have firm instructions from your people to make you comfortable," a *Harper's Bazaar* writer says to Brad Pitt, "so perhaps you should choose where you'd like to sit.") There is the disbelief on the part of both the celebrity and the author about how rich and famous and successful the movie star has become. In the end, it's not hard to see why Tom Cruise might not be essential to a Tom Cruise profile. With the pieces themselves as strictly styled as a geisha's makeup, the face behind them ceases to matter.

Start with the way the movie star looks. How should the aspiring plagiarist describe her? What should she be wearing? In *Esquire*, Winona Ryder was "in jeans, cowboy boots, and a clingy Agnes B.-type jersey," in *Life* she was "in jeans and a long-sleeved undershirt, "and in *In Style* she was "makeup-free, hair swept up in a headband." In *Harper's Bazaar*, Gwyneth Paltrow "is wearing jeans, a blue cotton-fleece sweatshirt. . . . Her hair is held back by a wide black headband," and in *Vanity Fair*, she wears "her long blond hair pulled back in a simple ponytail and no trace of makeup." Julia Roberts wears "Levi's, a snug blue top. . . . Her hair is pulled back" in *Vanity Fair* and "Levi's, a white shirt, boots, and no makeup" in *In Style*. In *Vanity Fair*, Renée Zellweger wears "jeans, a T-shirt, sneakers, and no makeup." A stripped-down wardrobe is offered as proof of the stars' unpretentiousness, their surprising accessibility.

If glossy magazines are to believed, movie stars also have a limited number   5 of character traits, one of which is vulnerability. Somebody in nearly every profile comments on that surprising aspect of the fabulous person's psyche, and if somebody else doesn't, the writer will. The mother of Jack Nicholson's child, for instance, is quoted in *Cosmopolitan* as saying, "'He's very strong yet very vulnerable.'" Julia Roberts is described in *Vanity Fair* as being "boldly vulnerable," and in *Cosmopolitan*, "her vulnerability brought Marilyn Monroe to mind," whereas in *Good Housekeeping*, "that same vulnerability that made her a star almost destroyed her." In *Rolling Stone*, she "show[s] some vulnerability." In *Vanity Fair*, Meg Ryan has a "compelling vulnerability," and Rupert Everett says of Madonna "'she has a lot of vulnerability'"; in *The New Yorker*, Regis Philbin is described by a fan as "'totally vulnerable.'" And why not? Vulnerability is the natural counterpoint to the sublime perfection that the profiler has gone out of his way to chronicle. It is a vague way of satisfying the need for the movie star to be "human" without detracting from her glamour with undue specificity.

And then there is the physical illustration of vulnerability: the mere presence of a magazine writer makes actresses turn every shade of red. In *Vanity Fair*, Renée Zellweger is "pink," and Meg Ryan's "face flushes." In *Harper's Bazaar*, Gwyneth Paltrow's "cheeks flush," in a *Vanity Fair* article, she "concedes with a blush," and in a *Vogue* article, "Paltrow turns crimson." *Esquire* reports a story in which Winona Ryder "turns scarlet." In *Newsweek*, the mention of her boyfriend's name causes Julia Roberts to blush and in *In Style* "reduced her to almost girlish blushes." Even Madonna blushes in *Vanity Fair*.

Not only do they blush; they glow. *Redbook* gushes, "It's really true: when you see Julia Roberts in person, she just . . . glows." *Vanity Fair* refers to her as "a lovely young woman glowing amid the flashbulbs," and *People* says, "[F]ans can't get enough of her glowing face." In *Newsweek*, the writer doesn't think Gwyneth Paltrow needs to lighten her hair because "[s]he's glowing already," and *Vogue* rhapsodizes about her "big, glowing smile." Other hackneyed phrases pop up regularly: in *Good Housekeeping* Julia Roberts is "like the proverbial deer caught in headlights," and in *Vanity Fair*, Meg Ryan "looked like a deer in headlights." There is no need in movie-star profiles to dispense with clichés—red carpet, flashbulbs, incandescence—are what stardom consists of: the role of the movie-star profile is to reinforce and sell that stardom, not to examine or undermine it. Which is also why almost all movie-star profiles from *People* to *The New Yorker* are peppered with superlatives—they add to the breathiness of the piece, the tone of worshipful trashy love and sheer commerce. *Cosmopolitan* calls Julia Roberts "the most desirable and successful actress in the world." *Redbook* calls her "the biggest female star on the planet." And *People* declares that "Roberts is, quite simply, the most appealing actress of her time." In *Vogue*, Gwyneth Paltrow is "The Luckiest Girl Alive," and in *Time* she is "the most beguiling actress of her young generation." In *The New Yorker*, Tom Hanks is "the most disarming and successful of American movie stars." In *People*, Brad Pitt is "Hollywood's hottest hunk," and Tom Cruise is "The Sexiest Man Alive." It is rare that one reads about a moderately successful actress, or the second sexiest man in Hollywood.

Every actress over the age of 20 is also depicted as girlish, childlike, or adolescent. Take the description of Julia Roberts in *Vanity Fair* ("[b]y turns childlike and sophisticated"), or Renée Zellweger (who has "little-girl moxie") in *Vanity Fair*, or Meg Ryan ("whose adult allure is redolent of adolescence") in *Vanity Fair*, or Sharon Stone (whose "childlike sexual greediness was perhaps the most eerily enticing quality about her [*Basic*] *Instinct* work") also in *Vanity Fair*. In *In Style*, the 28-year-old Winona Ryder is like a "defiant teen," and in *Life* she "sits like a kid." Fiftysomething Goldie Hawn, *In Style* informs us, looks as "youthful as a teenager," and a look of "childlike glee overtakes" Julia Roberts. *Cosmopolitan* compares Madonna to a "restless child," while *Vanity Fair* describes "the little girl . . . behind the woman." Male actors are invariably described as boyish. "Part of Hanks's appeal," *The New Yorker* explained, "is his boyishness." *GQ* talks about how Tom Cruise "projects a sexuality that is boyish." Even 61-year-old Warren Beatty appears "tousled and boyish" in the *New York Times Magazine*.

It often seems that the writers of magazine profiles have spent one too many Saturday nights watching *Breakfast at Tiffany's* on late-night cable, because nearly every movie star is compared to Audrey Hepburn or Holly Golightly, as Charlize Theron is in *Vanity Fair* and Julia Ormond is in the *New York Times Magazine*. In *Newsweek*, Gwyneth Paltrow's neck "brings Audrey Hepburn to mind," and other qualities of hers provoke the same comparison in *Vogue* and *In Style*. Julia Roberts is compared to Audrey Hepburn in both *In Style* and *Vanity Fair* (in 1993 and again in 1999), and *Redbook* reports that " 'she is the only actress now who can lay claim to Audrey Hepburn's mantle.' "

It is increasingly common for a magazine profile to include a pious denunciation or mockery of the tabloids, where, the highbrow writer points out, every little thing the celebrity does is being followed, every detail of what she eats and whom she dates is being observed—what an outrage to human dignity and privacy! And yet one wonders how the *Vanity Fair* or *Vogue* or *Entertainment Weekly* article is so wildly different. Indeed, it is often the same gossip, the same mundane details wrapped up and delivered in a different tone. But highbrow writers, and even not-so-highbrow writers, continue to be outraged by the tabloids, as if a slightly more literary turn of phrase changes the fundamental moral tenor and cultural worthiness of the venture. The anti-tabloid moment serves a definite function: it justifies the profile as more than just gossip. One writer in *Vanity Fair* makes fun of an item from the *New York Post* about Julia Roberts eating brunch with Benjamin Bratt at Caffe Lure on

Sullivan Street, and then proceeds to report in all seriousness that she shops for soy milk at Korean delis. The qualitative difference between these two observations is unclear. It may be a certain amount of self-contempt projected onto the "tabloids" for their invasive curiosity, or it may be that the highbrow writer really believes that his pursuit is more legitimate simply because it is juxtaposed with such psychological insights as "she's no shrinking violet," and printed on higher-quality paper.

There are certain stylistic guidelines that immediately present themselves to the aspiring plagiarist. One of the transparent rhetorical tricks employed by movie-star profilers across the country is a hip, *Bright Lights, Big City* second-person voice. A *Newsweek* profile of Julia Roberts states, "On the way to her house, [Julia] Roberts drags you into a lingerie shop and tries to persuade you to buy a nightgown for your wife." And in *Entertainment Weekly*, "As you walk in the door, Roberts tells you she's in her panic state." In *Rolling Stone*, "[y]ou opt to look out the trailer door and take in the view of the mountains. After a bit, Pitt joins you in contemplation." And again in *Rolling Stone*, "[w]hat really throws you is what happens when Cruise puts the pedal to the metal." This is a cheap way of drawing the reader into the encounter: offering the illusion that it is you who is admiring the view with the luminous cluster of glamour that is Brad Pitt. So much of the movie-star profile is premised on the perception of the reader's desperate desire to "meet" the movie star that it is no surprise that the fantasy should be so literally reflected in the style. The writer does not feel called upon to make the scene so vivid that we feel as if we are there; instead, he lazily types out three words: *You are there.*

One of the most important moments in the movie-star profile is the moment of intimacy. That is, the moment when the writer proves that he has really contacted his celestial subject and has forged a genuine connection, distinguishing himself from the sycophantish hordes and servers-up of celebrity fluff. In the *New York Times Magazine*, the profiler writes, "Minutes after the plane lands, Ormond and I are slumped in the backseat of a limousine. We're tired. We're angry. We are about to have our first fight." Or it can be something smaller, along the lines of this Julia Roberts profile in *Newsweek*: "Later she takes your arm. And crosses Union Square." Or this one in *Vogue*. "One last hug, Paltrow, after two hours of this fashion madness, smells very eau de fresh." Or it can be a flirtatious voice-mail message, like the one Regis Philbin leaves a *New Yorker* writer: "(The next day, I received a message on my voice mail: 'Spend a whole day with you. Sing my guts out onstage for you. Do everything I can for you, and not even a goodbye.')" The writer reports the flirtation, the few seconds of intimacy, the subtext of which is that he or she has really made an impression on the star, has penetrated the defenses. In the *New York Times Magazine*, the writer says that Warren Beatty "studied the artifacts of my life as if they were long-lost Mayan ruins." Julia Roberts says to a *Vanity Fair* writer, " 'You've got a pretty good pair of lips there yourself.' " These flirtations are never offered as evidence of the star's manipulative powers but rather suggest the ability of this particularly charming and attractive writer to get beyond the routine and glitter and impress the real person.

In a *Vanity Fair* profile of Renée Zellweger, "the look on her face is one that a grown woman gets that lets a man know that the night is now over." Often, the sexual overtone, the very datiness of the interview, is played up by the writer. It is fawning fandom taken to its logical extreme. There is a flirtation between the interviewer and the interviewee, a play of power, an adoration mingled with hostility that resembles nothing more than a 15-year-old's courtship. Here is *Vanity Fair*'s Kevin Sessums, the consummate highbrow profile writer and intellectual provocateur, with Julia Roberts: " '[Y]ou're famous because you're a good actress. You're *infamous* for the actors that you've f—ked,' I challenged, trying to shock a response from her. Roberts flashed her eyes at me the way she can flash them on-screen when someone has gotten her attention. Seduction lay in her unshockable stare; she cocked her head and waited." One can hear what he is saying to the reader: I have gotten Julia Roberts's attention! Seduction lay in her stare! But comments like this are often laced with a sadism—a certain resentment, perhaps, of having to sit there with an important person and record every minor dietary habit you are lucky enough to observe—that makes its way into the prose. Take the moment Sessums says to Meg Ryan " 'Cocaine may harden one's heart, but it makes one, well, less hard in other places,' I venture. 'If you were intimate with him—and I assume you were—how could you not know he was snorting coke?' "

Because fawning laced with irony somehow seems cooler and more palatable, the paradox of writers like Kevin Sessums—who has written more than 30 celebrity profiles for *Vanity Fair* alone—emerges. The tone is knowing and flirtatious and world-weary. But what is strange is how the world-weariness meshes with naïve fascination. It is, in a way, a perfect reflection of the culture—a faux intellectual distance masquerading as the real thing, irony that is really adoration in a new form. The complexities of the tone make celebrity worship less demeaning, giving it a kind of chic allure it would not otherwise have. These complexities allow the intelligent, critical reader to interest herself in the exact beige of the movie-star's furniture, to read about the blush and glow without shame. There is often a stunned incredulity, tinged with sexual attraction, that seems to render the writer comparatively speechless, so that the profile is dotted with banal statements of wonder that seem out of place in otherwise competent writing, as when a *Vanity Fair* reporter quotes Madonna as saying " 'I wanted to be *somebody*,' " and then adds, "And boy is she." That "boy is she" would not have made it into a piece about Alan Greenspan or Madeleine Albright or Al Gore; its wide-eyed wonderment would not have a place in any form of journalism other than that of the celebrity profile. It's as if the presence of Madonna had dazzled and almost drugged the writer (and the reader) into a haze of inarticulateness, a baby patter of awe.

But why are we willing to put up with it, to wade through the stock phrases,   15
to pick up the same article on the newsstand again and again? Because, in the
end, we are not interested in Winona Ryder; we are interested in fame: its
pure, bright, disembodied effervescence. And what these articles do is strip
down the particulars to give us the excitement itself. They provide us with the
affect of excitement, the sound and feel of it. It is a primitive thing, this form
of admiration, one that paints in fuzzy lines and speaks in hackneyed terms.
True mystery doesn't interest us; the statement "she had an aura of mystery"
does. The clichés are what we crave and continue to expect. What makes glamour, like lights on a marquee, is the repetition of the familiar sound of adoration, the same babble of fawning irony, the same vulnerable perfect creature
we don't really want to read about.

ANALYZING What the Writer Says

1. What does Roiphe cite as the dead giveaway that freelance writer Tom
   Kummer's celebrity profiles were bogus?

2. List the ingredients in the celebrity profile formula (or "ritual," as Roiphe calls it).

3. Pick out a single passage that answers this question: Why, if these pieces are all
   the same, do we continue to read them?

ANALYZING How the Writer Says It

1. Roiphe's title is obviously a takeoff on John F. Kennedy's *Profiles in Courage*.
   Comment, then, on the irony of the title.

2. Point out words and phrases that reveal Roiphe's attitude toward the genre
   about which she is writing.

3. Ten of the essay's fifteen paragraphs are laced with illustrations from articles in
   popular magazines. Comment on the effectiveness of this technique.

ANALYZING the Issue

1. Compare the kind of writing and fawning Roiphe describes to what you typically associate with tabloid journalism. How are they similar? Different? How do
   the celebrity profiles Roiphe describes compare to celebrity interviews on TV—
   brief chats on talk shows or more "in-depth" interviews by, say, Barbara Walters
   or Diane Sawyer?

2. What harm, if any, do celebrity profiles pose?

ANALYZING | Connections Between Texts

1. Compare and contrast Roiphe's points about why people love celebrity journalism to Reiss and Wiltz's about why people watch reality TV (p. 734).

"Granted, a living legend. But what has he done for his people?"

2. How does Joan Morgan's profile of Sean Combs ("The Bad Boy," p. 788) adhere to or depart from the "ritual" Roiphe describes?

3. In what way is Annie Leibovitz's treatment of celebrity in her photos of Liberace (p. 122) and of Jerry Hall (p. 94) similar to or different from what Roiphe describes?

YOUR TURN: Suggestions for Writing About "Spectacles and Spectators"

1. Compare Barbara Ehrenreich's analysis of why people watch family sitcoms to Reiss and Wiltz's thoughts about people watching reality TV. Write an essay in which you explain why people watch television, agreeing or disagreeing with Ehrenreich's and Reiss and Wiltz's points.

2. Television has become a daily ritual, turning family members into immobile couch potatoes, according to Barbara Ehrenreich. Write an essay in which you argue for or against the destructive influence of television on family life.

3. Jonah Goldberg ("Ozzy Without Harriet: What *The Osbournes* Tells Us About Drugs") argues that Ozzy Osbourne, the addled star of MTV's hit reality show *The Osbournes,* teaches viewers a lesson about the dangers of drug abuse. Other critics have argued that the show teaches lessons about parenting and family values as well, about love and sticking together against all odds. Watch a few episodes of the show and write an essay arguing whether or not *The Osbournes* teaches its viewers useful lessons.

4. For years, cultural critics have derided television for its mind-numbing effects, blaming it for everything from poor education to obesity. Write an essay, perhaps using Goldberg and Jeremiah Creedon ("The Greening of Tony Soprano") as sources, in which you argue that some television programs teach important lessons about our society.

5. Choose any of the reality TV shows currently on the air, watch several episodes of it, and write an essay in which you discuss the reasons viewers are attracted to this particular show. Use Reiss and Wiltz's "Why America Loves Reality TV" as a source.

6. In "Profiles Encouraged," Katie Roiphe analyzes the way celebrity journalists write about movie stars. She concludes that these pieces are all written according to the same formula. "In the end," she says, "we are not interested in Winona Ryder; we are interested in fame." Is this true? Do most people read celebrity portraits to fantasize about being famous? Write an essay in which you take a position on this issue.

7. Write an essay in which you analyze the images presented of women and men in one of the following music genres: heavy metal, rap, country, soul, rock, pop. Analyze videos, song lyrics, performers, and performances to support your points.

8. Write an essay in which you analyze the images presented of women and men in a particular sport. Analyze television, newspaper, and magazine coverage, including news stories, interviews, editorials, and feature writing to support your points.

9. Are larger-than-life figures treated fairly by the media? Do they owe their fame and success—and thus their privacy—to their fans? Write an essay in which you examine the cult of celebrity, considering what duty, if any, celebrities have to their fans and what role the media should play when it comes to celebrity.

"Great! O.K., this time I want you to sound taller,
and let me hear a little more hair."

10. The photograph of Allen Berner's "Linda" (p. 115) shows John DeAndrea's life-like sculpture of a nude woman being photographed by a man. Write an essay examining the commentary in Berner's photograph. Is the commentary demeaning to women—or is it simply commenting on the nature of art?

IMAGE GALLERY

L. BLANFORD

Roger Bannister Breaks the Four-Minute Mile

Blanford captures the moment Englishman Roger Bannister completes running a mile in under four minutes, on May 6, 1954. According to the original account in Time, *the athlete "tore the tape and collapsed unconscious" just seconds after the moment captured in the photograph. The announcement of his record time—3 minutes, 59.4 seconds—was eclipsed by the din of 1,500 cheering spectators.*

1. What do Roger Bannister's face and body language say about his athletic accomplishment?

2. How does the composition of the image enhance the significance of this moment? To what degree, do you think, is composition deliberate in sports photography?

3. Who are the people watching Bannister? Can you guess their professions by looking at them? Why do you think the photograph includes them, rather than taking the spectators on the other side of the track, in the shot?

BILLIE HOLIDAY

Billie Holiday's life (1915–59) was marked by personal tragedies: An illegitimate child, she was raped as a girl and worked as a prostitute when she was a teenager. She divorced three abusive husbands but could not shake her lifelong heroin addiction. Yet as dark as her life was, her career was brilliant: After her first record came out in 1933, Lady Day's contributions to jazz made her a legend. This 1943 photo captures a typically intense Holiday performance.

1. Even if you know nothing about Billie Holiday, what does this picture tell you about her music?

2. Look at the composition of the picture. Considering the crowd in the picture, how do you know that she is the star?

3. How does the photographer use light and shadow in this picture?

ELLIOTT ERWITT

Spectator

Paris-born Elliott Erwitt (b. 1928) has traveled the world since early childhood—and has been taking pictures almost as long. His work has been collected in several books, including the wildly popular Dog Dogs *(1998) and* Snaps *(2001), from which this photograph, snapped in 1961 in Brasilia, Brazil, comes.*

1. What kind of event does this photograph capture? How do you know?

2. What is the young woman in the foreground doing? How do you read her facial expression?

3. How does Erwitt arrange the subject matter in the three photographic planes—foreground, middle ground, and background? How do these compositional decisions contribute to the artistic effectiveness of his photograph?

4. How does Erwitt use light and shadow in this photograph?

5. Erwitt did not originally title this picture. What title would you give it? Why?

RALPH MORSE

Transfixing Experience

To Ralph Morse's 1948 photo, published in Life: Century of Change *(2000), the editors appended this humorous background story: "On the night that local station WICU went on the air, no one remembered to ring the retiring bell. So the sisters watched until sign-off at 11 p.m., two hours past their bedtime."*

1. Do you find this picture humorous? Why or why not?

2. What does the interior of the room say about the life these sisters lead?

3. What do the expressions on the sisters' faces say about their television experience? Does it matter that we do not know what program they are watching?

4. How does the picture's composition contribute to its overall effect? What setting that would be familiar to the nuns does the composition echo?

5. How does the photo's title reinforce the image?

18 | GENUS: GENIUS

Perhaps you have pondered what it is that sets some people apart, that perches them at the top of their professions or pushes them off the charts. Is genius born? Or is genius made? Is it a gift or a talent? Is it defined by the marketplace— or determined in the womb? Is there a gene for genius? Is genius simply our best, magnified?

"Genius is one percent inspiration and ninety-nine percent perspiration."

Thomas Alva Edison

Whether contemplating Einstein, a man whose very name, as Dennis Overbye writes, "has become a synonym for genius" or Martha Stewart, who, Joan

Didion argues, has tapped into every woman's fantasy, the writers featured in this unit explore the nuances of success—its glory, its consequences, its responsibilities. Richard Selzer and Malcolm Gladwell recognize genius in the surgeon's hands, but Gladwell also fixes his gaze on the otherworldly feats of great athletes. Golf prodigy Tiger Woods is Gary Smith's subject; his essay revisits the nature–nurture debate. Dave Hickey and Joan Morgan explore the cult of celebrity: Hickey's piece on the late Liberace examines the celebrity pianist's genius for marketing himself as a spectacle, as the Emperor *wearing* clothes; Morgan wonders, in a profile of supercelebrity Sean Combs, if pain is the price of fame.

Genius, this unit suggests, takes many forms. It is more than the IQ and eccentricity of conventional wisdom. It is both gift and burden. Absent unparalleled discipline, unparalleled gifts languish. Devotion to a vision, these writers would seem to agree, is even more important than the vision. Belief in your own thought, wrote nineteenth-century philosopher Ralph Waldo Emerson, "—that is genius." ✳

Everywoman.com

By Joan Didion

JOAN DIDION

A prolific essayist and keen observer of the cultural landscape, Joan Didion (b. 1934) examines the phenomenal success of Martha Stewart, a frequent target of criticism and parody before being convicted of lying to the government in March 2004. She argues that Stewart's genius is rooted in her understanding of Everywoman's fantasy— not mastery over the domestic domain but victory in the boardroom.

According to "The Web Guide to Martha Stewart— The UNOFFICIAL Site!," which was created by a former graduate student named Kerry Ogata as "a thesis procrastination technique" and then passed on to those who now maintain it, the fifty-eight-year-old chairman and C.E.O. of Martha Stewart Living Omnimedia L.L.C. ("MSO" on the New York Stock Exchange) needs only four hours of sleep a night, utilizes the saved hours by grooming her six cats and gardening by flashlight, prefers Macs in the office and a PowerBook for herself, commutes between her house in Westport and her two houses in East Hampton and her Manhattan apartment in a G.M.C. Suburban ("with chauffeur") or a Jaguar XJ6 ("she drives herself"), was raised the second-oldest of six children in a Polish-American family in Nutley, New Jersey, has one daughter, Alexis, and survived "a non-amicable divorce" from her husband of twenty-six years, Andrew Stewart ("Andy" on the site), who then "married Martha's former assistant who is 21 years younger than he is."

Contributors to the site's "Opinions" page, like good friends everywhere, have mixed feelings about Andy's defection, which occurred in 1987, while Martha was on the road promoting "Martha Stewart Weddings," the preface to which offered a possibly prescient view of her own 1961 wedding. "I was a naïve nineteen-year-old, still a student at Barnard, and Andy was beginning Yale Law School, so it seemed appropriate to be married in St. Paul's Chapel at Columbia in an Episcopalian service, mainly because we didn't have anyplace else to go," she wrote, and included a photograph showing the wedding dress she and her mother had made of embroidered Swiss organdy bought on West Thirty-eighth Street. On-line, the relative cases of "Martha" and of "Andy" and even of "Alexis," who originally took her mother's side of the divorce, get debated with startling familiarity. "BTW, I don't blame Andy," one contributor offers. "I think he took all he could. I think it's too bad that Alexis felt she had to choose." Another contributor, another view: "I work fifty hours a week and admit sometimes I don't have time to 'be all that I can be' but when Martha started out she was doing this part-time and raising Alexis and making a home for that schmuck Andy (I bet he is sorry he ever left her)."

Although "The UNOFFICIAL Site!" is just that, unofficial, "not affiliated with Martha Stewart, her agents, Martha Stewart Living Omnimedia, LLC or any other Martha Stewart Enterprises," its fairly lighthearted approach to its subject's protean competence ("What can't Martha do? According to Martha herself, 'Hang-gliding, and I hate shopping for clothes'") should in no way be construed as disloyalty to Martha's objectives, which are, as the prospectus prepared for Martha Stewart Living Omnimedia's initial public offering last October explained, "to provide our original 'how-to' content and information to as many consumers as possible" and "to turn our consumers into 'doers' by offering them the information and products they need for do-it-yourself ingenuity 'the Martha Stewart way.'" The creators and users of "The UNOFFICAL Site!" clearly maintain a special relationship with the subject at hand, as do the creators and users of other unofficial or self-invented sites crafted in the same spirit. "My Martha Stewart Page," say, or "Gothic Martha Stewart," which advises teen-agers living at home on how they can "goth up" their rooms without freaking their parents ("First of all, don't paint everything black") by taking their cues from Martha.

"Martha adores finding old linens and gently worn furniture at flea markets," users of "Gothic Martha Stewart" are reminded. "She sews a lot of her own household dressings. She paints and experiments with unusual painting techniques on objects small and large. She loves flowers, live and dried . . . and even though her surroundings look very rich, many of her ideas are created from rather simple and inexpensive materials, like fabric scraps and second-hand dishes." For the creator of "My Martha Stewart Page," even the "extremely anal" quality of Martha's expressed preoccupation with the appearance of her liquid-detergent dispenser can be a learning experience, a source of concern that becomes a source of illumination: "It makes me worry about her. . . . Of course it is just this strangeness that makes me love her. She helps me know I'm OK—everyone's OK. . . . She seems perfect, but she's not. She's obsessed. She's frantic. She's a control freak beyond my wildest dreams. And that shows me two things: A) no one is perfect and B) there's a price for everything."

There is an unusual bonding here, a proprietary intimacy that eludes con-   5
ventional precepts of merchandising to go to the very heart of the enterprise,

the brand, what Martha prefers to call the "presence": the two magazines (*Martha Stewart Living* and *Martha Stewart Weddings*) that between them reach ten million readers, the twenty-seven books that have sold eight and a half million copies, the weekday radio show carried on two hundred and seventy stations, the syndicated "AskMartha" column that appears in two hundred and thirty-three newspapers, the televised show six days a week on CBS, the weekly slot on the CBS morning show, the cable-TV show ("From Martha's Kitchen," the Food Network's top-rated weekly show among women aged twenty-five to fifty-four), the Web site (www.marthastewart.com) with more than one million registered users and six hundred and twenty-seven thousand hits a month, the merchandising tie-ins with Kmart and Sears and Sherwin-Williams (Kmart alone last year sold more than a billion dollars' worth of Martha Stewart merchandise), the catalogue operation (Martha by Mail) from which some twenty-eight hundred products (Valentine Garlands, Valentine Treat Bags, Ready-to-Decorate Cookies, Sweetheart Cake Rings, Heart Dessert Scoops, Heart Rosette Sets, Heart-Shaped Pancake Molds, and Lace-Paper Valentine Kits, to name a few from the on-line "Valentine's Day" pages) can be ordered either from the catalogues themselves (eleven annual editions, fifteen million copies) or from Web pages with exceptionally inviting layouts and seductively logical links.

These products are not inexpensive. The Lace-Paper Valentine Kit contains enough card stock and paper lace to make "about forty" valentines, which could be viewed as something less than a buy at forty-two dollars plus time and labor. On the "Cakes and Cake Stands" page, the Holiday Cake-Stencil Set, which consists of eight nine-inch plastic stencils for the decorative dusting of cakes with confectioner's sugar or cocoa, sells for twenty-eight dollars. On the "marthasflowers" pages, twenty-five tea roses, which are available for eighteen dollars a dozen at Roses Only in New York, cost fifty-two dollars, and the larger of the two "suggested vases" to put them in (an example of the site's linking logic) another seventy-eight dollars. A set of fifty Scalloped Tulle Rounds, eight-and-three-quarter-inch circles of tulle in which to tie up wedding favors, costs eighteen dollars, and the seam binding used to tie them ("sold separately," another natural link) costs, in the six-color Seam-Binding Ribbon Collection, fifty-six dollars. Seam binding sells retail for pennies, and, at Paron on West Fifty-seventh Street in New York, not the least expensive source, one-hundred-and-eight-inch-wide tulle sells for four dollars a yard. Since the amount of one-hundred-and-eight-inch tulle required to make fifty Scalloped Tulle Rounds would be slightly over a yard, the on-line buyer can be paying only for the imprimatur of "Martha," whose genius it was to take the once familiar notion of doing-it-yourself to previously uncharted territory: somewhere east of actually doing it yourself, somewhere west of paying Robert Isabell to do it.

* * *

This is a billion-dollar company the only real product of which, in other words, is Martha Stewart herself, an unusual business condition acknowledged in the prospectus prepared for Martha Stewart Living Omnimedia's strikingly successful October I.P.O. "Our business would be adversely affected if: Martha Stewart's public image or reputation were to be tarnished," the "Risk Factors" section of the prospectus read in part. "Martha Stewart, as well as her name, her image, and the trademarks and other intellectual property rights relating to these, are integral to our marketing efforts and form the core of our brand name. Our continued success and the value of our brand name therefore depends, to a large degree, on the reputation of Martha Stewart."

The perils of totally identifying a brand with a single living and therefore vulnerable human being were much discussed around the time of the I.P.O., and the question of what would happen to Martha Stewart Living Omnimedia if Martha Stewart were to become ill or die ("the diminution or loss of the services of Martha Stewart," in the words of the prospectus) remained open. "That was always an issue for us," Don Logan, the president of Time Inc., told the Los Angeles *Times* in 1997, a few months after Stewart managed to raise enough of what she called "internally generated capital," $53.3 million, to buy herself out of Time Warner, which had been resisting expansion of a business built entirely around a single personality. "I think we are now spread very nicely over an area where our information can be trusted," Stewart herself maintained, and it did seem clear that the very expansion and repetition of the name that had made Time Warner nervous—every "Martha Stewart" item sold, every "Martha Stewart Everyday" commercial aired—was paradoxically serving to insulate the brand from the possible loss of the personality behind it.

The related question, of what would happen if "Martha Stewart's public image or reputation were to be tarnished," seemed less worrisome, since in any practical way the question of whether it was possible to tarnish Martha Stewart's public image or reputation had already been answered, with the 1997 publication and ascension to the New York *Times* best-seller list of "Just Desserts," an unauthorized biography of Martha Stewart by Jerry Oppenheimer, whose previous books were unauthorized biographies of Rock Hudson, Barbara Walters, and Ethel Kennedy. "My investigative juices began to flow," Oppenheimer wrote in the preface to "Just Desserts." "If her stories were true, I foresaw a book about a perfect woman who had brought perfection to the masses. If her stories were not true, I foresaw a book that would shatter myths."

Investigative juices flowing, Oppenheimer discovered that Martha was "driv- 10 en." Martha, moreover, sometimes "didn't tell the whole story." Martha could be "a real screamer" when situations did not go as planned, although the case Oppenheimer makes on this point suggests, at worst, merit on both sides.

Martha was said to have "started to shriek," for example, when a catering partner backed a car over the "picture-perfect" Shaker picnic basket she had just
finished packing with her own blueberry pies. Similarly, Martha was said to
have been "just totally freaked" when a smokehouse fire interrupted the shooting of a holiday special and she found that the hose she had personally dragged
to the smokehouse ("followed by various blasé crew people, faux-concerned
family members, smirking kitchen assistants, and a macho Brazilian
groundskeeper") was too short to reach the flames. After running back to the
house, getting an extension for the hose, and putting out the fire, Martha,
many would think understandably, exchanged words with the groundskeeper,
"whom she fired on the spot in front of everyone after he talked back to her."

Other divined faults include idealizing her early family life (p. 34), embel-
lishing "everything" (p. 42), omitting a key ingredient when a rival preteen
caterer asked for her chocolate-cake recipe (p. 43), telling readers of *Martha
Stewart Living* that she had as a young girl "sought to discover the key to good
literature" even though "a close friend" reported that she had "passionately
devoured" the Nancy Drew and Cherry Ames novels (p. 48), misspelling "vil-
lainous" in a review of William Makepeace Thackeray's "Vanity Fair" for the
Nutley High School literary magazine (p. 51), having to ask what Kwanza was
during a 1995 appearance on "Larry King Live" (p. 71), and not only wanting a
larger engagement diamond than the one Andy had picked out for her at Harry
Winston but obtaining it, at a better price, in the diamond district (p. 101). "That
should have set off an alarm," a "lifelong friend" told Oppenheimer. "How
many women would do something like that? It was a bad omen."

This lumping together of insignificant immaturities and economies for conversion into character flaws (a former assistant in the catering business Martha
ran in Westport during the nineteen-seventies presents the damning charge
"Nothing went to waste. . . . Martha's philosophy was like someone at a restaurant who had eaten half his steak and tells the waiter 'Oh, wrap it up, and I'll
take it home'") continues for four hundred and fourteen pages, at which point
Oppenheimer, in full myth-shattering mode, reveals his trump card, "an eerie
corporate manifesto" that "somehow slipped out of Martha's offices and made
its way from one Time Inc. executive's desk to another and eventually from a
Xerox machine to the outside world. . . . The white paper, replete with what was
described as an incomprehensible flow chart, declared, in part":

> In Martha's vision, the shared value of the MSL enterprises are high-
> ly personal—reflecting her individual goals, beliefs, values and aspira-
> tions. . . . "Martha's Way" can be obtained because she puts us in direct
> touch with everything we need to know, and tells/shows us exactly what
> we have to do. . . . MSL enterprises are founded on the proposition that
> Martha herself is both leader and teacher. . . . While the ranks of
> "teaching disciples" within MSL may grow and extend, their authority
> rests on their direct association with Martha; their work emanates from

> her approach and philosophies; and their techniques, and products and
> results meet her test. . . . The magazine, books, television series, and
> other distribution sources are only vehicles to enable personal commu-
> nication with Martha. . . . She is not, and won't allow herself to be, an
> institutional image and fiction like Betty Crocker. . . . She is the cre-
> ative and driving center. . . . By listening to Martha and following her
> lead, we can achieve real results in our homes too—ourselves—just like
> she has. . . . It is easy to do. Martha has already "figured it out." She will
> personally take us by the hand and show us how to do it.

Oppenheimer construes this purloined memo or mission statement as sinister, of a piece with the Guyana Kool-Aid massacre ("From its wording, some
wondered whether Martha's world was more gentrified Jonestown than happy
homemaker"), but in fact it remains an unexceptionable, and quite accurate,
assessment of what makes the enterprise go. Martha Stewart Living
Omnimedia L.L.C. connects on a level that transcends the absurdly labor-
intensive and in many cases prohibitively expensive table settings and decorating touches (the "poinsettia wreath made entirely of ribbon" featured on
one December show would require of even a diligent maker, Martha herself
allowed, "a couple of hours" and, "if you use the very best ribbon, two or three
hundred dollars") over which its chairman toils six mornings a week on CBS.
Nor is the connection about her recipes, which are the recipes of Sunbelt
Junior League cookbooks (Grapefruit Mimosas, Apple Cheddar Turnovers,
and Southwestern Style S'Mores are a few from the most recent issue of
Martha Stewart Entertaining), reflecting American middle-class home cooking
as it has existed pretty much through the postwar years. There is in a Martha
Stewart recipe none of, say, Elizabeth David's transforming logic and assur-
ance, none of Julia Child's mastery of technique.

What there is instead is "Martha," full focus, establishing "personal communication" with the viewer or reader, showing, telling, leading, teaching,
"loving it" when the simplest possible shaken-in-a-jar vinaigrette emulsifies
right there onscreen. She presents herself not as an authority but as a friend
who has "figured it out," the enterprising if occasionally manic neighbor who
will waste no opportunity to share an educational footnote. "True," or
"Ceylon," cinnamon, the reader of *Martha Stewart Living* will learn, "originally came from the island now called Sri Lanka," and "by the time of the Roman
Empire . . . was valued at fifteen times its weight in silver." In a television segment about how to serve champagne, Martha will advise her viewers that the
largest champagne bottle, the Balthazar, was named after the king of Babylon,
"555 to 539 B.C." While explaining how to decorate the house for the holidays
around the theme "The Twelve Days of Christmas," Martha will slip in this
doubtful but nonetheless useful gloss, a way for the decorator to perceive herself as doing something more significant than painting pressed-paper eggs
with two or three coats of white semi-gloss acrylic paint, followed by another

two or three coats of yellow-tinted acrylic varnish, and finishing the result with ribbon and beads: "With the egg so clearly associated with new life, it is not surprising that the six geese a-laying represented the six days of Creation in the carol."

The message Martha is actually sending, the reason large numbers of Ameri-   15
can woman count watching her a comforting and obscurely inspirational expe-rience, seems not very well understood. There has been a flurry of academic work done on the cultural meaning of her success (in the summer of 1998, the *New York Times* reported that "about two dozen scholars across the United States and Canada" were producing such studies as "A Look at Linen Closets: Liminality, Structure and Anti-Structure in Martha Stewart Living" and locat-ing "the fear of transgression" in the magazine's "recurrent images of fences, hedges and garden walls"), but there remains, both in the bond she makes and in the outrage she provokes something unaddressed, something pitched, like a dog whistle, too high for the traditional textual analysis. The outrage, which reaches sometimes startling levels, centers on the misconception that she has somehow tricked her admirers into not noticing the ambition that brought her to their attention. To her critics, she seems to represent a fraud to be exposed, a wrong to be righted. "She's a shark," one declares in *Salon*. "However much she's got, Martha wants more. And she wants it her way and in her world, not in the balls-out boys' club realms of real estate or technology, but in the deli-cate land of doily hearts and wedding cakes."

"I can't believe people don't see the irony in the fact that this 'ultimate homemaker' has made a multi-million dollar empire out of baking cookies and selling bed sheets," a posting reads in *Salon*'s "ongoing discussion" of Martha. "I read an interview in *Wired* where she said she gets home at 11 PM most days, which means she's obviously too busy to be the perfect mom/wife/homemaker—a role which many women feel like they have to live up to because of the image MS projects." Another reader cuts to the chase: "Wasn't there some buzz a while back about Martha stealing her daughter's BF?" The answer: "I thought that was Erica Kane. You know, when she stole Kendra's BF. I think you're getting them confused. Actually, why would any man want to date MS? She is so frigid looking that my television actually gets cold when she's on." "The trouble is that Stewart is about as genuine as Hollywood," a writer in *The Scotsman* charges. "Hers may seem to be a nos-talgic siren call for a return to Fifties-style homemaking with an updated ele-gance, but is she in fact sending out a fraudulent message—putting pressure on American women to achieve impossible perfection in yet another sphere, one in which, unlike ordinary women, Stewart herself has legions of helpers?"

This entire notion of "the perfect mom/wife/homemaker," of the nostalgic siren call for a return to Fifties-style homemaking," is a considerable misun-derstanding of what Martha Stewart actually transmits, the promise she makes her readers and viewers, which is that know-how in the house will translate to can-do outside it. What she offers, and what more strictly professional shelter and food magazines and shows do not, is the promise of transferred manna, transferred luck. She projects a level of taste that transforms the often point-lessly ornamented details of what she is actually doing. The possibility of mov-ing out of the perfected house and into the headier ether of executive action, of doing as Martha does, is clearly presented: "Now I, as a single human being, have six personal fax numbers, fourteen personal phone numbers, seven car-phone numbers, and two cell-phone numbers," as she told readers of *Martha Stewart Living*. On October 19th, the evening of her triumphant I.P.O., she explained, on "The Charlie Rose Show," the genesis of the enterprise. "I was serving a desire—not only mine, but every homemaker's desire, to elevate that job of homemaker," she said. "It was floundering, I think. And we all wanted to escape it, to get out of the house, get that high-paying job and pay somebody else to do everything that we didn't think was really worthy of our attention. And all of a sudden I realized: it was terribly worthy of our attention."

Think about this. Here was a woman who had elevated "that job of home-maker" to a level where even her G.M.C. Suburban came equipped with a Sony MZ-B3 MiniDisc Recorder for dictation and a Sony ICD-50 Recorder for short messages and a Watchman FDL-PT22 TV set, plus phones, plus Power-Book. Here was a woman whose idea of how to dress for "that job of home-maker" involved Jil Sander. "Jil's responded to the needs of people like me," she is quoted as having said on "The UNOFFICIAL Site!" "I'm busy; I travel a lot; I want to look great in a picture." Here was a woman who had that very October morning been driven down to the big board to dispense brioches and fresh-squeezed orange juice from a striped tent while Morgan Stanley Dean Witter and Merrill Lynch and Bear, Stearns and Donaldson, Lufkin & Jenrette and Banc of America Securities increased the value of her personal stock in the company she personally invented to $614 million. This does not play into any "nostalgic siren call" for a return to the kind of "homemaking" that seized America during those postwar years when the conversion of industry to peace-time production mandated the creation of a market for Kelvinators, yet Martha was the first to share the moment with her readers.

"The mood was festive, the business community receptive, and the stock began trading with the new symbol MSO," she confided in her "Letter from Martha" in the December *Martha Stewart Living*, there between the lines was the promise from the mission statement: *It is easy to do. Martha has already "figured it out." She will personally take us by the hand and show us how to do it.* What she will show us how to do, it turns out, is a little more invigorating than your aver-age poinsettia-wreath project. "The process was extremely interesting, from deciding exactly what the company was (an 'integrated multimedia company' with promising internet capabilities) to creating a complicated and lengthy prospectus that was vetted and revetted (only to be vetted again by the Securities and Exchange Commission) to selling the company with a road show that took us to more than twenty cities in fourteen days (as far off as Europe)." This is getting out of the house with a vengeance, and on your own terms, the secret dream of any woman who has ever made a success of a PTA cake sale. "You could bottle that chili sauce," neighbors say to home cooks all over America. "You could make a fortune on those date bars." You could bottle it, you could sell it, you can survive when all else fails: I myself believed for most of my adult life that I could support myself and my family, in the catastrophic absence of all other income sources, by catering.

The "cultural meaning" of Martha Stewart's success, in other words, lies deep [20] in the success itself, which is why even her troubles and strivings are part of the message, not detrimental but integral to the brand. She has branded herself not as Superwoman but as Everywoman, a distinction that seems to remain unclear to her critics. Martha herself gets it, and talks about herself in print as if catching up her oldest friend. "I sacrificed family, husband," she said in a 1996 *Fortune* conversation with Charlotte Beers, the former C.E.O. of Ogilvy & Mather and a member of Martha Stewart Living Omnimedia's board of directors, and Darla Moore, the president of Richard Rainwater's investment firm and the inventor of "debtor in possession" financing for companies in bankruptcy. The tone of this conversation was odd, considerably more confessional than the average dialogue among senior executives who know they are being taped by *Fortune*. "Not my choice," Martha confided about her divorce. "His choice. Now, I'm so happy that it happened. It took a long time for me to realize that it freed me to do more things. I don't think I would have accomplished what I have if I had stayed married. No way. And it allowed me to make friends that I know I never would have had."

Martha's readers understand her divorce, both its pain and its up side. They saw her through it, just as they saw her through her dealings with the S.E.C., her twenty-city road show, her triumph on Wall Street. This relationship between Martha and her readers is a good deal more complicated than the many parodies of and jokes about it would allow. "While fans don't grow on fruit trees (well, some do), they can be found all over America: in malls, and Kmarts, in tract houses and trailer parks, in raised ranches, Tudor condos and Winnebagos," the parody Martha is made to say in HarperCollins' "Martha Stuart's Better Than You at Entertaining." "Wherever there are women dissatisfied with how they live, with who they are and who they are not, that is where you'll find potential fans of mine." These parodies are themselves interesting: too broad, misogynistic in a cartoon way (stripping Martha to her underwear has been a reliable motif of countless online parodies), curiously nervous ("Keeping Razors Circumcision-Sharp" is one feature in "Martha Stuart's Better Than You at Entertaining"), oddly uncomfortable, a little too intent on marginalizing a rather considerable number of women by making light of their situations and their aspirations.

Something here is perceived as threatening, and a glance at "The UNOFFICIAL Site!," the subliminal focus of which is somewhere other than on homemaking skills, suggests what it is. What makes Martha "a good role model in many ways," one contributor writes, is that "she's a strong woman who's in charge, and she has indeed changed the way our country, if not the world, views what used to be called 'women's work.'" From an eleven-year-old: "Being successful is important in life. . . . It is fun to say 'When I become Martha Stewart I'm going to have all the things Martha has.'" Even a contributor who admits to an "essentially anti-Martha persona" admires her "intelligence" and "drive," the way in which this "supreme chef, baker, gardener, decorator, artist, and entrepreneur" showed what it took "to get where she is, where most men aren't and can't. . . . She owns her own corporation in her own name, her own magazine, her own show."

A keen interest in and admiration for business acumen pervades the site. "I know people are threatened by Martha and Time Warner Inc. is going to blow a very 'good thing' if they let Martha and her empire walk in the near future," a contributor to "The UNOFFICIAL Site!" wrote at the time Stewart was trying to buy herself out of Time Warner. "I support Martha in everything she does and I would bet if a man wanted to attach his name to all he did . . . this wouldn't be a question." Their own words tell the story these readers and viewers take from Martha: Martha is *in charge*, Martha is *where most men aren't and can't*, Martha has *her own magazine*, Martha has *her own show*, Martha not only has *her own corporation* but has it *in her own name*.

This is not a story about a woman who made the best of traditional skills. This is a story about a woman who did her own I.P.O. This is the "woman's pluck" story, the dust-bowl story, the burying-your-child-on-the-trail story, the I-will-never-go-hungry-again story, the Mildred Pierce story, the story about how the sheer nerve of even professionally unskilled women can prevail, show the men; the story that has historically encouraged women in this country, even as it has threatened men. The dreams and the fears into which Martha Stewart taps are not of "feminine" domesticity but of female power, of the woman who sits down at the table with the men and, still in her apron, walks away with the chips.

ANALYZING What the Writer Says

1. What strikes Didion as unusual about the unofficial Martha Stewart Web sites and their users?

2. What, according to Didion, does Martha Stewart actually sell?

3. Cite one or two passages that reveal Didion's opinion of Jerry Oppenheimer, author of "Just Desserts," an unauthorized biography of Stewart.

4. Didion argues that Stewart's mission and her appeal are "not very well understood." In what ways is Stewart misunderstood? What, finally, is Stewart's mission?

5. What does Didion suggest is at the heart of the misunderstanding and criticism of Martha Stewart?

ANALYZING How the Writer Says It

1. Didion relies largely on quotes from unofficial Web sites to introduce Martha Stewart. What is the effect of her technique?

2. In one paragraph, the only one in which she includes parenthetical page numbers, Didion lists several examples of Stewart's "divined faults" from Jerry Oppenheimer's book. Why does Didion use page numbers in this paragraph, and what is the effect of these particular page numbers?

3. How does Didion's title encapsulate her thesis?

ANALYZING the Issue

1. What qualities are most often associated with business success? Do you think those qualities are more admired in men than in women?

2. Is Martha Stewart a feminist? Has she helped or hurt the feminist cause?

3. Analyze the relevance of Didion's argument in light of Martha Stewart's recent legal troubles.

ANALYZING Connections Between Texts

1. Joan Didion, Richard Selzer ("Imelda," p. 798), and Dennis Overbye ("He's Still Ready for His Close-Up," p. 794) all emphasize the quintessential *humanity* of their subjects: Despite her enormous success, Martha Stewart comes across as a friend to her readers; Dr. Franciscus performs plastic surgery on a dead girl to give her mother comfort; Einstein remains humbly focused on his science even after he has become a celebrity. Looking at these examples, do you think "true" genius is coupled with personal humility and a regard for one's fellow men? Or are these qualities that have nothing to do with genius? Explain.

2. In "Everywoman.com," Joan Didion suggests that Martha Stewart, the ultimate homemaker, embodies true feminism: She is tough, successful, in charge. Similarly, in "Polygamy Now!" (p. 143) Elizabeth Joseph argues that polygamy offers the "ultimate feminist lifestyle." Compare and contrast the two positions.

3. How does Didion's portrait of Martha Stewart compare to Timothy Greenfield-Saunders's in "Be It Ever So Humble" (p. 119)?

WARMING UP: *Do you know anyone who has an amazing athletic, artistic, or musical talent? Does that person have unusual habits or obsessions?*

The Physical Genius

BY MALCOLM GLADWELL

MALCOLM GLADWELL

In the following article, which first appeared in New York *in August 1999, a reporter tries to uncover the secrets of extraordinary physical prowess, arguing that geniuses, whether in a hockey rink or an operating room, share certain traits.*

Early one recent morning, while the San Francisco fog was lifting from the surrounding hills, Charlie Wilson performed his two thousand nine hundred and eighty-seventh transsphenoidal resection of a pituitary tumor. The patient was a man in his sixties who had complained of impotence and obscured vision. Diagnostic imaging revealed a growth, eighteen millimetres in diameter, that had enveloped his pituitary gland and was compressing his optic nerve. He was anesthetized and covered in blue surgical drapes, and one of Wilson's neurosurgery residents—a tall, slender woman in her final year of training—"opened" the case, making a small incision in his upper gum, directly underneath his nose. She then tunnelled back through his nasal passages until she reached the pituitary, creating a cavity several inches deep and about one and a half centimetres in diameter.

Wilson entered the operating room quickly, walking stiffly, bent slightly at the waist. He is sixty-nine—a small, wiry man with heavily muscled arms. His hair is cut very close to his scalp, so that, as residents over the years have joked, he might better empathize with the shaved heads of his patients. He is part Cherokee Indian and has high, broad cheekbones and large ears, which stick out at almost forty-five-degree angles. He was wearing Nike cross-trainers, and surgical scrubs marked with the logo of the medical center he has dominated for the past thirty years—Moffitt Hospital, at the University of California, San Francisco. When he was busiest, in the nineteen-eighties, he would routinely do seven or eight brain surgeries in a row, starting at dawn and ending at dusk, lining up patients in adjoining operating rooms and striding from one to the other like a conquering general. On this particular day, he would do five, of which the transsphenoidal was the first, but the rituals would be the same. Wilson believes that neurosurgery is best conducted in silence, with a scrub nurse who can anticipate his every step, and a resident who does not have to be told what to do, only shown. There was no music in the O.R. To guard against unanticipated disturbances, the door was locked. Pagers were set to "buzz," not beep. The phone was put on "Do Not Disturb."

Wilson sat by the patient in what looked like a barber's chair, manipulating a surgical microscope with a foot pedal. In his left hand he wielded a tiny suction tube, which removed excess blood. In his right he held a series of instruments in steady alternation: Cloward elevator, Penfield No. 2, Cloward rongeur, Fulton rongeur, conchatome, Hardy dissector, Kurze scissors, and so on. He worked quickly, and with no wasted motion. Through the microscope, the tumor looked like a piece of lobster flesh, white and fibrous. He removed the middle of it, exposing the pituitary underneath. Then he took a ring curette—a long instrument with a circular scalpel perpendicular to the handle—and ran it lightly across the surface of the gland, peeling the tumor away as he did so.

It was, he would say later, like running a squeegee across a windshield, except that in this case the windshield was a surgical field one centimetre in diameter, flanked on either side by the carotid arteries, the principal sources of blood to the brain. If Wilson were to wander too far to the right or to the left and nick either artery, the patient might, in the neurosurgical shorthand, "stroke." If he were to push too far to the rear, he might damage any number of critical nerves. If he were not to probe aggressively, though, he might miss a bit of tumor and defeat the purpose of the procedure entirely. It was a delicate operation, which called for caution and confidence and ability to distinguish between what was supposed to be there and what wasn't. Wilson never wavered. At one point, there was bleeding from the right side of the pituitary, which signalled to Wilson that a small piece of tumor was still just outside his field of vision, and so he gently slid the ring curette over, feeling with the instrument as if by his fingertip, navigating around the carotid, lifting out the remaining bit of tumor. In the hands of an ordinary neurosurgeon, the operation—down to that last bit of blindfolded acrobatics—might have taken several hours. It took Charlie Wilson twenty-five minutes.

Neurosurgery is generally thought to attract the most gifted and driven of medical-school graduates. Even in that rarefied world, however, there are surgeons who are superstars and surgeons who are merely very good. Charlie Wilson is one of the superstars. Those who have trained with him say that if you showed them a dozen videotapes of different neurosurgeons in action— with the camera focussed just on the hands of the surgeon and the movements of the instruments—they could pick Wilson out in an instant, the same way an old baseball hand could look at a dozen batters in silhouette and tell you which one was Willie Mays. Wilson has a distinctive fluidity and grace.

One of the most difficult of all neurosurgical procedures is aneurysm repair, where the surgeon sets out to seal, with a tiny titanium clip, a bulge in the side of an artery caused by the weakening of its wall. If the aneurysm bursts in the process—because the clip is applied incorrectly, or the surgeon inadvertently punctures one of the tributary vessels or doesn't see something critical on the underside of the aneurysm—the patient stands a good chance of dying. Aneurysm repair is bomb disposal. Wilson made it look easy. "After he'd dissected the whole aneurysm out, and when he had control of all the feeding vessels, I'd see him grasp it and flip it back and forth, because he somehow *knew* that if it popped he would still be able to clip it," says Michon Morita, who trained with Wilson at U.C.S.F. in the early nineties and now practices in Honolulu. "Most people are afraid of aneurysms. He wasn't afraid of them at all. He was like a cat playing with a mouse."

There are thousands of people who have played in the National Hockey League over the years. But there has been only one Wayne Gretzky. Thousands of cellists play professionally all over the world, but very few will ever earn comparison with Yo-Yo Ma. People like Gretzky or Ma or Charlie Wilson all have an affinity for translating thought into action. They're what we might call physical geniuses. But what makes them so good at what they do?

The temptation is to treat physical genius in the same way that we treat intellectual genius—to think of it as something that can be ascribed to a single factor, a physical version of I.Q. When professional football coaches assess the year's crop of college prospects, they put them through drills designed to measure what they regard as athleticism: How high can you jump? How many pounds can you bench press? How fast can you sprint? The sum of the scores on these tests is considered predictive of athletic performance, and every year some college player's stock shoots up before draft day because it is suddenly discovered that he can run, say, 4.4 seconds in the forty-yard dash as opposed to 4.6 seconds. This much seems like common sense. The puzzling thing about physical genius, however, is that the closer you look at it the less it can be described by such cut-and-dried measures of athleticism.

Consider, for example, Tony Gwynn, who has been one of the best hitters in baseball over the past fifteen years. We would call him extraordinarily coördinated, by which we mean that in the course of several hundred milliseconds he can execute a series of perfectly synchronized muscular actions—the rotation of the shoulder, the movement of the arms, the shift of the hips—and can regulate the outcome of those actions so that his bat hits the ball with exactly the desired degree of force. These are abilities governed by specific neurological mechanisms. Timing, for example, appears to be controlled by the cerebellum. Richard Ivry, a psychologist at the University of California at Berkeley, has looked at patients who suffered cerebellar damage as a result of a stroke. He had them pronounce the sounds "bah," "pah," and "dah." The difference between the "b" sound and the "p" sound is primarily a matter of timing. "To make the 'b' sound, you put your lips together and as you open them you immediately vibrate the vocal cords," Ivry said. "For 'p' you open the lips thirty to forty milliseconds before the vocal cords vibrate." Stroke patients with cerebellar damage, Ivry found, make lots of "b"–"p" mistakes: "baby" comes out "paby." Their timing is off. But they don't have trouble with "b" and "d" because the timing of lips and vocal cords for these two sounds is exactly the same. The difference is simply in the configuration of your tongue. "You never hear them say 'dady' instead of 'baby,'" Ivry said.

Force regulation appears to be controlled by another area of the brain entire- ly, the basal ganglia. "I like to think of the basal ganglia as a gate to the motor system," Ivry said, although he cautioned that the work on force regulation is still a good deal more speculative than the work on timing. "At any point in time, I have a few actions that I'm thinking about, and the basal ganglia are monitoring all the potential ones, then choosing one. The question is: How quickly does that gate open up?" He devised a study in which subjects were asked to press on a lever with their index finger over and over again, with the same degree of force each time. Patients with Parkinson's disease, which is a degenerative condition affecting the basal ganglia, had relatively little trouble with the timing of that movement, but they had terrible difficulty controlling the force of the tapping. At one moment they were pressing too hard, and the next they weren't pressing hard enough. Their "gate" wasn't working properly.

Stroke victims and Parkinson's patients, of course, are people who have actually suffered neurological impairment. But Ivry and Steven Keele, of the University of Oregon, suggest that in healthy people, too, there is probably a natural variation in the efficiency of these motor-control functions. They have done work on clumsy children, for example, that shows that what looks like a general lack of coordination can, in some cases, be broken down into either a basal-ganglia problem or a cerebellum problem. Clumsy kids are at one end of the coordination bell curve. "Maybe their neural connections or their branching isn't as well developed, or they don't have as many synaptic connections," Ivry suggests. And at the other end of the curve? That's where you find people like Tony Gwynn.

But being wonderfully coordinated isn't all there is to hitting. A ball thrown at eighty-nine miles per hour (which is a typical speed in the major leagues) takes roughly four hundred and sixty milliseconds to go from the pitcher's hand to home plate. Someone like Tony Gwynn, with all his finely tuned physiological hardware, takes about a hundred and sixty milliseconds to swing a bat. The decision about how to swing the bat, however, will take Gwynn between a hundred and ninety and four hundred and fifty milliseconds, depending on what the situation is and what he intends to do with the pitch. "Very good hitters base their decisions on past experience with certain pitchers, with the count, with the probabilities of certain types of pitches, with their own skills, and use very early cues in the pitcher's delivery to begin the swing," Janet Starkes, a professor of kinesiology at McMaster University, in Ontario, says.

What sets physical geniuses apart from other people, then, is not merely being able to do something but knowing what to do—their capacity to pick up on subtle patterns that others generally miss. This is what we mean when we say that great athletes have a "feel" for the game, or that they "see" the court or the field or the ice in a special way. Wayne Gretzky, in a 1981 game against the St. Louis Blues, stood behind the St. Louis goal, laid the puck across the blade of his stick, then bounced it off the back of the goalie in front of him and into the net. Gretzky's genius at that moment lay in seeing a scoring possibility where no one had seen one before. "People talk about skating, puck-handling, and shooting," Gretzky told an interviewer some years later, "but the whole sport is angles and caroms, forgetting the straight direction the puck is going, calculating where it will be diverted, factoring in all the interruptions." Neurosurgeons say that when the very best surgeons operate they always know where they are going, and they mean that the Charlie Wilsons of this world possess that same special feel—an ability to calculate the diversions and to factor in the interruptions when faced with a confusing mass of blood and tissue.

When Charlie Wilson came to U.C. San Francisco, in July of 1968, his first case concerned a woman who had just had a pituitary operation. The previous surgeon had done the one thing that surgeons are not supposed to do in pituitary surgery—tear one of the carotid arteries. Wilson was so dismayed by the outcome that he resolved he would teach himself how to do the transsphenoidal, which was then a relatively uncommon procedure. He carefully read the medical literature. He practiced on a few cadavers. He called a friend in Los Angeles who was an expert at the procedure, and had him come to San Francisco and perform two operations while Wilson watched. He flew to Paris to observe Gerard Guiot, who was one of the great transsphenoidal surgeons at the time. Then he flew home. It was the equivalent of someone preparing for a major league tryout by watching the Yankees on television and hitting balls in an amusement-arcade batting cage. "Charlie went slowly," recalls Ernest Bates, a Bay-area neurosurgeon who scrubbed with Wilson on his first transsphenoidal, "but he knew the anatomy and, boom, he was there. I thought, My God, this was the first? You'd have thought he had done a hundred. Charlie has a skill that the rest of us just don't have."

This is the hard part about understanding physical genius, because the source of that special skill—that "feel"—is still something of a mystery. "Sometimes during the course of an operation, there'll be several possible ways of doing something, and I'll size them up and, without having any conscious reason, I'll just do one of them," Wilson told me. He speaks with a soft, slow drawl, a remnant of Neosho, Missouri, the little town where he grew up, and where his father was a pharmacist, who kept his store open from 7 A.M. to 11 P.M., seven days a week. Wilson has a plainspoken, unpretentious quality. When he talks about his extraordinary success as a surgeon, he gives the impression that he is talking about some abstract trait that he is neither responsible for nor completely able to understand. "It's sort of an invisible hand," he went on. "It begins almost to seem mystical. Sometimes a resident asks, 'Why did you do that?' and I say"—here Wilson gave a little shrug— "'Well, it just seemed like the right thing.'"

There is a neurosurgeon at Columbia Presbyterian Center, in Manhattan, by the name of Don Quest, who served two tours in Vietnam flying A-1s off the U.S.S. Kitty Hawk. Quest sounds like the kind of person who bungee jumps on the weekend and has personalized license plates that read "Ace." In fact, he is a thoughtful, dapper man with a carefully trimmed mustache, who plays the trombone in his spare time and quite cheerfully describes himself as compulsive. "When I read the *New York Times*, I don't speed-read it," Quest told me. "I read it carefully. I read everything. It drives my wife crazy." He was wearing a spotless physician's coat and a bow tie. "When I'm reading a novel—and there are so many novels I want to read—even if it's not very good I can't throw it away. I stick with it. It's quite frustrating, because I don't really have time for garbage." Quest talked about what it was like to repair a particularly tricky aneurysm compared to what it was like to land at night in rough seas and a heavy fog when you are running out of fuel and the lights are off on the carrier's landing strip, because the skies are full of enemy aircraft. "I think they are similar," he said, after some thought, and what he meant was that they were both exercises in a certain kind of exhaustive and meticulous preparation. "There is a checklist, before you take off, and this was drilled into us," Quest said. "It's on the dashboard with all the things you need to do. People forget to put the hook down, and you can't land on an aircraft carrier if the hook isn't down. Or they don't put the wheels down. One of my friends, my roommate, landed at night on the aircraft carrier with the wheels up. Thank God, the hook caught, because his engine stopped. He would have gone in the water." Quest did not seem like the kind of person who would forget to put the wheels down. "Some people are much more compulsive than others, and it shows," he went on to say. "It shows in how well they do their landing on the aircraft carrier, how many times they screw up, or are on the wrong radio frequency, or get lost, or their ordinances aren't accurate in terms of dropping a bomb. The ones who are the best are the ones who are always very careful."

Quest isn't saying that fine motor ability is irrelevant. One would expect him to perform extremely well on tests of the sort Ivry and Keele might devise. And, like Tony Gwynn, he's probably an adept and swift decision maker. But these abilities, Quest is saying, are of little use if you don't have the right sort of personality. Charles Bosk, a sociologist at the University of Pennsylvania, once conducted a set of interviews with young doctors who had either resigned or been fired from neurosurgery-training programs, in an effort to figure out what separated the unsuccessful surgeons from their successful counterparts. He concluded that, far more than technical skills or intelligence, what was necessary for success was the sort of attitude that Quest has—a practical-minded obsession with the possibility and the consequences of failure. "When I interviewed the surgeons who were fired, I used to leave the interview shaking," Bosk said. "I would hear these horrible stories about what they did wrong, but the thing was that they didn't *know* that what they did was wrong. In my interviewing, I began to develop what I thought was an indicator of whether someone was going to be a good surgeon or not. It was a couple of simple questions: Have you ever made a mistake? And, if so, what was your worst mistake? The people who said, 'Gee, I haven't really had one,' or, 'I've had a couple of bad outcomes but they were due to things out of my control'—invariably those were the worst candidates. And the residents who said, 'I make mistakes all the time. There was this horrible thing that happened just yesterday and here's what it was.' They were the best. They had the ability to rethink everything that they'd done and imagine how they might have done it differently."

What this attitude drives you to do is practice over and over again, until even the smallest imperfections are ironed out. After doing poorly in a tournament just prior to this year's Wimbledon, Greg Rusedski, who is one of the top tennis players in the world, told reporters that he was going home to hit a thousand practice serves. One of the things that set Rusedski apart from lesser players, in other words, is that he is the kind of person who is willing to stand out in the summer sun, repeating the same physical movement again and again, in single-minded pursuit of some fractional improvement in his performance. Wayne Gretzky was the same way. He would frequently stay behind after practice, long after everyone had left, flipping pucks to a specific spot in the crease, or aiming shot after shot at the crossbar or the goal post.

And Charlie Wilson? In his first few years as a professor at U.C.S.F., he would disappear at the end of the day into a special laboratory to practice his craft on rats: isolating, cutting, and then sewing up their tiny blood vessels, and sometimes operating on a single rat two or three times. He would construct an artificial aneurysm using a vein graft on the side of a rat artery, then manipulate the aneurysm the same way he would in a human being, toughening its base with a gentle coagulating current—and return two or three days later to see how successful his work had been. Wilson sees surgery as akin to a military campaign. Training with him is like boot camp. He goes to bed somewhere around eleven at night and rises at 4:30 A.M. For years, he ran upward of eighty miles a week, competing in marathons and hundred-mile ultra-marathons. He quit only after he had a hip replacement and two knee surgeries and found himself operating in a cast. Then he took up rowing. On his days in the operating room, at the height of his career, Wilson would run his morning ten or twelve miles, conduct medical rounds, operate steadily until six or seven in the evening, and, in between, see patients, attend meetings, and work on what now totals six hundred academic articles. One of his former residents says, with a laugh, that when he was on Wilson's rotation he developed a persistent spasm of his upper eyelid and it did not go away until he moved on to train with someone else. Julian Hoff, the chairman of neurosurgery at the University of Michigan and a longtime friend of Wilson's, says, "The way he would communicate with people in the office is that he would have a little piece of paper and he would put your name with an arrow next to it, and two words saying what he wanted you to do." Once, when a new head of nursing at U.C.S.R. wanted to start rotating nursing teams in neurosurgery, instead of letting Wilson work with the same team every day, he stopped operating for a week in protest. New nurses, he explained, would mean more mistakes—not fatal mistakes but irregularities in the flow of his operating room, such as someone's handing him the wrong instrument, or handing him an instrument with the blade up instead of down, or even just a certain hesitation, because to Wilson the perfect operation requires a particular grace and rhythm. "In every way, it is analogous to the routine of a concert pianist," he says. "If you were going to do a concert and you didn't practice for a week, someone would notice that, just as I notice if one of my scrub nurses has been off for a week. There is a fraction-of-a-second difference in the way she reacts."

"Wilson has a certain way of positioning the arm of the retractor blade"—an [20] instrument used to hold brain tissue in place "so that the back end of the retractor doesn't stick up at all and he won't accidentally bump into it," Michon Morita told me. "Every once in a while, though, I'd see him when he didn't quite put it in the position he wanted to, and bumped it, which caused a little bit of hemorrhage on the brain surface. It wasn't harming the patient, and it was nothing he couldn't handle. But I'd hear 'That was stupid,' and I'd immediately ask myself, What did I do wrong? Then I'd realize he was chastising himself. Most people would say that if there was no harm done to the patient it was no big deal. But he wants to be perfect in everything, and when that perfection is broken he gets frustrated."

This kind of obsessive preparation does two things. It creates consistency. Practice is what enables Greg Rusedski to hit a serve at a hundred and twenty-five miles per hour again and again. It's what enables a pianist to play Chopin's double-thirds Étude at full speed, striking every key with precisely calibrated force. More important, practice changes the *way* a task is perceived. A chess master, for example, can look at a game in progress for a few seconds and then perfectly reconstruct that same position on a blank chessboard. That's not because chess masters have great memories (they don't have the same knack when faced with a random arrangement of pieces) but because hours and hours of chess playing have enabled them to do what psychologists call "chunking." Chunking is based on the fact that we store familiar sequences—like our telephone number or our bank-machine password—in long-term memory as a single unit, or chunk. If I told you a number you'd never heard before, though, you would be able to store it only in short-term memory, one digit at a time, and if I asked you to repeat it back to me you might be able to remember only a few of those digits—maybe the first two or the last three. By contrast, when the chess masters see the board from a real game, they are able to break the board down into a handful of chunks—two or three clusters of pieces in positions that they have encountered before.

In "The Game of Our Lives," a classic account of the 1980–81 season of the Edmonton Oilers hockey team, Peter Gzowski argues that one of the principal explanations for the particular genius of Wayne Gretzky was that he was hockey's greatest chunker. Gretzky, who holds nearly every scoring record in professional hockey, baffled many observers because he seemed to reverse the normal laws of hockey. Most great offensive players prefer to keep the rest of the action on the ice behind them—to try to make the act of scoring be just about themselves and the goalie. Gretzky liked to keep the action in front of him. He would set up by the side of the rink, or behind the opposing team's net, so that the eleven other players on the ice were in full view, and then slide the perfect pass to the perfect spot. He made hockey look easy, even as he was playing in a way that made it more complicated. Gzowski says that Gretzky could do that because, like master chess players, he wasn't seeing all eleven other players individually; he was seeing only chunks. Here is Gzowski's conclusion after talking to Gretzky about a game he once played against the Montreal Canadiens. It could as easily serve as an explanation for Charlie Wilson's twenty-five-minute transsphenoidal resection:

> What Gretzky perceives on a hockey rink is, in a curious way, more simple than what a less accomplished player perceives. He sees not so much a set of moving players as a number of situations. . . . Moving in on the Montreal blueline, as he was able to recall while he watched a videotape of himself, he was aware of the position of all the other players on the ice. The pattern they formed was, to him, one fact, and he reacted to that fact. When he sends a pass to what to the rest of us appears an empty space on the ice, and when a teammate magically appears in that space to collect the puck, he has in reality simply summoned up from his account of knowledge the fact that in a particular situation, someone is likely to be in a particular spot, and if he is not there now he will be there presently.

For a time, early in his career, Charlie Wilson became obsessed with tennis. He took lessons from Rod Laver. He joined three tennis clubs, so he could be absolutely assured of having court time whenever he wanted it. He had his own ball machine, and would go out early in the morning, before anyone else was on the court, and hit bucket after bucket of balls. He was in great shape. He could play any number of sets. He had a serve that he says was a beauty, a great backhand, and—as he put it—"a very expensive" forehand. But Wilson never turned into the kind of tennis player he wanted to be. Julian Hoff recalls, "There was this guy in the neurosurgery department, John Adams, who was a former tennis champion. An older guy. Arthritic. Rickety. Looked terrible. Charlie decided that he had to beat John Adams. But he never could. It drove him crazy."

It is easy to understand Wilson's frustration. He was a superb athlete—as a teen-ager he had been an excellent basketball player, and he attended college on a football scholarship—and a surgeon who could make life-or-death decisions in a split second. And yet, for all his focus and determination, he could not respond effectively to an old man shuffling toward the ball twenty feet across the net from him. "A good player knows where the ball is going," Wilson says. "He anticipates it. He is there. I just wasn't." What Wilson is describing is a failure not of skill or of resolve but of the least understood element of physical genius—imagination. For some reason, he could not make the game come alive in his mind.

When psychologists study people who are expert at motor tasks, they find that almost all of them use their imaginations in a very particular and sophisticated way. Jack Nicklaus, for instance, has said that he has never taken a swing that he didn't first mentally rehearse, frame by frame. Yo-Yo Ma told me that he remembers riding on a bus, at the age of seven, and solving a difficult musical problem by visualizing himself playing the piece on the cello. Robert Spetzler, who trained with Wilson and is widely considered to be the heir to Wilson's mantle, says that when he gets into uncharted territory in an operation he feels himself transferring his mental image of what ought to happen onto the surgical field. Charlie Wilson talks about going running in the morning and reviewing each of the day's operations in his head—visualizing the entire procedure and each potential outcome in advance. "It was a virtual rehearsal," he says, "so when I was actually doing the operation, it was as if I were doing it for the second time." Once, he says, he had finished a case and taken off his gloves and was walking down the hall away from the operating room when he suddenly stopped, because he realized that the tape he had been playing in his head didn't match the operation that had unfolded before his eyes. "I was correlating everything—what I saw, what I expected, what the X-rays said. And I just realized that I had not pursued one particular thing. So I turned around, scrubbed, and went back in, and, sure enough, there was a little remnant of tumor that was just around the corner. It would have been a disaster."

The Harvard University psychologist Stephen Kosslyn has shown that this [25] power to visualize consists of at least four separate abilities, working in combination. The first is the ability to generate an image—to take something out of long-term memory and reconstruct it on demand. The second is what he calls "image inspection," which is the ability to take that mental picture and draw inferences from it. The third is "image maintenance," the ability to hold that picture steady. And the fourth is "image transformation," which is the ability to take that image and manipulate it. If I asked you whether a frog had a tail, for example, you would summon up a picture of a frog from your long-term memory (image generation), hold it steady in your mind (image mainte-nance), rotate the frog around until you see his backside (image transforma-tion], then look to see if there was a tail there (image inspection). These four abilities are highly variable. Kosslyn once gave a group of people a list of thir-teen tasks, each designed to test a different aspect of visualization, and the results were all over the map. You could be very good at generation and main-tenance, for example, without being good at transformation, or you could be good at transformation without necessarily being adept at inspection and maintenance. Some of the correlations, in fact, were negative, meaning that sometimes being good at one of those four things meant that you were likely to be bad at another. Bennett Stein, a former chairman of neurosurgery at Columbia Presbyterian Center, says that one of the reasons some neuro-surgery residents fail in their training is that they are incapable of making the transition between the way a particular problem is depicted in an X-ray or an M.R.I., and how the problem looks when they encounter it in real life. These are people whose capacities for mental imaging simply do not match what's required for dealing with the complexities of brain surgery. Perhaps these peo-ple can generate an image but are unable to transform it in precisely the way that is necessary to be a great surgeon; or perhaps they can transform the image but they cannot maintain it. The same may have been true for Charlie Wilson and tennis. Somehow, his particular configuration of imaging abilities did not fit with the demands of the sport. When he stopped playing the game, he says, he didn't miss it, and that's not surprising. Tennis never quite got inside his head. Neurosurgery, of course, is another matter.

"Certain aneurysms at the base of the brain are surrounded by very impor-tant blood vessels and nerves, and the typical neurosurgeon will make that dis-section with a set of micro-instruments that are curved, each with a blunt end," Craig Yorke, who trained with Wilson and now practices neurosurgery in Topeka, recalls. "The neurosurgeon will sneak up on them. Charlie would call for a No. 11 blade, which is a thin, very low-profile scalpel, and would just cut down to where the aneurysm was. He would be there in a quarter of the time." The speed and the audacity of Wilson's maneuvers, Yorke said, would some-times leave him breathless. "Do you know about Gestalt psychology?" he con-tinued. "If I look at a particular field—tumor or aneurysm—I will see the gestalt after I've worked on it for a little while. He would just glance at it and see it. It's a conceptual, a spatial thing. His use of the No. 11 blade depended on his ability to construct a gestalt of the surgical field first. If just anybody had held up the eleven blade in that way it might have been a catastrophe. He could do it because he had the picture of the whole anatomy in his head when he picked up the instrument."

If you think of physical genius as a pyramid, with, at the bottom, the raw components of coordination, and, above that, the practice that perfects those particular movements, then this faculty of imagination is the top layer. This is what separates the physical genius from those who are merely very good. Michael Jordan and Karl Malone, his longtime rival, did not differ so much in their athletic ability or in how obsessively they practiced. The difference between them is that Jordan could always generate a million different scenarios by which his team could win, some of which were chunks stored in long-term memory, others of which were flights of fancy that came to him, figuratively and literally, in midair. Jordan twice won championships in the face of unexpected adversity: once, a case of the flu, and, the second time, a back injury to his teammate Scottie Pippen, and he seemed to thrive on these obstacles, in a way Karl Malone never could.

Yo-Yo Ma says that only once, early in his career, did he try for a technically perfect performance. "I was seventeen," he told me. "I spent a year working on it. I was playing a Brahms sonata at the 92nd Street Y. I remember working really hard at it, and in the middle of the performance I thought, I'm bored. It would have been nothing for me to get up from the stage and walk away. That's when I decided I would always opt for expression over perfection." It isn't that Ma doesn't achieve perfection; it's that he finds striving for perfection to be banal. He says that he sometimes welcomes it when he breaks a string, because that is precisely the kind of thing (like illness or an injury to a teammate) that you cannot prepare for—that you haven't chunked and, like some robot, stored neatly in long-term memory. The most successful performers improvise. They create, in Ma's words, "something living." Ma says he spends ninety per cent of his time "looking at the score, figuring it out—who's saying this, who wrote this and why," letting his mind wander, and only ten per cent on the instrument itself. Like Jordan, his genius originates principally in his imagination. If he spent less time dreaming and more time playing, he would be Karl Malone.

Here is the source of the physical genius's motivation. After all, what is this sensation—this feeling of having what you do fit perfectly into the dimensions of your imagination—but the purest form of pleasure? Tony Gwynn and Wayne Gretzky and Charlie Wilson and all the other physical geniuses are driven to greatness because they have found something so compelling that they cannot put it aside. Perhaps this explains why a great many top neurosurgeons are also highly musical. Robert Spetzler, Wilson's protégé, seriously considered a career as a concert pianist. Craig Yorke made his debut as a violinist at sixteen with the Boston Pops. Quest, of course, plays the trombone. As for Wilson, he is a cellist and, when he was a student in New Orleans, he would play jazz piano at Pat O'Brien's, in the French Quarter. Music is one of the few vocations that offer a kind of sensory and cognitive immersion similar to surgery: the engagement of hand and eye, the challenge of sustained performance, the combination of mind and motion—all of it animated by the full force of the imagination. Once, in an E-mail describing his special training sessions on rats, Wilson wrote that he worked on them for two years and "then trailed off when I finally figured that I was doing it for fun, not for practice." For fun! When someone chooses to end a twelve-hour day alone in a laboratory, inducing aneurysms in the arteries of rats, we might call that behavior obsessive. But that is an uncharitable word. A better explanation is that, for some mysterious and wonderful reason, Wilson finds the act of surgery irresistible, in the way that musicians find pleasure in the sounds they produce on their instruments, or in the way Tony Gwynn gets a thrill every time he strokes a ball cleanly through the infield. Before he was two years old, it is said, Wayne Gretzky watched hockey games on television, enraptured, and slid his stockinged feet on the linoleum in imitation of the players, then cried when the game was over, because he could not understand how something so sublime should have to come to an end. This was long before Gretzky was any good at the game itself, or was skilled in any of its aspects, or could create even the smallest of chunks. But what he had was what the physical genius must have before any of the other layers of expertise fall into place: he had stumbled onto the one thing that, on some profound aesthetic level, made him happy.

Charlie Wilson says that only once in his career has he allowed himself to 30 become emotionally attached to a patient—attached to the point where the patient's death felt like that of a family member. "It was this beautiful girl who had a spinal tumor," he told me. "She was always bringing me cookies. It was a malignant tumor. She became a paraplegic, and then she got married." Wilson was talking softly and slowly. "It just tore me up. I couldn't help myself. I remember operating on her and crying, right there in the O.R." Charlie Wilson is a man who, when he operates, does not permit music or extraneous talking or the noise of beepers or phones, who is attuned to even the slightest hesitation on the part of his scrub nurse, who admits, in his entire life, to just one day of depression, and who has the audacity and the control to take a No. 11 blade and slice down—just like that—to the basilar artery. But she was young, and it was tragic, and there was nothing he could do, and he has a daughter, too, so perhaps it touched a chord. He was sitting, as he talked, in his office at Moffitt Hospital with his Nike cross-trainers and surgical scrubs, thinking back to a moment when all certitude and composure escaped him. His performance on the day he operated on the girl's spinal tumor must have been compromised by his grief, he admitted. But what did it matter? This was not a procedure that required great judgment or technical mastery. "It was an ugly operation," he said, pronouncing the word "ugly" with a special distaste. "Maybe that was part of it." Of course, it was. Charlie Wilson is one of the world's great neurosurgeons because he can find some beauty in what he does even in the midst of terrible illness. There was nothing beautiful there. "This lovely, lovely girl." He looked away. "Such a heart."

ANALYZING What the Writer Says

1. What sets Charlie Wilson apart in the operating theater? How is he different from other neurosurgeons?

2. Although studies have identified some of the neurological reasons for differences in motor skills and physical coordination, Gladwell points to other characteristics as well. What are some of those?

3. In what specific ways are Charlie Wilson and Wayne Gretzky alike?

4. What has the sociologist interviewed by Gladwell discovered about the attitudes of unsuccessful doctors in neurosurgery programs?

5. Why is Charlie Wilson unable to become the tennis player he wants to be?

6. What three components of physical genius does Gladwell identify as common to all superstars?

ANALYZING How the Writer Says It

1. What kinds of evidence does Gladwell use to support his theory of physical genius?

2. Why do you think Gladwell closes his piece with an anecdote about Charlie Wilson that is uncharacteristic of the man? What is the effect of the last sentence?

ANALYZING the Issue

1. Do you think a person can *become* a prodigy through focus, concentration, and training? Or do you agree with Gladwell that part of it is simply gift? Explain.

2. Is genius something that can be codified—or is mystery or mysticism intrinsic to genius? Explain.

ANALYZING Connections Between Texts

1. Both Malcolm Gladwell and Richard Selzer ("Imelda," p. 798) write about doctors whose enormous professional success may have spoiled their "bedside manner"; they have trouble relating to their patients and the patients' families as human beings. How important is bedside manner to a doctor? Does it matter if doctors are rude and condescending so long as they save lives? Explain.

2. Compare the description of Malcolm Gladwell's performing surgery on a
   patient to the description of (similar) procedures in Keith D. Mano's "Plastic
   Surgery" (p. 238). In what ways do the authors' attitudes toward surgery and
   surgeons resemble each other? In what ways do they differ?

3. Walter Iooss Jr.'s photograph of Michael Jordan (p. 121) shows the basketball
   star soaking his sprained ankle in a bucket, surrounded by the splendor of a
   fancy hotel room. Compare this depiction of Jordan to Malcolm Gladwell's
   description of Charlie Wilson's spending countless hours in the lab to perfect
   his technique of repairing a brain aneurism. How do Iooss and Gladwell alter
   the popular myth of genius as a God-given talent that emerges without much
   effort? Are geniuses born? Or are they made through relentless work and
   training? Explain.

WARMING UP: *Are you bothered when "theater rock" artists (David Bowie in the seventies, Marilyn Manson in our day) wear clothes and makeup traditionally worn by women? Why or why not?*

A Rhinestone as Big as the Ritz

BY DAVE HICKEY

DAVE HICKEY

Dave Hickey has enjoyed a variety of occupations: gallery owner, editor, songwriter, art critic, and writer. Currently a professor of art criticism and theory at the University of Nevada, Las Vegas, Hickey analyzes Liberace's flamboyant style in "A Rhinestone as Big as the Ritz," from his 1997 essay collection Air Guitar: Essays on Art & Democracy. *It first appeared as "A Rhinestone as Big as the Ritz: Liberace and His Amazing Museum" in 1992 in* Art issues.

The balcony of my apartment faces west toward the mountains, overlooking the Las Vegas Strip; so, every evening when the sky is not overcast, a few minutes after the sun has gone down, the mountains turn black, the sky above them turns this radical plum/rouge, and the neon logos of The Desert Inn, The Stardust, Circus Circus, The Riviera, The Las Vegas Hilton, and Vegas World blaze forth against the black mountains—and every night I find myself struck by the fact that, while The Strip always glitters with a reckless and undeniable specificity against the darkness, the sunset, smoldering out above the mountains, every night and without exception, looks bogus as hell. It's spectacular, of course, and even, occasionally, sublime (if you like sublime), but to my eyes that sunset is always fake—as flat and gaudy as a Barnett Newman and just as pretentious.

Friends of mine who visit watch this light show with different eyes. They prefer the page of the landscape to the text of the neon. They seem to think it's more "authentic." I, on the other hand, suspect that "authenticity" is altogether elsewhere—that they are responding to nature's ability to mimic the sincerity of a painting, that the question of the sunset and The Strip is more a matter of one's taste in duplicity. One either prefers the honest fakery of the neon or the fake honesty of the sunset—the undisguised artifice of culture or the cultural construction of "authenticity"—the genuine rhinestone, finally, or the imitation pearl. Herein I take my text for the tragicomedy of Liberace and the anomaly of his amazing museum.

As its emblem, I cite my favorite *objet* in his collection—its keystone, in fact—the secret heart and sacred ark of Las Vegas itself: "The World's Largest Rhinestone," 115,000 karats revolving in a circular vitrine, dazzling us all with its plangent banality. It weighs 50.6 pounds and is fabricated of pure lead glass. It was manufactured by Swarovski Gem Company, the rhinestone people of Vienna (where else?), and presented to Liberace as a token of appreciation for his patronage, for the virtual fields of less substantial rhinestones he had acquired from them over the years to endow his costumes, his cars, his furniture, and his pianos with their ersatz spiritual dazzle. In my view, this was money well spent, for, within the confines of the Liberace Museum, dazzle they certainly do.

Within these three large showrooms, spaced around a shopping center on East Tropicana Boulevard, dazzle rules. Everything fake looks bona fide. Everything that Liberace created or caused to be created as a function of his shows or of his showmanship (his costumes, his cars, his jewelry, his candelabra, his pianos) shines with a crisp, pop authority. Everything created as a consequence of his endeavor (like the mega-rhinestone) exudes a high-dollar egalitarian permission—while everything he purchased out of his rising slum-kid appetite for "Old World" charm and *ancien régime* legitimacy (everything "real," in other words) looks unabashedly phoney.

Thus, in the Liberace Museum, to paraphrase Ad Reinhardt, authenticity is ₅ something you bump into while you're backing up to look at something that interests you. And there is much of interest there, because Liberace was a very interesting man. He did interesting things. When I think of him today, I like to imagine him in his Palm Springs home sitting before his most "priceless antique": a full-tilt Rococo, inlaid and ormolued Louis xv desk once owned by Czar Nicholas ii. He is wearing his Vegas-tailored "Czar Nicholas" uniform. (He said he never wore his costumes off-stage, but you *know* he did.) He is making out his Christmas list. (He was a *fool* for Christmas.) There is a handsome young "hillbilly" (as his mother called them) lounging nearby.

In this scene, everything is "real": The entertainer, the "hillbilly," the white, furry shag carpet, the Vegas-Czarist uniform, the red ink on the Christmas list, even *Palm Springs* is real. Everything is real except that silly desk, which is fake just for his owning it, just for his wanting to own it—fake, finally, for his not understanding his own radicality. He had, after all, purchased the 1962 Rolls Royce Phantom v Landau sitting out in the driveway (one of seven ever made), then made it disappear—let it dissolve into a cubist dazzle of reflected desert by completely covering it with hundreds of thousands of tiny mirrored mosaic tiles—a gesture comparable to Rauschenberg erasing a de Kooning. But Lee didn't get that.

He was an innocent, a pop naïf, but he was more than that. Most prominently, Liberace was, without doubt and in his every facet, a genuine rhinestone, a heart without malice, whose only flaw was a penchant for imitation pearls—a certifiable neon icon, a light unto his people, with an inexplicable proclivity for phony sunsets. Bad taste is real taste, of course, and good taste is the residue of someone else's privilege; Liberace cultivated them both in equal parts and often to disastrous effect. But if, by his reactions—his antiques and his denials—he reinforced a tattered and tatty tradition of "Old World" respectability, then by his actions his shows and his "showmanship" (that showed what could not, at that time, be told)—he demonstrated to m-m-m-my generation the power of subversive theatricality to make manifest attitudes about sex and race and politics that could not, just for the mo', luv, be explicitly avowed.

In Liberace's case, they were never avowed. He never came out of the closet; he lived in it like the grand hypocrite that he was, and died in it, of a disease he refused to acknowledge. But neither, in fact, did Wilde come out of it, and he, along with Swinburne, and their *Belle Époque* cronies, probably *invented* the closet as a mode of subversive public/private existence. Nor did Noel Coward come out of it. He tricked it up with the smoke and mirrors of leisure-class ennui and cloaked it in public-school double entendre. What Liberace did do, however, was Americanize the closet, democratize it, fit it out with transparent walls, take it up on stage and demand our complicity in his "open secret."

In-crowd innuendo was not Liberace's game; like a black man in black-face, he took it to the limit and reveled in the impertinence of his pseudo-masquerade. He would come striding onto the stage in a costume that was, in his description, "just one tuck short of drag." He would stop under the big light, do a runway turn, and invite the audience to *"Hey, look me over!"* Then, flinging his arms upward in a fountain gesture, like a demented Polish-Italian diva, he would shoot his hip, wink, and squeal, *"I hope ya' like it! You paid for it!"* And the audience members would signify their approval and their complicity by their applause. They not only liked the dress, they were happy to have bought it for him. So, unlike Coward, whose veiled naughtiness remained opaque to those not "in the know," Liberace's closet was as democratically invisible as the emperor's new clothes, and just as revolutionary. *Everybody* "got it." But nobody said it.

Even my grandfather got it, for Chris'sake. I can remember sitting before the flickering screen of an old Emerson at my grandparents' house, watching *Liberace*, which was one of my grandmother's "programs." At one particularly saccharine moment in the proceedings my grandfather leaned forward, squinting through his cataract lenses at the tiny screen.

"A bit like cousin Ed, ain't he," my grandfather said. Getting it but not saying it.

"Yes, he is," my grandmother said, with an exasperated sniff. "And just as nice a young man, I'm sure." She got it, too. She didn't say it, either. And my point here is that, if my grandmother and grandfather (no cosmopolitans they) got it, if they perceived in Wladziu Valentino Liberace's performance, in his longing gaze into the television camera, a covert acknowledgment of his own sexuality—and if they, country people to the core, covertly accepted it in him, then "the closet" as a social modality was, even then, on the verge of obsolescence. All that remained was for Liberace and the people who accepted him to say the words. But for the most part they never did and some, recalcitrant to the last, never have.

Those who got it and didn't accept it, however, never stopped yelping. Liberace's career from first to last was beleaguered by snickers, slimy innuendo, and plain invective with regard to his sexuality . . . and his bad taste. The two, perhaps not surprisingly, seem so inextricably linked in attacks on his persona that you get the feeling they are, somehow, opposite sides of the same coin. At any rate, he was so regularly attacked for dramatizing his sexual deviation while suppressing the formal deviations of Chopin and Liszt, you get the impression that, had he purveyed a little more "difficult" art, he would have been cut a little more slack with regard to his behavior.

He chose not to do either, and, as a consequence, if Liberace had been a less self-confident figure, a more fragile and self-pitying soul, it would be all too easy now to cast him in the loser's role, as a tragic and embattled sexual outlaw. But beneath the ermines and rhinestones, Wladziu Liberace was a tough cookie and a high-roller—a positive thinker and an American hero. He came to the table to take away the money, so he cashed in the invective and, in his own immortal phrase, "cried all the way to the bank." His response to the virulent accusations that dogged his progress was always impudent passive-aggression: aggrieved, tearful, categorical denials followed immediately by further and even more extravagant behavior. So, by the end, he was gliding through the showplaces of the Western World with his handsome young "hillbillies" in tow, wearing that outrageous denial like an impregnable invisible shield. Like an old bootlegger smuggling legal booze, he continued to brandish the hypocrisies that he himself had helped make obsolete, just for the thrill of it.

Honesty is nice, they say, but transgression is sexier. So, in his final days, he 15 must, like Wilde, have decried "the decay of lying." It was what he did best, and over the years he took some shots for it—the best and most lucrative of which he took on his first tour of the British Isles in 1956, at the peak of his television and movie celebrity. In the autumn of that year, he and his manager, Seymour Heller, decided to skim a little cash off his brimming European popularity and so set sail, with Mom and brother George in tow, on the Queen Mary for an initial round of engagements in London. His reception, as they say in show business, both fulfilled his wildest dreams and confirmed his worst suspicions.

He was greeted at Southampton by a squadron of press and a gaggle of cheering fans all of whom trooped aboard the chartered "Liberace Special" for the train ride to Waterloo. There, his reception, in volume and hysteria, outstripped anything hitherto experienced in the category of pop celebrity welcomings. An unnerving crush of little old ladies and teenage bobby-soxers screamed, giggled, fainted, waved signs, and scattered paper rosepetals (thoughtfully provided) in his path. Chauffeurs and footmen bowed as his party approached the pair of Daimlers rented to "whisk them to their hotel." Then, as he was about to step into one of the limousines, a reporter shouted above the crowd,

"Do you have a normal sex life?"

Liberace, looking blandly back over his shoulder, said, "Yes. Do you?"

That night at the Royal Festival Hall, he was greeted by hostile pickets outside ("Down with Liberace!") and by a standing room audience inside that reacted to his every remark with enthusiastic shrieks and shouts and responded to every number with thunderous and unruly cheers. The press reaction, needless to say, was uniformly uncomplimentary—ranging from bored, Cowardesque dismissal, a wave of the napkin, "Take it away, please, it's corked," to hostility that bordered on panic. The masterpiece of this latter category was produced by Cassandra (William Conner) for the tabloid *Daily Mirror*, with a national circulation of 4.5 million. I quote it at length here because it is world-class screed—but also because I would like to think that, in its little way, it changed the world.

> He is the summit of sex—the pinnacle of masculine, feminine and neuter. Everything that he, she, and it can ever want. I spoke to . . . men on this newspaper who have met every celebrity coming from America for the past thirty years. They said that this deadly, winking, sniggering, snuggling, chromium plated, scent-impregnated, luminous, quivering, giggling, fruit-flavored, mincing, ice-covered heap of mother love has had the biggest reception and impact on London since Charlie Chaplin arrived at the same station, Waterloo, on September 12, 1921 . . .
>
> He reeks with emetic language that can only make grown men long for a quiet corner, an aspidistra, a handkerchief, and the old heave-ho. Without doubt, he is the biggest sentimental vomit of all time. Slobbering over his mother, winking at his brother, and counting the cash at every second, this superb piece of calculating candy floss has an answer for every situation.
>
> Nobody since Aimee Scruple McPherson has purveyed a bigger, richer and more varied slag heap of lilac-colored hokum. Nobody anywhere has made so much money out of high speed piano play with the ghost of Chopin gibbering at every note.
>
> There must be something wrong with us that our teenagers longing for sex and our middle-aged matrons fed up with sex alike should fall for such a sugary mountain of jingling claptrap wrapped up in such a preposterous clown.

Liberace would ultimately sue the *Mirror* for impugning his manhood and, 20
all evidence to the contrary, win £40,000 in damages. But what intrigues me
about Cassandra's invective is the possibility that it just might mark the official beginning of the "Sixties," as we call them. Because Liberace had this great
idea. He had touched a jangling nerve, and I like to imagine young John and
Paul up in Liverpool, young Mick and Keith down in London, little David
Bowie, and the soon-to-be Elton John, in their cloth caps, all full of ambition
and working-class anger, looking up from their *Daily Mirrors* with blinking
lightbulbs in talk balloons above their heads.

At this point, I would like to think, the rhetoric of closet homosexuality as
practiced by Wilde, Coward, and Liberace is on the verge of being appropriated for a broader attack upon the status quo, demonstrating the fact that it was
never, in the hands of its masters, a language of disguise, but a rhetoric of deni-
able disclosure—a language of theatrical transgression that had its own content. This strategy of theatrical subversion would eventually resonate throughout the entire culture and would end, I suggest, very near where it began with
Wilde, whose "effeminacy" was regarded as indicative of his dissent and cultural disaffection, rather than the other way around.

By the time we reach the watershed marked by the heterosexual drag of The
New York Dolls, I think, this re-reversal has taken place in American popular
culture. Sexuality is no longer a mere matter of biology and whim. It *means*
something. The battle for sexual tolerance has moved on to other, more political, battlefields, and, in view of this transformation, I think we can regard the
Liberace Museum as having some general historical significance beyond the
enshrining of a particularly exotic entertainer. Its artifacts, genuine rhinestones, and imitation pearls alike mark an American moment—the beginning
of the end of the "open secret." So the cars and the costumes and the silly
pianos might be seen as more than just the memorabilia of an exotic saloon
singer: because they are, in fact, the tools with which Liberace took the "rhetoric of the closet" public, demonstrated the power of its generous duplicity,
and changed the world.

I would like to think that Liberace knew this, somehow, in some way, as he
stood in the sunny parking lot of his Las Vegas shopping center on Easter
Sunday, 1979, with the mayor and other dignitaries in attendance, and opened
his amazing museum. Maybe it's sentimental of me, but I would like to think
that, as he stood there, the guy had some sense of his own authenticity. The
reporters noted that he was wearing a pink, blue, and yellow checkered jacket
with matching yellow shirt and slacks. A large gold cross hung around his
neck and six diamond rings adorned his fingers.

"Welcome to the Liberace Museum!" he cried to the assembled multitude.
"I don't usually wear diamonds in the afternoon, but this is a special occasion!"

ANALYZING What the Writer Says

1. Hickey opens his essay with a description of a Nevada sunset, backdrop to the neon landscape of Las Vegas. How is this image related to Liberace, the subject of his essay?

2. In what way is the huge rhinestone symbolic of Liberace?

3. What is the thesis of the essay?

4. What does Hickey mean when he says that Liberace "democratized the closet"?

5. Toward the end of his essay, Hickey claims that Liberace "changed the world." What does he mean by this statement?

ANALYZING How the Writer Says It

1. Hickey makes frequent references in his essay to popular culture. What do these references say about his intended audience?

2. Hickey starts the essay with a description of a "flat and gaudy" Las Vegas sunset and ends it with a description of an outrageous Liberace outfit. What effect does he accomplish by framing the essay in these images?

ANALYZING the Issue

1. Hickey claims that (at least in contemporary art and entertainment) the real and the fake are often hard to distinguish, that there is no essential difference between the sublime and the tacky. Do you agree with this assertion? Is there ultimately no significant difference between the *Mona Lisa*, say, and a velvet painting of Elvis or a Disney World snow globe? Why do you agree or disagree? If you think that "art" is different from "kitsch," define the terms very carefully.

2. Liberace, by being outrageous and flamboyant in an era that did not openly acknowledge homosexuality, had a liberating effect for artists that came after him. How might the antics of some of the more outrageous rock bands (or other artists) today have a similarly liberating effect?

ANALYZING Connections Between Texts

1. Joan Morgan ("The Bad Boy," p. 788) claims that Sean Combs "owes much of his success to his penchant for self-promotion." Liberace seems to possess the same talent. Does a talent for marketing oneself as a star qualify as genius? Why or why not?

2. Deborah Tannen argues in "Marked Women" (p. 521) that men have a choice about whether or not they will be marked. Clearly the Liberace Hickey describes not only marks himself but deliberately makes a spectacle of himself. How does he thus, wittingly or unwittingly, liberate himself from the closet other gays of his era could not escape?

"Mostly Mozart, nothing. It's all Mozart or no Mozart."

3. How does Annie Leibovitz's photograph of Liberace (p. 122) illustrate Dave Hickey's point that glitz and glamour in show business can be the "real thing," the essence of an artist's art?

WARMING UP: *Do you think celebrities are treated fairly by the media? Do you think many celebrities are able to control the media images of themselves?*

The Bad Boy

By Joan Morgan

JOAN MORGAN

In a 1997 Essence *profile of Sean "Puffy" Combs (who currently prefers the nickname "P-Diddy"), Joan Morgan considers the man behind the meteoric rise, suggesting that his carefully cultivated bad boy image is a pose and that Combs "is a poster boy for the few, the proud, the elite—pure Black royalty."*

What's the difference between mogul Sean "Puffy" Combs and the average Black man? Oh, about $100 million. Though his rise to fame and fortune has been shadowed by death, Puff Daddy still reigns supreme.

Back in 1992, when money in Black entertainment was plentiful and new, and hip-hop wasn't quite innocent but was still unscarred, then-Uptown Records prez Andre Harrell used to throw these ridiculously fly house parties. In his palace in the New Jersey suburbs, the YBF (Young, Black and Fabulous—or those aspiring to be) would sip champagne, dance to Kid Capri, eat nouvelle soul food and get high on the exhilarating ability to be both "ghetto" and "fabulous" at the same time. Rush played basketball, Andre ate barbecue, and Veronica Webb swam laps in the pool. While the rest played, Uptown's VP of A&R—a skinny, well-dressed and palpably ambitious 22-year-old named Sean Combs (aka Puff Daddy)—made moves. Briefcase in hand, he was busy showing off the logo for the company he dreamed he'd have one day. Said he'd call it Bad Boy.

Five summers later, Combs has a palace of his own, and his mentor, Harrell, has tumbled to earth. It is Combs, baseball-capped, bare-chested and glistening with sweat—Biggie's name tattooed above his right breast and a diamond-encrusted Jesus medallion resting protectively over his heart—who dominates newsstands across America. *Rolling Stone* magazine declared him "The New King of Hip-Hop."

The fact that Combs's company, Bad Boy Entertainment, has sold more than $100 million worth of music makes him a major contender. And his emergence as "Puff Daddy," CEO as rap star, cinched the title. His debut album, No Way Out, reached the top of the Billboard charts, with two hit singles, "Can't Nobody Hold Me Down" and "I'll Be Missing You," the latter becoming one of the biggest songs of the year. The ultimate coup: Combs signed a deal with Arista Records, which reportedly includes a $50 million credit line, a $6 million cash advance and a salary of $700,000 a year with the option to buy the company outright in the year 2001. By all accounts, Sean "Puff Daddy" Combs is primed to be one of the youngest and most successful moguls in Black music.

His reign represents a kind of new Black power. The multimillionaire status of Russell Simmons and Andre Harrell was proof positive that the Buppie—prep-school—Ivy League college-investment-banker route was not the quickest way to the lucchini at the end of the rainbow. Hip-hop's billion-dollar success meant it was not only possible but crazy lucrative to market the culture that White folks and integrationist-minded elders once convinced us to assimilate out of.

For this gang of Black nouveau riche (which includes Rowdy Records' Dallas Austin, So-So Def's Jermaine Dupri, Vibe's Keith Clinkscales and Violator Record's Chris Lighty), success means simultaneously keeping a finger firmly on the pulse of Black street culture, while infiltrating the upper levels of lily-White corporate America. As members of the first generation to grow up with all the gains of the Civil Rights Movement and the first to see them erode, they are acutely aware that America has long recovered from her racial guilt. For them, it's less about arguing for affirmative action than hustling to make those Benjamins by any means necessary. And the brothers are doing it lovely.

Combs's rise to fame, however, has been as rocky as it has been meteoric. For the 27-year-old wunderkind, the old adage rings painfully true—it's an uneasy head that wears the crown. "One of the saddest things about me is that people really don't know me," says Combs. "And they won't know me until I'm gone."

Against the backdrop of his Long Island, New York, oceanside home, sur-rounded by his Bad Boy family and other members of the new Black entertain-ment elite—LL Cool J, Missy, Veronica Webb and John Singleton, to name a few—an MTV-style beach jam is in full swing, and Combs seems at ease, fully in charge of getting his thing on. It is easy, then, to see why people forget he is in mourning for the Notorious B.I.G., Bad Boy's undisputed star and his ally and best friend. Later, however, when the cameras are gone and Puff Daddy has left the spotlight, Combs downshifts into that disarmingly soft "Sean voice," and his pain is palpable. He searches for words to describe his loss.

"Biggie was somebody who came into my life right on time," says Combs. "When I met him, I had this dream of a company, and all he wanted to do was be a rapper. I thanked God, not because he sent me a dope rapper, but because he sent me somebody who cared for me. I needed that.

"I miss him, but his presence is so strong. I still talk to him—like I'm crazy. ¹⁰
I used to do s— like touch his big face—and now I feel his face in my hands
all the time. I still pray I'm in a coma, that I'm having this long dream. I pray
that I'm going to wake up."

This isn't Combs's first brush with the Dark Angel. During his ascendancy
he has made repeated trips to the abyss and always managed to struggle back.
While a freshman at Howard (where he was already starting to gain renown as
a party promoter), Combs hustled his way to an internship at Uptown Records.
At 21, he got Harrell to hire him as vice-President of A&R. With a wizardlike
touch, Combs pooled his talents as A&R man, producer, stylist and video
director to give birth to hip-hop soul—sending the careers of megaplatinum
sellers such as Jodeci and Mary J. Blige soaring. He soon found himself producing everyone from TLC to Michael Jackson and Mariah Carey. When he
wasn't creating music that rocked urban behinds, he was hosting parties that
did. His hip-hop party, Daddy's House, was known as the flava on both coasts.
The general rule in hip-hop then: "If Puff Daddy throws it, they'll come." For
a while, he seemed indomitable.

The first of several calamities hit in 1991. As promoter of a highly publicized
celebrity basketball tournament staged at the City College of New York, Combs
was accused of overselling tickets and inadequately controlling the crowd after
the event resulted in a stampede that claimed nine lives. Although he was
eventually cleared of criminal negligence, there are still folks who will not
absolve him of guilt, claiming Combs's insatiable greed and ego were to
blame. Then in 1993, at the seeming height of his career, Harrell fired him
from Uptown. (There is much speculation about the whys of all this—chalk it
up to that old African saying, "Two rams can't drink from the same watering
hole.") Arista Records, however, offered him a $15 million distribution deal,
and Bad Boy Entertainment was born. And then in March of this year, Biggie
was murdered.

To add to the documented troubles are the ever-persistent rumors. They
range from the mundane—"He's power-hungry, plays dirty, can't be trusted,
would sell his own mama if it meant winning"—to the trifling—"Girl, did you
hear Wendy Williams [New York City's Hot 97 radio personality and relentless
gossip] said Puffy's gay?"

And the sinister: In a jail-cell interview, Tupac Shakur accused both Combs
and Biggie of being responsible for the highly publicized attempt on his life.
Adding fuel to an already incendiary situation, Death Row's Suge Knight—self-
appointed Bad Boy nemesis—accused Combs of commandeering the murder
of one of his boys. And when Tupac was murdered last year, both the media and
detractors implied once again that Combs could possibly have blood on his
hands. The most sinister of all, however, are the rumors swearing Combs was
responsible for Biggie's murder—with the supposed motive of jealousy—
because he allowed Biggie to be in a clearly Biggie-hostile environment without

enough protection from bodyguards. There are even those who laughingly claim his days are numbered, in the same matter-of-fact tone one reserves for the weather. Others callously await his demise. For every fan who admires Combs's phoenix-like ability to come back better, harder and stronger, there is a detractor who despises his seemingly unnatural resiliency.

And Combs is by no means immune to the criticism; he takes it hard. 15 Responding to the heat, he seems downright depressed. He sounds more like the hurt little middle-class "good boy" raised by his mother in Mount Vernon, New York, than the bad-boy, sunglasses-wearing, media-savvy rapper. "It hurts to do three and four years of busting your ass and have all your fame be about Biggie and Tupac's death. But that's a reality for me.

"I know what they say about me, that I'm just this guy who doesn't think about what he's doing, doesn't give a f—, only on a mission. I can't take that people think that about me. What gets me through is that God knows the truth."

It's a Sunday afternoon in Astoria, Queens, and Puffy is not happy. The correct clothes weren't at the video shoot, and he's being asked too many questions. He needs his staff to take more initiative so he can free up some space in a head that's crowded with the monumental responsibilities of being both a CEO and pop star.

But being in charge also means coming down hard on some folks, a role Combs is not comfortable with: He likes being Mr. Nice Guy. On this day, his manager, Benny Medina (who also works with box-office honey Will Smith and with Babyface) is doing the dirty work. His job is to make sure that Combs does not allow Puff Daddy, the very lucrative, chart-making artist, to get lost in the shuffle. Medina's priority is efficiency, and he doesn't mince words about Combs's dream to have a company full of young, hungry kids learning the ropes—as he once was. "I know seasoned experts," says Medina, "who know exactly what to do with this level of celebrity."

Although it's clear Combs agrees (Medina was hired for his knowledge of the celebrity game), his body language is a clear indication that he's not having fun. He's slouched and petulant and whining a little. "This is all too stressful for me. I don't want to be an artist no more," he says. Anyone in earshot smirks at the BS inherent in this comment. Puffy has always wanted to be a star.

Truth be told, he owes much of his success to his penchant for self- 20 promotion. Working both the media and pop culture's obsession with celebrity, Combs emblazoned himself into our consciousness. If he produced a record, then he spoke on it. If the artists were doing a video, best believe he'd have a cameo. As a result, Puffy emerged as not only a hot producer and A&R man, but he was also a personality. Introducing the masses and hip-hop to some of the finer things in life—Cristal champagne, designer suits and a jet-skiing, golfplaying, action-adventure lifestyle—Puffy is a Black Blake Carrington for a generation weaned on eighties excess and Dynasty. And they can't get enough of him.

He is a poster boy for the few, the proud, the elite—pure Black royalty. But while kings may be admired and envied, they are rarely universally loved. And stars become stars because that's what they need most of all—very public, large displays of unconditional love. It's the times this love is present that Combs seems most at ease. Like when he's talking about the marvel of his 3-year-old son, Justin, or his mother and grandmother or reminiscing about Biggie, or when he introduces Kim, the lady in his life, with a smile that stretches from ear to ear. Whether he's performing on Letterman or for a few hundred Black and Latino kids at Daddy's House Boys and Girls Club (part of his nonprofit corporation for urban youths that's run by Sista Souljah), Combs is notably gracious with his fans. He acknowledges every squealing hello or request for a hug, picture or autograph with genuine warmth and sincerity. Still these moments are not enough to completely ameliorate the pain and loneliness he confesses permeate his life.

"You know, it ain't really fly to be successful in young Black America," he says. "You're hated. It's like you walk in the spot, and you got the cake, and niggas is feeling like 'I'm working and this nigga just wake up in the morning and shoot a video.'

"There are times when the loneliness just gets to you. I just break down and start crying—just to get it out of my system. It hurts for people to think you have so much, and I do have a whole lot, but I wish I could have this much and be treated regular."

But Puff—Sean "Puffy" Combs—isn't regular. He may get paid because he has an incisive understanding of what regular heads want—the music they need, the fantasies they thrive on—but he is not one of them. Regular twentysomethings will never know his level of drive or focus or what it means to run a hugely successful multimillion-dollar business. They cannot employ their own people or open trust funds and restaurants in their sons' names. They'll never know what it means to be onstage or walk down the street and invoke love from absolute strangers. And while regular people are likely to experience the depths of his pain, most do not possess his capacity for survival.

Instead of sharing the thought, I ask hip-hop's reigning king about an old 25
African perspective that says each of us examines the possibilities of a number of lives and then we choose the one we want: "Is this the life you would have chosen, Puff?"

"Yes," he answers a bit too quickly. "But without the tragedies. I mean the pain that I've seen, it just ain't worth. . . ."

I don't think that would have been a choice. And then, slowly, it seems to dawn on him what the other choice may have been. A pain-free lifetime of regular. "That's ill. You mean I chose this?" he says incredulously. Then he kinda half-smiles.

Maybe he realizes that it wasn't a bad choice. Maybe it was just a brave one.

ANALYZING | What the Writer Says

1. What, according to Morgan's piece, drives Sean "Puffy" Combs?

2. What is the source of Combs's genius? What do Combs and his counterparts market, according to Morgan?

3. Is the author's portrait of Combs balanced? Give examples to back up your answer.

4. Referring to Combs's life, Morgan writes, "Maybe he realizes that it wasn't a bad choice. Maybe it was just a brave one." What does she mean?

ANALYZING | How the Writer Says It

1. Who is Morgan's intended audience? What techniques suggest a particular audience?

2. Morgan uses words like "king" and "royalty" and "elite" throughout her piece. What are the connotations of the language she uses of such word choice?

3. What is the effect of Morgan's opening sentences?

ANALYZING | the Issue

Morgan points to a contradiction between the street culture that Combs has marketed successfully and the world in which he lives. Do you think Combs exploits a social class to which he does not belong? Explain.

ANALYZING | Connections Between Texts

1. Compare Joan Didion's argument about the way Martha Stewart has marketed herself (p. 754) to Joan Morgan's about the way Sean Combs has marketed himself. Do the two super-celebrities have anything in common?

2. In "Ring Leader" (p. 223) Natalie Kusz admits to crafting an in-your-face image so that *she*, rather than those who would judge her against conventional standards of beauty, controls her own image. To what extent does Sean Combs use similar tactics to control his persona?

3. Walter Iooss's photograph of Michael Jordan (p. 121) deliberately exposes a vulnerable side of the superstar, metaphorically cutting him down to (human) size. Is Morgan's portrait of Combs similarly sympathetic? Point to passages in Morgan's article that reveal her attitude toward Combs.

WARMING UP: *Do you know any people whose extraordinary talent or intellect isolates them?*

He's Still Ready for His Close-Up

BY DENNIS OVERBYE

DENNIS OVERBYE

A science editor for the New York Times, *Dennis Overbye (b. 1944) studied physics at MIT before becoming a full-time writer. Responding to an interviewer's question about his penchant for coupling love and the cosmos, the author of the critically acclaimed* Lonely Hearts of the Cosmos (1992) *and* Einstein in Love (2000) *asks, "What else is there? Sex and physics." In "He's Still Ready for His Close-Up," published in the* New York Times Magazine *shortly after the release of Einstein's FBI file, Overbye reminds readers of his more ordinary qualities, of his flaws and his humanity.*

Albert Einstein, so the story goes, was playing the violin with a bunch of friends in a chamber group one afternoon, and it wasn't going well. Finally, after several false starts, the conductor turned to him scowling and asked: "Einstein! Can't you count?"

It's my favorite Einstein story, simply because I have heard it so many times, invariably recounted by a friend or relative of someone who was there, that I have had to conclude either that conductors bawled him out about once a month, or that he and his friends played in stadium-sized living rooms. It's an endearing anecdote (and maybe even true), one that we mortals cling to, perhaps out of wishful thinking that nature is somehow fair and democratic: surely what it gives to one man in the form of brains, it would take away in other ways. Einstein might have been the master of space-time, but here on Earth he was a naïve bumbler, the absent-minded professor, the kindly sockless wizard. We want there to be a price—preferably tragic—for genius.

That cuddly cosmic image has amazingly endured despite the ruthless grilling of history in the last 20 years, including revelations of an illegitimate daughter, a nasty divorce, girlfriends and lawsuits between his descendants, among other things. Yet the stream of calendars, coffee mugs and T-shirts keeps flowing.

In 1919, British astronomers returning from an eclipse expedition reported that they had measured the bending of light rays, thus confirming Einstein's revolutionary new theory, known as general relativity, which described gravity as the warping of space-time. At that moment, Einstein caught a wave that had been building for decades. The world was exhausted, materially, morally and intellectually, from World War I, a catastrophe that shattered the faith in progress and reason that had guided European civilization since the Enlightenment. Everyone was ready for something new. Einstein gave them a whole new universe.

And although few understood his theory, everybody could understand that the stars in the sky—the most ancient symbols of order in the universe—had apparently moved. "Lights All Askew in the Heavens" read part of a headline in this newspaper on Nov. 10, 1919.

Einstein proclaimed that the universe was not three-dimensional but had a fourth dimension, namely time. As it happened, the notion of a fourth dimension of space had been the object of mystical fascination since the late 19th century, even affecting modern art. As popularized by the writer Charles Hinton, among others, it was an ethereal realm where the bounds of ordinary space and time were transcended, a so-called astral plane where spirits dwelled.

The public already knew, then, that they weren't supposed to understand the fourth dimension, only to celebrate it. And so it was with relativity and its enigmatic creator, a sort of cosmic medium who was suddenly staring out of newspaper photos with dark eyes that seemed to look farther and deeper than mortals ever could. In touching him, the public was able to touch the cosmic mystery itself. It was a bonus that Einstein was a German whose theory had been confirmed by the arduous and dangerous efforts of Britons, thus helping to knit the tattered framework of international science.

The reporters came and never left. Virtually every word that left his lips (and a few that didn't) were written down, accounting for the abundance of Einstein aphorisms on all those calendars and posters. It helped that he wore his fame lightly, with humor and a cute accent, and without a trace of arrogance. He wasn't out for money or power—or even a good restaurant seat. All he wanted was to do his science. He liked to say that fate had punished him for his youthful disdain for authority by making him an authority himself.

It is still Einstein's universe. Some 47 years after his death, he continues to make headlines, whether it's because of the revelations about his 1,500-page F.B.I. file reported last week, or because of news that modern science has confirmed yet another of his strange ideas. The dark energy that astronomers now think is blowing the universe apart, for example, was first postulated by him in desperation back in 1917 (and later renounced as a blunder) to explain why the cosmos did not collapse of its own weight.

His name has become a synonym for genius—"He's smart, but he's no Einstein"—in a way that Darwin and Freud, to cite two contemporaries, have not. In fact, neuroscientists are still studying his brain, and Hollywood has reportedly optioned the film rights to a book about his gray matter's posthumous travels.

But it is his humanity, with all its newfound flaws (and perhaps amplified by them), that ultimately binds us to Einstein. By the time he became famous, he was 40 and notorious in Germany as a pacifist. He was willing to invest his new celebrity in that and other causes, like a drive to set up a Hebrew university in Jerusalem. He was the original peacenik, and when he left Nazi Germany for the United States in 1933, the Wandering Jew as well. His outspoken desire that America live up to its ideals of tolerance and freedom made J. Edgar Hoover fear that the stars were going askew.

And then there is the bomb. Einstein forsook his pacifism in 1939 to write a letter nudging the United States into an atomic bomb project because he was afraid Germany might do it first. Later, he publicly rued that action and campaigned for nuclear disarmament, but the damage was done, and the full measure of haunted humanity, the last quantum step in his progress toward being Everyman, had overtaken him. In his later years, the eyes that saw farther than anyone could imagine seemed bagged by mushroom clouds and Promethean guilt: he became a symbol of both cosmic and moral mystery.

In the end, that weather-beaten face reveals a lonely soul, unsatisfied by his marriages and tumultuous personal life, isolated by fame and by the secret knowledge that makes the stars dance.

As Charlie Chaplin is said to have told him in 1931, when the pair attended the premiere of "City Lights" in Los Angeles and was besieged by mobs of adoring fans: "They cheer me because they all understand me, and they cheer you because no one understands you."

ANALYZING What the Writer Says

1. Why does Overbye open with an anecdote about Einstein that he suggests may be exaggerated if not entirely untrue?

2. Did Einstein like the status his genius afforded him? What does Overbye suggest he really wanted?

3. What single act haunted Einstein, according to Overbye? Why did he do it?

4. How does the comment Charlie Chaplin reportedly made to Einstein illustrate Overbye's thesis?

ANALYZING How the Writer Says It

1. What techniques does Overbye use in his attempt to humanize Einstein?

2. What words or phrases help to retain Einstein's enigmatic quality?

ANALYZING the Issue

To what extent do the public (or the media) dictate the image of famous people?

ANALYZING Connections Between Texts

1. Compare Overbye's piece on Einstein to Richard Selzer's "Imelda" (p. 798). What techniques do the writers employ to humanize their subjects, both brilliant, larger-than-life figures operating in scientific environments?

2. Compare Overbye's portrait of Einstein to Rebecca Mead's profile of Shaquille O'Neal in "A Man-Child in Lotusland" (p. 717). Could Mead's title apply to Overbye's piece? Why or why not?

3. How does Overbye's essay reinforce or challenge the visual message in Ernest Hamlin Baker's painting of Einstein (p. 120)?

WARMING UP: *Do you know, or have you known, people so good at what they do that they seem to have little room for anything or anyone else in life? Have you ever been surprised when such a person made an unusual gesture?*

Imelda

BY RICHARD SELZER

RICHARD SELZER

Turning to writing well after forty to shake the surgeon's image as "someone who is out of touch with his humanity," Richard Selzer (b. 1928) soon realized he could not maintain the dispassion necessary to surgery and practice the passion of writing. He chose, at 58, to become a writer. "Imelda" recounts an incident in which one of Selzer's medical professors—a surgical genius distanced emotionally from colleagues, students, and patients—performs an incredible act of compassion.

I heard the other day that Hugh Franciscus had died. I knew him once. He was the Chief of Plastic Surgery when I was a medical student at Albany Medical College. Dr. Franciscus was the archetype of the professor of surgery—tall, vigorous, muscular, as precise in his technique as he was impeccable in his dress. Each day a clean lab coat monkishly starched, that sort of thing. I doubt that he ever read books. One book only, that of the human body, took the place of all others. He never raised his eyes from it. He read it like a printed page as though he knew that in the calligraphy there just beneath the skin were all the secrets of the world. Long before it became visible to anyone else, he could detect the first sign of granulation at the base of a wound, the first blue line of new epithelium at the periphery that would tell him that a wound would heal, or the barest hint of necrosis that presaged failure. This gave him the appearance of a prophet. "This skin graft will take," he would say, and you must believe beyond all cyanosis, exudation and inflammation that it would.

He had enemies, of course, who said he was arrogant, that he exalted activity for its own sake. Perhaps. But perhaps it was no more than the honesty of one who knows his own worth. Just look at a scalpel, after all. What a feeling of sovereignty, megalomania even, when you know that it is you and you alone who will make certain use of it. It was said, too, that he was a ladies' man. I don't know about that. It was all rumor. Besides, I think he had other things in mind than mere living. Hugh Franciscus was a zealous hunter.

Every fall during the season he drove upstate to hunt deer. There was a glass-front case in his office where he showed his guns. How could he shoot a deer? we asked. But he knew better. To us medical students he was someone heroic, someone made up of several gods, beheld at a distance, and always from a lesser height. If he had grown accustomed to his miracles, we had not. He had no close friends on the staff. There was something a little sad in that. As though once long ago he had been flayed by friendship and now the slightest breeze would hurt. Confidences resulted in dishonor. Perhaps the person in whom one confided would scorn him, betray. Even though he spent his days among those less fortunate, weaker than he—the sick, after all—Franciscus seemed aware of an air of personal harshness in his environment to which he reacted by keeping his own counsel, by a certain remoteness. It was what gave him the appearance of being haughty. With the patients he was forthright. All the facts laid out, every question anticipated and answered with specific information. He delivered good news and bad with the same dispassion.

I was a third-year student, just turned onto the wards for the first time, and clerking on Surgery. Everything—the operating room, the morgue, the emergency room, the patients, professors, even the nurses—was terrifying. One picked one's way among the mines and booby traps of the hospital, hoping only to avoid the hemorrhage and perforation of disgrace. The opportunity for humiliation was everywhere.

It all began on Ward Rounds. Dr. Franciscus was demonstrating a cross-leg flap graft he had constructed to cover a large fleshy defect in the leg of a merchant seaman who had injured himself in a fall. The man was from Spain and spoke no English. There had been a comminuted fracture of the femur, much soft tissue damage, necrosis. After weeks of debridement and dressings, the wound had been made ready for grafting. Now the patient was in his fifth postoperative day. What we saw was a thick web of pale blue flesh arising from the man's left thigh, and which had been sutured to the open wound on the right thigh. When the surgeon pressed the pedicle with his finger, it blanched; when he let up, there was a slow return of the violaceous color.

"The circulation is good," Franciscus announced. "It will get better." In several weeks, we were told, he would divide the tube of flesh at its site of origin, and tailor it to fit the defect to which, by then, it would have grown more solidly. All at once, the webbed man in the bed reached out, and gripping Franciscus by the arm, began to speak rapidly, pointing to his groin and hip. Franciscus stepped back at once to disengage his arm from the patient's grasp.

"Anyone here know Spanish? I didn't get a word of that."

"The cast is digging into him up above," I said. "The edges of the plaster are rough. When he moves, they hurt."

Without acknowledging my assistance, Dr. Franciscus took a plaster shears from the dressing cart and with several large snips cut away the rough edges of the cast.

"*Gracias, gracias.*" The man in the bed smiled. But Franciscus had already moved on to the next bed. He seemed to me a man of immense strength and ability, yet without affection for the patients. He did not want to be touched by them. It was less kindness that he showed them than a reassurance that he would never give up, that he would bend every effort. If anyone could, he would solve the problems of their flesh.

Ward Rounds had disbanded and I was halfway down the corridor when I   10 heard Dr. Franciscus's voice behind me.

"You speak Spanish." It seemed a command.

"I lived in Spain for two years," I told him.

"I'm taking a surgical team to Honduras next week to operate on the natives down there. I do it every year for three weeks, somewhere. This year, Honduras. I can arrange the time away from your duties here if you'd like to come along. You will act as interpreter. I'll show you how to use the clinical camera. What you'd see would make it worthwhile."

So it was that, a week later, the envy of my classmates, I joined the mobile surgical unit—surgeons, anesthetists, nurses and equipment—aboard a Military Air Transport plane to spend three weeks performing plastic surgery on people who had been previously selected by an advance team. Honduras. I don't suppose I shall ever see it again. Nor do I especially want to. From the plane it seemed a country made of clay—burnt umber, raw sienna, dry. It had a deadweight quality, as though the ground had no buoyancy, no air sacs through which a breeze might wander. Our destination was Comayagua, a town in the Central Highlands. The town itself was situated on the edge of one of the flatlands that were linked in a network between the granite mountains. Above, all was brown, with only an occasional Spanish cedar tree; below, patches of luxuriant tropical growth. It was a day's bus ride from the airport. For hours, the town kept appearing and disappearing with the convolutions of the road. At last, there it lay before us, panting and exhausted at the bottom of the mountain.

That was all I was to see of the countryside. From then on, there was only   15 the derelict hospital of Comayagua, with the smell of spoiling bananas and the accumulated odors of everyone who had been sick there for the last hundred years. Of the two, I much preferred the frank smell of the sick. The heat of the place was incendiary. So hot that, as we stepped from the bus, our own words did not carry through the air, but hung limply at our lips and chins. Just in front of the hospital was a thirsty courtyard where mobs of waiting people squatted or lay in the meager shade, and where, on dry days, a fine dust rose through which untethered goats shouldered. Against the walls of this courtyard, gaunt, dejected men stood, their faces, like their country, preternaturally solemn, leaden. Here no one looked up at the sky. Every head was bent beneath a widebrimmed straw hat. In the days that followed, from the doorway of the dispensary, I would watch the brown mountains sliding about, drinking the hospital into their shadow as the afternoon grew later and later, flattening us by their very altitude.

The people were mestizos, of mixed Spanish and Indian blood. They had flat, broad, dumb museum feet. At first they seemed to me indistinguishable the one from the other, without animation. All the vitality, the hidden sexuality, was in their black hair. Soon I was to know them by the fissures with which each face was graven. But, even so, compared to us, they were masked, shut away. My job was to follow Dr. Franciscus around, photograph the patients before and after surgery, interpret and generally act as aide-de-camp. It was exhilarating. Within days I had decided that I was not just useful, but essential. Despite that we spent all day in each other's company, there were no overtures of friendship from Dr. Franciscus. He knew my place, and I knew it, too. In the afternoon he examined the patients scheduled for the next day's surgery. I would call out a name from the doorway to the examining room. In the courtyard someone would rise. I would usher the patient in, and nudge him to the examining table where Franciscus stood, always, I thought, on the verge of irritability. I would read aloud the case history, then wait while he carried out his examination. While I took the "before" photographs, Dr. Franciscus would dictate into a tape recorder:

"Ulcerating basal cell carcinoma of the right orbit—six by eight centimeters—involving the right eye and extending into the floor of the orbit. Operative plan: wide excision with enucleation of the eye. Later, bone and skin grafting." The next morning we would be in the operating room where the procedure would be carried out.

We were more than two weeks into our tour of duty—a few days to go— when it happened. Earlier in the day I had caught sight of her through the window of the dispensary. A thin, dark Indian girl about fourteen years old. A figurine, orange-brown, terra-cotta, and still attached to the unshaped clay from which she had been carved. An older, sun-weathered woman stood behind and somewhat to the left of the girl. The mother was short and dumpy. She wore a broad-brimmed hat with a high crown, and a shapeless dress like a cassock. The girl had long, loose black hair. There were tiny gold hoops in her ears. The dress she wore could have been her mother's. Far too big, it hung from her thin shoulders at some risk of slipping down her arms. Even with her in it, the dress was empty, something hanging on the back of a door. Her breasts made only the smallest imprint in the cloth, her hips none at all. All the while, she pressed to her mouth a filthy, pink, balled-up rag as though to stanch a flow or buttress against pain. I knew that what she had come to show us, what we were there to see, was hidden beneath that pink cloth. As I watched, the woman handed down to her a gourd from which the girl drank, lapping like a dog. She was the last patient of the day. They had been waiting in the courtyard for hours.

"Imelda Valdez," I called out. Slowly she rose to her feet, the cloth never leaving her mouth, and followed her mother to the examining room door. I shooed them in.

"You sit up there on the table," I told her. "Mother, you stand over there, please." I read from the chart:

"This is a fourteen-year-old girl with a complete, unilateral, leftsided cleft lip and cleft palate. No other diseases or congenital defects. Laboratory tests, chest X ray—negative."

"Tell her to take the rag away," said Dr. Franciscus. I did, and the girl shrank back, pressing the cloth all the more firmly.

"Listen, this is silly," said Franciscus. "Tell her I've got to see it. Either she behaves, or send her away."

"Please give me the cloth," I said to the girl as gently as possible. She did not. She could not. Just then, Franciscus reached up and, taking the hand that held the rag, pulled it away with a hard jerk. For an instant the girl's head followed the cloth as it left her face, one arm still upflung against showing. Against all hope, she would hide herself. A moment later, she relaxed and sat still. She seemed to me then like an animal that looks outward at the infinite, at death, without fear, with recognition only.

Set as it was in the center of the girl's face, the defect was utterly hideous— a nude rubbery insect that had fastened there. The upper lip was widely split all the way to the nose. One white tooth perched upon the protruding upper jaw projecting through the hole. Some of the bone seemed to have been gnawed away as well. Above the thing, clear almond eyes and long black hair reflected the light. Below, a slender neck where the pulse trilled visibly. Under our gaze the girl's eyes fell to her lap where her hands lay palms upward, half open. She was a beautiful bird with a crushed beak. And tense with the expectation of more shame.

"Open your mouth," said the surgeon. I translated. She did so, and the surgeon tipped back her head to see inside.

"The palate, too. Complete," he said. There was a long silence. At last he spoke.

"What is your name?" The margins of the wound melted until she herself was being sucked into it.

"Imelda." The syllables leaked through the hole with a slosh and a whistle.

"Tomorrow," said the surgeon, "I will fix your lip. *Mañana*."

It seemed to me that Hugh Franciscus, in spite of his years of experience, in spite of all the dreadful things he had seen, must have been awed by the sight of this girl. I could see it flit across his face for an instant. Perhaps it was her small act of concealment, that he had had to demand that she show him the lip, that he had had to force her to show it to him. Perhaps it was her resistance that intensified the disfigurement. Had she brought her mouth to him willingly, without shame, she would have been for him neither more nor less than any other patient.

He measured the defect with calipers, studied it from different angles, turning her head with a finger at her chin.

"How can it ever be put back together?" I asked.

"Take her picture," he said. And to her, "Look straight ahead." Through the eye of the camera she seemed more pitiful than ever, her humiliation more complete.

"Wait!" The surgeon stopped me. I lowered the camera. A strand of her hair   35
had fallen across her face and found its way to her mouth, becoming stuck there by saliva. He removed the hair and secured it behind her ear.

"Go ahead," he ordered. There was the click of the camera. The girl winced.

"Take three more, just in case."

When the girl and her mother had left, he took paper and pen and with a few lines drew a remarkable likeness of the girl's face.

"Look," he said. "If this dot is A, and this one B, this, C, and this, D, the incisions are made A to B, then C to D. CD must equal AB. It is all equilateral triangles." All well and good, but then came X and Y and rotation flaps and the rest.

"Do you see?" he asked.   40

"It is confusing," I told him.

"It is simply a matter of dropping the upper lip into a normal position, then crossing the gap with two triangular flaps. It is geometry," he said.

"Yes," I said. "Geometry." And relinquished all hope of becoming a plastic surgeon.

In the operating room the next morning the anesthesia had already been administered when we arrived from Ward Rounds. The tube emerging from the girl's mouth was pressed against her lower lip to be kept out of the field of surgery. Already, a nurse was scrubbing the face which swam in a reddish-brown lather. The tiny gold earrings were included in the scrub. Now and then, one of them gave a brave flash. The face was washed for the last time, and dried. Green towels were placed over the face to hide everything but the mouth and nose. The drapes were applied.

"Calipers!" The surgeon measured, locating the peak of the distorted   45
Cupid's bow.

"Marking pen!" He placed the first blue dot at the apex of the bow. The nasal sills were dotted; next, the inferior philtral dimple, the vermilion line. The A flap and the B flap were outlined. On he worked, peppering the lip and nose, making sense of chaos, realizing the lip that lay waiting in that deep essential pink, that only he could see. The last dot and line were placed. He was ready.

"Scalpel!" He held the knife above the girl's mouth.

"O.K. to go ahead?" he asked the anesthetist.

"Yes."

He lowered the knife.   50

"No! Wait!" The anesthetist's voice was tense, staccato. "Hold it!"

The surgeon's hand was motionless.

"What's the matter?"

"Something's wrong. I'm not sure. God, she's hot as a pistol. Blood pressure is way up. Pulse one eighty. Get a rectal temperature." A nurse fumbled beneath the drapes. We waited. The nurse retrieved the thermometer.

"One hundred seven . . . no . . . eight." There was disbelief in her voice.   55

"Malignant hyperthermia," said the anesthetist. "Ice! Ice! Get lots of ice!" I raced out the door, accosted the first nurse I saw.

"Ice!" I shouted. "*Hielo!*[1] Quickly! *Hielo!*" The woman's expression was blank. I ran to another. "*Hielo! Hielo!* For the love of God, ice."

"*Hielo?*" She shrugged. "*Nada.*"[2] I ran back to the operating room.

"There isn't any ice." I reported. Dr. Franciscus had ripped off his rubber gloves and was feeling the skin of the girl's abdomen. Above the mask his eyes were the eyes of a horse in battle.

"The EKG is wild . . ."   60

"I can't get a pulse . . ."

"What the hell . . ."

The surgeon reached for the girl's groin. No femoral pulse.

"EKG flat. My God! She's dead!"

"She can't be."   65

"She is."

The surgeon's fingers pressed the groin where there was no pulse to be felt, only his own pulse hammering at the girl's flesh to be let in.

It was noon, four hours later, when we left the operating room. It was a day so hot and humid I felt steamed open like an envelope. The woman was sitting on a bench in the courtyard in her dress like a cassock. In one hand she held the piece of cloth the girl had used to conceal her mouth. As we watched, she folded it once neatly, and then again, smoothing it, cleaning the cloth which might have been the head of the girl in her lap that she stroked and consoled.

"I'll do the talking here," he said. He would tell her himself, in whatever Spanish he could find. Only if she did not understand was I to speak for him. I watched him brace himself, set his shoulders. How could he tell her? I wondered. What? But I knew he would tell her everything, exactly as it had happened. As much for himself as for her, he needed to explain. But suppose she screamed, fell to the ground, attacked him, even? All that hope of love . . . gone. Even in his discomfort I knew that he was teaching me. The way to do it was professionally. Now he was standing above her. When the woman saw that he did not speak, she lifted her eyes and saw what he held crammed in his mouth to tell her. She knew, and rose to her feet.

---

[1] Ice. (Editor's note)

[2] Nothing. (Editor's note)

"*Señora*," he began, "I am sorry." All at once he seemed to me shorter than 70
he was, scarcely taller than she. There was a place at the crown of his head
where the hair had grown thin. His lips were stones. He could hardly move
them. The voice dry, dusty.

"No one could have known. Some bad reaction to the medicine for sleeping.
It poisoned her. High fever. She did not wake up." The last, a whisper. The
woman studied his lips as though she were deaf. He tried, but could not control a twitching at the corner of his mouth. He raised a thumb and forefinger
to press something back into his eyes.

"*Muerte*,"[3] the woman announced to herself. Her eyes were human, deadly.

"*Sí, muerte*." At that moment he was like someone cast, still alive, as an effigy
for his own tomb. He closed his eyes. Nor did he open them until he felt
the touch of the woman's hand on his arm, a touch from which he did not
withdraw. Then he looked and saw the grief corroding her face, breaking it
down, melting the features so that eyes, nose, mouth ran together in a distortion, like the girl's. For a long time they stood in silence. It seemed to me that
minutes passed. At last her face cleared, the features rearranged themselves.
She spoke, the words coming slowly to make certain that he understood her.
She would go home now. The next day her sons would come for the girl, to
take her home for burial. The doctor must not be sad. God has decided. And
she was happy now that the harelip had been fixed so that her daughter might
go to Heaven without it. Her bare feet retreating were the felted pads of a great
bereft animal.

The next morning I did not go to the wards, but stood at the gate leading
from the courtyard to the road outside. Two young men in striped ponchos
lifted the girl's body wrapped in a straw mat onto the back of a wooden cart. A
donkey waited. I had been drawn to this place as one is drawn, inexplicably, to
certain scenes of desolation—executions, battlefields. All at once, the woman
looked up and saw me. She had taken off her hat. The heavy-hanging coil of
her hair made her head seem larger, darker, noble. I pressed some money into
her hand.

"For flowers," I said. "A priest." Her cheeks shook as though minutes ago a 75
stone had been dropped into her navel and the ripples were just now reaching
her head. I regretted having come to that place.

"*Sí, sí*," The woman said. Her own face was stitched with flies. "The doctor
is one of the angels. He has finished the work of God. My daughter is beautiful."

What could she mean! The lip had not been fixed. The girl had died before
he would have done it.

"Only a fine line that God will erase in time," she said.

---

[3]Dead. (Editor's note)

I reached into the cart and lifted a corner of the mat in which the girl had been rolled. Where the cleft had been there was now a fresh line of tiny sutures. The Cupid's bow was delicately shaped, the vermilion border aligned. The flattened nostril had now the same rounded shape as the other one. I let the mat fall over the face of the dead girl, but not before I had seen the touching place where the finest black hairs sprang from the temple.

"*Adiós, adiós. . . .*" And the cart creaked away to the sound of hooves, a tinkling bell. 80

There are events in a doctor's life that seem to mark the boundary between youth and age, seeing and perceiving. Like certain dreams, they illuminate a whole lifetime of past behavior. After such an event, a doctor is not the same as he was before. It had seemed to me then to have been the act of someone demented, or at least insanely arrogant. An attempt to reorder events. Her death had come to him out of order. It should have come after the lip had been repaired, not before. He could have told the mother that, no, the lip had not been fixed. But he did not. He said nothing. It had been an act of omission, one of those strange lapses to which all of us are subject and which we live to regret. It must have been then, at that moment, that the knowledge of what he would do appeared to him. The words of the mother had not consoled him; they had hunted him down. He had not done it for her. The dire necessity was his. He would not accept that Imelda had died before he could repair her lip. People who do such things break free from society. They follow their own lonely path. They have a secret which they can never reveal. I must never let on that I knew.

How often I have imagined it. Ten o'clock at night. The hospital of Comayagua is all but dark. Here and there lanterns tilt and skitter up and down the corridors. One of these lamps breaks free from the others and descends the stone steps to the underground room that is the morgue of the hospital. This room wears the expression as if it had waited all night for someone to come. No silence so deep as this place with its cargo of newly dead. Only the slow drip of water over stone. The door closes gassily and clicks shut. The lock is turned. There are four tables, each with a body encased in a paper shroud. There is no mistaking her. She is the smallest. The surgeon takes a knife from his pocket and slits open the paper shroud, that part in which the girl's head is enclosed. The wound seems to be living on long after she has died. Waves of heat emanate from it, blurring his vision. All at once, he turns to peer over his shoulder. He sees nothing, only a wooden crucifix on the wall.

He removes a package of instruments from a satchel and arranges them on a tray. Scalpel, scissors, forceps, needle holder. Sutures and gauze sponges are produced. Stealthy, hunched, engaged, he begins. The dots of blue dye are still there upon her mouth. He raises the scalpel, pauses. A second glance into the darkness. From the wall a small lizard watches and accepts. The first cut is made. A sluggish flow of dark blood appears. He wipes it away with a sponge.

No new blood comes to take its place. Again and again he cuts, connecting each of the blue dots until the whole of the zigzag slice is made, first on one side of the cleft, then on the other. Now the edges of the cleft are lined with fresh tissue. He sets down the scalpel and takes up scissors and forceps, undermining the little flaps until each triangle is attached only at one side. He rotates each flap into its new position. He must be certain that they can be swung without tension. They can. He is ready to suture. He fits the tiny curved needle into the jaws of the needle holder. Each suture is placed precisely the same number of millimeters from the cut edge, and the same distance apart. He ties each knot down until the edges are apposed. Not too tightly. These are the most meticulous sutures of his life. He cuts each thread close to the knot. It goes well. The vermilion border with its white skin roll is exactly aligned. One more stitch and the Cupid's bow appears as if by magic. The man's face shines with moisture. Now the nostril is incised around the margin, released, and sutured into a round shape to match its mate. He wipes the blood from the face of the girl with gauze the he has dipped in water. Crumbs of light are scattered on the girl's face. The shroud is folded once more about her. The instruments are handed into the satchel. In a moment the morgue is dark and a lone lantern ascends the stairs and is extinguished.

Six weeks later I was in the darkened amphitheater of the Medical School. Tiers of seats rose in a semicircle above the small stage where Hugh Franciscus stood presenting the case material he had encountered in Honduras. It was the highlight of the year. The hall was filled. The night before he had arranged the slides in the order in which they were to be shown. I was at the controls of the slide projector.

"Next slide!" he would order from time to time in that military voice which had called forth blind obedience from generations of medical students, interns, residents and patients.

"This is a fifty-seven-year-old man with a severe burn contracture of the neck. You will notice the rigid webbing that has fused the chin to the presternal tissues. No motion of the head on the torso is possible. . . . Next slide!"

"Click," went the projector.

"Here he is after the excision of the scar tissue and with the head in full extension for the first time. The defect was then covered. . . . Next slide!"

"Click."

". . . with full-thickness drums of skin taken from the abdomen with the Padgett dermatome. Next slide!"

"Click."

And suddenly there she was, extracted from the shadows, suspended above and beyond all of us like a resurrection. There was the oval face, the long black hair unbraided, the tiny gold hoops in her ears. And that luminous gnawed mouth. The whole of her life seemed to have been summed up in this photograph. A long silence followed that was the surgeon's alone to break. Almost at once, like the anesthetist in the operating room in Comayagua, I knew that something was wrong. It was not that the man would not speak as that he could not. The audience of doctors, nurses and students seemed to have been infected by the black, limitless silence. My own pulse doubled. It was hard to breathe. Why did he not call out for the next slide? Why did he not save himself? Why had he not removed this slide from the ones to be shown? All at once I knew that he had used his camera on her again. I could see the long black shadows of her hair flowing into the darker shadows of the morgue. The sudden blinding flash . . . The next slide would be the one taken in the morgue. He would be exposed.

In the dim light reflected from the slide, I saw him gazing up at her, seeing not the colored photograph, I thought, but the negative of it where the ghost of the girl was. For me, the amphitheater had become Honduras. I saw again that courtyard littered with patients. I could see the dust in the beam of light from the projector. It was then that I knew that she was his measure of perfection and pain—the one lost, the other gained. He, too, had heard the click of the camera, had seen her wince and felt his mercy enlarge. At last he spoke.

"Imelda." It was the one word he had heard her say. At the sound of his voice I removed the next slide from the projector. "Click" . . . and she was gone. "Click" again, and in her place the man with the orbital cancer. For a long moment Franciscus looked up in my direction, on his face an expression that I have given up trying to interpret. Gratitude? Sorrow? It made me think of the gaze of the girl when at last she understood that she must hand over to him the evidence of her body.

"This is a sixty-two-year-old man with a basal cell carcinoma of the temple   95 eroding into the bony orbit . . ." he began as though nothing had happened.

At the end of the hour, even before the lights went out, there was loud applause. I hurried to find him among the departing crowd. I could not. Some weeks went by before I caught sight of him. He seemed vaguely convalescent as though a fever had taken its toll before burning out.

Hugh Franciscus continued to teach for fifteen years, although he operated a good deal less, then gave it up entirely. It was as though he had grown tired of blood, of always having to be involved with blood, of having to draw it, spill it, wipe it away, stanch it. He was a quieter, softer man, I heard, the ferocity diminished. There were no more expeditions to Honduras or anywhere else.

I, too, have not been entirely free of her. Now and then, in the years that have passed, I see that donkey-cart cortège, or his face bent over hers in the morgue. I would like to have told him what I now know, that his unrealistic act was one of goodness, one of those small, persevering acts done, perhaps, to ward off madness. Like lighting a lamp, boiling water for tea, washing a shirt. But, of course, it's too late now.

ANALYZING What the Writer Says

1. How do Selzer and his medical school colleagues view Dr. Franciscus? How do they account for his remoteness?

2. How does Dr. Franciscus's initial treatment of Imelda contrast to his final treatment of her? Or does it?

3. At the time of the incident, why, according to Selzer, does Dr. Franciscus repair Imelda's lip? How—and why—does Selzer's perspective change?

4. What is the significance of the lesson in the amphitheater? Why do you think Dr. Franciscus includes the slides of Imelda?

5. Does Selzer think Dr. Franciscus is a good doctor?

6. Who is the real subject of the essay? Why is the essay titled "Imelda"?

ANALYZING How the Writer Says It

1. Selzer peppers his essay with several quotes from Dr. Franciscus in which he barks orders or dictates flatly, in medical jargon, descriptions of his patients' medical situations. How do these quotes affect your understanding of Dr. Franciscus?

2. Consider the first two sentences of the essay. Why do you think Selzer opens this way? Given that Dr. Franciscus dominates much of Selzer's account, what is the effect of the casual "I knew him once"—and how does it help shape the portrait of Franciscus that emerges? Of Selzer?

3. The concluding sentence of the essay may strike some as unnecessarily sentimental, others as dismissive, a linguistic shrug of the shoulders. What *is* the effect of that sentence? What point or points in the essay does it reinforce?

ANALYZING the Issue

1. Cite examples of professions in which you think detachment from subjects, patients, clients, and the like is necessary, as well as those in which you think emotional engagement is necessary. Explain.

2. Should training in "bedside manner" or "people skills" be a required component of all medical programs? Other professional programs? Why or why not?

ANALYZING Connections Between Texts

1. Dispassion, some would argue, is necessary for total focus—whether one is a champion athlete, a brilliant surgeon, a great lawyer. Richard Selzer and Malcolm Gladwell (p. 765) l write about doctors so focused on their surgical

skills that they forget—or seem to others to forget—the feelings of their patients. Both Selzer's and Gladwell's subjects, however, have pivotal experiences with patients during which they are unable to maintain emotional distance. Compare Selzer's treatment of Hugh Franciscus to Gladwell's of Charlie Wilson. Are the doctors' failures at dispassion viewed as weakness? Strength? Explain.

2. Both Keith D. Mano ("Plastic Surgery," p. 238) and Roy Selby, Jr. ("A Delicate Operation," p. 246) write about surgery: Mano writes a graphic description of plastic surgery, highlighting the paradox of the almost violent procedure performed for the sake of vanity; Selby is awed by a miraculous brain surgery. Consider the different attitudes toward surgery and its purposes. Compare and contrast the writers' attitudes toward surgery, surgeons, and patients.

3. What comparisons can you draw between Selzer's depiction of Dr. Franciscus and Walter Iooss's photograph of Michael Jordan (p. 121)? Make a list of similar techniques despite the different mediums.

WARMING UP: *Think of your favorite sports hero. What, for you, makes this person so special?*

The Chosen One

BY GARY SMITH

GARY SMITH

Award-winning sports journalist and senior writer for Sports Illustrated *Gary Smith examines the various pressures Tiger Woods has faced, both from his father and from "the machine." This essay first appeared in* Sports Illustrated *in December 1996.*

It was ordinary. It was oh so ordinary. It was a salad, a dinner roll, a steak, a half potato, a slice of cake, a clinking fork, a podium joke, a ballroom full of white-linen-tablecloth conversation. Then a thick man with tufts of white hair rose from the head table. His voice trembled and his eyes teared and his throat gulped down sobs between words, and everything ordinary was cast out of the room.

He said, "Please forgive me . . . but sometimes I get very emotional . . . when I talk about my son. . . . My heart . . . fills with so . . . much . . . joy . . . when I realize . . . that this young man . . . is going to be able . . . to help so many people. . . . He will transcend this game . . . and bring to the world . . . a humanitarianism . . . which has never been known before. The world will be a better place to live in . . . by virtue of his existence . . . and his presence. . . . I acknowledge only a small part in that . . . in that I know that I was personally selected by God himself . . . to nurture this young man . . . and bring him to the point where he can make his contribution to humanity. . . . This is my treasure . . . Please accept it . . . and use it wisely. . . . Thank you."

Blinking tears, the man found himself inside the arms of his son and the applause of the people, all up on their feet.

In the history of American celebrity, no father has ever spoken this way. Too many dads have deserted or died before their offspring reached this realm, but mostly they have fallen mute, the father's vision exceeded by the child's, leaving the child to wander, lost, through the sad and silly wilderness of modern fame.

So let us stand amidst this audience at last month's Fred Haskins Award ₅ dinner to honor America's outstanding college golfer of 1996, and take note as Tiger and Earl Woods embrace, for a new manner of celebrity is taking form before our eyes. Regard the 64-year-old African-American father, arm upon the superstar's shoulder, right where the chip is so often found, declaring that this boy will do more good for the world than any man who ever walked it. Gaze at the 20-year-old son, with the blood of four races in his veins, not flinching an inch from the yoke of his father's prophecy but already beginning to scent the complications. The son who stormed from behind to win a record third straight U.S. Amateur last August, turned pro and rang up scores in the 60s in 21 of his first 27 rounds, winning two PGA Tour events as he doubled and tripled the usual crowds and dramatically changed their look and age.

Now turn. Turn and look at us, the audience, standing in anticipation of something different, something pure. Quiet. Just below the applause, or within it, can you hear the grinding? That's the relentless chewing mechanism of fame, girding to grind the purity and the promise to dust. Not the promise of talent, but the bigger promise, the father's promise, the one that stakes everything on the boy's not becoming separated from his own humanity and from all the humanity crowding around him.

It's a fitting moment, while he's up there at the head table with the audience on its feet, to anoint Eldrick (Tiger) Woods—the rare athlete to establish himself immediately as the dominant figure in his sport—as *Sports Illustrated*'s 1996 Sportsman of the Year. And to pose a question: Who will win? The machine . . . or the youth who has just entered its maw?

Tiger Woods will win. He'll fulfill his father's vision because of his mind, one that grows more still, more willful, more efficient, the greater the pressure upon him grows.

The machine will win because it has no mind. It flattens even as it lifts, trivializes even as it exalts, spreads a man so wide and thin that he becomes margarine soon enough.

Tiger will win because of God's mind. Can't you see the pattern? Earl Woods ₁₀ asks. Can't you see the signs? "Tiger will do more than any other man in history to change the course of humanity," Earl says.

Sports history, Mr. Woods? Do you mean more than Joe Louis and Jackie Robinson, more than Muhammad Ali and Arthur Ashe? "More than any of them because he's more charismatic, more educated, more prepared for this than anyone."

Anyone, Mr. Woods? Your son will have more impact than Nelson Mandela, more than Gandhi, more than Buddha?

"Yes, because he has a larger forum than any of them. Because he's playing a sport that's international. Because he's qualified through his ethnicity to accomplish miracles. He's the bridge between the East and the West. There is no limit because he has the guidance. I don't know yet exactly what form this will take. But he is the Chosen One. He'll have the power to impact nations. Not people. Nations. The world is just getting a taste of his power."

Surely this is lunacy. Or are we just too myopic to see? One thing is certain: we are witnessing the first volley of an epic encounter, the machine at its mightiest confronting the individual groomed all his life to conquer it and turn it to his use. The youth who has been exposed to its power since he toddled onto *The Mike Douglas Show* at 3, the set of *That's Incredible!* at 5, the boy who has been steeled against the silky seduction to which so many before him have succumbed. The one who, by all appearances, brings more psychological balance, more sense of self, more consciousness of possibility to the battlefield than any of his predecessors.

This is war, so let's start with war. Remove the images of pretty putting   15 greens from the movie screen standing near the ballroom's head table. Jungle is what's needed here, foliage up to a man's armpits, sweat trickling down his thighs, leeches crawling up them. Lieut. Col. Earl Woods, moving through the night with his rifle ready, wondering why a U.S. Army public information officer stationed in Brooklyn decided in his mid-30s that he belonged in the Green Berets and ended up doing two tours of duty in Vietnam. Wondering why his first marriage has died and why the three children from it have ended up without a dad around when it's dark like this and it's time for bed—just as Earl ended up as a boy after his own father died. Wondering why he keeps plotting ways to return to the line of fire—"creative soldiering," he calls it—to eyeball death once more. To learn once again about his dark and cold side, the side that enables Earl, as Tiger will remark years later, "to slit your throat and then sit down and eat his dinner."

Oh, yes, Earl is one hell of a cocktail. A little Chinese, a little Cherokee, a few shots of African-American; don't get finicky about measurements, we're making a vat here. Pour in some gruffness and a little intimidation, then some tenderness and some warmth and a few jiggers of old anger. Don't hold back on intelligence. And stoicism. Add lots of stoicism, and even more of responsibility—"the most responsible son of a bitch you've ever seen in your life" is how Earl himself puts it. Top it all with "a bucket of whiskey," which is what he has been known to order when he saunters into a bar and he's in the mood. Add a dash of hyperbole, maybe two, and to hell with the ice, just whir. This is one of those concoctions you're going to remember when morning comes.

Somewhere in there, until a good fifteen years ago, there was one other ingredient, the existential Tabasco, the smoldering why? The Thai secretary in the U.S. Army office in Bangkok smelled it soon after she met Earl, in 1967. "He couldn't relax," says Kultida (Tida) Woods. "Searching for something, always searching, never satisfied. I think because both his parents died when he was young, and he didn't have Mom and Dad to make him warm. Sometimes he stayed awake till three or four in the morning, just thinking."

In a man so accustomed to exuding command and control, in a Green Beret lieutenant colonel, *why?* has a way of building up power like a river dammed. Why did the Vietcong sniper bracket him that day (first bullet a few inches left of one ear, second bullet a few inches right of the other) but never fire the third bullet? Why did Earl's South Vietnamese combat buddy, Nguyen Phong—the one Earl nicknamed Tiger, and in whose memory he would nickname his son—stir one night just in time to awaken Earl and warn him not to budge because a viper was poised inches from his right eye? What about that road Earl's jeep rolled down one night, the same road on which two friends had just been mutilated, the road that took him through a village so silent and dark that his scalp tingled, and then, just beyond it . . . hell turned inside-out over his shoulder, the sky lighting up and all the huts he had just passed spewing Vietcong machine-gun and artillery fire? He never understands what is the purpose of Lieutenant Colonel Wood's surviving again and again. He never quite comprehends what is the point of his life, until . . .

Until the boy is born. He will get all the time that Earl was unable to devote to the three children from his first marriage. He will be the only child from Earl's second marriage, to the Thai woman he brought back to America, and right away there are signs. What other 6-month-old, Earl asks, has the balance to stand in the palm of his father's hand and remain there even as Daddy strolls around the house? Was there another 11-month-old, ever, who could pick up a sawed-off club, imitate his father's golf swing so fluidly, and drive the ball so wickedly into the nylon net across the garage? Another 4-year-old who could be dropped off at the golf course at 9 A.M. on a Saturday and picked up at 5 P.M., pockets bulging with money he had won from disbelievers ten and twenty years older, until Pop said, "Tiger you can't do that"? Earl starts to get a glimmer. He is to be the father of the world's most gifted golfer.

But why? What for? Not long after Tiger's birth, when Earl has left the mil- [20] itary to become a purchaser for McDonnell Douglas, he finds himself in a long discussion with a woman he knows. She senses the power pooling inside him, the friction. "You have so much to give" she tells him, "but you're not giving it. You haven't even scratched the surface of your potential." She suggests he try EST, Erhard Seminars Training, an intensive self-discovery and self-actualizing technique, and it hits Earl hard, direct mortar fire to the heart. What he learns is that his overmuscular sense of responsibility for others has choked his potential.

"To the point," says Earl, "that I wouldn't even buy a handkerchief for myself. It went all the way back to the day my father died, when I was 11, and my mother put her arm around me after the funeral and said, 'You're the man of the house now.' I became the father that young, looking out for everyone else, and then she died two years later.

"What I learned through EST was that by doing more for myself, I could do much more for others. Yes, be responsible, but love life, and give people the space to be in your life, and allow yourself room to give to others. That caring and sharing is what's most important, not being responsible for everyone else. Which is where Tiger comes in. What I learned led me to give so much time to Tiger, and to give him the space to be himself, and not to smother him with dos and don'ts. I took out the authority aspect and turned it into companionship. I made myself vulnerable as a parent. When you have to earn respect from your child, rather than demanding it because it's owed to you as the father, miracles happen. I realized that, through him, the giving could take a quantum leap. What I could do on a limited scale, he could do on a global scale."

At last, the river is undammed, and Earl's whole life makes sense. At last, he sees what he was searching for, a pattern. No more volunteering for missions—he has his. Not simply to be a great golfer's father. To be destiny's father. His son will change the world.

"What the hell had I been doing in public information in the army, posted in Brooklyn?" he asks. "Why, of course, what greater training can there be than three years of dealing with the New York media to prepare me to teach Tiger the importance of public relations and how to handle the media?"

Father: Where were you born, Tiger?   25

Son, age 3: I was born on December 30, 1975, in Long Beach, California.

Father: No, Tiger, only answer the question you were asked. It's important to prepare yourself for this. Try again.

Son: I was born in Long Beach, California.

Father: Good, Tiger, good.

The late leap into the Green Berets? "What the hell was that for?" Earl says.   30 "Of course, to prepare me to teach Tiger mental toughness."

The three children by the first marriage? "Not just one boy the first time," says Earl, "but two, along with a girl, as if God was saying, 'I want this son of a bitch to really have previous training.'"

The Buddhist wife, the one who grew up in a boarding school after her parents separated when she was 5, the girl who then vowed that her child would know nothing but love and attention? The one who will preach inner calm to Tiger simply by turning to him with that face—still awaiting its first wrinkle at 52? Whose eyes close when she speaks, so he can almost see her gathering and sifting the thoughts? The mother who will walk every hole and keep score for Tiger at children's tournaments, adding a stroke or two if his calm cracks? "Look at this stuff!" cries Earl. "Over and over you can see the plan being orchestrated by someone other than me because I'm not this damn good! I tried to get out of that combat assignment to Thailand. But Tida was meant to bring in the influence of the Orient, to introduce Tiger to Buddhism and inner peace, so he would have the best of two different worlds. And so he would have the knowledge that there were two people whose lives were totally committed to him."

What of the heart attack Earl suffered when Tiger was 10 and the way the retired lieutenant colonel felt himself floating down the gray tunnel toward the light before he was wrenched back? "To prepare me to teach Tiger that life is short," Earl says, "and to live each day to the maximum, and not worry about the future. There's only now. You must understand that time is just a linear measurement of successive increments of now. Anyplace you go on that line is now, and that's how you have to live it."

No need to wonder about the appearance of the perfect childhood coach, John Anselmo: the perfect sports psychologist, Jay Brunza; the perfect agent, Hughes Norton; the perfect attorney, John Merchant; and the perfect pro swing instructor, Butch Harmon. Or about the great tangle of fate that leads them all to Tiger at just the right junctures in his development. "Everything," says Earl, "right there when he needs it. Everything. There can't be this much coincidence in the world. This is a directed scenario, and none of us involved in the scenario has failed to accept the responsibility. This is all destined to be."

His wife ratifies this, in her own way. She takes the boy's astrological chart ³⁵ to a Buddhist temple in Los Angeles and to another in Bangkok and is told by monks at both places that the child has wondrous powers. "If he becomes a politician, he will be either a president or a prime minister," she is told. "If he enters the military, he will be a general."

Tida comes to a conclusion. "Tiger has Thai, African, Chinese, American Indian, and European blood," she says. "He can hold everyone together. He is the Universal Child."

This is in the air the boy breathes for twenty years, and it becomes bone fact for him, marrow knowledge. When asked about it, he merely nods in acknowledgment of it, assents to it; of course he believes it's true. So failure, in the rare visits it pays him, is not failure. It's just life pausing to teach him a lesson he needs in order to go where he's inevitably going. And success, no matter how much sooner than expected it comes to the door, always finds him dressed and ready to welcome it. "Did you ever see yourself doing this so soon?" a commentator breathlessly asks him seconds after his first pro victory, on October 6 in Las Vegas, trying to elicit wonder and awe on live TV. "Yeah," Tiger responds. "I kind of did." And sleep comes to him so easily; in the midst of conversation, in a car, in a plane, off he goes, into the slumber of the destined. "I don't see any of this as scary or a burden," Tiger says. "I see it as fortunate. I've always known where I wanted to go in life. I've never let anything deter me. This is my purpose. It will unfold."

No sports star in the history of American celebrity has spoken this way. Maybe, somehow, Tiger can win.

The machine will win. It must win because it too is destiny, 5 billion destinies leaning against one. There are ways to keep the hordes back, a media expert at Nike tells Tiger. Make broad gestures when you speak. Keep a club in your hands and take practice swings, or stand with one foot well out in front of the other, in almost a karate stance. That will give you room to breathe. Two weeks later, surrounded by a pen-wielding mob in La Quinta, California, in late November, just before the Skins Game, the instruction fails. Tiger survives, but his shirt and slacks are ruined, felt-tip-dotted to death.

The machine will win because it will wear the young man down, cloud his judgment, steal his sweetness, the way it does just before the Buick Challenge in Pine Mountain, Georgia, at the end of September. It will make his eyes drop when the fans' gaze reaches for his, his voice growl at their clawing hands, his body sag onto a sofa after a practice round and then rise and walk across the room and suddenly stop in bewilderment. "I couldn't even remember what I'd just gotten off the couch for, two seconds before," he says. "I was like mashed potatoes. Total mush."

So he walks. Pulls out on the eve of the Buick Challenge, pulls out of the Fred Haskins Award dinner to honor him, and goes home. See, maybe Tiger can win. He can just turn his back on the machine and walk. Awards? Awards to Tiger are like echoes, voices bouncing off the walls, repeating what a truly confident man has already heard inside his own head. The Jack Nicklaus Award, the one Jack himself was supposed to present to Tiger live on ABC during the Memorial tournament last spring? Tiger would have blown it off if Wally Goodwin, his coach at Stanford during the two years he played there before turning pro, hadn't insisted that he show up.

The instant Tiger walks away from the Buick Challenge and the Haskins dinner, the hounds start yapping. See, that's why the machine will win. It's got all those damn heel-nippers. Little mutts on the PGA Tour resenting how swiftly the 20-year-old was ordained, how hastily he was invited to play practice rounds with Nicklaus and Arnold Palmer, with Greg Norman and Ray Floyd and Nick Faldo and Fred Couples. And big dogs snapping too. Tom Kite quoted as saying, "I can't ever remember being tired when I was twenty," and Peter Jacobsen quoted, "You can't compare Tiger to Nicklaus and Palmer anymore because they never [walked out]."

He rests for a week, stunned by the criticism—"I thought those people were my friends," he says. He never second-guesses his decision to turn pro, but he sees what he surrendered. "I miss college," he says. "I miss hanging out with my friends, getting in a little trouble. I have to be so guarded now. I miss sitting around drinking beer and talking half the night. There's no one my own age to hang out with anymore because almost everyone my age is in college. I'm a target for everybody now, and there's nothing I can do about it. My mother was right when she said that turning pro would take away my youth. But golfwise, there was nothing left for me in college."

He reemerges after the week's rest and rushes from four shots off the lead on the final day to win the Las Vegas Invitational in sudden death. The world's waiting for him again, this time with reinforcements. Letterman and Leno want him as a guest; GQ calls about a cover; Cosby, along with almost every other sitcom you can think of, offers to write an episode revolving around Tiger, if only he'll appear. Kids dress up as Tiger for Halloween—did anyone ever dress up as Arnie or Jack?—and Michael Jordan declares that his only hero on earth is Tiger Woods. Pepsi is dying to have him cut a commercial for one of its soft drinks aimed at Generation Xers; Nike and Titleist call in chits for the $40 million and $20 million contracts he signed; money managers are eager to know how he wants his millions invested; women walk onto the course during a practice round and ask for his hand in marriage; kids stampede over and under ropes and chase him from the 18th hole to the clubhouse; piles of phone messages await him when he returns to his hotel room. "Why," Tiger asks, "do so many people want a piece of me?"

Because something deeper than conventional stardom is at work here, something so spontaneous and subconscious that words have trouble going there. It's a communal craving, a public aching for a superstar free of anger and arrogance and obsession with self. It's a hollow place that chimes each time Tiger and his parents strike the theme of father and mother and child love, each time Tiger stands at a press conference and declares, "They have raised me well, and I truly believe they have taught me to accept full responsibility for all aspects of my life." During the making of a Titleist commercial in November, a makeup woman is so moved listening to Earl describe his bond with Tiger that she decides to contact her long-estranged father. "See what I mean?" cries Earl. "Did you affect someone that way today? Did anyone else there? It's destiny, man. It's something bigger than me." 45

What makes it so vivid is context. The white canvas that the colors are being painted on—the moneyed, mature, and almost minority-less world of golf—makes Tiger an emblem of youth overcoming age, have-not overcoming have, outsider overcoming insider, to the delight not only of the 18-year-olds in the gallery wearing nose rings and cornrows, but also—of all people—of the aging insider haves.

So Tiger finds himself, just a few weeks after turning pro at the end of August, trying to clutch a bolt of lightning with one hand and steer an all-at-once corporation—himself—with the other, and before this he has never worked a day in his life. Never mowed a neighbor's lawn, never flung a folded newspaper, never stocked a grocery shelf; Mozarts just don't, you know. And he to act as if none of this is new or vexing because he has this characteristic—perhaps from all those years of hanging out with his dad at tournaments, all those years of mixing with and mauling golfers five, ten, twenty, thirty years older than he is—of never permitting himself to appear confused, surprised, or just generally a little squirt. "His favorite expression," Earl says, "is, 'I knew that.'" Of course Pop, who is just as irreverent with Tiger as he is reverent, can say, "No, you didn't know that, you little s—." But Earl, who has always been the filter for Tiger, decides to take a few steps back during his son's first few months as a pro because he wishes to encourage Tiger's independence and because he is uncertain of his own role now that the International Management Group (IMG) is managing Tiger's career.

Nobody notices it, but the inner calm is beginning to dissolve. Earl enters Tiger's hotel room during the Texas Open in mid-October to ask him about his schedule, and Tiger does something he has never done in his twenty years. He bites the old man's head off.

Earl blinks. "I understand how you must feel," he says.

"No, you don't," snaps Tiger.

"And I realized," Earl says later, "that I'd spent twenty years planning for this, but the one thing I didn't do was educate Tiger to be the boss of a corporation. There was just no vehicle for that, and I thought it would develop more slowly. I wasn't presumptuous enough to anticipate this. For the first time in his life, the training was behind the reality. I could see on his face that he was going through hell."

The kid is fluid, though. Just watch him walk. He's quick to flow into the new form, to fit the contour of necessity. A few hours after the outburst he's apologizing to his father and hugging him. A few days later he's giving Pop the O.K. to call a meeting of the key members of Tiger's new corporation and establish a system, Lieutenant Colonel Woods in command, chairing a two-and-a-half-hour teleconference with the team each week to sift through all the demands, weed out all the chaff, and present Tiger five decisions to make instead of five hundred. A few days after that, the weight forklifted off his shoulders, at least temporarily, Tiger wins the Walt Disney World/Oldsmobile Classic. And a few weeks later, at the Fred Haskins Award dinner, which has been rescheduled at his request, Tiger stands at the podium and says, "I should've attended the dinner [the first time]. I admit I was wrong, and I'm sorry for any inconvenience I may have caused. But I have learned from that, and I will never make that mistake again. I'm very honored to be part of this select group, and I'll always remember, for both good and bad, this Haskins Award; for what I did and what I learned, for the company I'm now in and I'll always be in. Thank you very much." The crowd surges to its feet, cheering once more.

See, maybe Tiger can win. He's got the touch. He's got the feel. He never writes down a word before he gives a speech. When he needs to remember a phone number, he doesn't search his memory or a little black book; he picks up a phone and watches what number his fingers go to. When he needs a 120-yard shot to go under an oak branch and over a pond, he doesn't visualize the shot, as most golfers would. He looks at the flag and pulls everything from the hole back, back, back . . . not back into his mind's eye, but into his hands and forearms and hips, so they'll do it by feel. Explain how he made the preposterous shot? He can't. Better you interview his knuckles and metacarpals.

"His handicap," says Earl, "is that he has such a powerful creative mind. His imagination is too vivid. If he uses visualization, the ball goes nuts. So we piped into his creative side even deeper, into his incredible sense of feel."

"I've learned to trust the subconscious," says Tiger. "My instincts have never lied to me."

The mother radiates this: the Eastern proclivity to let life happen, rather than the Western one to make it happen. The father comes to it in his own way, through fire. To kill a man, to conduct oneself calmly and efficiently when one's own death is imminent—a skill Earl learns in Green Beret psychological training and then again and again in jungles and rice paddies—one removes the conscious mind from the task and yields to the subconscious. "It's the more powerful of the two minds," Earl says. "It works faster than the conscious mind, yet it's patterned enough to handle routine tasks over and over, like driving a car or making a putt. It knows what to do.

"Allow yourself the freedom of emotion and feeling. Don't try to control them and trap them. Acknowledge them and become the beneficiary of them. Let it all outflow."

Let it all because it's all there: the stability, almost freakish for a close-of-the-millennium California child—same two parents, same house all his twenty years, same best friends, one since second grade, one since eighth. The kid, for god's sake, never once had a baby-sitter. The conditioning is there as well, the two years of psychological boot camp during which Earl dropped golf bags and pumped cart brakes during Tiger's backswings, jingled change and rolled balls across his line of vision to test his nerves, promising him at the outset that he only had to say "Enough" and Earl would cut off the blowtorch, but promising too that if Tiger graduated, no man he ever faced would be mentally stronger than he. "I am the toughest golfer mentally," Tiger says.

The bedrock is so wide that opposites can dance upon it: the cautious man can be instinctive, the careful man can be carefree. The bedrock is so wide that it his enticed Tiger into the habit of falling behind—as he did in the final matches of all three U.S. Junior Amateur and all three U.S. Amateur victories—knowing in his tissue and bones that danger will unleash his greatest power. "Allow success and fame to happen," the old man says. "Let the legend grow."

To hell with the Tao. The machine will win, it has to win, because it makes 60 everything happen before a man knows it. Before he knows it, a veil descends over his eyes when another stranger approaches. Before he knows it, he's living in a walled community with an electronic gate and a security guard, where the children trick-or-treat in golf carts, a place like the one Tiger just moved into in Orlando to preserve some scrap of sanity. Each day there, even with all the best intentions, how can he help but be a little more removed from the world he's supposed to change, and from his truest self?

Which is . . . who? The poised, polite, opaque sage we see on TV? No, no, no; his friends hoot and haze him when they see that Tiger on the screen, and he can barely help grinning himself. The Tiger they know is perfectly a fast-food freak who never remembers to ask if anyone else is hungry before he bolts to Taco Bell or McDonald's for the tenth time of the week. The one who loves riding roller coasters, spinning out golf carts, and winning at cards no matter how often his father accuses him of "reckless eyeballing." The one who loves delivering the dirty joke, who owns a salty barracks tongue just a rank or two beneath his father's. The one who's flip, who's downright cocky. When a suit walks up to him before the Haskins Award dinner and says, "I think you're going to be the next great one, but those are mighty big shoes to fill," Tiger replies, "Got big feet."

A typical exchange between Tiger and his agent, Norton:

"Tiger, they want to know when you can do that interview."

"Tell them to kiss my ass!"

"All right, and after that, what should I tell them?"   65

"Tell them to kiss my ass again!"

"O.K., and after that . . ."

But it's a cockiness cut with humility, the paradox pounded into his skull by a father who in one breath speaks of his son with religious awe and in the next grunts, "You weren't s— then, Tiger. You ain't s— now. You ain't never gonna be s—."

"That's why I know I can handle all this," Tiger says, "no matter how big it gets. I grew up in the media's eye, but I was taught never to lose sight of where I came from. Athletes aren't as gentlemanly as they used to be. I don't like that change. I like the idea of being a role model. It's an honor. People took the time to help me as a kid, and they impacted my life. I want to do the same for kids."

So, if it's a clinic for children instead of an interview or an endorsement for   70
adults, the cynic in Tiger gives way to the child who grew up immersed in his father's vision of an earth-altering compassion, the 7-year-old boy who watched scenes from the Ethiopian famine on the evening news, went right to his bedroom and returned with a $20 bill to contribute from his piggy bank. Last spring busloads of inner-city kids would arrive at golf courses where Tiger was playing for Stanford, spilling out to watch the Earl and Tiger show in wonder. Earl would talk about the dangers of drugs, then proclaim, "Here's Tiger Woods on drugs," and Tiger would stagger to the tee, topping the ball so it bounced crazily to the side. And then, presto, with a wave of his arms Earl would remove the drugs from Tiger's body, and his son would stride to the ball and launch a 330-yard rocket across the sky. Then Earl would talk about respect and trust and hard work and demonstrate what they can all lead to by standing ten feet in front of his son, raising his arms and telling Tiger to smash the ball between them—and, *whoosh*, Tiger would part not only the old man's arms but his haircut too.

They've got plans, the two of them, big plans, for a Tiger Woods Foundation that will fund scholarships across the country, set up clinics and coaches and access to golf courses for inner-city children. "I throw those visions out there in front of him," Earl says, "and it's like reeling in a fish. He goes for the bait, takes it, and away he goes. This is nothing new. It's been working this way for a long time."

"That's the difference," says Merchant, Tiger's attorney and a family friend. "Other athletes who have risen to this level just didn't have this kind of guidance. With a father and mother like Tiger's, he has to be real. It's such a rare quality in celebrities nowadays. There hasn't been a politician since John Kennedy whom people have wanted to touch. But watch Tiger. He has it. He actually listens to people when they stop him in an airport. He looks them in the eye. I can't ever envision Tiger Woods selling his autograph."

See, maybe Tiger can win.

Let's be honest. The machine will win because you can't work both sides of this street. The machine will win because you can't transcend wearing sixteen Nike swooshes, you can't move human hearts while you're busy pushing sneakers. Gandhi didn't hawk golf balls, did he? Jackie Robinson was spared that fate because he came and went while Madison Avenue was still teething. Ali became a symbol instead of a logo because of boxing's disrepute and because of the attrition of cells in the basal ganglia of his brain. Who or what will save Tiger Woods?

Did someone say Buddha?   75

Every year near his birthday, Tiger goes with his mother to a Buddhist temple and makes a gift of rice, sugar, and salt to the monks there who have renounced all material goods. A mother-of-pearl Buddha given to Tiger by his Thai grandfather watches over him while he sleeps, and a gold Buddha hangs from the chain on his neck. "I like Buddhism because it's a whole way of being and living," Tiger says. "It's based on discipline and respect and personal responsibility. I like Asian culture better than ours because of that. Asians are much more disciplined than we are. Look how well behaved their children are. It's how my mother raised me. You can question, but talk back? Never. In Thailand, once you've earned people's respect, you have it for life. Here it's, what have you done for me lately? So here you can never rest easy. In this country I have to be very careful. I'm easygoing, but I won't let you in completely. There, I'm Thai, and it feels very different. In many ways I consider that home.

"I believe in Buddhism. Not every aspect, but most of it. So I take bits and pieces. I don't believe that human beings can achieve ultimate enlightenment, because humans have flaws. I don't want to get rid of all my wants and desires. I can enjoy material things, but that doesn't mean I need them. It doesn't matter to me whether I live in a place like this"—the golf club in his hand makes a sweep of the Orlando villa—"or in a shack. I'd be fine in a shack, as long as I could play some golf. I'll do the commercials for Nike and for Titleist, but there won't be much more than that. I have no desire to be the king of endorsement money."

On the morning after he decides to turn pro, there's a knock on his hotel room door. It's Norton, bleary-eyed but exhilarated after a latenight round of negotiations with Nike. He explains to Tiger and Earl that the benchmark for contract endorsements in golf is Norman's reported $2^1/$_2$ million-a-year deal with Reebok. Then, gulping down hard on the yabba-dabba-doo rising up his throat, Norton announces Nike's offer: $40 million for five years, 8 mil a year. "Over three times what Norman gets!" Norton exults.

Silence.

"Guys, do you realize this is more than Nike pays any athlete in salary, even   80
Jordan?"

Silence.

"Finally," Norton says now, recalling that morning, "Tiger says 'Mmmm-hmmm,' and I say, 'That's it? Mmmm-hmmm?' No 'Omigod.' No slapping five or 'Ya-hooo!' So I say, 'Let me go through this again, guys.' Finally Tiger says, 'Guess that's pretty amazing.' That's it. When I made the deal with Titleist a day later, I went back to them saying, 'I'm almost embarrassed to tell you this one. Titleist is offering a little more than $20 million over five years.'"

On the Monday morning after his first pro tournament, a week after the two megadeals, Tiger scans the tiny print on the sports page under Milwaukee Open money earnings and finds his name. Tiger Woods: $2,544. "That's my money," he exclaims. "I earned this!"

See, maybe Tiger can win.

How? How can he win when there are so many insects under so many   85
rocks? Several more death threats arrive just before the Skins Game, prompting an increase in his plainclothes security force, which is already larger than anyone knows. His agent's first instinct is to trash every piece of hate mail delivered to IMG, but Tiger won't permit it. Every piece of racist filth must be saved and given to him. At Stanford he kept one letter taped to his wall. Fuel comes in the oddest forms.

The audience, in its hunger for goodness, swallows hard over the Nike ad that heralds Tiger's entrance into the professional ranks. The words that flash on the screen over images of Tiger—"There are still courses in the United States I am not allowed to play because of the color of my skin. I've heard I'm not ready for you. Are you ready for me?"—ooze the very attitude from which many in the audience are seeking relief. The media backlash is swift: the Tiger Woods who used to tell the press "The only time I think about race is when the media ask me"—whoa, what happened to him?

What happened to him was a steady accretion of experiences, also known as a life. What happened, just weeks before he was born, was a fusillade of limes and BBs rattling the Woods house in Cypress, California, one of the limes shattering the kitchen window, splashing glass all around the pregnant Tida, to welcome the middle-class subdivision's first non-Caucasian family.

What happened was a gang of older kids seizing Tiger on his first day of kindergarten, tying him to a tree, hurling rocks at him, calling him monkey and nigger. And Tiger, at age 5, telling no one what happened for several days, trying to absorb what this meant about himself and his world.

What happened was the Look, as Tiger and Earl came to call it, the uneasy, silent stare they received in countless country-club locker rooms and restaurants. "Something a white person could never understand," says Tiger, "unless he went to Africa and suddenly found himself in the middle of a tribe." What happened was Tiger's feeling pressured to leave a driving range just two years ago, not far from his family's California home, because a resident watching Tiger's drives rocket into the nearby protective netting reported that a black teenager was trying to bombard his house.

What happened was the cold shoulder Earl got when he took his tyke to play 90 at the Navy Golf Course in Cypress—"a club," Earl says, "composed mostly of retired naval personnel who knew blacks only as cooks and servers, and along comes me, a retired lieutenant colonel outranking 99 percent of them, and I have the nerve to take up golf at 42 and immediately become a low handicap and beat them, and then I have the audacity to have this kid. Well, they had to do something. They took away Tiger's playing privileges twice, said he was too young, even though there were other kids too young who they let play. The second time it happened, I went up to the pro who had done it and made a bet. I said, 'If you'll spot my 3-year-old just one stroke a hole, nine holes, playing off the same tees, and he beats you, will you certify him?' The pro started laughing and said, 'Sure.' Tiger beat him by two strokes, got certified, then the members went over the pro's head and kicked him out again. That's when we switched him to another course."

Beat them. That was his parents' solution for each banishment, each Look. Hold your tongue, hew to every rule, and beat them. Tiger Woods is the son of the first black baseball player in the Big Seven, a catcher back in the early '50s, before the conference became the Big Eight. A man who had to leave his Kansas State teammates on road trips and travel miles to stay in motels for blacks; who had to go to the back door of restaurant kitchens to be fed while his teammates dined inside; who says, "This is the most racist society in the world—I know that." A man who learned neither to extinguish his anger nor spray it but to quietly convert it into animus, the determination to enter the system and overcome it by turning its own tools against it. A Green Beret explosives expert whose mind naturally ran that way, whose response, upon hearing Tiger rave about the security in his new walled community, was, "I could get in. I could blow up the clubhouse and be gone before they ever knew what hit them." A father who saw his son, from the beginning, as the one who would enter one of America's last Caucasian bastions, the PGA Tour, and overthrow it from within in a manner that would make it smile and ask for more. "Been planning that one for twenty years," says Earl. "See, you don't turn it into hatred. You turn it into something positive. So many athletes who reach the top now had things happen to them as children that created hostility, and they bring that hostility with them. But that hostility uses up energy. If you can do it without the chip on the shoulder, it frees up all that energy to create."

It's not until Stanford, where Tiger takes an African-American history course and stays up half the night in dormitories talking with people of every shade of skin, that his experiences begin to crystallize. "What I realized is that even though I'm mathematically Asian—if anything—if you have one drop of black blood in the United States, you're black," says Tiger. "And how important it is for this country to talk about this subject. It's not me to blow my horn, the way I come across in that Nike ad, or to say things quite that way. But I felt it was worth it because the message needed to be said. You can't say something like that in a polite way. Golf has shied away from this for too long. Some clubs have brought in tokens, but nothing has really changed. I hope what I'm doing can change that."

But don't overestimate race's proportion in the fuel that propels Tiger Woods. Don't look for traces of race in the astonishing rubble at his feet on the Sunday after he lost the Texas Open by two strokes and returned to his hotel room and snapped a putter in two with one violent lift of his knee. Then another putter. And another. And another and another—eight in all before his rage was spent and he was ready to begin considering the loss's philosophical lesson. "That volcano of competitive fire, that comes from me," says Earl. A volcano that's mostly an elite athlete's need to win, a need far more immediate than that of changing the world.

No, don't overestimate race, but don't overlook it, either. When Tiger is asked about racism, about the effect it has on him when he senses it in the air, he has a golf club in his hands. He takes the club by the neck, his eyes flashing hot and cold at once, and gives it a short upward thrust. He says, "It makes me want to stick it right up their asses." Pause. "On the golf course."

The machine will win because there is so much of the old man's breath in 95 the boy . . . and how long can the old man keep breathing? At 2 A.M., hours before the second round of the Tour Championship in Tulsa on October 25, the phone rings in Tiger's hotel room. It's Mom. Pop's in an ambulance, on his way to a Tulsa hospital. He's just had his second heart attack.

The Tour Championship? The future of humanity? The hell with 'em. Tiger's at the old man's bedside in no time, awake most of the night. Tiger's out of contention in the Tour Championship by dinnertime, with a second-round 78, his worst till then as a pro. "There are things more important than golf," he says.

The old man survives—and sees the pattern at work, of course. He's got to throw away the cigarettes. He's got to quit ordering the cholesterol special for breakfast. "I've got to shape up now, God's telling me," Earl says, "or I won't be around for the last push, the last lesson." The one about how to ride the tsunami of runaway fame.

The machine will win because no matter how complicated it all seems now, it is simpler than it will ever be. The boy will marry one day, and the happiness of two people will lie in his hands. Children will follow, and it will become his job to protect three or four or five people from the molars of the machine. Imagine the din of the grinding in five, ten, fifteen years, when the boy reaches his golfing prime.

The machine will win because the whole notion is so ludicrous to begin with, a kid clutching an eight-iron changing the course of humanity. No, of course not, there won't be thousands of people sitting in front of tanks because of Tiger Woods. He won't bring about the overthrow of a tyranny or spawn a religion that one day will number 300 million devotees.

But maybe Pop is onto something without quite seeing what it is. Maybe it   100
has to do with timing: the appearance of his son when America is turning the corner to a century in which the country's faces of color will nearly equal those that are white. Maybe, every now and then, a man gets swallowed by the machine, but the machine is changed more than he is.

For when we swallow Tiger Woods, the yellow-black-red-white man, we swallow something much more significant than Jordan or Charles Barkley. We swallow hope in the American experiment, in the pell-mell jumbling of genes. We swallow the belief that the face of the future is not necessarily a bitter or bewildered face; that it might even, one day, be something like Tiger Woods' face: handsome and smiling and ready to kick all comers' asses.

We see a woman, 50-ish and Caucasian, well-coiffed and tailored—the woman we see at every country club—walk up to Tiger Woods before he receives the Haskins Award and say, "When I watch you taking on all those other players, Tiger, I feel like I'm watching my own son" . . . and we feel the quivering of the cosmic compass that occurs when human beings look into the eyes of someone of another color and see their own flesh and blood.

ANALYZING What the Writer Says

1. Does Smith share the vision Tiger Woods's father has of Tiger Woods? How do you know?

2. In what way is Tiger Woods a "new manner of celebrity"?

3. Look at all of Smith's references to "the machine." In your own words, what is the machine to which he refers?

4. Using Tiger Woods as the illustration, define genius.

ANALYZING the Writer's Techniques

1. What is the purpose of the portrait of Tiger Woods's father at the beginning of the essay? How would the piece have been different had it been only about the son?

2. Smith repeats statements like "Tiger Woods will win" and "the machine will win" throughout the essay. What is the purpose of these statements?

ANALYZING the Issue

1. Smith presents Tiger Woods as a child prodigy in danger of being crushed by the relentless machine of celebrity, the sports industry that markets (and corrupts) individual athletic talent through endorsements and other commercial ventures. Can you think of any famous athletes who have succumbed to "the machine"? Do you think Tiger has a chance of beating the system?

2. "Show me the money," Cuba Gooding Jr.'s character tells his agent in the movie *Jerry Maguire*. Are professional sports all about money, leaving little room for humanity and greatness of character? Cite examples (fictional or real) to support your answer.

ANALYZING Connections Between Texts

1. Analyze Smith's profile of Tiger Woods in the context of Gladwell's concept of the "Physical Genius" (p. 765). Are there indications that Woods fits Gladwell's definition?

2. Several pieces in Chapter 9 concern the hopes and dreams of parents for their children. None of the parent-child relationships featured in Anndee Hochman's "Growing Pains: Beyond 'One Big Happy Family'" (p. 131), Caroline Hwang's "The Good Daughter" (p. 139), and E. B. White's "Once More to the Lake" (p. 178) is as public as that of Tiger Woods; none of the children are prodigies. How do all these relationships, however, parallel that of the Woodses? In what significant ways, if any, are they different?

3. The *New Yorker* cartoon above and Gary Smith's "The Chosen One" both depict parents who actively push their children toward success. Do "stage mothers" (or fathers) promote their children's happiness this way, or are they trying to live vicariously through their children? Explain. Look at the example of Tiger Woods and/or other child prodigies.

YOUR TURN: Suggestions for Writing About "Genius: Genius"

1. Gladwell, in "The Practical Genius," takes a rather unconventional approach to the term "genius." Write an essay in which you define what the term means to you.

2. Write an essay in which you define what "genius" means, using the readings in this unit and your personal experience as sources.

3. Annie Leibovitz's photograph of Liberace illustrates Dave Hickey's point ("A Rhinestone as Big as the Ritz") that glitz and glamor in show business can be the "real thing," the essence of an artist's art. Think about some showy performances of our time and age (in music, sports, or the arts) and argue that the real talents of these artists/athletes lie less in their music or their athletic or artistic talent than in the spectacle they make of themselves. Or argue that a particular artist or performer *does* have talent that goes beyond the spectacle.

4. Thomas Edison once said, "Genius is ten percent inspiration, ninety percent perspiration." Using the readings in this unit and your own experience as sources, write an essay in which you show this observation to be true or false.

5. Do you think child prodigies (or children with some degree of talent) benefit from parents who relentlessly push them toward success? Research a prominent figure in sports, entertainment, or some other profession and demonstrate how his/her success is due to ambitious parental guidance—or the lack thereof.

6. Using Gladwell's and Selzer's essays and your own experience as sources, write an essay on the importance of "bedside manner" in physicians. Imagine your audience as a group of young medical students whose training in medical school focuses mainly on acquiring the physical and medical skills to be good doctors.

7. The surgeons in Gladwell's "The Physical Genius" and Selzer's "Imelda" share qualities of medical brilliance, meticulousness, and emotional detachment. Write an essay in which you define what makes a good doctor, or if you wish, specifically a good surgeon. In your essay, discuss whether dispassion is an important attribute—or a shortcoming.

8. Consider an outstanding public figure you admire and show how this person achieved his/her standing by thinking differently.

9. In his famous essay "Self Reliance," Ralph Waldo Emerson writes that to be great is to be misunderstood. Write an essay in which you use one or more of the people from the readings in this unit to illustrate his point. Or apply the idea to some other famous (or not-so-famous) person.

10. Dennis Overbye, in "He's Still Ready for His Close-Up," mentions the contro-
    versy surrounding Einstein: at some point in his career, he promoted the
    development of the atomic bomb. His research enabled Robert J.
    Oppenheimer to build the first bomb, which led to the build-up of a nuclear
    arsenal that could destroy the world several times over. (Not surprisingly, the
    painting by Ernest Hamlin Baker pictures the famous physicist with an atomic
    cloud in the background.) More recently, scientists experimenting with genetic
    engineering have been caught in a similar dilemma: to what degree is a scien-
    tist responsible for the outcome of his/her discoveries? Should scientists halt
    their research once they realize its potentially dangerous and/or unethical
    results?
11. Using Overbye's "He's Still Ready for His Close-Up" and other research if
    necessary, write an analysis of Ernest Hamlin Baker's painting of Einstein,
    relating Baker's visual message to what you learn about Einstein in your read-
    ing.
12. Several of the essays in this unit make reference to "Everyman" or
    "Everywoman." How do different authors use the concept of Everyperson to
    define genius?
13. Many of the essays in this unit depict people who have made their marks by
    thinking (or doing something) different. To what degree does being different
    define genius?
14. Find a "typical" sports photograph of Michael Jordan or some other athlete in
    action. Write a contrastive analysis in which you point out the difference
    between a dynamic action picture of an athlete and Ioss's meditative portrait
    of the injured Jordan. Make sure you show how the visual elements in each
    picture support the overall message the picture is trying to convey about sports
    and/or athletes.
15. Consider Annie Leibovitz's portrait of Liberace, looking carefully at composi-
    tion, color, details. Write an essay analyzing the photographer's attitude
    toward her subject.

IMAGE GALLERY 👁

KEVIN LEIGH

Computer Baby

This photograph by Kevin Leigh shows a young computer user hard at work— or play.

1. Does the baby "working" on the computer strike you as odd? Why or why not?

2. What does this photograph suggest about computers in our society?

3. The photographer did not title this picture. What would you call it? Explain your choice.

4. What connections do you see between this picture and any of the readings in "Genus: Genius"?

JEFF CHRISTIANSEN

Bill Gates

A twenty-year-old college dropout, Bill Gates founded Microsoft in 1975; he is still the head of the company, its chief software designer, and the richest man in the world. His phenomenal success and the personality behind it continue to intrigue people.

1. Does Bill Gates's appearance fit our expectations of "genius"? Why or why not? Explain your answer.

2. How do you read his facial expression and his hand gestures in this photograph?

3. How does the photographer use lighting effectively in the picture?

Renee Graham
"Can Hollywood Kick the Habit?" by Renee Graham from THE BOSTON GLOBE, August 20, 2002. Copyright © 2002. Reprinted by permission of The Boston Globe, via Copyright Clearance Center.

Fred E. Hahn
From TESTED ADVERTISING METHODS, 5th Edition by Fred E. Hahn. Copyright © 1999 Reprinted with permission of Prentice Hall Direct, an imprint of Pearson Education Co.

Stephen S. Hall
"The Bully in the Mirror" by Stephen S. Hall from THE NEW YORK TIMES Magazine, August 22, 1999. Copyright © 1999, Stephen S. Hall. Reprinted by permission.

Harper's Magazine
"Passed by a Hair." Copyright © 2000 by HARPER'S Magazine. All rights reserved. Reproduced from the October issue by special permission.

Harper's Magazine
"Joystick Jihad." Copyright © 2002 by HARPER'S Magazine. All rights reserved. Reproduced from the October issue by special permission.

Dave Hickey
"A Rhinestone As Big As the Ritz" by Dave Hickey. Copyright ©1997 The Foundation for Advanced Critical Studies, Inc. Originally published in ART ISSUES #22 (March/April 1992) and reprinted in AIR GUITAR: Essays on Art & Democracy (Art Issues Press, Los Angeles, 1997). Reprinted by permission.

Dave Hickey
"The Kids Are All Right: After the Prom" by Dave Hickey from NORMAN ROCKWELL: Pictures for the American People by Maureen Hart Hennesey and Anne Knutson, eds. Published by Harry N. Abrams, Inc., New York. All rights reserved.

Jack Hitt
"The Hidden Life of SUVs" by Jack Hitt from MOTHER JONES, July/August 1999. Copyright © 1999 Foundation for National Progress. Reprinted by permission.

Anndee Hochman
"Growing Pains: Beyond 'One Big Happy Family'" from EVERYDAY ACTS AND SMALL SUBVERSIONS by Anndee Hochman. Copyright © 1994 by Anndee Hochman. (Portland, OR: The Eighth Mountain Press, 1994). Reprinted by permission of the publisher.

Arianna Huffington
"The Coming SUV Wars" by Arianna Huffington as appeared on Salon.com. Reprinted by permission of Arianna Huffington.

Langston Hughes
"Theme for English B" from THE COLLECTED POEMS OF LANGSTON HUGHES by Langston Hughes, copyright © 1994 by The Estate of Langston Hughes. Used by permission of Alfred A. Knopf, a division of Random House, Inc.

Caroline Hwang
"The Good Daughter" by Caroline Hwang from NEWSWEEK, September 23, 1998. Copyright © 1998 Newsweek. All rights reserved. Reprinted by permission.

Molly Ivins
"How 1984 and 2002 Add Up To Trouble" by Molly Ivins from FORT WORTH STAR-TELEGRAM, November 24, 2002. Reprinted by permission of Creators Syndicate.

Elizabeth Joseph

"Polygamy Now!" by Elizabeth Joseph. Copyright © 1998 by HARPER'S Magazine. All rights reserved. Reproduced from the February issue by special permission.

Paul Keegan

"Culture Quake" by Paul Keegan from MOTHER JONES, November/December 1999. Copyright © 1999 Foundation for National Progress. Reprinted by permission.

Adnan R.Khan

"Bordering on Panic: Post–9/11" by Adnan R. Khan as appeared in MACLEAN'S, November 25, 2002. Reprinted by permission of the author.

Michael Kinsley

"Orwell Got It Wrong" by Michael Kinsley as appeared in READER'S DIGEST, June 1997.

Charles Krauthammer

"The Case for Profiling" by Charles Krauthammer from TIME Magazine, March 18, 2002. Copyright © 2002 Time Inc. Reprinted by permission.

Natalie Kusz

"Ring Leader" by Natalie Kusz. Copyright © 1996 by Natalie Kusz. Originally appeared in ALLURE, February 1996. Reprinted by permission of Brandt and Hochman Literary Agents, Inc. All rights reserved.

Lewis H. Lapham

"Audible Silence" by Lewis H. Lapham. Copyright © 2002 by HARPER'S Magazine. All rights reserved. Reproduced from the November issue by special permission.

Lewis H. Lapham

"Regime Change" by Lewis H. Lapham. Copyright © 2003 by HARPER'S Magazine. All rights reserved. Reproduced from the February issue by special permission.

C.S. Lewis

GOD IN THE DOCK by C.S. Lewis. Copyright © C.S. Lewis Ptd. Ltd. 1971, 1979. Extract reprinted by permission of The C.S. Lewis Company Ltd.

William Lutz

"Weasel Words" from DOUBLESPEAK by William Lutz. Reprinted from Doublespeak: From Revenue Enhancement to Terminal Living. Copyright © 1980 by St. Martin's Press.

Nancy Mairs

From CARNAL ACTS by Nancy Mairs. Copyright © 1990 by Nancy Mairs. Reprinted by permission of Beacon Press, Boston.

Farhad Manjoo

"Everything Is Watching You" by Farhad Manjoo from Salon.com. Reprinted by permission.

D. Keith Mano

"Plastic Surgery" by D. Keith Mano from NATIONAL REVIEW, November 13, 1981. Copyright © 1981 by National Review, Inc., 215 Lexington Avenue, New York, NY 10016. Reprinted by permission.

Katherine Mansfield

"Miss Brill" from THE SHORT STORIES OF KATHERINE MANSFIELD by Katherine Mansfield, copyright 1923 by Alfred A. Knopf, a division of Random House, Inc. and renewed 1951 by John Middleton Murry. Used by permission of Alfred A. Knopf, a division of Random House, Inc.

Scott Russell Sanders

"Under the Influence" by Scott Russell Sanders. Copyright © 1989 by HARPER'S Magazine. All rights reserved. Reproduced from the November issue by special permission.

Anton Scalia

"Dissent to Lawrence et al vs. Texas" by Anton Scalia.

Eric Schlosser

"Introduction" from FAST FOOD NATION: The Dark Side of the All-American Meal by Eric Schlosser. Reprinted by permission of Houghton Mifflin Company. All rights reserved.

Julie Schlosser

"Scandal 101: Lessons from Ken Lay" by Julie Schlosser from FORTUNE Magazine, September 2, 2002. Copyright © 2002 Time Inc. All rights reserved.

David Sederais

"Me Talk Pretty One Day" from ME TALK PRETTY ONE DAY by David Sedaris. Copyright © 2000 by David Sedaris. By permission of Little, Brown and Company, (Inc.)

Roy Selby, Jr.

"A Delicate Operation" by Roy Selby, Jr. Copyright © 1975 by HARPER'S Magazine. All rights reserved. Reproduced by special permission.

Richard Selzer

"Imelda" from LETTERS TO A YOUNG DOCTOR by Richard Selzer. Copyright © 1982 by David Goldman and Janet Selzer, Trustees. Reprinted by permission of Georges Borchardt, Inc., Literary Agency.

Gary Smith

Reprinted courtesy of SPORTS ILLUSTRATED: "The Chosen One" by Gary Smith, December 23, 1996. Copyright © 1996, Time Inc. All rights reserved.

Deborah Sontag

"Fierce Entanglements" by Deborah Sontag from THE NEW YORK TIMES Magazine, November 17, 2002. Copyright © 2002, Deborah Sontag. Reprinted by permission.

Amy Tan

"Mother Tongue" by Amy Tan. Copyright © 1990 by Amy Tan. First appeared in THE THREEPENNY REVIEW. Reprinted by permission of the author and the Sandra Dijkstra Literary Agency.

Deborah Tannen

"Marked Women" by Deborah Tannen from THE NEW YORK TIMES Magazine, June 20, 1993. Copyright © 1993, Deborah Tannen. Reprinted by permission.

Melanie Thernstrom

"The Inheritance That Got Away" by Melanie Thernstrom from THE NEW YORK TIMES Magazine, June 9, 2002. Copyright © 2002, Melanie Thernstrom. Reprinted by permission.

John Taylor Tierney

"Playing the Dozens" by John Taylor Tierney from THE NEW YORK TIMES Magazine, May 15, 1994. Copyright © 1994, John Taylor Tierney. Reprinted by permission.

Leigh Turner

"The Media and the Ethics of Cloning" by Leigh Turner from CHRONICLE OF HIGHER EDUCATION, September 26, 1997. Reprinted by permission of Leigh Turner.

PHOTO AND ILLUSTRATION CREDITS

COLOR IMAGE GALLERY

Color Plate 1   "After the Prom" by Norman Rockwell. *Saturday Evening Post*, May 27, 1957. Printed by permission of the Norman Rockwell Family Agency © 2004 the Norman Rockwell Family Entities. Photo from Curtis Publishing Company.

Color Plate 2   "Wedding Dress" Credit: Yann Arthus-Bertrand

Color Plate 3   "Close-up: James Carville" Credit: Richard Ellis/Liaison/Time, Inc./Getty Images

Color Plate 4   "Jerry Hall and Gabriel Jagger, Model and Her Son" Credit: Annie Leibovitz/Contact Press Images Inc.

Color Plate 5   "Amy Foote and Paul Neis as exercise partners" Credit: Arthur Grace/Zuma Press

Color Plate 6   "Ashleigh, 13, with Her Friends and Parents, Santa Monica" Copyright © 2004 Lauren Greenfield Photography

Color Plate 7   "Lenda Murray, Ms. Olympia 1990-1995" Credit: Annie Leibovitz/Contact Press Images Inc.

Color Plate 8   "Cowboy Mike Hunter with his family buying meat at grocery store." Credit: Chris Johns/National Geographic Image Collection

Color Plate 9   "Lunch at Uncle Antonio's" Credit: Stephanie Maze/Woodfin Camp & Associates

Color Plate 10   "Lucky Dog," Bourbon Street, New Orleans. Credit: Kerri McCaffety

Color Plate 11   "Home schooling, Topsham, Maine in 1990" Credit: Steve Liss/Time Inc./Getty Images

Color Plate 12   "The Problem We All Live With," by Norman Rockwell. Oil on canvas 36 × 58 inches. *Look* Magazine story Illustration January 14, 1964. Credit: Collection of The Norman Rockwell Museum at Stockbridge © 2004 The Norman Rockwell Family Trust

Color Plate 13   "Reaching for Help" Credit: Max Aguilera-Hellweg/Time, Inc./Getty Images

Color Plate 14   "Computer in Society" TIME cover dated April 2, 1965 Credit: Time Life Pictures/Getty Images Art by Boris Artzybasheff

Color Plate 15   "Three Mile Island nuclear power station" #ab26215 Credit: John McGrail/Taxi/Getty Images

Color Plate 16   "Talk the Talk" Credit: Inge Fink

Color Plate 17   "Rebecca Denison, Executive Director of Organization of Women with AIDS, San Francisco, California" Credit: Annie Leibovitz/Contact Press Images Inc.

Color Plate 18   "The Gossips," by Norman Rockwell. Oil on canvas *The Saturday Evening Post* cover March 6, 1948. Credit: Collection of The Norman Rockwell Museum At Stockbridge © 2004 The Norman Rockwell Family Agency

Color Plate 19   Former Seal of the Office of Total Information Awareness. From www.conspiracyarchive.com.

Color Plate 20   Office of Emergency Management, "He's Watching You" Credit: David Pollack © K.J. Historical/Corbis

Color Plate 21   "99 Cent" by Andreas Gursky Credit: © 2004 Andreas Gursky/Artists Rights Society (ARS), New York/VG Bild-Kunst, Bonn. Courtesy the Artist and Matthew Marks Gallery, New York.

Color Plate 22   "In the Pits" #784807-001 Credit: Paul Chesley/Stone/Getty Images

Color Plate 23   "Medicine shopping cart" Credit: © Comstock Images

Color Plate 24   "Money. It's just not what it used to be." Copyright © 2000 by Phoenix Home Life Mutual Insurance Company. Courtesy of The Phoenix Companies, Inc.

Color Plate 25   "Linda" 1983 sculpture by John DeAndrea at the Denver Art Museum. Credit: Alan Berner

Color Plate 26	"Cassius Clay Beats Sunny Liston" Lewiston, Maine May 25, 1965 Credit: Neil Leifer/*Sports Illustrated*
Color Plate 27	"The Connoisseur" by Norman Rockwell. *Saturday Evening Post*, September 13, 1962. Credit: Printed by permission of the Norman Rockwell Family Agency © 2004 the Norman Rockwell Family Entities. Photo from Curtis Publishing Company
Color Plate 28	"Tiger Woods on the 18th hole in the file round of The Masters, April 2001" Credit: Fred Vuich/*Sports Illustrated*
Color Plate 29	"Martha Stewart" Credit: Timothy Greenfield-Sanders
Color Plate 30	"Albert Einstein & Atom Bomb" TIME cover dated July 1, 1946. Credit: Time Life Pictures/Getty Images
Color Plate 31	"Michael Jordan" © Walter Iooss
Color Plate 32	"Liberace and Scott Thorson" October 1, 1981. Credit: Annie Leibovitz/Contact Press Images Inc.

INDEX